Anatomy of a Train Wreck

Anatomy of a Train Wreck

The Rise and Fall of Priming Research

Ruth Leys

The University of Chicago Press
Chicago and London

The University of Chicago Press, Chicago 60637
The University of Chicago Press, Ltd., London
© 2024 by The University of Chicago
All rights reserved. No part of this book may be used or reproduced in any manner whatsoever without written permission, except in the case of brief quotations in critical articles and reviews. For more information, contact the University of Chicago Press, 1427 E. 60th St., Chicago, IL 60637.
Published 2024
Printed in the United States of America

33 32 31 30 29 28 27 26 25 24   1 2 3 4 5

ISBN-13: 978-0-226-83693-5 (cloth)
ISBN-13: 978-0-226-83695-9 (paper)
ISBN-13: 978-0-226-83694-2 (e-book)
DOI: https://doi.org/10.7208/chicago/9780226836942.001.0001

Library of Congress Cataloging-in-Publication Data

Names: Leys, Ruth, author.
Title: Anatomy of a train wreck : the rise and fall of priming research / Ruth Leys.
Description: Chicago : The University of Chicago Press, 2024. | Includes bibliographical references and index.
Identifiers: LCCN 2024019026 | ISBN 9780226836935 (cloth) | ISBN 9780226836959 (paperback) | ISBN 9780226836942 (ebook)
Subjects: LCSH: Priming (Psychology) | Psychology—Research. | Causation.
Classification: LCC BF371 .L46 2024 | DDC 150.72/4—dc23/eng/20240509
LC record available at https://lccn.loc.gov/2024019026

♾ This paper meets the requirements of ANSI/NISO Z39.48-1992 (Permanence of Paper).

To Michael and Anna

Contents

Acknowledgments xi

Introduction 1
Prime Time in Social Psychology 1
The Replication Crisis 7
"If you want to understand any scientific work properly, you need to know its history" 14
Basic Assumptions 20
Outline of the Book 34

1 The Rise of Attribution Research 40
Fritz Heider and the Causes of Social Interaction 40
The Contributions of Edward E. Jones and Keith E. Davis to Attribution Research 46
Harold Kelley and the Situation/Disposition Debate 50
The Growth of Attribution Research 53
"Telling More Than We Can Know": Attribution and the Limits of Introspection 57
The "Why" Question: Are Reasons Causes? 63

2 Intentions and Causes 67
"Baseball and Hot Sauce" 67
Reasons versus Causes 72
Anscombe versus Davidson on Intentional Action 79

Agent Causation versus Event Causation *83*
Does Social Psychology Need a New Paradigm? *87*
The Two Social Psychologies, or, Whatever Happened
    to the Crisis? *91*

3   John Bargh's Approach to Automaticity *97*
Subliminal Perception Becomes "Unconscious Priming" *97*
Is Automaticity Its Own Thing, and If Not, What Is the Recipe? *98*
A Features or Graded Approach to Automaticity? *106*
Bargh's Auto-motive Theory, or, How Intentions and Goal Pursuits
    Came Apart *115*
Prinz's Ideomotor Theory of Automaticity *121*
Does the Environment Trigger Goal Pursuits Independently of
    Intentions? *124*
The Elderly Priming Experiment *128*

4   "The Unbearable Automaticity of Being" *131*
Bargh's Manifesto *131*
The Automaticity of Everyday Life *135*
Automaticity, Attention, and Control *143*
Skilled Action *152*
Must Automatic Actions Be Inflexible? *158*

5   The Chameleon Effect *164*
Postural Mimicry and Automaticity *164*
Imitation as an Intentional-Communicative Action *168*
Imitation When We Are Alone *173*
How Bargh and Chartrand Misunderstood Bavelas's
    Experiments *175*
The Limits of Contagion *180*
Emotional Mimicry *187*
The Contextual Sensitivity of Mimicry *193*
The Sociality of Chameleons, or, The Watching Eyes Effect *196*
Alan Alda's Intentions *202*

6   A Theory in Crisis? *204*

Unconscious Thought Theory   *204*
The "One-to-Many" or "Many Effects of One Prime" Problem   *209*
Bargh under Fire and the Problem of Selectivity   *214*
The Power of the Situation   *218*
Agency and the Legacy of Cognitive Psychology   *224*

7   The Fate of Priming   *228*

Doyen et al.'s (2012) Failed Replication and Its Aftermath   *228*
Hidden Moderators: "The Ultimate Attribution Error"?   *240*
The Historical Sensitivity of Priming Outcomes   *244*
"There might be deep and substantive limits to both the replicability and the generalizability of . . . social priming effects"   *259*

8   "Behavioral Priming: It's All in the Mind, but Whose Mind?"   *267*

Experimenter Expectancy   *268*
What Explains Experimenter Expectancy and Demand Effects?   *273*
Kenneth Bowers's "Dissociated Control" Theory of Hypnosis   *277*
"The question 'Why' has and yet has not application"   *282*
Bargh on Priming and Hypnosis   *287*
Priming and Expectancy Effects   *290*
The Long Legacy of Nisbett and Wilson (1977): What Is Consciousness For?   *292*
Consciousness as Rationalization   *298*

Conclusion: The Two Camps   *309*

Appendix: Bargh on Unconscious Intentionality   317
References   327
Index   389

Acknowledgments

For their support, discussions of topics central to my book, and helpful comments on certain parts of this text, I am grateful to Jennifer Ashton, Walter Benn Michaels, Robert Pippin, and Lisa Siraganian. I owe a special thanks to Alan Fridlund and Michael Fried for reading the entire manuscript and generously providing me with scrupulous feedback on my arguments and presentation. My warm thanks also to Karen Merikangas Darling, executive editor at the University of Chicago Press, who shepherded my book throughout the entire editorial process and gave me excellent advice, help, and support. I also thank James C. Welling, art photographer and friend, who kindly gave me permission to make use of one of his extraordinary series of railroad track photographs for the cover of my book.

About the title of my book: In my introduction, I quote Nobel Prize winner Daniel Kahneman as warning in a letter in *Nature* that he saw a "train wreck looming" in the field of priming research, owing to doubts about the robustness of priming results and the recent failure of researchers to replicate certain iconic experiments. This train wreck is exactly what happened, and my book is an account of how the wreck occurred.

Introduction

Prime Time in Social Psychology

"It's prime time in social psychology for studying primes, a term for cues that go unnoticed but still sway people's attitude and behavior," science journalist Bruce Bower wrote in a 2012 article in *Science News*:

> Primes have been reported to influence nearly every facet of social life, at least in lab experiments. Subtle references to old age can cause healthy college students to slow their walking pace without realizing it. Cunningly presented cues about money can nudge people to become more self-oriented and less helpful to others. And people holding a hot cup of coffee are apt to judge strangers as having warm personalities . . .
>
> Yale University psychologist John Bargh likens primes to whistles that only mental butlers can hear. Once roused by primes, these silent servants dutifully act on a person's pre-existing tendencies and preferences without making a conscious commotion . . . People can pursue actions on their own initiative, but mental butlers strive to ease the burden on the conscious lord of the manor. (Bower 2012, 26)

At the time, John Bargh was widely regarded as the most influential priming researcher in the United States. Several years earlier, he had defined *priming* in the more scientific language of his field. Priming, he wrote, is the "incidental activation of knowledge structures, such as trait concepts and stereotypes, by the current situational context. Many studies have shown that the recent use of a trait construct or stereotype, even in an earlier or unrelated situation, carries over for a time to exert an unintended, passive influence on the interpretation of behavior" (Bargh, Chen, and Burrows 1996, 230). Bargh had given this definition in the course of describing a particular priming experiment on the influence of words relevant to stereotypes regarding the elderly, one of the experiments mentioned by Bower. In that experiment, as part of an ostensible language-proficiency test, Bargh and his research team had asked thirty male and female New York University students majoring in psychology to sort, as fast as possible, thirty sets of five-word scrambled sentences; the task for the participants was to compose a grammatically correct four-word sentence for each set by dropping the odd word that did not belong (Bargh, Chen, and Burrows, 1996).

The participants took the test one at a time; half of them had been randomly selected to receive words in the scrambled sentences associated with stereotypes of the elderly (for example, *worried, Florida, old, forgetful, lonely,* although all references to slowness were excluded); the other half of the students had been given "neutral" words (for example., *thirsty, clean,* and *private*).[1]

The experimenter had kept himself blind to the priming conditions by prepackaging the various scrambled-sentences sets and selecting the packages randomly when handing them to the students. After completing the word-sorting tasks, the participants had been partially debriefed, thanked for their participation, and told to leave via an elevator down the hallway. Unknown to them, a confederate of the experimenter—sitting in a chair and apparently waiting to talk to a professor—had recorded with a hidden, handheld stopwatch the amount of time it took each participant to walk a specific length of the corridor.

Bargh, along with his junior co-authors Mark Chen and Lara Burrows, had reported that the students in the elderly priming condition had walked significantly more slowly than the students in the neutral priming condition. The participants had voluntarily participated in the experiment and

---

1. The words relevant to the elderly in the scrambled sentence or word-sorting task were *worried, Florida, old, lonely, grey, selfishly, careful, sentimental, wise, stubborn, courteous, bingo, withdraw, forgetful, retired, wrinkle, rigid, traditional, bitter, obedient, conservative, knits, dependent, ancient, helpless, gullible, cautious,* and *alone*. These priming words were obtained from previous research that had examined the components of the elderly stereotype (Brewer, Dull, and Lui 1981; Harris and Associates 1975; McTavish 1971; see also Perdue and Gurtman 1990). Bargh, Chen, and Burrows gave only three examples of the neutral words used in the experiment (*thirsty, clean, private*). These words may have been neutral to Bargh and his team but perhaps not to the participants, some of whom might have found the words quite charged. Bargh had to hope that this variability would wash out in the group analyses.

were conscious of reading the primes in the word-sorting task. But they were not informed of the general purpose of the experiment, and Bargh and his co-authors stated that, on their debriefing after the experiment, participants had been unaware of the reason for the study: none of them had discerned a connection between the words in the scrambled-sentences test and their walking speed, nor had they been aware that their walking speed had been measured. A replication of the experiment involving another thirty students confirmed that participants primed with words connoting old age walked more slowly than the controls. A third replication involving nineteen students and more-thorough debriefing methods also corroborated the finding that the participants were unaware of the connection between the priming manipulation and their walking speeds. In other words, the mere exposure to socially relevant stimuli appeared to activate, or "prime," a stereotype and a behavior without the individual's awareness or intention. A further experiment appeared to rule out the possibility that the words relating to the elderly stereotype induced in participants a sad mood, which might have been the reason they walked more slowly.

Bargh, Chen, and Burrows (1996) had also reported the results of other priming experiments using different priming cues. In one experiment, some participants were primed with words connoting rudeness while others were primed with words connoting politeness. The participants primed with rudeness words subsequently interrupted a confederate more quickly than those primed with politeness words. In another variant, based on their videotaped facial reactions recorded by a hidden camera, White participants subliminally primed with photographs of African American faces reacted with more hostility to an annoying request by an experimenter than did unprimed participants.[2]

Bargh had predicted the outcome of these experiments on the basis of his "auto-motive" or "direct perception-behavior" theory of automaticity. According to Bargh's theory, the perception of stimuli from the environment, regardless of context and a person's intentions or motives, automatically and nonconsciously activated, or made more accessible in memory, certain internal cognitive processes and constructs, such as stereotypes

---

2. Bargh reported that the elderly priming experiment was originally carried out in 1991, but that he and his team did not publish their findings until after certain conceptual replications had been obtained in different laboratories—notably by Steele and Aronson (1995) and Dijksterhuis and van Knippenberg (1998)—because they knew that the effect would be surprising to many (Bargh 2012b).

about the elderly, and this activation then triggered the behavior. Priming was thus the experimental technique that validated Bargh's automaticity theory according to which, as he later put it, the environment directly determined the "internal cognitive processes involved in perception, judgment, behavior and goal pursuits" (Bargh 2011, 629).

In the ensuing years, many other experiments suggested that complex automatic actions could be determined by causes outside awareness. Stimuli associated with the concept of *library* appeared to cause people to make less noise (Aarts and Dijksterhuis 2003); material objects, such as backpacks and briefcases, primed cooperation and competitiveness respectively (Kay et al. 2004); scents, such as cleaning fluids, primed cleanliness goals (Holland, Hendriks, and Aarts 2005); reading money-related words made people volunteer more and donate less (Vohs, Mead, and Goode 2006); holding a warm cup of coffee made people judge a target person as having a warmer personality (Williams and Bargh 2008); seeing the American flag made US voters more favorably disposed to politically conservative points of view (Carter, Ferguson, and Hassin 2011); and so on (see Morsella, Dennehy, and Bargh 2013 for a partial list of such findings). Semantic priming effects, according to which, for example, hearing the word *doctor* enhances the speed of association to the word *nurse*, had long been considered an empirically robust phenomenon. But the effects of fleeting exposure to priming words, images or other stimuli on behaviors, as reported by Bargh and colleagues, were dramatically larger and appeared to be more long-lasting than those seen in semantic priming, and accordingly they aroused great interest.[3]

Indeed, within the social sciences and beyond, Bargh's pioneering elderly priming experiment was regarded as so remarkable that in 2003 it was described as a "new classic" and as one of the "most admired" experiments in the previous decade of social psychology research (Baumeister and Vohs 2003, 194; see also Fiske 2003, 206–7). In a sign of its fame, the experiment had been singled out by Nobel researcher Daniel Kahneman, in his best-selling book, *Thinking, Fast and Slow* (2011), as a major advance in priming studies, because it demonstrated that primes unconsciously influenced not just people's use of concepts or attributions but also their actual behavior. "You cannot know this from conscious experience, of

---

3. In a large literature, for discussions of the longevity of semantic versus behavioral priming effects, see for example Förster, Liberman, and Friedman 2009; Moutsopoulou et al. 2019; and Messenger 2021.

course," Kahneman had observed with reference to Bargh's experiment, "but you must accept the alien idea that your actions and your emotions can be primed by events of which you are not even aware" (Kahneman 2011, 53). In his discussion of the "marvels of priming," Kahneman had cited such priming effects as crucial evidence in favor of his view that two independent mental processing or systems, System 1 and System 2, governed the way we think. Dual-system (or dual-process) theories had had a long history in psychology, and Kahneman drew on various popular models in the course of his argument.[4] According to him, System 2 governed slow, effortful, or deliberate mental activities demanding complex computational processes, and its operations were associated with the subjective experience of agency and choice. But it was System 1, operating automatically, quickly, and intuitively, with little or no effort or sense of voluntary control, that he declared the "hero" of his book (Kahneman 2011, 21).[5]

Kahneman was not the only person to jump on the bandwagon of priming: claims for the "automaticity of everyday life" (Bargh 1997) made their way into many popular accounts of the ways in which we humans are governed by unconscious, automatic processes (for example, Gladwell 2005). But his reliance on Bargh's priming work was upended when, at the start of 2012, some Belgian researchers, headed by Stéphane Doyen, reported that they had been unable to replicate Bargh, Chen, and Burrows's (1996) iconic elderly experiment (Doyen et al. 2012). Social scientists were already absorbing the fact that, the year before, the well-known researcher

---

4. Kahneman borrowed the terms *System 1* and *System 2* from Stanovich and West (2000) (see Kahneman 2011, 450, n1). For other dual-system theories he also cited Evans and Frankish (2009) and Evans (2008). Although Kahneman did not explicitly say so, many researchers such as Bargh regarded System 2 as operating consciously and intentionally, and System 1 as operating unconsciously and unintentionally (as noted by Schlosser 2019b; De Neys 2021). For recent discussions of the status of these different dual- and single-process models, see Keren and Schul 2009; Kruglanski and Gigerenzer 2011; and De Neys 2021. See also the appendix of this book for a critical analysis of Melnikoff and Bargh's (2018a) recent critique of dual-system theories.

5. In their best-selling book *Nudge* (2021), Nobel Prize–winning behavioral economist Richard H. Thaler and Cass R. Sunstein renamed Kahneman's System 1 and System 2 the "Automatic System" and the "Reflective System" (Thaler and Sunstein 2021, 41). They used Kahneman's distinction between the two systems to explain how certain simple "choice architectures," or "nudges," could be deployed non-coercively to alter people's decisions and behaviors. Thaler and Sunstein's work has had an enormous impact on the field of behavioral economics and behavioral research more generally, as well as on many government policies. However, Maier et al. (2022) have recently reported that, after adjusting for publication bias, there is no evidence that nudges are effective as tools for behavior change (my thanks to Leif Weatherby for alerting me to this last citation).

Daryl Bem had thrown the field of social psychology into disarray by publishing a paper ostensibly proving the validity of extrasensory perception (Bem 2011). In addition, in 2011 a large body of research by Dutch social psychologist Diederik Stapel, some of it on social priming, had been exposed as fraudulent (Vogel 2011). Moreover, at the start of 2012 another Dutch researcher, Dirk Smeesters, who also worked on priming, had to resign when questions were raised about the integrity of his data (Yong 2012a; Simonsohn 2013). The failed replication of Bargh and colleagues' elderly study added to the sense of crisis in the field. The situation became ugly when Bargh attacked Doyen and his colleagues in a series of caustic blog posts, some of which he later deleted, accusing them of methodological and other faults (Bargh 2012a; 2012b; 2012c).[6]

Bargh was particularly incensed when, on the basis of Doyen et al.'s suggestions about the possible influence of experimenter expectancy on Bargh's original findings, the well-regarded science journalist Ed Yong compared Bargh's experimental subjects to the mathematical horse Clever Hans, and Bargh himself to the horse's owner, Mr. von Osten. As described in sensational reports at the start of the twentieth century, Clever Hans had appeared to be able to perform basic arithmetic by stomping his hooves in response to questions from von Osten and others. But it had then been demonstrated by the scientist Otto Pflueger that the horse had been picking up the correct answer from the ultra-subtle bodily movements made by the owner or other questioners, who knew the answers. One implication that might have been drawn from those findings was that the horse was an extraordinarily sensitive reader of such cues (Despret 2015a; 2015b). But that inference had been lost in the general sense that Hans's owner and the other humans caught up in the phenomenon had been duped. All those years later, the implication of Yong's comparison was that, like Clever Hans's owner, in his elderly priming experiment Bargh's expectations and beliefs, or those of his confederates, had been communicated to and subtly influenced the participants' walking speed. Priming existed, but the priming influence stemmed from the behavior of Bargh and his confederates during the experiment, not the priming words connoting old age (Yong 2012a; 2012b; 2012c; 2012d).

The influence of one person on another had long been linked to hypnotic suggestion, the nature of which remained as much of a mystery in

---

6. Many of the findings described in Kahneman's *Thinking, Fast and Slow* (2011) have now also been found to be non-replicable. On this point see especially Schimmack 2020.

2012 as it had in the past. Although Bargh himself had made the connection between his claims about automaticity and theories of suggestion and hypnotism, he did not appreciate Yong's comparison between his work and the story of Clever Hans, hinting, as it did, that he had not adequately controlled for what psychologists call *demand characteristics*. These are the ways in which experimenters can inadvertently influence their participants toward desired responses. The extent to which experimenters' own behaviors, both verbal and behavioral, exerted such effects had been as hot a topic for psychology in the 1970s as priming was in 2012 (see Rosenthal 1966 and Rosenthal and Rosnow 2009 for a review of studies).

In 2012 the controversy over Bargh, Chen, and Burrows's elderly priming study was so devastating that, later the same year, Kahneman himself entered the fray. He published an open letter in *Nature* addressed to Bargh and other priming researchers, warning them of a "train wreck looming," urging them to stop adopting a posture of "defiant denial," and recommending that they work together to restore confidence by creating protocols designed to guarantee the replicability of priming results (Kahneman 2012). He later admitted that in his book *Thinking, Fast and Slow* (2011) he had overrated the validity of priming claims. "'The experimental evidence for the ideas I presented . . . was significantly weaker than I believed . . . This was simply an error: I knew all I needed to know to moderate my enthusiasm . . . but did not think it through'" (cited in Ritchie 2020, 28).

Even before 2012, trouble had been brewing over the legitimacy of claims by Bargh and like-minded priming researchers regarding the outsized role they attributed to stimulus-driven, automatic, non-intentional, unconscious determinants of behavior. To some critics it had begun to seem obvious that the theory of automaticity on which Bargh's elderly study and related experiments was based was problematic. In response, Bargh had already begun to try to accommodate his critics' concerns by revising his claims in various ways. The controversy generated by the 2012 report of the failed replication of his elderly priming study helped precipitate a very public reckoning not only with Bargh's most famous experiment and priming research but with the entire field of psychology (see, for example, Singal 2021).

The Replication Crisis

There is now a very large literature on the twenty-first-century replication crisis in the psychological sciences. As several commentators have observed, the notion of *crisis* has a long history in psychology, even if the meaning of the term has proven hard to pin down.[7] Much of the debate following Doyen et al.'s 2012 failed replication of Bargh, Chen, and Burrows's elderly priming study focused on methodological problems, or what came to be called "questionable research practices." In the case of Bargh and colleagues' (1996) elderly priming study, those problems included whether (a) experimenter expectations had been effectively controlled for by double-blind procedures; (b) proper tests had been in place to evaluate the participants' awareness of the effect of the primes; and (c) using a handheld stopwatch to measure the participants' speed of walking had biased the measurements.

There were also more general debates on a multitude of concerns, including whether (a) sample sizes and statistical methods, such as "null hypothesis significance testing," were justified; (b) "conceptual" replications were sufficient to stop the proliferation of false results or "direct" replications were instead a requirement of good scientific practice; (c) confirmation bias distorted research claims; (e) journal editorial bias led to the publishing of only positive results; (f) experimenters who found negative priming results chose not to submit their papers for publication (the "file drawer" problem); (g) there was post-hoc hypothesizing after the results were known, or HARKing; (h) there was abuse of "researcher degrees of freedom," which is to say, ways in which scientists could tweak their data and analyses using various statistical and other methods to make them confirm their hypotheses; and so on.[8]

---

7. For discussions of the meaning of the term *crisis* in the sciences, including its use by Thomas Kuhn in his analysis of scientific revolutions, as well the history of the use of the term in the psychological sciences in which crises have been declared with great regularity, in a very large literature see Kuhn 1970a; Sturm and Mülberger 2012; and Goertzen 2008.

8. In scientific research the *null hypothesis* states that there is no relationship between the two sets of variables being examined. Roughly speaking, a *direct replication* tries to reproduce the conditions governing an experiment as exactly as possible, whereas a *conceptual replication* attempts to test the underlying hypothesis of a former experiment without trying to duplicate exactly the variables and methodology. The *file drawer problem* refers to the tendency of researchers not to publish but put away in a drawer any findings that fail to show statistically significant effects or reproduce the findings of others. *HARKing*, or hypothesizing after the results are known, is the practice of altering the experimental hypothesis of a study after researchers have analyzed the data, in order to pretend that they had predicted results which were, in reality, unexpected. *Researchers' degrees of freedom* refers to the flexibility researchers have in making a variety of decisions during their analyses of the data in ways that can be abused by generating results attractive to journals. See Chambers 2017 and Bakker, van Dijk, and Wicherts 2012.

The controversy extended well beyond priming research because subsequent developments revealed similar problems in the sciences more broadly, including the life and biomedical sciences (see for example Ioannidis 2005; 2012; Szucs and Ioannidis 2017; Nelson et al. 2022).[9] Proposed solutions to these problems, which remain contested, include (a) the preregistration of experiments before data are collected, including the hypotheses to be tested, the research design, and the design analysis; (b) increased sample sizes; (c) improved statistical methods; and (d) the adoption of large-scale, multi-laboratory efforts for the replication of certain well-known experiments (Ioannidis 2014; Gilbert et al. 2016; Chambers 2017; Gigerenzer 2018; Mirowski 2018; Ritchie 2020; Flis 2022; Morawski 2022).

Concerns about poor experimental standards in psychology had been raised before. Already in 1967 in a well-known statement, the influential psychologist Paul Meehl discussed the inadequate methods of research practices in the field. Among those inadequacies he included

> a fairly widespread tendency to report experimental findings with a liberal use of *ad hoc* explanations for those that didn't "pan out." This last methodological sin is especially tempting in the "soft" fields of (personality and social) psychology, where the profession highly rewards a kind of "cuteness" or "cleverness" in experimental design, such as a hitherto untried method for inducing a desired emotional state, or a particularly "subtle" gimmick for detecting its influence upon a behavioral output. The methodological price paid for this highly-valued "cuteness" is, of course . . . an unusual ease of escape from *modus tollens* refutation.[10]

For, the logical structure of the "cute" component typically involves use

---

9. The debate has also revealed cases of actual cheating by certain well-known scientists, and the conclusion of some recent investigations now is that most scientific results are false; see, e.g., Szucs and Ioannidis 2017 and Gigerenzer 2018. But I think it is important to distinguish between cases of outright fraud by behavioral scientists such as Diedrick Stapel, Francesca Gino, and Daniel Ariely (see Lewis-Kraus 2023) and cases of sloppy research practices of the kind suggested by Doyen et al. (2012) in their discussion of Bargh's elderly priming experiment, although the dividing line between deliberate misconduct and carelessness can sometimes be difficult to draw. For an interesting recent discussion of the prevalence of scientific fraud and the role of the Retraction Watch Database in publicizing and monitoring retractions of findings, see Ritchie 2020 (chapter 3).

10. *Modus tollens* is a mode of reasoning from a hypothetical proposition according to which, if the consequent is denied, the antecedent is denied (thus: if A is true, B is true; but if B is false, A is therefore false).

of complex and rather dubious auxiliary assumptions, which are required to mediate the original prediction and are therefore readily available as (genuinely) plausible "outs" when the prediction fails. (Meehl 1967, 113–14)

Meehl described how this state of affairs could lead a clever (or cynical) researcher to "slowly wend his way through a tenuous nomological network" (that is, a system of related psychological constructs), by performing a long series of related experiments that

> appear to the uncritical reader as a fine example of an "integrated research program," *without ever once refuting or corroborating so much as a single strand of the network* . . . Meanwhile our eager-beaver researcher, undismayed by logic-of-science considerations and relying blissfully on the "exactitude" of modern statistical hypothesis-testing, has produced a long publication list and been promoted to a full professorship. In terms of his contribution to the enduring body of psychological knowledge, he has done hardly anything. (Meehl 1967, 114; his emphasis; cf. Meehl 1978; 1990a)

It is an open question whether Meehl's account of flimsy practices in psychology accurately describes Bargh's research enterprise.[11] To ask this question in the more general, Kuhnian-Lakatosian terms with which Meehl was familiar: Could priming research be considered part of "normal" science in Thomas Kuhn's sense of the term, which is to say a progressive "research program" in Imre Lakatos's formulation, proceeding by the solution of problems on the basis of shared exemplars and sound disciplinary practices, and capable of tolerating anomalies? Or was it instead a "pre-paradigmatic" enterprise (Kuhn 1970a) or "degenerative" research program (Lakatos 1970), characterized by competing schools of thought, debates about methodology, and endemic disputes over first principles that left little room for cumulative progress and consensus?[12] These are

---

11. For an important critique of psychologists' routine dependence on the "null ritual" in psychological research, in which Meehl is quoted for calling that dependence "'one of the worst things that ever happened in the history of psychology,'" see Gigerenzer 2018 (591), citing Meehl 1978 (817).

12. In 1970 Kuhn substituted the term *disciplinary matrix* or *exemplar* for the concept of the *paradigm*, the term he had earlier used to characterize the theoretical assumptions and experimental standards governing well-established sciences. As he observed, the

not questions I seek to answer definitively, but they are ones I aim to bear in mind when assessing the history of priming research and responses to the crisis precipitated by Doyen et al.'s announcement (2012) that Bargh, Chen, and Burrows's famous elderly priming experiment could not be replicated.

Although during the replication crisis commentators traced problems in psychology back to its earliest foundations as a science, critics also identified certain distinct features of the crisis that was precipitated in 2012. Some attempted to link the crisis to specific economic developments. They focused on the status of academic labor under neoliberalism, including the precarious working conditions of nontenured adjunct faculty and postdocs who carry out much of the technical research work—working conditions that had been exacerbated by the financial crisis of 2008–2009. They argued that the ensuing economic stresses had led to ever-increasing competition for dwindling research grants, an unhealthy emphasis on the importance of positive findings, and the consequent institutionalization of journal biases against publishing negative results, and so on—all factors that had encouraged scientists to use sloppy research methods (Mirowski 2018; Morawski 2022; Callard 2022; see also Adams et al. 2019; Gjorgjioska and Tomicic 2019).

More broadly, with occasional reference to debates over the notion of Popperian falsification associated with the work of Kuhn (1970a), Lakatos (1970), Harry Collins (1985), and other philosophers of science, commen-

---

change deprived him of recourse to the phrase *pre-paradigm sciences*, which in his opinion included the social sciences. In explaining his reasons for this change of terminology, Kuhn acknowledged that paradigms have been possessed by many scientific communities, including those he had previously called pre-paradigmatic. But the change in terminology did not alter his description of the maturation process of the sciences: "The early stages in the development of most sciences are characterized by the presence of a number of competing schools. Later, usually in the aftermath of a notable scientific achievement, all or most of these schools vanish, a change which permits a far more powerful professional behaviour to the members of the remaining community" (Kuhn 1970b, 272, n1). Kuhn also used the term *proto-sciences* for those fields, such as the modern social sciences, in which "incessant criticism and continual striving for a fresh start are primary forces, and need to be. No more than in philosophy and the arts, however, do they result in clear-cut progress" (Kuhn 1970a, 24; see also Masterman 1970, 70–72). For a thoughtful discussion of Kuhn's views on the status of the social sciences in light of his discussion of scientific revolutions, paradigms, and normal science, see Sharrock and Read 2002 (especially chapter 3). See also Leahey 1992 and Greenwood 1999 for critical analyses of claims for the revolutionary status of the changes that took place in America as introspectionist approaches gave way first to behaviorism and then to cognitivism.

tators also pointed out that, compared to the basic sciences, replications in the social sciences were performed infrequently (Makel, Plucker, and Hegarty 2012).[13] Moreover, as several critics emphasized, failed replications were rarely decisive in and of themselves, though they might be "informative"—especially if enough disconfirmatory evidence accumulated to undermine confidence among even the most die-hard believers in the original findings (Collins 1985; Mahoney 1985; Schmidt 2009; Brandt et al. 2014; Open Science Collaboration 2015; Earp and Trafimow 2015; see also Zammito 2004, for a valuable examination of post-Kuhnian controversies over the question of the underdetermination of theories by empirical data).

In the course of the post-2012 debates over replication it was therefore not unexpected that those defending their findings adopted the familiar tactics of (a) arguing that subtle methodological differences between their original experiments and failed replication attempts accounted for confirmation failures; and (b) making various adjustments to their loosely formulated theoretical claims in order to account for unwelcome new findings. Moreover, some psychologists also argued that the complexity of human behavior meant that it was likely to vary across a wide range of individual differences and experimental contexts, and that these complexities would make replication difficult or impossible. As priming researcher Joseph Cesario stated, "absent well-developed theories for specifying such variables, the conclusions of replication failures will be ambiguous" (Cesario 2014, 41, cited in Earp and Trafimow 2015, 3; see also Iso-Ahola 2017).

Cesario was nonetheless sanguine about the absence of such well-developed theories. He suggested that while direct replication was a necessity, critics' expectations that priming effects should be widely invariant were inconsistent with what was known about the nature of the mind and the sensitivity of priming effects to a variety of individual and situational differences. According to him, the complexity of the priming

---

13. On the basis of an overview of replications in psychological research since 1900, Makel, Plucker, and Hegarty (2012) reported that only 1.6 percent of all psychology publications used the term *replication* in the text. A more thorough analysis of five hundred randomly selected articles revealed that only 68 percent of articles using the term *replication* were actual replications, resulting in an overall replication rate of 1.07 percent. The authors also noted that while the majority of the direct and conceptual replications reported in psychology journals were said to be successful, replications were significantly less likely to be successful when there was no overlap in authorship between the original and the replicating articles.

situation and the lack of adequate theories capable of specifying the relevant variables involved had been largely responsible for the uncertainty of priming outcomes. Cesario did not deny the importance of replication efforts in social psychology. But he defended the lack of replication results in priming research on the grounds of the immaturity of the field: if priming theories had been deficient, he argued, this was because the research domain was still young. He therefore concluded that, although the relevant theories had yet to emerge, "with better practice on the part of priming researchers, we will get there" (Cesario 2014, 45).

But others were less optimistic about the theoretical potential of priming research. Even before the crisis, the well-known bounded-rationality and heuristics researcher Gerd Gigerenzer had suggested that, unlike other fields—such as evolutionary biology, genetics, and physics, where the unification of theories has been a valued goal—psychology had always suffered from a theoretical malaise whose main symptom had been a proliferation of theories that were frequently poorly formulated and lacked adequate attempts at integration (Gigerenzer 2010). The shortcomings of theorizing became an important theme in the post-2012 debates over replication (Fiedler 2017; Strack 2017; Szollosi and Donkin 2021; Eronen and Bringmann 2021; Grahek, Schaller, and Tackett 2021; Gervais 2021; Proulx and Morey 2021). For example, Ivan Flis suggested that the "indigenous" epistemology of cognitive psychology, involving a new take on "rationality," had guided attempts to restructure the psychological sciences in the wake of the replication crisis. According to that indigenous epistemology, which had developed in the United States in the post–World War II period, human inferences and thinking didn't conform to the rules of formal logic and probability but operated in a biased way. (As we shall see in the chapters that follow, this picture of biased rationality indeed informed Bargh's priming research from the start.) Flis observed in this regard that, since researchers recognized that they were not immune to bias, the question became how to eliminate bias in the scientists themselves. That was why there were calls for better experimental protocols designed to sequester thinking from bias, as well for institutional structures to enforce those strategies (Flis 2019).

But in Flis's view, even the reformers in psychology were simply too beholden to an old, compromised "logic" of science—a confused blend of hypothetico-deductive models and inductive practices—to offer a genuine way forward. Instead, he argued that they needed to embrace a different, more historical understanding of the nature of psychology as a science of the kind emanating from Kuhn's account of the structure of scientific revolutions—an account that emphasized the contingencies of scientific development. In a somewhat similar spirit, Bradford Wiggins and Cody Christopherson suggested that the reform movement in psychology had implicitly accepted what the authors called "objectivist" epistemologies, which presumed that values and biases were inherently problematic and that "reality is underlain with fundamental universal laws, principles, and truths" that are unchangeable from one situation to the next (Wiggins and Christopherson 2019, 211–12). Reform, Wiggins and Christopherson argued, required very different epistemologies and ontologies of the kind associated with phenomenology, hermeneutics, critical theory, and feminist epistemology. In fact, as we shall see in chapter 2, debates in the 1970s and 1980s about the status of social psychology, driven by the claims of attribution researchers, had already raised pivotal questions about whether social psychology should be treated as a scientific enterprise or whether it was better understood as a historical or ethnographic-hermeneutic undertaking in which the search for causes was replaced by an emphasis on the meaning of social behavior.

"If you want to understand any scientific work properly, you need to know its history"[14]

Whatever one may think of the proposals for improved theorizing made by reformers Flis, Wiggins, Christopherson, and others, from my perspective their principal shortcoming is that they have tended to remain too general to provide much illumination of the stakes involved. Danielle Navarro, a former mathematical-computational cognitive scientist and now a data analyst, has recently co-authored an article criticizing the reformers' reasons for stressing the requirement of the preregistration of experiments designed to test hypotheses as a tool for solving various statistical and other problems (Szollosi et al. 2020). She is skeptical of the emphasis on hypothesis testing on the grounds that most hypotheses are too imprecise to warrant checking. "In almost all cases our measurement instruments are proxies—we are *never* measuring the actual thing we care about, and our models are fantasies," she writes. "It is very rare that our data are tightly linked to the phenomenon of interest and even rarer for the model to bear any strong connection to the theoretical claim we wish

---

14. The title of this section is taken from Navarro 2020.

to assert." In her opinion, there is no point in the preregistration of experiments if hypotheses provide merely the illusion of rigor or, worse, serve to ossify scientific practices (Navarro 2020; see also Scheel et al. 2021).

But Navarro justifies preregistration on other grounds, specifically its importance as a tool for providing "transparency" in the scientific process, especially to colleagues. "If you want to understand any scientific work properly," Navarro argues, "you need to know its history." By this she means the immediate history of the scientist's project, including an account of where the data are coming from, what inferences the experiment was designed to support, what mechanisms were posited, and any other details concerning the paths the scientist pursued in carrying out her work (Navarro 2020). She suggests that preregistration, carried out for this purpose, functions like a kind of "critique," allowing others to understand and possibly question the decisions that the researcher has made.

Navarro is of course a practicing scientist, so she restricts her sense of the historical enterprise to an account of the development and rationale of a single experiment. My intentions in this book are also historical, but I understand history to include the study of several decades of experimental and theoretical work. More precisely, my goal is to supplement the all-important literature on the methodological problems in the psychological sciences by providing a hitherto-missing, critical account of the vicissitudes of priming research from its beginnings in the late 1970s to the replication crisis of 2012 and its aftermath, in an effort to make clear both the experimental and the conceptual-theoretical stakes involved.

Although most researchers grappling with the problems revealed by the replication crisis have raised various methodological and theoretical and criticisms, others have suggested that criticism is misguided. Among the latter camp is psychologist and historian of psychology Jill Morawski, who appears to disagree with the need for critique. She was recently asked about her views concerning the philosophical issues central to the replication crisis, and about how studies in the theory and philosophy of psychology might contribute to their resolution. She replied that, on listening to the "cacophony" of the many voices in the debate, including those of psychologists, journalists, statisticians, and philosophers, it became clear to her that

> the actors' perspectives, psychologists' voices, are crucial to engaging the questions put to me. To proceed otherwise (by either foregrounding outsiders' talk or backgrounding insiders') is to suppose that there is

something critical that the actors are unaware of or about which they are aware yet choose not to address, thereby intimating the workings of subterranean forces or adopting a "hermeneutics of suspicion (Sedgwick, 2002)" [*sic*, 2003]. Above all, listening to the actors is essential to establishing more constructive relationships between researchers directly engaged with the crisis and those studying the philosophy and theory of psychology. (Morawski 2019, 219)

To which she adds:

The present review thus begins with the actors' accounts and then takes an "anti-forensic" purchase . . . that employs science and technology studies (STS) to connect the crisis concerns with knowledge about the structure and practices of science. *The aim is not critique* . . . Like many studying the philosophy and theory of psychology who are situated as insider–outsiders, my aspirations are *reparative*. As described by Simmons (2016), reparative work requires reassembling the problem at hand and undertaking "the essential critical work of thinking with care and anxiety . . . it means staying with and caring for the trouble" . . . Reparation is best begun, then, by close attention to and elucidation of the "symptoms" and exploring their performative effects, not their dysfunctions or hidden drivers (Fleissner, 2009). Commitment to repair and care entails simultaneously practicing skepticism and involvement. (Morawski 2019, 219, my emphasis)[15]

15. It seems that Morawski does not conceptualize the symptom in the psychoanalytic sense as a disguised representation of a hidden or repressed desire, or in the neuropsychiatric sense as a natural sign of an underlying cause. Rather, she cites and appears to rely on the definition suggested by literary critic Jennifer Fleissner (Morawski 2019, 219, citing Fleissner 2009), for whom the symptom is the surface manifestation of desire, which is to say, following Slavoj Zizek's Lacanian interpretation of Freud, the form through which the subject can "organize his enjoyment." This Zizekian-Lacanian understanding of the symptom leads Fleissner to propose that in reading a text symptomatically, "the point is not the symptom's cause . . . the point is the energy invested in it, which in turn generates its elaboration, its effects—on . . . the text as such, and on us as we read" (Fleissner 2009, 390). Fleissner's claim resonates with a post-critique emphasis on the idea that the interpretation of a text or the viewing a work of art involves a relationship between the work and the viewer or reader, a relationship that has the potential to transform both the meaning of the work, independently of the author's or artist's intentions, and the subjective experience of the recipient (see also Felski 2020). It remains unclear what relevance these ideas have for understanding the replication crisis in the psychological sciences.

It is difficult to know what to make of Morawski's remarks. As her references in these passages indicate, her rejection of critique is in part indebted to literary critic Eve Sedgwick's influential attack on critique (Sedgwick 2003), by which term Sedgwick meant the routine way in which, under the impact of Foucault, deconstruction, and related developments, it had become mandatory for critics to read texts symptomatically and suspiciously in order to expose the powerful underlying forces that are held to be the real causes of their meaning.[16] In reaction against what she decried as a fatalistic and paranoid mode of interpretation, Sedgwick promoted the adoption of "reparative reading," a form of reading that, in the words of literary critic Rita Felski, an advocate of Sedgwick's ideas, "looks to a work of art for solace and replenishment rather than viewing it as something to be interrogated and indicted" (Felski 2015, 151). More broadly, Sedgwick's arguments have been taken up and further elaborated by Felski and others in a movement known as "post-critique," in which the aim of interpretation is not to look "behind a text for its hidden cause, determining conditions, and noxious motives," but to appreciate that text's fecundity and pleasures, as well as its status as a "co-actor: as something that makes a difference, that helps makes [sic, make] things happen" (Felski 2015, 12). Thus, the dismissal of critique involves a form of "post-critical" reading that declines to "subject a text to interrogation" (Felski 2015, 173). In a post-critical approach, reading is conceptualized as a "co-production between actors rather than an unraveling of manifest meaning, a form of making rather than unmaking" (Felski 2015, 12).

The idea that such inanimate things as texts or works of art can be considered co-actors or "active mediators" (Felski 2015, 164) that collaborate with readers or viewers to help "shape outcomes and influence actions" (Felski 2015, 164) stems in turn from the work of French sociologist Bruno Latour. He is one of the founders of the "science and technology studies" (STS) movement mentioned by Morawski in the passages cited above. In 2004 Latour influentially suggested that critique had run out of steam and called instead for modes of engagement that did not depend on debunk-

---

16. As her references in these passages show, Morawski is also indebted to a publication by the historian of science and technology, Dana Simmons, who in her history of the concept of the *imposter syndrome* likewise draws on the same work of Sedgwick (2003). Simmons rejects what she calls a hermeneutics of suspicion or a "paranoid" reading of the past, in order to pursue a "reparative history," defined as revolving around the "desire to heal the self through the care of others" (Simmons 2016, 108, 124).

ing (Latour 2004; Fluck 2019). In the course of developing his critique of critique, Latour proposed that objects of all kinds can be treated as actors or "actants" that have the capacity for agency on a par with that of human beings. But the agency Latour attributes to objects is not the agency traditionally associated with consciousness and intention. Rather, agency is conceived as a pre-subjective, prelinguistic "force" that is not specific to humans or even nonhuman animals but can also be attributed to works of art, metals, minerals, microbes, mugs, and so on, defined as anything that "modifies a state of affairs by making a difference" (Felski 2015, 163).

It is not clear how any of these ideas could serve the purpose of understanding the crisis precipitated by the failed replication of Bargh, Chen, and Burrows's famous elderly priming study. Whereas, in the study of literature, the substitution of reparative reading for critique leads to the idea of taking pleasure in novels, there is nothing analogous to this outcome in not criticizing experimenters who get their data wrong.[17] At the very least, we can ask how a "caring" but "skeptical" approach to the replication crisis in psychology of the kind advocated by Morawski could be undertaken without the interpreter (psychologist, philosopher, or historian) making some kinds of critical judgments concerning the issues at stake. Somewhat contradictorily, perhaps, Morawski also recommends a "stepping back" from local scientific undertakings in order to "assess the larger, longer life of psychology's objects. Genealogical methods in particular enable tracing how objects come into being, how they are supported, nourished, travel, used, survive or pass away" (Morawski 2019, 230). In short, she recommends a genealogical approach to psychology—an approach that I contend goes hand in hand with critique. I have adopted exactly such an approach in this book, in an effort to critically assess the vicissitudes of experimental and theoretical work on automaticity and priming in the post–World War II period to the present.

It is worth emphasizing in this connection that I reject the relativism associated with the science and technology studies (STS) invoked by Morawski, a relativism that makes the question of the correctness or

---

17. It would take me too far afield to dismantle the ontological and related claims associated with the arguments of Felski, Latour, and others. But see Posnock 2016; Leys 2012; 2017; Robbins 2017; and Michaels 2022. I should add that my criticisms of the terms in which Morawski (2019) has staged her intervention in the replication crisis are not meant to detract from the great value of many of her observations concerning the role that certain key words, such as *crisis* and *epistemology* (or its synonym, *philosophy of science*), have played in discussions of that replication crisis.

incorrectness of scientific claims irrelevant. Historians of science "do not doubt the distinctive character of science," as Lorraine Daston has put it in her analysis of the reasons why such scholars gave up their initial enthusiasm for science studies (Daston 2009, 807). Just so, I am interested in how that distinctive character of science has been formed, and in the extent to which certain claims do or do not live up to certain standards. In principle, scientific inquiry is aspirational: It aims to verify and to discard what cannot be verified according to consensual methods and practices. Only verified knowledge about rocketry could enable a successful rocket launch, and that knowledge came only after decades of failures of theorizing and hypothesis testing in rocket chemistry, orbital mechanics, and flight dynamics. Theories that led nowhere were discarded. As I have observed, it is an open question whether the psychological sciences have ever lived up to this ideal of scientific practice or have ever achieved the status of a "normal science," in Thomas Kuhn's influential sense of the term.

More generally, in contrast to many kinds of causal history, my approach as an intellectual historian trained in the history of science focuses on the genealogy of hypotheses and experimental protocols per se, and not as offshoots of the wider historical landscape. Of course, the larger historical context matters. Questions concerning the institutional structures that support scientific methods are important, as are no doubt questions concerning events in the lives of individual researchers that push them in one direction or another. To take an example, pre–World War II physicists were riven by contrasting views about whether electrons were particles or waves. Claims were made and tested experimentally, and a shaky resolution, quantum theory, emerged from the battles. It is certainly interesting to consider whether the "particle" and "wave" partisans were influenced by their own cosmological and metaphysical intuitions, and, in some cases, religious and cultural backgrounds, or whether their views were related to general societal forces and trends. But the heart of the battle concerned the claims, hypotheses, and experiments. In this book I focus on the specifics of the history of priming research—how psychologists structured their experiments, interpreted their data, and defended (or failed to defend) their work against critics—in the belief that such an approach provides a more granular view of the research assumptions and practices involved.

But it is not just my concern for the specifics of conceptualization and of laboratory methods alone that characterizes my approach. What I also aim to show is that researchers' theoretical assumptions and experimental methods cannot be separated from each other: those assumptions inform how scientists proceed in the laboratory every step of the way, even if often they don't admit or recognize this fact. (One reason they don't is that career incentives are designed to advance empirical projects rather than to examine the conceptual underpinnings of those projects.) The entanglement between theory and laboratory practice makes it nearly impossible to separate conceptual assumptions from empirical claims in the work of Bargh and his contemporaries, which makes it imperative for the historian to study both the assumptions and the empirical claims. As a first step, in the next section I list some of the basic presuppositions that have informed experiments in the field of priming. The inventory is not meant to be comprehensive, but it will allow me to identify the issues I regard as among the most significant if we are to understand the shape and trajectory of Bargh's experimental and theoretical enterprise.

Basic Assumptions

One could characterize Bargh's priming project as having been motivated by a general desire to undermine the tendency of psychologists and laypeople alike to assume that our actions and responses to the world are necessarily under our conscious, intentional control. As he stated in his reflections on the premises of cognitive science that governed his research project: "In the attempt to address the ways in which the mind worked in conjunction with the environment, cognitive science did not need to invoke concepts such as consciousness, intention, or free will" (Bargh and Ferguson 2000, 928).

In addition to the intrinsic interest and field-specific importance of Bargh's work on priming and automaticity, Bargh is "good to think with," or should I say—anticipating my arguments in this book—against. That is, his assumptions and claims exemplify dominant trends in American psychology during recent decades, and the questions raised by his research throw light not only on problems intrinsic to his field but also on larger philosophical topics concerning the mind, especially the nature of human agency in an age increasingly seen as pervaded by automaticity. In that sense the intellectual focus of this book is only instrumentally on the work of Bargh and his colleagues (and critics): what I hope to show is that the debates over priming illuminate a nested set of issues that remain fundamental in present-day psychology.

1. One of the most central assumptions guiding much of post–World

War II research on the mind was that automatic actions, or what used to be called *habits*, could be contrasted with intentional actions, or what used to be called *actions of the will*. The idea was that automatic actions competed with intentional ones, because some responses were so strongly associated with particular stimuli that they could be triggered by them even in opposition to the subject's conscious will or intentions. Many dual-process or dual-systems theories of cognition of the kind proposed by Kahneman thus differentiated between two discrete systems, one of which subserved nonconscious and automatic actions, and the other of which governed conscious and controlled actions. On the basis of such assumptions, automaticity came to be viewed as an independent domain of research.

But the trouble with the distinction between automatic and intentional actions was that it could not be sustained: it was apparent to at least some investigators that the two forms of action did not refer to alternative modes of control but were so intertwined as to be indissociable. As researchers put it, the two processes were on a continuum. From this perspective, intentional and automatic behaviors were not in conflict with each other and attempts to provide clear-cut criteria to distinguish them were bound to fail. Indeed, as I will show throughout this book, it turned out that automaticity was so imbricated in intentional action that their dissociation from each other was impossible to maintain. Moreover, the recognition of this point weakened the notion of automaticity itself, because it became evident to some researchers that properties such as people's consciousness or unconsciousness of stimuli, or the extent of their influence over their behaviors, were not categorical but matters of degree (Hommel 2019).

At the start of his career, Bargh accepted the fact that most of the actions widely considered to be automatic in priming research, such as the learned skills of typing, driving, and playing the piano, were intentional and controllable, even if with practice and routinization they often appeared to occur without deliberation or the individual's conscious attention.[18] But over time, and especially after he had entered what he called his "feisty" period in the late 1990s, when he pursued the idea of the pervasiveness of automaticity in everyday life, Bargh tended to contrast automatic processes with intentional agency, as if the kinds of automatic actions of

---

18. Reflexes have been taken as prototypical automatic actions, but the question at stake in most discussions of automaticity concerns intentional actions that have become routinized or automatic through practice and habit.

most concern to him implied the absence of all conscious control. Or perhaps it would be more accurate to say that throughout his career, Bargh wavered between adopting a continuum or "gradual" approach to automaticity versus espousing a dual-system approach, with all the confusions that this wavering entailed.

One legacy of the dual-system approach was the effort to ascertain the features by which automatic processes could be distinguished. Bargh contributed to that effort, calling those features the "four horsemen of automaticity" and identifying them as: (1) *the absence of consciousness*; (2) *the lack of intentionality*; (3) *the lack of control*; and (4) *the presence of "efficiency"* (by which he meant that automatic processes tended to be insensitive to context: they went to completion without further conscious guidance or input and, in contrast to intentional processes, used minimal cognitive capacity). Although Bargh did not think these features necessarily co-occurred or formed a unity, his features approach nevertheless tended to strengthen the idea that automaticity constituted a research category in its own right, with properties that distinguished it from conscious, intentional actions.

2. The decisive influence in the development of Bargh's ideas about automaticity was the rise of cognitive science, with its assumption that mental functions could be explained in cybernetic-computational terms. In the years after the Second World War, American psychologists were looking for ways to bring the mind and purpose back into psychology, from which behaviorism had banished it. Cybernetics was attractive in this context because it suggested that intentionality could be theorized, in effect recast, in strictly mechanical terms (Edwards 1996, esp. chapter 7; Shanker 1998; Crowther-Heyck 1999; Mindell 2002). In their widely read book *Plans and the Structure of Behavior* (1960), George Miller, Eugene Galanter and Karl Pribram claimed that the cybernetic hypothesis, or feedback loop, was the fundamental building block of the nervous system and human behavior (Miller, Galanter and Pribram 1960). At the center of their approach was the idea that the mind was made up of mental representations—variously called "plans," "programs," "models," or "schemas"—that functioned as hierarchically organized information-processing systems. "The notion of a Plan that guides behavior is," Miller, Galanter, and Pribram wrote, "... quite similar to the notion of a program that guides an electronic computer" (Miller, Galanter and Pribram 1960, 2). According to this cybernetic picture, mental representations of various kinds mediated between the environmental stimulus and the organism's actions or behavior, and

positive or negative feedback regulated the human "servomechanism" in the same way that an automatic thermostat controlled the temperature of a room. As Hunter Crowther-Heyck has put it, "purpose was reintroduced, not in rats or men, but in machines" (Crowther-Heyck 1999, 50).

Ulric Neisser consolidated the cybernetic approach to mental states in his "manifesto" of the cognitive revolution, *Cognitive Psychology* (Neisser 1967). But although Neisser depicted the majority of cognitive functions in information-processing terms, he excluded from his analysis the "executive" operations associated with the higher mental functions, such as intentional-purposive processes themselves, which were depicted as a kind of "black box" of functions that the computational system could not yet accommodate or explain. Over time, however, Bargh interpreted Neisser's work to mean that the scope of the "executive" could be reduced by attributing all, or almost all, its functions to automatic systems. As he observed:

> For Neisser, as for the cognitive scientists who followed him . . . one important goal of cognitive science was to shrink the size of the black box of executive control processes by discovering ever more internal mechanisms. The social-cognitive research on the automaticity of higher order processes . . . represents one attempt to shrink this black box. It has reopened the behaviorists' hypothesis that the higher order responses of human beings can be directly put in motion by environmental stimuli. However, unlike the behaviorist approach, it makes full use of internal psychological processes as explanatory mechanisms in testing this hypothesis. (Bargh and Ferguson 2000, 928)

In the course of this attempt at shrinkage, the contents of the black box of executive control were dispersed into subsystems of various kinds. On this model, many situational influences bypassed the consciousness "bottle-neck," thereby eliminating the need for an agentic self in the selection of behavioral responses. Eventually, Bargh suggested that all human actions and behaviors could be treated as if they occurred "*without the direct participation of man*'" (Bargh and Ferguson 2000, 932; their emphasis, citing Aizerman 1963, 1), with the result that an individual's sense of agency came to be viewed as an illusion (Wegner and Bargh 1997; Wegner 2002). A related outcome of these developments was that Bargh and his colleagues reinforced tendencies to "situationism" in American psychology, as represented by Stanley Milgram's notorious "obedience" studies

(Milgram 1974), according to which actions and behaviors reflect the triggering, automatic effect of the situation or external cues much more than they reflect a person's good or bad "character."

There has recently been a renewed historical and philosophical engagement with the complex role of cybernetics in creating modern, automated systems of governance, regulation, and control, or what Stiegler calls the "automatic society" (Stiegler 2016). From my perspective, of special interest in this wide-ranging literature are those works that focus on the concerns of thinkers such as Hannah Arendt with the human capacity for decision-making, spontaneity, and political freedom in a post–World War II period that saw the potential and threat of emerging global, automated systems. The apprehensions of such thinkers can be seen to parallel those of the critics in psychology and philosophy discussed in this book, who opposed the claims of Bargh and other priming researchers concerning the pervasiveness of automaticity in everyday life by emphasizing the importance of intentionality and agency in human behavior.[19] A related background context to the developments I analyze is the emergence by the 1970s of what Hunter Heyck (2015) has called a mainstream "high modern social science" or "bureaucratic worldview" in the human sciences, such as anthropology, economics, political science, and sociology, all of which reconceptualized their central object of study as "a nested set of complex, hierarchic systems (a treelike structure), with the most interesting systems having the additional characteristic of being adaptive—that is, of being environmentally sensitive" (Heyck 2015, 21). As Heyck makes clear, the cognitive sciences, which decisively shaped Bargh's approach to automaticity, belonged to this development.

3. Bargh's views about the non-intentionality of automatic actions had several consequences. In particular, he frequently suggested that when people focus conscious attention on their own habitual actions, they inevitably lose control of them. He therefore made it difficult to see how skilled performers, such as athletes or musicians, can successfully adjust their habitual actions from moment to moment by paying attention to them—as, of course, they routinely do.

An important debate begun in 2005 between the philosophers Hubert

---

19. In the large recent literature on the history and meaning of the cybernetic movement I am indebted especially to Bates (2015, 2020); Carr (2020); Geroulanos and Weatherby (2020); Guilhot (2011, 2020); Kline (2015, 2020); Mindell (2002); Rid (2016); Rindzevičiūtė (2016); and Stiegler (2016).

Dreyfus and John McDowell focused precisely on the issue of the intentional character of skilled coping. In his influential book *Mind and World* (1994a) and in numerous other publications, McDowell rejected a "bald" or restricted naturalism that, he argued, had marginalized the intact person with his or her intentions and meanings and had raised intractable questions about how concepts could be added to a raw "given" of nonconceptual mental contents and processes. In place of such a bald or restricted naturalism, McDowell defended the idea of a "liberal" naturalism that took in its stride the idea that types of mindedness, such as intentional mental states, were part of the natural world and not alien or external to it, as post-Cartesian forms of naturalism, such as modern cognitive psychology, assumed. For McDowell, accordingly, the mind in the form of concepts and intentions was pervasive in human action, including in the performance of habits and practical skills (McDowell 1994a).

However, in his 2005 presidential address to the American Philosophical Association, Dreyfus accused McDowell of overestimating the influence of mindedness on our ordinary actions, arguing that skilled actions of the kind we perform in our everyday copings are non-intentional and as such nonconceptual (Dreyfus 2005, 2007a, 2007b, 2013).[20] The disagreement between Dreyfus and McDowell had important implications for understanding the nature of human agency. If learned skills—the principal actions studied in priming experiments—are intentional in origin and character, as McDowell argued (McDowell 2007a, 2007b, 2013), they are meaningful to the individual and as such are capable of being explained rationally, which is to say, by reasons. From this perspective, the copings of the kind that occur when agents are immersed in their habits and skills might be unreflective, in the sense that in the moment they do not depend on deliberate thinking, yet they are enacted for a reason. Thus, according to McDowell, the chess master's absorption in a game does not preclude her from knowing what she is up to or prevent her from giving reasons for making the moves that she does (Schear 2013). (Unconscious intentions form a special case, because, owing to some form of psychological dysfunction, or a neurological "ownership" syndrome such as "Alien-hand syndrome," or a mechanism like repression, an agent may fail to understand her reasons for acting unless some therapeutic treatment brings

---

20. On the other hand, Dreyfus does not deny that we are responsible for the performance of our skills even as he argues that the "ego" or self is not involved in absorbed coping (Dreyfus 2007b, 374).

those reasons into conscious awareness, thereby allowing her to take possession of them as her reasons for behaving in the way she has done.)

But if, as Dreyfus as well as Bargh argued, learned skills are direct bodily responses to stimuli and the affordances of the situation and as such don't require intentions or concepts, they must occur outside the domain of reason and rationality. As Dreyfus maintained: "One can easily accept that in *learning* to be wise we learn to follow general reasons as guides to acting appropriately. But it does not follow that, once we have gotten past the learning phase, these *reasons* in the form of habits still *influence* our wise actions" (Dreyfus 2005, 51; his emphasis). Or, as he also observed: "Mindedness is the enemy of embodied coping" (Dreyfus 2007a, 353). One of the questions Dreyfus's picture of automatic actions raised, therefore, was how the contents of nonconceptual automatic behaviors could be converted into intentional-conceptual contents. It was not obvious that authors adopting Dreyfus's position had the philosophical resources needed to explain how this transformation might be achieved. As Dreyfus himself acknowledged: "Phenomenologists lack a detailed and convincing account of how rationality and language grow out of nonconceptual and nonlinguistic coping" (Dreyfus 2005, 61).

Undeterred by such considerations, Bargh extended his ideas about automaticity to the topic of imitation, which became a major research interest, as it did for his student Tanya Chartrand. But we shall see that Bargh's and Chartrand's insistence on the non-intentional, automatic nature of mimicry turned out to be unsustainable in the face of evidence demonstrating that imitation was highly sensitive to contextual cues in ways suggesting that it was in fact an intentional-strategic-communicative action.

4. Another important aspect of these developments was that cognitive psychologists treated intention as a mental process or state that was distinct from the physical act that followed it, as if these were two discrete happenings or processes. Priming researchers occasionally recognized that there was no consensus over how intentionality ought to be conceptualized, thereby preventing a clear discussion of the critical issues (Ferguson and Mann 2014, 35; see also my appendix). But they agreed generally, as did cognitive scientists more broadly, that intentions were private, internal mental "representations," "plans," or "programs," that were separated by a gap from the publicly observable motor behaviors and movements to which they were connected; that gap was held to be closed by the causal relationships obtaining between these two processes or happenings. Miller, Galanter, and Pribram (1960) provided an early,

influential statement of this idea. "What does it mean when an ordinary man has an ordinary intention?" they asked, and answered: "It means that he has begun the execution of a Plan and that his intended action is a part of it . . . The term is used to refer to the *uncompleted parts of a Plan whose execution has already begun*" (Miller, Galanter, and Pribram 1960, 61; their emphasis). For these and most cognitive psychologists, intentions were thus internal "plans" or mental states that were causally realized by the publicly observable movements which followed. In short, intentional actions were a "compound of metaphysically independent inner psychical and outer material elements joined by a generic bond of causality" (Lavin 2015, 609). The task of cognitive science, accordingly, was to discover the psychological mechanisms and processes that "translate intentions into actions" (Gollwitzer 1993, 142).

But the philosopher Elizabeth Anscombe, recognized today by many philosophers of mind as *the* outstanding post–World War II philosopher of intentionality, argued that intention and action could not be separated into distinct components in this way (Anscombe 2000 [1957]; Hornsby 2011). She regarded it as a mistake to view intentions as private mental states existing prior to, or alongside, publicly observable physical actions. For her, intentions are intrinsic to action, which is to say that they are not distinct from the actions in which they inhere. Her position on this point led her to emphasize that intentional actions are "the ones to which the question 'Why' is given application" (Anscombe 2000 [1957], 24), by which she meant that they are actions for which people's reasons for acting are a relevant focus of interest.[21] In brief, for Anscombe the relationship between intention and action is not causal in the Humean-empirical sense of that term, nor psychological, but conceptual and logical. I will have more to say about these issues in chapter 2.

Like other cognitive psychologists, however, Bargh depicted intentions as private, internal mental states or representations in the mind-brain that are separated by a gap from the relevant motor representations and

---

21. Lisa Siraganian usefully glosses Anscombe's thought here by observing: "Intentional actions, then, are the ones to which the question 'Why' is given application, not in the sense of the answer providing evidence or stating a cause, but of an answer that mentions past history, interprets the action, or implies something about the future" (2020, 48). I note that although Anscombe defined intention in terms of human language—that is, in terms of the question "Why?"—she nevertheless argued that there was no difficulty in ascribing intentions to nonhuman animals by introducing the notion of "intention-dependent" concepts for that purpose (see Wiseman 2016, 156).

behaviors. As he put it: "Conscious intention and behavioral (motor) systems are fundamentally dissociated in the brain" (Bargh, 2005, 43). Social psychologist Peter Gollwitzer, a co-author of various papers with Bargh, likewise stated that the aim of much of his own work was to "scrutinize the processes which translate intentions into action" by determining the different "consecutive action phases" that realize the goals of intentions (Gollwitzer 1993, 142, 149).

However, it is important to emphasize that over time, Bargh came to argue that many or even most of our goals can be directly activated by the perception of external stimuli without involving intentions of any kind. "In my opinion, there are many cases in which goal-directed behavior is *not* intentional or desired," Bargh wrote. "To be intentional and to be goal directed are two separate things, and it is better to leave them as two separate concepts than to obfuscate the true state of affairs by assuming they are isomorphic" (Bargh1990b, 249, 250; his emphasis). Bargh eventually multiplied the number of possible goal representations or constructs that could be directly activated by the environment to the point that he conceptualized the mind as an assemblage of many such representations, each of which was understood to operate unintentionally yet "selfishly" in its own interests, sometimes to the disadvantage of the individual's conscious, intentional goals (Huang and Bargh 2014).

It also needs stressing that there was a fundamental ambiguity about the meaning attached to the notion of *goals* in cognitive psychology throughout this period. In ordinary language, the terms *goals* and *goal pursuit* are commonly used to refer to people's intentions to achieve some meaningful end. But when the concepts of goals and goal pursuit were translated into the language of information processing, they referred to computational events that lacked meaning and intentionality—as Shannon made clear when he gave his well-known definition of the cybernetic concept of *information*.[22] Psychologists tended to gloss over the difference between

---

22. Shannon's cybernetic theory of information has nothing to do with meaning in the ordinary, everyday sense of that term. It is a non-semantic, mathematical theory of the capacity of communication channels to transmit data. A bit (binary digit) of information tells the receiver which of two equally probable alternatives has been selected (Dreyfus 1979, 165). As Shannon observed, the semantic aspects of communication "are irrelevant to the engineering problem" (Shannon 1948, 379). N. Kathleen Hayles has recently urged the importance of the notion of the "Cognitive Nonconscious," claiming that although computer programs understand nothing about semantic content, they nevertheless possess the capacity for cognition, interpretation, and choice and are capable of making meaning (Hayles 2017). Siraganian has recently placed Hayles's views in the context of

the pursuit of goals in the information-processing sense and the pursuit of goals in the ordinary, everyday sense of the term *intentional*. Thus, at one moment they presented their findings about the automatic pursuit of goals within the framework of the concepts of information processing and even suggested that the pursuit of goals could occur independently of intentionality. But at another moment the same investigators implicitly relied on the everyday meaning of the concepts of goals and goal pursuits to suggest that such actions were performed intentionally. It is necessary for the historian to be alert to these slippages when evaluating claims about the nature of automaticity.

Furthermore, although at first Bargh regarded habitual automatic actions as inflexible, over time he began to suggest that they were capable of functioning flexibly and strategically because they appeared to be sensitive to context. Automatic processes were generally treated as actions that, once triggered, rigidly progressed to completion. But Bargh's experiments seemed to show that certain effects of priming were more plastic and variable than he had first recognized. The question of how to handle the context sensitivity of automatic actions within the non-intentional terms proposed by Bargh became an increasing focus of concern. We will see that it was difficult for him and like-minded researchers to come up with successful solutions to that problem.

5. One of Bargh's favorite examples of the non-intentionality of automatic actions was what happens when people make slips of the tongue and similar errors, errors that he regarded as unintended behaviors triggered directly by the environment. As a case in point, Bargh cited William James's story of the man who was sent upstairs to his bedroom by his wife to change for dinner but instead got into his pajamas and went to sleep (Bargh 1990b, 250; James 1950 [1890], vol. 1, 115). In the postwar years, Bargh and many other researchers treated such action slips as automatic behaviors that occurred when an original intention was sidetracked, as when a mother followed the route she usually followed to pick up a child at school, when in fact she intended to drive to the mall. Instead of con-

---

legal scholars' attempt to use literary-theoretical arguments to support the claim that computer-generated speech is meaningful language that ought to be protected by the First Amendment, arguments Siraganian convincingly rebuts on the grounds that these authors misunderstand the nature of language and intention (2021). For an illuminating discussion of the relationship between large language models (LLMs or chatbots), meaning, and intentionality, see Kirschenbaum et al. 2023, especially the contributions of Knapp and Michaels, and Siraganian.

sidering such slips as the result of a conflict between two competing intentions (one of which might be below the threshold of awareness), Bargh and most cognitive psychologists treated the resulting actions as unintentional (Norman 1981; Reason 1984; Motley 1985; Monsell 1996). As Bargh observed: "These are unintended acts that occur when the presence of environmental cues relevant for a habitual action 'capture' one's behavior even though the habitual action is inappropriate this particular time" (Bargh 1990b, 249–50). We shall see that he came to regard pathological cases of the kind described by the clinician Lhermitte (1986), in which patients with frontal-lobe lesions uncontrollably and automatically reacted to various stimuli in their environment, as providing important insights into the dissociation between intentional and automatic actions, to the point of suggesting that people's daily lives were lived in a state of more or less complete automatism.

6. Bargh's ideas about the non-intentionality of behaviors such as "action slips" led him to systematically misrepresent Sigmund Freud's concept of the *unconscious*. According to Freud, slips of the tongue and other "parapraxes" are not accidental events but are intentional actions, albeit unconscious intentional ones. But Bargh misunderstood Freud on this point, erroneously stating that "the traditional definition of the *unconscious*, as used by . . . Freud, was in terms of unintentional processes" (Bargh 2011, 636; his emphasis; see also Hassin, Uleman, and Bargh 2005; Bargh and Morsella 2008, 74).[23] Because of his commitment to the tenets of cognitive science, Bargh's notion of the unconscious was also radically different from Freud's. Freud's unconscious was a dynamic psychic state in which repressed contents were constantly seeking expression, as manifested in neurotic symptoms, dreams, parapraxes, and related phenomena. Bargh's "new" or "cognitive" unconscious (Bargh 2005)—and that of the cognitive sciences more generally—was a smoothly running, efficient, and adaptive entity, or set of entities, held to be capable of carrying out much or indeed most of our thinking for us, with little or no input from consciousness (Shevrin and Dickman 1980; Kihlstrom 1987;

---

23. Similarly, Bargh stated that "nearly all the examples given in [Freud's] *The Psychopathology of Everyday Life* involve unintended behavior, the source or cause of which was unknown to the individual . . . And this equation of *unconscious* with *unintentional* is how unconscious phenomena have been conceptualized and studied within social psychology for the past quarter century or so" (Bargh and Morsella 2008, 74; their emphasis).

Wilson 2002, 7).[24] One way of expressing the differences between these two conceptions is to say that for Freud the unconscious was an *interpsychic* mental state that originated in and was constituted by the infant's conflicted relationship, at once identificatory and erotic, with significant others, especially its parents or caretakers. From the start, the Freudian unconscious was thus inherently interpersonal or social. By contrast, the cognitive unconscious was understood by Bargh and his peers as an *intrapsychic* mental state involving information processes located inside the individual mind-brain. We shall see in chapter 5 and elsewhere in this book that one of the complaints voiced by critics was that Bargh and colleagues reinterpreted in individualistic-cognitivist terms evidence demonstrating the interpersonal-communicative nature of automatic behavior, such as motor mimicry, and thereby missed its social-situational character.[25] Furthermore, Freud claimed that the repressed unconscious could be brought into consciousness in the "talking cure," whereas Bargh and the cognitivists tended to assume that once actions had become automatic through practice, they became non-intentional and inaccessible to consciousness (Wilson 2002, 23).

7. Even before Doyen et al. (2012) raised the possibility that experimenter' expectations and participant compliance to those expectations might have influenced the outcome of Bargh, Chen, and Burrows's (1996) famous elderly priming experiment, Bargh himself had noted the similarity between the effects of priming and of hypnotic suggestion. Post–World War II debates over the nature of hypnosis had pitted social psychological or "role-playing" theorists, who had emphasized the intentionality of the hypnotized subject's actions, against "special-state" or "dissociation" theorists, who had stressed the non-intentional and involuntary nature of the behaviors of subjects in the trance state. By endorsing a recent version of "special-state" theory, Bargh implied that the behavioral effects

---

24. Although the particular vision of the unconscious in current theories of the "cognitive unconscious" originated in the approaches to computing in the middle of the twentieth century, this story belongs to a far longer history of theories of mental automaticity going back to at least the seventeenth century, as noted by Bates (2015).

25. For detailed analyses of the identificatory-disidentifactory, or mimetic-antimimetic, constitution of the Freudian unconscious, see Leys 2000 and Borch-Jacobsen 1988. For an interesting discussion of the methodological, empirical, and rhetorical practices and strategies by which the work of the "social" has been rendered implicit and therefore largely invisible in the development of the implicit (or unconscious) social-cognition paradigm, see Steele and Morawski 2002.

seen in his experiments, such as the slow walking pace of participants in his iconic elderly priming experiment, had nothing to do with the participants' compliance with the experimenter's suggestive influence, as Doyen et al. (2012) seemed to suggest, but were the result of genuine alterations in the participants' mental state caused by the direct influence of the priming words.

Not that Bargh's views about the similarity between the effects of hypnosis and of priming, understood as causally induced mental states, were successful in staving off worries about the role of expectancy effects in his elderly priming study. Rather, it's as if, at the center of the 2012 replication crisis in psychology, the validity of cognitive science's attempt to eliminate the role of the person—by treating his or her actions as the product of direct causal links between perception and behavior—was called into question. In other words, when reports emerged that Bargh's iconic elderly priming study could not be replicated, it began to seem that it was precisely his effort to get rid of the influence of the person (with his or her beliefs, intentions, expectations, and desires) in his account of human behavior that might be at fault. In short, it began to seem that such influences were inherent in social interaction and were therefore ineliminable.[26] The implication was that psychologists such as Bargh had been deluding themselves all along in thinking that role of the person could be expelled from the experimental situation and from the science of cognition.

8. Over time Bargh began to argue that non-intentional, automatic behaviors are so pervasive in everyday life that human consciousness serves little or no purpose. The question then posed was: If humans are essentially automatons, what is the function of consciousness? The answer for Bargh was that consciousness had evolved in humans in order to provide them with rationalizations for actions for which they could not be held responsible—because those actions were the unconscious, unintended outcome of the direct link between the perception of stimuli and the resulting behavior. Bargh therefore continued an influential line of argument by cognitive psychologists that the mind was powerless to actually intend or control human actions, because those actions were determined

---

26. Martin Orne, who in the 1950s along with Rosenthal first made the issue of experimenter expectancy and demand characteristics a central concern in experiments in psychology, observed that in spite of all attempts to reduce experimenter bias by eliminating the role of the experimenter altogether and using only mechanical procedures, demand characteristics would still be present: "Subjects will always be in a position to form hypotheses about the purpose of an experiment" (Orne 2009, 114).

by unconscious, automatic operations. Accordingly, the reasons people gave for their actions were concocted after the fact, just as subjects later attempted to rationalize the bizarre, automatic behaviors they had performed when in a trance state by fabricating explanations for them.

Bargh's further proposal was that by offering such rationalizations, people were able to put a positive spin on the actions they had "accidentally" performed but did not intend, thereby making their behaviors acceptable to the social group. In short, consciousness served a kind of public-relations function and nothing more. His argument was consistent with the cognitive-science presuppositions that had informed his research all along, and the fact that such an impoverished account of the role of consciousness could find a ready audience within psychology testifies to how entrenched those presuppositions had become.

9. At first sight a certain skepticism would seem to be justified when hearing the claim that briefly exposing people in a laboratory to a few words often used to describe the elderly, or to images of the flag of the Unites States, will automatically and unconsciously cause those people to walk more slowly, or increase conservatism among American participants. It hardly seems possible that these simple techniques could be a stand-in for the real world, where we would go mad if we had to react to every single one of the myriad influences and stimuli that buffet us each day. Indeed, as we shall see, there were critics in the research community who opposed claims for the kind of direct unconscious influence posited by priming experts. Their skepticism received support from the fact that, during the replication crisis, it emerged that many outcomes of psychology experiments were false positives and that priming results were especially difficult to reproduce.

But one could argue differently. One could adopt the position that unconscious influence is real but that explaining its effects would take more than Bargh's notion of automatic relationships between fleeting stimuli and behavioral responses. A satisfactory explanation might require a different, more complex picture of the mind, perhaps one similar to the depth psychology of the kind Freud posited (as well as a more complex picture of the situational contexts in which people found themselves). In this connection, in support of the view that unconscious influence is real, one could cite the widely accepted and routinely demonstrated fact that experimenter expectations can unconsciously shape the behavior of experimental subjects in ways that are difficult to explain or control—hence the need for double-blind experimental procedures. Accordingly, for this and other reasons, I will proceed on the assumption that unconscious influence is a genuine phenomenon. The question I raise in this book is whether the theories proposed by Bargh and his colleagues and the experiments they performed were adequate to the topic.

Outline of the Book

I have divided my book into eight chapters and a conclusion (plus a brief appendix). I note that this book is an intellectual history of research on priming and automaticity. The work I examine took place against the backdrop of numerous social, political, and economic developments in America that lie outside the scope of my analysis. One development, though, is so germane to my project that it deserves a brief mention here. As I briefly noted earlier, Bargh began his priming research at the moment when the hegemony of Cold War views of rationality—stretching from 1945 to the 1970s—came to a close. The Cold War ideal was of a formal, algorithmic, rule-following, universal kind of rationality, modeled on computation and abstracted from persons, history, and context, that promised to provide optimal solutions to human problems (Erickson et al. 2013). But that ideal was challenged in the late 1970s and early 1980s by social psychologists and heuristics-and-bias researchers who argued that human judgment and decision-making were often biased and human behaviors highly irrational. The "collapse of Cold War Rationality" (Erickson et al. 2013, 159) set the stage for Bargh's work on the role of automaticity in everyday life. Nevertheless, the formal-computational premises of that ideal of rationality remained intact in ways that from the start were decisive in determining how the concept of automaticity should be formulated and understood.

In chapter 1, I discuss the history of attribution research in social psychology in the years after World War II. The aim of attribution research was to undertake experiments designed to reveal how individuals identified the causes of the behavior of others and of their own actions, a process that was conceptualized as one of making "inferences" about the relative contributions of the agent and of the situation to which the agent was responding. Attribution research formed the backbone of Bargh's theory of automaticity, and the concepts and research strategies developed by attribution researchers set the stage for Bargh's claims regarding the causal impact of automatic processes in human judgment and behavior.

In the course of this chapter, I pay special attention to Richard Nisbett and Timothy Wilson's influential paper, "Telling More Than We Can

Know" (Nisbett and Wilson 1977), in which the authors claimed that, when attempting to judge the cause of some action or event, subjects were often unaware of the existence of a stimulus, or of their responses to it, or of how the stimulus had influenced their reactions. In Nisbett and Wilson's view, this lack of awareness stemmed from subjects' lack of access to the unconscious, sub-personal information-processing events that actually determined their judgments, attributions, and actions. The result was that, when asked to report on their own perceptions and cognitions, they based their introspections on invented or implicit theories about the extent to which a particular stimulus plausibly explained a given response. In effect, Nisbett and Wilson claimed that people were bound to make up reasons for their attributions and judgments after the fact because of the opacity of their cognitive systems to self-knowledge. They therefore called into question the status of individuals as intentional creatures capable of accurately identifying the reasons for their own intentions or for their judgments of others.

It is almost impossible to overstate the significance of Nisbett and Wilson's paper on the development of American social psychology. Their article of 1977 represented a crucial moment when social psychology was tempted to repudiate explanations of human action based on intentional considerations and instead made causal-mechanical information-processing explanations the norm for all aspects of human cognition. Thereafter, the logic of cognitive psychology appeared to require a completely mechanistic account of mindedness. This development did not occur without debate. Indeed, it was in the context of attribution research, and especially of Nisbett and Wilson's article, that the issue of intentional versus causal approaches to mindedness and action was largely fought out, with enormous consequences for priming research and theories of automaticity.

In chapter 2, I focus on that debate. On one side of the controversy were researchers who questioned the value of intentional explanations and emphasized instead the need for a causal science of human action and behavior. On the other side were psychologists and others who accused cognitive scientists such as Nisbett and Wilson of failing to recognize the significance of the distinction between reasons and causes. In effect, such critics accused attribution theorists of reducing a person's normative evaluations and judgments, with whose truth other people might agree or disagree, to the status of causally produced reactions that it made no sense to regard as either correct or incorrect. At the heart of the controversy was thus the question of the nature of intentional explanation itself, as several of the participants recognized when they invoked the work of Ludwig Wittgenstein, Anscombe, and other philosophers on that topic. The overarching issue was how or whether the social sciences could be properly scientific if issues of intentionality and meaning were to be given a fundamental place in the enterprise. Not surprisingly, the two sides could not come to any agreement, with the result that the conflict ended in an impasse.

In chapter 3, I turn to Bargh's work on automaticity in order to trace the development of his approach from its beginnings in the early 1980s up to 1997, when he radicalized his views by arguing that automaticity was pervasive in all social interactions. My aim is to provide the reader with a sense of the stakes involved as Bargh started to elaborate his ideas about the nature of automatic action. The story concerns the steps by which he began to reduce the scope of the executive or higher cognitive functions by theorizing more and more of them in information-processing terms, thereby expanding the role of automaticity in everyday life. In the course of this chapter, I discuss graded versus category approaches to automaticity; Bargh's auto-motive model of automaticity; Prinz's related ideomotor theory; Bargh's dissociation between goal pursuits and intentions; and the details of Bargh, Chen, and Burrows's famous elderly priming experiment of 1996.

In chapter 4, I describe the further development of Bargh's work on automaticity during his "feisty" period when, starting in 1997, he argued, with some incoherence and even contradiction, that automaticity was a pervasive feature of everyday life. Among the topics I discuss are the role of attention and control in automatic behavior; the nature of skilled action; Bargh's ideas about the role of "moderators" in automatic behaviors; and his emerging recognition of the flexibility of automatic actions.

Chapter 5 is devoted to the work of Bargh and his former student Tanya Chartrand on mimicry. Their findings on this topic appeared to confirm the validity of Bargh's theory of automaticity, according to which people's imitations were the product of a direct link between perception and behavior. Accordingly, Bargh and Chartrand interpreted imitation as a process that occurred blindly, as it were, because the imitator copied the model unconsciously and automatically, without intending to do so. Bargh and Chartrand's interpretation directly contradicted the claims of the psychologist Janet Bavelas and her colleagues, who had proposed that mimicry was a form of intentional-strategic communication between the imitator and the model. The focus of this chapter is therefore on the conflict between these competing views of imitation. In particular I will show that Bargh and Chartrand continually misunderstood and misrepresented Bavelas's findings. I will also demonstrate the ways in which Chartrand eventually modified her views in light of Bavelas's work and of the accumulating evidence that made her and Bargh's original position unsustainable. I end with a discussion of recent studies of emotional mimicry that, not without confusion, have emphasized the contextual sensitivity of facial displays in ways that call into question the validity of Chartrand's and Bargh's claims about the automaticity of imitation.

In chapter 6, I focus on the events leading up to the crisis precipitated by Doyen et al.'s paper of 2012 which announced a failure to replicate Bargh, Chen, and Burrows's iconic elderly priming study. Even before 2012, various developments in the field of automaticity research had begun to shine a critical spotlight on Bargh's claims for a direct perception-behavior connection. These developments included the emergence of: (a) "Unconscious Thought Theory," which suggested that much thinking was best left to unconscious processes and which occasioned a strenuous debate over the validity of such claims; (b) concerns about the "one-to-many problem" in priming research, by which was meant the difficulty of explaining why primes caused a specific response among so many possible outcomes; and (c) theories concerning the situatedness of cognition, which emphasized that priming responses were more sensitive to the total affordances of the priming situation than Bargh's direct perception-behavior link had appeared to recognize.

In chapter 7, I analyze the debate that was precipitated by the publication of Doyen et al.'s paper. In particular I focus on the intellectual strategies adopted by the different parties to the dispute to shore up their competing theoretical and empirical claims. I am especially interested in how Bargh and other defenders of priming now appealed to hitherto unidentified or hidden "moderators" internal to the context of the original experiments to explain failures to replicate certain priming results. The argument that hidden moderators influenced priming outcomes led to arguments for the inherent historical or cultural sensitivity of priming phenomena. But those same arguments posed a dilemma for defenders of priming claims because they raised the question: If priming effects are so context-sensitive, how is it possible to develop general laws or systematic predictions about primed behavior? Researchers might be able to identify the moderators that influenced priming outcomes in certain particular cultural settings involving specific participant populations at a particular time and place, but how could the findings be extended to other situations, other participant populations, and other times? The answer to replicability failures, based on the contextual and historical sensitivity of priming effects, raised awkward questions about the scientific status of the entire priming enterprise.

The chief concern of chapter 8, the last chapter, is the topic of experimenter expectancy. As I have observed, that issue was placed at the center of the replication crisis by Doyen et al. (2012) when, in their attempt to repeat Bargh's elderly priming experiment, they demonstrated that the manipulation of experimenters' expectations regarding the speed at which participants would walk influenced the experimental outcome. Doyen et al. thus raised questions, not only about whether Bargh had adequately controlled for experimenter expectancy in his original elderly priming experiment, but about the nature of expectancy itself—which is to say, about the nature of suggestive influence. In this chapter I will discuss why Bargh adopted a causal theory of hypnotic suggestion according to which hypnotic responses are not the product of the hypnotized subject's intentional efforts to perform the hypnotic role, but rather are the outcome of genuine alterations in the subject's cognitive powers and functions. On such a causal approach, hypnotized subjects can't give reasons for their actions performed in the trance state because those actions have been executed in a changed mental state of unconsciousness caused by the hypnotic induction itself. In short, hypnotized subjects behave exactly as Nisbett and Wilson claimed experimental subjects do when, lacking introspective knowledge of the actual hidden, information-processing causes of their behaviors, they make up reasons after the fact to account for their actions (Nisbett and Wilson 1977).

In the course of this chapter, I will consider Anscombe's similarly causal approach to hypnosis (Anscombe 2000 [1957]). I will also attempt to show how such a causal approach to hypnosis served Bargh's purposes by proposing that the actions performed by hypnotic and priming subjects were not the result of the participant's obedience to the hypnotist's or the experimenter's expectations. Rather, they were the result of the disconnect between the subject's conscious executive functions and the various subsystems responsible for automatic behavior, a disconnect causally triggered by the hypnotic induction procedure or by the unconscious influence of the priming words or stimuli. In effect, by adopting a causal view of hypnosis, Bargh made the agency and expectations of the experimenter disappear as the source of priming responses. The same argument led Bargh to adopt a view of the function of consciousness as merely providing rationalizations for behaviors we perform automatically and that lie outside our individual control. Inevitably, questions about the nature of moral responsibility were raised by claims for the pervasiveness of unconscious automaticity in human behavior. Although these questions lie outside the main purview of this book, I will touch on some of them.

Finally, in a brief conclusion, I provide a broad overview of the debate over priming and over the experimental procedures and methods that have supported its claims. That debate is ongoing. The question posed by this book as a whole is whether the present proposals for reform in psychology will prove adequate to handle the issue of intentionality that has haunted the priming field from first to last.

The Rise of Attribution Research

> The broad outlines of contemporary attribution theory... were first sketched by Heider (1944, 1958) and developed in greater detail by Jones and Davis (1965), Kelley (1967) and their associates... These theorists emphasized two closely related tasks confronting the social observer. The first task is causal judgment: the observer seeks to identify the cause, or set of causes, to which some particular effect (i.e., some action or outcome) may most reasonably be *attributed*. The second task is social inference: the observer of an episode forms inferences about the *attributes* of relevant entities, that is, either the dispositions of actors or the properties of situations to which those actors have responded.
> —L. ROSS (1977, 10, 175; his emphases)

Fritz Heider and the Causes of Social Interaction

This statement by Lee Ross, one of the leading attribution theorists in the United States, neatly captures Fritz Heider's role in influencing the direction of attribution research in the decades that followed the appearance of his book *The Psychology of Interpersonal Relations* (Heider 1958). To figures such as Ross and his colleagues in social psychology, and the same would also be true of Bargh, the assumption that their job was to study the causes of human behaviors was so basic as to be incontrovertible. Wasn't it obvious that people wish to understand the causes of behavior? What else could they possibly want? The idea expressed by Ross in this passage, that the judgment of causes was a matter of "inference," was also fundamental to the majority of social scientists. They believed, as Ross put it, that individuals behave like "intuitive psychologists" seeking to identify the causes of their own behavior or those of others by making inferences from the observational "data"—although, Ross argued, people are not effective at doing so because they tend to make irrational or biased attributions.

In this chapter I plan to analyze the history of attribution research in social psychology in the years after World War II. The concepts and research strategies developed in this field provided the background for Bargh's arguments regarding the powerful role of automaticity in human behaviors. In essence, attribution research established the causal assumptions informing Bargh's work. In the course of this chapter, I will briefly examine the most significant publications that shaped attribution research. I will end the chapter by discussing Nisbett and Wilson's influential paper, "Telling More Than We Can Know" (1977), which helped set the stage for major debates over intentional versus causal approaches to human action, the topic of chapter 2.

Fritz Heider (1896–1988) was born in Vienna, and after obtaining his PhD at the University of Graz, where he studied the causal structure of perception, he went to Berlin to learn about Gestalt psychology from Koehler, Wertheimer, and Lewin. In 1930 he moved to the United States, ending up at the University of Kansas, where he remained for the rest of his career. In 1958 he published *The Psychology of Interpersonal Relations*, which offered a new approach to the study of interpersonal relations. Scholars dispute the extent to which Heider should be held responsible for some of the more rigid causal attribution theories subsequent researchers developed out of his work (Malle and Ickes 2000). But I think it is fair to say that in this book Heider pushed American social psychology toward making the causal origin of attributions a central focus of attention.

At the risk of simplifying a complex text, I will single out four features of Heider's work that I believe were especially significant for the subsequent growth of attribution theory and research in the Unites States.

The first feature concerns Heider's attitude toward everyday language. Heider emphasized that psychology ought to start with the study of commonsense psychology and indeed with the insights about interpersonal relations as embodied in the language of fables, novels, and other forms of literature. But he also maintained that ordinary language lacked the kind of systematic order that was necessary for science. As he stated: "The psychologist must first, however, translate the basic outlines of the nonscientific propositions into a language of more use to scientific investigations"

(Heider 1958, 7). In pursuing this goal, Heider explicitly linked his project to the philosopher Rudolf Carnap's logical-positivist attempt to render everyday terms more exact. As he commented: "Carnap (1953)... points out that making more exact a concept that is used 'in a more or less vague way either in every-day language or in an earlier stage of scientific language' is often important in the development of science and mathematics" (Heider 1958, 9; his emphasis; see also Malle and Ickes 2000).

On this basis, Heider criticized the philosopher Gilbert Ryle for paying too-close attention to everyday language use in his famous book *The Concept of Mind* (1949) (Heider 1958, 12). Heider acknowledged that Ryle's work contained similarities to his own concern with "naïve psychology." But he objected that, although Ryle's book contained many stimulating ideas of great value, it was not always immediately applicable to the work of psychologists:

> In contrast to the present approach, he is mainly concerned with the actual meaning of words in ordinary usage with all their ambiguities, whereas our main purpose is to make explicit the system of concepts that underlies interpersonal behavior, and the analysis of words and situations is considered only a means to this end. We want to find a reality that lies beyond this rough sketch language gives us, and are not so much concerned with the sketch as such. (Heider, 1958, 12)

In other words, Heider was not satisfied with understanding people's interactions in the everyday terms they themselves deployed but sought to extract from ordinary language usage a set of underlying concepts that could serve the purposes of a scientific social psychology. As he put it, the task facing the social psychologist was to translate everyday language into such concepts, concepts which would then "provide the nodal points in terms of which the event can be described most economically, which allow for the extrapolation to other possible events and which allow for prediction" (Heider 1958, 33). In line with his scientific ambitions, Heider emphasized the predictive possibilities of his approach.

The second feature of Heider's approach that deserves emphasis is the importance he attached to the concept of *cause* in the study of interpersonal relations. "Of great importance for our picture of the social environment," Heider wrote, "is the attribution of events to causal sources." Heider sometimes appeared to distinguish between *causes* and *intentions*, as when he observed that "it makes a real difference . . . whether a person discovers that the stick that struck him fell from a rotting tree or was hurled by an enemy. Attribution in terms of impersonal and personal causes, and with the latter, in terms of intent, are everyday occurrences that determine much of our understanding of and reaction to our surroundings." But he went on to equate personal intent with causation when he added: "An additional fact of importance is that personal causation not only effects changes in the physical environment, as when a man winds his watch; it also has social implications. Thus 'benefiting' means that a person has caused change that is agreeable or positive in another person. Also, one person can cause another person to cause a change by asking him to do something, or commanding him, etc." (Heider 1958, 16).

In passages such as these, Heider tended to fudge the distinction that was widely held to be of fundamental significance in the philosophy of mind—the distinction between someone having a reason for performing an action and someone who is caused to act in a certain way (see also Malle 2008). There are many nuances that philosophers have raised concerning this distinction, some of which I will address in the next chapter. But for the moment, it is enough to observe that Heider sidestepped or downplayed the importance of understanding people's normative reasons for their actions in favor of an analysis of the scientifically defined causal determinants of their behaviors. On the one hand, he argued that "in most cases we cognize a person's traits, and especially his wishes, sentiments, or intentions from what he does and says, and we know considerably less when we are limited to what we can see of him as a static object." On the other hand, he paid little attention to people's stated intentions or reasons for their actions. Instead, he declared: "In the interest of conceptual clarification . . . we shall use the term intention to refer to *what* a person is trying to do, that is to the goal or action outcome, and not to *why* he is trying to do it. The latter applies more particularly to the reasons behind the intention" (Heider 1958, 39, 110–11; his emphases).

Heider's emphasis in this statement on action outcomes and his indifference to people's reasons for acting are evident in many other passages of his book. Even in the important chapter on "The Naïve Analysis of Action," in which we might have expected him to offer a systematic discussion of the concept of intention, his remarks on the topic remained unsystematic and scattered. Instead, he constantly displaced attention away from the notion of intention to the question of the causal relationship between a person's underlying, personal "dispositions" and the environmental situation. In a characteristic passage, Heider described the task of analyzing action as requiring

> a description of the causal nexus of an environment which contains not only the directly observable facts about the behavior of another person, but also their connection with the more stable structures and processes underlying that behavior. It is an important principle of common-sense psychology, as it is of scientific theory in general, that man grasps reality, and can predict and control it, by referring transient and variable behavior and events to relatively unchanging underlying conditions, the so-called dispositional properties of his world. (Heider 1958, 79)

On this basis Heider immediately turned to a discussion of the "relatively unchanging" personal and situational dispositions that, according to him, made possible a "more or less stable, predictable, and controllable world" (Heider, 1958, 80).

The third significant feature of Heider's thought was precisely the importance he attached to the notion of *disposition*. This concept has had a long and complex history in philosophy (Choi and Fara 2018). But for my purposes it is sufficient to observe that, like many other psychologists, Heider defined dispositions as the relatively constant "mental" characteristics of an individual. (He also used the word *traits* as a synonym for *dispositions*.) "In social perception," Heider remarked, "the direct impressions we form of another person, even if they are not correct, refer to dispositional characteristics" (Heider 1958, 30). And in another statement that is worth citing at length, he observed of these dispositional characteristics that

> at least relative to the events that mediate these impressions, the characteristics show a high degree of intrinsic invariance. For instance, the impression that a person is friendly, which may be conveyed in any number of ways, points to a relatively enduring characteristic of the person. In fact, any personality trait refers to something that characterizes the person, that is, holds over time in spite of irregularities of circumstance and behavior. As a dispositional property, a personality characteristic enables one to grasp an unlimited variety of behavioral manifestations by a single concept, e.g., friendliness. A description of a manifold of interpersonal

relations becomes far more systematically simple by reference to such enduring characteristics. Furthermore, insofar as personal dispositions are connected in lawful ways with other features, predictions about behavior of the other person become possible . . . Without the aid of such psychological, dispositional properties, the behavior of persons mediated by the proximal stimuli would remain largely unintelligible. (Heider 1958, 30–31)

I note that Heider counted environmental features among the dispositions, as when he stated that the study of dispositions included the "dispositional properties of environmental contents, properties that show invariant relations with possible events and are themselves relatively enduring" (Heider 1958, 31). This framing meant that the study of interpersonal relations was a matter of analyzing the relationship between personal and environmental "dispositions" defined as fairly permanent dimensions of self and the world.

It was partly because of the importance Heider attached to the analysis of dispositions that he ignored the analysis of reasons. He gave as an example the social interaction between person A who likes person B and wants to do B a favor. A goes through with his action and B is overjoyed. Heider commented: "[B] concludes that A, about whose attitudes he has been in doubt, really likes him; he appreciates especially the tactful way in which A handled the matter." Furthermore:

> Descriptions of this kind seem to capture the essential features of an interpersonal event. One might go even further and try to discover the reasons why A likes B, or why B was questioning A's sentiments; or one might try to assess the personality characteristics that played a role in this event. Though the description as it stands does not go far back into the history of the relation between A and B, nor into deep psychological motivations, within its limits it is a meaningful episode. (Heider 1958, 33)

In this passage Heider suggests or implies that, for the purposes of a scientific psychology, a person's reasons for acting in a particular way could be ignored: the interaction between A and B could be analyzed independently of the reasons that might have motivated the actions of the two individuals by focusing on the more or less fixed personal and situational dispositions causing the individuals to behave in certain ways.

A fourth feature of Heider's approach is the way in which his dispositional analysis inevitably tended to set up a simple distinction between environmental and personal "causes" of behavior. As the passage just quoted suggests, Heider encouraged attribution theorists to assume that the proper goal of research was to determine whether a specific social interaction was a function of either "external" (environmental-situational) or "internal" (personal) dispositions or causes. It would later appear to critics that this either-or approach in attribution research was naïve, since typically there was no simple answer to the question, "Was this behavior internally or externally caused?" (Sabini, Siepmann, and Stein 2001, 8). The answer usually was that the behavior in question was caused by both personal and external factors (Malle et al. 2000, 319; see also White 1991). In the prolonged debate over attribution theory that began in the 1970s and has persisted to the present day, critics have argued that attribution researchers have tended to make too stark a division between a person's dispositions as the cause of behavior versus environmental or situational causes. Some critics have gone even further by suggesting that attribution theorists designed their experiments in such a way as to deprive their subjects of the opportunity to give their reasons for making attributions, with the result that these studies yielded findings that could have been determined in advance. There is more to be said about this topic, to which I shall return shortly.

The Contributions of Edward E. Jones and Keith E. Davis to Attribution Research

Heider's book was a fertile source of ideas for American social psychologists. Starting in the 1960s, attribution scientists in a series of publications laid the groundwork for a flourishing research field largely dominated by the features of Heider's work that I have just described. One of the first important post-Heider texts was a long paper by Edward E. Jones and Keith E. Davis in which the authors declared that "the kind of systematic, conceptual structure" that was needed in the study of interpersonal behavior had to involve an analysis of "the determinants and consequences of attributing causation for particular actions." The authors acknowledged their debt to Heider by observing that "at the heart of Heider's analysis of naïve or 'common sense psychology' is the distinction between personal and impersonal causality" (Jones and Davis 1965, 220). Jones and Davis handled the question of a person's reasons for acting in the following way:

> We assume that the person-perceiver's fundamental task is to interpret or infer the causal antecedents of action. The perceiver seeks to find *sufficient reason* why the person acted and why the act took on a particular form. Instead of the potentially infinite regress of cause and effect which characterizes an impersonal scientific analysis, the perceiver's explanation comes to a stop when an intention or motive is assigned that has the quality of being reason enough . . . The cognitive task of establishing sufficient reason for an action involves processing available information about, or making assumptions about, the links between stable individual dispositions and observed action. (Jones and Davis 1965, 220; their emphasis)

This passage contains many of the essential ingredients of attribution theory. It presumes that a perceiver's basic aim in any social interaction is to discover the causes of another person's or actor's behavior. Thus, although Jones and Davis described the perceiver as seeking to find a "sufficient reason" why an actor behaved in some way, their experimental methods were designed to help the perceiver answer the "why" question by asking participants to locate the cause of an actor's response in his or her personal dispositions. The actor was viewed as the depository of a set of fairly enduring personal traits, and although Jones and Davis defined the goal of the perceiver as deciding which actions were "intended by the actor," it was those personal dispositions or traits that were the focus of their analysis. As they wrote: "Intentions are the data for inferring dispositions" (Jones and Davis 1965, 220, 224). The shift of focus from intentions to the underlying dispositions is evident in the authors' statement that

> all actions have effects on the environment. From the perceiver's point of view, any effect of another person's actions is a potential reason why this person has engaged in that action. To infer that the action occurred for X reason is to specify the actor's intention and, indirectly, an underlying disposition. Both intentions and dispositions are attributes of the person. The perception of a link between a particular intention or disposition and a particular action may therefore be called an attribute-effect linkage (Jones and Davis, 1965, 224)

The authors provided a figure depicting the causal sequence involved, tracing the system back from an actor's behavior to its origins in personal dispositions, or tracing it forward from the dispositional origin as the "first cause" leading to the behavioral outcome. Like Heider, they emphasized that the perceiver's main purpose in attributing dispositions to an actor was to be able to generate "reasonably precise predictions" about the actor's future behavior (Jones and Davis 1965, 230).

Moreover, for Jones and Davis the effort to determine the links between an actor's behavior and its causes required the perceiver to make "inferences" from the observed behavior to the dispositions. Such inferences were required because, on an assumption not always stated but widely held at the time by both philosophers and psychologists, an agent's mental states—thoughts and feelings—were held to be hidden and private and therefore inaccessible to an observer's direct perception. Accordingly, those mental states had to be inferred from the actor's publicly observable behaviors, with the result that personal dispositions were treated as unobservable constructs whose inferred existence, moreover, might be erroneous. As Jones and Nisbett put this point: "Like the actor's feeling states, his intentions can never be directly known to the observer . . . [T]he observer may infer intentions from the actor's expressive behavior and from the 'logic' of the situation. But, as with feeling states, knowledge of intentions is indirect, usually quite inferior, and highly subject to error" (Jones and Nisbett, 1972, 84). This common presupposition about the privacy of mental states was open to the objection, made on Wittgensteinian and related grounds by several critics in social psychology and philosophy, that, on the contrary, the meaningful aspects of people's actions are manifested directly to us without the need for mediation or inference.

A new note in Jones and Davis's 1965 article was their use of the language of information processing to describe how the perceiver went about inferring the links between an actor's behavior and various dispositions. To repeat the authors' comment, already cited above: "The cognitive task of establishing sufficient reason for an action involves processing available information about, or making assumptions about, the links between stable individual dispositions and observed action" (Jones and Davis 1965, 220). The language of information processing was of course derived from cognitive science's analysis of cognition in terms of the computation of bits of information, and its use here indicates the integration between social psychology and cognitive science that was occurring at this time.

Another important feature of Jones and Davis's paper was their discussion of the use of rating scales designed to measure the strength of a disposition or trait displayed by an actor. Such rating scales introduced a means by which an actor's intentions, or dispositions, could be treated as a quantifiable component of the attribution process and could be used to compare findings across subjects and experimental contexts. In a typical attribution experiment, participants might be given a brief, written description of some piece of behavior by an individual. The wording of the behavior descriptions could be varied in certain ways to embody conditions or circumstances of interest to the investigator, such as whether the behavior portrayed was highly distinctive, whether it was the sort of behavior that almost everyone might perform, or whether the behavior was consistent with past performances. Participants would be asked to read the description and choose among several options listed in a questionnaire designed to ascertain whether they thought the behavior reflected something about the person or about the circumstances, or some combination of those factors, and their responses in the form of quantifiable measurements could then be compared to those of others in the experiment.

More generally, Jones and Davis presented the attribution process as occurring in several stages. The first stage occurred when the observer of an actor's behavior assigned a "probability" value to each action as a candidate for "launching an inference," which then determined the likely goal of the action. The probability value of an action or effect was held to vary directly with the assumed desirability of the goal and inversely as a function of the other actions competing for the observer's attention. The second stage of the attribution process involved attaching personal significance to the action. "In short, what does the action reveal about this particular actor that sets him apart from other actors?" (Jones and Davis 1965, 228). The greater the desirability of the effect in question, the less warrant there was for a rating of the relative extremity of a disposition or an attribute in the actor. Hence the authors' formulation:

> An inference from action to attribute is correspondent as an inverse function of (a) the number of noncommon effects following the action, and (b) the assumed social desirability of these effects. This relationship may be stated in simpler terms as a near tautology: the more distinctive reasons a person has for an action, and the more these reasons are widely shared in the culture, the less informative that action is concerning the identifying attributes of the person. (Jones and Davis 1965, 228; their emphasis)

The authors labeled their conceptual framework the "correspondent inference theory." In 1967, Jones and co-author Victor Harris published the results of several attribution experiments informed by this theory, experiments that appeared to demonstrate that participants found it difficult to assign the appropriate weight to the influence of the situation on behavior because the performance of the *actor* tended to "engulf the total field." This phrasing was Heider's formulation of the idea that observers were less than fully rational when judging the behavior of others, because they tended to overestimate the influence of a person's "internal" dispositions and underestimate the impact of "external" or situational factors. The implication was that observers were often biased in their attributions when assessing the relative influence of the internal (personal) versus the external causes of behavior (Jones and Harris 1967). Jones and Harris's experiments were widely regarded as a milestone in the investigation of this bias.

Harold Kelley and the Situation/Disposition Debate

Jones and Davis concluded their 1965 article with the hope that their framework would encourage systematic thinking about the processes involved in inferring dispositions (Jones and Davis 1965, 265). In 1967, social psychologist Harold E. Kelley took up that challenge by attempting to further systematize and formalize the causal analysis of attribution. Kelley presented his approach as an extension of Heider's and Jones and Davis's analyses of the attribution process (Kelley 1967, 192). His aim was to propose a model for disentangling which effects in any social interaction were to be attributed to the external situation and which were to be attributed to the properties or dispositions of the self.

To illustrate his approach, Kelley gave the following example, in this case an example of self-attribution:

> Am I to take my enjoyment of a movie as a basis for an attribution to the movie (that it is intrinsically enjoyable) or for an attribution to myself (that I have a specific kind of desire relevant to movies)? The inference as to where to locate the dispositional properties responsible for the effect is made by interpreting the raw data (the enjoyment) in the context of subsidiary information from experiment-like variations of conditions. A naïve version of J. S. Mills' method of difference provides the basic analytic tool. The effect is attributed to that condition which is present when the effect is present and which is absent when the effect is absent. This

basic notion of covariation of cause and effect is used to examine variations over (1) entities (movies), (b) persons (other viewers of the movie), (c) time (the same person on repeated exposures), and (d) modalities of interaction with the entity (different ways of viewing the movie). (Kelley 1967, 194)

Put simply, on Kelley's model people attributed a behavior to whatever co-varied with it. He described what was involved in deciding whether one's own response was caused by the external object or by personal dispositions in the following way:

> The attribution to the external thing rather than to the self requires that I respond *differentially* to the thing, that I respond *consistently* over time and over modality, and that I respond *in agreement* with the consensus of other person's responses to it. In other words, the movie is judged enjoyable if I enjoy only it (or at least, not all movies), if I enjoy it even the second time, if I enjoy it on TV as well as at the drive-in theater, and if others also enjoy it. If these conditions are not met, there is indicated an attribution to the self (I enjoy all movies, or I alone have a weakness for this particular type) or to some juxtaposition of circumstances (I was in an especially susceptible mood on the one occasion). (Kelley 1967, 194; his emphases)

More formally, Kelley suggested that there were three significant sources informing causal attributions: consistency information (the extent to which most people behave in the same way in a given situation); distinctiveness information (the extent to which behavior varies across different situations); and consensus information (whether most people engage in the behavior in a particular situation).

An important aspect of Kelley's theory was the idea that, in making attributions, people functioned like "naïve psychologists" who used a version of the method of science—which is to say a version of the analysis of variance (ANOVA)—in their conceptualization of the attribution process, albeit an unsophisticated version of that method because of their tendency to biases of various kinds. As Kelley observed: "The assumption is that the man in the street, the naïve psychologist, uses a naïve version of the method used in science. Undoubtedly, his naïve version is a poor replica of the scientific one—incomplete, subject to bias, ready to proceed on incomplete evidence, and so on. Nevertheless, it has certain general properties in common with the analysis of variance as we behavioral scientists use it" (Kelley 1973, 109).[1]

There were some differences between Kelley's approach and that of Jones and Davis. As Jones and Davis observed, they wanted to explain how attributions to the person could be made by ruling out environmental explanations; whereas Kelley wanted to show how people decided whether an actor's response was caused by the environmental object or situation or by some idiosyncratic feature of personality. Thus, the research emphases were slightly different. But the similarities were more important than the differences. Both approaches treated people's actions as caused by internal or external factors and hence presented the task of attribution as a matter of a person's deciding between situational and personal-dispositional causes of behavior. The researchers' aim was to prove in the laboratory that individuals made their causal allocations in the same way as the "man on the street" (Jones 1976, 300).

I think it is fair to say that Jones, Davis, and Kelley shared an extremely abstract, unrealistic, and impoverished picture of actual persons. This truth is especially evident in Kelley's work. In his commitment to science, he reduced all the complex reasons people have for responding to others and the world to a simple choice between two mutually exclusive causal factors: the "external" event or situation versus the "internal" attributes of the self (the personal dispositions). I can think of no other attribution theorist whose work better represents, or gives a starker sense of, what was lost when social psychology turned the ordinary ways in which people understand each other's behaviors, including understanding the reasons that motivated their actions, into an effort to subject all those reasons to a certain kind of causal analysis.

Take for example Kelley's hypothetical scenario involving the case of Paul who is captivated by a painting in a museum. "Consider the following information, (adapted from McArthur 1972)," Kelley writes. "'Paul is enthralled by a painting he sees at the art museum. Hardly anyone who

---

1. As Gigerenzer critically observed: "Some of the most popular theories and research programs [in the "probabilistic revolution"] owed their genesis to an analogy between social cognition and 'intuitive statistics.' In 1967, for instance, Harold Kelley proposed that the layperson attributes a cause to an effect in the same way as a statistician of the Fisherian school would, by (unconsciously) calculating an analysis of variance (ANOVA). Research on the ANOVA mind soon became mainstream social psychology" (Gigerenzer 1991, 84).

sees the painting is enthralled by it. Paul also is enthralled by almost every other painting. In the past, Paul has almost always been enthralled by the same painting.'" "Given that information," Kelley continues,

> the subject is asked what probably caused this event—Paul's being enthralled by the same painting—to occur? Was it something about Paul (person), something about the painting (entity), something about the particular circumstances (time), or some combination of these factors? ... The effect occurs only for ... Paul ... but it occurs for him at various times and for various entities. This pattern suggests that the effect, "enthrallment," is dependent on Paul. It is "caused" by Paul—some property, characteristic, or predisposition of him. (Kelley 1973, 110)

The implication of Kelley's remarks is that if an art critic is the only person in the world to admire the work of a particular painter, and if she does so consistently over time without regard to other people's judgments, her evaluation can't be attributed to the quality of the painting but only to her personal-subjective idiosyncrasies. But what kind of model of the human being, or indeed of the enterprise of aesthetic criticism, is that? On Kelley's approach to attribution, no critic's judgments could ever be given any weight if they happened to contradict the consensus.

The Growth of Attribution Research

This question is only one of many that could be asked about Kelley's attribution theory and the approach of other attribution researchers. In the meantime, though, the attribution field grew rapidly. Among the publications playing an especially significant role in its development was Jones and Nisbett's discussion of the different perspectives of the actor and the observer in the attribution process (Jones and Nisbett 1972). Building on the work of Heider and Kelley and on various experimental findings, Jones and Nisbett argued that actors and observers looked for the causes of behavior in different places. In particular, actors tended to stress situational causes of their own behavior, whereas observers tended to attribute the same actors' behaviors to personal-dispositional causes. As the authors stated: "*There is a pervasive tendency for actors to attribute their actions to situational requirements, whereas observers tend to attribute the same actions to stable personal dispositions*" (Jones and Nisbett, 1972, 80, their emphasis; see also Nisbett et al. 1973). The result was that actors and observers were systematically biased in their judgments. Jones and Nisbett's publications added further support for the emerging picture of human beings as less than perfect, indeed somewhat irrational, judges of their own and others' behaviors—not so much because of misleading motivational factors but because of non-motivational, informational, cognitive, and perceptual biases.[2]

A number of other publications reinforced these trends. They included *Cognition and Social Behavior,* a collection of symposium conference papers edited by John S. Carroll and John W. Payne (Carroll and Payne 1976) and singled out by Bargh as the "breakthrough" shot in the "insurrection" against the model of the rational man that had previously prevailed in social psychology (Bargh 1984, 1). The chief message of this book, as an exercise in cognitive science resting on the assumption that individuals were "limited information processors" (Carroll and Payne 1976, x), was that people's evaluations were not a function of people's reasons but of their cognitive processes of categorization and judgment, which could be treated as distinct from and independent of their "motivations."[3] Another message was that, in part because of the alleged limitation of cognitive capacity and other cognitive frailties, human beings were much less effective processors of information, and much more biased in their judgments, than had previously been recognized. Worth noting, too, was the reference by one of the contributors to Daniel Kahneman and Amos Tversky's first paper on judgment heuristics and biases, a paper that helped consolidate the idea that laypeople were fallible decision-makers as measured against the standards of formal inferential conventions and the rules of probability (Carroll and Payne 1976, 114; Kahneman and Tversky 1973; see also Tversky and Kahneman 1974).

In an influential article two years later, Ross gave the name the "funda-

---

2. Drawing in part on Walter Mischel's recent critique of the entire apparatus of personality theory and its commitment to the notion of personality dispositions or traits, Jones and Nisbett even suggested that personality traits were an "illusion," existing "more in the eye of the beholder than in the psyche of the actor" (Jones and Nisbett 1972, 89; and Mischel 1968; 1969; 1971).

3. However, the problem of motivation returned to haunt the field when Edward E. Jones attributed some discrepancies in the attribution evidence to motivational factors—factors that potentially eliminated or reversed the predicted attributional differences. But even if motivations were viewed as of considerable interest in their own right, some commentators felt free to ignore them because they were not held to be directly relevant to the basic attribution hypothesis; Jones himself simply proposed that motives could be an area of further research (Jones 1976, Watson 1982).

mental attribution error" to Jones and Nisbett's finding that observers of the behaviors of others tended to underestimate the impact of situational factors and to overestimate the role of dispositional (or personal) factors in the individual's control of behavior (Ross 1977, 1). Interestingly, however, in the same article Ross acknowledged a basic problem in attribution theory. The problem was that the alleged dichotomy between "external" and "internal" causes of behavior on which attribution theory was based was fundamentally ambiguous and unstable, since many of the behaviors that participants in attribution experiments were asked to judge cut across the situation-person divide. Ross gave as an example the statement, "Jack bought the house because it was secluded." As he observed, in an attribution experiment this sentence would be typically coded as a *situation* attribution. Whereas the statement, "Jill bought the house because she wanted privacy," would be coded as a *personal* attribution. Ross noted that the rationale for these codings seemed straightforward: the statement about Jack located the cause of his behavior in the situation, whereas the statement about Jill seemed to be about her need for privacy and hence located the cause of her behavior in her personal disposition.

But as Ross went on to suggest, a closer examination of these statements revealed that they were ambiguous and that the causal attributions assigned to them were problematic. On the one hand, statements that explicitly cited situational cues implicitly conveyed something about the actor's dispositions. Thus, in accounting for Jack's purchase of a house, the situation explanation ("because it was secluded") also implied a disposition on Jack's part to favor seclusion. "Indeed," Ross stated, "the explanation provided is no explanation at all unless one *does* assume that such a disposition controlled Jack's response." On the other hand, the dispositional explanation of Jill's purchase ("because she likes privacy") clearly implied "something about the house" (its capacity to provide such privacy), and hence pointed to a situational factor that, in turn, governed Jill's behavior. As Ross remarked, "the content of both sentences, notwithstanding their differences in form, communicates the information that a particular feature of the house exists and that the purchaser was disposed to respond positively to that feature. In fact, the form of the sentences could have been reversed without altering their content to read 'Jack bought the house because he wanted seclusion' and 'Jill bought the house because it provided privacy'" (Ross 1977, 176; his emphasis).

As Bertram Malle and colleagues would comment more than twenty years later, this "puzzle" was frequently mentioned by attribution researchers but never resolved (Malle et al. 2000, 319; see also Malle 2006a; 2006b). Ross himself did not recommend abandoning the fundamental dichotomy between personal and situational causes. Rather, he proposed various more local solutions to the interpretive dilemmas facing attribution researchers, solutions that did not challenge the general contours of attribution theory itself. One of Ross's proposals was to shift attention from the task of assigning causes to the investigation of how people make inferences. As he observed: "The interpretation of causal statements . . . is obviously a difficult undertaking and many investigators may favor the second attribution task, i.e., the formation of social inferences. This task, at first glance, seems to offer a far less forbidding but no less rewarding research target" (Ross 1977, 177).

This was exactly the solution favored by Nisbett and Ross in their widely cited book *Human Inference: Strategies and Shortcomings of Social Judgment* (1980). The major message of this influential text was that ordinary people's attributions and judgments were irrational because they were ignorant of formal scientific procedures for solving inferential problems and making valid predictions. The authors attributed such inferential failures to various factors, especially to "cold," non-motivational perceptual and cognitive errors and biases, as opposed to "hot" motivational-emotional influences. "We argue," they wrote, "that many phenomena generally regarded as motivational (for example, self-serving perceptions and attributions, ethnocentric beliefs, and many types of human conflict) can be understood better as products of relatively passionless information-processing errors than of deep-seated motivational forces" (Nisbett and Ross 1980, 12).

Nisbett and Ross used the normative methods of inference, adopted by trained social scientists such as themselves, to evaluate the ways in which ordinary people's attributions manifested certain errors. Those errors were said to include mistakes in probabilistic reasoning, such as overconfidence bias, base-rate neglect, and mistakes about samples and representativeness of the kind discussed by Daniel Kahneman and Amos Tversky, to whose influence the authors acknowledged a major debt. The psychologist Gerd Gigerenzer would later emerge as the most important critic of Kahneman's and Tversky's claims. He argued that most so-called errors in probabilistic reasoning were not in fact violations of probability theory, and he persuasively questioned the use by social scientists such as Nisbett and Ross of Kahneman's and Tversky's "normative principles of statistical prediction" to find fault with the ways people made predictions in their everyday lives (Gigerenzer 1991). But that is another story (Elio 2002; Erickson et al. 2013, ch. 6).

"Telling More Than We Can Know": Attribution and the Limits of Introspection

It is against the background of these developments in attribution theory that the enormous impact of Nisbett and Wilson's famous—to its critics, infamous—paper entitled "Telling More Than We Can Know" (1977) must be understood. In an important sense their paper took the trends internal to attribution theory to their inevitable terminus. The text became well-known for numerous reasons, above all for its skeptical conclusions concerning the relevance of the commonsense assumption that people's agency, intentions, and reasons make a real difference in how they behave (for critiques, see also Leys 2017; Schlosser 2019b). Bargh was not alone in regarding Nisbett and Wilson's paper as among the most consequential of the many publications emerging from attribution research, one that decisively shaped not only his own thinking about priming and automaticity but also the further development of American social psychology.

In their paper Nisbett and Wilson radicalized attribution theory by claiming not only that ordinary individuals were often mistaken about the causes of their own behavior, as other attribution theorists had already argued, but that they were *in principle incapable of identifying them* because the workings of their own minds were unavailable to introspection. This claim was indeed far-reaching, because social scientists routinely depended on participants' self-reports to provide information about their experiences. But now Nisbett and Wilson were questioning the use of self-report as a reliable research method—even though such self-reports remained an important source of information in social psychology research as a means of verifying participants' lack of awareness of the influence of primes on their behavior.[4] The authors proceeded to raise their questions by first invoking a key premise of cognitive science, that the contents of mental states are the product of hidden, unconscious

---

4. Of course, this moment was not the first one of crisis for this research mode. In a large literature of the history of the role of introspection in scientific psychology, see the valuable overview of the topic in Schwitzgebel 2019. For the debate between the leading academic psychologist at the start of the twentieth century, Edward Bradford Titchener, and the Swiss American psychiatrist Adolf Meyer concerning the validity of introspection as a methodology, see also Leys and Evans 1990.

information-processing events that are unreachable by consciousness. Nisbett and Wilson quoted several cognitive psychologists to this effect. "'It is the *result* of thinking, not the process of thinking, that appears spontaneously in consciousness,'" they quoted George Miller as stating (Miller 1962, 56; his emphasis; Nisbett and Wilson 1977, 232). They also quoted Neisser's assertion that "'the constructive processes [of encoding perceptual sensations] themselves never appear in consciousness, their products do'" (Neisser 1967, 301; Nisbett and Wilson 1977, 232). To these they added several characteristic statements by George Mandler: "'The analysis of situations and appraisal of the environment... goes on mainly at the nonconscious level'" (Mandler 1975, 241; Nisbett and Wilson 1977, 232). "'There are many systems that cannot be brought into consciousness, and probably most systems that analyze the environment in the first place have that characteristic. In most of these cases, only the products of cognitive and mental activities are available to consciousness'" (Mandler 1975, 241, 245; Nisbett and Wilson 1977, 232). Or again: "'Unconscious processes... include those that are not available to conscious experience, be they feature analyzers, deep syntactic structures, affective appraisals, computational processes, language production systems, [or] action systems of many kinds'" (Mandler 1975, 230; Nisbett and Wilson 1977, 232).

For Nisbett and Wilson, then, self-reports were likely to be an inadequate method for detecting the causes of behavior, either one's own or that of others, because we are only able to report on the "contents" or "products" of our cognitions, but not on the cognitive "processes" themselves. This conclusion implied in turn that we are better able to report correctly *what* we are thinking and feeling than *why* we are. Nisbett and Wilson also argued that, even on those occasions when we do give correct testimony about our higher mental processes, that testimony is not the result of direct introspective awareness but of the "incidentally correct employment of a priori causal theories" about the connection between stimulus and response (Nisbett and Wilson 1977, 233).

In support of their claims, Nisbett and Wilson reviewed various empirical findings casting doubt on the ability of individuals to accurately report their cognitive processes, including especially the accumulating evidence from attribution research. For example, in what became a frequently cited study, passersby ostensibly participating in a consumer survey had been invited to evaluate four pairs of nylon stockings laid out in a row, side by side. The participants were asked to say which pair was the best quality and to explain their selections. In actuality, all four pairs were identical.

Nisbett and Wilson reported that, by a factor of four to one, the individuals surveyed had a pronounced tendency to favor the rightmost pair of stockings, although no participants spontaneously mentioned that the position of the stockings had played a role in their choices. When asked directly whether a position effect could have influenced their decisions, nearly all the subjects denied this possibility, "usually with a worried glance at the interviewer suggesting that they felt either that they had misunderstood the question or were dealing with a madman." Nisbett and Wilson therefore argued that, unknown to the participants, the position of the stocking pairs was the decisive cause of their selections, adding: "Precisely why the position effect occurs is not obvious. It is possible that subjects carried into the judgment task the consumer's habit of 'shopping around,' holding off on choice of early-seen garments on the left in favor of later-seen garments on the right" (Nisbett and Wilson 1977, 244).

The authors concluded on the basis of this and other experiments that, on the whole, people were unable to identify accurately the causes of their own behavior. Pointing to the fact that we can proficiently perform skilled actions without being able to articulate how we do it, philosopher Michael Polanyi had previously argued that because of our possession of tacit knowledge, "we can know more than we can tell." Now, Nisbett and Wilson were claiming that the converse was also true: we "sometimes tell more than we can know" (Nisbett and Wilson 1977, 247).

Nisbett and Wilson also suggested that people's erroneous reports about their own cognitive processes and the causes of their behavior were not "capricious or haphazard" but "regular and systematic." The evidence for this assertion came from the fact that "observer" subjects, who did not participate in attribution studies but simply read verbal descriptions of the same situations as the experimental subjects, made predictions about how they would react that were remarkably similar to the (inaccurate) reports given by the actual participants (Nisbett and Wilson 1977, 247). This finding suggested to the researchers that both experimental subjects and observers were drawing on implicit, a priori causal theories about the extent to which a particular stimulus was a plausible cause of a given response. For example, in an experiment described by Nisbett and Wilson, when a word association experiment was described to mere observers,

> the judgments of probability that particular word cues would affect particular target responses were positively correlated with the original subjects' "introspective reports" of the effects of the word cues on the

target responses . . . Thus, whatever capacity for introspection exists, it does not produce accurate reports about stimulus effects, nor does it even produce reports that differ from predictions of observers operating with only a verbal description of the stimulus situation. (Nisbett and Wilson 1977, 247–48)

Nisbett and Wilson therefore concluded that

if the reports of subjects in such experiments did not differ from those of observers, then it is unnecessary to assume that the former are drawing on "a fount of privileged knowledge" . . . It seems equally likely that subjects and observers are drawing on a similar source for their verbal reports about stimulus effects. (Nisbett and Wilson 1977, 248)

That "similar source," they suggested, was the set of explicit or implicit theories about causal relations embedded in the culture or subculture to which participants and observers alike belonged.

Such theories, added Nisbett and Wilson, might well include the "representativeness heuristic" described by Tversky and Kahneman according to which, in making judgments about the probability that an individual is, say, a librarian, one compares information about the individual with stereotypes about librarians, and if the given information is representative of the stereotype, then one deems it "probable" that the individual is a librarian. "Information that is more pertinent to a true probability judgment, such as the proportion of librarians in a population, is ignored. We are proposing that a similar sort of representativeness heuristic is employed in assessing cause and effect relations in self-perception" (Nisbett and Wilson 1977, 249). Nisbett and Wilson argued that other heuristics described by Tversky and Kahneman, such as the availability heuristic, were undoubtedly involved in the (mistaken) attribution of cause-and-effect relationships.

It is important to note that Nisbett and Wilson's arguments depended on a major shift in psychology's understanding of unconscious processes. Prior to the cognitive revolution, unconscious processes were treated in Freudian terms as mental states or events that were not present to consciousness because they had been actively repressed. Moreover, in Freud's conception unconscious and conscious processes were governed by different rules or laws: for instance, unlike people's ordinary consciousness of events, the unconscious knew no time and made no distinction between reality and fantasy. In addition, the psychoanalytic unconscious was dynamic and conflictual, involving the role of an ego capable of banishing the subject's unacceptable desires and thoughts from conscious awareness. Freud's conception did not mean that the unconscious was inaccessible to consciousness: the purpose of the Freudian "talking cure" was to provide a method whereby the patient's unconscious thoughts could be brought into consciousness. In addition, and crucially, for Freud unconscious mental states were intentional: their contents were infantile erotic intentions and desires that were blocked from consciousness because of their prohibited nature.

But with the rise of cognitive science and information-processing theories of mental function, Freud's dynamic theory was abandoned. Unconscious activities were now viewed as forms of automatic, nonconscious, non-intentional information processing that occurred in computational subsystems capable of acting independently of the mind's conscious control. In the process of this transformation in the understanding of the unconscious, the dynamic-conflictual dimension of the psychoanalytic unconscious was lost as mental actions were converted into nonconscious, mechanically filtered, adaptive processes and events.

That these attempts at reformulation were motivated by a lack of comfort with the very notion of intention was spelled out by Matthew Hugh Erdelyi, one of the leading figures in this development. Commenting on the Freudian notion of "defense," Erdelyi observed that "the ultimate problem with defense, as with so many other constructs in psychology, is that it is anchored to the notion of intention and purpose and is thus problematic on both philosophical and methodological grounds ... [W]e have yet no explicit methodology of purpose." As a solution to this problem, he suggested that the phenomenon of defense and other processes could be accounted for differently as "the nondefensive disruption of perception and memory by emotion or by any other attention-disrupting event" (Erdelyi 1990, 85). In 1987, Kihlstrom gave the name "cognitive unconscious" to the unconscious formulated in information-processing terms, with the result that for majority of psychologists the triumph of the computer model of the mind seemed virtually complete (Kihlstrom 1987; see also Hassin, Uleman, and Bargh 2005).

Nisbett and Wilson's (1977) paper quickly achieved the status of a classic. It also contributed to one of the most sustained and divisive controversies in the postwar period about the direction of the social psychology as a field. It was apparent to many critics that the authors' claims trenched on long-standing philosophical debates about the explanation of behavior. In particular, opponents asserted that the authors' arguments—and indeed attribution theorists' similar contentions about the weakness and irrationality of the individual's grasp of causal processes—amounted to an indictment of intentionality (Buss 1978; 1979; Smith and Miller 1978; White 1980; 1988; Adair and Spinner 1981; McClure 1983). Nisbett and Wilson's suggestion was that human behavior was determined by causes external to the person as an intentional agent, indeed that individuals were not advantaged over observers in their knowledge of their own intentions, because the causes of their behavior were sub-personal information-processing mechanisms over which they had no conscious control. By making the causes of behavior, whether environmental or personal-dispositional, the focus of interest rather than the reasons individuals gave for their actions, attribution theorists lent support to the idea that people's intentions and reasons could not be explanatory at all. The issue was not just that people held many false beliefs and reasons for their actions: they were wrong in thinking they had reasons of any kind.

In short, Nisbett and Wilson's arguments were influential because of their skeptical conclusions concerning the relevance of the commonsense assumption that people's agency, intentions, and reasons make a real difference in how they behave. Their views fed into and reinforced an ongoing debate over the best ways in which to approach the study of social psychology, one in which the conflict between causal and intentional explanations occupied center stage. Many commentators focused their criticisms on Nisbett and Wilson's stocking experiment, particularly the claim that the participants' tendency to prefer the rightmost pair of identical stockings was based on the stockings' position alone. Objections included the argument that the participants had reasons for thinking that there were differences among the stocking pairs, and that they were not mistaken about their reasons: they necessarily knew what their reasons were. Indeed, without such reasons they would not have made the choices they did. Moreover, such critics argued, even if in this particular experiment the participants' reasons might appear to be rationalizations because the position of the stocking pair influenced their decisions in ways of which they were unaware, it did not therefore follow that all reasons were explanatorily nugatory (Locke and Pennington 1982). The net result of such critiques was to insist on the significance of the distinction between *performing an action for reasons* versus *being caused to behave in some particular way*.

The "Why" Question: Are Reasons Causes?

In her book *Intention*, the philosopher Elizabeth Anscombe asked: "What distinguishes actions which are intentional from those which are not?" and replied: "The answer that I shall suggest is that they are the actions to which a certain sense of the question 'Why?' is given application: the sense is of course that in which the answer, if positive, gives a reason for acting" (Anscombe 2000 [1957], 9). Several years later, attribution theorist Harold Kelley observed that "attribution theory is a theory about how people make causal explanations, about how they answer questions beginning with 'why'? It deals with the information they use in making causal inferences, and with what they do with this information to answer causal questions" (Kelley 1973, 107).

As these statements indicate, Anscombe and Kelley gave fundamentally different rejoinders to the question why individuals act in the ways they do. As Anscombe scholar Rachel Wiseman has recently put it, for Anscombe what a person with the concept of intention can do is "take part in the highly sophisticated 'Why'-Because . . .' language game," a game in which a person's *reasons* for acting are the focus of interest (Wiseman 2017, 539). On this view, if we want to determine whether someone is doing something intentionally, we can simply ask her. From an Anscombean perspective, questions about the first-person experience of consciousness or the causal role of mental states or events (such as beliefs and desires) are irrelevant to discussions of the epistemological status of intentional action. One way of putting this is to say that Anscombe's is a conceptual view of intentionality, not an empirical, psychological, or phenomenological one.

But as we have seen in this chapter, for attribution theorist Kelley the goal of social psychology was not to ask participants in experiments to give the reasons for their actions or those of others. Rather, the aim was to ask them to make a choice between, say, attributing an individual's liking for a painting either to the effect of the person's individual "dispositions" or to the impact of the painting itself, conceived as a "situational" cause. In short, for Kelley people's judgments were the effect of either "internal" or "external" *causes*.

For researchers in social psychology debates in the 1970s and 1980s over how to handle the question of intentionality and meaning in the social sciences, the divide between "reason" versus "causal" approaches was so great as to be virtually unbridgeable. We will see in chapter 2 that Anscombe's work was taken up by certain important social psychologists involved in the controversy over the role of intention in behavior. This fact is striking because Anscombe's book was long neglected by many philosophers. There are several reasons for this neglect, including the sheer difficulty of a work that many scholars now regard as the most significant discussion of intentionality in post–World War II Anglo-American philosophy. But another reason was that Anscombe's views on intention were largely mediated, and in an important sense eclipsed, by the writings of philosopher Donald Davidson. Davidson influentially argued that reasons could be causes, and as a result led scholars caught up in the attempt to naturalize intentionality in a causal direction that was radically different from Anscombe's (Davidson 1963). Thus, with a few notable exceptions, it was from the writings of Davidson rather than Anscombe that the majority of philosophers obtained their orientation in the philosophy of intentionality.

As has emerged in this chapter, the foundational text of post–World War II American social psychology, Fritz Heider's *The Psychology of Interpersonal Relations* (1958), likewise treated intentionality as a matter of identifying causal processes in terms that made Anscombe's emphasis on reason explanations appear to many researchers to be beside the point. Heider's ideas decisively influenced generations of attribution researchers, even as those ideas helped fuel a major debate over the nature of explanation in social psychology. The rise of cognitive science and its commitment to the project of naturalizing the philosophy of mind by treating intentionality as the outcome of the processing of information on the model of computational processes also encouraged social psychologists to treat the mind in physical-causal terms.

Such trends within social psychology came to a climax of sorts with the publication of Nisbett and Wilson's "Telling More Than We Can Know" (1977). Their article set in motion a discussion that revealed deep fissures in the social sciences generally, and especially in social psychology. The controversy set to a boil a dispute that had already been simmering for some time about the methods and assumptions of the field, a dispute that touched on some of the most fundamental epistemological and ontological issues at stake in the study of interpersonal relations. Among important works in that debate were Peter Winch's *The Idea of a Social Science and Its Relation to Philosophy* (1958), a Wittgensteinian critique of the claims of social psychology to scientific status; Martin Orne's (1962) and Robert Rosenthal's (1963; 1966) revelations concerning the complex "psychology of the psychology experiment," in which the relationship between experimenter and participant was shown to be influenced by unconscious expectations, biases, demands, and motives (Morawski 2015); Meehl's searing indictments of the use of null-hypothesis significance testing in psychology (Meehl 1967; 1978; 1990a; 1990b); and Milgram's famous experiments on participant obedience (Milgram 1974). These and related works had already contributed to the sense that social psychology was in a state of crisis and that its paradigms were inadequate to the tasks confronting it.[5]

I use the word *paradigm* deliberately, because some of the contributors to the debates over the status of social psychology in the 1970s and beyond were influenced by Kuhn's (1970a) examination of the nature of scientific revolutions. The speed with which some psychologists adopted Kuhn's term, *paradigm*, suggests that the attribution of a "paradigm" to psychology gave a sense of legitimacy to a field that had been repeatedly undermined by quarrels over fundamentals. The issue became whether the social sciences as a whole conformed to Kuhn's account of established sciences—such as physics and chemistry, in which robust paradigms or "research exemplars" subtended the accumulation of research findings—or whether instead, as Kuhn (1970b) himself suggested, the social sciences were better described as "pre-paradigmatic" or "proto-sciences" in which "incessant criticism and continual striving for a fresh start" were primary forces, with the result that they failed to produce clear-cut progress.[6]

---

5. Among secondary sources regarding the "crisis" in social psychology reaching back to the early history of the field, see Gjorgjioska and Tomicic 2019; and Morawski 2015; 2019; 2020. I note that Meehl (1978) cited intentionality as one of the features of the psychology of humans that made psychology hard to "scientize."

6. For debates at this time over whether psychology constituted a "normal" science in Kuhn's sense of the term, see Palermo 1971; Warren 1971; 1974; Briskman 1972; Mackenzie 1972; Weimer and Palermo 1973; 1974; and Weimer 1974. In her analysis of the crisis in American psychology which began in the late 1950s and early 1960s, Faye (2012) states that by the end of the 1970s the sense of crisis had largely dissipated. In a related spirit, Cohen-Cole (2014) argues that when the cognitive revolution displaced behaviorism, thereby legitimating renewed attention to mental states, the effect was to redirect attention away from the troubling questions of experimenter expectancy in favor of a picture of humans as autonomous, flexible, and rational. Picking up on Cohen-Cole's analysis, Morawski (2015) likewise suggests that by the 1970s the experimental anxieties precipitated by the discovery of the influence of experimenter expectancy and demand on experimental outcomes had been alleviated by the political-ontological transformation of subjects and experimenters. These analyses are interesting and valuable. But there are problems not only with Cohen-Cole's claim that cognitive psychology offered a picture of the subject as autonomous, but also with the suggestion that the resolution of the crisis in the social sciences occurred in the 1970s, not least because, after the demise of behaviorism, critics continued to raise the same epistemological and ontological questions about cognitive psychology that they had

It is against the background of this long-standing dispute that the significance of Nisbett and Wilson's influential paper (1977) needs to be assessed. The fact that, in the short term, the critics of Nisbett and Wilson's claims and of attribution theory more generally were defeated did not mean that the issues those critics raised were permanently routed. On the contrary, I will argue that those criticisms were largely correct, which is why in the end Bargh's experiments on automaticity would eventually turn out to be non-replicable, based as they were on precisely the mistaken causal premises informing Nisbett and Wilson's work.[7] In the next chapter I propose examining the alternative ways of accounting for human action as they surfaced in the 1970s in the important if unresolved debates that ensued over the direction of social psychology.

---

earlier raised against behaviorism. On this last point see Adair 1991. Faye is right, though, to suggest that over time the larger epistemological problems of central concern to critics of the social sciences tended to be marginalized by mainstream psychology, as the conclusion of my chapter 2 demonstrates.

7. The philosopher Eric Mandelbaum takes Nisbett and Wilson's 1977 paper as showing that our minds are opaque to us because our thought processes are not available to introspection, but he appears to be unaware of the controversy that Nisbett and Wilson's paper generated at the time of its publication or indeed of the more recent debate over the validity of priming-research findings, a field that he has recently described as "thriving" (Mandelbaum 2014, 76; see also Mandelbaum 2010). For related discussions of the relevance of Bargh's priming experiments to philosophy, see also Gendler 2008a; 2008b; 2010; 2012; and Mandelbaum 2013.

2

Intentions and Causes

"Baseball and Hot Sauce"

As emerged in the previous chapter, Nisbett and Wilson challenged the view that people's self-reports based on introspection gave a reliable picture of the cognitive mechanisms causing their own behavior or that of others. They claimed that all that individuals were capable of doing was to give an account on the "contents" of their minds, not the cognitive "processes" that ostensibly accounted for those contents. Nisbett and Wilson defended their claims by appealing to a combination of empirical evidence and theoretical arguments. They cited the findings of attribution experiments appearing to demonstrate that, as "intuitive psychologists," participants tried to identify the causes of behavior but did this task poorly because they were liable to attribution errors and biases. According to Nisbett and Wilson, this liability arose because the causes of people's behavior were information processes in the mind-brain that were in principle unavailable to consciousness. As a result, people were only able to report the "products" of these unconscious events (the mental "contents"), not the processes themselves. The authors further argued that individuals were no better than observers at reporting the causes of their own actions, a claim that challenged the traditional view of introspection as providing unique access to personal experience. The net effect of Nisbett and Wilson's paper was not only to deliver a blow to introspection as a reliable research methodology but to call into question the function of consciousness itself. That is why they claimed that, for the most part, people were in the condition of telling more than they could know.

Nisbett and Wilson's paper generated an extraordinary outpouring of commentary that drew attention to the range of issues at stake in attribution research. One of the most brilliant critiques was offered by social psychologists John Sabini and Maury Silver, who challenged the validity of the fundamental distinction the authors made between cognitive "content" and cognitive "processes" (Sabini and Silver 1981a).[1] Indeed, Sabini and Silver called into question the whole idea of introspectable *cognitive processes* being the kind of thing to which people don't have access. The authors first discussed what it means for a person to give a description of a behavioral process, such as baking a cake, in order to demonstrate that the person requires much more than "access to his baking process." To describe the event accurately, the person has to understand what counts as irrelevant among all the things she does while producing the cake (for example, answering the telephone, closing the door, scratching a knee, and so on) and what counts as relevant (turning on the oven, mixing the ingredients, placing the cake in the oven, removing it, and so on). In other words, according to Sabini and Silver, Nisbett and Wilson were wrong to think that having access alone ensures that people will be able to answer the "why" question, because they have to be forearmed with an understanding of what it means to bake a cake in order to make use of the access available to them. As the authors put it: "To report accurately on someone's process of baking a cake (as well as to give causes of baked cakes), one must know when to start the report and what to include in it. Mere access, without criteria of starting and inclusion and knowledge of how to apply them, does not ensure an accurate report" (Sabini and Silver 1981a, 178). They applied the same analysis to cognitive processes, selecting as their example the case of perfect introspective access to a cognitive process, in this case a computer's program, since computer programs had become prevalent in cognitive-psychology models of cognitive processes.

The upshot of Sabini and Silver's argument was that Nisbett and Wilson's picture of individuals introspecting their minds to discover the causes of their behavior was a mistake, because to make sense, any report of one's cognitions cannot just be a report of putative internal processes but has to involve a reference to the objective circumstances in the world in which the performance takes place. Knowing the world in all its conventional, rule-governed, everyday public aspects is part of what knowing a process is. In sum, with a brief mention of Wittgenstein's account of rule-following

---

1. The next two paragraphs repeat the account of Sabini and Silver's (1981a) paper given in Leys 2017 (214–15).

(Wittgenstein 1953), the authors proposed that the standards, rules, and conventions governing our actions are not a matter of individual mental contents inside the head or brain but are shared social products, a conclusion implying that the program of cognitive psychology, with its emphasis on introspecting internal causal processes or mechanisms, was misguided.

In related publications, Sabini and Silver criticized attribution theory itself. Not only did they attack the "fundamental attribution error" as based on a false dichotomy between external-situational causes versus internal-dispositional ones. They objected to the whole tendency of attribution theorists to substitute causal analyses of human actions when reason analyses were called for. In a paper amusingly entitled "Baseball and Hot Sauce: A Critique of Some Attributional Treatments of Evaluation," Sabini and Silver complained that attribution theorists reduced people's attributions to matters of taste or personal preference when they were actually normative decisions about whether things were good or bad, decisions that could be evaluated objectively and potentially disputed (Sabini and Silver 1980). We might put it that, according to Sabini and Silver, attribution theorists converted people's disagreements about their beliefs and evaluative judgments into merely subjective responses or personal preferences, about which it made no sense to disagree.

To bring out the difference between evaluations and mere reactions, Sabini and Silver compared a dispute between two people about the merits of the baseball player Tommy Ryle (in real life a semiprofessional player with a brief career in the game) versus a conversation about eating hot sauce. In the hot sauce case, two people who have different reactions to the sauce are not really attempting to prove the superiority of their judgments. "Each accepts that the other had the reaction that he said he had . . . How could someone be mistaken about whether he had heartburn? . . . They might say as a summary of their discussion of hot sauce, 'Well, you had one reaction I had another.' And we and they can see that this summary is fair." But in the baseball case, each person treats the other's judgment about the merits of Ryle as a baseball player as mistaken—and mistaken about an object in the world. "But on the other hand, would it be a fair summary of the argument about baseball to say 'Well you had one reaction and I had another?' In the baseball case this is a clear evasion, not a summary. In the hot sauce case there is nothing to evade or resolve; in the baseball case there is—who is wrong about Tommy Ryle." To describe or explain the Tommy Ryle example in a straightforward manner, Sabini and Silver added, "one would have to include these features that made the controversy over the evaluations reactions different from the discussion of the gastric reactions" (Sabini and Silver 1980, 85–86).

Sabini and Silver argued that it was precisely the distinction between reactions (or the effects of causes) and evaluations (or normative judgments) that attribution theorists such Kelley, Jones, Nisbett, and Wilson failed to recognize:

> They suggest that the only, or at least the most important way commonsense actors treat evaluations is to search for their causes; and *this follows from the description of evaluations as reactions, since reactions cannot be true or false or much else except caused.* We propose that the search for causes is more appropriate to understanding heartburn, which cannot sensibly be said to be correct or incorrect, than for reactions like, "he's a great ballplayer," which can. (Sabini and Silver 1980, 87; their emphasis)

The problem with attribution theory, then, was that it converted disagreements about truth and falsity—which is to say, disagreements about the meaning of an intended action, performance, utterance, or work of art—into a concern with causally determined reactions or effects, which might be different in different people but are neither right nor wrong.

As Sabini and Silver recognized, this conversion took place in Kelley's approach to attribution. According to Kelley, when we react to a movie with laughter and claim we do so because it is funny, we are claiming that the movie is an external cause of the laughter. We are predicting that not only we ourselves but nearly everyone else will react to this "stimulus" by laughing, no matter how often it is presented or in what medium. "Stating that the movie is funny," Sabini and Silver commented, "is [for Kelley] 'really' a shorthand way of making a prediction of the popularity of 'funniness reactions' over people, time, and mode of presentations ... So we are left with consensus" (Sabini and Silver 1980, 88–89).

And that was precisely the problem. Such an account was "terribly oversimplified," Sabini and Silver stated (Sabini and Silver 1980, 89). Referring to the baseball player Tommy Ryle again, they observed that, even if only a single fan argued that Ryle was a great player, consensus would not show him to be wrong, because consensus was not a guarantor of truth in such matters. Kelley's approach was "not a description of *how* people decide truth and falsity," they argued, nor was it "an adequate account of what it means for an evaluation to be true or false" (Sabini and Silver 1980, 89, 90; their emphasis).

Sabini and Silver further insisted that when we make evaluations, we are not making merely personal or subjective assessments of some object in the world, we are rendering judgments that we believe are objectively true. They noted that both "interpretive sociology" and the "symbolic interactionists," by which they meant figures such as Harold Garfinkel, Émile Durkheim, George Herbert Mead, and others, "take as their first principle that people treat social facts, including evaluations, as real, *objective*, beyond their will, interests, and moods" (Sabini and Silver 1980, 91; their emphasis). They contrasted ordinary language treatments of evaluations of the kind proposed by philosophers Ludwig Wittgenstein and John Austin with those offered by social psychologists:

> Analytic philosophers in the traditions of Wittgenstein (1953) and Austin (1961), also analyse evaluations as meaningful utterances, as having meaning within a shared form of life . . . [But] while these philosophers look for the meaning of terms, for the significance of utterances, not in their being individual reactions, but in their actual *use* in social life, i.e., they look at the *shared* forms of social life that evaluations are part of, social psychologists, who ought by virtue of their particular discipline to be *most* concerned with the relation of individual thought and action to "shared forms of life," treat evaluations as subjective, personal, biased, not to be understood as either "real" or social. (Sabini and Silver 1980, 91; their emphasis)

In sum, Sabini and Silver reproached Nisbett and Wilson, and attribution theorists more generally, for proceeding as if beliefs and actions could not be defended by reasons and arguments because they were merely the effect of sub-personal, material processes in the brain. By failing to distinguish between normative evaluations and causally determined reactions, attribution theorists treated ethics and aesthetics as merely "branches of internal medicine," the grading of students as simply "exercises in personal bias," and the evaluation of the worth of a person as just an "abreaction" (Sabini and Silver 1981b, 100). In effect, Sabini and Silver criticized attribution theorists for treating reasons as explanatorily impotent or mere epiphenomena, as if the only real causal work were carried out by computational processes in the mind-brain.[2]

---

2. Sabini and Silver went on to publish several more articles critiquing attribution theorists and certain moral philosophers (e.g., Flanagan 1991; Harman 1999; Doris 2002)

Reasons versus Causes

Sabini and Silver were not alone in criticizing Nisbett and Wilson and the attribution theorists for failing to respect the distinction between reasons and causes. Their arguments strike me as particularly acute, but many others also took Nisbett and Wilson to task for similar errors and mistakes. Indeed, the debate concerning the role of reasons versus causes in social explanation was so widespread that it seems unlikely that a psychologist such as Bargh could have been unaware of the controversy.[3] Whether he grasped the import of the stakes involved in the dispute is another question.

Critics in the debate over the distinction between reasons and causes appealed to a variety of philosophical authorities. We have seen that Sabini and Silver cited both Wittgenstein and Austin in their discussions of Nisbett and Wilson's 1977 paper and attribution research. Similarly, in 1978 psychologist Allan Buss placed the well-known statement in Wittgenstein's *Philosophical Investigations* (1953) about the conceptual confusions in psychology at the beginning of his own response to Nisbett and Wilson's claims.[4] It was precisely those conceptual confusions that concerned Buss when he insisted on the difference between "causal" explanations and "reason" explanations. "Behavior that happens *to* a person—that is non-intentional, that a person 'suffers'—is an *occurrence* and is explained by both actors and observers with causes," Buss declared. "Behavior that is done *by* a person—that is intended, that has a goal or purpose—is an *action* and is explained by the actor with reasons. The observer may use causes and/or reasons in explaining action" (Buss 1978, 1311; his emphasis). He added:

---

for overestimating the role of situational factors in human behavior while underestimating the role of people's inherent dispositions and intentions. Sabini and Silver's general position was that attribution theorists and the "situationists" tried to enforce too stark a choice between the *environment as cause* and the *person as cause* (which is to say, the person as an intentional agent), instead of realizing that people's actions are always the outcome of a mix of such influences (Sabini and Silver 1983, 2005).

3. For a useful evaluation of the literature on this dispute and of the various objections raised against Nisbett and Wilson's 1977 paper, see White 1988.

4. "'For in psychology,'" Buss quoted Wittgenstein as stating, "'there are experimental methods and *conceptual confusion* . . . The existence of the experimental method makes us think we have the means of solving the problems which trouble us; though problem and method pass one another by'" (Buss 1978, 1311; emphasis in the original).

Thus, the kinds of attributions made depend upon what kind of behavior is to be explained (occurrences or actions) and the status of the explainer (observer or actor) . . . Attribution theorists have tended to project an exclusively causal framework onto the lay explanation of all behavior and all explainers and are thus confused and confusing regarding causes and reasons . . . Attribution theorists need to become more self-conscious about the correct use of the terms *cause* and *reason* in the explanation of behavior. (Buss 1978, 1311; his emphasis)

Buss dismissed those who argued that the problems facing attribution theory were primarily empirical (Harvey and Tucker 1979). For him, as for Sabini and Silver, those problems were conceptual through and through (Buss 1979, 1458). And the most fundamental conceptual problem concerned the failure of attribution theorists to recognize that, as Buss put it, "causes and reasons are logically distinct categories for explaining different aspects of behavior." He ascribed the mistake of attribution theorists in this regard to the influence of Heider. "Heider, unfortunately, did not distinguish between causes and reasons—the two different kinds of explanations that have their basis in ordinary language," he remarked. "Lay explanation for Heider was assumed to be entirely causal in nature, in spite of the fact that he gave considerable attention to the commonsense use of such reason concepts as purpose, motive, and intention in the explanation of action. It has been the perpetuation of Heider's exclusively causal interpretation of action that has contributed to some of the serious conceptual confusion in the field" (Buss 1978, 1311, 1313).

In his critique of attribution theory, Buss referred to a range of authorities. Among these he included Aristotle, for his four different uses of the term *cause* (efficient, final, material, and formal); Charles Taylor's *The Explanation of Behaviour* (1964); Gilbert Ryle's *The Concept of Mind* (1949); R. S. Peters's *The Concept of Motivation* (1958); Peter Winch's *The Idea of Social Science* (1958); and analytic philosopher K. S. Donnellan's "excellent discussion" in his entry "Reasons and Causes" in the *Encyclopedia of Philosophy* (1967).[5] From a consideration of these sources, he concluded that causal and reason explanations of behavior were conceptually

---

5. Donnellan (1967) listed Anscombe and Wittgenstein among philosophers who favored the distinction between reasons and causes, and Davidson among those critical of the distinction.

distinct and were "different ways of talking about different kinds of behavior" (Buss 1978, 1314). He observed of the philosophy of Wittgenstein and Ryle:

> The major cases involving reason explanations of human action include (a) justifying, evaluating, or appraising the action; (b) stating the goal, end, or intention of the action; and (c) stating the means or instrumentality of the goal, end, or intention of the action. All of these reason-type explanations help to make an action intelligible by attaching *meaning* to the action in terms of the rules for social behavior and, as such, are not causal explanations. By causal behavior one refers to lawfulness and predictability, where an event is explained by reference to a general principle. While there are many controversial issues surrounding the causality notion . . . for present purposes it will suffice to associate this kind of explanation with such connotative "attributes" as lawfulness, determinism, antecedent-consequent relationship, predictability, and replicability. With respect to explaining behavior, causes are necessary when dealing with either (a) unintelligible or irrational intended behavior or (b) unintended behavior. (Buss 1978, 1314; his emphasis)

Buss therefore denied Jones and Nisbett's (1972) claim that both actors and observers were concerned to identify the causes of behavior, as if the only difference was that actors mistakenly tended to attribute the causes of their own actions to external situations, whereas observers mistakenly tended to attribute those same actions to causes inherent in the actors' personal dispositions. Instead, Buss argued that actors, like students, eyewitnesses, and politicians, were engaged in attempting to *justify* their actions, to provide a *rationale* for them, to make their actions *intelligible* to others, and to offer a *moral* explanation for their behavior. As he stated:

> In short, they are in a situation where a *reason*, and not a causal explanation of their action, is required. To construe an actor's self-explanation to be fundamentally causal in nature, where the actor supposedly divides his or her causal attributions disproportionately to self and the environment, is to make a serious category mistake . . . In asking an actor to explain his or her action, the "why" is a request to make rational, intelligible, his or her action vis-à-vis society's norms for "proper" conduct.

The actor's "because" statements consist of giving his or her reasons for an action, that is, matters that weighed in on his or her deliberation. (Buss 1978, 1315; his emphasis)

The upshot of Buss's discussion was that actors and observers did not occupy identical positions, and thus that an observer could not have exactly the same claim to understand an actor's responses as the actor himself or herself. He cited Donnellan on this point:

"First, the agent seems to have a privileged position concerning the reasons for his actions . . . He does not, at any rate, utilize evidence and empirical investigation in the normal case to establish what his reasons are. Second, we seem to accept reason explanations, without supposing the necessity for some generalization to a larger class of cases. If a man acts from certain reasons in this instance, we may, but do not have to, suppose that either he or others will act in this way when they have these reasons in other cases. These two facts . . . seem foreign to causal explanations." (Buss 1978, 1316; citing Donnellan 1967, 88)

On this basis, Buss criticized Jones and Nisbett for suggesting that the only difference between actor and observer concerned differences in their sources of information and modes of information processing.[6] Buss ended by suggesting that the terms *cause* and *reason* had been used so incorrectly by those working in attribution theory that the search for causes had become a totalizing ideology in the social sciences.

One ambitious work of criticism, to which Buss drew attention in his critique of Nisbett and Wilson's paper, was Rom Harré and P. F. Secord's *The Explanation of Social Behavior* (1972). The authors, a philosopher and psychologist respectively, had argued even before Nisbett and Wilson's

---

6. Buss even suggested that the term *actor*, as used by attribution theorists, was a misnomer because it implied an agency that the subject lacked, according to the attribution theorists. He suggested that *sufferer* would be a better term for what attribution theorists were concerned with, and that *occurrences* would be a better term than *actions* for their behaviors (Buss 1978, 1317). The substitution of the name *participant* for the experimental *subject* in psychology in recent years can be seen as the attempt to restore some measure of personhood and agency to the subjects of experiments, although social psychology has remained largely committed to treating the behaviors of participants as if they were the passive products of causal forces. Morawski has recently commented in this regard that "the more recent replacement of the designation 'subject' with 'participant' seems not to have affected experimental relations much" (Morawski 2015, 573 n19).

1977 article that the underlying reason for the increasing dissatisfaction with the state of psychology at that time was "a continued adherence to a positivist methodology, long after the theoretical justification for it, in naïve behaviorism, has been repudiated." They had added:

> In such a vacuum it is still possible to carry on empirical studies which make sense only if people are conceived of in the mechanical tradition as passive entities whose behavior is the product of "impressed forces," and whose own contribution to social action is the latent product of earlier impressed experience. A methodology of experiment survives in which the typical investigation is recommended to be the manipulation of "variables," and the typical result a correlation in the manner of Boyle's Law. (Harré and Secord 1972, 1)

Harré and Secord's book is especially interesting because of the authors' belief that social psychology had reached a crossroads. One of their targets was Robert Zajonc, who was to become Bargh's doctoral thesis supervisor. Harré and Secord rebuked Zajonc for sticking to what, in reference to Kuhn's discussion of the structure of scientific revolutions, they called "the Old Paradigm" in social psychology. "The Old Paradigm," they wrote,

> involves the conception of a theory as a deductive structure from which the empirically ascertained laws are to be derived by strict logical inference... This assumption is thought to be justified in turn by the general principle that the aim of science is to discover correlations between changes in the properties of systems. In the farthest background lies Hume's theory of causality according to which such correlations *are* causal laws. The Old Paradigm... is particularly well exemplified in social psychological contexts by the work of experimentalists such as R. B. Zajonc. (Harré and Secord 1972, 19–20; their emphasis).

Harré and Secord focused attention on "cognitive dissonance theory" and Zajonc's response to critiques of that theory, critiques which gestured toward the "New Paradigm" that Zajonc rejected. Cognitive dissonance theory, which was part of emerging attribution theory and research, proposed that a situation involving conflicting attitudes, beliefs, or behaviors produced subjective feelings of mental dissonance and distress. The theory suggested that this distress led subjects to change certain of their attitudes, beliefs, or behaviors in order to reduce discomfort and restore balance. Harré and Secord's general complaint was that the experimental protocols informing studies of cognitive dissonance, and the kind of cognitive-science research Zajonc championed, destroyed the possibility of studying the very features which were essential to social behavior in its natural setting. They argued that the experiments conducted under the Old Paradigm presented to the experimental participants descriptions of "stimulus" persons in terms of "absurdly limited information" (such as a few attitude statements purported to be theirs) and treated experimental subjects as "severely restricted" in the form of the attribution judgments they might make. "Common to all types of overly-restrictive experiments," Harré and Secord observed, "is the conception of people as information-*processing* machines, rather than information-seeking and information-generating agents. Thus information is deliberately restricted, and *inter*action prevented" (Harré and Secord 1972, 44; their emphasis).

In opposition to what they considered the "Old Paradigm" in social psychology, Harré and Secord proposed as a "New Paradigm" an alternative "anthropomorphic" vision of what a social psychology of the future should look like. Above all, they argued, the New Paradigm in social psychology should attempt to explain human behavior "according to the meaning ascribed to the situation." As they wrote: "At the heart of the explanation of social behavior is the identification of the meanings that underlie it. Part of the approach to discovering them involves the obtaining of *accounts*—the actor's own statements about why he performed the acts in question, what social meanings he gave to the actions of himself and others." Or as they also asserted: "We are going to have to put the person back into experimental psychology" (Harré and Secord 1972, 9, 61–62; their emphasis).

As these statements indicate, putting the person back into psychology meant attending to the "why" question, understood as the question that concerned the meaning of people's actions, a question that could only be answered by listening to people's reasons for their performances and behaviors: "The things that people say about themselves and other people should be taken seriously as reports of data relevant to phenomena that *really exist* and which are *relevant* to the explanation of behavior." Or as they also observed: "It is through reports of feelings, plans, intentions, beliefs, reasons and so on that the meanings of social behavior and the rules underlying social acts can be discovered" (Harré and Secord 1972, 7; their emphasis).

Here we reach a major theme of Harré and Secord's book, namely, the nature of intentional action and the associated question of the difference between reasons and causes. "The distinction between reasons and causes has been thoroughly debated by philosophical psychologists," they remarked, "and has, it seems to us, reached a definite conclusion. There can be no doubt that the concepts are distinct" (Harré and Secord 1972, 159). They considered and rejected the supposition of some philosophers that reasons were a special class of cause. They especially emphasized the role reasons played in justifications of action, observing that reasons were "logically related to the propriety of the actions and not to the existence or occurrence of the action, which in one and the same episode may be causally explained." They observed:

> What is deceptive here is that both reason and cause are answers to a single question, "Why did he do it?" What is overlooked is that this question can be answered in two conceptually independent contexts. In terms of reasons, the consideration is of an active agent making a decision in a normative or justificatory context; in terms of causes, the consideration is of a passive agent exposed to certain circumstances and conditions, both internal and external. That both are answers to the same form of the question—namely "Why?"—sometimes leads to the two forms of explanation to be confused with each other.
>
> It would be a serious mistake to treat reasons offered in a justificatory context as if they were causes. This could be looked upon with some justification as one of the most serious defects of the methodology of traditional psychology. This treatment is implicit in the various attempts that have been made to treat both motives and intentions as special classes of causes. We shall not go any further into this matter at this point, since the . . . conceptual impropriety of a thoroughgoing identification of intentions with part of the causal conditions of action seems to be a clear consequence of the study of intentions by G. E. M. Anscombe. (Harré and Secord 1972, 161)[7]

---

7. For other critiques of social-psychology assumptions framed in terms of the distinction between reasons and causes, see Beck 1975; Strickland, Aboud, and Gergen 1976; and Malle 2006a.

Anscombe versus Davidson on Intentional Action

It seems to me that Harré and Secord were right to attribute to the philosopher Elizabeth Anscombe the view that there is a clear distinction between reason explanations and causal explanations. Moreover, they were not alone in citing Anscombe's work: for example, Kenneth Gergen also made use of Anscombe's analysis of intention in his criticisms of social psychology (Gergen 1982, 63, 87, 185, 212). As I observed at the end of chapter 1, the use of Anscombe's work on intention by certain social psychologists who were caught up in the debate over the status and methods of social psychology is especially noteworthy, given the tendency of many philosophers to neglect her work. But the issue requires further discussion.

I noted at the end of chapter 1 that Anscombe's account of intention tended to be mediated by the writings of Donald Davidson. We can come to grips with the issues at stake here by considering the difference between Donaldson's approach to intentionality and that of Anscombe. Davidson recognized Anscombe's *Intention* as "'the most important treatment of action since Aristotle'" (cited by Stoutland 2011, 1) but, rejecting her arguments, explicitly defended the view that reasons could be causes (Davidson 1963).[8] Thus for him, an intentional action was done for reasons if it was caused by the right mental states and events in the right way.[9] Davidson was not a dualist in the sense of positing an interaction between two substances, mind and body, as in the classical Cartesian picture. Rather, as the philosopher Jennifer Hornsby, one of the best guides to Anscombe's

---

8. Stoutland (2011) provides a useful account of the philosophical context in which Davidson attempted (unsuccessfully) to integrate Anscombe's notions of intentionality with a causal account of action and of how Davidson's views came to be understood and interpreted in the now widely accepted "standard" theory of intentionality. It is only recently, thanks to the work of Hornsby (2011) and others (Thompson 2008; Wiseman 2016; Schwenkler 2019; Michaels 2019), that the differences between Davidson's and Anscombe's views have become clear.

9. As the large literature on "deviant causal chains" or counterexamples demonstrates, it is always possible that the relevant mental states and events cause the relevant action in a deviant way. For example, in Davidson's example, a climber intends to rid himself of the weight and danger of holding another person on a rope by loosening his grip, but the intention unnerves him, and he inadvertently loses his grip on the rope. "Although his bodily movements were caused by his belief and desire, they were not his action: they did not cause his movements in the right way" (Stoutland 2011, 14). See also Davidson 2001, 79–81; Schlosser 2019a.

thinking, has stressed, Davidson posited a dualism of two happenings according to which there is a gap between the mental happening (the intention) and the consequent happening (the action itself), considered as two separate events. "Donald Davidson propounded a Principal of Causal Interaction," Hornsby observes, "which says that 'at least some mental events interact causally with physical events'" (Hornsby 2015, 126; citing Davidson 1970, 88). Indeed, as I observed in the introduction, most cognitive psychologists thought of intentionality exactly in this way, as involving two events separated by a gap between them—the intention (the mental state) and the consequent action (the behavioral event or effect). Bargh pictured intention in this way. Moreover, many philosophers took Davidson to authorize an empirical approach to issues of intention precisely because he treated agency in causal terms.[10]

But it was not Davidson's belief that reasons can be causes that troubles Anscombean critics, such as Hornsby. Their criticism is, rather, that Davidson adhered to a wrong, Humean account of causes according to which causes are external to, or independent of, the intentional action itself, instead of internal to it. As Hornsby argues in favor of Anscombe's views and against Davidson's position: "The properly causal aspect of agency is not accounted for using a relation 'cause' obtaining between pairs of items" (Hornsby 2015, 125). Hornsby illustrates Anscombe's thinking on this issue by giving as an example Ann's carrying a suitcase. "When Ann is carrying the suitcase—when she is in the process of carrying it, so that her action is occurring—there seems to be no candidate for an event that her action is causing." That is, one does not see two events, a person intending to carry a suitcase and the suitcase being carried. "So long as Ann is carrying the suitcase," Hornsby writes, "the only event in which the suitcase participates is its being carried. The causality here is internal to an event: Ann's carrying the suitcase *is* the event of its being carried. As Anscombe herself might put it: 'Ann does what happens'" (Hornsby 2011, 107; her emphasis).

She notes in this regard that Anscombe would say of such an intentional action, "gainsaying Hume, that 'efficacy is plainly discoverable to the mind'" (Hornsby 2011, 108). The efficacy is "evident," Hornsby comments,

---

10. I note, however, that according to Frey, Davidson thought it was a mistake to hold that action explanation—while causal in his sense—was reducible to the kinds of explanation found in the sciences (Frey 2013, 51).

"not because one sees two happenings, nor yet because one sees a person and a happening that she causes, but because one sees a happening that *is* the person's causing. If you focus on the suitcase, you may see it being carried; if you focus on her, you may see her carrying. But there is only one event of carrying to be seen, and so, *mutatis mutandis*, in the other cases. In seeing this event, you see causality in operation; and that is because what you see is *her at work*—her causing this or that." She observes that for Anscombe "causality can be internal to an action" and suggests that there is "no need to deny that there is a genuine causal element in 'making it happen that one's arm is up.' For raising one's arm (in the usual case) is surely a matter of non-mediately causing" (Hornsby 2011, 108, 109, 113; her emphasis). This claim leads Hornsby to state that "neo-Aristotelians [such as Anscombe and herself] do not treat *cause* as everywhere a relation—neither as a relation between two events, nor between two objects, nor between an object and an event" (Hornsby 2015, 131; her emphasis).[11]

In short, according to Hornsby, Anscombe did not deny that agents have causal powers, but believed, rather, that their causal powers do not conform to the Humean picture of causality (for Anscombe's anti-Humean views, see also Wiseman 2016, 82, 94–96, 102).[12] As Hornsby states: "The

11. See also Michael Thompson's (2008) neo-Aristotelian analysis of intentional action.
12. One way in which Anscombe herself put this point was to say that our intentional actions are known to us non-inferentially and "without observation," by which she meant that we have an immediate awareness or knowledge of our own intentions: I don't have to observe my arm moving to know I'm moving it; moreover, as an intentional action I move it for a reason, and so my action is open to the question, Why? In a famous crux in *Intention*, Anscombe asks: What do I say I am doing if I start writing "I am a fool" in ink on a piece of paper, or with chalk on a blackboard, while my eyes are shut? (Anscombe 2000 [1957], ¶29, 53; ¶46, 83). All sorts of things might go wrong with the writing—the words might become unintelligible; I might go on writing after my pen runs out of ink; my chalk might break—but, as Michaels has recently argued, according to Anscombe the account I would give of what I am doing would not be a description of separate events or movements, such as how I hold the pen or chalk or move my arms. Even if I were to fail to write legibly, Michaels suggests, I would not think of what I am doing as moving my hands in such a way as "to cause there to be a word," but as writing (Michaels 2016a). He quotes Anscombe as stating in this regard that "'the term intentional has reference to a form of description of events,'" and he comments on her meaning by adding "that form is distinguished by its inclusion of purpose (that's part of the description of an act)" (Michaels 2019, 4–5). For an important exchange about this crux in Anscombe's *Intention*, see Michaels 2016a; 2020; and Schwenkler 2020. See Wiseman 2016 (65–72) for a valuable discussion of what Anscombe meant when she stated that "an action may be intentional

initial anti-Humean thought may be that the very various phenomena which attract the label 'causation' cannot all be brought under the head of 'cause' if this is understood as a relation between events. More specifically, the suggestion may be that a different understanding is required in order that *agency*—a phenomenon in which something *acts*—should be recognized as the causal phenomenon it is" (Hornsby 2015, 129–30; her emphasis). Recognizing agency as the causal phenomenon it is also requires understanding that what distinguishes intentional actions is that they are, as Anscombe famously stated, "actions to which a certain sense of the question "Why" is given application: the sense is of course that in which the answer, if positive, gives a reason for acting" (Anscombe 2000 [1957]). In other words, an agent's capacity to act intentionally is a capacity to act for reasons. As Hornsby argues, "one can provide a causal explanation of what an agent does by saying what her reasons for doing it were" (Hornsby 1998, 382 n16).[13]

This argument suggests that for Anscombe, reasons can be considered causes in the sense that agents have a causal role to play in intentional action: it's just that the cause here can't be considered external to, or independent of, the action as Davidson would have it. Commenting on the difference between Anscombe's and Davidson's views in this regard, Hornsby remarks:

> Given Anscombe's avowed anti-Humeanism, we can assume that she would find it obvious that we often do something non-mediately. Davidson, on the other hand, thought that everything we do . . . we always do mediately. If someone has brought it about that something is squashed, for example, then Davidson would say that that can only be because that person's action caused an event by virtue of whose occurrence the thing came to be squashed . . . Davidson's idea was that we take people to cause things only because we take them to inherit properties that accrue to their actions by dint of the operation of event causality. But once it is

---

under one description and not intentional under another" (Anscombe 1979, 210; Anscombe 2000 [1957], ¶23–26, 37–47), or that "one and the same action (or other event) may have many descriptions" (Anscombe 1979, 210), as when I intend to sign a piece of paper but not to scratch the table in the process of doing so.

13. However, on Wittgensteinian and related grounds Hornsby rejects the charge that agent causality presumes Cartesian substance dualism, implying an interaction between two different substances, mind (or soul) and body, in intentional action. On this point, see Hornsby 1998, (391).

accepted that causality can be internal to an action, it is evident that we need a different idea (Hornsby 2011, 109)

For Hornsby, the "different idea" that is needed in contrast to "event causality" is what she calls "agent causality," about which she comments:

> a generic notion of an agent's causing something embraces both mediately causing and non-mediately causing. Using this idea, we allow for a variety of different specific ways in which an agent may be related to such things as she causes. We then take *agent* causality for granted, as Anscombe surely did. Taking it for granted, she saw no need to *speak* of agent causality: she didn't herself attempt to unearth an underlying "cause" from the causative verbs. (Hornsby 2011, 110; her emphasis)

Hornsby adds: "One way to be clear how different the two notions are is to notice that the doctrine of agent causation makes a specific claim about the agency of human beings (or, as it may be, of beings who enjoy a peculiar kind of freedom), whereas not all the agents that cause things in the sense of [event] 'cause' . . . are human" (Hornsby 2011, 110).

Agent Causation versus Event Causation

The difference between Anscombe's and Davidson's views concerning causation is now standardly described as a difference between "agent causation" (Anscombeans) and "event causation" (Davidsonians) (Hornsby 2011, 110; Schlosser 2011, 2019a). The two positions represent different approaches and have different implications.[14] Anscombe calls into question the relevance of attempts to provide an explanation of intentional action based on event causation, whether involving mental states or states of the nervous system. Instead, in the spirit of agent causation she treats people's reasons for performing an intentional action as a crucial conceptual (or logical) issue that cannot be reduced to the kind of empirical considerations basic to the modern cognitive sciences.

It might seem that Anscombe's position entails a rejection of natural-

---

14. In addition to publications by Hornsby and other authors already cited, in a large literature I have found the following works especially helpful for their arguments about causal theories of intentional action: Wilson 1989; Mele 1997; Sehon 2000; Ginet 2001; Thompson 2008; and Satiya 2018.

istic approaches to the problem of intentionality, which is to say that it might seem that she rejects explanations that fall within the purview of scientific investigation. But it would be more accurate to say that those who defend an Anscombean approach to intentional action do not reject naturalism as such. Hornsby, for example, follows McDowell in endorsing a "liberal" or "naïve" naturalism that takes in its stride the idea that forms of mindedness, such as intentional actions, are through and through a part of the natural world and not alien to it, as a post-Cartesian naturalism of the kind informing the modern cognitive sciences assumes (Hornsby 1997b; see also McDowell 2009). Like Anscombe, Hornsby adopts an irreducible, non-event-based account of agent causation. As she argues against the Davidsonian event-causal theory of intentional action, "*the story leaves agents out*. Human beings are ineliminable from any account of their agency, and, in any of its versions, the standard story is not a story of agency at all" (Hornsby 2004, 2; her emphasis).

It follows that according to Hornsby we cannot account for agency from an external standpoint, as event-causal theories do, but only from the perspective of the agent herself in light of the reasons she gives for her actions and intentions. For Hornsby such an accounting does not mean attempting to locate the agent inside the ostensibly private workings of the mind, as cognitive scientists try to do. Rather, it means breaking completely with the idea, as the philosopher Michael Thompson has put it in his neo-Aristotelian discussion of intentional action, that intending (and wanting and other such "acts of will") are properly defined as internal psychological or mental states at all (Thompson 2008, 92). His point resonates with Sabini and Silver's claim that the rules governing our behavior are not a matter of individual mental contents inside the head or brain but are shared social products.

The significance of the question of agency has emerged in several domains, one of which is in discussions of the nature of human powers or, more specifically, the nature of human dispositions. This topic is of special interest to my project because of the central role the concept of dispositions has played in attribution research, as we have seen. Once again, recent philosophical discussions of dispositions offer a valuable orientation. To repeat Hornsby's observation quoted earlier: "Neo-Aristotelians [such as herself or Anscombe] do not treat *cause* as everywhere a relation— neither as a relation between two events, nor between two objects, nor between an object and an event," to which she immediately adds: "Neo-Aristotelians find fault with the empiricists' treatment of dispositional properties as analyzable away in favour of counterfactual conditionals which introduce relations between events" (Hornsby 2015, 131; her emphasis). By this claim she means that philosophers like Anscombe and herself do not accept an approach to dispositions which assumes that for every disposition, such as a fragile object's disposition to shatter, there is a relation between two separate terms or events: a "stimulus" and the disposition's "manifestation."

In a valuable analysis cited by Hornsby, E. J. Lowe traces the "stimulus-manifestation" approach to dispositions back to the radical empiricism of the philosopher Rudolf Carnap, whose aim was to construct an empiricist language in which all meaningful sentences, including dispositional ones, could be analyzed in observational and extensional-logical terms. Carnap claimed that such analysis could be done by analyzing dispositional statements in terms of conditional statements that defined "predicates expressing 'unobservable' properties in terms of predicates expressing 'observable' ones." As Lowe reports, Carnap offered the "infamous" example of salt, which manifests its disposition to dissolve when it makes contact with the "stimulus" of water. He asked whether the dispositional predicate "soluble in water" could be defined conditionally in terms of a predicate "'is placed in water (at a time t) and dissolves (at t),' which he took to be observational" (Lowe 2011, 20).

Lowe demonstrates that Carnap's attempts to answer this question quickly ran into difficulties, such as being unable to explain how it is that a piece of common salt which is never placed in water is nonetheless soluble in water. Numerous problems of this and related kinds have been raised over the years without receiving satisfactory solutions. Nevertheless, as Lowe notes, those problems have not deterred philosophers from continuing to hanker after such conditional analyses of disposition statements. "One gets the impression," Lowe remarks, "that many of them think that somehow, if only the world were ordered aright, such an analysis would be forthcoming and that it is just a tiresome nuisance that messy concrete reality seemingly conspires to frustrate their hopes of achieving one" (Lowe 2011, 19).

Lowe argues, however, that the situation is "beyond repair." The problem, he persuasively argues, is precisely the empirical approach to dispositions, specifically, the basic idea that for every disposition, there is a "stimulus" and a "manifestation." His point is that dispositions always have "manifestations," but they don't always have "stimuli," at least not in the way the dispositional theorists typically conceive of such stimuli. "The *manifestation* of a disposition is something that is built into the disposition's very *nature*," Lowe states, "for ... a disposition is always a disposition *to* such-and-such, where the 'such-and-such' is its manifestation. But the notion of a 'stimulus' is *not*, I would urge, similarly built into the very nature of any disposition" (Lowe 2011, 23). Thus, the notion of "disposition" or "power" is irreducible to a stimulus-manifestation, or an if-then analysis, which is to say that it does not conform to a cause-and-effect analysis. As Lowe puts this point:

> What is customarily described as the "stimulus" of a disposition and customarily regarded as being one [of] the causes of that disposition's "manifestation," is in fact just *a logically necessary condition* of the (properly described) manifestation's taking place at all. And this, indeed, is why it is so easy for us to come up with a putative "stimulus" in so many cases, since we merely need to call upon our understanding of the meaning of the (transitive) verb (properly) used to describe the disposition's manifestation. (Lowe 2011, 29; his emphasis)

Lowe concludes his paper by suggesting that "we should learn to accept the language of dispositional predication—the language of *powers*—for what it is: perfectly intelligible in its own terms" (Lowe 2011, 32; his emphasis). Hornsby likewise rejects an empirical, causal approach to dispositions: she regards the term *disposition* as simply another word for an object's "powers," defined as intrinsic properties that inhere in things as potentialities of various kinds. In the case of humans, one such crucial intrinsic power is the capacity to act, the power of agency. As Hornsby writes: "We must give *agents* the central place in a story, and allow that agents have powers to affect things and that what they bring about intentionally is shaped by their reasoning" (Hornsby 2011, 125; her emphasis). She cites the recent growth of neo-Aristotelian treatments of these topics as proof of the contemporary relevance of such work to the philosophy of mind.

More generally, we can say that Anscombean and other critics of the Humean-causal approach to reason and of Davidson's event-causal theory of intentional action accuse their opponents of transforming intentional actions into events that merely happen to us as passive creatures, which is to say, they accuse them of leaving out the agency of human beings. The problem has come to be called the problem of the "disappearing agent."

Does Social Psychology Need a New Paradigm?

All this has direct bearing on the crisis in social psychology triggered by Nisbett and Wilson's "Saying More Than One Can Know." Anscombe's agent-causal account of intentional action called into question the scientism that many followers of Davidson accept as inherent in the latter's approach to intentional action. As the philosopher Markus Schlosser has recently remarked in this regard, a commitment to Davidson's event-causal framework is "tantamount to a commitment to a very minimal and widely-endorsed kind of naturalism, according to which any appeal to irreducible substance-causation or teleology is to be avoided" (Schlosser 2019b).[15] Schlosser accepts the Davidsonian view of reason as a form of causation and accordingly dismisses the concept of agent causation as a controversial metaphysical doctrine that is also empirically inadequate (Schlosser 2012, 139–40). In short, although on various empirical and other grounds, Schlosser pushes back against Nisbett and Wilson's claims about the non-intentionality of much human behaviors, he does not question the causal assumptions informing such work.

But for those who, in the 1970s, on Anscombean, Wittgensteinian, or other grounds held that there was a radical difference between reason and event-causal explanations, the consequences for the conduct of their field were more radical. Their conceptual commitments called into question the entire framework governing experimental social psychology. These conceptual commitments included the following:

1. A rejection of Humean-causal approaches to the investigation of social life in favor of a focus on the intentions and meanings of human action. Already in 1958, Winch had set the pattern when, inspired by Wittgenstein's discussions of rule-following in *The Philosophical Investigations*, he rejected the assimilation of the social sciences to the model of the natural sciences. As he had argued in the second edition of his famous text *The Idea of a Social Science and Its Relation to Philosophy*, "our understanding of natural phenomena is in terms of the notion of cause, while our understanding of social phenomena involves the categories of *motives* and *reasons* for actions." To this argument he added that "whereas the category of cause involves generality by way of empirical generalizations,

---

15. As Schlosser (2019b) observes, Davidson's event-causal framework has prevailed in spite of the serious problem of deviant causal chains.

that of a reason for action involves generality by way of rules. And these notions—of generalization and of rule—differ from each other in important logical respects" (Winch 2008 [1958], xi; his emphasis). He therefore refused a causal approach to dispositions, asserting that "a dispositional, just as much as a causal, statement, is based on generalizations from what has been observed to happen. But a statement about an agent's motives is not like that: it is better understood as analogous to setting out the agent's *reasons* for acting thus" (Winch 2008 [1958], 76; his emphasis). In the same vein, he argued that people don't give their reasons as *evidence* for their actions but to *justify* their intentions (Winch 2008 [1958], 76).[16] For Winch, the social sciences had to look elsewhere than the natural sciences for guidance as to how to proceed.

We have seen that the distinction between intentional explanations and causal explanations (in the sense of Hume) was also central to Harré and Secord's criticisms of social psychology (Harré and Secord, 1972), as it was to the objections of Buss, Sabini, and Silver to the formulations of attribution theorists. Several of these critics went on to suggest that, because of the centrality of intention, meaning, and reasons to understanding human behavior, it was necessary to investigate social relations outside the causal framework of the natural sciences.[17]

2. An emphasis on human agency as a power that is irreducible to an analysis in terms of Humean causality. How agency was to be theorized in non-reductive, non-Humean-causal terms, which is to say in non-event-causal terms, is an important topic in its own right, one that within philosophy has generated an enormous literature covering diverse views. In

---

16. In the second edition of his book Winch criticized himself for not making it clear that his main target in rejecting the application of the notion of cause to human behavior was Hume's account of cause, and that the term *cause* could be used in a non-Humean way to explain human motives (Winch 2008 [1958], xii). For the best recent treatment of Winch's views from a sympathetic and informed perspective see Hutchinson, Read, and Sharrock 2008.

17. Another important figure in these debates was the psychologist Jerome Bruner, who was instrumental in the cognitive revolution but who subsequently accused cognitive science of betraying the impulses that had originally animated it, namely, to provide a place for "mind" in the sense of intentional states, such as believing, desiring, or grasping a meaning (Bruner 1990). For valuable discussions of the issues at stake in Bruner's criticisms of cognitive science and his search for alternative approaches that placed meaning-making at the center of psychology, see Shanker 1992; 1993; Bruner 1992; and Bakhurst and Shanker 2001.

social psychology, Harré and Secord (1972) rejected conceptualizations of human agency formulated in mechanical-causal terms as a passive tendency to suffer change because of the effect of external conditions and contingencies. Instead, in an explicitly anti-Humean spirit, the authors conceived of human agency as irreducible to a mechanical cause-and-effect analysis and instead identified its intrinsic property as "the power of self-direction and spontaneous action. They argued that "'having the power' involves being in a certain state, and in the case of human individuals, being an agent" (Harré and Secord 1972, 247). It was crucial to Harré and Secord's analysis that to attribute a power or disposition to somebody or something was to attribute to it a property that it has independently of conditions, so that people and things possess powers even when they are not exercising them (Harré 1970). In *Causal Powers: A Theory of Natural Necessity* (1975), Harré and Edward Madden pursued such arguments further by defending the concept of "natural necessity," according to which, as agent-causality theorist Timothy O'Connor has put it, there is a "necessary connection between an object's instantiating a certain set of properties and its possession of a causal power or powers" (O'Connor 2003, 259). Harré and Madden denied that they appealed to occult powers since they attributed the potency of particular things to a "quite unproblematic basis in chemical, physical, or genetic natures of the entities involved" (Harré and Madden 1975, 5).

3. The need to adopt new paradigms in social psychology. As we have seen, Harré and Secord made clear from the outset of their critique of the positivist assumptions of social psychology that some other approach must take its place. Instead of the "Old Paradigm" associated with the cognitive sciences, such as cognitive-dissonance theory or Zajonc's social-psychology investigations, they proposed as a "New Paradigm" an alternative "anthropomorphic" vision of what a social psychology of the future should look like. Their position was that in order to understand people's intentions one had to ask them what those intentions were, or why they had acted in a particular way. In short, Harré and Secord emphasized the importance of taking seriously people's account of their reasons for acting in the way they did and of the need to identify the nature of the powers, rules, and conventions governing those actions. It goes without saying that skepticism about self-reports of the kind expressed by Nisbett, Wilson, Bargh, and others was alien to Harré and Secord's approach to social psychology, even as the latter explained that their views concerning the

nature of the person left room for the possibility of deception and self-correction in ascribing mental attributes—even room for unconscious intentions (Harré and Secord 1972, 8).

In their positive methodological proposals, Harré and Secord suggested the need to focus on field studies rather than laboratory experiments; to pay close attention to conceptual foundations; to emphasize descriptive approaches; to undertake comparative investigations among different peoples of the world; to be alert to the role of cultural influences in people's social interactions; and above all to abandon the picture of the human subject as a passive recipient of stimuli and to acknowledge instead the role of agency in social life. From their perspective, the usual statistical and experimental methods of social psychology were of no use in this enterprise, precisely because they eliminated the idiosyncratic and particular features of people's specific reasons and actions.[18]

Harré and Secord regarded both Harold Garfinkel's ethnomethodology (Garfinkel 1967) and Erving Goffman's approach in his book *The Presentation of Everyday Life* (1959) as exemplifying the kinds of investigation in social psychology that needed to be carried out (Harré and Secord 1972, 216). They were especially impressed by Goffman's dramaturgical standpoint because of its emphasis on the active role of the participant in social interactions and also because thinking of social performances in dramatic terms focused attention on the actors' reasons for their actions. They stressed in this regard that the experiment itself constituted a social-performative space in which, as Rosenthal and Orne's discussions of the influence of experimenter expectancy and experimental demand had demonstrated, both experimenters and participants played various roles, each with their own set of expectations and biases.

Harré also opposed the tendency of experimentalists in psychology to think that a computational process must be occurring "behind" the overt social performances, of which the performances were the outcome. "That is the temptation we wish to resist," Harré observed:

> The explanatory use of rules is itself a category of social episode, through which what we do is rendered intelligible and warrantable. We can

---

18. See also Strickland, Aboud, and Gergen (1976) for discussions by Harré, Secord, Gergen, McGuire, and others about the status of social psychology, including an exchange between Robert Zajonc, who defended his positivist approach in social psychology, and Alan Moffitt, who offered a rebuttal.

exercise our social skills, our know how, in doing things and in displaying those things as the correct thing to do or to have done in the circumstances. Nothing is hidden. There are no information processing mechanisms behind what we are doing, doing those things for us! Rules and scripts are not the causes of actions. They are what we use to present our actions as correct or incorrect. The metaphor of causation is out of place. It leads to the fantasy of hidden processors that we are only too ready to entertain . . . The only causes of actions are persons [. . .] In the context of social psychology causal power resides in people. (Harré 1993, 97–98)

The Two Social Psychologies, or, Whatever Happened to the Crisis?

It is not surprising that incomprehension and downright hostility characterized the response of social psychologists when challenged by Harré and other critics about the epistemological and methodological norms of their field. This reaction is strikingly evident in an exchange of papers that occurred at a conference held in Paris in 1988 expressly to consider "the two psychologies" and the possibilities of a rapprochement between them. The meeting was organized by psychologists John Rijsman and Wolfgang Stroebe and included contributions by leading representatives of the positions that had been debated in earlier discussions of the crisis in social psychology (Rijsman and Stroebe 1989). Robert Zajonc and Jozef M. Nuttin defended the "old" paradigm or positivist approach associated with the hypothetico-deductive method and the standard of experimental testability (Zajonc 1989; Nuttin 1989). Wille Doise and Serge Moscovici defended what the organizers identified as "psychological constructivism" (Doise 1989; Muscovi 1989). And Harré and Gergen upheld the "new" paradigm associated with strong "social constructivism" (Harré 1989; Gergen 1989). The social constructionist Kenneth Gergen, a former student of attribution theorist Edward Jones, was well known for an earlier article (Gergen 1973) in which he had argued that the kinds of things social psychology studied, such as attitudes, were highly sensitive to cultural context, with the result that it was impossible to derive general, universal rules from their study. In short, Gergen had suggested that psychology was fundamentally a historical discipline that could not and should not be considered a scientific enterprise on the model of the physical sciences.[19]

19. In a valuable analysis, Stam, Radtke, and Lubek (2000) identify four strains or tensions in the post–World War II development of social-psychological methods texts

Zajonc led off the proceedings. He cast the dispute between social psychologists over how to tackle problems in their field as a matter of a preference for one "style" of explanation over another. According to him, some stylistic preferences were without significant consequences for the growth of the field. Since he had long argued that preferences (including emotions) were dissociated from cognition, the implication was that the explanatory "preferences" of critics of social psychology, such as Harré, Gergen and others, were not a matter of reasoned evaluations but were merely personal and subjective reactions. Zajonc's tactic therefore seemed designed to render innocuous the differences between himself and critics of social psychology by treating such differences as not substantive but a question of merely personal taste. In a note he dismissed expressions of "epistemological malaise" by Gergen and other critics as of no importance because they were "entirely without heuristic consequences." He nevertheless complained, however, that those expressions of malaise had been "outright destructive and paralyzing for social psychology" because they had discouraged promising students from entering the field and granting agencies from increasing social-psychology research budgets (Zajonc 1989, 347).

Zajonc aimed some of his strongest criticisms at the work of Harré, who had previously mentioned his personal discomfort over the discrepancy between his own experience of social life and the descriptions of that life found in the writings of social scientists, as a motive for his attempts

---

and their prescriptions for experimentation: the rational experimenter versus the intuitive one; the proselytizer versus the insecure experimenter; the docile subject versus the "underhanded" (or disruptive) undergraduate subject; the sober experimenter versus the practitioner of playful experimentation. These strains, Stam and coauthors argue, reflected the impossibility of producing the desired development of a self-perpetuating technology of experimentation in social psychology, even as the public development of a standard form of the experimental method took root in the English-language (largely American) social-psychology journals. Rijsman and Stroebe's (1989) paper receives a passing mention in Stam, Radtke, and Lubek's analysis (Stam, Radtke, and Lubek 2000, 369). In an equally interesting article, Danziger (2000) demonstrates that the practice of social psychological experimentation changed over time from an emphasis chiefly on correlation studies to a stress on various models of investigation involving actual experimental controls and manipulations of independent and dependent variables, as in the study of social attitudes and conformity experiments. This development was accompanied by the ontological presupposition that the social situation was composed of "separate, unambiguously denotable, elements and their essentially additive interconnections" (Danziger 2000, 344). These methodological and ontological assumptions were profoundly at odds with those of Harré and Gergen.

to find other methods of research (Harré 1993 [1979]). Zajonc dismissed Harré's concerns as simply personal "intuitions" that ought not to be trusted because they could be "fatally misleading" (Zajonc 1989, 358). He also characterized Harré's statement, that the experimental style Zajonc himself exemplified was too restrictive and impoverished, as a form of irrational anti-scientism which denied that the laboratory was part of reality (Zajonc 1989, 359). And he contrasted what he deemed the meager results of ethnomethodology, whose approach Harré admired, with the positive achievements, as he saw it, of the standard laboratory methods used in research in the social sciences.[20]

As for Harré himself, he offered a characteristically philosophical critique of social psychology in terms, at once ontological and epistemological, so far removed from Zajonc's positivist approach as to seem to come from a different universe.[21] Harré was joined in the "strong" social-constructionist camp by Gergen, who criticized the positivist, cognitivist approach in social psychology on several familiar grounds, especially for creating several "intractable" conceptual difficulties or "inescapable cul de sacs." In terms not unlike those of Harré, Gergen singled out three particular problems generated by cognitive psychology's main assumptions: the individualizing of cognition to the point of lapsing into solipsism and the consequent "disappearance of the social world";[22] an "impasse of origin," by which he meant the inability of cognitive psychology to give a plausible account of the origins of human concepts, representations and categories; and what Gergen called "the impasse of action" (Gergen 1989, 469), namely, the difficulty cognitive psychology had in explaining the relationship between cognition and subsequent behavior. As he commented: "The theoretical edifice begins to buckle under the strain of its own weight" (Gergen 1989, 471). In short, social psychology had undergone the "wrong revolution" when it adopted cognitive, information-processing explanations of human action.

20. In effect, Zajonc proceeded against Harré as if his own preference for the standard experimental methodologies of social psychology was ontologically and epistemologically unproblematic or neutral.
21. For a recent discussion of Harré's approach in social psychology, see Van Langenhove 2021.
22. As Gergen put it, "the cognitive perspective reduces the social world to a projection or an artifact of the individual cognizer... There is no group worth studying in itself for 'groupness' is essentially an attribute projected onto the social world by the individual. And so is the fate of all other so-called 'social phenomena'" (Gergen 1989, 465).

Gergen ended his paper by sketching the social epistemology view he thought should replace cognitive social psychology. He advocated an approach that would take into account the work of historians and philosophers of science, such as Kuhn, Paul Feyerabend, social anthropologists, and even literary theorists, work that he argued had already constituted a revolution in the intellectual world. In particular he stressed that, as a result of that revolution, it was now understood that the locus of knowledge could no longer be taken to be the individual mind, as cognitive psychology held, but rather that it inhered in patterns of social relatedness.[23]

But neither Harré nor Gergen received much satisfaction from their colleagues. Gadenne's defense of cognitive psychology's mentalistic, information-processing presuppositions against Harré's attempts at correction suggested that the divide between the two positions could not be bridged (Gadenne 1989). Stroebe and Kruglanski offered a somewhat more sympathetic hearing to Gergen, but they also pushed back at his critique, in part because, they claimed, he offered no solutions to the problems he had specified.[24] They rejected Gergen's "social epistemology" as unacceptable to most empirical social psychologists. And they criticized his views for being too vague, for lacking sufficient rigor, and for being "nihilistic" in their implications. Nevertheless, Stroebe and Kruglanski attempted to smooth over the profound epistemological and indeed ontological differ-

---

23. Interesting as Harré's and Gergen's attempts to restore meaning to psychology are, the kinds of constructivism they and others adopted are vulnerable to various critiques, of which that offered by the philosopher David Bakhurst is especially interesting. Bakhurst recognizes the attractiveness of many of the assumptions influencing those, such as Gergen (and Harré, whom Bakhurst does not mention), who espouse a social-constructionist approach to the mind (Bakhurst 2011; cf. Bakhurst and Shanker 2001). He is sympathetic to Gergen's desire to acknowledge the influence of culture and history in the development of categories such as categories of the mental. But he is skeptical of the value of social constructionism in illuminating the nature of human mindedness. In particular, Bakhurst does not accept the relativism and "irrealism" inherent in constructionism. Instead, Bakhurst favors a different, realist approach, "one effecting a post-Cartesian reconciliation of mind and world that appreciates the profound socio-historical forces at work in shaping both, while preserving the idea of an independent reality and respecting the integrity of individual minds" (2011, 29). He finds in the work of the philosopher John McDowell the resources to effect this reconciliation and does so in ways that strike me as illuminating. But see also Sebastian Rödl's instructive McDowellian corrective to Bakhurst's own attempt to use McDowell's ideas about "first" and "second" nature to explain how human reason develops in infancy and childhood (Bakhurst 2016a; 2016b; Rödl 2016).

24. I note that in 1981–1982, Kenneth Gergen spent a term at the University of Marburg and during that period co-authored an article with Stroebe (see Stroebe et al. 1982, 87).

ences between social psychologists by adopting a bland pluralism suggesting that such differences did not really matter. Many of the theoretical clashes of the seventies, they observed, had finally been resolved "by accepting that all of these theoretical positions are valid and that we have to focus on the conditions under which one mechanism dominates over the others... Instead of letting ourselves be forced into a choice between two opposing camps, astute psychologists will take advantage of both types of approach to further their understanding of social conduct" (Stroebe and Kruglanski 1989, 489).

As the organizers of the conference, Rijsman and Stroebe took a similar tack in their introduction to the conference papers. On the one hand, they acknowledged that there were substantial differences among the disputants. On the other hand, they argued that, unlike the darkest moments of the earlier postwar crisis in social psychology, the two positions had now reached a peaceful coexistence in which neither side needed to take into account the views of the other. As the organizers saw it, the old crisis in social psychology had been resolved by splitting the discipline into two: "We have now two social psychologies," they observed, "which exist side by side with very little interaction" (Rijsman and Stroebe 1989, 341). In their view, the differences between the old and new paradigms could be viewed simply as different voices functioning in counterpoint to each other and together capable of producing lovely music. As they commented in their introduction to the various contributions to the conference, it had now become

> harder and harder indeed to remember and, for younger generations, even to imagine that the first critical remarks about the epistemological status of experimental social psychology had such an unsettling effect upon many of our colleagues. Just looking ahead at the different papers and comments in this issue, one would rather feel sorry if a "crisis" of that kind were not possible in our discipline, but then the word "crisis" is probably not the best choice to indicate a scholarly controversy about the "social" in social psychology. If we just turn our mind in that direction then maybe the voices which we will hear in this issue will not sound like the ominous toll of a bell, but rather as a beautiful exercise in counterpoint, a good formula one would say, not only for good music, but for discipline as well. So, why not for our discipline? (Rijsman and Stroebe 1989, 342)

Zajonc offered a less conciliatory statement at the end of his conference paper when he aggressively defended the experimental methods of the "old" positivist paradigm in social psychology. The question to examine, he wrote, was not whether a given procedure revealed or duplicated reality but "whether the controlled and standard environments and the procedures that they employ are capable of revealing the *essential* aspects of fundamental social psychological processes. The fact that replications of laboratory experiments in the field or in free observations are seldom in contradiction with each other suggests that rather little is lost" (1989, 360; his emphasis). Just so: that was indeed *the* question. But as the 2012 failed replication in the case of Bargh's famous elderly priming study would demonstrate, what was at stake in that study was precisely the role of the person and his or her intentions whose influence and importance had been so systematically excluded by the methods advocated by Zajonc, Bargh, and the other "old"-paradigm social psychologists. From the perspective of that subsequent development, Zajonc's confidence in cognitive psychology's ability to reveal the fundamental social psychological processes would turn out to be misplaced.

In the next chapter, I turn to the origins and development of Bargh's priming experiments and his approach to the topic of automaticity.

3

John Bargh's Approach to Automaticity

Subliminal Perception Becomes "Unconscious Priming"

Bargh's approach to automaticity was the product of several developments in the social sciences after the Second World War, including crucially the work of attribution theorists. Like them, he was also decisively influenced by the cognitive revolution in psychology which, rejecting the strictures of behaviorism, had made it respectable to study mental phenomena once again. The paradox was that, although Bargh's work on automaticity developed in the context of the cognitive revolution and its assumptions, he nevertheless came to echo behaviorism's stress on the direct influence of the environment on behavior in terms that were so mechanical that he created the impression that not much had changed in the social sciences. But in an important sense the paradox was only apparent: cognitive scientists were themselves so captive to assumptions about the computational-mechanical nature of information processing and to the importance of situational-environmental influences on individual judgment and behavior, that the role of the person with his or her intentions, beliefs, and agency in behavior largely disappeared.[1] It was therefore almost a foregone conclusion that, not without hesitation and contradiction, Bargh would come to argue that all human behavior could be analyzed in automatic, perception-behavior terms.

Bargh's views were attacked in a series of articles by psychologist

---

1. However, it appears that, while social and cognitive psychology were captured by mechanism and situationism, personality psychology continued to thrive, as is shown by a PubMed search.

John Kihlstrom, who—many years after Bargh's debut in the field of automaticity—excoriated what he called the "automaticity juggernaut" (Kihlstrom 2008). As Kihlstrom described it, the problem stemmed precisely from Bargh's assumptions concerning the overwhelming importance of environmental or situational influences on social behavior:

> The doctrine of situationism in social psychology found a natural affinity with the behaviorism that dominated elsewhere in academic psychology... Behaviorism, with its emphasis on stimulus and response, did not survive the cognitive revolution, but the "positivistic reserve"... that was part and parcel of behaviorism is still with us. As a result, we grudgingly accept intervening mental states and processes as necessary to the explanation of behavior—but we want them to be as mechanical as possible. We've replaced both the black box and the ghost in the machine with a clockwork mechanism that is as close to reflex activity as we can get and still pay lip service to cognitivism... In a theoretical environment in which social behaviors are automatically generated by mental states that may be preconscious, and which in turn are evoked automatically by cues in the social situation (Bargh 1990) [*Bargh 1990a*], interpersonal behavior may not be precisely mindless, but it might just as well be. We had a cognitive revolution for this—only to be told that Skinner had it right after all? (Kihlstrom 2004, 348)

This critique offered an acute diagnosis of the general thrust of Bargh's influential research. But it is necessary to recognize that Kihlstrom had played an important role in advocating the same information-processing approach that also informed Bargh's work. The difference was that, in his work on automaticity, Bargh carried the logic of the cognitive sciences to its mechanical-causal conclusion to an extent Kihlstrom refused to go.

In this chapter I will chart the development of Bargh's approach to automaticity from its beginnings in the 1980s up to the moment when, in 1997, he argued in favor of a strictly deterministic approach to all human action.

Is Automaticity Its Own Thing, and If Not, What Is the Recipe?

Bargh was born in Champaign, Illinois, and attended the University of Illinois as an undergraduate and the University of Michigan as a postgraduate, working under the supervision of psychologist Robert Zajonc. After obtaining his doctorate in 1981, he went on to hold positions at New York University and then at Yale, where he remains.

When Bargh went to Michigan, Zajonc was already well known for his experiments on the "exposure effect" and, more generally, on processes occurring outside consciousness. The exposure effect was the name for the psychological phenomenon according to which people tend to develop a preference or liking for previously unfamiliar objects simply because they have been repeatedly exposed to them. Starting in the 1960s, Zajonc had carried out a series of laboratory experiments on the exposure effect using a variety of test stimuli, including drawings, facial expressions, nonsense words, Japanese ideographs, and "meaningless" Chinese characters, and in each case had appeared to demonstrate the influence of "mere" exposure. Even the subliminal exposure of images on a tachistoscope produced the same effects. His studies were the start of his career-long interest in the operation of affective processes, or personal preferences, outside a person's knowledge, cognition, or awareness. Zajonc proposed that such preferences must occur independently of cognition or meaning, a view that was contested by several psychologists, such as emotion researcher Richard Lazarus, but was endorsed by many others, including Bargh (see Lazarus 1999 for a summary of the debate, and Leys 2017 for the postwar history of these competing models of the emotions).

Bargh's early research work likewise explored the influence of stimuli of whose effects participants were unaware, using experimental setups of the kind developed in priming studies. As noted in the introduction, the term *priming* refers to an experimental method aimed at demonstrating the ways in which individuals who are exposed to various stimuli automatically respond to them, without being aware that their responses have been influenced by those stimuli, or primes. In a standard priming study, experimental participants are first exposed supraliminally (consciously) or subliminally (unconsciously) to unsorted sets of words that include the primes (today usually presented on a computer screen) and are then asked to sort those words into meaningful sentences (usually one of the words in the set does not fit grammatically and has to be left out). They are then requested to perform an apparently unrelated task, such as to make a trait judgment of persons based on written descriptions of those persons' attributes. The purpose of the experiment is to determine whether the participants' judgments on the second task are influenced by the prime words contained in the first task. Control participants are exposed to sets of words that are similar to those given the experimental participants but lack the primes. Debriefing involves questioning the participants, often undergraduates majoring in psychology, concerning their degree of awareness of the purpose of the study. It is worth emphasizing that in many priming experiments in which the priming stimuli are presented supraliminally, participants are of course aware of the words they are asked to sort; the point of interest for researchers is whether the primes exert an influence on some target response, such as participants' subsequent judgments or behaviors, an influence of which participants appear to be unaware.[2]

Bargh later attributed the first use of the term *priming* to a paper by psychologist Karl Lashley dealing with the problem of how serial response sequences, as in speech production, flow so quickly and apparently effortlessly (Bargh and Chartrand 2000, 313; Lashley 1951). He credited Storms (1958) with the first demonstration of passive priming when the latter accidentally discovered that words given to students to memorize were more likely to be given as associations in a subsequent free-association task; and he credited Segal and Cofer (1960) with being the first to use the term *priming* to refer to the effect of the recent use of a concept in one task on the likelihood of its use in a subsequent unrelated task. After their paper, Bargh reported, priming began to be used as an experimental technique, especially in the study of implicit and explicit memory (Bargh and Chartrand 2000, 313).

According to Bargh, however, it was the "groundbreaking" study by E. Tory Higgins, Williams Rholes, and Carl Jones (1977) that ushered in modern priming research in social psychology by demonstrating that exposing participants to different personality-trait terms influenced their responses in an unrelated experiment in which the same participants were asked to evaluate the description of a man who behaved in ways ambiguously related to the primed traits. Participants primed with words such as "adventurous" and "independent" formed more positive impressions of the man than did those primed with words such as "reckless" and "aloof," even though none of the subjects evidenced any awareness of having been influenced by the primes (Bargh and Chartrand 2000, 314; see also Förster, Liberman, and Friedman 2009).

Against this background, Bargh commenced his career as a researcher of priming in a study of 1982 in which he and his co-author asked participants to perform a vigilance task during which they were unknowingly

---

2. For useful statements about how priming developed, see also Srull and Wyer 1980 and Bargh and Gollwitzer 1994.

exposed to subliminally presented words displayed on a computer screen, relating to hostility in various proportions (that is, either 0 percent, 20 percent, or 80 percent of the priming words were semantically related to hostility). The subliminal method involved a very brief presentation of the prime and its immediate masking by another stimulus. In an ostensibly unrelated second task, the participants read a behavioral description of a stimulus person—a description that was ambiguous regarding hostility— and were asked to rate the stimulus person on several trait dimensions. The authors reported that the amount of processing subjects gave to hostile information and the negativity of their ratings were reliably related to the proportion of hostile words with which they had been primed. Assessments confirmed that the participants had not consciously perceived the stimulus words (Bargh and Pietromonaco 1982). The purpose of Bargh's experiments was to ensure that the original findings of priming experiments by Higgins, Rholes, and Jones (1977) and Srull and Wyer (1979, 1980) were not the result of experimental demand or active strategies on the part of the experimental participants. Presenting the primes subliminally was understood by Bargh to conclusively rule out the participants' conscious awareness of the primes, thereby confirming that the effects were the result of a purely passive, automatic activation of the hostility construct (Bargh and Pietromonaco 1982; Bargh and Chartrand 2000).

In 1984, Bargh was invited to publish a paper reviewing the literature on automaticity (Bargh 1984). As he was well aware, interest in automatic behavior could be traced back to late nineteenth-century studies of hypnotism, automatic writing, spiritualism, hysteria, and the unconscious by such figures as William Carpenter, William James, and Pierre Janet. But in his paper Bargh singled out two particular developments for their decisive role in renewing interest in the topic of automaticity in the post–World War II period. The first was the turn in the middle 1970s "away from the model of rational, scientific man and towards a model of man as cognitively limited and subject to all sorts of distortions as a result" (Bargh 1984, 1). Bargh ascribed this "insurrection" largely to the experimental work of attribution theorists Edward Jones, Richard Nisbett, Lee Ross, and others whose findings had fostered the widely held belief that people have only a limited conscious involvement with their social environment (Bargh 1984, 2). In other words, according to attribution theorists, people were not very good at judging the true causes of their own behavior or that of others.

More specifically, as we have seen in chapter 1, attribution theorists claimed that when individuals judged the causes of other people's behavior, they tended to underestimate the influence of situational factors and overestimate the sway of personal traits and dispositions. Conversely, individuals erred in the opposite direction when they considered the causes of their own behavior: here they tended to attribute too little to the influence of their own individual traits and dispositions and to overestimate the role of situational factors. The upshot of attribution research was a rejection of the picture of humans as fundamentally rational. Rather, people were held to be inherently liable to irrational biases, because their behavior was largely shaped by causes of which they were unaware and over which they had no control. The work of Kahneman and Tversky on the biases and heuristics of decision-making influenced attribution theory in the same general direction (for example Tversky and Kahneman 1973 and 1974; Nisbett and Ross 1980, cited by Bargh 1984, 1–2; and chapter 1).[3]

According to Bargh, the second development that shaped post–World War II work on automaticity was the mid-1970s emergence of models of attention in the context of cognitive psychology's information-processing assumptions about the nature of the mind. By 1984, those theories of attention tended to distinguish between two modes of information processing. One form of processing, later called Type 2 or System 2 processing, was held to be conscious, inefficient or effortful, intentional, and controlled. The other form of processing, later called Type 1 or System 1 processing, was held to be unconscious, efficient (or effortless), non-intentional, and uncontrolled, which is to say that it occurred automatically unless it was checked by attentional resources (Posner and Snyder 1975; Schneider and Shiffrin 1977; Shiffrin and Schneider 1977; Kahneman's Systems 1 and 2 mentioned in the introduction are versions of the same dual-process or dual-system theories). The opposition between conscious-intentional and unconscious-non-intentional processes was linked to notions of cognitive capacity. The claim was that conscious cognitive capacity was limited, an idea that originated in the work of George Miller who had famously stated that the capacity of conscious awareness, or rather short-term (or working) memory, was restricted to about seven units of information (Miller 1956). In contrast, unconscious processing was held to be far less

---

3. Bargh and his colleagues did not appear to recognize the paradox that they depended on the participants' self-reports for evidence concerning their awareness of the influence of primes on their behaviors, while accepting the view, associated especially with Nisbett and Wilson's influential claims (Nisbett and Wilson 1977), that participants' self-reports could not be relied on as evidence because they were liable to biases and inaccuracies.

demanding of capacity and hence unconstrained by capacity limitations. Unconscious systems were therefore conceptualized as efficient, effortless processes that could occur alongside other automatic processes without interference.[4] These views led to various dual-process or dual-system theories according to which automatic processes occurred in information processing channels that were separate from those for conscious, intentional processing.[5]

As Bargh observed in his 1984 review, the outcome of such ideas about information processing was an increased concern with automatic processes themselves. The problem was that it was unclear whether the dichotomy between automatic versus nonautomatic processes could be sustained, as researchers constantly ran up against the problem of assigning behaviors to one or other of these categories in clear and unambiguous ways. The result was a widespread use of the *automaticity* label without any consensus about what its boundaries were. For example, as Bargh noted, many everyday automatic skills and habits, such as driving, typing, playing the piano and so on, were highly controllable: they had to be intended and one could usually stop them whenever one wanted to. Similarly, Stroop interference effects, which had been held to be unintentional and uncontrollable, were found to be attention-dependent because those effects could be diminished when participants' attention was diverted

---

4. *Capacity* came to be defined by automaticity theorists as the amount of information transmitted in bits per second, although this definition was later criticized on the grounds that Miller's units were "chunks" of information, not "bits" (González-Vallejo et al. 2008; see also Shiffrin and Nosofsky 1994). For a discussion of the widespread assumption in the early years of cognitive science that the human mind was a machine with limited capacities and that accordingly human rationality was "bounded" or "limited," a view which led to an explosion of research on decision-making, see Heyck 2015 (ch. 4).

5. In another paper also published in 1982, Bargh reported the results of an experiment on the automaticity of participants' responses to a dichotic listening task in which subjects were asked to attend to, or to ignore or reject, self-relevant stimuli. The experiment was designed to evaluate models of attention according to which there were two types of mental processing that occurred concurrently: flexible but capacity-limited control processes that regulated the contents of conscious awareness, and relatively inflexible, unlimited-capacity, automatic processes that were held to be responsive to stimuli without the subject's conscious awareness or intention. The results of the experiment appeared to demonstrate that, relative to neutral words, self-relevant stimuli required less attentional resources when presented to the attended channel but more attentional resources when presented to the ignored or rejected channel. The differential capacity allocation occurred despite the fact that the participants were unaware of the contents of the rejected channel. Bargh therefore interpreted his findings as supporting the existence and interaction of two processes of attention (Bargh 1982).

from the targets.[6] Moreover, individuals were generally aware of engaging in their skilled activities, even though such routine actions did not require active attention. Thus, it was exceedingly difficult to delimit the features that distinguished automatic behaviors from nonautomatic ones, because no individual feature appeared to belong exclusively to either the automatic or the nonautomatic category.

Bargh also observed that since nearly all of a person's cognitive processes occurred without the person being aware of them, the vast majority of cognitive processes had to be considered automatic, with the result that the automatic-conscious distinction risked losing all meaning (Bargh 1984, 3–4). Bargh's claim for the pervasiveness of unconscious cognitive processes in everyday life depended in part on the arguments made by Nisbett and Wilson in their influential paper of 1977. As discussed in chapter 1, Nisbett and Wilson distinguished between the "contents" of the mind, which subjects are able to identify in self-reports, versus the sub-personal, unconscious, unintentional cognitive "processes" that actually cause behaviors but are unavailable to introspection or consciousness (Nisbett and Wilson 1977). Their general conclusion was that nearly all cognitive functions are the product of sub-personal, automatic processes of which the subject is unaware. Nevertheless, Bargh was not yet prepared to accept the more radical conclusions about the constitutive pervasiveness of automaticity in everyday life that Nisbett and Wilson drew in their paper of 1977. Instead, he endorsed claims regarding the limits placed on automaticity by the so-called executive function of the mind, a function that, according to Neisser (1967) and other cognitive psychologists, controlled conscious, intentional processes (Bargh 1984, 5–6).

On this basis, Bargh criticized claims that a great deal of human behavior was the product of unconscious automatic processes. For example, in the late 1970s and early 1980s the social psychologist Ellen Langer declared that many of our apparently mindful social interactions go on in

---

6. As Logan observed, the major evidence that automatic processes were uncontrolled derived from the Stroop effect in its various guises (Logan 1985, 378). In the Stroop effect, unattended aspects of a stimulus interfere with the processing of attended aspects. Thus, given the task of naming the *ink color* of words in a Stroop-effect test, when that color was used to spell the name of a different color, participants intended to avoid reading the actual words, but found it impossible to do so completely. The idea was that once automatic processes were activated by an appropriate stimulus, they ran to completion despite the participants' attempts to inhibit them. Thus, automaticity and control were viewed as distinct processes. See Isen and Diamond 1989 (128) and Hommel and Wiers 2017.

the absence of mindedness and emphasized instead the mindlessness of ostensibly thoughtful action (Langer 1978). As psychologist Daniel T. E. Gilbert would subsequently describe the impact of Langer's work:

> Langer (1978) quite colorfully articulated a widespread discontent when she urged attribution theorists to "rethink the role of thought in social interaction." She pointed out that social inference is not always a conscious and deliberate act; rather, it is often the province of mindless automata. Attribution theories (according to Langer) have been too quick to assume that perceivers engage conscious processes in order to achieve their causal conclusions. This clarion call was widely appreciated, and if Langer did not quite set the stage for a psychology of unconscious social inference, she at least rented the theater . . . [W]hen theorists such as LaBerge and Samuels (1974), Posner and Snyder (1975), Shiffrin and Schneider (1977), and Hasher and Zacks (1979) began to explicate the parameters of automatic "off-line" processes in a computer-based vernacular, the ghost somehow fled the machine. All this is to say that there has, in recent years, been a discernible shift in the wind: The role of awareness and control in the social inference process has been appropriately questioned, and the role of unconscious and unintentional processes has been approved for exploration. (Gilbert 1989, 192)

Thus, in a series of influential experiments Langer had claimed to show that behaviors that had become routinized through habit were not the result of conscious thought but were managed by unconscious, overlearned mental representations or "scripts." In one of her experiments, participants using a copying machine were interrupted by a confederate of the experimenter, who asked them to let him or her use the machine before they did. The request was to make either a small or a large number of copies, and various reasons for the request were given. The results showed that, when a small number of copies was involved, the form of the reason for request ("because I have to make copies" versus "because I am in a rush") made no difference to the rate of the participants' compliance to the appeal, although compliance was lower if no reason at all was given. But when the request was for a large number of copies, the form of words used to make the appeal did influence the rate of compliance (Langer 1978; Langer and Weinman 1981).

On the basis of this experiment and related investigations Langer argued that, as long as the effort involved in acceding to a request was low, as in the small-number-of-copies condition, and the reasons given conformed to the expected "scripts" or norms of politeness, the request was processed "mindlessly" and the compliance behavior was automatic. The necessity of higher effort expenditure, as in the larger copying condition, or the failure of the wording of the request to follow normal verbal conventions, activated the participant's conscious attention, in which case the quality of the reason given for the request made a difference in the rate of compliance (Langer, Blank, and Chanowitz 1978).

But in his 1984 article, Bargh challenged Langer's claims on the grounds that it was difficult to rule out conscious involvement in the compliance condition. He observed that Robert Abelson, who had been the first to develop the script concept, emphasized the role of conscious enactment. He quoted Abelson as stating of Langer's work: "'The present concept of scripts does not necessarily imply total automaticity of performance and is not equivalent to Langer's concept of 'mindless' behavior. One obvious way in which 'mindful' behavior enters scripts is that acts of thinking can appear explicitly in the specified event sequence'" (Bargh 1984, 34; Abelson 1981, 723). Bargh went on to argue that in none of Langer's studies was there sufficient evidence to rule out the conscious direction of behavior:

> In fact, what they *do* indicate is that well-learned scripts function as do any other mental representation or schema, and direct the search of the environment for needed information. That is, the features of the situation automatically activate the relevant script, which then directs the *conscious* process of searching for further cues to verify the script as an adequate model of the situation . . . The result is that certain pieces of information are selected by the script over others that may actually be more relevant and useful in the current situation, but which are not part of the script. Such a model can account for the results of other "mindlessness" studies as well . . . Thus, experiments that Langer has considered to be evidence of "automatic" social behavior can be seen instead as good support for a processing model in which an automatic analysis of the social environment is followed by a consciously directed exploration and response production. (Bargh 1984, 35; his emphasis)

A Features or Graded Approach to Automaticity?

Bargh later observed that when he was a graduate student it was Langer's work on the "mindless" enactment of interaction scripts that had aroused his interest in "things automatic" (Bargh 2003, 218). But as we have seen, in his 1984 review of automaticity research he was not prepared to accept Langer's conclusions about the mindlessness of automatic actions, at least not yet. Instead, he focused his efforts on identifying the specific features associated with automaticity. As Agnes Moors and Jan De Houwer observed in a later conceptual analysis, in the 1970s, capacity models of information processing assumed that automatic processes required only minimal capacity resources, whereas nonautomatic processes were understood to draw on substantial capacity. Most proponents of the capacity approach also regarded automatic and nonautomatic processes as constituting a continuum. But the capacity approach eventually gave way to the view that automatic and nonautomatic processes represented two opposed ways of processing, each characterized by a fixed set of features, although researchers differed about the number and nature of the features involved (Moors and De Houwer 2006, 298).

Bargh adopted a features approach and identified the following as the "four horsemen of automaticity": lack of consciousness, unintentionality, uncontrollability, and efficiency (processes requiring minimal capacity, attentional requirements, or effort). However, he rejected the idea that those features constituted a single, unified package. According to him, automatic behaviors might exhibit several properties, but those properties did not necessarily hang together, just as the features associated with consciousness also lacked a unitary character. As he commented: "Attention, awareness, intention, and control do not necessarily occur together in an all-or-none fashion. They are to some extent independent qualities that may appear in various combinations. As there is ample evidence that automatic processing is not unitary, such that all of its component properties do not co-occur, so also there is no compelling theoretical reasons to believe in its unitary nature" (Bargh 1989, 6, citing Zbrodoff and Logan 1986; see also Bargh 1994). On this basis, Bargh was understood as offering a critique of theories which assumed that automatic modes of processing hung together in an all-or-nothing fashion and as such were strictly opposed to nonautomatic or controlled processes (Bargh 1992; Moors and De Houwer 2006, 298).

As Bargh noted in this regard, attempts to treat automatic and nonautomatic processes as involving mutually exclusive features ran into logical difficulties. Those difficulties arose because, as Cowan had indicated (Logan and Cowan 1984), nearly all the mundane examples of automatic processes, such as reading, driving, walking, and typing, were in truth highly controlled. One must intend to engage in any of these activities, and one can stop them whenever one wants. Also, the individual is usually aware of engaging in the activity, even though such routine action sequences do not require active attention (i.e., they are autonomous). These well-learned activities do not fall neatly into one classification or the other: They are intentional but autonomous: they are quite efficient (minimally demanding of processing resources), but one is aware of them. And they are controllable . . . [T]he automated responses that characterize driving, typing, and so on do not occur without the overarching goal to engage in the activity. (Bargh 1992, 183)

In other words, many of the automatic processes of interest to Bargh were consciously intended—a point of considerable importance in discussions of automaticity, as we shall see. More generally, Bargh argued, as did several other researchers at the time (for example, Isen and Diamond 1989), that cognitive science ought to proceed on the assumption that the processing features of automaticity were orthogonal to, or independent of, each other unless proven otherwise. Since most mental processes were a mix of automatic and controlled processing features, it was time to get rid of the all-or-nothing approach to automatic and nonautomatic processes because it was causing "confusion and misunderstanding" (Bargh 1994, 3). Thus, according to Moors and DeHouwer, "Bargh (1992) pushed independence between features to the extreme, suggesting that for any random combination of features (some automatic, others nonautomatic), a process can be found that fits the description. He also suggested that a process matching the pure case of automaticity may be encountered only rarely" (Moors and DeHouwer 2006, 299).

Bargh described his approach as one of "decomposition" because he proposed that the properties held to be associated with automaticity could be decomposed into separate, independent features or qualities (Bargh 1994). The one feature that, in the early years of his career, he explicitly identified as common to all automatic phenomena was their "autonomy," by which he meant that, however they were instigated, once started, automatic processes tended to run to completion without further conscious guidance or input. As he observed: "This appears to be the core of the concept for cognitive psychologists—that once the process is put in motion (and this could be by an intentional choice or by a triggering stimulus in the environment) . . . it runs off by itself without the need for conscious monitoring" (Bargh1992, 186).[7] In addition, Bargh suggested that automatic processes were "conditional," by which he meant that they depended on a set of operating preconditions (Bargh 1989; 1992). He proposed that, although automatic processes could be endowed with almost any combination of features, most automatic processes fell into three broad classes, depending on the conditions they required. Thus, "preconscious" automatic actions did not need any conscious input or intention, which is to say, they operated "uncontrollably, autonomously, involuntarily, and nearly effortlessly" (Bargh, 1989, 11). Indeed, as Bargh noted, philosopher Jerry Fodor (Fodor 1983, 55) had likened such preconscious processes to reflexes, because they were automatically triggered by the relevant environmental stimuli (Bargh 1989, 11). Examples of such preconscious automatic processes included certain priming effects. "Postconscious" automatic processes or behaviors depended on the individual having a particular conscious processing goal at the start, but the outcome of the processing might or might not be intended (certain priming studies also belonged to this category). Finally, "goal-dependent automaticity" required that the individual had a particular goal, but the outcome of the processing might be intended, or it might occur unintentionally. For Bargh, all this meant that the specific set of enabling or triggering conditions for an autonomous process to occur became the focus of research interest (Bargh 1989, 7).

In their subsequent evaluation of the theorization of automaticity, Moors and De Houwer granted that according "autonomy" the status of a minimal criterion of automaticity had "considerable conceptual appeal"

---

7. Zbrodoff and Logan defined a process as "autonomous" if (a) if it could begin without intention and (b) it could run to completion without intention. Applying various empirical criteria for determining whether various processes conformed to these two criteria, the authors concluded in the case of performing simple arithmetic that the process was only partially autonomous, suggesting that "there may be a continuum of autonomy, ranging from completely autonomous to completely nonautonomous" (Zbrodoff and Logan 1986, 118). Bargh cited Zbrodoff and Logan's (1986) paper when arguing that automatic processing was not unitary, which is to say that the various properties associated with it did not necessarily co-occur. He noted that on these grounds Zbrodoff and Logan had concluded that it would be more profitable to investigate individual properties separately (Bargh 1989, 6). In 2018, Bargh acknowledged his debt to Zbrodoff and Logan (1986) on this point (Melnikoff and Bargh 2018a, 284). See also Saling and Phillips's criticism of Bargh's attempt to define automaticity by the property of "ballisticity"—or autonomy—on the grounds that such a definition reinstated the idea that automatic processes were independent of attention or intention, whereas it had been shown, among other findings, that the apparently automatic Stroop effect could be prevented from going to completion by contextual manipulations (Saling and Phillips 2007, 9).

(Moors and De Houwer 2006, 302). But they questioned why Bargh had singled out this particular quality as the one feature common to all forms of automaticity. Was it because it allowed the greatest variety of processes to be included under its rubric, thereby providing Bargh with a solution to the problem of how to draw a line between automatic and nonautomatic processes (Moors and De Houwer 2006, 301–2; see also Moors and De Houwer 2007)? Moors and De Houwer agreed with Bargh in rejecting an approach that treated automatic and nonautomatic processes as absolutely distinct. But they also argued that the concept of automaticity retained its value as an independent research field, in spite of Regan's view that it ought to be abandoned because it was so internally inconsistent (Regan 1981). Instead, in line with Bargh's views, Moors and De Houwer recommended a "features" approach to automaticity as the most cautious and scientifically sound position.

But given the uncertainty about which features should be regarded as essential to automaticity, Moors and De Houwer stated that they were also drawn to a "gradual" approach. According to the gradual approach, the traits associated with automatic actions could be viewed as on a gradient or, as Logan put it, "a continuum or a set of ordered states ranging from nonautomatic to automatic" (Logan 1985, 374). On this approach, attributes such as the speed or efficiency with which processes occurred, or people's awareness or unawareness of stimuli, or the extent of their control over behaviors, were not considered categorical but matters of degree. As Logan argued, the properties of habitual or automatic behaviors changed more or less continuously as a function of practice, so that the attribution of automaticity was itself relative to the state of a learned skill: at the start, learning a new skill was laborious and effortful, but with practice it became increasingly effortless (Logan 1985).[8]

It might seem obvious that trying to combine a "gradual" with a "features" approach to automaticity, as Moors and De Houwer appeared to recommend, risked making the concept of automaticity unmanageable. Not only was it a challenge to isolate certain features of automaticity and investigate them separately, but, as Moors and De Houwer noted, the

---

8. Although I cannot pursue the topic here, it is worth noting that there were powerful historical precedents in the work of Maine de Biran, Félix Ravaisson, William James, Paul Ricoeur, Maurice Merleau-Ponty, and others for treating automatic and nonautomatic processes as on a continuum in this way. See Carlisle 2010; 2014; and Fried 1990 (182–84); 2012 (63–71, 82–86).

gradual approach tended to weaken the notion of automaticity itself. "As a gradual concept," they observed, "automaticity loses its ability to distinguish one type of process (automatic) from another (nonautomatic), for any process can be labeled automatic to some degree" (Moors and De Houwer 2006, 300). In other words, the gradual approach could not provide criteria by which the various feature pairs, such as conscious or unconscious, could be distinguished. As Moors and De Houwer remarked: "An important weakness of the gradual approach is that it does not provide objective criteria for distinguishing between the automatic and the nonautomatic member of each feature pair: Every process is uncontrolled, efficient, unconscious, and fast, to some degree" (Moors and De Houwer 2006, 321). Or as Moors in a 2014 discussion of dual-process theories stated: "Although I believe the gradual approach to automaticity is theoretically the most cautious approach, it does not provide an objective criterion for the diagnosis of a process as automatic or nonautomatic" (Moors 2014, 26). In short, if automatic and nonautomatic processes were on a continuum, attempts to carve out an independent domain of automaticity for research purposes were bound to fail.

In the same paper of 2014, Moors proposed, as a solution to the difficulties of such attempts, that researchers install "intersubjective dividing lines between the two terms of the dichotomy" (Moors 2014, 30). By this proposal she appeared to mean that researchers should try to reach a consensus about the set of operational criteria to be used for deciding whether a process could be considered automatic or nonautomatic. She wrote:

> This problem can be dealt with by specifying the sense in which (i.e., the feature according to which) one considers a process to be automatic or nonautomatic, and by making relative conclusions or choosing an intersubjective criterion (i.e., convention) for calling some process controlled or uncontrolled, conscious or unconscious, efficient or nonefficient, and fast or slow [...] Rather than calling a process more or less automatic... the community of researchers may come to an agreement about a set of operational criteria that determines when they consider a process as automatic. (Moors 2014, 26–30)

Even in the case of certain features that some researchers continued to deny were continuous or gradual, Moors argued that those features might still "not escape gradual treatment," by which she appeared to mean that they would turn out to occur on a continuum. Hence her conclusion that "the fate of dual-process models may be gradual and/or a matter of convention" (Moors 2014, 30).

It is hard to see how these tortuous proposals could solve the formidable problems facing scientists investigating automatic processes. In the case of those who favored a continuum or gradual approach to automatic and nonautomatic actions, it was not feasible to separate the features of the two hypothesized systems: the principle of continuity ruled out the possibility of isolating automaticity from nonautomatic behaviors as an independent field of research. As Moors noted, the result was that gradualist definitions of the mechanisms involved in processing were actually "unimodels" (Moors 2014, 30)—that is, models of mental functioning that rejected the idea that there were two distinct modes of processing. Thus, a logical step taken by several critics of dual-process or dual-system theories over the years was to abandon altogether the effort to dichotomize the features of automaticity and nonautomaticity on the grounds that such an attempt was empirically and theoretically unsound. Instead, those critics insisted on, and claimed greater validity for, a single-system framework in which ostensibly opposing features, such as automatic (or uncontrolled) versus nonautomatic (or controlled) processes occurred on a continuum and hence existed on a single dimension (see for example Gigerenzer and Regier 1996; Newstead 2000; Keren and Schul 2009; Kruglanski and Gigerenzer 2011; Osman 2004; Hommel and Wiers 2017).[9] As Keren remarked of the logic underlying the rejection of dual-process systems: "If a particular dimension (e.g., automatic versus controlled) is continuous, where is the cutting line that separates the two systems? This is a major drawback that makes the theory untestable" (Keren 2013, 259).

But within the features approach to automaticity, the problems facing researchers were daunting. Indeed, Bargh might have realized that, according to the logic of his own argument for the lack of co-occurrence between the features of automaticity, almost any combination of properties might exist such that various alignments between the hypothetical automatic and nonautomatic processing systems were bound to occur. That is, qualities on either side of any proposed duality of processing might be

---

9. Over the years, dual-process or dual-system theorists aligned a variety of different features on either side of the proposed dichotomy of processes. Much of the discussion focused on the alleged distinction between rational or rule-based versus associative reasoning. But other proposed oppositions were between cognition and emotion, intentional and unintentional actions, automatic versus nonautomatic processes, and so on.

combined in any number of ways. Not only might intentional processes be conscious, but they might also be unconscious; unconscious processes might be efficient, but they might also be inefficient (or effortful); inefficient processes might sometimes be controllable but sometimes uncontrollable; effortful, inefficient processes could be intentional, but they could also be unintentional; unintentional processes could sometimes be uncontrollable but might also be controllable; and so on. There was no a priori rationale for ruling out any particular combination of features.[10]

Yet it would be decades before Bargh recognized the merits of this argument. In particular, he tended to reject the combination of unconsciousness and intentionality: to his way of thinking, consciousness implied intentionality and the notion of unconscious intentionality was a contradiction in terms. His position on this point was not unusual. On the contrary, it was shared by the majority of his contemporaries. Thus, as Fiedler and Hütter observed in a later discussion of the limits of automaticity, the chief criterion of automaticity in priming research had always been that automatic actions must not be subject to intentional control. The implication was that, since such actions were performed effortlessly or automatically and often without the individual's conscious attention or awareness, they must therefore be unintentional (Fiedler and Hütter 2014).[11] But Bargh's career-long inability to accept the idea of unconscious intentionality came at a considerable cost: for example, as we shall see in chapter 5, it lay behind his failure to grasp that apparently unconscious, automatic imitations were not independent of intentionality but were forms of intentional, interpersonal communication.

For the moment, though, Bargh did not grapple with such problems.

---

10. Thus Uleman (1999) argued that three of the features Bargh called the "four horsemen of automaticity"—lack of awareness, lack of control, and efficiency—were also continuous or a matter of degree. Uleman suggested that only intention was the clearest candidate for a dichotomy on which to base a dual-process theory: either one intends to do something or one does not. Uleman therefore distinguished sharply between intentional and unintentional processes, leaving the clear impression that one cannot intend and not intend to do something at the same time, but that one can intend something consciously or unconsciously, and that similarly, one can be conscious or unconscious of performing an unintentional action.

11. Bargh was by no means alone in assuming that lack of consciousness equated with lack of intentionality: it was the default position of the earliest post–World War II theories of automaticity and of most cognitive scientists thereafter. Fiedler and Hütter, however, stated that there was compelling evidence demonstrating that automatic actions were subject to strategic, intentional-voluntary control (Fiedler and Hütter 2014, 497, 504).

Instead, in 1984 he proceeded with the task of identifying the features he associated with automaticity, such as lack of intentionality and lack of consciousness, while also arguing that such features did not cohere in an all-or-none fashion. He also retained a role for intention and consciousness in social behavior. On the one hand, he gradually began to align his thought more closely with that of Langer. For example, in 1989 he and Uleman acknowledged that their own investigations had followed in the line of research opened by Langer's work on the "mindlessness" of typical social interactions by addressing "the extent to which impressions of others are formed and dispositional attributions are made without the person's intention that such processing occurs" (Bargh and Uleman 1989, xv).

On the other hand, Bargh rejected the idea that, because people's tendency to stereotype others was automatic in the sense of efficiency and ease of activation, it must also be completely uncontrollable. He resisted this proposal on the grounds that it was empirically incorrect and because of its implications for the absence of responsibility in discrimination cases. Thus, he accepted Susan Fiske's arguments against the claim that, since people were "wired" to stereotype others, they could not be held responsible for their behaviors (Bargh 1989, 6). As Fiske stated: "That stereotyping is unintentional and perhaps inevitable is a mistaken assumption at worst, and an inadequately examined one at best [...] [T]here is potential for damage due to misinterpretations of cognitive approaches to stereotyping as necessarily implying a lack of intent on the part of the social categorizer" (Fiske 1989, 254–55). Thus, on the basis of evidence demonstrating a capacity for control in the case of even the most automatic of stereotyped reactions, Fiske defended the concept of intentionality as a necessary concept in social psychology, one that had been "out of scientific fashion lately" in spite of the fact that psychology had returned to cognitive explanations (Fiske 1989, 257).[12]

Similarly, although Bargh compared the influence of automatic input on judgment, decisions, and behavior to that of the "ambitious royal advisor upon whom a relatively weak king relies heavily," he nevertheless affirmed that "the actual power of decision always rests with the king, who by no means has to follow the proffered advice" (Bargh 1989, 40). He reached the same conclusion from priming experiments he performed with Lombardi and Higgins, which suggested that consciousness

---

12. Experimental approaches to the phenomenon of stereotyping (or of implicit bias) have generated a very important literature that, however, lies outside the scope of this book.

of a prime at the moment information of the event was retrieved from memory made a qualitative difference to the effect of the prime (Lombardi, Higgins, and Bargh 1987). In short, his position was that stimuli could automatically influence early attentional and perceptual processing without the individual's awareness. But they could not directly determine responses to the situation because those responses ultimately depended on the individual's current intentional purposes and goals. As he later recalled: "Faced with this situation, Bargh (1989) was ready to pack up shop and call it quits regarding the extent of automatic influences of the environment. They seemed, as Neisser (1967) had originally argued, to be limited to early attentional and perceptual processes (pattern detection, figural synthesis) with an asymptotic limit at directly controlling any actual responses" (Baumeister and Bargh 2014, 39).

Bargh's Auto-Motive Theory, or, How Intentions and Goal Pursuits Came Apart

But Bargh did not pack up shop. Instead, he began to revise his position. In a series of publications in the years after 1989, he expanded the reach of automaticity until he was ready to declare that, in principle, all human behavior was automatic. According to him, not only were most judgments and decisions regulated automatically, so were goal pursuits which had formerly been attributed to conscious intentions. Emboldened by his findings, he shrugged off his initially cautious opinion that all effects of automatic and unconscious processes depended on influencing conscious processes in order to enact behavior. He began to speculate that most behavior, and perhaps nearly all of it, was the product of unconscious, unintentional, automatic processes. In 1997 he would therefore make the case that "much of everyday life—thinking, feeling, and doing—is automatic in that it is driven by current features of the environment (i.e., people, objects, behaviors of others, settings, roles, norms, etc.) as mediated by automatic cognitive processing of those features, without any mediation by conscious choice or reflection" (Bargh 1997, 2).

It took Bargh a few steps before he was ready to "shrink the domain of the homunculus," or the "executive," to the point that it could (almost) be made to disappear. As he later put it, "one last chance" of direct environmental control had to be examined before closing the books on the potential automaticity of all higher mental processes. He asked: "What if the goals themselves could be triggered and put into motion directly by environmental stimuli?" (Baumeister and Bargh 2014, 39). In the spring of 1989, Bargh made a sabbatical visit to Germany during which he hoped to be able to identify a mechanism to explain the automatic activation of goals. "I had been pondering any and all possible ways in which the external situation or environment could directly produce behavior," he later recalled; "that is, without the need for any intervention by conscious intention or construal processes. What were the possible automatic routes from environment to behavior?" (Bargh 2003, 217).

An encounter with researcher Peter Gollwitzer and others during his visit to Germany led to a solution. This solution was Bargh's "auto-motive" theory (Bargh 1990a), according to which goals could be pursued independently of intentions. Bargh conceded that much of the time, with sufficient motivation and effort, people could intentionally prevent themselves from reacting automatically to the environmental triggering of their stereotypes, traits, and other mental constructs. Nevertheless, he suggested that many goal-setting activities were not under executive control but were initiated directly by the relevant external stimuli. Bargh's argument depended on the cognitive-science assumption that, just as stereotypes and other constructs could be represented in the mind as independent components, so an individual's goals could likewise take the form of discrete, internal mental representations. Those represented goals could then be directly activated by the stimuli with which they had become associated. As he argued:

> The mechanism proposed here by which the social environment may control judgments, decisions, and behavior is the formation of direct and automatic mental links between representations of motives and goals in memory (and consequently the goals and plans associated with them) and the representations of the social situations in which those motives have been frequently pursued in the past. The result of this automatic associative link is that the motive-plan structure becomes activated whenever the relevant triggering situational features are present in the environment. The activated goals and plans then presumably guide the social cognition and interaction of the individual, without the person's intention or awareness of the motive's guiding role. (Bargh 1990a, 100)

In other words, Bargh now claimed that "goals" or "goal pursuits" were constituents of internal mechanisms that explained purposive action without appealing to the idea of intentionality in Brentano's sense of the term (which is to say, the idea of intention as a property of mental states which are directed at real or imagined objects or at some state of affairs). The information-processing models of mental functioning that Bargh adopted encouraged him to transfer the capacity for the pursuit of goals from the intentionality of the agent to putative internal information-processing systems in the mind-brain and to model those systems in such a way that goal pursuits could be treated as if they occurred independently of intention.

In presenting his auto-motive theory in 1990, Bargh cited in support of his views both Miller, Galanter, and Pribram's (1960) earlier effort to explain intentionality and purpose in information-processing terms, and Robert Wilensky's more recent *Planning and Understanding: A Computational Approach to Human Reasoning* (1983) (Bargh 1990a, 103–4). In his well-known critique of computational approaches to the mind, Hubert Dreyfus had observed that cognitive scientists and researchers in artificial intelligence mistakenly assumed that human understanding consisted in the forming and use of symbolic representations built up out of primitive, disembodied, context-free facts, elements, and features, and that explicit rules for manipulating the latter could be determined. But Dreyfus had countered on Wittgensteinian, Heideggerian, and phenomenological grounds that human understanding did not work in that way: rather, it depended on background "knowhow," ordinary coping skills, personal experience, and knowledge that could not be represented in formal rules of that kind. In short, Dreyfus had argued that the mind's sense of the relevance of the situation and cues was holistic, not atomistic: its processes resisted capture by the context-independent and digitalized formulations of artificial-intelligence researchers (Dreyfus 1979). On this basis, he had predicted that efforts to create artificial intelligence modeled on the computer were bound to fail.

In citing Wilensky's book in support of his auto-motive model, however, Bargh aligned his views with those of the computer scientists and artificial-intelligence researchers who had been the target of Dreyfus' critique. Wilensky dismissed Dreyfus's book in three lines, even though his only solution to the problem of how goal pursuits were enacted was to posit a hypothetical "Goal Detector" composed of mechanisms he termed the "Noticer," the "Plan Proposer," the "Projector" and the "Executor." Acting together, these mechanisms were said to be able to "recognize" whether a particular situation merited the selection and activation of a goal and then could proceed to perform the specified action. However, Wilensky's proposals appeared to simply restate in information-processing language the very problems of intention, recognition, and selection the model was supposed to explain. To the question "How does the mind recognize a situation as affording possibilities for choosing and activating the relevant goals?" the answer seemed to be: "Because it has a Goal Detector, a Plan Proposer, a Projector, and an Executor that make such recognition possible." (For a brief discussion of the conceptual and philosophical problems associated with the topic of recognition, especially in infant development, see Leys 2020, 26–27).

But such concerns did not deter Bargh. Instead, he deployed Wilensky's claims to support the hypothesis that environmental stimuli could directly activate goal pursuits without the intervention of intentions, the implication being that intentions and goal pursuits could come apart. Indeed, in a debate over the nature of intentionality, also published in 1990, Bargh explicitly defended this idea (Bargh 1990b). That debate was anchored by developmental psychologist Michael Lewis, who proposed a broad account of intentionality in order to suggest that not only did the behaviors of infants and adults exist on a continuum, but intentionality was present in any goal-directed, purposive phenomenon, such as a plant's movement toward the sun, or even behavior at the cellular level. In the case of humans, Lewis proposed the existence of various levels of intention, from the simplest intentions observed in very young infants through various more-complex levels as the infants matured into adulthood (Lewis 1990).

Lewis's argument was chiefly motivated by the worry that Jean Piaget's view that infants only develop intentional behavior in the fourth stage of sensorimotor development raised difficult questions concerning where intentions came from—specifically, how could intentionality be derived from non-intentional processes? As Lewis saw it, the problem with Piaget's theory was: "How can the infant discover intentions if it does not already possess them?" (Lewis 1990, 233). Lewis suggested that this problem of origins could be solved by adopting the idea that all living, goal-directed systems were already intentional, as it were. On his proposal, intentions were assumed to exist in all forms of life and to develop through an ascending series of levels of complexity. Lewis's claims reflected ongoing debates within the field of infant development over how to characterize the behavior of very young children, as well as his understanding of recent contributions to the topic of intentionality by philosophers such as John Searle (1984) and Daniel Dennett (1987).

One of the more interesting responses to Lewis's paper was by psychologist Joseph Rychlak, who criticized Lewis for failing to appreciate that intentionality was a teleological concept that couldn't be handled coherently with efficient-causal models, as Lewis tried to do, or by combining machine- or information-processing talk with "meaning" talk. Rychlak pointed out that, according to the "father of information theory," Claude Shannon, information in a cybernetic sense had nothing to do with the meaning of the message being transmitted. Information in this engineering sense did not convey "knowledge" at all, as Lewis's mixing of models suggested it did. On these and related grounds, Rychlak rejected Lewis's proposals (Rychlak 1990).

As for Bargh, he too rejected Lewis's arguments, but for very different reasons. Above all, he denied Lewis's equation between intentionality and goal-directed behavior. "In my opinion, there are many cases in which goal-directed behavior is *not* intentional or desired," he wrote, giving the example of traumatized people who compulsively and uncontrollably ruminate about their traumas but do not desire or wish to do so.[13] Bargh also mentioned "action slips," such as slips of the tongue, as examples of this kind. "These are unintended acts that occur when the presence of environmental cues relevant for a habitual action 'capture' one's behavior," he wrote, "even though the habitual action is inappropriate this particular time." In support of his position, Bargh also mentioned the findings of experiments on priming, cognitive dissonance, bystander interventions, and persuasion to claim that "individuals are being manipulated to behave in ways inconsistent with their desires and intentions... To be intentional and to be goal directed are two separate things," he concluded, "and it is better to leave them as two separate concepts than to obfuscate the true state of affairs by assuming they are isomorphic" (Bargh 1990b, 249–50; for a subsequent iteration of these and related claims see also Chartrand and Bargh 2002).

In their later discussion of automaticity Moors and De Houwer also dissociated intentions from goal pursuits, writing:

Intentional(ity) refers to a property of mental phenomena by which they are directed at or about some state of affairs outside of themselves (Bren-

---

13. Bargh here stated that goal-pursuits occurring independently of intention were those that were not desired (Bargh 1990b, 249–50). In later attempts to explain how it was that ostensibly non-intentional goal-pursuits could also be highly flexible and sensitive to contextual cues, he would smuggle "desires," "wishes," and even "beliefs" back into his description of the nature of such goal-directed actions in ways that were closer to certain standard intentionalist approaches (Baumeister and Bargh 2014, 36).

tano, 1874) ... We need to delineate the concept intentional from the concepts goal directed and goal dependent. Because the core meaning of *intentional* is directed, one would expect a strong overlap between the terms *intentional* and *goal directed*. On closer consideration, however, it is evident that the source and the terminus of the directedness relation are different. In an intentional act, it is the person (source) that is directed onto the act (terminus), whereas in a goal-directed act, it is the act (source) that is directed onto a further goal (terminus).

Although acts often combine the features intentional and goal directed, both features can, in principle, occur independently. Not all intentional acts are directed at a further goal, and not all acts that are directed at a goal are intentional. (Moors and De Houwer 2006, 303; their emphasis)

Moors and De Houwer applied the distinction between intentional and goal-directed actions to the phenomenon of driving. They argued that the intention to drive a car gives rise to many subsidiary acts, such as changing gears, which they depicted as goal-directed but unintentional. They conceded that these goal-directed subsidiary actions would not have occurred without the overarching intention to drive. Nevertheless, they reasoned that the intentional act could be divided into separate components: the proximate goal, which was intentional, and the remote goal, which was unintentional. Actions could thus be described at various levels, where low-level descriptions concerned the physical movements and high-level descriptions concerned overarching intentions. They identified three ingredients as the formal criteria needed to classify an action as intentional: intention, act, and causal connection (Moors and De Houwer 2006, 303, 306). In other words, they assumed the existence of independent, private mental states of intention that were separated by a gap from their (behavioral, motor, or other) manifestations or effects, a gap which was closed by the causal relationship between the two. In short, they adopted a causal account of intentionality in terms derived from the philosopher Donald Davidson that was compatible with the causal claims of the cognitive sciences but at odds with an Anscombean treatment of intentionality, as discussed in chapter 2.[14] (I shall have more to say about the example of driving in chapter 4 and the appendix.)

---

14. Moors and De Houwer thus defined an intentional act as

one that was caused by the goal to engage in it. This definition contains three ingredients: (a) the intention or goal to engage in the act, (b) the act (bodily motion or

Prinz's Ideomotor Theory of Automaticity

Bargh's auto-motive mechanism was not the only mechanism proposed at this time to explain how goal-directed behaviors could be completely and automatically determined by environmental cues. An encounter during the same visit to Germany with Wolfgang Prinz and his ideas about ideomotor action suggested to Bargh a related but somewhat different possibility. The term *ideomotor* had been used by the British authors Thomas Laycock and William Benjamin Carpenter in the mid- to late nineteenth century to express the notion of a direct relationship between ideas and movements, as when, for example, a person imagines acting in some way, or a hypnotist commands a subject to carry out certain imitations, and the movements then follow. The proposal was that the mere spontaneous or suggested act of thinking about, or idea of, behaviors increases a person's tendency to automatically perform them. Ideomotor theory also had roots in a German tradition of research influenced by the work of Friedrich Herbart, Hermann Lotze, and others. The theory was taken up by William James but soon fell out of favor because in the eyes of many psychologists it was tainted by its connection with suggestion and other "occult" phenomena such as Ouija boards, divining rods, and "automatic writing" by psychics and seers (Greenwald 1970; 1971; Greenwald and Banaji 1995; Prinz 1987; 1990; 1997b; 2002; 2005; Stock and Stock 2004; Shin et al. 2010).

Prinz was one of a small number of investigators who in the post-World War II period attempted to recast the ideomotor theory in terms deemed more acceptable to science. Two features of Prinz's approach deserve special emphasis. The first was his proposal that, when individuals mimicked the actions of others, as when they involuntarily and unconsciously copied the movements of a sports player or a movie actor, their imitations were the result of a similarity or overlap between the mental representations of the motor action itself and the action as the viewer perceived it. He therefore argued that, through the effects of association, there developed a commonality between the individual's perceptual and motor codes. In making this point, Prinz deliberately broke with a long

---

mental process), and (c) the causal connection between the goal and the act (Davidson, 1980; Searle, 1983), with the goal being the cause and the act being the effect [...] The three ingredients—intention, act, and causal connection—can be regarded as the formal criteria needed to classify an act as intentional... An act is unintentional when it is not caused by an intention (or when it is not in the right way). (Moors and De Houwer 2006, 306)

tradition in psychology according to which perceptual (or sensory) and motor codes were incommensurable. He suggested instead that it was the similarity or overlap between the codes that mattered and that held the key to the match between perceived actions and their imitation (Prinz 1987; 2002; 2005; see also Leys 2020). As Bargh stated when he recalled his first encounter with Prinz's views:

> [Prinz's] basic idea was that there was an overlap or even isomorphism between the (perceptual) representations one uses to perceive an action and the (motor) representations used to produce it oneself, so that perceiving an action also made the corresponding motor-behavioral representation active (i.e., more accessible).
>
> Here was a second potential mechanism or route by which the external social environment could directly affect social behavior—through its effect on perception. According to this logic of a direct and passive (automatic) connection between perception and action, then, the same priming manipulations many of us had used in the 1980s to influence social perception (e.g., impression formation) should also influence the perceiver's own social behavior. (Bargh 2003, 217)

Prinz was especially interested in the implications of his ideomotor model for imitation, since it suggested a solution to the well-known "correspondence problem," namely, how sensory input generated by observing another person's actions was converted into a recognizably similar or mirroring behavior on the part of the beholder, an enigma that has been described as "arguably the central scientific puzzle in imitation research" (Nehaniv and Dautenhahn 2002, 41). It is not surprising that, in the course of developing his ideas, Prinz drew support from Andrew Meltzoff and M. Keith Moore's similar, influential arguments regarding the existence of a "supramodal system," or common representational domain for perception and action, in order to explain their claims for the existence of newborn imitation (Prinz 1987, 68). Meltzoff and Moore had argued that an active matching process between perception and action could occur because of the similarity between perceptual and motor codes. I note, however, that the consensus today is that the capacity to integrate information across the senses is not an innate or inherent feature of the newborn's brain but develops through experience in postnatal life (Stein and Meredith 1993, x, 11–15, 21; Stein, Stanford, and Rowland 2014, 521). Moreover, claims for newborn imitation had always been questioned by some researchers and have been seriously undermined by a recent meta-analysis of the evidence (Davis et al. 2021; for a critical history of the claims made for newborn imitation see also Leys 2020).

As we can see from Bargh's comments, another important feature of the ideomotor theory was the emphasis Prinz gave to "perceptions" as the instigators of ideomotor actions rather than James's or the hypnotist's "ideas" (or "suggestions"). He argued that, in the case of "perceptual induction," all that was required to instigate an imitation was the mere perception of someone's action. As Prinz and his colleagues put it: "Perceptual induction implies that people tend to perform the movements they see" (Knuf, Aschersleben, and Prinz 2001, 780). According to Prinz, even in the case of what he called "intentional induction," where the imitations were generated by ideas and therefore understood as intentional and voluntary, the intentions themselves depended on the prior perception of ongoing events. The perception-behavior link was therefore a central component of Prinz's ideomotor theory. Indeed, it can plausibly be argued that the purpose of Prinz's reframing of ideomotor action as a matter not of the direct influence of *ideas* on action, as in the case of the hypnotist's commands to the hypnotized subject, but of *common codes between perception and action*, was precisely to try and strip the phenomenon of its historical association with the uncanny phenomenon of hypnotic or suggestive influence.

Moreover, by substituting perceptions for ideas as the instigators of ideomotor action, Prinz also contributed to the tendency to eliminate considerations of intention and meaning from the understanding of such movements. He rejected the notion that a mental state (an "idea") could cause a bodily movement, which he dismissed as an unfortunate holdover from Cartesian dualism, in favor of what he considered a strictly causal explanation. According to him, all that was required to instigate an imitation was the direct interaction between a "percept," defined as a stimulus input, and the relevant, commonly coded motor structures. As Prinz argued:

> Our considerations only refer to perceptual guidance of movements and do not include what Carpenter and James called "ideational guidance," i.e., the guidance of movements by corresponding images, conceptions, or thoughts. There are three reasons for this restriction. First, it is suggested by the scope of this book. Second, for obvious reasons most

of the experimental literature refers to perceptual rather than ideational guidance. Third, when extented [*sic, extended*] to include ideational guidance, the notion of ideo-motor action becomes overexpanded and therefore quite diffuse in its meaning... According to James, body movement is a natural, direct effect of specific feelings and representations, and it occurs entirely by itself, unless it is impeded by other, simultaneously effective ideas and their corresponding impulses: "Drop this idea (i.e., the competing idea), think of the movement purely and simply, with all brakes off; and presto! it takes place with no effort at all" (James, 1890, II, p. 527).

Though the magic spell of James's words may be tempting we resist their lure and confine ourselves to the case of perceptual guidance of movements. (Prinz 1987, 54–55)[15]

Or, as Bargh and Chartrand later put the same point: "Because perceptual activity is largely automatic and not under conscious or intentional control ... perception is the route by which the environment directly causes mental activity—specifically, the activation of internal representations of the outside world ... In short, the 'ideo' in ideomotor effects could just as well come from outside the head as within it" (Bargh and Chartrand 1999, 465).

Does the Environment Trigger Goal Pursuits Independently of Intentions?

Bargh promoted both his auto-motive hypothesis and Prinz's ideomotor theory in various subsequent research papers. His auto-motive hypothesis informed a paper with Gollwitzer in 1994 that Bargh later cited as offering the first demonstration of nonconscious, non-intentional goal pursuit. In this paper the authors acknowledged that goal-directed behavior was derived from, or dependent on, the existence of prior intentions. They observed:

15. By tracing the origin of ideomotor behaviors to perceptions, Prinz aligned his position with determinism in science. As he objected to the notion of free will: "An important consequence of using the jargon of free will is the *cutting short of explanatory chains*" (1997a, 158; his emphasis). He therefore proposed that the focus of psychological explanations of imitation should not be an inquiry into people's reasons for their actions but the investigation of the assumed sub-personal perceptual processes that generated the behavior.

This behavior is intentional in that it was repeatedly and deliberately selected in the past. Eventually, we postulate, this selection or choice becomes just another routine and invariant feature of the situation to the mental system, and is thus bypassed. The same principle of routinization can be found in models of skill acquisition ... proceduralization ... and script operation ... Therefore, it would be appropriate to say that automatic behavior due to the operation of enduring goals or motives is unintentional at the time but intentional in the sense that the choice of the behavior was made in the past, not in the present. (Bargh and Gollwitzer 1994, 82)

One might object, however, that the authors were wrong to characterize such behaviors as having become unintentional through routinization or overlearning. It seems likely, rather, that if the participants were asked *why* they had performed certain actions in carrying out a routine skill, they would have been able to give their reasons for doing so.

Bargh and Gollwitzer's discussion of what they called "implementation intentions" is revealing in this regard. In the case of implementation intentions, they wrote,

the individual intentionally turns to environmental control to further goal achievement. Implementation intentions, in effect, create a contingency between a future (usually the short-term or immediate future) set of circumstances and the behavior one has decided to enact when those circumstances occur ... However, this behavior is also automatic, because at the time of behaving, the effect of the triggering environmental features is direct and immediate and requires no intervening conscious choice, intention, or awareness at that time. (Bargh and Gollwitzer 1994, 72–73)

This account offers a strange explanation of how intention is linked to action. It's as if, in an example given by the authors, I deliberately decide in advance that I will pick up my daughter from school at an earlier time than usual, which is to say that I form an "implementation intention." Because of the link between the particular situational context and the goal, at the specified time environmental cues will automatically trigger the required actions without my having to intend them. One could plausibly argue, however, that since I would be able to give reasons for my actions in collecting my daughter at the earlier time, and could presumably change my plans if the circumstances were warranted, it is difficult to understand why the fulfillment of my intention should be regarded as if it had been carried out by an entirely non-intentional, automatic mechanism independently from my intentional agency (nor would Bargh and Gollwitzer's arguments explain why I might forget to pick up my daughter).

Bargh and Gollwitzer's account depended on the assumption that the intentional system could relegate the instigation of an action to future events that then triggered the required action, presumably when the person perceived that the time was right. As Gollwitzer put this point: "The underlying theory is that by forming implementation intentions people pass on control of goal-directed activities from the self to the environment. The intended behavior is subjected to external control through the environmental cues specified in one's implementation intention ... When these cues (occasions or opportunities) or means are encountered, they are expected to prompt the intended behavior" (Gollwitzer 1993, 153). Such a picture of how the mind works would not be thinkable without the cognitive-science idea that the mental state of the representation of intention is separated by a gap from the intended action. Nor would it be plausible without the proviso that intentions translate into action via a subordinate sequence of processes running in an automatic manner from the perception of the triggering "stimulus" through the associations between internal, cognitive representations and motor representations to the desired actions.

The experiments Bargh and Gollwitzer described in their 1994 paper in support of their views were classical priming experiments. For example, they described an experiment in which participants were first asked to carry out a scrambled-sentence test containing prime words connoting assertiveness or politeness. The participants then had to listen to an ongoing conversation between the experimenter and another subject (actually a confederate of the experimenter) that held up the start of the next experiment. The authors reported that participants primed with assertiveness words interrupted the conversation more quickly than did a control group of participants who had been primed with words for politeness. For Bargh and Gollwitzer, the findings suggested that goals could be activated directly by social situations "without the subject consciously choosing or intending the behavior" (Bargh and Gollwitzer 1994, 85).[16] A second ex-

---

16. Bargh reported more details of this experiment in Bargh, Chen, and Burrows 1996. Katzko argued that Bargh, Chen, and Burrows did not explain why the "time to interrupt" a conversation was defined as rudeness, especially since the manner of interruption was

periment tested the differential importance of achievement versus affiliation primes in situations in which, after priming, the participants were asked to perform with others as a team a series of word-search puzzles. The experiment appeared to show a "sizable" difference in the performance on the puzzles, depending on which goal had been primed (Bargh and Gollwitzer 1994, 86).[17]

In order to demonstrate that even chronic goals could be activated directly by the environment in this way, Bargh and Gollwitzer undertook another experiment designed to test the persistence of environmentally activated goals. In the study, three participants at a time, who were partitioned from each other's view, were primed with either "achievement" or "neutral" words. Then in an ostensibly independent task, they were asked to find as many words as they could in a rack of eight Scrabble letter tiles within the short time span of two minutes. The experimenter told the participants that she had to leave in order to go to another experiment down the hall and that, if she could not return in time, over the intercom she would give the signal to stop. She then told the participants to begin their test and left the room.

Unknown to the participants, a video camera was hidden in a box at the front of the room, and their behaviors were monitored. After two minutes the experimenter gave the stop command, and the video camera recorded how long the participants continued with their tasks in her absence. According to Bargh and Gollwitzer, the results showed a "powerful" effect of the priming manipulation on the dependent task variable of persistence. Over 50 percent of the subjects in the achievement priming condition—more than twice as many than in the neutral priming condition—continued to work on the Scrabble test after the signal to stop had been given. The authors emphasized that the primed goal caused the participants to ignore the instructions to stop. Bargh and Gollwitzer inter-

---

"'to say anything to the experimenter, such as 'Excuse me' or 'Sorry, but...'" (Bargh, Chen, and Burrows 1996, 234; Katzko 2006, 217 n5). For more on this point see chapter 6.

17. In their paper, Bargh and Gollwitzer contested Carver et al.'s claim that the effects observed in such priming studies activated various behavioral schemas or goals stored in the individual's memory that were relevant to the subsequent situation, thereby permitting the subject to consciously choose how to behave (Carver et al. 1983). Against Carver, Bargh and Gollwitzer argued that enduring goals and motives were "*directly* triggered by the environment without any intervening conscious choice among alternatives" (Bargh and Gollwitzer 1994, 90; their emphasis).

preted this result to mean that priming manipulations influenced not just the participants' cognitions but also their chronic goals.[18] Their general conclusion was that persistent goals could be triggered by familiar situations and implemented in a "mindless" way, which is to say, entirely without the subject's awareness or intention (for similar claims see also Chartrand and Bargh 1996; Bongers and Dijksterhuis 2009; for an overview of such claims see Fishback and Ferguson 2007; Ferguson and Cone 2013).

The Elderly Priming Experiment

In 1996, Bargh, Chen, and Burrows published a paper on the automaticity of social behavior that included the results of their experiment demonstrating that participants primed with words chosen to connote the elderly automatically slowed their walking pace when they left the laboratory. The findings were presented in the light of both Bargh's auto-motive model and Prinz's ideomotor framework, as proof that not just social judgments but actual behavior could be initiated by the mere presence of the relevant situational features. In support of their claims regarding the existence of a direct perception-behavior link, the authors also cited Daniel Wegner's studies of "ironic" processes (Wegner 1994), Meltzoff and Moore's studies of imitation in newborns (Meltzoff and Moore 1977; 1983), and Leonard Berkowitz's theory of the contagion of mass violence (Berkowitz 1984; Bargh, Chen, and Burrows 1996, 231). The authors argued:

> The influence of perception on behavioral tendencies is automatic in that it is passive, unintentional, and nonconscious . . . [R]ecent evidence of automatic influences in social perception, such as the automatic activation of stereotypes and priming effects on impression formation . . . implies that there may be behavioral consequences of automatic social perception for the perceiver. For it is precisely when the individual is not aware of a perceptual process that conscious control over it is not possible . . . maximizing the possibility of the passive perception-behavior effect. (Bargh, Chen, and Burrows 1996, 233)

---

18. The authors did not include information on debriefing the participants. More generally, their discussions of these experiments were not formal scientific reports, but informal accounts and claims, lacking the detail needed to assess the likely validity or replicability of their findings.

The first experiment the authors reported appeared to be a variation of the "persistence" experiment as described by Bargh and Gollwitzer in 1994. Participants were asked to sort into sentences sets of scrambled words that included priming words connoting rudeness or politeness, or scrambled-word sets without the two kinds of primes. The length of time it took them to interrupt a (staged) conversation between the experimenter and a confederate was then surreptitiously measured by the confederate using a stopwatch. Once participants either interrupted the conversation or waited a maximum of ten minutes, they were led into an adjacent room and asked to complete an anagram puzzle task that took no more than two minutes to complete. They were then partially debriefed and questioned using a funnel procedure to determine how they thought the scrambled-sentence task might have influenced the rest of the experiment.[19] Bargh, Chen, and Burrows reported that no participant showed any awareness or suspicion that the scrambled-sentence task might have influenced their interruption behavior (Bargh, Chen, and Burrows 1996, 234). A further survey of the participants was conducted as they left the building to make sure that the experimenter had behaved in a courteous and polite way at all times and had not behaved in ambiguous ways that might have affected the results. The findings were that participants in the rude priming condition interrupted significantly faster than did participants in the neutral or polite priming conditions. The experiment seemed to show that priming a single trait could indeed influence subsequent social behavior. The next experiments tested the direct effects of priming words connoting old age and words connoting African American stereotypes, already described in the introduction.

The general conclusion of the paper was that, across all the experiments, the activation of a trait construct or a stereotype in one context resulted in behavior consistent with it in a subsequent context. According to Bargh, Chen, and Burrows, the participants were not aware of the influence, or potential influence, of the priming words on their behavior.

---

19. Bargh, Chen, and Burrows's funnel debriefing procedure involved probing participants in a systematic way for any suspicions they might have had about the intended effect of the primes on their subsequent performance in the experiment, and included questions concerning whether they had noticed or suspected any relation between the scrambled-sentence task and the concept of old age (Bargh, Chen, and Burrows 1996, 237). For further details concerning the funnel debriefing procedure, see also Chartrand and Bargh 1996; Bargh and Chartrand 2000.

The authors explained their findings as the result of behavioral responses that had become automatically linked to representations of familiar social situations. At the time, the size of the behavioral effects of priming was a surprise, because they were so much larger than those of previous priming effects on social-perceptual variables such as impressions. Bargh later reported that he and his team had been in no rush to publish their results, even after replicating them several times, because they wanted to be sure of them. It was therefore a "great and happy relief" when Dijksterhuis and van Knippenberg (1998) and others had begun to carry out related experiments that conceptually replicated the findings. As he testified: "We need not have worried, as it turned out—the effect has since proven to be very robust" (Bargh 2003, 216).

One puzzling question raised by Bargh, Chen, and Burrows was why the results were so easily obtained, when subliminal advertising did not work in anything like such a simple way. Their suggestion was that the primed behaviors in their experiments were relevant and appropriate in the experimental situation in which the participants were placed, whereas in, say a movie theater, an advertisement for Pepsi-Cola drinks had to influence a person in the context of many other possible competing goals, such as not disturbing others in the audience. On the other hand, the evidence for the strength and compulsory nature of these primed effects also suggested that unless people were aware of various influences impacting them, were motivated to control them, and had sufficient attentional capacity at the time to do so, then such automatic behaviors were likely to occur. (The issue at stake here concerned the selectivity of priming influences, a topic that I will have more to say about in chapter 4.)

In sum, Bargh's view of automatic actions in 1996 was that they were compulsory, perception-driven behaviors occurring in the absence of intentional influences owing to the close associations that had built up over time between perceptual and motor representations in the mind-brain. Left somewhat unclear in these developments was the extent of automaticity in everyday behavior. Bargh understood automatic actions to occur in the absence of the people's awareness of the true causes of their behavior, as Nisbett and Wilson had argued in their famous attribution studies. But how pervasive was automaticity in the economy of human life? It is to Bargh's answer to that question that I turn in the next chapter.

4

"The Unbearable Automaticity of Being"

> Our sense of agency is an inference, not incorrigible evidence that intentions cause actions.
> —J. S. ULEMAN (2005, 7)

Bargh's Manifesto

In 1997, in a deliberately provocative keynote address on the "automaticity of everyday life," Bargh made the case for the pervasiveness of automaticity in social interactions. Bargh claimed that the automatic effects of priming were not limited to the activation of judgments and traits but extended to all human behaviors. Drawing on his auto-motive hypothesis, Prinz's ideomotor theory, claims for the existence of newborn imitation, the imitative-contagious effects of media representations of violence, the results of priming experiments such as his elderly priming study, and other evidence, Bargh proposed that in principle all aspects of social interaction were the result of automatic links between perception and behavior.

Bargh would later describe this moment in his career as his "feisty period," when he shrugged off his "initial, cautious view" that "all effects of automatic and unconscious processes depended on influencing conscious processes in order to reach behavior" and began to speculate that "the majority of behavior, and perhaps close to all of it," was the product of unconscious processes rather than conscious ones (Baumeister and Bargh 2014, 37). In this chapter I propose to examine Bargh's arguments for the automaticity of everyday life and to trace the further development of his

---

The title of this chapter is taken from the title of a paper by Bargh and Chartrand (1999).

claims for what he called "the unbearable automaticity of being" (Bargh and Chartrand 1999).

In his 1997 keynote address, bearing the title "Manifesto" and with a quotation at the start from the behaviorist B. F. Skinner on the methodological necessity of determinist assumptions in the science of human behavior, Bargh stated:

> The more we know about the situational causes of psychological phenomena, the less need we have for postulating internal conscious mediating processes to explain those phenomena . . . [I]t is hard to escape the forecast that as knowledge progresses regarding psychological phenomena, there will be less of a role played by free will or conscious choice in accounting for them. In other words, because of social psychology's natural focus on the situational determinants of thinking, feeling, and doing, it is inevitable that social psychological phenomena will be found to be automatic in nature. That trend has already begun . . . and it can do nothing but continue. (Bargh 1997, 1)

Bargh went much further than even Langer had done in claiming the "mindlessness" of social behavior (see also Bargh 1999). Bargh acknowledged that Skinner had been wrong to argue that mental processes or cognitions played no part in the regulation of behavior. But according to him, the fact that mental (or "cognitive") processes mediated the effects of environmental and social stimuli on judgmental and behavioral responses did not make those responses any less determined. He quoted approvingly the psychologist Lawrence Barsalou as stating, "'Like behaviorists, most cognitive psychologists believe that the fundamental laws of the physical world determine human behavior completely. Whereas behaviorists view control as only existing in the environment, however, cognitive psychologists view it as also existing in cognitive mechanisms . . . The illusion of free will is simply one more phenomenon . . . that cognitive psychologists must explain'" (Bargh 1997, 2, citing Barsalou 1992, 91). Or as Bargh also stated: "So it may well be that there ultimately is no future role for conscious processing in accounts of the mind, in the sense of free will and choice" (Bargh 1997, 52). "My thesis," he wrote, "is that because social psychology, like automaticity theory and research, is also concerned with phenomena that occur whenever certain situational features or factors are in place, social psychological phenomena are essentially automatic. Which of the different varieties of automaticity a given phenomenon corresponds to depends on the nature of the situational (including internal cognitive) preconditions" (Bargh 1997, 3).

No wonder Kihlstrom later complained that the "positivistic reserve" inherent in cognitive psychology meant that Bargh's position was no different from that of behaviorism (Kihlstrom 2004). It seemed that automaticity effects were expected to "go to completion" directly, from the perception of the external stimulus to the internal mental cognitive representations to the response, without regard to differences between individuals, their intentions, desires, or beliefs, or the role of motivational-contextual factors. As Bargh wrote: "An *automatic mental phenomenon* occurs reflexively whenever certain triggering conditions are in place" (Bargh 1997, 3; his emphasis).

In his "Manifesto," Bargh mostly discussed the evidence for his claims derived from studies of automatic phenomena of the kind seen in many priming experiments, but he also proposed that many other situations might have their "if-then" reflexive effects. He argued: "If the situation activates the same goal in nearly everyone so that it is an effect that generalizes across individuals, and can be produced with random assignment of experimental participants to conditions, the only preconditions for the effect are the situational features" (Bargh 1997, 3). Bargh therefore analyzed goal pursuits in terms of postulated "goal" constructs and representations held to mediate between the stimulus and the behavioral output in a completely automatic processing sequence:

> Goals and behavioral responses do not exist in some mysterious ether, but correspond to mental representations in much the same way as do attitudes and perceptual structures . . . And because they are mental representations, the same principle of automatization that produces automatic perceptual interpretations, for instance, should apply to them as well . . . [I]f an individual has the same goal and intention within a given social situation repeatedly over time, then that goal representation, with its associated plans to attain that goal . . . will become active automatically whenever those situational features are present. (Bargh 1997, 7–8)[1]

---

1. I note that Bargh here appeared to assume that the hypothesized mental representations of the mind are isomorphic with the perceived scenes, as if the relevant information were totally contained in just the scene independently of the social context in which the scene occurred. But we know that this isophormism between perception and situations is not true, even with simple perceptual illusions, e.g., the Müller-Lyer illusion, which shows cultural effects.

Moreover, Bargh argued that evidence for the intervention of conscious intentions in social-behavioral research was frequently inadequate or lacking. Bystander research, for instance, had explained the failure of witnesses to help someone in need by suggesting that a group of several bystanders experienced a diminished sense of responsibility for the unfolding events. But Bargh suggested that for the effect to occur with regularity among a range of spectators, "the feeling of less responsibility and the decision not to help, and so on, are also automatic reactions to the situational information across different individuals" (Bargh 1997, 4). He cast doubt on claims regarding the role of conscious processes in such bystander research on the grounds that psychologists had only inferred the presence of consciousness from behavioral measures.

More generally, he argued that doubters like himself about the role of consciousness and intention in behavior had unfairly been made to jump through methodological hoops to establish nonconsciousness in automaticity beyond any reasonable doubt. It was time, Bargh suggested, for social psychology to adopt the same level of healthy skepticism about models that included a role for conscious intervention. He asserted: "The assumption of conscious mediation should be treated with the same scientific scrutiny as the assumption of automaticity." Indeed, he claimed that whenever conscious mediators had been proposed, subsequent evidence had always reduced their importance and scope. "I emphatically push the point that automatic, nonconscious processes pervade all aspects of mental and social life," he remarked, "in order to overcome what I consider dominant, even if implicit, assumptions to the contrary" (Bargh 1997, 5, 50).

The immediate response of most of Bargh's commentators was one of resistance to his overarching conclusion that automatic processes would eventually take over psychology. Some years earlier, Walter Mischel had played an influential role in the rise of "situationism" in social psychology—the idea that behavior was entirely determined by the environmental situation—but had subsequently modified and softened his claims. While characterizing Bargh's 1997 statement as a "tour de force," he now questioned whether Bargh really meant to resurrect in cognitive-science terms the old behaviorist claims about the reflexivity of behavior. "Bargh sounds like he is resurrecting, in cognitivized form, the concept of the automatic stimulus control of behavior," he remarked, "and one wonders if he really means it." But Mischel doubted that Bargh was sincere, pointing out that, in an apparent contradiction of his own arguments, Bargh had stated in his "Manifesto" that a precondition of goal-dependent automaticity was "'the individual intending to perform the mental function.'" But "such talk of intentionality and goal-dependence and psychological (rather than objective) situations," Mischel remarked, "sounds not even remotely like the behaviorist concept of stimulus control" (Mischel 1997, 182, 183). He observed:

> In everyday life, as well as in the laboratory, people can and do modify and transform the power and impact of the stimuli they encounter and create, persisting in pursuit of long-term, difficult goals even in the face of potential barriers and temptations along the route ... These phenomena (as when the habitual smoker gives up tobacco, and the difficult new year's resolution to exercise is actually executed) may be rare events, but it is their importance for being human, not their frequency, that is at issue. Surely this is part of what psychologists must explain in a comprehensive account of what is significant in everyday life.
>
> In summary, the prevalence and significance of the automaticity of *if-then* links in everyday life that Bargh so elegantly demonstrates is not diminished (it may even be enhanced) by the concurrent recognition of the field's other major conclusion: Regardless of its frequency, humans do engage at least some of the time and under some circumstances in self-regulatory behavior in pursuit of their long-term goals and values. In these moments, they manage to purposely modify, transform, and even overcome the power of the immediate stimulus, interjecting their own personal agendas between the external "*if*" and the observable external "*then*," in ways that reveal their distinctive personality signatures. (Mischel 1997, 185; his emphasis)

Mischel therefore suggested that Bargh had deliberately overstated his arguments. Nor was he alone in criticizing Bargh's radical claims, even though the force of the criticisms raised by Bargh's commentators was somewhat weakened by their commitment to the same information-processing assumptions that had led Bargh to such an extreme position.

The Automaticity of Everyday Life

But Bargh held his ground. He acknowledged that his claims for the automaticity of everyday life might have been "more tactical than heartfelt," but he insisted on the overwhelming dominance of automaticity.

"Bloodied but unbowed," he responded, "I gamely concede that the commentators did push me back from a position of 100% automaticity—but only to an Ivory soap bar degree of purity in my beliefs about the degree of automaticity in our psychological reactions from moment to moment" (Bargh 1997, 231, 244). As Kihlstrom later noted for readers too young to understand Bargh's reference, Ivory soap was perennially advertised as 99.4 percent pure, and Bargh therefore insisted that cognitions and actions were 99.4 percent automatic (Kihlstrom 2008, 161).

Nevertheless, in the years after 1997, Bargh's statements about the role of automaticity in everyday life exhibited several ambiguities and inconsistencies. On the one hand, he qualified his more extreme views about the automaticity of everyday life by remarking that "*sometimes*" goal pursuits occurred without conscious awareness, or that "*many*" (and hence not all) of the goals that an individual pursued were the result of conscious deliberation and choice, and so on (Chartrand and Bargh 2002, 14, 15; my emphases). Moreover, since most of his findings and theories concerned skilled behaviors that had been acquired through learning and habit, it remained an open question—as he himself sometimes noted—whether those behaviors were the result of intentions and as such derivatively intentional and therefore controllable and sensitive to the intentions from which they had originated, or instead were fundamentally unintentional and environmentally driven, as his auto-motive model proposed.

On the other hand, Bargh also expressed a strong commitment to determinism in psychology, leaving the distinct impression that, in spite of hesitations and qualifications, he believed that "mindless" automaticity was the entire story of human behavior. Thus in 1998 he teamed up with Daniel Wegner, soon to become famous for his experiments purportedly demonstrating the illusion of free will, to suggest that all mental events, including the conscious experience of intentionality, were entirely determined by sub-personal information-processing systems. As Wegner and Bargh stated: "The way in which people control their behavior is no less determined than the way in which their automatic behavior occurs. Control is merely one conduit by which the determinants of behavior express their influence. Far from the ghost in the machine, then, the process of control is a particularly interesting *machine* in the machine" (Wegner and Bargh 1997, 450; their emphasis).[2]

---

2. The authors were referring here to the work of the philosopher Gilbert Ryle (1949). In critiquing the idea of the mind as a "ghost" in the machine, in the spirit of Wittgenstein's

Wegner and Bargh appealed to the role of feedback mechanisms to justify their position. Referring to computational approaches to problems of control in Norbert Wiener's *Cybernetics* (1948), they observed:

> The use of self-guiding mechanisms had swept the field of engineering in the years before and after World War II, and it was a natural next step to consider how such control systems might model human thought and behavior ... Simple mechanical gadgets such as the thermostat, the engine governor, and the logic circuit could be given goals ... and they could then regulate the behavior of systems such that those goals could be met. Although it seems perfectly natural now to describe humans as intelligent machines containing control systems, this was a revolutionary idea at the time, as it broke down Ryle's and other behaviorists' objections to the study of a "ghost" that behaved in accord with unobservable purposes and goals. Eventually, this break-through produced a large literature on control in humans. (Wegner and Bargh 1997, 450)

On this basis, Wegner and Bargh proposed that the setting of goals by individuals was the product of various control systems that did the work of selecting the relevant target for them. They argued that "*mental control* involves a *mental state selection process* that functions to set us in pursuit of particular mental states. So, for instance, when we get it into our heads that we want to avoid thinking about an old flame, that we want to fall asleep, or that we want to stop being angry, these goals are often set for us by a higher-level process that decides that a certain mental state would be good in that particular situation" (Wegner and Bargh 1997, 453; their emphasis). Bargh and Melissa Ferguson expressed the same idea:

> Although the currently pervasive distinction in cognitive science between automatic and controlled mental processes makes it perhaps difficult to conceive of automatic control, we note that the term has been common in engineering for nearly 50 years ... and means the same thing there that we mean by it here: autonomous systems interacting with environmental information over time to attain a goal, without any need of

---

rejection of the idea of a private language, Ryle was attacking the idea of the mind as a private, internal mental state. But the conclusion Wegner and Bargh drew from Ryle's critique was that there was no "ghost" (or mind) at all, only mechanical, deterministic processes, a view that was very far from Ryle's position.

intervention from outside that closed system to do so. It is not necessary to invoke the idea of free will or a nondetermined version of consciousness as a causal explanatory mechanism in accounting for higher mental processes in humans. (Bargh and Ferguson 2000, 939)

It's as if Bargh and his colleagues believed that individuals are unable to intend their own goals, but instead depend on the pursuit of goals set for them by computational control processes, presumably in response to yet other control processes even higher up in the hierarchical chain in the mind-brain, control processes that are responding in turn to environmental cues as the ultimate instigators of action. Left unexplained was how exactly, among the myriad environmental cues the individual encountered all the time, only certain ones were selected as the relevant ones for association with the internal cognitive representations that were linked in turn to the relevant motor representations. Bargh thus appeared to beg the fundamental question of the selectivity of human responses—the human ability to decide among a myriad of situational cues which actions to perform—a topic to which I will return in a moment.

In their paper, Wegner and Bargh also drew on Benjamin Libet's famous experiments ostensibly showing that there was a half-second delay between the start of brain activation and its completion in the form of various apparently voluntary or intentional actions, suggesting that unconscious cerebral processes initiated such actions before conscious intentions were activated, even if, as Libet had proposed, the brain fooled us into thinking that we consciously decided matters for ourselves (Libet 1985). On the basis of Libet's and related findings, Wegner and Bargh concluded that "conscious intentions are not the causes of action we had always hoped them to be" (Wegner and Bargh 1997, 455; see also Wegner 2002).

Given the philosophical and ethical importance of the free-will problem, it is not surprising that several investigators raised questions about the conceptual and empirical bases of Wegner's and Libet's arguments (for example, Kihlstrom 2004; 2008). More generally, I think it is fair to say that the issues at stake in Wegner and Bargh's claims could not be solved by empirical findings alone but depended on highly contentious theoretical-philosophical presuppositions (in a large literature on Libet's experiments and related topics, see Pockett, Banks, and Gallagher 2006; Mele 2009; Schlosser 2012; Nahmias 2014; Leys 2017, 324–29). Nevertheless, rejection of the commonsense conception of human agency was widespread in the cognitive sciences, because for many researchers the empirical evidence seemed valid and because the claims for determinism were part of the scientific zeitgeist, with all the complications entailed for considerations of morality and jurisprudence.[3] Thus Bargh and Chartrand (1999) argued that cognitive functions were (almost?) completely determined by information-processing mechanisms in the absence of any conscious control:

> Given one's understandable desire to believe in free will and self-determination, it may be hard to bear that most of daily life is driven by automatic, nonconscious mental processes—but it appears impossible, from these findings, that conscious control could be up to the job [...] What the recent research has demonstrated ... is that "environment to perception to behavior" operates as efficiently and smoothly in producing social behavior as the legendary Chicago Cubs infielders did in producing double plays. (Bargh and Chartrand 1999, 464–68)

Implicit in this statement was the idea that skilled actions, such as the performance of double plays in baseball, are carried out entirely unconsciously and unintentionally because they have become completely automatic. Bargh and Chartrand further proposed that conscious deliberation prevented the successful performance of routine actions, such that "the longer one consciously deliberates about one's preferences and judgments, the less accurate and predictive they become." With a nod to his former teacher Zajonc, Bargh and Chartrand also included emotional responses (or "preferences") in their assessment by remarking: "We know that ... evaluations are made constantly without any intention to make them ... and so, as Zajonc (1980) first argued, our preferences and many

---

3. To take just one example, with reference to Bargh's work on automaticity among many other studies, Lieberman, Schreiber, and Ochsner (2003) argued that political cognition was a habit or skill, like riding a bicycle, a view that reduced people's reasons for their political beliefs and decisions to the play of unconscious, automatic processes. Olivier Klein, one of the co-authors of Doyen et al.'s (2012) failed replication of Bargh, Chen, and Burrows's 1996 elderly priming study, criticized Lieberman, Schreiber, and Ochsner (2003) and Bargh (1999), among others, for substituting mechanical for reason-based explanations. Klein was especially concerned with the ethical implications of such arguments. He asked: "If supporting fascist political parties is equivalent to riding a bicycle, who should be blamed for doing so?" (Klein 2009, 94). See also Leys 2017 (chapter 7) for a critique of similar "neuropolitical" arguments based on claims about the non-intentional nature of emotion and affect.

other judgments may be made literally before we know it" (Bargh and Chartrand 1999, 475). As I have argued elsewhere, however, by 1999 there were already strong arguments against the idea of the independence of emotions, or preferences, from intention (Leys 2017), although those arguments were ignored by Bargh and his colleagues, as we will see in chapter 5.

On the basis of these and related considerations, in subsequent papers Bargh emphasized the similarity between the assumptions of cognitive psychology and of behaviorism. On the one hand, as he noted, unlike behaviorism, cognitive psychology emphasized the importance of internal mental representations in behavior. On the other hand, he argued that cognitive psychology shared with behaviorism the same commitment to determinism and that, accordingly, the similarities greatly outweighed the differences. The main difference was that, according to the tenets of cognitive psychology, habitual or automatic actions were not behaviors linked directly to the environment, as in behaviorism's stimulus-response psychology, but were instead connected to higher-order mental representations mediating between environmental stimuli on the input side and motor reactions on the output side. Thus, as Bargh's auto-motive hypothesis proposed, the activation of internal mental representations could be triggered by environmental events without the intervention of conscious choice or reasoning processes (Bargh and Ferguson 2000, 928). It is not surprising in this regard that some researchers characterized the ideas of Bargh and other like-minded automaticity researchers as "neo-behaviorist" (Fiedler and Hütter 2014, 506).

One sign of the lengths Bargh was willing to go to defend the idea of the pervasiveness of automaticity in daily life was the use he made of French physician F. Lhermitte's account of the behavior of two patients with frontal-lobe lesions (Lhermitte 1986). As described by Lhermitte, the patients' pathological condition affected their planning and control functions with the result that they could not help responding to, or imitating, the suggestions emanating from whatever situations they found themselves in. Thus, when one of the patients was in Lhermitte's office, without being asked to do so she made use of the available medical instruments to give the physician himself a physical examination (Lhermitte accompanied his account of the behavior of these frontal-lobe patients with interesting photographs of their behaviors). Or after Lhermitte had casually mentioned the word "museum" to them, the patients scrutinized the paintings and objects in his apartment as if they were in a museum and were examining everything in it as works of art. When the male patient entered the apartment bedroom, he saw the bed and immediately undressed, got into the bed, and prepared to go to sleep. When the female patient noticed a sewing box, she began to sew two pieces of cloth together; and so on. The patients also showed a loss of inhibitions, as when one of them urinated against a public wall, or, without being asked to do so, undressed completely in front of the physician.

Neither of the patients appeared to be aware of anything unusual in their behaviors and they never seemed to notice the film crew, cameraman, and photographer who were recording their actions. At the same time, the patients retained certain specific features of their personalities, which gave an individual aspect to their compulsive actions. Lhermitte named their medical condition the *environmental dependency syndrome* (now known as "Lhermitte's syndrome"), a condition he characterized as one in which frontal-lobe patients experienced a radical loss of autonomy: "For the patient, the social and physical environments issue the order to use them, even though the patient 'himself' or 'herself' has neither the idea nor the intention to do so." He reported that such patients were "powerless in the face of influences from the outside world" (Lhermitte 1986, 342; see also Lhermitte, Pillon, and Serdaru 1986).[4]

---

4. Dijksterhuis and Bargh (2001) had earlier cited Lhermitte's (1983) observations concerning "utilization behaviors" (along with imitation understood by him as precursors to, or the core symptoms of, the "environmental dependency syndrome") as evidence that in these patients the normal inhibitory functions of the frontal lobes had been damaged, with the result that patients automatically responded to the demands of environmental cues of various kinds. Using an alternative to Lhermitte's research methodology, Shallice et al. (1989) distinguished between Lhermitte's "induced" form of utilization behavior, so called because the behavior was provoked by the examiner's behavior or environmental cues, and an "incidental" form that occurred when patients were carrying out other cognitive tasks that did not draw their attention to the objects in their vicinity. Shallice et al. interpreted the "incidental" form of utilization behavior in information-processing terms as actions that were automatically triggered by perceptual inputs when the hypothesized Supervisory Attentional System located in the frontal lobes was impaired (see this chapter, below, for a further discussion of Shallice and Norman's theory of attention).

For valuable recent discussions of the enigmatic "environmental dependency syndrome," see Besnard et al. 2010; 2011 and Iaccarino, Chieffi, and Iavarone 2014. The syndrome remains puzzling for numerous reasons, including the clinical and anatomical heterogeneity of the phenomena observed, such as the contradictory results obtained by the different methodologies used to instigate utilization and imitative behaviors. There remain disagreements, too, about whether the observed behaviors are entirely automatic or whether patients retain a degree of intentional control over their actions. Lhermitte's observations are somewhat ambiguous in this regard. Thus, he described the patients'

In 2005, Bargh equated the behavior of Lhermitte's patients with the responses of normal undergraduates participating in his priming experiments because, he argued, actions by patients and normal students were controlled by external stimuli, not by intentions and acts of will (38). "People are often unaware of the reasons and causes of their own behavior," he wrote:

> In fact, recent experimental evidence points to a deep and fundamental dissociation between conscious awareness and the mental processes responsible for one's behavior; many of the wellsprings of behavior appear to be opaque to conscious access. That research has proceeded somewhat independently in social psychology, ... cognitive psychology ... and neuro-psychology ... All three lines of research have reached the same general conclusions despite the quite different methodologies and guiding theoretical perspectives employed.
>
> This consensus has emerged in part because of the remarkable resemblance between the behavior of patients with some forms of frontal lobe damage and (normal) participants in contemporary priming studies in social psychology. In both cases, the individual's behavior is being "controlled" by external stimuli, not by his or her own consciously accessible intentions or acts of the will. Both sets of evidence demonstrate that action tendencies can be activated and triggered independently and in the absence of the individual's conscious choice or awareness of those causal triggers ... [F]or Lhermitte's (1986) patients as well as our undergraduate experimental participants (Bargh, Chen, and Burrows, 1996), individuals were not aware of the actual causes of their behavior. (Bargh 2005, 37–38)

Bargh acknowledged that there were key differences between Lhermitte's patients and normal undergraduates. Notably, he did not deny that undergraduates retained the ability to act autonomously in ways Lhermitte's patients did not. Nevertheless, he took Lhermitte's cases to reinforce his general claim regarding the tendency to automaticity in ordinary human behaviors. As he added: "Yet the priming and the patient studies do complement and support each other by demonstrating the same two

---

behaviors as voluntary and, as such, distinct from automatic behaviors and reflexes, but as we see in the statement quoted above, he simultaneously held that frontal lobe patients did not intend to imitate (Lhermitte 1986, 331, 342).

principles: that an individual's behavior can be directly caused by the current environment, without the necessity of an act of conscious choice or will; and that this behavior can and will unfold without the person being aware of its external determinants" (Bargh 2005, 39). In short, Bargh normalized the implications of Lhermitte's report by taking it to mean that, like frontal-lobe patients, ordinary humans tended to live their everyday lives rather like somnambulists, controlled by forces of which they were unaware.

Automaticity, Attention, and Control

If normal people are so susceptible to the contagious effects of stimuli, if they can even be compared to Lhermitte's patients who copied everyone and everything with whom they interacted, how can they effectively live their lives? Would it be remotely adaptive for humans to be the merely passive "victims" of every stimulus they encounter? A system or process of control would seem to be required to override or inhibit the tendency to automaticity, otherwise humans would be vulnerable to constant buffeting by the momentary currents in the social and physical environment. What could those systems or processes of control be, especially if, as appeared to be the case, Bargh was committed to eliminating any appeal to the role of intentionality? What system would the cognitive psychologist propose that could put the brakes on indiscriminate imitation?

The question of the control of automatic actions went back to the post–World War II work on information processing by Neisser (1967), Posner and Snyder (1975), Shiffrin and Schneider (1977), and others. Those investigators had posited a distinction between the information-processing system governing unconscious automatic behavior and the "executive control system" mediating selective attention. More recently, Alan Baddeley had argued that there must be a component of working memory, which he called the "central executive," that allowed information to be controlled and manipulated (Baddeley 1986; Baddeley, Sala, and Robbins 1996). In a related proposal, Donald Norman and Tim Shallice had suggested that there were two complementary control systems for the regulation of action: a lower-order, decentralized, "content scheduling" system that took care of routine actions without conscious control, and a higher-order "supervisory attentional system" that could override automatic responses in favor of scheduling behavior on the basis of plans and intentions (Norman and Shallice 1986; Shallice 1988).

C. Neil Macrae and Lucy Johnston (1998) incorporated these suggestions by proposing that "attention" held the key to the control and regulation of automatic actions. Specifically, they made use of Norman and Shallice's ideas to argue that, in situations where various behavioral schemas competed for control, the attentional system assumed executive authority in order to determine the best course of action. As they argued:

> According to Norman and Shallice (1986) . . . behavior is controlled either by the automatic operation of preexisting action schemas (when everything is going to plan), or else by a Supervisory Attentional System (SAS) that assumes executive authority when novel task environments are encountered or higher-order processing objectives are operating. Behavior is typically regulated by the automatic activation of action schemas . . . However, when perceivers are confronted with novelty, or conscious processing objectives are in place, the inflexible products of implicit action schemas are no longer appropriate, so behavioral control is passed instead to the SAS. At any point of time, therefore, one will simultaneously be entertaining a variety of behavioral options, some triggered by environmental cues, others by one's current processing objectives. Ultimately, it is the action schema with the strongest activation level that triumphs in this battle for cognitive supremacy and guides one's behavior. (Macrae and Johnston 1998, 404)

Macrae and Johnston observed that in the experiments on automatic behavior by Bargh and others, mental battles for action control had been circumvented by placing the student participants in task environments in which primed behavioral responses did not encounter any situational or cognitive impediments. In contrast, Macrae and Johnston deliberately set up priming situations in which various internal or external obstructions to action were present, in order to see what happened when conflicting automatic responses were activated. Adopting Norman and Shallice's (1986) theory of attention, they predicted that the competition between conflicting behaviors would be resolved in favor of the strongest goal states.

To test this prediction, Macrae and Johnston used a scrambled-sentence test to prime a group of participants with stimuli related to "helpfulness." When the experimenter, who was blind to condition, began to leave the laboratory, she "accidentally" dropped some pens from the top of a pile of things she was carrying. As expected, the primed participants were more helpful in helping her pick up her dropped things than the participants who had not been primed in this way. But when leaking pens were dropped, there was a dramatic reduction in helping behavior and no effect of the prime was observed. Macrae and Johnston attributed this result to the inhibitory impact of the messy, leaking pens on the automatic elicitation of action. The experiment thus confirmed the moderating effect of the task environment on automaticity. A second experiment was designed to test the moderating effects of internal impediments to automatic action. The researchers predicted that when primed tendencies conflicted with a participant's conscious goal states, "executive operations" would inhibit the instigation of the automatic action processes. Macrae and Johnston quoted Shallice and Burgess as stating: "'The supervisory system ... modulates the operation of contention scheduling by providing additional activation or inhibition of schemas competing in the lower-level mechanism'" (Macrae and Johnston 1998, 408–9; Shallice and Burgess 1993, 172).

To test this claim, the researchers replicated their first experiment with a couple of modifications after the initial priming for helpfulness. When participants had finished the scrambled-sentence test, the experimenter explained that they should leave the laboratory to go to the Department of Psychology, where another researcher would be waiting for them. As the experimenter gave her instructions, she looked at her watch and explained to half the participants that the experimental session was running on time, and to the other half that it was running late. The experimenter then collected her belongings and opened the laboratory door so that the participants could leave. As she did so, she "accidentally" dropped regular pens from the pile of items she was carrying. The prediction was that the participants who had been told the experiment was running on time would help the experimenter pick up the dropped things, whereas the participants who had been told the experiment was running late would simply leave the laboratory without providing any assistance. The prediction was confirmed.

Two years after Macrae and Johnston published their findings, Bargh and colleagues likewise proposed that "focal attention" held the key to the control of automatic actions (Dijksterhuis, Bargh, and Miedema 2000). In their paper, Bargh and his co-authors endorsed an evolutionary view of the organization of brain structures according to which the more recent cortical layers of the human brain had simply been layered on top of the preexisting older brain structure, the so-called limbic brain, which was held to govern the noncognitive processes that humans shared with fish and other species.[5] On the basis of the idea that "the fish . . . is still in us," Bargh and his colleagues compared the tendency of humans to imitate others with the imitative behavior of fish who synchronize their behavior with the other fish in the school, thereby treating automaticity as an atavism. They noted that many years earlier Le Bon (1895) and Tarde (1903) had argued that a form of passive imitation was the main driving force of crowd behavior (Dijksterhuis, Bargh, and Miedema 2000, 37, 38).[6] They argued that in the case of both fish and humans, a powerful perception-behavior link mediated such mimetic responses, as when, in Bargh, Chen, and Burrows's elderly priming experiment (1996), activation of the elderly stereotype caused the primed participants to walk more slowly on leaving the experimental session.

The authors went on to state, however, that such automatic processes had an important limitation: they were *inflexible*. Hence, Bargh and his co-authors suggested that there needed to be a mechanism capable of controlling them. They compared such a control mechanism to a smart inspector in a clothing factory who, by paying conscious attention, could override the mindless automatic behavior of the "'dim little tailors'" who only knew how to make one size of each garment (Dijksterhuis, Bargh, and Miedema 2000, 40, citing Gilbert 1989, 206–7). With reference to Macrae and Johnston's (1998) experiments and to Norman and Shallice's "Supervisory Attentional System," Bargh and his colleagues now hypothesized that "if attention is directed toward one's ongoing behavior, the direct and automatic effects of perception on this behavior . . . are inhibited or eliminated" (Dijksterhuis, Bargh, and Miedema 2000, 41).

On this basis, they reported the results of experiments designed to manipulate the degree of consciousness in participants primed in various ways. In one experiment, some of the participants were primed with the stereotype of politicians as long-winded, using the standard scrambled-sentence test. The participants were then asked to write an essay about a political topic. In addition, the participants were divided into two groups,

---

5. But Dijksterhuis, Bargh, and Miedema (2000) were mistaken: the so-called limbic brain is just as human as the brainstem and neocortex; we don't have ancestor brain-parts inside us. See Fridlund 1994 (294); Feldman Barrett 2006 (46); and Leys 2017 (274).

6. In his influential late-nineteenth-century account of the laws of imitation, Gabriel Tarde had stressed the importance of the absolute subject or "leader" who, exceptionally, remained immune to the imitative influences that dominated the life of others (Tarde 1903). But Tarde's solution to the problem of how imitation was regulated and controlled was too arbitrary and dogmatic for the modern psychologist (Leys 1993).

one of which was seated in front of a mirror in order to raise the level of self-awareness or attention, while the other group was not seated in front of a mirror. The prediction was that participants primed with the long-winded stereotype of politicians would write longer essays than the unprimed control participants, but only in the non-mirror condition (in which a focus on the self was held to be absent). These predictions were confirmed.

In a second study, some participants were primed with either stereotypes of professors or stereotypes of soccer "hooligans" (or troublemakers) and were then asked to answer forty-two multiple-choice general-knowledge questions (taken from the game "Trivial Pursuit"). Professor-primed participants performed better and hooligan-primed participants performed worse than unprimed controls. As in the previous experiment, some participants faced a mirror throughout the experiment and others did not. Under the mirror condition, the effect of the stereotype activation on intellectual performance completely disappeared. Two more variations on these experiments were carried out, and the findings again appeared to confirm the role of focal attention in controlling automatic responses to primes. The authors therefore concluded that when participants are offered the chance to become aware of their actions, they are capable of inhibiting the behavioral representations associated with the activated stereotype. "Perception does determine behavior, but not inevitably—at least not for human beings," they said (Dijksterhuis, Bargh, and Miedema 2000, 45, 49).

Only the year before, Bargh had explicitly made the case against the controllability of automatic stereotype effects. He had argued:

> It would be *nice* if stereotypes were found not to be activated automatically. It would be *nice* if, failing that and stereotypes were found to be automatically activated, then it was found that an individual could prevent this activation by having conscious, counter-stereotypic expectancy. It would be *nice* if, even if automatic activation could not be shown to be prevented in this (or any other) way, individuals were found to be indeed cognizant of the possibility of being nonconsciously influenced, and when aware of that influence, to have the motivation and the time to effortfully control it. (Bargh 1999, 366; his emphasis)

"All of this would indeed be nice—if it were true," Bargh had stated. "But the relevant research evidence largely contradicts this rosy picture"

(Bargh 1999, 366). Yet now Dijksterhuis, Bargh, and Miedema (2000) seemed to be saying the opposite, by appealing to the role of conscious control or attention in regulating the tendency to automaticity. As Klaus Fiedler and Mandy Hütter commented several years later on Dijksterhuis, Bargh, and Miedema's claims: "Apparently, 'automatic' behavior shared by humans and mackerels can be easily overridden by metacognitive shifts of attention" (Fiedler and Hütter 2014, 506).

The contradiction between Bargh's (1999) rejection of the idea that consciousness could play a controlling part in mental life, and Dijksterhuis, Bargh, and Miedema's (2000) appeal to the role of the attentional system capable of supervising automatic behaviors, reflected strains or ambiguities that were inherent in all cognitive theories of attention at the time. As several commentators have remarked, most theorists attributed selective power to attention as a causal entity capable of biasing the individual toward picking out certain stimuli and neglecting others. Yet even though much empirical and theoretical effort had been directed at establishing the distinction between automatic and controlled processes, based on dual-systems theories, attention itself had rarely been defined and its mechanisms seldom researched. In particular, in a critical evaluation of the literature on attention, William Johnston and Veronica Dark (1986) had observed that most theorists of attention had implicitly relied on the commonsense idea of attention as an intelligent agent, even as those same theorists were committed to denying such a conceptualization:

> In reviewing the literature on attention we were struck by several observations. One was a widespread reluctance to define attention. Another was the ease with which competing theories can accommodate the same empirical phenomena. A third observation was the consistent appeal to some intelligent force or agent in explanations of attentional phenomena. These observations are likely to be causally connected. It is difficult to conceptualize a process that is not well defined, and it is difficult to falsify empirically a vague conceptualization, especially one that relies on a homunculus. (Johnston and Dark 1986, 43)

Or as they had also stated of dual-system theorists' account for the phenomenon of selective attention:

> The basic explanation given for the variable automaticity with which subjects detect targets . . . is that subjects are equipped with [an] . . .

"attention director" that detects targets with variable automaticity. This explanation introduces an infinite regress because the same questions that were asked about how individuals pay attention now have to be asked about how the attention director pays attention . . . [I]f a psychological construct is to explain the intelligent and adaptive selection powers of the organism, then it cannot itself be imbued with those powers. (Johnston and Dark 1986, 68)

Evidently the attempt to put a stop to the infinite regress implicit in theories of attention by relying on the work of an inner homunculus, or intelligent agent, capable of selectively attending to environmental stimuli, had been felt by Johnston and Dark to be a general weakness in such theorizing. These authors had pessimistically concluded that they were "left wondering if the attempt to elucidate the nature of selective attention empirically is ultimately a futile one" (Johnston and Dark, 1986, 70).[7] The philosopher Daniel Dennett also ridiculed Norman and Shallice's attentional system as "an ominously wise overseer homunculus who handles the hard cases in the workshop of consciousness" (Dennett 1998, 288). In other words, for these critics, attention theorists smuggled in appeals to first-person agency in ways that were deemed incoherent in terms of their adherence to cognitive, information-processing theories of the mind.

From the point of view of those committed to an Anscombean approach to intentionality the problem of attention is somewhat different. As Naomi Eilan and James Roessler have put it: "A common complaint against the idea of a 'supervisory attentional system' is that it credits an information-processing system with the causal powers of a rational agent . . . On one reading, the complaint here is that the theory lacks explanatory force—it does not tell us *how* the operation of the supervisory attentional system carries out the kinds of functions we associate with intentional agency" (Eilan and Roessler 2003, 11). The issue, as Jennings has observed, is who or what is responsible for the mental act of selection (Jennings 2012, 537). Is the act of attention an ability that belongs to the agency of the person, or is it the outcome of internal information-processing mechanisms?

---

7. Johnston and Dark ended by commenting: "We suspect that it would be instructive to see how much we can understand about selective attention without appealing to a processing homunculus. Still, a dull, sinking feeling comes with the acknowledgment that James was much brighter than we and that he eventually abandoned psychology altogether" (Johnston and Dark 1986, 70). See also Allport 1993; 2008; Mole 2009; and Wu 2014.

Dennett (1969) offered one solution to the difficulties posed in this domain, when he introduced a distinction between personal and sub-personal levels of explanation. As Hornsby has demonstrated, at first the difference between these two levels preserved the autonomy of the person-level of explanation, with its view of humans as intentional, rational beings, from the encroachments of the sub-personal level of explanation, which concerned the material properties of information-processing systems. Over time, however, Hornsby has argued, Dennett allowed the "objective materialist third-person standpoint" (Hornsby 1997a, 169) to prevail, thereby threatening the autonomy of the person-level of perspective by assimilating it to the level of sub-personal processes in the brain.

Indeed, as McDowell maintained in a critique of Dennett's views, it was a mistake for the latter to assume that one could derive personal-level meaning from putative internal, sub-level computational-mechanical operations (McDowell 1994b). Adopting Dennett's terminology, McDowell observed that intact animals are "semantic engines" whereas sub-personal information-processing mechanisms are "syntactic engines" and argued:

> And nobody knows how to make sense of an animal's internal control mechanism, and connect it conceptually to the competence it is supposed to explain, except by describing it *as if* it were, what we know it is not really, a semantic engine, interpreting inputs as signs of environmental facts and, as output, directing behavior so as to be suitable to those facts in the light of the animal's needs or goals. (McDowell 1994b, 199; his emphasis)

McDowell did not object to sub-personal explanations. But he suggested that Dennett flew in the face of his own understanding that information-processing machines are only syntactic engines if he thought it was possible to derive the semantic-personal level from the syntactic, which is to say to derive meaning from digital "information." For McDowell, the "as if" talk was fine—as long as that was all it was. As he pointed out, the question posed was: "What enables us animals to be the semantic engines we are"? (McDowell 1994b, 199). It was precisely this question that Dennett could not answer. Thus McDowell quoted Dennett as stating: "'*Somehow*, the syntactical virtuosity of our brains permits us to be interpreted at another level as semantic engines—systems that (indirectly) discriminate the significance of impingements on them'" (McDowell 1994b, 200, quoting Dennett 1982, 26; emphasis mine). In this statement, Dennett implicitly conceded that the process of converting the syntactic to the semantic (meaning) was mysterious ("somehow"): his was just an "as-if" way of talking that papered over all the difficulties. As McDowell commented:

> The "sub-personal" account of a sensory system, which treats it as an information-processing device that transmits its informational results to something else inside the animal, cannot adequately characterize what its sensory systems are for the animal (as opposed to what they are, metaphorically speaking for the internal parts that receive the results of the information-processing): namely, modes of sensitivity or openness to features of the environment—not processors of information, but collectors of it. (McDowell 1994b, 197)

Nearly all theorists of attention were equivocal on precisely this point: they tried to explain attention in terms of the sub-personal, computational processing of internal representations, all the while implicitly relying on the commonsense idea that attention is a person-level achievement. This equivocation or ambiguity was present in Norman and Shallice's theory of attention, which simultaneously presented the "supervisory attentional system" as an information-processing mechanism for avoiding conflicts between competing automatic behavioral responses, while under the radar attributing the ultimate source of the control of automaticity to the individual's conscious plans and goals. Indeed, a few years earlier Bargh had noted that Norman and Shallice had seemed to trace the origins of behavioral control to the individual's intentions:

> In Norman and Shallice's (1986) model, environmental stimuli can control behavior, but only given that the overarching source goal has been activated (e.g., the intention to drive home). The activation for the source goal itself is said to come either from a "supervisory attentional system" (SAS; Norman and Shallice 1986), *clearly the source of intentional and conscious control*, or from "motivational factors" . . . that are said to bias the SAS "toward the long-term goals of the organism by activating source schemas." (Bargh 1990a, 103; my emphasis)

But in their appeal to the role of focused attention in controlling and regulating the default tendency to automaticity, Bargh and colleagues exploited the same ambiguities inherent in the theorizing of such attentional systems (Dijksterhuis, Bargh, and Miedema 2000). It appeared to themselves and others that they had proposed a mechanism capable of carrying out the selection process independently of intentions. But they implicitly relied on an ordinary understanding of the role of human intentional agency in doing the work of selecting among competing behavioral options.

Skilled Action

A further problem with Dijksterhuis, Bargh, and Miedema's analysis of the role of attention in regulating automaticity was the way in which they continued to conceptualize automatic actions and conscious control systems in dichotomous terms. Bargh often repeated his view that skilled, automatic actions occurred in the absence of intention, almost as if they were a kind of reflex. Although he recognized that driving a car depended on the person intending to drive in the first place, he described the routine actions we perform when driving as automatic and unintentional. As he stated:

> The classic example of automatic processes such as typing and driving were, of course, dependent on the person wanting to type something or to drive somewhere in the first place; once that goal was active, then the movement of the fingers to type or the complicated attentional-motoric processes involved in driving operated automatically. Traveling a bit too fast around a curve and suddenly seeing a stop sign ahead causes one's right foot to kick out and slam on the brakes without any need for conscious intention or decision. But viewing that same stop sign while meandering on a pleasant walk along the sidewalk does not cause one's leg suddenly to kick out, fortunately for any fellow pedestrians nearby. The same stimulus (stop sign) has dramatically different effects depending on one's currently active goals. (Baumeister and Bargh 2014, 38–39)

But this account strikes me as problematic. When I am driving and suddenly hit the brake pedal, I intend to do so because I understand that the stop sign means I must halt the car. I may act very quickly and "automatically," but my response is not unintentional. I know that if I don't slam on the brakes, I might cause an accident. The situation is no different when I refrain from kicking out my foot on seeing the same stop sign when I am taking a walk. In both cases, I understand the meaning of the sign and intentionally respond to it in ways that are appropriate for the situation.

What is at stake in these two scenarios is precisely the meaning the stop sign has for me in different contexts.[8]

Moreover, we have seen that Bargh emphasized not only the lack of intention when we perform automatic, skilled actions but also our tendency to perform such actions without being aware of doing so, which is to say that for him automaticity and the absence of consciousness tended to be aligned. Drivers commonly have the experience, when driving long distances without a pause, of suddenly becoming conscious of the fact that they have been at the wheel for long stretches of time, automatically carrying out all the actions necessary to stay in their lanes, to avoid other cars, to accelerate or brake when required, and so on, without having been conscious of doing all these things. It might be argued against Anscombe's theory of intentional action, discussed in chapter 2, that such automatic, unconscious actions lack intentionality because, without awareness, such persons are unable to answer the "Why?" question by giving reasons for their behaviors. But in commenting on Anscombe's views on the topic of the relationship between consciousness and intentionality, Schwenkler has helpfully observed that

> "awareness" in the sense Anscombe uses it in *Intention* is simply equivalent to "knowledge," and . . . does not have any implications for what a person's *conscious* mental life must be like at the time she acts. Just as one may "come to" the realization that one knows a certain fact, say that Trenton is the capital of New Jersey, even if she has known this for a long time, so the phenomenon of "coming to" the realization that she has been doing something does not show that she was doing it unknowingly. (Schwenkler 2019, 23)

In other words, Anscombe appears to have accepted the idea of unconscious knowledge (or intentions) in the sense specified by Schwenkler, as on various grounds do various other philosophers (for Davidson, see Schlosser 2019b, 38, 44–54). Whereas Bargh tended to treat unconscious

---

8. In his interesting book on Wittgenstein's remarks on the foundations of AI, Shanker observes that what distinguishes our behavior when driving a car from genuinely automatic behavior, such as autonomic processes or reflexes, is that unlike the latter, which we explain in causal terms, driving a car is a normative action, which means that we can justify or explain our actions by reference to the rules or conventions we are following (or fail to observe). As he also notes, the fact that we might follow such rules unreflectingly does not license the conclusion that our actions are noncognitive (1998, 31).

intentions as a contradiction in terms: for him, if we perform certain actions without awareness, they must be unintentional.

Another mistake made by Bargh and his colleagues was to suggest that conscious attention inevitably interferes with skilled, automatic actions: "*If attention is directed elsewhere and for some reason shifts towards one's current behavior, producing a metacognitive awareness of what one is doing,*" they wrote, "*this in itself can be enough to eliminate the influence of activated percepts on that behavior*" (Dijksterhuis, Bargh, and Miedema 2000, 41; their emphasis; citing experiments among others by Baumeister 1984; and Baumeister and Showers 1986). As they stated:

> It is not just that attention focused on the self is not needed for the execution of these automatized actions; it is that the absence of such self-consciousness—that is, the absence of consciously experiencing such actions—is actually necessary for their execution." (Dijksterhuis, Bargh, and Miedema 2000, 41)

Nor were Dijksterhuis and his colleagues alone in proposing that consciously attending to a skilled action interferes with its performance. Indeed, according to Montero, in their classic text on the psychology of skilled performance Fitts and Posner (1967) argued that once a skill is learned it acquires an autonomy from cognition, such that paying attention to the details of the movements hinders its execution: "'If the attention of a golfer is called to his muscle movements before an important putt, he may find it unusually difficult to attain his natural swing'" (cited in Montero 2013, 306). Similarly, in a defense of the scientific status of the unconscious that made many references to cognitive-science findings, such as Bargh's experiments on automaticity, Drew Westen asserted that "the surest way for a pianist to make a mistake on a complex piece is to think about what she is doing" (Westen 1999, 1066).

The trouble is that the examples frequently cited in support of such claims involved skilled performances in which participants were described or imagined as having to pay close attention to muscle movements or processes that were normally carried out without the person's awareness, just as skilled pianists are not usually consciously aware of the innumerable muscle movements their fingers must make in the course of a performance. To ask performers to focus on movements of this kind imposes a highly artificial or indeed an impossible requirement on them, with the result that a smooth performance is likely to be derailed. Thus, it did *not* necessarily follow from several of the experiments on skilled actions cited by Dijksterhuis, Bargh, and Miedema that "the absence of . . . self-consciousness—that is, the absence of consciously experiencing such actions—is actually necessary for their execution" (Dijksterhuis, Bargh, and Miedema 2000, 41), as if the successful performance of such skills depended on agents being completely unaware of what they were doing.[9] Indeed, Logan had earlier rejected such views, attributing them to the tendency to adopt false oppositions in psychology:

> The close relation between automaticity and skill suggests that automatic processes may not be difficult to control. Skilled performers are usually able to control their performance better than unskilled performers, even though their performance is likely to be more automatic. That is why we prefer to fly with experienced pilots rather than novices . . . It appears that the general belief that automaticity and control are opposites may be mistaken, or at least, overstated.
>
> The contrast between automaticity and control may be an artifact of our usual style of theorizing in psychology rather than a theoretical necessity forced upon us by the data. Psychologists often characterize the phenomena they study as dichotomies. (Logan 1985, 379)[10]

---

9. Researchers in favor of the view that awareness impedes the efficient performance of skills have appealed to the case of the visual agnosia patient D. F., who suffered from vision impairments owing to carbon monoxide poisoning. D. F. was able to grasp objects but without being able to point to and identify them, the implication being that she had a bodily understanding but not a cognitive or conceptual understanding of space and spatial features. The further suggestion was that there are two different streams of visual-information processing in the brain, a dorsal ("where"), fast-acting, unconscious stream geared to action, and a ventral ("what"), slower, sometimes-conscious stream subserving perceptual judgments. The two-stream theory has fed into and reinforced dual-systems theories which dissociate unconscious, automatic actions from conscious-intentional actions. However, recent research on the interplay between dorsal and ventral processes has raised questions about the posited dissociation between them. In a large literature, see Goodale and Milner (1991; 1992; 2003; 2008); Jeannerod and Jacob (2005); McIntosh and Schenk (2009); Clark (2009); Himmelbach, Boehme, and Karnath (2012); Montero (2013); and Rossetti et al. (2017).

10. Logan (1985) offered some interesting suggestions for future research on automaticity, such as that it should be studied in a broader range of contexts than the experimental paradigms in use in the field, paradigms that tended to use automaticity trials lasting less than two seconds and were often boring to perform, whereas most skills were continuous, might contain sequential dependencies that took hours of experience to discover, and were usually enjoyable to perform. See also Saling and Phillips (2007) for their criticisms of automaticity theory, especially their reasons for rejecting the idea that skilled performances are "mindless."

In a recent debate over the nature of skilled action, the philosopher Hubert Dreyfus took exactly the same position as did Dijksterhuis, Bargh, and Miedema by proposing that conscious mentation disrupted the smooth execution of the expert (Dreyfus 2005). According to Dreyfus, when athletes are absorbed in the "flow" and performing well, they are not paying any attention to their skilled performances. He used the well-known story of the problems in throwing to first base of the second baseman, Chuck Knoblauch, to illustrate his contention, on the grounds that when Knoblauch began to think about the mechanics of his ball-throwing skills, his performance radically deteriorated. To Dreyfus, the Knoblauch case showed that mindedness was the enemy of expertise. Dreyfus therefore rejected John McDowell's influential account of the mindedness of human actions, including the mindedness of routine skilled performances. But for McDowell, all that the Knoblauch case demonstrated was that "when mindedness gets detached from immersion in activity, it can be the enemy of embodied coping (to echo Dreyfus's wording). It cannot show that mindedness is not in operation when one is immersed in embodied coping" (McDowell 2007b, 367; see also Dreyfus 2007a; 2007b; 2013; Schear 2013).[11]

Nor is McDowell the only person to question Dreyfus's claim that conscious attention is necessarily detrimental to a skilled performance. Indeed, several commentators have emphasized that, in order for athletes, dancers, or other performers to improve their skills, focused attention to and awareness of their own performances can be highly beneficial and indeed necessary (Sutton 2007; Montero 2010; Smith 2013). In *Zidane: A Twenty-First Century Portrait* (2006), a film by Douglas Gordon and Philippe Parreno, the great soccer player Zinédine Zidane was filmed in the course of a regular Spanish league match by seventeen cameras trained exclusively on him; in addition, there were eighty thousand spectators in the stands as well as a television audience of millions. So, in the film there is no question but that throughout the match Zidane is conscious of the crowd and of being seen—how could he not be? (At one point he is quoted in a subtitle as saying, "You are never alone.") And yet we viewers of the film never for a moment doubt Zidane's absorption in the match, which is to say that, as the art critic Michael Fried has argued, there is not the slightest sense of a conflict between Zidane's consciousness of being

---

11. Anyway, Knoblauch started to have problems with his throws to first base before he started "thinking" about them.

seen and his being caught up in the "flow" of his performance (Fried 2006; see also Smith 2013).[12]

In short, it can be argued that an either-or analysis of skilled behavior based on the opposition between conscious attention versus the unconscious performance of automatic actions, as proposed by Dijksterhuis, Bargh, and Miedema (2000), lacks adequate empirical and theoretical support.[13] To make this point is not to deny that certain individuals may choke under pressure in situations where the presence of an audience draws attention to themselves or their performances in unwanted ways. But it is to deny the validity of Dijksterhuis, Bargh, and Miedema's stark opposition between consciousness of the self or of what one is doing, and skilled behavior. We might say that, just as the absence of self-awareness cannot guarantee a good performance, attention on the self or one's performance cannot as such predict choking.

---

12. Fried writes:

A major part of the conceptual brilliance of [the film] Zidane consists in the fact that its protagonist's sustained feat of absorption is depicted as taking place before an audience of eighty thousand spectators, with millions more watching via TV. Thus throughout the film there is the unmistakable implication that Zidane himself—as we see him—could not have been other than acutely aware that literally untold numbers of viewers had their eyes on him. (In fact, he knew too that seventeen movie cameras were following his every move.) And yet the viewer's conviction of the athlete's total engagement in the match is not thereby undermined. Instead, the film lays bare a hitherto unthematized relationship between absorption and beholding—more precisely, between the persuasive representation of absorption and the apparent consciousness of being beheld—in the context of art, a relationship that is no longer simply one of opposition or complementarity but that allows a sliding and indeed an overlap. (Fried 2006, 333)

Indeed, as Fried goes on to note, by the use of subtitles and other devices, the directors of the film made a point of Zidane's consciousness of the crowd.

13. N. Kathleen Hayles has offered a critique of the McDowell-Dreyfus debate that amounts to little more than a depreciation of these philosophers for not making use of empirical evidence concerning the role of what she calls the computational or "cognitive nonconscious" in skilled copings (2017; see also Hayles 2019). But her arguments depend on experimental findings that are by no means as settled as she believes, as well as on various related claims, especially regarding the limited capacity of conscious functions compared to the unrestricted capacity of unconscious (or nonconscious) processes. Those claims in turn are associated with dual-process theories of cognitive function the validity of which is a highly debated topic. In short, Hayles assumes as solid various proposals regarding the nature of cognition, unconscious processes, and consciousness that remain open to contestation within cognitive science and among philosophers and others. For these and related reasons, her claims fall short.

Must Automatic Actions Be Inflexible?

A further issue raised by Bargh's approach to automaticity was whether the kinds of automatic actions studied in priming experiments were inflexible responses to perceptual inputs or whether such responses were malleable behaviors that were sensitive to situational features and context. As Clare Carlisle has recently observed, in the long history of philosophical reflection on the topic, habit has been widely recognized as intrinsically double, in that it is simultaneously a source of constancy and resistance to change, *and* a source of plasticity, creativity, and freedom (Carlisle 2014). To take a simple example, as Nathan Brett observed some years ago, on the one hand walking is a learned skill that we normally do effortlessly, repetitively, and automatically, day in and day out. Yet it is also clear that even a daily walk along a familiar path may present obstacles of various kinds which require the ability to intentionally change one's course. In short, uniformity and alteration are both integral features of habits (Brett 1981, 368).

We have seen that in 2000, Dijksterhuis, Bargh, and Miedema characterized automatic behaviors as inflexible. When comparing men and mackerels they had stated that "the effects of perception on behavior have an important limitation: *they are inflexible*" (Dijksterhuis, Bargh and Miedema 2000, 40; my emphasis). Likewise, in standard dual-process theories of mental functioning, conscious processes were contrasted with automatic processes: controlled processes were held to be conscious, intentional, and flexible, whereas automatic processes were considered unintentional, nonconscious, and "autonomous" or "ballistic," by which was meant that, once started, they ran to completion without any further conscious direction or guidance (Hassin, Bargh, and Zimerman 2009, 21). Similar views were pervasive in personality theory and social psychology. As Ran Hassin, Bargh, and Zimerman commented when summarizing the literature on this topic, even Timothy Wilson, in his "excellent book" *Strangers to Ourselves: Discovering the Adaptive Unconscious* (2002), appeared to endorse the view that automatic processes were relatively inflexible in nature (Hassin, Bargh, and Zimerman 2009, 21).

But it became clear over time that automatic actions of various kinds were sensitive to the situational contexts in which they occurred and accordingly displayed more flexibility than Bargh's direct perception-behavior theory had appeared to recognize. As Bargh himself observed, research appeared to show that nonconscious goal pursuits operated flexibly and adaptively to sudden changes in situation; he cited Hassin's use of the Wisconsin Card Sorting Task to demonstrate the flexible response of participants when the sorting rule was altered (Bargh 2006, 149, referring to Hassin 2005). More generally, when participants in priming experiments were presented with stimuli strongly related to a goal such as achievement or cooperation using the standard scrambled-sentence test, they tended to act in line with the primed goal construct while reporting no awareness of the influence of the primes on their behaviors. The same participants in those studies also exhibited signs of motivated behavior, such as persistence, the resumption of a goal pursuit after an interruption, and increased pursuit following a delay. The conclusion was that unconsciously induced goal pursuits operated as flexibly as consciously induced ones (McCullough et al. 2008).

In 2009, Hassin, Bargh, and Zimerman conducted experiments that appeared to confirm the idea that automatic behaviors exhibited a combination of automaticity and flexibility. The authors staged their findings as a contribution to the question of whether dual-system theories, which posited a distinction between a conscious, intentional, and effortful system of control that required flexibility in choosing goals and making decisions, and an unconscious, unintentional, and inflexible system that governed automatic processes, could do justice to the need for flexibility in the automatic pursuit of goals. They argued that, given the capacity limitations of conscious system, which meant that conscious resources could only be used infrequently, in order to be truly beneficial automatic goal pursuits *needed* to be flexible. Their new experiments appeared to demonstrate this point (Hassin, Bargh, and Zimerman 2009).

In their first experiment, Hassin, Bargh, and Zimerman primed forty-two participants with an achievement goal, while other participants remained unprimed, and then the researchers used the Wisconsin Card Sorting Test to examine the participants' adaptation to changing environmental conditions. The Wisconsin Card Sorting Test involves showing participants cards that differ by the number of symbols, types of symbol, and color of symbols they display. The examiner lays out one card of each type in a different pile and then gives the examinee the rest of the cards one by one, asking him or her to put each card in the "correct" pile. The trick is that only the examiner knows the rules and moreover can change them at will. So, if the test subject is given a card with three red diamonds, should she put the card in the pile of cards with red symbols, with diamond shapes, or with the three symbols? Only by the examiner's "right" or "wrong" feedback is the subject able to guess the rule, and it takes multiple trials to abstract it (Berg 1948). This task is a test of frontal-lobe function—which is to say, of cognitive skills, including the ability to shift cognitive strategies in response to changing environmental conditions or rules.

In Hassin, Bargh, and Zimerman's study, words connoting high performance, such as *win, compete, succeed, strive, attain, achieve,* and *master*, were used to prime some of the participants, while the controls were not primed in this way. The Wisconsin Card Sorting Test was then administered and the scores analyzed and compared. Hassin, Bargh, and Zimerman used a computerized version of the test using 128 cards, and the test was continued until the participants had finished sorting them all. The results appeared to show that the primed participants performed better than the unprimed participants, who were simply exposed to neutral words. The primed subjects made fewer perseverative errors during the test, which is to say, they caught on more easily to changes in the rules than did the control participants. On debriefing, only one participant guessed the purpose of the word-search task in the priming phase and noticed that many words were associated with achievement. His data were excluded from the analyses. Hassin, Bargh, and Zimerman interpreted the findings to mean that the participants primed for achievement performed more flexibly than the unprimed participants, because they were better able to adapt to the changing rules, even though they were unaware of the influence of the primes on their performance.

In the next experiment, the researchers used the Iowa Gambling Task to test the flexibility of the participants, again comparing participants primed for achievement with unprimed participants. In the Iowa Gambling Test participants are presented with four virtual decks of cards on a computer screen. They are told that each deck holds cards that will either reward or penalize them, using game money. The goal of the game is to win as much money as possible. The decks differ from each other in the balance of reward versus penalty cards. Thus, some decks are "bad decks," and other decks are "good decks," because some decks will tend to reward the player more often than the other decks. Most normal participants sample cards from each deck, and after about forty or fifty selections are fairly effective at identifying and sticking to the good decks. However, patients with various deficits continue to persevere with the bad decks, even though they sometimes know that they are losing money overall.

Hassin, Bargh, and Zimerman introduced a variation in the Iowa Gambling Task: unknown to the participants, the location of the decks was altered halfway through the test, so that the "good" deck with relatively big but infrequent losses was moved from the left-hand deck position to the right-hand deck position. Participants' behavior on these kinds of tests clearly show that they have a favorite deck on this test: it is the deck with the infrequent but relatively large losses. The question posed by the study was how successfully the primed participants would respond to the new deck environment as compared with the unprimed participants. The evidence appeared to show that the unprimed participants hardly changed their behavior at all in response to the altered deck environment. But the primed participants were more flexible, as was shown by the fact that the latter more successfully disengaged from their "favorite" deck location following such changes. Only two out of the total of sixty-four participants guessed the nature and purpose of the experiment on debriefing after the test, and their data were excluded from the analyses. Two other participants did not finish their debriefing, and their data were also excluded. No differences were found between the primed and the unprimed condition in the participants' ratings of how important it was to them to succeed in the task or in the meaning they attached to success in the task.

Hassin, Bargh, and Zimerman did not deny that the participants in these studies were probably consciously pursuing multiple goals, some of which might have been related to the task. Nevertheless, they argued that the effects they reported were the result of nonconscious, non-intentional goal pursuits. They based their claim on the fact that when they debriefed their subjects, none of them were aware of having been primed or of the consequences of the priming on their subsequent performances. Moreover, a measure of goal commitment in the second experiment yielded no differences between the primed and the unprimed participants. On this basis, the authors argued that, although priming led to the behavioral effects they had documented, it did so without altering conscious goal commitments. They therefore concluded that their experiments provided strong evidence for automaticity, nonconsciousness, and non-intentionality in the flexible pursuit of goals.

Of course, in large measure the plausibility of the authors' interpretation of their findings depended on how the notions of *goal* and *goal pursuits* were understood.[14] They defined a goal as "a mental representation of

---

14. There are also problems with the authors' use of the notion of flexibility. Following the Oxford English Dictionary, they defined *flexibility* as the capacity for ready adaptation to various purposes or conditions, noting that flexibility of this kind might have cognitive

a future state that one *wishes* to attain, and that one *believes*—consciously or not—that she knows how to attain... Simply, if one does not wish (in one sense or another) to attain a certain future state then this future state is not one's goal; and if one does not even think s/he knows how to promote goal achievement then the wish is more fantasy than a goal" (Hassin, Bargh, and Zimerman 2009, 22; my emphases). The trouble with this definition is that it smuggled the person's "wishes" and "beliefs" back into the explanation of goal pursuits in ways that made it seem that such pursuits must be intended after all—because, at least according to Donald Davidson's influential arguments, an agent's intentions are explained in terms of causation by the agent's desires and beliefs (Davidson 1963; Schlosser 2019b).[15] Yet Hassin, Bargh, and Zimerman continued to treat such goal pursuits as if they occurred without intention. As they stated: "While, on its own, none of the measures we report guarantees that goal pursuit is automatic or nonconscious, their combination serves as strong evidence for automaticity and nonconsciousness. We conclude, then, that priming results in goal pursuit that is unintentional and nonconscious" (Hassin, Bargh, and Zimerman 2009, 32)—yet flexible.

As Keren and Schul observed the same year in a critical assessment of dual-system theories, such a combination of automaticity and flexibility contradicted a basic assumption of such theories according to which automatic processes belonged to System 1 and as such were held to be not only unconscious and automatic but also inflexible (Keren and Schul 2009). But this contradiction was one that for the moment Hassin, Bargh, and Zimerman were unable to resolve:

---

components (e.g., realizing that a rule governing the environment has changed), behavioral components (e.g., altering one's behaviors accordingly), and affective elements (e.g., not resenting the new rule just because it is new). They elucidated the superior performances of their primed participants on the Wisconsin Card Sorting Test and the Iowa Gambling Test in terms of participants' ability to be flexible according to this definition. But their use of the term *flexible* seems rather arbitrary. There are many ways one could explain such superior performances: why not attribute them to intelligence, resourcefulness, skills at pattern recognition, and so on? Moreover, Hassin, Bargh, and Zimerman did not establish participants' "before" and "after" test-performance levels but based their claims only on a comparison between the primed and unprimed student participants (2009).

15. I note that Bratman (1987) has argued—successfully according to some commentators—against Davidson's claim that acting for a reason is to be explained in terms of causation and rationalization by the agent's desires and intentions. See also Schlosser 2019b.

In light of the research presented herein, how shall we go about thinking about the dichotomy between automatic and controlled processes? One way would be to stick with the rigid definition of automaticity (and control), and pronounce every flexible process as not automatic. If we follow this route, we may end up with a new category of processes that are unintentional, unconscious, ballistic and effortful, yet flexible. This seems unwarranted because it is an ad-hoc category that, to the best of our understanding, serves nothing but the wish to maintain a "pure" category of automatic and flexible processes.

Alternatively, we may be more pliable and argue that under certain circumstances automatic processes may well be flexible... This conclusion seems to create a contradiction because... automatic processes are widely held to be inflexible (and pliability is regarded as one of the main advantages of controlled processes). This quasi-contradiction, we think, sends us back to the drawing table, to redraw the lines that separate automatic processes from controlled ones. Given the centrality of this dichotomy in the cognitive sciences... this road promises to be fascinating, challenging, and rewarding. (Hassin, Bargh, and Zimerman 2009, 33)

More than ten years later, Schlosser would seize on this apparent contradiction for dual-system theories and attempt to find a solution. In the process he redefined as forms of unconscious but intentional actions most of the automatic yet flexible goal pursuits that Hassin, Bargh, and Zimerman had described as non-intentional behaviors. In doing so, he challenged years of Bargh's theorizing on this topic (Schlosser 2019b). The surprising fact is that, unknown to Schlosser, the previous year Bargh had himself come to a similar conclusion, finally arguing—against the general tendency of his thinking up to that time—that the notion of unconscious intentional action was not a contradiction in terms (Melnikoff and Bargh 2018a). I will return to this topic in the appendix to this book.

But Bargh wasn't only interested in priming. Throughout his career he also explored the topic of imitation, theorizing it in the same automatic perception-behavior terms he applied to his priming results. He and his student, Tanya Chartrand, made imitation another major focus of automaticity research. It is to Bargh's and Chartrand's work on this topic that I turn in the next chapter.

5

The Chameleon Effect

Postural Mimicry and Automaticity

In 1999, Chartrand and Bargh published a paper in which they presented evidence ostensibly demonstrating that postural and other forms of human mimicry were the result of unintentional, automatic processes. Their findings appeared to confirm the validity of Bargh's theory of automaticity, according to which such behavioral effects were the product of a direct perception-behavior link (Chartrand and Bargh 1999). In the course of their paper, Chartrand and Bargh contradicted the claims of the psychologist Janet Bavelas and her colleagues, who had suggested that postural mimicry was a form of interpersonal communication that served to convey messages from the imitator to the model (Bavelas et al. 1986; 1987; 1988). The emphasis in Bavelas's et al.'s work fell on the strategic, intentional nature of such mimetic interactions. But Chartrand and Bargh explicitly denied this strategic-intentional interpretation. They regarded postural and other forms of imitation as automatic, perception-driven, passive behavioral responses that occurred without the person's awareness or intention.

In this chapter I propose to examine the evolution of Chartrand and Bargh's work on imitation in the context of Bavelas's competing approach. We shall see that, over time, Chartrand and Bargh were obliged to revise their assertions regarding the automaticity of mimicry as evidence accumulated that their original position was unsustainable. They were forced to concede that such imitations were more flexible and variable than they had first assumed. They did so by adding the influence of various "moderators," such as social motives, in the selection, facilitation, or inhibition of mimetic responses, while clinging to their previous views about automaticity and non-intentionality. I will argue that in the process Chartrand and Bargh tied themselves into various knots trying to square the evidence for the strategic nature of imitations with their claims for the non-strategic, non-intentional, automatic nature of such actions or behaviors.

Chartrand made the study of imitation a major focus of her research career, extending her early findings on postural matching to include all kinds of mimicry, including the well-known studies of facial mimicry in newborns by Andrew Meltzoff and M. Keith Moore; the emotional contagion observed when people copy the facial expressions of others; the contagion of yawning; and the imitative effects of unconscious priming. I shall be paying close attention to Chartrand's many articles on this theme from 1999 to the present and shall also track related contributions by Bargh and other researchers. I shall bring the story of Chartrand and Bargh's handling of imitation up to the period of the general crisis over replication that, starting in 2012 with the failed replication of Bargh's famous elderly priming experiment, undermined their long-standing claims regarding the nature and scope of automatic imitation.[1]

Chartrand was a graduate in psychology at New York University who had recently completed her dissertation under Bargh's supervision when, in 1999, she co-authored with him a paper with the title "The Chameleon Effect: The Perception-Behavior Link and Social Interaction." As they observed, the term "chameleon effect" was meant to convey the idea that, like chameleons, and like Woody Allen in the movie *Zelig* who could not help take on the behavior, personality, and values of whomever he was with, in ordinary life people automatically copy the accents, speech patterns, and even mannerisms of their interaction partners, without any awareness that they are doing so. Chartrand and Bargh began their article by observing that such imitations had generally been considered intentional, goal-directed responses. But they argued that, on the contrary, the existence of a direct, passive effect of perception on social behavior had been demonstrated by Bargh, Chen, and Burrows in their recent elderly priming experiment and related investigations (Bargh, Chen, and Burrows 1996). According to Chartrand and Bargh, those studies demonstrated that imitative behaviors were "unintended and not in the service of any

---

1. Certain portions of this chapter have appeared in various guises in Leys 2017 and Leys 2020, but they are here developed in greater detail and taken in new directions.

discernible purpose." Common to all such cases, they claimed, was that "one typically does not notice doing these things—if at all—until after the fact" (Chartrand and Bargh 1999, 893).

Before presenting their experiments on this topic, Chartrand and Bargh discussed the idea that mimicry was an automatic response. The authors' opinions were of course familiar to those who had been following Bargh's publications since the 1980s. Chartrand and Bargh noted the harmony between Prinz's ideomotor theory and Bargh's direct perception-behavior theory. They also briefly described previous experiments suggesting the validity of the ideomotor hypothesis. They went on to survey research results held to prove the existence of automatic, unintended, and passive effects of perceptions on behavior, such as Bargh, Chen, and Burrows's (1996) elderly priming study and its conceptual replication by Dijksterhuis and van Knippenberg (1998) and others. They then turned to the main topic of their paper, which concerned postural mimicry.

As Chartrand and Bargh observed, research on postural mimicry had started back in the 1960s, when motion-picture recordings were used to study the role played by bodily imitations observed during interactions between patients and their therapists. Subsequently, several researchers had gone on to study postural mimicry in more experimental settings (for example, LaFrance 1979; 1982; LaFrance and Broadbent 1976). But in their 1999 paper Chartrand and Bargh argued that the minimal conditions in which imitation takes place had not been adequately tested. They were especially interested in finding out whether postural mimicry occurred between partners who were unknown to each other. Some earlier studies had raised the question of the connection between the imitator's copying behavior and the feeling of rapport or affiliation between mimic and model. Were imitations motivated by the imitator's desire to establish rapport with the model? Or did the imitation come first and produce the affiliation?

Chartrand and Bargh reasoned that if, as they hypothesized, postural mimicry was the result of an entirely passive, preconscious automatic process that did not depend on motivation or an intentional goal, then the response should occur even between strangers. They also predicted, on the basis of the same reasoning, that the Chameleon Effect should take place independently of any purpose on the part of imitators, such as the aim of getting along with, or being liked by, those with whom they were interacting.

In order to evaluate their ideas experimentally, Chartrand and Bargh arranged for each of several test subjects to look at and describe the contents of various photographs while in the company of someone they did not know. The latter was actually the experimenters' confederate. The experimenters took several steps to ensure that rapport would not develop between the participants and the confederates used in the experiments. The confederates were told not to make eye contact with, or smile at, the participants at any point during the brief sessions; one of them was told not to smile at all during the experiment, but instead to show a negative and bored expression. Chartrand and Bargh assumed that if participants had a default tendency to try to affiliate with a confederate and create a sense of rapport, this tendency would be overridden by the confederate's unfriendly behavior.

During the shared photo-describing sessions, which were secretly videotaped, the confederates quietly performed either face-rubbing or foot-shaking movements. The results of those sessions demonstrated that the participants rubbed their faces more in the presence of the face-rubbing confederate and shook their feet more in the presence of the foot-shaking confederate. Moreover, Chartrand and Bargh reported that, at the debriefing after the experiment was over, participants were "often stunned" to learn that they had been performing these imitations. The researchers interpreted this last fact to confirm the idea that the Chameleon Effect occurred without the participants' awareness or purpose. In short, the findings appeared to support the hypothesis that subjects passively and automatically copied the mannerisms, behaviors, and expressions of those around them without any intention to do so.

In a follow-up experiment the direction of the imitation was reversed, so that this time the confederates were directed to unobtrusively imitate the gestures made by the participants during a shared photo-description task. After the session, the participants were asked how much they liked their partners in the test, and the results appeared to show that being imitated made them like the confederates more. Chartrand and Bargh therefore argued that social affiliation was the result of imitation and not the other way around: mimicry came first as the cause and possibility of any subsequent empathy or liking. The function of imitation was to therefore to produce *by* automatic contagion the "social glue" that bound individuals together. As such, automatic mimicry could be seen to be an adaptive mechanism with beneficial social consequences. In their discussion of these findings, Chartrand and Bargh compared the behavior of the participants who unconsciously imitated the confederate's behavior to the hypnotized subject who, as Hilgard had proposed, owing to a suspension of the will characteristic of the induced hypnotic state, passively responds to the hypnotist's suggestions (Hilgard 1965; Chartrand and Bargh 1999, 906; I pursue the topic of the relationship between priming effects and hypnotic responses further in chapter 8).

In a related paper, Bargh and Chartrand defended the view that the behaviors of everyday life are largely automatic. What recent research had demonstrated, they wrote in a passage I already quoted in chapter 4, was that "'environment to perception behavior' operates as efficiently and smoothly in producing social behavior as the legendary Chicago Cubs infielders did in producing double plays" (Bargh and Chartrand 1999, 468). The implication was that imitations and skilled behaviors are in a fundamental sense performed entirely mindlessly and automatically, because they are performed without awareness or guidance by "higher-order cognition" (Chen et al. 1998, 686). Bargh and Chartrand defended the adaptive value of such learned, automatic processes on the grounds that they serve people's best interests. As they wrote with a personifying flourish: "They are, if anything, 'memory butlers' who know our tendencies and preferences so well that they anticipate and take care of them for us, without having to be asked" (Bargh and Chartrand 1999, 476).

Imitation as an Intentional-Communicative Action

But Chartrand and Bargh's conclusions about the automaticity of mimicry conflicted with research on postural imitation that had been undertaken by certain other psychologists a few years earlier. Starting in the late 1980s, on the basis of an ingenious series of investigations, Janet Bavelas and her colleagues had suggested that motor mimicry was not a simple reflex or automatic behavior but was sensitive to social and communicative contexts.[2] First, Bavelas and her team had demonstrated experimentally that the pattern and timing of wincing at a participant's seeing an experimental confederate's pain was strongly dependent on the witness's eye contact with the ostensible sufferer. In those experiments, an injury sequence of behaviors was embedded in a complex set of procedures and interactions with participants, such that during the study an experimenter-confederate was ostensibly injured by accidentally dropping a large television moni-

---

2. See Bavelas (2013) for an account of the development of her interest in nonverbal communication and her reasons for rejecting information-processes theories of communication.

tor on his apparently already injured finger. The confederate wore a fully taped finger splint throughout the experiment to indicate he had already hurt his finger. In one experimental condition, at the moment he appeared to injure his finger again because he had accidentally dropped the television monitor on his hand, the confederate deliberately glanced at and made brief eye contact with the participant as he winced in pain and rolled his head back. In the other experimental condition, he again dropped the TV monitor on his already injured hand and winced, but he did not glance at or make eye contact with the participant (Bavelas et al. 1986).

The results of the experiments, as revealed in videotaped recordings, indicated that participants winced in imitation of the confederate's painful expression, but only when eye contact was made. "As the probability of eye contact with the receiver increased, motor mimicry not only increased generally but was available at the best 'delivery point.' When, on the other hand, it became less and less probable that the victim could see the expression, motor mimicry either faded away quickly or did not occur at all. These observers' faces seemed to go on hold, apparently waiting for eye contact that never happened" (Bavelas et al. 1986, 325). In other words, the experiments showed that whether the participant winced did not depend on the visibility of the wincing expression of the confederate per se but on the presence or absence of eye contact between the two interactants. This point needs emphasis because, as we shall see, it was repeatedly misunderstood by the majority of researchers.

On the basis of these experiments, Bavelas proposed an intentional-communicative explanation of human mimicry. Bavelas et al. did not deny that, in wincing, participants might have felt the emotion of the apparently injured confederate. But even if the participants did feel the pain, it was not responsible for the motor mimicry. They argued that the motor mimicry itself was not a derivative of the subject's vicariously experienced emotional state, but a parallel, independent process of communication or representation by which the participant-mimic intended to communicate to the confederate-model:

> Expressive behaviors . . . are not an inadvertent by-product of a private experience but are primarily and precisely interactive; they are constant evidence that in our social behavior we are intricately and visibly connected to others. For these reasons we propose that the overt behavior of motor mimicry is primarily communicative and that, moreover, it conveys a message fundamental to our relationships with others: I am like

you, I feel as you do. Thus the centuries-old puzzle of motor mimicry—and perhaps many other behaviors—may be solved by looking beyond the individual to the immediate interpersonal context in which the behavior occurs. (Bavelas et al. 1986, 328)[3]

In another study by Bavelas et al. (1988), participants who listened face-to-face to stories recounted by a confederate predictably mimicked the movements of the storyteller when she deliberately punctuated her performance with brief movements to her right or left. Bavelas and her team reasoned that if the listeners' movements were empathy-induced readouts of an internal state, then their movements should be identical in "form" to those of the storyteller. In other words, they reasoned that when the storyteller moved to her *right*, the listeners facing her should also move to *their* right, as if the listeners had mentally and emotionally rotated themselves in order to occupy the same role as the storyteller and hence to adopt her inner affective state. Instead, however, the listeners' movements were genuine mirror reflections of the storyteller: when the storyteller moved to her *right*, the listeners facing her moved to their *left* (in order, as Bavelas and her co-authors suggested, to maintain an empathic relationship with her). Once again, Bavelas et al.'s conclusion was that

> motor mimicry is not the manifestation of a vicarious internal state, but a *representation* of that state to another person . . . [M]otor mimicry should not be equated with the state it represents . . . We do not agree with theories that, in effect, assume that the overt behavior is a "spill over" from an inner vicarious experience. We propose that it has a function of its own, a communicative one. (Bavelas et al. 1988, 278–79; their emphasis)

Or as they also put this point:

> We propose that the observer is not having the other's reaction but is portraying it. He or she is sending the message. "It is *as if* I feel as you

---

3. Bavelas et al. (1986) did not speculate further about why eye contact was the key variable in their experiment, beyond stressing its role in the interpersonal communicative process. It is possible that the confederate who winced in pain while also making eye contact with the participant-observer was understood as seeking an involved, empathic wincing response from the latter.

do." In other words, the motor mimicry is an encoded representation quite different from, say, actual pain. (Bavelas et al. 1987, 329; their emphasis)[4]

The implication of Bavelas et al.'s research was that, although someone witnessing another's pain (or grief, or effort, or success) might experience similar personal feelings, we should not conclude that this will necessarily happen, or that a feeling will inevitably be the cause of the person's mimetic display. In the standard Basic Emotion Theory associated with the work of Sylvan Tomkins and Paul Ekman, a paradigm to which Chartrand and Bargh adhered, emotions are internal mental states that can involuntarily leak out to others in the form of signature facial expressions and related autonomic processes and bodily movements. On this paradigm, under the right circumstances or conditions a person automatically and unintentionally transmits the truth of her emotional state. Thus, if people mimetically wince at someone else's expression of pain, or cringe when they see another's fear, it is because they read or automatically respond to the other person's emotions as their own, and accordingly match their feelings and expressions with the other (see Leys 2017 for a critical discussion). As Ross Buck, an adherent of the Basic Emotion Theory, explained:

> The primary role of the display is . . . to "inform other members of the species about the sender's emotional state" . . . The display is innate—a phylogenetic adaptation . . . The receiver "knows the meaning" of the display directly as a kind of inherited knowledge.
> The result is a spontaneous communication process that is, in effect, a conversation between limbic systems. It answers the problem of "other minds" posed by philosophers: we know certain feelings and desires in others directly because they are constructed to display those states and we are constructed, given attention, to know the meaning of those displays just as directly . . . In spontaneous communication the sender and receiver constitute literally a biological unit. (Buck 1991, 158–59)[5]

---

4. Thus, according to Bavelas and Chovil, facial displays are "nonliteral in the sense that the individual is not necessarily claiming to have the reaction being depicted . . . They are selective in the sense of being partial portrayals rather than faithful reproductions" (Bavelas and Chovil 2000, 173).
5. As Chovil and Fridlund remarked in rejecting Buck's arguments: "Buck's idea of limbic systems in intimate communication precludes the possibility of deception or misinterpretation" (Chovil and Fridlund 1991, 166).

But Bavelas and her colleagues argued that if an observer sees someone wincing from pain and imitatively winces "as if" in the place of the injured person, she does not necessarily do so because she herself is feeling pain. The observer's mimicry is not necessarily an involuntary leakage of a vicariously aroused and experienced emotion but a communication that is appropriate to the situation of the model, rather than to the observer's own. Bavelas and her colleagues therefore argued that "I *show* how you feel" by wincing at your pain, not because I actually feel your pain but because I wish to communicate my sympathy with you, which is to say that the imitation is a meaningful referential gesture (Bavelas et al. 1986). These researchers proposed that in their wincing experiment the injured confederate's behavior played a critical role in such mimetic effects because, as microanalyses of the videotaped interactions between the "injured" confederate and the observer demonstrated, the pattern and timing of the observer's motor mimicry were significantly influenced by the eye contact established by the confederate's glance of pain.

For Chartrand and Bargh, the fact that their own experimental participants were clueless about their mimicry was evidence that it was unintentional. They equated consciousness with intentionality and therefore assumed that all behaviors performed without awareness must be unintentional, which is to say, automatic. We have seen that, in theory, Bargh denied that any single feature or property was necessarily characteristic of automaticity. But in practice his attachment to the equation between consciousness and intentionality was so basic that, for him and Chartrand, any behaviors that occurred without a person's awareness had to be nonintentional. As Jessica Lakin, Chartrand, and Robert Arkin commented: "Nonconscious mimicry . . . is an easy prosocial behavior that is not an intentional act of regaining favor . . . [I]t is an efficient and effective attempt to readjust to a perceived drop in one's status with members of one's in-group" (Lakin, Chartrand, and Arkin 2008, 821; see also van Baaren et al. 2009). But for Bavelas and her team, the fact that mimicry was fleeting and remained "in the background"—out of conscious awareness—did not disprove its communicative-intentional function. They held this position because Bavelas rejected the equation between intentionality and consciousness that governed Chartrand and Bargh's analyses. She and her colleagues therefore stressed the intentional-symbolic communicative meaning of motor mimicry (Bavelas and Coates 1992).

Imitation When We Are Alone

In their research, Bavelas and her group raised a fundamental question: If facial displays are a function of the relationship between interactants and the social context, why do people make faces when they are alone and no other person is present? In fact, solitary facial expressions do occur, and that fact was routinely cited as definitive evidence that emotional expressions are not strategic forms of social signaling or interpersonal communication but spontaneous readouts of internal emotional states. For example, Buck stated: "When a sender is alone . . . he or she should feel little pressure to present a proper image to others, and any emotion expression under such circumstance should be more likely to reflect an actual motivational-emotional state" (Buck 1984, 20; cited by Fridlund 1994, 158). Similarly, Ekman remarked that "facial expressions of emotion do occur when people are alone . . . and contradict the theoretical proposals of those who view expressions solely as social signals" (Ekman, Davidson, and Friesen 1990, 351; cited by Fridlund 1994, 158).

But it is important to recognize that the idea that the truth shows itself on someone's face when a person believes he or she is alone is what might be called a "theoretical" claim—one for which there is no compelling, confirming evidence. Put slightly differently, it does not follow from the fact that the face for us is a privileged site of such expressions that, if only it could be seen in solitude, it would tell us the deep truth about ourselves. To believe so is to surrender to the fiction that we can draw an absolute distinction between the masks we allegedly put on for others and the genuine faces we wear when we are alone and no one is watching—as if it is impossible to discover the truth about other people in the course of interacting with them in daily life; or by observing how they respond to an emergency; or on the basis of intimate conversations over a period of time; or by any other means than coming across them in circumstances when they believe themselves to be unobserved.

In discussions of the topic, Bavelas proposed that just because we are alone in a room or in a laboratory space does not mean that we are alone psychologically. Rather, she considered facial movements in the "alone" condition to be a function of an implicit sociality because of the presence of imagined interlocutors and interactants of various kinds. As she and her colleagues pointed out, we often act as if others are present even when they are not, as when we talk back at TV shows or movies or conduct conversations in our heads with imagined friends or others. "The occurrence of motor mimicry... when alone is the nonverbal equivalent of talking to oneself," they observed. "Just as we represent our thoughts in words that sometimes spill over into muttering to ourselves, we might represent some thoughts in nonverbal actions that are not always suppressed" (Bavelas et al. 1986, 328).

In a similar line of research Alan Fridlund also championed a social-communicative view of facial signaling, which he called the Behavioral Ecology View. A former disciple of Ekman and an expert on the electromyographic study of facial muscles, Fridlund in the late 1980s had come to see that Ekman's Basic Emotion Theory was erroneous. On the basis of the "new ecology" associated with the work of Richard Dawkins, John Krebs, W. John Smith, and others, he argued that facial displays and other forms of nonverbal signaling could not have evolved to provide information detrimental to the signaler: "Displayers must not signal automatically, but only when it is beneficial for them to do so, that is, when signaling serves... motives. Automatic readouts or spillovers of drive states (i.e., 'facial expressions of emotion') would be extinguished early in phylogeny in the service of deception, economy, and privacy" (Fridlund 1994, 132; see also Crivelli and Fridlund 2018).

From this argument it followed that facial displays could not be regarded as leakages of internal affective states, as Tomkins and Ekman had argued, but rather were intentional gestures serving various social motives. This meant that such displays were not only responsive to proximate elicitors, they were also sensitive to those who were present, the displayer's aims toward them, and the nature and context of the interaction. In short, Fridlund argued that facial expressions were not surefire, automatic signals of the truth of someone's inner affective state but strategic-intentional forms of social communication. He had backed up his claims by reviewing the enormous literature in the emotion field, by critiquing and reinterpreting some of Ekman's iconic experiments, and by reporting important new experimental results (Fridlund 1994; Leys 2017).

Among the many changes in perspective brought about by Fridlund's challenge to the Basic Emotion Theory was an emphasis on the ways in which human and nonhuman displays varied with the presence of interactants and with the relationship between those interactants and the displayer. Fridlund (1991) conducted a study in which participants watched an amusing video under conditions of increasing levels of sociality: (a) alone; (b) alone but believing a friend was doing another task; (c) watching while the friend was present. Smiling increased with the level of sociality, despite there being no differences in self-reported emotion. The same year, Nicole Chovil, a doctoral student of Bavelas's, carried out a similar study (Chovil 1991), finding that imitative wincing in response to a story about a harrowing close situation increased with the degree of sociality involved, such as whether participants heard the story alone from an audiotape recording; from another person separated by a partition; alone, over the telephone; or talking to another subject face-to-face (I shall return to Chovil's study later in this chapter).

Like Bavelas, Fridlund also argued that just because participants are alone they are not alone psychologically. Rather, he considered facial movements in the "alone" or solitary condition a function of an implicit sociality because of the presence of imagined interlocuters and interactants of various kinds. In other words, we often act as if others are present even when they are not, so that implicit audiences function as mediators of our so-called solitary faces.[6]

How Bargh and Chartrand Misunderstood Bavelas's Experiments

So far as I am aware, Chartrand never cited Fridlund's publications and Bargh did so rarely (for example, Ackerman and Bargh 2010).[7] Both of them, however, were aware of Bavelas et al.'s research on postural mimicry. Yet for many years the significance of that research was lost on them. Instead, they repeatedly denied that imitation was governed by intentional-

---

6. Using electromyography to measure subtle movements of the relevant facial muscles, Fridlund demonstrated that the incidence of smiling in solitary viewers watching a videotape was not correlated with self-reports of happiness but varied according to the imagined presence of friends. In this way he proved that the smiling by viewers who believed a friend was in a nearby room was not only greater than that which occurred when the subjects simply viewed alone but was nearly equal to the smiling that took place in the actual presence of the friend. Fridlund's experiments not only corroborated the hypothesis that solitary facial displays are mediated by imaginary interactants but also demonstrated the actual separability of subjective-emotional experience and communicative signaling in terms that, once again, challenged the readout view of affective expression and transmission. See Fridlund et al. 1990; Fridlund 1994 (157–68); and Bavelas et al. 1986 (327–28).

7. Ackerman and Bargh interpreted the communicative nature of facial displays in terms of the coordination between the actor's and the observer's "internal states," an explanation at odds with Fridlund's Behavioral Ecology View of the strategic-intentional character of such signals and consistent with Ekman's Basic Emotion Theory (Ackerman and Bargh 2010, 337, citing Fridlund 1997). In the course of their discussion Ackerman and Bargh cited a paper by Wicker et al. (2003) on the imitation of disgust expressions that was based on Ekman's Basic Emotion Theory (Ackerman and Bargh 2010, 340); for a critique of Wicker et al. 2003 see Leys 2014.

strategic motives and considerations. For example, in a paper reviewing the evidence in favor of Bargh's theory of the "perception-behavior expressway," Dijksterhuis and Bargh rejected Bavelas et al.'s views regarding the communicative-strategic nature of mimicry:

> Bavelas and colleagues ... accounted for their findings with a motivational communicative perspective. They argue that participants imitate in order to show the confederates that they are empathizing with them, that they are "feeling their pain." And if there is more eye contact between the confederates and the participants, the participants imitate more because they know that the confederates are better able to see their expression. In other words, they interpret the imitation as motivated, strategic behavior to create an empathic bond with the other person. (Dijksterhuis and Bargh 2001, 14–15)

Dijksterhuis and Bargh asserted instead that

> there is no evidence at all for the strategic nature of the imitation effects ... whereas the support for the automatic and unintentional nature of imitation is evident ... Chartrand and Bargh (1999) showed that even minimal interaction with a complete stranger led to imitation ... [I]n the experiments reviewed above, people did not imitate because they wanted to imitate. Instead, they imitated for no other reason than they are designed to do so. ((Dijksterhuis and Bargh 2001, 15)

In this way, Bargh and Dijksterhuis interpreted the findings of Bavelas's wincing experiment to mean that the participants copied the wincing expression of the confederate because they automatically felt the same emotions as the model. Chartrand and Lakin understood Bavelas's findings in the same way. "Bavelas et al. (1986) have argued that mimicry serves a communicative function," they wrote, "because mimicry of pained expressions is more likely when eye contact is made; this suggests that feelings are being shared between interaction partners, which is characteristic of empathy" (Chartrand and Lakin 2013, 293).

But these statements reveal that these researchers did not grasp—and therefore misrepresented—Bavelas's position. As I have already observed, Bavelas and her colleagues did not regard the imitator's wincing as necessarily an expression of an imitatively aroused, vicariously felt inner emotional state. They argued that the observer was not necessarily feeling the pain of the confederate-model but through her mimicry was conveying a communication or representation. To repeat what Bavelas et al. stated: "We propose that the observer is not having the other's reaction but is portraying it. He or she is sending the message, 'It is *as if* I feel as you do.' In other words, the motor mimicry is an encoded representation, quite different from, say, actual pain" (Bavelas et al. 1987, 329). But it was precisely the idea of the *as if* communicative nature of the imitation that Dijksterhuis and Bargh, and Chartrand and Lakin, failed to grasp.

Moreover, for Bavelas the role of the wincing confederate's staged gaze was to elicit a matching communication from the participant in the form of a mimetic wincing response. The importance of the gaze was demonstrated by the fact that participants winced more frequently when the wincing victim made eye contact with them than in the control condition, when there was no eye contact. But for Chartrand and like-minded researchers, all that mattered in the experiment was the mere visibility of the confederate's wincing expression. As Dijksterhuis and Bargh observed of Bavelas et al.'s studies:

> In their experiments, a confederate was the victim of a painful injury that occurred in the presence of the participants. As expected, the participants imitated the expressions of the confederate, which can best be described as a big wince. Interestingly, they [Bavelas and her colleagues] also manipulated the visibility of the expression of the confederate. In one condition, the expression of the confederate was easier to see than in a second condition. As a result, the degree to which participants imitated the expression varied as well. More visible expression led to more imitation; that is, the easier it was to perceive the expression, the greater the effect on one's own behavior. (Dijksterhuis and Bargh 2001, 11)

Dijksterhuis, Chartrand, and Aarts similarly remarked:

> During [Bavelas et al.'s] research studies participants witnessed a painful accident to a confederate which resulted in a wince. It was found that the participants imitated the expressions of the confederate, especially when the wince was more visible to the participant. The more visible the expression of the confederate was to the participant, the more the participant imitated the expression. In other words, the easier it was to perceive the expression, the greater the effect of their own behavior. (Dijksterhuis et al. 2007, 64)

But these statements misdescribed Bavelas's views. Why would eye contact make the pain expression of the confederate more visible and easier to perceive? Dijksterhuis, Bargh, Chartrand and their co-authors don't and can't say. In fact, Bavelas et al. had deliberately structured the wincing experiments so that the confederate's face was equally visible to participants in both the eye-contact and the no-eye-contact condition. In reporting their wincing experiment, Bavelas et al. (1986) had explicitly considered (in order to rule it out) an alternative explanation of their findings, which was that the information conveyed by the confederate to the participants in the eye-contact versus the non-eye-contact condition was not the same. As they had noted, it could be argued that, because the confederate's face was visible longer in the eye-contact condition, his injury appeared more serious and painful than in the non-eye-contact condition, and this augmented visibility increased the probability of the participants' mimetic wincing responses.

Precisely because they deemed this to be a strong alternative explanation, Bavelas et al. had devoted considerable planning to make the possibility less likely. They had made sure that most aspects of the two conditions were identical, including the injury itself, the full view of the injury, the sharp intake of breath, the pronounced bodily reaction, and so on. The stimulus configurations at the time of the injury were also almost identical. "In brief," they had reported, "everything was scripted to make the injury in the no-EC [no Eye Contact] condition appear at least as painful, if not more, than the injury in the EC [Eye Contact] condition" (Bavelas et al. 1986, 325). Or as Bavelas, in a detailed discussion of the same experiment, later emphasized: "The experimenter's facial display of pain was identical and equally visible in both conditions" (Bavelas 2007, 137).

The difference between the two situations was therefore a function of eye contact alone. For Bavelas et al. the wincing experiment thus proved that imitation was a specific form of communication between the observer and the victim based on a shared gaze. These effects were labeled "audience effects" by Fridlund in his related analyses of facial signaling (Fridlund 1994, 145–46). We might therefore put it that Dijksterhuis, Chartrand, and Aarts missed the role of audience effects in Bavelas's communicative-representational view of imitation.

Also striking was Bargh's and Chartrand's failure to grasp Bavelas et al.'s arguments concerning the nature of imitations performed when people are alone. I noted above that Bavelas and her colleagues invoked the idea of implicit sociality to defend their communicative view of mimicry against the criticism that people make imitations in solitary situations. Their point was that even when we are ostensibly alone, social motives and intentions are not rendered inoperative. But Bargh, Chartrand, and their like-minded colleagues were unable to comprehend this point. In the paper by Dijksterhuis and Bargh cited above, the authors mentioned that Roland Neumann and Fritz Strack (2000) had obtained evidence that participants responded to the emotional tone of someone's voice with a similar mood, even when the person being imitated was a stranger and was not even present to the experimental subject (Dijksterhuis and Bargh 2001, 14). Neumann and Strack therefore proposed that vocally expressed emotions elicited congruent mood states in the listener, without any intention on the part of the participant to share or communicate the target's feelings. In short, because imitation occurred when the listener was alone, it must have been unintentional (Neumann and Strack 2000).

In the same interpretive spirit, in 2005 Chartrand, Maddux, and Lakin pointed to the existence of facial imitation, in so-called solitary subjects observing photographs of happy and angry faces, as evidence against the social-communicative function of such motor mimicry. In a statement that I am sure would have sounded naïve to Bavelas, the authors wrote:

> Although Bavelas and her colleagues argue that facial mimicking functions as a communication tool, there is also evidence that we mimic facial expressions even when we have no need to communicate. For example, researchers have shown that viewers mimic the facial expressions of people on television ... [F]acial mimicry ... is even more common than we think. Unobservable to the naked eye, facial mimicry also occurs at the micro level, involving tiny facial muscles that are used for smiling and frowning ... [T]he fact that the micromimicry occurs when looking at photographs—that is, in the absence of real social interaction or even the presence of another person—suggests that mimicry need not function as a communicative tool that relays the message "I like you" to others. Even when no such function is served, and even when no person is present, it still occurs. (Chartrand, Maddux, and Lakin 2005, 338–39)

The authors seemed to think that, when people are alone, they shed the cultural conventions that control public displays of feelings, which is to say that, in response to looking at photographs in a solitary situation, their authentic feelings and facial expressions involuntarily leak out.[8] Here too, Chartrand and her colleagues simply failed to understand Bavelas's arguments.

The Limits of Contagion

After 1999, several developments boosted Chartrand's claims about the unconscious, unintentional nature of imitation. Priming research, from which Chartrand's work on mimicry emerged, flourished during the first decade of the twenty-first century, expanding its claims in ways that seemed to further confirm the validity of her approach. Theories of psychic contagion were easily assimilated to the idea of the automaticity of mimicry (Hatfield, Cacioppo, and Rapson 1994; Hatfield et al. 2014). Claims for the existence of newborn imitation, first made by Meltzoff and Moore in 1977, appeared to demonstrate that some imitations were innate and present at birth, and those claims were taken up by imitation researchers. Starting in 2004, advocates of Unconscious Thought Theory, such as Dijksterhuis and colleagues, not only suggested that unconscious thought was the default form of thinking, but that many unconscious decisions were more intelligent and effective than those made by the conscious mind (Dijksterhuis 2004; see also chapter 6 for a further discussion of Unconscious Thought Theory). Also, as I noted in the previous chapter, in the 1980s Libet had appeared to show that there was unconscious brain activity a half-second before we become conscious of our intentions to act, suggesting that unconscious brain processes were the true instigators of our actions and behaviors (Libet 1985). Libet's findings and claims converged with Daniel Wegner's experiments ostensibly proving that the brain makes our decisions for us and that free will is an illusion (Wegner 2002).

Throughout the same period and since, some of these claims have unraveled in a rather spectacular fashion (for example, experiments purporting to demonstrate the existence of newborn imitation have been put in question by replication failures; see Leys 2020). But in the first decade of the twenty-first century, the dominant research atmosphere was one of

---

8. Similarly, van Baaren et al. premised a study of the effects of mood on mimicry on the idea that when participants were alone in the testing room, although they mimicked the movements of performers they saw on a TV screen, they could not be doing so for communicative purposes, because there was no one there with whom to communicate. The researchers therefore treated the participants' imitations as unconscious and unintentional (Van Baaren et al. 2006, 432).

enthusiasm for theories of automaticity, and this enthusiasm reinforced Chartrand's claims for the unconscious, non-intentional, and automatic character of imitation.[9]

Moreover, the discovery of mirror neurons, which more or less coincided with Chartrand's and Bargh's earliest discussions of the Chameleon Effect, were important to theorists of mimicry because those neurons appeared to offer precisely the kind of neuronal mechanism required to explain imitative effects. As is well known, mirror neurons constitute a unique class of cells that fire both when an animal enacts a particular movement, such as grasping or manipulating an object, and when the animal merely observes the same action performed by someone else. Proponents argued that mirror neurons have sensory and motor properties that allow a person to "mirror" the behavior of others by a kind of simulation or resonance. Mirror neurons were first detected in the 1990s by a group of scientists in Parma, Italy, in experiments using electrodes directly implanted in the premotor cortex of macaque monkeys. More recent evidence for the existence of mirror neurons in humans is somewhat equivocal, but even critics of mirror neuron theorists do not doubt that mirror neurons are present in the human brain (Leys 2014, 2020).

From the start, the function of mirror neurons has been the topic of much speculation and controversy. Many researchers have claimed that mirror neurons provide the mechanism for an animal's ability to grasp the motor actions of others. Mirror neurons have also been used to explain why humans are capable of being empathically attuned to someone else's facial expressions and feelings. Similarly, some theorists have suggested that mirror neurons enable humans to read the minds of others, so that dysfunction in the mirror neuron system is thought to explain mindreading failures associated with autism and other abnormal states. Mirror neurons are also held to account for the impact of artworks on the beholder. And many theorists have appealed to mirror neurons to explain the mechanism of imitation.

It is easy to understand why mirror neurons are so alluring to researchers. If people's interpersonal relationships are a matter of the automatic

---

9. For example, citing Chartrand and Bargh (1999) among other sources, Alex Pentland of the MIT Media Lab has claimed that mimicry is a form of signaling which honestly, automatically, and unconsciously communicates the truth of a person's bodily states to others (Pentland 2008, 10). Hayles has welcomed Pentland's ideas, describing Pentland's "sociometer" device as an exteriorization of the "cognitive nonconscious" (Hayles 2016b, 43; see also Hayles 2014; 2016a).

resonance between subjects, then mirror neurons would seem to offer an explanation of how that resonance might occur. Chartrand and Bargh thus referred to mirror neuron research in order to claim that perceiving someone else engaging in a behavior was neurologically similar to performing that behavior (Chartrand, Maddux, and Lakin 2005; Bargh 2003; 2011). Vittorio Gallese, one of the co-discoverers of mirror neurons, likewise suggested that the Chameleon Effect could be explained by the operation of these cells (Gallese 2011).

Nevertheless, all imitation theorists have had to confront a fundamental question: *Why does mimicry have its limits*? Why is it that we don't imitate every behavior or movement or emotional expression that we perceive but select and adapt our imitations according to the setting or context or social circumstances? From the start of their work on imitation, Chartrand and Bargh acknowledged this fact. In their 1999 launch paper on the "Chameleon Effect," they emphasized the automaticity of imitation according to the perception-behavior model. But they also abruptly observed that "emotional contagion has its limits" because certain circumstances inhibit its transmission. As they stated: "Although we may pick up emotions from friends, family, or even strangers, our opponents may not have such an easy time infecting us—the tendency to mimic may be over-ridden by general negative emotions" (Chartrand, Maddux, and Lakin 2005, 343). Indeed, it was often recognized that we would soon go mad if we spent our days resonating nonselectively, immoderately, and automatically to whatever facial and other signals we encountered.

I think it is fair to say that Chartrand and her colleagues struggled to account for this fact. Their response was to admit the selectivity of imitation while also defending its non-intentional nature—not an easy maneuver to pull off. The problem these imitation theorists faced was identical to the problem Bargh confronted when trying to explain the selectivity of automaticity. We have seen that Chartrand and Bargh rejected Bavelas's idea that postural imitations were strategic-intentional signals. The fact that, according to their own experiments, imitation occurred even between strangers, appeared to them to prove that imitations lacked strategic intentionality. So did the fact that individuals made imitations even when they were alone when, Chartrand and Bargh argued, there was no one there with whom to communicate. They were deaf to Bavelas's arguments concerning the existence of an implicit audience in the alone condition, and they failed to notice Fridlund's related arguments concerning the strategic-social-communicative nature of facial signaling.

But as it became clear that the problem of the selective nature of imitation had to be met, Chartrand, Bargh, and other researchers tried to respond to the challenge. They did so by invoking the role of various "moderators" capable of influencing imitative outcomes—all the while denying the influence of intentional-strategic intentions in controlling the "perception-behavior expressway" and defending instead the automaticity of imitative reactions. For example, Dijksterhuis and Bargh wrote that "the only real precondition of imitation of observable behavior is the perception of the behavior. We emphasize that our explanation of an innate express route between perception and action is supported by [the] evidence, as our explanation would lead one to predict all the reviewed effects to be automatic and nonstrategic as opposed to other explanations that claim these effects to be strategic and intentional" (Dijksterhuis and Bargh 2001, 15).

But the authors also recognized that people do not mindlessly mimic every stimulus they encountered: imitation is not always obligatory and can be countermanded. As they observed: "Humans are flexible and they can override direct effects of perception on behavior. We do possess a set of moderating modules clearly separating us from fish and frogs" (Dijksterhuis and Bargh 2001, 28). They invoked one kind of moderator—liking someone—to explain why this trait increased a person's tendency to imitate another. But they explicitly denied that the imitations they observed in their experiments were due to conscious, strategic motivations or intentions:

> It should be noted that although the relation between liking and imitation has often been regarded as a strategic one—people want to be liked and therefore mimic more—this does not have to be the case. It is possible that the more people like each other, the more they pay attention to each other, or, in other words, the more they look at each other. It is possible, therefore, that *liking simply leads to stronger perceptual effects and to a higher activation level of the perceptual representation and therefore to more pronounced behavioral effects*. (Dijksterhuis and Bargh 2001, 31–32; my emphasis)

The cunning of this interpretation was the way in which it suggested that liking someone merely enhanced the imitator's attention to the model, thereby intensifying the activation of perceptual effects that augmented the tendency to imitation. In this way, Dijksterhuis and Bargh attempted to forestall an appeal to the role of intentional-strategic intentions or motives in producing such behavioral reactions.

The authors' use of the notion of "modules" in the phrase cited above, "*We do possess a set of moderating modules clearly separating us from fish and frogs,*" is also significant (Dijksterhuis and Bargh 2001, 28; my emphasis). They appear to have taken the term *module* from Fodor's influential book *The Modularity of Mind* (1983). According to Fodor, the mind was largely modular in structure. By this claim he meant that many of the most important mental systems, such as perception, were highly specialized, informationally encapsulated, domain-specific modules involving computational mechanisms that operated sub-personally and independently of higher cognitive functions. In adopting the concept of "moderating modules," such as the moderating influence of liking someone, Bargh and Dijksterhuis suggested that such moderators functioned as autonomous, computational representations in the mind-brain, working alongside all the other mental representations and computational processes they regarded as the engines of behavior. They offered a picture of the individual as a compendium of such modules, all of which functioned as non-intentional, nonconscious, sub-personal, information-processing systems. On this picture of the mind, the self was regarded as an aggregate of numerous independent modules that Bargh characterized as "selfish" because, he argued, each of them automatically and unconsciously pursued its own aims and end states without regard to the goals of all the others (Bargh and Huang 2009, 138; see also Bargh, Green, and Fitzsimons 2008).

Note that Bargh and Chartrand treated the moderators held to influence the outcome of automatic responses as add-ons to, or qualifiers of, perception-behavior sequences, not as intrinsic to automatic reactions. They understood moderators as contextual influences that occurred at a late stage in the sequence of information processing, influences that in an important sense obscured the more basic functions of importance, namely, the automatic, unintentional processes themselves. I shall have more to say about this topic in chapter 7. There we will see that Bargh appealed to the role of moderators as a way of deflecting criticism when confronted with questions concerning the robustness of his priming findings. It was always open to him or his colleagues to attribute replication failures not only, or not just, to slight differences in the experimental methods or procedures used, but to differences due to the influence of hitherto unidentified moderators in the original studies. But of course, the more it emerged that priming results appeared to be sensitive to such moderating contingencies, the less predictable were research findings, which made it hard to make generalizations from priming experiments.

In accounting for variations in imitation outcomes, Chartrand and her colleagues adopted similar strategies to those of Bargh and colleagues. They defended the default importance of the perception-behavior link in explaining the automaticity of mimicry, but also invoked the role of moderators to explain why it was that humans did not imitate everyone all the time. Thus, in a paper of 2003, Lakin and Chartrand reported findings allegedly proving that the desire to affiliate with someone increased participants' tendency to mimicry. They dismissed as unlikely the idea that these findings were due to intentional-motivational factors, appealing to the fact that significant postural mimicry occurred even among strangers. They therefore concluded that increased mimicry was due to a strengthened perception-behavior link, owing to the moderating influence of attention:

> Activating the desire to affiliate temporarily strengthened the perception-behavior link. Specifically, the desire to affiliate may cause people to pay more attention to what occurs in their social environments (i.e., they perceive more), which would result in a stronger relationship between perception and behavior. To the extent that this explanation is true, the perception-behavior link would mediate the effects demonstrated in the present studies. (Lakin and Chartrand 2003, 338)[10]

Over time Chartrand and her colleagues also invoked the influence of many other moderators to explain why imitation might not only be facilitated, but also sometimes inhibited. The moderators they identified included: the desire to be liked; the goal to affiliate; various self-construals; the role of gender differences in mimicry; and so on (for examples, see Chartrand and Jeffers 2003; Cheng and Chartrand 2003; Chartrand, Maddux, and Lakin 2005; van Baaren et al. 2009; Dalton, Chartrand, and Finkel 2010; Leander, Chartrand, and Wood 2011). Chartrand and her colleagues even began to use the word *strategy* to describe the way in which people used imitations flexibly in order to achieve certain goals. But in their hands the term *strategy* did not refer to the intentional use of certain tactics or schemes but to non-intentional, automatic processes. As Lakin, Chartrand, and Arkin put this point in a study of the effect of social

---

10. For related arguments about the role of attention in mimicry, see van Baaren et al. 2003a; 2003b; and Lakin, Chartrand, and Arkin 2008.

exclusion on the tendency to mimicry: "Although social interactions may always trigger some mimicry . . . selective mimicry following [social] exclusion would mean that mimicry is flexible and strategic despite the fact that it occurs without conscious awareness or intent" (Lakin, Chartrand, and Arkin 2008, 818). They added:

> The fact that mimicking happens automatically, without conscious awareness or intention, is evidence of the evolutionary criticality of the need to belong; this need is so pervasive that if belongingness could not have been pursued automatically, human ancestors might not have had enough cognitive resources to accomplish other important tasks . . . [N]on conscious mimicry . . . is an easy prosocial behavior that is not an intentional act of regaining favor, and it is an efficient and effective attempt to readjust a perceived drop in one's status with members of one's in-group [. . .] People whose need to belong is threatened do not necessarily mimic the first person they see; they take into account aspects of the situation and act accordingly, all unconsciously. (Lakin, Chartrand, and Arkin 2008, 821; see also Lakin and Chartrand 2003; Lakin et al. 2003; Chartrand, Maddux, and Lakin, 2005).

For these authors, as was also the case for Bargh and many other automaticity researchers, intentions and goal pursuits came apart as two independent processes or events. The authors therefore increasingly emphasized the flexibility and "strategic" nature of automatic behaviors when people pursued various goals, all the while insisting on the non-intentional character of those responses (Dalton et al. 2010; Leander, Chartrand, and Wood 2011; Leander, Chartrand, and Bargh 2012).[11]

---

11. An interesting challenge to the argument for the intentional-communicative nature of imitation, one that supports the general tendency of Chartrand and others to treat mimicry as unintentional, comes from the work of Leighton et al. (2010). In this paper, co-authored by Cecilia Heyes among others, the claim was made that "pro-social" priming had a larger effect on mimicry than did antisocial priming, that this effect was direct, and that it occurred without intention or conscious awareness. Leighton et al.'s experiments were designed to address three outstanding questions about the relationship between social attitudes and mimicry: (a) Do social attitudes influence mimicry directly, or indirectly by modulating the amount of attention given by the participant to the body movements of the model? The latter suggestion was of course Chartrand and Bargh's explanation, designed to counter Bavelas's intentional-communicative explanation of mimicry, with whose views, however, Leighton et al. did not engage; (b) How specific are these imitative effects: Do social attitudes influence the frequency with which participants or observers copy the specific movements of a model or merely the frequency with which they move the same part of the body? (c) Does mimicry that is modulated by social attitudes occur even when it is counter

Emotional Mimicry

Not surprisingly, Chartrand and her co-researchers continued to reject Bavelas's communicative explanation for postural mimicry, invoking the finding that mimicry occurred between strangers and when people were alone as decisive evidence against the latter's explanation (Chartrand, Maddux, and Lakin 2005, 339, 351; see also van Baaren et al. 2006, 432–33). They also continued to misunderstand and misrepresent Bavelas's wincing experiment: they failed to see the significance of the crucial role played by eye contact between the confederate and the participant in inducing imitation, and instead attributed the participant's mimicry simply to the enhanced visibility of the confederate's wincing expression. To repeat a passage quoted earlier, as Chartrand and colleagues observed in reference to Bavelas et al.'s experiment:

> During their research studies participants witnessed a painful accident to a confederate which resulted in a wince. It was found that the participants imitated the expressions of the confederate, especially when the wince was more visible to the participant. The more visible the expression of the confederate was to the participant, the more the participant imitated the expression. In other words, the easier it was to perceive the expression, the greater the effect of their own behavior. (Dijksterhuis, Chartrand, and Aarts 2007, 64)

Similarly, in a paper of 2009, Chartrand and van Baaren again attributed the participant's imitation of the experimenter's wincing behavior to the fact that, when the experimenter was turned toward the participant, the latter could perceive the victim better and accordingly winced in imitation because she vicariously experienced the same painful feelings (Chartrand and van Baaren 2009, 256–57).

But as we have seen, and as Bavelas herself pointed out in 2007 in a

---

to the participant's intention? It lies beyond the scope of this chapter to offer a detailed critique of Leighton et al.'s experiments and claims. Suffice it to say here that it is not obvious that the hand movements they studied by the "stimulus-response compatibility, reaction time paradigm" (Leighton et al. 2010, 906) were imitations; nor is it obvious that the movements studied were non-intentional. Bargh et al. (2012) cited Leighton et al.'s (2010) paper as providing support for the idea that, although several forms of automaticity were driven by the direct perception of environmental stimuli, moderators such as self-construals or social attitudes often intervened to mediate between perception and automatic responses.

devastating critique of all those researchers, such as Bargh and Chartrand, who had misdescribed and misunderstood her wincing experiment over the years, it was not the *visibility* of the wincing as such that played a determining role in the participant's tendency to imitate, but specifically the *eye-contact* condition: if the confederate performed the accident in such a way as to avert his eyes at the moment of pain, the participants observing the scene could see the confederate wincing but tended not to mimic his expression (Bavelas 2007).[12] To put this another way: If Chartrand's automatic mimicry theory had been correct, the participant's responses would have been the same regardless of the eye-contact condition: all that would have mattered was whether participants saw the experimenter's grimace of pain, which was identical in both conditions and equally visible. It was the eye contact between the experimenter and the participant that made the difference in the responses of the participants: the latter winced in the same way as the confederate if they exchanged glances with him. This point is what Chartrand and her colleagues failed to grasp when they argued that eye contact made the experimenter's wincing expression *more visible*, which is to say, easier for participants to *perceive*.

In her critique, Bavelas attributed the failure of Chartrand, Bargh and so many other imitation researchers to correctly report the findings of her wincing experiment to false "individualistic" theories of facial displays based on the assumptions of cognitive science (Bavelas 2007, 140–42; see also Bavelas and Coates 1992). Instead of understanding the communicative-strategic and social-interpersonal nature of such signals, she maintained, theorists wrongly attributed the effect of the latter to the automatic triggering of the observer's individual affective processes and hence treated the imitator's facial expressions as involuntary leakages or

12. Bavelas reported that only five out of thirty-nine publications correctly described the procedures and findings of her wincing experiment (if the procedures were described at all); of these five, two were by Fridlund and colleagues. Fridlund agreed with Bavelas that facial signals, including facial mimicries, were communicative signals that were sensitive to the social context in which they occurred, hence his grasp of the importance of eye contact in Bavelas's wincing experiment (Bavelas 2007, 137). Bavelas also pointed out that the behaviors regarded as motor mimicry in her studies were much more varied than literally imitative displays, because, in keeping with historical definitions of motor mimicry, she and her colleagues counted as imitative responses any behaviors indicative of pain, including vocalizations and certain head movements. She also noted that participants in the eye-contact condition sometimes included smiles mixed with their pain displays, which she and her team interpreted as forms of communication, "that is, as reassuring or face-saving smiles to the experimenter" (2007, 138).

"readouts" of their own matching internal emotional states. This insight was shrewd on Bavelas's part, because as we are about to see, when Chartrand and colleagues finally conceded that, exceptionally from the point of view of their automatic imitation theories, *emotional mimicry* could be considered an intentional-strategic and communicative signal after all, they did so in terms of Ekman's Basic Emotion Theory, which was premised on precisely such individualistic assumptions. In other words, in framing their new interpretation of emotional mimicry, Chartrand and her co-authors incoherently appealed to Ekman's Basic Emotion Theory of facial expression, a theory that was at odds with Bavelas's intentional-communicative understanding of postural signaling (and also at odds with Fridlund's behavioral-ecology approach to facial signaling).[13]

For example, in 2009 Chartrand and Rick van Baaren mentioned the work of researchers Kraut and Johnson, who had emphasized the role of audience effects in support of their claim that nonverbal behaviors served a communicative function (Chartrand and van Baaren 2009, 256; see also Chartrand and Dalton 2009, 471).[14] As far back as 1979, Robert Kraut and Robert Johnson had published the results of a study showing that bowlers smiled when they were socially engaged by observers but did not necessarily smile just because they had scored a strike. The authors had reported similar audience effects in other sports settings. The implication of those studies was that facial expressions served an interpersonal, social-communicative function, independently of what the actors were

13. Bavelas remarked in this regard: "I propose that it is primarily the tendency to see the individual as a natural unit of analysis that prevents our seeing the micro-social context that surrounds and profoundly influences each individual. Focusing on the individual creates an implicit border . . . which seems to limit our perceptual or conceptual field to mental rather than social processes. Even when researchers briefly step outside and notice what is happening around and in interaction with the individual, the focus soon retreats to the isolated individual. Both language and social interaction have been predominantly attributed to mental processes not just in the broader domains of linguistics and psychology, but even in those that one might expect to be especially interested in face-to-face dialogue, such as psycholinguistics and social psychology" (2007, 140). Bavelas quoted Kurt Danziger's remark that psychology's experimental methods "'isolated individuals from the social context of their existence and sought to establish timeless laws of individual behavior by analogy with the laws of natural science. Shared social meanings and relations were automatically broken up into the properties of separate individuals [versus] features of an environment that was external to each of them . . . Anything social became a matter of external influence that did not affect the identity of the individual under study'" (2007, 140–41, quoting Danziger 1990, 186–87).

14. In yet another publication Chartrand again failed to recognize the role of eye contact in Bavelas et al.'s wincing experiment (Chartrand and Dalton 2009, 472).

themselves feeling (Kraut and Johnson 1979). The significance of Kraut and Johnson's experiments had long been understood by Bavelas and Fridlund, both of whom had made use of them to justify their interpretations of facial behaviors as social-communicative signals (Bavelas et al. 1986; Fridlund 1994; see also Russell and Fernández-Dols 1997, in which contributors frequently cited Kraut and Johnson's experiments for the light they shed on the sociality and strategic-intentional nature of facial expressions).

Now Chartrand and van Baaren (2009) belatedly added the names of Kraut and Johnson to those of Bavelas and others who had stressed the importance of audience effects in ways that contradicted the view that mimicry was a passive, automatic response serving no communicative function. Chartrand and van Baaren tried to resolve the apparent discrepancy between these two positions by arguing that, *alone among forms of mimicry*, "emotional mimicry" could be considered a communicative phenomenon and hence an exception to their view that, since mimicry occurred in solitary situations, fundamentally it must be a non-communicative process. As they wrote:

> The results discussed previously ... — that mimicry does in fact communicate liking and understanding to the person being mimicked — further support the notion of mimicry as a communication tool. However, there are also studies that find mimicry among individuals who are alone and watching a videotape ... Why does mimicry occur under these circumstances? *The key to reconciling this apparent discrepancy may lie in whether the behavior being mimicked is related to feelings or emotions. When it comes to emotional contagion, there may be a strong communicative reason behind our tendency to imitate. In fact, the communication function may be limited to instances when emotions are involved.* In the videotape studies, the mimicry was not emotional in nature. Thus, although mimicry may result in increased empathy, liking, rapport and prosociality, it also occurs in situations where there is no human present (e.g., looking at a photograph or TV-screen). There needs to be an additional, more fundamental reason for mimicking that goes beyond a solely strategic communicative one. (Chartrand and van Baaren 2009, 257; my emphasis)

In this convoluted statement, Chartrand and van Baaren attempted to defuse the implications of findings concerning the communicative nature of imitation by a series of maneuvers:

First, they restricted claims for the communicative function of facial and postural displays to "emotional" mimicry, to the exclusion of other forms of imitation.

Second, in line with Ekman's Basic Emotion Theory, they treated the form of communication in emotional mimicry as involving leakages or readouts of internal emotional states.[15] The point at issue was that, on Ekman's Basic Emotion Theory, the emotions were held to be innate "affect programs" in the mind-brain that, under the right conditions, were involuntarily and unintentionally triggered to discharge signature behaviors, feelings, autonomic reactions, and above all facial expressions. On this model, facial expressions functioned as innately determined signals with whose meaning the receiver immediately resonated. Thus, according to Chartrand and van Baaren, when people experienced an emotion, especially a strong emotion, they were bound to leak it out in the form of micro-expressions and transmit it to others. This understanding was a far cry from the meaning of communication in Bavelas's or Fridlund's sense of the term, since for them communication was an intentional, strategic, and social interaction and as such not an obligatory, involuntary reaction.[16]

Third, Chartrand and van Baaren suggested that the imitations that had been captured when participants watched videotapes in the alone condition proved that such imitations were not emotional and hence could not be regarded as having a communicative function. To repeat their statement: "In the videotape studies, the mimicry was not emotional in nature" (Chartrand and van Baaren 2009, 257). It is difficult to disentangle this last

15. Chartrand and van Baaren (2009) did not cite Ekman, but all the papers they cited on facial and emotional mimicry, including neonatal imitation, were informed by Ekman's Basic Emotion Theory, which was the dominant emotion paradigm at this time.

16. In a discussion of emotional expressions as nonverbal communications, Lakin contrasted Ekman's Basic Emotion Theory and Fridlund's Behavioral Ecology View as alternative approaches to facial displays. She correctly observed of Fridlund's position that "this perspective suggests that facial displays do not reflect expressions of discrete, internal, emotional states but rather are messages that signal people's intentions within a particular context." But she then muddied the waters by continuing: "Fridlund (1994) argues that displays of facial expressions have evolved to meet specific selection pressures and that because they reveal information about people's intentions, they are displayed to serve people's social motives. Although this approach offers a different explanation for what "emotional" facial expressions mean, this perspective also suggests that facial expressions have evolved to serve specific purposes, can occur quickly within a particular context, and often occur without conscious intention or awareness" (Lakin 2006, 65). The last words in this passage embody the ambiguities that have haunted the discourse of automaticity throughout its recent history: did Lakin mean that facial displays could be forms of unconsciously intentional actions, or did she mean that because they occur outside conscious awareness, they must be considered non-intentional?

claim. The authors seemed to depend on a theoretical claim to the effect that, because people made facial imitations when they were alone, such imitations could not be communicative because there was no one there with whom to communicate. As such, they could not be emotional either, as per their stipulation that only emotional mimicries served a communicative function. Of course, Bavelas and Fridlund, among others, had a different interpretation of the performance of imitation in the alone condition, one that preserved the social-intentional framework for understanding these actions by assuming the existence of an implicit audience. But Chartrand and Bargh also seemed to depend on an empirical claim to the effect that, according to various laboratory studies of participants watching videotapes when alone, their mimicries of what they saw were not in fact emotional in nature. The trouble was that the laboratory studies they cited either contradicted or failed to prove their point.[17]

Fourth and finally, according to Chartrand and van Baaren's reasoning, because mimicry occurred in the alone condition and therefore served no communicative function, they concluded that there needed to be an "additional, more fundamental reason for mimicking that goes beyond a solely strategic communicative one" (Chartrand and van Baaren 2009, 257). The fundamental reason they had in mind was the idea that, primordially, mimicry was not a communicative action but a passive, nonintentional, automatic behavior that depended on the direct perception-behavior link posited by Chartrand and Bargh ten years earlier. As the authors went on to state:

> Chartrand and Bargh (1999) argued that nonconscious mimicry is a passive and automatic response. They based this argument on the results of funnel debriefings at the end of the experiments that were designed to probe for awareness of the mimicry. Participants indicated no awareness

---

17. Of the studies Chartrand and van Baaren cited, Bavelas et al. (1986) did not rule out the possibility that the observers' wincing at the sight of the ostensibly wounded confederate might have had an emotional component, but they did insist on the independent communicative function of the imitation; Hsee et al. (1990) was an experimental study of emotional contagion in which the facial expressions of the participants were videotaped and evaluated for their emotional content as they responded to various actual or taped affective scenarios, so it is hard to see in what sense this publication supported Chartrand and van Baaren's claim for the nonemotional nature of videotaped imitations; Lakin and Chartrand (2003) was a study of mimicry that did not attempt to evaluate the participants' emotional reactions; and the reference to van Baaren et al.'s paper (2007), given in the text, was not provided in the paper's bibliography, and I have been unable to identify it.

that they mimicked their interaction partners. Moreover, mimicry occurred in their studies under minimal conditions, among strangers with no goal to affiliate with each other. Thus, they concluded that mimicry must not depend on the presence of a communication or affiliation goal during the interaction. They suggested that a "perception–behavior link" might be the mechanism driving mimicry, at least under these "minimal conditions." That is, mimicry may be an automatic result of how our brains are wired. They argued that due to a strong link between perception and action, observing a behavior increases the chances of overtly or covertly copying it. (Chartrand and van Baaren 2009, 257)

In short, by the first decade of the 2000s, Chartrand and her colleagues were finding ways to accommodate new findings about "emotional" imitation without undermining their perception-behavior theory's basic premises. However, they would soon find matters closing in on them as opposing views of imitation began to disturb their claims.

The Contextual Sensitivity of Mimicry

Some hints of the disturbances to come emerged from within the priming field itself, when on the basis of experiments demonstrating the influence of individual motivation on priming outcomes, the well-established researcher Joseph Cesario and colleagues questioned Bargh's direct perception-behavior theory. Cesario, Plaks, and Higgins extended their critique to Bargh and Chartrand's explanation of mimicry, suggesting that here, too, the Chameleon Effect was not the result of a simple resonance between primes and behavior but depended on the overall context of the situation, including the participants' overriding goals as well as the affordances of the environment (Cesario, Plaks, and Higgins 2006). I will have more to say about this development in the next chapter.

Other findings during the same period brought the question of the validity of Bargh and Chartrand's perception-behavior approach even closer to home. In particular, several emotion researchers began to focus on the contextual sensitivity of facial displays in ways that raised critical questions about the viability of the Chartrand-Bargh perception-behavior theory. Among important publications in this development was a paper in which emotion scientist Brian Parkinson undertook a detailed comparison between Ekman's Basic Emotion Theory and Fridlund's Behavioral Ecology View, concluding that the preponderance of the evidence favored

Fridlund's position (Parkinson 2005). Parkinson thereby helped stimulate a revival of interest in the question of the intentional-strategic nature of facial displays. He also paid attention to Bavelas's long-misrepresented experiments on mimicry, including her wincing experiment, which he described correctly by noting the crucial role of eye contact between confederate and participant in determining whether or not the participant imitated the confederate's facial expression of pain.

Parkinson's paper gave a boost to the intentional-communicative view of facial expression as proposed by Bavelas and Fridlund. Unfortunately, the significance of their work was somewhat lost on various emotion researchers as they began to investigate more closely the social context of emotional displays. The trouble was that, almost without exception, those researchers tried to *combine* Ekman's Basic Emotion Theory with Fridlund's and Bavelas's competing intentional-communicative view of facial displays in ways that were fundamentally incoherent. For instance, Parkinson himself never broke completely with the assumptions of Ekman's theory. The result was that, even after grappling with Fridlund's views, his publications continued to present a fusion of incompatible ideas (see Parkinson, Fischer, and Manstead 2005; Parkinson 2011, Parkinson and Simons 2012; Leys 2017, 279–80, 286–88). The same was true of other emotion researchers in this period. If one followed Ekman in believing that authentic, spontaneous facial expressions were involuntary readouts of discrete, internal emotional states, then it was not clear how, without contradiction, one could also claim that facial displays were not emotional readouts but forms of intentional-strategic communication. But several emotion researchers tried to amalgamate these irreconcilable positions.

Among psychologists committed to a contradictory blend of Ekman's Basic Emotion Theory and Fridlund's opposing Behavioral Ecology View of facial displays were Agneta Fischer, Shlomo Hareli, and Ursula Hess. Together and separately, these researchers began to argue, as Chartrand and van Baaren (2009) had done, that "emotional mimicry" had a special status among imitations because it was an intentional-communicative form of expression. On this basis they challenged Chartrand and Bargh's "classic" or "standard" perception-behavior theory of imitation, or what Hess and Fischer called the Matched Motor Hypothesis (Hess and Fischer 2013, 143). Hess and Fischer rested their arguments on this point on an assumed convergence between Ekman's Basic Emotions Theory and the more social-communicative approach to certain facial displays proposed by Bavelas and Fridlund, with all the confusions that such an approach entailed. As a result,

Hess and Fischer fudged certain important issues, such as what they meant by the term *emotion* independently of facial displays, or how they distinguished between genuine versus false expressions of emotion—issues that Fridlund had decisively analyzed in his critique of Ekman's approach to the emotions (Fridlund 1994) but whose arguments these authors ignored.

Hess and Fischer (2013) made a distinction between "emotional mimicry" and "behavioral" mimicry in ways that echoed the distinction Chartrand and van Baaren (2009) had already suggested. According to that distinction, emotional mimicry was intentional and communicative in ways that other behavioral mimicries, such as the foot-tapping and face-touching imitations discussed by Chartrand and Bargh (1999), were not. The distinction had the unfortunate effect of implying that the kinds of postural mimicries Bavelas had studied were not intentional—precisely the opposite of Bavelas's position. So, in essential ways Hess and Fischer's challenge to Chartrand and Bargh on the nature of imitation fell short.[18]

Nevertheless, muddled and incoherent as their analyses were, their publications served the purpose of raising questions about Chartrand and Bargh's approach to mimicry by emphasizing the importance of social context and the communicative-intentional nature of some behavioral displays, specifically emotional mimicry. With reference to Bargh's and Chartrand's work, Hess and Fischer commented:

> It has been implicitly assumed that emotional mimicry can be considered simply one of the different forms of behavioral mimicry . . . thus implying that the perception of a specific emotion display leads to the imitation of that display, the only difference being that in emotional mimicry the imitated behavior represents an emotional signal . . . Following the Matched Motor Hypothesis, the movements of the face are spontaneously copied, independently of the intentions of the observer and the expresser. (Hess and Fischer 2013, 143)

But the authors rejected those assumptions on the grounds that, unlike behavioral mimicry, emotional expressions are "intrinsically meaning-

---

18. Hess's attempts to synthesize Ekman's Basic Emotion Theory and Fridlund's Behavioral Ecology View of facial displays went back to the 1990s. See for example Hess, Banse, and Kappas (1995); Hess, Philippot, and Blairy (1998). Bavelas (2007) included Hess et al. 1998 among the list of publications that had given an inaccurate description of her eye-contact wincing experiment.

ful . . . [W]hen a person shows an emotion, information about the person's interpretation of the event and his or her behavioral intentions is also transmitted . . . We contend that the dispositions and intensions of the expressers are crucial to emotional mimicry." On this basis, the authors argued that "emotion recognition naturally occurs within a social context. We suggest that emotional mimicry is related to the understanding of an emotion in context and is involved in regulating one's relation with the other person, rather than being the synchronization of meaningless individual muscle actions" (Hess and Fischer 2013, 143, 144–46).[19] In an overview of the literature on emotional mimicry, these authors repeated these claims, stating that emotional mimicry was "not a process based on the blind copying of observed facial actions but on inferences about the emotional intentions of others . . . In other words, emotional mimicry involves the interpretation of signals, conveying emotional intentions in a specific context" (Hess and Fischer 2014, 51–52).[20]

The Sociality of Chameleons, or, The Watching Eyes Effect

There is a sense in which, in advocating an intentional-communicative view of emotional signaling, Hess, Fischer, and their associates were merely reinventing a wheel devised by others many years before, adding little in the way of usable empirical findings because of the confusions inherent in their work, and providing even less in the way of theoretical insights. Their publications on this topic have involved such a tissue of poorly formulated claims that it would be a thankless task to try and sort them out, and impossible to do so within the confines of this chapter.

19. I note that Hess and Fischer (2013, 147) mentioned that eye contact between the expresser and the observer was required for the imitation of an emotional expression, although they did not cite Bavelas's wincing experiment in proof of this view, but an unpublished paper by Rychlowska, Zinner, and Niedenthal (2011) (it appears this paper was never published). I note also that, in now acknowledging that eye contact was crucial for emotional mimicry, Hess and Fischer (2013) ignored the fact that mimicry also occurs in the solitary condition; they therefore appeared to reject the idea of an implicit audience. We might put it that they literalized the idea of audience effects in terms that were at odds with both Bavelas's and Fridlund's views. Throughout their paper, they endorsed the idea of discrete, basic emotions, an assumption that rendered their arguments incoherent.

20. The authors cited Cesario, Plaks, and Higgins's (2006) motivated view of automatic behavior, among other sources, in support of their position (Hess and Fischer 2014). See also Hess and Hareli 2016; 2017; 2018; and Hess and Fischer 2017, in which these authors continued to offer confused analyses of the sociality of facial signals in terms that showed they had learned very little from Fridlund's work.

Their work is of interest, however, because of the pressure it began to exert on Chartrand and her colleagues. In particular, in 2015 we find Korrina Duffy and Chartrand agreeing with Hess and Fischer (2013) that emotional mimicry must be an intentional-communicative action:

> *Emotional mimicry* occurs when someone mimics the emotional expression(s) of another. Although emotional mimicry occurs automatically and nonconsciously, it is moderated by affiliation goals [Hess and Fischer, 2013; Hess and Fischer, 2014; Fischer, Becker, and Veenstra 2012]. For example, offensive facial expressions are typically not mimicked, perhaps because they do not serve affiliative goals (i.e., watching someone smell a disgusting odor does not elicit mimicry of the disgust reaction, but watching someone receive a compliment does elicit mimicry of the complimented person's smile) [Fischer, Becker, and Veenstra 2012]. These findings suggest that emotional mimicry is not solely based on mere perception but also on the emotional intentions within a specific context [Hess and Fischer 2013]. This is consistent with behavioral mimicry research that suggests that mimicry is not merely a consequence of the link between perception and behavior, but rather a nonconsciously activated behavior motivated by affiliation goals. (Duffy and Chartrand 2015, 112; their emphasis)[21]

Moreover, Duffy and Chartrand finally appeared to understand the significance of eye contact in Bavelas's wincing experiment. "Eye contact facilitates motor mimicry," they observed with a reference to Bavelas et al.'s wincing experiment, adding:

> But exactly why this happens has only recently been explored [Wang and Hamilton 2014; Bateson, Nettle, and Roberts 2006]. In a voluntary mimicry paradigm, participants were instructed to mimic the hand movements of a filmed actress [Wang and Hamilton 2014]. Automatic mim-

---

21. Duffy and Chartrand (2015) implied that Chartrand, Maddux, and Lakin (2005) had viewed imitations as the product of "motivations" and therefore as intentional-communicative actions. But Chartrand, Maddux, and Lakin had explicitly defended the opposite position: they had rejected Bavelas's views of the intentional-communicative view of postural mimicry (Bavelas et al. 1986; Bavelas et al. 1987), arguing that the mere perception or act of seeing another person had direct "unmediated" effects on behavior, causing "unintentional, nonconscious" mimetic effects (Chartrand, Maddux, and Lakin 2005, 334, 338–39).

icry of the hand movement was enhanced if the actress gazed directly ahead at the participant immediately before the hand action [Wang and Hamilton 2014]. However, if the actress averted her gaze or gazed to [*sic*, at] the acting hand immediately before the hand action, then mimicry was not enhanced [Wang and Hamilton 2014]. The authors suggest that this eye contact enhancement of mimicry is similar to an audience effect and may come from a goal to maintain a prosocial reputation [Wang and Hamilton 2014]. (Duffy and Chartrand 2015, 113)

In fact, two years earlier Chartrand and Lakin had also cited experiments by Judith Holler and Katie Wilkin (2011), Suresh Ramanathan and Ann McGill (2007), and Yin Wang, Roger Newport, and Antonia Hamilton (2011) on the question of how eye contact affected mimicry (Chartrand and Lakin 2013, 293).[22] Among the several references to the influence of eye contact on behavior cited by Chartrand and her colleagues, Melissa Bateson, Daniel Nettle, and Gilbert Roberts (2006) had reported that an image of a pair of eyes, posted in a psychology department coffee room, led members of the department to pay nearly three times as much for their drinks compared to when there was no such image. The conclusion was that the sense of being seen—if only by an image of eyes—was sufficient to induce the members to act differently (Bateson, Nettle, and Roberts 2006). In another of Duffy and Chartrand's references, in the course of presenting findings by themselves and others on the role of gestures as accompaniments to speech in face-to-face encounters, Holler and Wilkin (2011) had emphasized the influence of being seen by another in a person's tendency to imitate. Along similar lines, Ramanathan and McGill (2007) had demonstrated that participants' tendency to mimicry, when watching a video, was influenced by whether they were alone during the experience, in the "mere" presence of another person, or in the full social presence and actual sight of another. These researchers had concluded

22. Thus, Chartrand and Lakin had observed: "Bavelas et al. (1986) have argued that mimicry serves a communicative function because mimicry of pained expressions is more likely when eye contact is made; this suggests that feelings are being shared between interaction partners, which is characteristic of empathy" (Chartrand and Lakin 2013, 293). But once again Chartrand and Lakin misdescribed the import of Bavelas et. al.'s 1986 paper on wincing. Bavelas et al. had not suggested that in the wincing experiment, feelings or emotions were being shared owing to the effect of eye contact between confederate and participant. Rather, they had argued that the participant's mimicry of the confederate's facial wincing occurred as a result of eye contact because it served to communicate the participant's message: "I *Show* How You Feel" (Bavelas et al. 1986).

that participants' shared experiences, based on eye contact and being seen by another, caused a convergence of judgment between the interactants through processes of imitation and emotional contagion.

Likewise, Wang, Newport, and Hamilton (2011) had presented evidence concerning the influence of eye contact in boosting people's social standing. And in a related study, Wang and Hamilton (2014) had again emphasized the influence of eye contact on mimicry. They had shown the different effects on participants' tendencies to imitation when they were interacting with a model, depending on whether the model's gaze was aimed directly at them or averted during her performance of hand movements. The experiments showed that a model's direct gaze significantly facilitated the participants' hand imitations as compared to an averted gaze. Further experiments suggested that the effects could not be attributed to attention alone but that eye contact was the crucial component driving the mimicry (Wang and Hamilton 2014, 5). According to Wang and Hamilton, as reported by Duffy and Chartrand, "this eye contact enhancement of mimicry is similar to an audience effect and may come from a goal to maintain a prosocial reputation" (Duffy and Chartrand 2015, 113).

In the studies on eye contact cited by Duffy and Chartrand, only Holler and Wilkin (2011) and Wang and Hamilton (2014) referred to Bavelas's experiments on the influence of eye contact on postural and facial displays, and only Holler and Wilkin (2011) cited Fridlund's related work. The other psychologists whose work on eye contact I have mentioned tended to conduct their experiments in ignorance of the rich history of research on audience effects that had been conducted by Bavelas, Fridlund, and others.[23] This ignorance is a pity because, had they been aware of such work, it might have saved those researchers from certain analytic errors. Among them was a tendency to literalize the presence of the beholder. By saying so I mean the following: It is of course the case that in many of the reported experiments on eye contact and mimicry, increased sociality led to a greater frequency or intensity of displays. For example, when Ramanathan and McGill (2007) assessed the differences in participants' moment-to-moment retrospective evaluations of an experience depend-

---

23. I note that Wang and Hamilton (2014) attributed to Bavelas et al. (1986) the view that the enhancement of mimicry under the influence of the gaze increased the participants' prosociality and empathy, which was not Bavelas et al.'s argument (Wang and Hamilton 2014, 749). Holler and Wilkin (2011), however, understood the import of both Bavelas's and Fridlund's communicative-intentional analysis of affective communication.

ing on whether they were alone or in the presence of another person, they found that exposure to the sight of another person yielded the greatest degree of rapport among the participants. Similarly, Wang, Newport, and Hamilton (2011) demonstrated that a direct gaze had a prosocial effect by potentiating the participants' spontaneous mimicry of hand movements.[24]

But many years earlier, Chovil and Fridlund had argued that the augmentation of such effects was not inevitable. In a 1991 paper Chovil, who had been co-author with Bavelas in several studies of the communicative function of mimicry, had presented the results of an experiment in which she had controlled for differing degrees of sociality when participants listened to a particularly harrowing story in one of four conditions: (a) alone, from an audiotape recording; (b) from another person, separated from view by a partition; (c) alone, over the telephone; and (d) talking to another subject, face-to-face. The participants' facial displays—largely wincing and grimacing—were recorded using visible facial coding. Chovil had then obtained sociality ratings of the recordings from the four conditions by asking a separate group of raters to estimate the "psychological presence" afforded by each condition, where the conditions were ordered according to their estimated degree of sociality. Her results showed that the mimicry of facial displays increased with rated sociality, thereby providing evidence in favor of a communicative view of facial displays (Chovil 1991).

In her paper, Chovil had suggested that the readout paradigm of facial expressions associated with Ekman's views, and the communicative view of facial displays associated with Bavelas's position, offered different predictions about the impact of interpersonal contexts and audiences on facial behavior. She had argued that on the readout model, the presence of other people might make participants moderate or inhibit otherwise "spontaneous" expressions of emotion of the kind we make when we are alone, suggesting that in the presence of others the intensity and frequency of facial mimicries and displays would be *reduced*. In contrast, the

---

24. The effects of "watching eyes" on people's "prosocial" (i.e., cooperative) behaviors have been the topic of many experiments appearing to demonstrate that images of eyes trigger feelings of being observed and hence cause participants to behave more prosocially, as measured by the generosity of their performances in dictator games or other kinds of social interaction. But several recent studies have failed to replicate such "watching eyes" findings (see Rotella et al. 2021 for a recent failed replication and discussion). My takeaway from the mixed results of such experiments is that contextual factors of various kinds, including individual sensitivity to cues of observation, the degree of participants' preexisting prosociality, and other variables influence the effects of being observed, as Chovil and Fridlund (1991) argued many years before (see above).

communicative view predicted that, on the whole, there would be fewer facial movements in the unobserved situations (though not none) than in those in which an amenable addressee or audience was present, suggesting that in the presence of others the intensity and frequency of facial displays would be facilitated or *enhanced*. Her findings confirmed the latter prediction.

Buck, whose readout views of emotions I have already mentioned, had contested Chovil's claims because he took her to mean that sociality always boosted facial displays; he had cited evidence that contradicted this view (Buck 1991). But as Chovil and Fridlund in a jointly authored response to Buck had observed, the communicative view of displays, including imitative displays, did not predict that such displays must always increase in number and intensity with increased sociality. In Chovil's study, increased sociality led to greater frequency of displays because, Chovil and Fridlund had suggested, the more-social situations were closer to face-to-face encounters (Chovil and Fridlund 1991). But as Fridlund had gone on to emphasize, in other social contexts, such as the social setting of a game, where being able to maintain a poker face can be important, the intensity of facial displays might decrease (Fridlund 1994, 164). In short, Fridlund had made clear that it is important not to be too literal about the relationship between facial behavior and sociality: the nature of facial displays always depends on the context of the interaction as well as on the nature of the relationship between the interactants, with the result that, while in some social conditions the intensity of facial movements might be reduced, in other ones they might be potentiated.

But such nuances seem to have been lost on most of the researchers who later began studying audience effects, specifically the influence of eye contact on mimicry. Their findings were interesting and important, even if, without their realizing it, in some cases they were merely repeating the kinds of experiments that had been performed long ago. But owing to their narrow research programs and ignorance of long-standing work on the role of audience effects in interpersonal communication, they did not confront alternative ways of thinking about such topics, with the result that, from the perspective of those other alternatives, their theoretical formulations were riddled with confusions and errors.[25] Such failings were

25. See for example papers by Ponari et al. (2012); Rychlowska et al. (2014); and Krumhuber, Likowski, and Weyers (2014), cited by Duffy and Chartrand (2015), each of which relied on Ekman's Basic Emotion Theory in experiments on the relationship

certainly true of Chartrand herself: whatever adjustments she has made in recent years to her understanding of imitation, she has been so shaped by Bargh's claims regarding the existence of a direct perception-behavior link that, even when she tries to revise her position toward a more intentional-communicative framework, she seems unable to make a clean break with the former paradigm.[26]

What can be said, however, is that through the recent emphasis on the role of eye contact and audience effects by imitation researchers such as Chartrand and others, there is a sense in which Bavelas and Fridlund's intentional-communicative views have at last begun to receive some sort of recognition and even vindication.

Alan Alda's Intentions

An inadvertently comic moment occurred in the course of Chartrand and Bargh's work on imitation when the basic claims they were making about the automatic, unintentional nature of mimicry were directly contradicted in plain sight. In a video made for the PBS series *The Human Spark*, the actor Alan Alda participated in a replica of one of the postural studies on which Chartrand and Bargh had built the case for the Chameleon Effect (Chartrand and Bargh 1999). In the experiment, Alda is seen participating with a stranger, actually one of Chartrand's confederates, in the task of describing the contents of some photographs together. Although Alda was not aware of this at the time, and viewers themselves might not notice it, during one of the shared photo-description tasks, the confederate quietly mimics Alda's mannerisms, postures, and gestures. When the photograph task is over, Alda is invited to leave the room and to sit on any one of four chairs lined up in a row in the corridor. Someone's backpack and a sweater occupy a chair at one end, and Alda chooses a chair two seats away.

---

between emotions and facial mimicry, without any acknowledgment or apparent awareness that a debate over the validity of Ekman's claims had been ongoing for several years.

26. Thus, Duffy and Chartrand argued that unconscious imitation helped produce trust, liking, rapport, emotional empathy, social bonds, and other positive effects, and in doing so played an important role in the development and maintenance of moral behavior (Duffy and Chartrand 2017a, 455–56). It is hardly surprising that the two scholars invited to comment on Duffy and Chartrand's views were skeptical about such claims, largely because of the obvious fact that imitation can have negative as well as positive effects on people's emotions and behavior (Goodwin 2017, 466; Nahmias 2017, 478; see also Duffy and Chartrand 2017b).

When Chartrand joins Alda a few moments later, she tells him that what she wanted to see was where he sat, whether he would choose a chair close to the one with the backpack and sweater on it, or whether he would sit on a chair further away. Alda of course had chosen a seat further away. He asks Chartrand: "Would you like to know why I chose that chair?" and when Chartrand says "Sure," he says: "To make a better shot for the cameraman!" Chartrand laughs nervously, and Alda adds: "You can't bring in an actor to do this!" Chartrand replies: "A good point, I didn't anticipate this!" Alda states that his first impulse was that he wasn't going to sit next to the chair with the personal clothing "because they were someone's personal things and then I would have to be next to a real person later, you know, and I don't want that." Chartrand laughs again, and Alda goes on: 'No, but the main reason . . . was that if I sat in that chair all the way over then he [the cameraman] could get a shot that didn't include the messy chair, which would be better for the scene, you know.'"

Chartrand again laughs and says: "You are not our typical participant, to be honest." She explains that she and the confederate had expected Alda to sit near the backpack because, according to the Chameleon Effect theory, Alda's being mimicked during the photo-description task should have made him experience prosocial feelings, causing him to want to sit closer to the already occupied chair. But instead, as a professional actor Alda intentionally selected a chair that avoided being near another person and, just as important, gave the cameraman a clean shot of him.

In short, Alda had good reasons for acting in the way he did, reasons and intentions that had nothing to do with being mimicked and whose influence was precisely what Chartrand's theory denied—evidence, if more were needed, that the Chameleon Theory was based on false premises.

In the next chapter I discuss various developments in social psychology in the first decade of the twenty-first century, prior to the publication of Doyen et al.'s (2012) experiment challenging the findings of Bargh, Chen, and Burrows's (1996) famous elderly priming study. My aim is to analyze the criticisms that began to be raised about the basic presuppositions of Bargh's theory of automaticity. My chapter title—"A Theory in Crisis?"—is meant to convey the growing sense that priming theory had entered a period of trouble. The question that interests me is how Bargh began to respond to the challenges he faced.

6

A Theory in Crisis?

Unconscious Thought Theory

An important development in social psychology bearing on the theme of automaticity was the rise of Unconscious Thought Theory. If, as automaticity theorists claimed, relegating so many actions and behaviors to nonintentional, automatic unconscious processes was actually an adaptive and efficient thing for the mind to do, why not include all the complex higher mental functions among those processes? Was it possible that the unconscious mind was better at solving complex problems than the conscious mind? Received opinion held that unconscious processes were intellectually much simpler than conscious ones. But if, as was widely accepted, the conscious mind had limited processing capacity, then it would make sense that for much of our thinking and actions we would rely instead on our unconscious processes, which were held to suffer from no such capacity restrictions. The general idea was that analyzing the reasons for our decisions can make us focus attention on nonoptimal criteria, whereas letting our unconscious thought system make the choices for us produces superior outcomes. This notion was what the Dutch psychologists Ap Dijksterhuis and Loran Nordgren set out to demonstrate.

At the start of his career, Dijksterhuis had undertaken a series of priming studies whose results challenged "rational choice theories" that attributed human behavior to conscious intentions or reasons. His research was influenced by Bargh's claims regarding the existence of an automatic link between perception and behavior. Thus, Dijksterhuis and colleagues

I have borrowed the title of this chapter from Chivers 2019.

conducted several experiments on the behavioral effects of primes on stereotypes, mental abilities, and behaviors. Among those experiments was one that appeared to confirm Bargh, Chen, and Burrows's elderly priming study (Dijksterhuis et al. 1998) — although as we shall see in a moment, there were questions about whether it indeed did so (Katzko 2006). One of Dijksterhuis's best-known studies claimed that participants exposed to primes associated with the idea of intelligence, such as the word "professor," performed better on a Trivial Pursuit test of intelligence than participants primed with words connoting a lack of intelligence, such as the words "soccer hooligan" (Dijksterhuis and van Knippenberg 1998). In another experiment, Dijksterhuis primed habitual and unhabitual bicycle users with the goal to travel. The participants were then asked to respond to various location words on a computer screen (for example, the word *university*), each followed by words connoting a method of transportation (for example, the word *bicycle*). The participants' task was to indicate as quickly and accurately as possible whether the method of transportation constituted a realistic mode of travel to the previously presented location. The results appeared to show that habitual cyclists responded more rapidly to the word *bicycle* than unhabitual bike users, but only after being activated with the goal to travel. The findings were interpreted to mean that habitual behaviors were linked to environmental events via the mental representations of the higher goals they served, in accordance with Bargh's views (Aarts and Dijksterhuis 2000a; cf. Aarts and Dijksterhuis 2000b; see also Dijksterhuis and Bargh 2001; Bargh and Ferguson 2000; and Chartrand and Bargh 2002).

On the basis of these and related studies, in 2004 Dijksterhuis sketched what he came to call "Unconscious Thought Theory." His hypothesis was that conscious thinking was "maladaptive when making complex decisions" compared to unconscious processes, which enjoyed unlimited cognitive capacity. He therefore challenged the "fashionable" view that the unconscious was a relatively stupid system that could not perform in an efficient way (Dijksterhuis 2004, 586). In his paper, Dijksterhuis reported the results of several new experiments in support of his claims. In these, participants were presented with a complex decision problem, such as deciding on the basis of a substantial list of features of apartments, potential roommates, and automobiles, which alternatives they preferred, where what counted as the right or "best" decision was based on the normative judgment of "experts" in the relevant domain. In one condition, the randomly assigned participants were asked to make their decisions immediately after being presented with the various features; in a second, "conscious thought" condition, participants were given a few minutes to think about the features before making their choices; and in a third, "unconscious thought" condition, participants were distracted for a few minutes before they made their selections, the idea being that the process of distraction prevented them from making their decisions on the basis of conscious thought. The findings appeared to show that the unconscious thinkers made the best decisions because, Dijksterhuis suggested, unconscious thought led to "clearer, more polarized, and more integrated representations in memory" (Dijksterhuis 2004, 586).[1]

In his 2004 paper Dijksterhuis did not go so far as to propose that the unconscious mind could be left to deal with making hard decisions while the conscious mind tackled easier problems, nor did he suggest that consciousness was rather stupid and the unconscious was smart. He argued instead that too much depended on the kinds of problems to be solved to make such claims. But he did conclude that the unconscious was good at making complex decisions and recommended: "When faced with complex decisions such as where to work or where to live, do not think too much consciously. Instead, after a little initial conscious information acquisition, avoid thinking about it consciously. Take your time and let the unconscious deal with it" (Dijksterhuis 2004, 597). By 2006, however, these reservations were set aside when Dijksterhuis and Nordgren formally launched their Unconscious Thought Theory. They challenged traditional views concerning the superiority of conscious deliberation in decision-making by arguing that decisions about complex matters were best left to the unconscious (Dijksterhuis and Nordgren 2006).

Although Dijksterhuis and Nordgren's claims were taken up and informed many research projects, there was an immediate pushback against

---

1. See Dijksterhuis (2004, 589) for a description of the distraction task designed to block conscious thinking after participants saw the list of features but before they made their decisions. Note that, in the study of apartment decisions, Dijksterhuis reported that the hypothesized unconscious effect was not always found, and indeed in his first two experiments Dijksterhuis himself reported no statistically significant differences in findings between the primed and the unprimed conditions (González-Vallejo et al. 2008, 238). His experiments followed on from studies by Wilson and Schooler, who had tested the responses of participants to the task of evaluating various strawberry jams under various conditions, such as whether they were allowed time to analyze the reasons for their selections or not, and had concluded that conscious thinkers made less accurate evaluations (Wilson and Schooler 1991). This is the same Timothy Wilson who published with Richard Nisbett the famous (or infamous) article "Telling More Than We Can Know" (1977).

their work, and several of the criticisms raised—at once empirical, methodological, and conceptual—anticipated the charges that would subsequently be leveled against Bargh's priming research. Among the complaints were:

1. Unconscious Thought Theory made too stark an opposition between conscious and unconscious processes. This opposition was inherent in many dual-system (or dual-process) theories of the kind that already existed and that Kahneman would propose in 2011. For some time, critics of such dual-system theories had objected that the proposed systems dichotomy could not be sustained and that a "unimodal" or single mental system explained the phenomena better (see Melnikoff and Bargh 2018a for a recent summary of the relevant literature). González-Vallejo et al. (2008) added to the critical literature by noting that Richard Shiffrin, one of the architects of the distinction between conscious-intentional and unconscious-non-intentional or automatic processing, had observed that it was impossible to make a definitive differentiation between the two processes because tasks were never fully conscious (or attentive) or fully automatic (González-Vallejo et al. 2008, 284; Shiffrin 1997).

2. Unconscious Thought Theory's interpretation of the capacity principle, according to which unconscious thought had a much larger capacity than conscious thought, was based on a misunderstanding of Miller's original discussion of human capacity (Miller 1956). Dijksterhuis and Nordgren calculated that the processing capacity of consciousness was limited to about 40–60 bits per second, whereas the total processing capacity of conscious and unconscious processes combined was an enormous 11,200,000 bits (Dijksterhuis and Nordgren 2006). It followed from such calculations that the unconscious had almost unlimited capacity. The authors based their claims on George Miller's earlier discussion of the limited capacity of short-term memory (Miller 1956). But according to critics, Dijksterhuis and Nordgren failed to realize that Miller's units of information were "chunks," not bits (González-Vallejo et al. 2008, 286), so that Dijksterhuis and Nordgren's calculations were way off the mark. In any case, as Shiffrin had argued (1997), capacity arguments were insufficient for differentiating unconscious from conscious thought (González-Vallejo et al. 2008, 285–86).

3. Several of the experiments performed by Dijksterhuis and his colleagues could not be replicated (Acker 2008; Newell, Wong, and Cheung 2009; Payne et al. 2008; Warroquier et al. 2009). The defenders of Unconscious Thought Theory countered by arguing that replication attempts

generally found no difference between the decision quality of conscious versus unconscious thought (Nordgren and Dijksterhuis 2011, 626–627; Bargh 2011, 639). But this reply did not address the question of whether decisions performed by unconscious thought were actually superior to those carried out consciously, the major claim of Unconscious Thought Theory.

4. There were problems with the methods used by the Unconscious Thought theorists to assess the lack of awareness during the participants' decision-making process. In effect, critics suggested that the Unconscious Thought effect was an artifact of experimental design, because participants quickly formed "online" impressions of the decision alternatives while they received the information, as opposed to forming the evaluations during the distraction period (Lassiter et al. 2009; Warroquier et al. 2009; for counterarguments see Strick et al. 2011). Critics also objected to the researchers' dependence on the evaluations of "experts" to assess the quality of the participants' various decisions, arguing that those experts often used standards of utility and optimality which did not reflect the factors influencing real-life choices.

5. The application of the null-hypothesis significance testing was erroneous in some of the experiments cited as evidence.

6. The idea that unconscious thought did not follow the strict rules of conscious thought was questionable, as were the claims that unconscious thought was superior to conscious thought in solving creative tasks (González-Vallejo et al. 2008).

In 2011, a special issue of the well-known journal *Social Cognition* was devoted to the topic of Unconscious Thought Theory. The special issue was put together by Nordgren and Dijksterhuis, so it is not surprising that most of the contributors defended the theory, even as some of them attempted to complicate claims about the role of unconscious thought, for example by identifying several moderators that helped explain the mixed results across various studies (Strick et al. 2011). The lone exception to the general support for the theory was a paper by Ben Newell and Tim Rakow (2011) in which the authors reported the results of a Bayesian reanalysis of sixteen experiments, only one of which found any significant advantages to unconscious thought. Their conclusion was that the period of distraction used to prevent conscious thought in the decision-making process did not improve decision-making—a finding that the editors reported without comment, except to note the finding that the period of distraction did not benefit *or hinder* decision-making.

The leadoff paper in the issue was by Bargh, who adopted an uncompromising defense of Unconscious Thought Theory in terms that anticipated his defiant response to the subsequent crisis over the failed replication of his elderly priming experiment. Bargh characterized Unconscious Thought Theory as the "latest and possibly last extension of automaticity within cognitive science," one that was fully congruent with his views. He defined automaticity as "the direct environmental control over internal cognitive processes involved in perception, judgment, behavior, and goal pursuits" (Bargh 2011, 629) and placed the claims for unconscious thought in the tradition of automaticity research of the kind he had pursued for nearly thirty years.

Notable in Bargh's brief account of the events leading to the development of Unconscious Thought Theory was his continued misunderstanding of Freud's thought by characterizing unconscious processes as non-intentional. Moreover, even though Bargh recognized that most of the skilled actions that concerned him had been acquired through intentional learning, he argued that, once they had become routinized and could be performed without the individual's awareness, they could be considered unintentional. Bargh backed up his claims for the centrality of unintentional, unconscious automatic behaviors in daily life by offering a Darwinian account of the early evolution of unconscious processes with a view to refuting all those critics who claimed that decision-making and goal pursuits must be conscious processes. In his picture, goal pursuits in the form of unconscious, non-intentional (yet purposive) behaviors developed in nonhuman animals and humans prior to the arrival of conscious thought (Bargh 2011, 636). He argued that the similarity between the outcomes and processing stages, as well as the phenomenal qualities of conscious versus unconscious goal pursuits, justified this claim. He therefore suggested that models of judgment and decision-making based on the hypothesis of exclusively conscious influences were out of step with recent findings. He dismissed all the theoretical, methodological, and empirical criticisms that had been raised against the priming experiments performed by Dijksterhuis and his colleagues, attributing failed attempts at replication to small methodological variations.

The "One-to-Many" or "Many Effects of One Prime" Problem

The Unconscious Thought Theory debate was not the only issue that impinged on Bargh's work in the years leading up to the 2012 crisis over the validity of his elderly priming study. The same year that Dijksterhuis and Nordgren formally launched their claims, the psychologist Michael Katzko, who had received his PhD in theoretical psychology at the University of Alberta at Edmonton, Canada, published a critique of the arguments commonly used in psychological research, using Bargh, Chen, and Burrows's 1996 elderly priming experiment as exemplary of the problems that concerned him. He called the fundamental weakness of such research the "one-to-many" problem and argued that it was deeply institutionalized in psychological experimentation.

As Katzko observed, Bargh, Chen, and Burrows's elderly priming study had been hailed as a "'modern classic,'" as "'perhaps the most elegant,'" "'provocative'" and the "'most dramatic demonstration of the priming effect,'" and as providing "'potent'" empirical evidence for the "'powerful effects'" of unconscious activation (Katzko 2006, 212). But according to Katzko, Bargh's experiment was based on a simple but common error, namely, that numerous intervening conditions or representations could be associated with the independent variable in any particular experiment, so that the same priming stimulus could produce several possible responses. As he wrote:

> The difficulty is that the theory being invoked at the substantive level sets logical demands on what needs to be elaborated at the research and experimental levels of the empirical argument. The problem is how to get from the general framework to predicting specific events in the real world. This problem has long been recognized in the research tradition built on models of association. Deese (1965, p. 19) summarized it thus: "The principles of organization that come from association theory itself imply almost complete anarchy . . . anything can be associated with anything else with about equal ease."

Katzko added:

> The phenomenon itself is overdetermined. One stimulus may lead, through any one of several mediating representations (each with a variety of associated behaviors) to any one of several possible responses, and any one behavioral response can be caused by a large number of initiating stimuli. The observation is repeated in a critical review of the recent research on automaticity where "the fact that multiple mechanisms are possible and not been sufficiently distinguished . . . has highlighted the

mediational ambiguity that has characterized much of the prior research in this domain" [citing Wheeler and Petty 2001, 819]. (Katzko 2006, 214–15)

Applying this argument to Bargh, Chen, and Burrows's elderly priming experiment, Katzko noted that the scrambled-sentence test involving words connoting old age could in principle yield several different effects. Why had Bargh decided that a slower walking speed was the likely response of participants to being primed with words associated with being old? Wouldn't some other behavioral reactions have been possible? Katzko warned: "The empirical problem does not center on confirming substantive generalizations such as 'perception affects behavior' or the concept that the mediating events could be automatic (sub- or preconscious). The empirical problem centers on accounting for the circumstances under which specific associations between stimulus and response—or perception and behavior—are made from all available associations" (Katzko 2006, 215).

But according to Katzko, this problem was precisely the one that Bargh, Chen, and Burrows had failed to solve. As he complained: "No rationale is provided for why variation in walking speed was expected rather than any other behavior associated with the elderly. The results are nonetheless described as if such a rationale had been provided" (Katzko 2006, 215). He therefore implied that it was a matter of luck that Bargh, Chen, and Burrows had hit upon the dependent variable, walking speed, that happened to express the stereotype regarding old people held by the student participants at New York University at the time of the experiment, namely, that the elderly tended to walk slowly. In short, Bargh, Chen, and Burrows had simply assumed the truth of their argument's premises: they had set up their elderly priming experiment looking for a particular behavior as evidence for the elderly stereotype and their interpretation of the findings had then been taken at face value by the research community. They had selected a behavioral response to a prime that happened to coincide with one means of interacting with a stereotype of the elderly. But other responses were possible.

Katzko aimed a similar criticism at an experiment by Macrae et al. (1998) that had purported to demonstrate an effect of a prime on the speed of a behavioral response of the kind documented in Bargh, Chen, and Burrows's elderly priming experiment. He accused the researchers of simply assuming without further justification that the name of the Formula 1 racing driver, Michael Schumacher, embedded in the title of a reading test, would automatically cause participants to speak a list of words more quickly. Katzko noted that "speedy racer" was simply assumed to be the most salient of all potential behavioral responses to the name, Michael Schumacher, in contrast to "arrogant," "confident," or "skillful." He made the same kind of criticisms of Dijksterhuis and van Knippenberg's claims (1998) regarding the influence of the words "professor" and "hooligan" on their experimental participants (Katzko 2006, 217–18).

To the question "How else can one explain the results?" Katzko answered that it was not even apparent what it was about the data that required an explanation. As he observed, Bargh, Chen, and Burrows's (1996) findings were presented in a terminology that already matched the language of the research hypothesis, so the argument was a tautology. It will be recalled that, in the first of the experiments reported by Bargh, Chen, and Burrows in their 1996 study, participants had been primed either with words connoting rudeness or politeness or with "neutral" words, and the time it took them to interrupt a (staged) conversation between the experimenter and a confederate had been surreptitiously measured with a stopwatch by the confederate. The researchers had reported that participants in the rude priming condition interrupted significantly faster than did participants in the neutral or polite priming conditions. But as Katzko remarked, no reason had been given for why the "time to interrupt" a conversation was defined as rudeness, especially since the manner of interruption was "to say anything to the experimenter, such as 'Excuse me' or 'Sorry, but . . .'" (Bargh, Chen, and Burrows 1996, 234). "This sort of reasoning labels an effect at the operational level in terms of the *assumed* cause at a more general theoretical level," Katzko objected (Katzko 2006, 217n5; his emphasis). He remarked in this regard that other improbable explanations for such priming effects could be found in the history of priming manipulations.

Katzko emphasized the need to carry out many replication experiments in order to confirm the validity of priming claims—replications that, he implied, were likely to fail. In fact, as he observed, in a repeat of Bargh, Chen, and Burrows's elderly study, Dijksterhuis and van Knippenberg (1998) had found that participants walked *more quickly*, not more slowly, in response to elderly priming words. The researchers had attributed this result to slight methodological differences in the way they had carried out their experiment, particularly the fact that participants were required to perform a judgment task subsequent to the priming and before they

A Theory in Crisis? 213

walked away from the laboratory, a variation on Bargh, Chen, and Burrows's (1996) experiment that, the researchers claimed, might have wiped out the expected priming effects (Dijksterhuis and van Knippenberg 1998, 867). But this explanation did not satisfy Katzko. "If differences in procedure undermine the capacity to generalize from one experiment to the next," he maintained, "then by the same argument, there is little ground for making broad generalizations from individual experiments to the world at large" (Katzko 2006, 220). One of Katzko's conclusions in this regard was that, when priming experiments were carried out with the required degree of precision about the hypothesis to be tested, the interpretation of the results should be limited to the actual experimental situation, including as a primary factor the personal significance of the priming words to the specific group of participants that had been deliberately selected for their expected sensitivity to just those words. He contrasted the correct experimental strategies pursued by several priming researchers with Bargh, Chen, and Burrows's poorly rationalized studies.

More generally, Katzko accused Bargh and colleagues of frequently committing the fallacy of confirmation bias: they imposed on their research findings a selective interpretation of the data in accord with their hypotheses and jettisoned evidence that did not fit their prior beliefs. He also suggested that this confirmation bias was encouraged by the institutional conventions and styles of reasoning to which published research articles had to conform. In a detailed analysis of citation patterns, Katzko decried the way so many researchers had failed to detect the fallacies inherent in Bargh's arguments and instead had uncritically endorsed his findings and claims. The strong implication of Katzko's critique was that the selection of which behavioral outcome in the elderly priming experiment to focus on had been so arbitrary that replication attempts were likely to fail. In the light of Doyen et al.'s (2012) subsequent inability to replicate Bargh's elderly priming study, Katzko's complaints about Bargh's interpretation of the results of his famous elderly priming study appear to have been on the mark.

In 2010, Gerd Gigerenzer, well-known for his work on the use of heuristics in decision-making and for his critique of Tversky and Kahneman's work on this topic, approvingly cited Katzko's paper (2006) in an article criticizing poor theory construction in psychology. Labeling the problem in psychology as one of offering "surrogates for theory," Gigerenzer recalled Molière's parody of the Aristotelian doctrine of substantial forms. "Why does opium make us sleepy?" he asked, and answered: "Because of its dormative properties" (Gigerenzer 2010, 737–38). Gigerenzer called this kind of empty explanation "circular restatements of the phenomenon" (Gigerenzer 2010, 733) and included among examples Dijksterhuis and van Knippenberg's 1998 experiment ostensibly proving that a "professor" stereotype primed more intelligent behavior (Gigerenzer 2010, 738), a finding that later studies would fail to replicate (Shanks et al. 2013; O'Donnell et al. 2018). Gigerenzer quoted Dijksterhuis and van Knippenberg's explanation of their finding: "'In concrete terms, activation of the professor stereotype is expected to result in intelligent behavior because activation of the professor stereotype leads to activation of intelligence'" (Gigerenzer 2010, 738; Dijksterhuis and van Knippenberg 1998, 872). Gigerenzer suggested that there was nothing wrong with being unable to explain how priming effects worked. What he deplored was the use of circular statements that pretended to offer explanations, thereby distracting from the task of proposing an actual explanatory model. As he commented: "Restatements both create a theoretical void and cover it up" (Gigerenzer 2010, 738).

Bargh under Fire and the Problem of Selectivity

But Bargh himself did not view matters in this way. So far as I have been able to determine, Bargh never referred to Katzko's or Gigerenzer's critiques. But he was alert to the "one-to-many problem" in priming research. The same year in which Katzko's article appeared, Bargh himself commented on the skepticism among cognitive psychologists about the power of priming in social psychology and identified the "many effects of one prime" (what Katzko called the "one-to-many") problem as a key challenge in automaticity research. He even admitted that his choice of the dependent variable, walking speed, in his elderly priming study had been a matter of luck. As he observed, the effect of the prime in these various types of studies "just depends on which dependent variable the experimenter happens to be interested in." Or again: "The quality of the obtained effect depends only on the happenstance of the experimenter's choice of D[ependent] V[ariable]" (Bargh 2006, 152).

But unlike Katzko, who regarded the "one to many" as a major problem, Bargh optimistically presented the difficulty as a normal "second-generation" research question of the kind that was to be expected in science as disciplines matured. Moreover, he was confident that the problem could be addressed. As in the case of Bargh and Chartrand's handling of the complexities of imitation, Bargh's solution took the form of adding to the putative internal, information-processing representations various "moderators" governing social behaviors that had previously been excluded from his theoretical analysis. As Bargh explained, the question posed was how the many possible psychological effects of a single prime could be reduced to a single response, a problem especially salient in the real world where we are bombarded by so many stimuli, any one of which might function as a prime. He illustrated the problem in the following way:

> For example, say while walking down lower Broadway I come across a small boy sitting by himself on the curb, crying to himself. The *behavioral* priming effect here, through the perception-behavior link, should cause me to imitate the boy—that is, to sit down next to him and start crying myself. Happily, this does not usually happen—but why not? Because there are other responses primed as well. The situational norm or goal of helping someone so clearly in need . . . would also be activated . . . and dominate the nonmotivational priming influence. (Bargh 2006, 159; his emphasis)

This problem was one of the selectivity of responses to multiple cues and stimuli, namely, how did the individual—or rather, for cognitive psychologists such as Bargh, how did the cognitive system—select which, among all the stimuli impinging on it, it ought to react to? As we saw in chapter 4, Macrae and Johnston (1998) had raised this question when they invoked the role of attention in the selection process. As Bargh in his 2006 paper noted:

> Macrae and Johnston (1998) were the first to pit such competing priming influences against each other; participants were primed with helping related stimuli and were then presented, in the elevator leaving the experimental session, with a chance to help. A confederate in the elevator dropped some pens, and helping-primed participants were more likely than a control group to pick up the pens for the confederate—unless the pens were leaky and messy. Helping behavior in that case would conflict with a stronger goal to avoid dirt and contamination . . .
>
> The general principle seems to be that one's current goal or motivational state will "win out" over other potential influences when they are

in conflict [...] Recent work in social cognition also shows that active goals can override even effects that have long been understood as obligatory or uncontrollable. (Bargh 2006, 159)

In other words, as Macrae and Johnson had suggested, perhaps the absence of any competing behavioral options explained why the participants primed with the elderly stereotype in Bargh, Chen, and Burrows's famous study had walked more slowly on leaving the laboratory. One might note in this regard that Bargh, Chen, and Burrows's participants were undergraduates at New York University, where Bargh then taught. They were enrolled in the Introductory Psychology course and had participated in the experiment in partial fulfillment of a course requirement. It seemed likely that they were therefore motivated to conform to the limited behavioral options of the experimental situation in ways that ruled out the influence of other goals that could have competed with the requirements of the experiment and laboratory setting.

In fact, Bargh had previously acknowledged that the results obtained in his elderly experiment might have been different if the primed participants had entertained alternative motives (although, of course, they were not asked). "In an earlier experiment, participants were induced to walk slower by the activation of the stereotype of the elderly," Dijksterhuis, Bargh, and Miedema had commented:

> In the absence of any competing behavioral cues, people indeed walked more slowly. However, we hypothesize that when people focus their attention on their behavior, alternative behavioral cues become salient ("I have to go to the dentist," "I'm thirsty," "Let's go shopping."). This creates the need for a selection process, an active control process that inhibits the access of passive "default" cues to the motorium. The selection process itself, in other words, inhibits the effects of the activated stereotype on people's walking speed. (Dijksterhuis, Bargh, and Miedema 2000, 44).

This statement is noteworthy for several reasons. One of its implications was that Bargh, Chen, and Burrows's elderly priming study might not be easily replicable in other laboratories because a variety of hitherto unidentified mediating factors might intervene to alter the results. This implication suggested in turn that the outcome of such experiments might be less predictable than Bargh's theory of the direct perception-behavior link had implied. As the cognitive scientist Barsalou would later comment: "The modulation issue is much more extreme than imagined previously, because virtually any element of a situation can modulate social priming, not just those noted so far in the literature" (Barsalou 2016, 9). On the other hand, the fact that moderating factors capable of affecting the outcome of priming experiments were increasingly seen as important could be turned to Bargh's advantage. It suggested a way for him to hold on to his claims for the unconscious, non-intentional nature of automatic behaviors and the default tendency for them to occur, while also proposing that variables of all kinds—including but not limited to attention—could influence the course of automatic behaviors, with the result that the outcomes of priming experiments could be portrayed as more flexible and more sensitive to context than they had tended to be on the past. To take one example, in 2002 Hull and colleagues performed a replication of Bargh, Chen, and Burrows's elderly priming study and reported that slow walking after priming for an elderly stereotype only occurred in highly self-conscious participants and not in participants with low self-consciousness (Hull et al. 2002).

In 2012, in a paper evidently written before, but published several months after, Doyen et al.'s failed replication was announced, Bargh et al. cited Hull et al.'s (2002) findings among many others in an overview of automaticity in social-cognitive processes (Bargh et al. 2012). Here Bargh reiterated his commitment to the existence of forms of automatic processing that were "effortlessly" and preconsciously determined by perceptions, according to his theory of the direct perception-behavior link. For Bargh et al., such behaviors were primed by the "relevant situational features" operating outside of conscious awareness or control (Bargh et al. 2012, 593). Without questioning the underlying claims for the importance of the direct perception-behavior link, Bargh et al. also referred to the many experiments that had demonstrated the role of moderators in constraining and limiting priming effects. The mechanisms underlying these effects were as yet unknown.

Bargh et al. suggested that some automaticity effects, such as the reduction of body temperature consequent on feelings of social exclusion, might be hard-wired. The authors were also intrigued by recent imaging studies that attempted to link priming effects to specific locations and organs in the brain. But the details remained to be worked out. As S. Christian Wheeler and Kenneth DeMarree observed: "Explanations for these [priming] effects all center on processes involving construct accessibility. Specifically, features of the environment make some constructs more accessible in memory, and this accessibility somehow translates into behavior" (Wheeler and DeMarree 2009, 566). It was the *"somehow"* that was mysterious. In their contribution to this topic Wheeler and DeMarree provided a picture of the possible mechanisms involved, with boxes and arrows representing the primes, the activated constructs, and the pathways to the behavioral effects, but the figure was just a representation, not a formal model (Wheeler and DeMarree 2009, 567). As the authors suggested, even in the case of the simplest kinds of priming effects, a large number of behavioral representations could presumably be activated by any single prime: even the elderly stereotype was associated with several different behaviors, not just walking slowly but forgetting, and so on. According to them, the strength of the association between the construct activation and the behavioral representation appeared to be the factor that influenced which of several possible priming effects would occur. But as they acknowledged, the proposal had not been tested. In the case of more-complex pathways between perception and behavior involving several intermediate steps, many different moderating variables seemed to play important roles. But neither the full range of boundary conditions nor the mechanisms involved had been identified.

The Power of the Situation

A further development that complicated Bargh's direct perception-behavior model of automaticity in the years leading up to the replication crisis was the emergence of what might be called the "situated cognition" movement. In response in part to the "many effects of one prime" problem, it became clear to some researchers that priming responses were more sensitive to the total affordances of the priming situation than Bargh's theory of a direct link between perception and behavior had appeared to recognize. We have seen that when Bargh was confronted with evidence that priming effects were less rigid and inflexible than he had originally assumed, he accommodated the findings by including "moderators" in the mix of the internal perceptual and motoric representations held to govern such responses, moderators that were held to facilitate or inhibit priming effects in various ways. But in his view, such moderators were merely "add-ons" to already established perception-behavior sequences. He did not regard the various environmental or situational cues as internal to the situation of the agent, but simply as qualifiers of a more primordial response.

On his model, the individual reacted automatically and in a purely passive way to the environment, and whatever influence moderators exerted was held to occur at a late stage in the information-processing perception-behavior sequence. Bargh thus treated the perception-behavior pathway as the fundamental unit of interest and as such, an automatic response that lacked any inherently strategic aspect.

But some researchers began to question those assumptions by suggesting that situational influences operated at such an early stage in the processing sequence as to be essentially intrinsic to it from the start. Their revisions led to a reconceptualization of the priming situation itself. Instead of making the subject merely a passive conduit for links between environmental stimuli, internal representations, and motor behaviors, the results of priming were now said to depend on the agent's social motives and goals within the range of contextual affordances and possibilities.

Publications on this topic by Eliot Smith and Gun Semin are especially relevant (2004; 2007). These authors rejected the classical computational picture of the mind as made up of fixed knowledge structures or static mental representations encapsulated within the brain, structures that could be activated automatically and independently of the perceiver's goals by the mere perception of an appropriate stimulus person. Instead, they argued that people's apprehensions or cognitions of the world were inseparable from their actions, as such actions were adaptively performed in the context of specific motivational, communicative, social, and physical situations. The shift in perspective meant that the malleability of the individual's responses to the demands of the situation became the focus of interest.

Smith and Semin drew attention in this regard to priming studies demonstrating the adaptiveness of cognition to the current situation and the communicative context. For example, Ara Norenzayan and Norbert Schwarz (1999) demonstrated in a priming experiment that participants' assessments of the causes of a mass murder, as described in a newspaper report, were sensitive to the interests of the researcher conducting the experiment(Norenzayan and Schwarz 1999). When the letterhead of the questionnaire used to gauge the participants' evaluations suggested that the researcher was a social scientist, participants tended to attribute the murders to situational causes; but when the letterhead suggested that the researcher was a personality psychologist, they tended to attribute the murders to more dispositional or individual causes. In effect, the participants tailored their responses according to the researcher's presumed or inferred academic affiliation: a letterhead that read "Institute for Social Research" implied that the researcher was a social scientist likely to be interested in social-contextual variables, whereas a letterhead that read "Institute of Personality Research" suggested that the researcher was interested in personality features.

Norenzayan and Schwarz rejected the idea that priming alone could explain their findings because researchers had already established that priming effects only occurred when priming stimuli were presented *before* the information participants were asked to assess, not if they were presented afterward. But Norenzayan and Schwarz demonstrated that the impact of the researchers' affiliation on participants' situational and dispositional attributions was unchanged, or if anything became stronger, when the affiliation was introduced *after* the participants had already read the story. The researchers did not rule out an explanation in terms of Orne's concept of experimenter demand characteristics, according to which the participants were specifically motivated by the desire to substantiate the researchers' expectations. In other words, they did not discount the possible role of suggestion or "influence"—however these phenomena were to be understood (more on this topic in chapter 8). But they favored a Gricean conversational analysis according to which people strove to be cooperative communicators in any interpersonal situation, not just in experimental settings (Norenzayan and Schwarz 1999, 1018, citing Grice 1975).[2] They concluded that the attribution process, long viewed as the outcome of context-free universal forms of judgment, was in fact "a process which is embedded in the social and communicative context in which it occurs" (Norenzayan and Schwarz 1999, 1019).

2. As Norenzayan and Schwarz explained, Orne's concept of demand characteristics differs from a conversational analysis by postulating motivations that are specific to the role of research participants and are driven by a desire to substantiate the researchers' expectations. In contrast, in a conversational analysis based on Grice's work, research participants are not trying to tell researchers what they "want to hear" but rather what they "want to know." "Nevertheless," the authors added "we cannot say for sure to what extent motivations that may be specific to research participants contributed to cooperative conversational conduct, over and above conversational inferences. Hence, a demand explanation for our findings cannot be ruled out" (Norenzayan and Schwarz 1999, 1018). Norenzayan and Schwarz 's analysis gave the appearance of resonating with Bavelas's' similar Gricean analysis of imitation as a form of interpersonal communication (Bavelas 1995; 1998). Although both Norenzayan and Schwarz and Bavelas cited the same text by Grice (1975), we shall see in chapter 7 that Norenzayan's and Schwarz's views were rather remote from those of Bavelas. For an overview of Grice's work, including his ideas about the nature of conversational interaction, see Grandy and Warner 2021.

In a related study, also cited by Smith and Semin, Irene Blair (2002) documented the fact that since 1999 nearly fifty investigations had demonstrated the malleability of stereotypes and the responsiveness of experimental subjects to a wide range of strategic, social, and contextual influences. "Automatic" stereotyped reactions—defined according to Bargh by the absence of awareness, lack of intention, and uncontrollability—had turned out not to be so automatic after all. In her general discussion, Blair suggested that the entire conceptualization of attitudes and stereotypes as stable, context-independent representations that could be stored and retrieved in much the same form at a later time, needed to be revised in favor of the view according to which they were temporary constructions or states formed in response to the current situation.[3]

On the basis of the findings I have just described and related studies, Smith and Semin (2002) rejected the idea that context sensitivity could be viewed merely as a kind of "noise" or inessential barrier to the study of putatively invariant representations, considered by so many social psychologists to be the most fundamental causes of social judgment and behavior. They argued instead that the mutual interdependence between person and context ought to be the center of research, and rejected the idea that cognition was simply an abstract, amodal form of information processing.

Along somewhat similar lines, priming researcher Cesario and his colleagues criticized Bargh's "direct expression" (or direct perception-behavior) model of automatic action by accentuating instead the role of contextual factors, especially the influence of motives, in influencing priming outcomes. They argued that priming responses were not simply determined by the overlap between the areas of the brain governing perception and those controlling motor behavior, as Bargh and Prinz had claimed, but by the degree to which behavior fulfilled the person's goals and intentions in the light of situational possibilities (Cesario, Plaks, and Higgins 2006). In a replication of Bargh, Chen, and Burrows's (1996) elderly priming experiment using subliminal priming, Cesario, Plaks, and Higgins demonstrated that the priming effect was significant only among

---

3. Blair took issue with Bargh's claims published before the latter had attempted to complicate his account of priming responses by adding the influence of various putative moderators. Thus, she quoted him as having stated in 1997 that "an automatic mental phenomenon occurs reflexively whenever certain triggering conditions are in place . . . It does not matter where the current focus of conscious attention is, what the individual was recently thinking, or what the individual current intentions and goals are" (Blair 2002, 242–43; Bargh 1997, 3).

participants who had positive attitudes toward old people, not among participants with negative attitudes.

On the one hand, Cesario, Plaks, and Higgins presented their views and findings as a logical extension of Bargh, Chen, and Burrows's auto-motive model of priming, which proposed that features of the environment could activate mentally represented goals that then automatically triggered the goal pursuit process (Cesario, Plaks, and Higgins 2006, 894). The implication was that priming with words connoting old age would activate participant behaviors based on their personally relevant attitudes toward the elderly—in this case, as their experiment demonstrated, the participants' positive attitudes toward the elderly. On the other hand, Cesario, Plaks, and Higgins explicitly contrasted their own emphasis on the role of personal motivation and attitudes in determining priming responses with Bargh's more mechanical, direct perception-behavior theory, stressing the divergent predictions involved, since Bargh's model made no allowance for the influence of motivational factors on priming outcomes.

As I observed in chapter 5, Cesario, Plaks, and Higgins applied their insights to the phenomenon of mimicry. It will be recalled that when confronted with evidence of the influence of the desire to affiliate on imitation, Bargh and Chartrand maintained the perception-behavior model by arguing that the desire to imitate simply caused participants to attend more to perceptual cues, thereby increasing the strength of the perception-behavior link. Cesario, Plaks, and Higgins argued, however, that mimicry was not a function of a direct perception-behavior link but served strategic-motivational purposes (Cesario, Plaks, and Higgins 2006). As Cesario and colleagues subsequently proposed, "any behavior similarly functional for goal fulfilment could be executed following priming... Similarly, different social-category primes could produce an identical behavioral response if the motivational significance of the categories is the same (e.g., people to distance myself from)" (Cesario et al. 2010, 1316).

In their paper of 2010 Cesario et al. reported the results of another replication of one of Bargh, Chen, and Burrows's 1996 experiments in which non–African American participants worked on a boring computer task while being subliminally primed with pictures of Black or White men. After ten minutes, the computer crashed and the participants were provoked by the experimenter to start again. Participants primed with pictures of Black men responded with greater aggression than participants primed with pictures of White men. Bargh, Chen, and Burrows had offered a "direct-expression" explanation of this finding by proposing that there was an automatic link between the increased accessibility of the participants' aggression construct primed in this way and the participant's aggressive behavior. But Cesario et al. showed that the results of the priming varied according to the contingencies of the participants' physical situation: if participants were seated in an enclosed booth that prevented flight, they exhibited increased accessibility of *fight*-related action semantics; but if they were seated in an open field where distancing behavior was possible, they showed increased accessibility of *flight*-related action semantics (Cesario et al. 2010). Cesario et al. concluded, with reference to Smith and Semin's papers on situated cognition (Smith and Semin 2004; 2007), that an understanding of automaticity had to consider its situated nature. "In our account," they wrote, "the relevance of a behavioral response is not determined by the degree of feature overlap between that behavior and the information contained in the primed category. Instead, relevance is determined by the degree to which a behavior fulfills a person's interaction goal" (Cesario et al. 2010, 1316).

In a related development, Chris Loersch and B. Keith Payne proposed a "situated inference" approach to priming. Characterizing the "theoretical mystery" of the "many effects from one prime" as a major problem confronting scientists engaged in priming research, Loersch and Payne stressed the idea that how perceivers interpreted the meaning of any situation was a crucial factor in determining priming outcomes (Loersch and Payne 2014, 235). These researchers argued that priming stimuli did not usually produce an automatic reaction in the form of judgments or behaviors, as Bargh's direct perception-behavior theory claimed. Instead, priming altered the accessibility of prime-associated mental content in ways that produced divergent downstream results depending on the individual's motivations and the affordances of the situation. Because different situations afforded very different questions and concerns, the meaning of the prime-related content and the inferences the individual drew about the situation could vary greatly, with the result that one prime could produce disparate effects on judgment, motivation, and behaviors.

Loersch and Payne proposed a single mechanism to explain how a wide variety of situations affected priming outcomes. They suggested that, depending on how easily the primed content was confused with individuals' own cognitive responses, the individuals mistakenly attributed the information derived from primes to their own internal thought processes; they then used the misattributed information flexibly to produce (often biased) answers to the most salient questions afforded by the situation. Because different situations afforded different options for judgment or behavior, the inferred meaning of any misattributed prime-related information could vary greatly. "It is in this way," Loersch and Payne argued, "that the general construct accessibility resulting from a single prime can differentially produce downstream changes in judgment, behavior, and motivation [. . .] [T]he way in which a perceiver uses prime-related information should be able to drastically alter the prime's effect, causing a single prime to sometimes lead to assimilation, sometimes lead to contrast, and sometimes lead to no effect at all" (Loersch and Payne 2011, 237, 240). That was why there were many effects from one prime.

In comparing their model of priming to that of Bargh, Loersch and Payne emphasized two chief differences. The first was that Bargh's model traced priming effects to the interplay of internal representations encapsulated in the head or brain, whereas Loersch and Payne's model placed more emphasis on the richness of the social environment. The second difference between the two models was that Bargh's priming model was analogous to late-selection models of attention, according to which many streams of input information were processed to a high level of semantic analysis in parallel, before attention intervened to select one among those fully processed streams to allow access to consciousness and action. But Loersch and Payne's model was more like early-selection models of attention, according to which unattended information received scant processing, and attentional selection was necessary at an early stage to permit a stream of information to reach a high level of analysis. "In contrast to models that assume primes directly activate behaviors or goals," they wrote, "the situated inference model predicts that metacognitive judgments about the meaning and validity of thoughts are critical . . . If one's thoughts are viewed as invalid, nondiagnostic, or otherwise inappropriate for use in the inference process, then priming will have no effect on subsequent judgment, behavior, or motivation" (Loersch and Payne 2011, 245). For these authors, the main value of their particular model was that it could account for the role of moderators in producing variable priming results. The authors described some testable predictions that they thought could help to decide between Bargh's and their own approach (Loersch and Payne 2011; see also Loersch and Payne 2012).

Agency and the Legacy of Cognitive Psychology

When Loersch and Payne (2011) referred to the role of metacognitive judgments about meaning in the priming process, it appeared that these researchers were denying the idea that there were automatic effects of thoughts on behavior of the kind advocated by Bargh. During the post-2012 crisis over replication and priming, Ben Newell and David Shanks (2014b) would thus interpret Loersch and Payne's position to signify that thoughts were only instrumental if they were interpreted as valid reasons for behavior. Accordingly, Newell and Shanks suggested that there were few if any strictly automatic, unconscious processes of the kind Bargh had claimed, and that the activation of behavior was not a passive and obligatory phenomenon (Newell and Shanks 2014b). In other words, it seemed to Newell and Shanks that Loersch and Payne had reintroduced an emphasis on the necessary role of reason and intention in behavior that Bargh had rejected. But Loersch and Payne denied the validity of Newell and Shanks's interpretation of their work, emphasizing instead the very lack of intentionality in priming behaviors that their situated cognition model had appeared to question (Payne, Brown-Iannuzzi, and Loersch 2016; for a rebuttal see Shanks 2017).

More generally, in spite of their critiques of Bargh's direct-expression account of priming, "situated-cognition" theorists tended to remain so committed to information-processing theories of the mind that they were unable to address the fundamental question: how do we account for the meaning of the experimental priming situation to the participants involved? The task for any cognitive-science approach to the mind is to solve the frame problem, which is to say, to show how a computational system is capable of selecting the relevant cues among a host of situational ones. In 1972, Dreyfus had identified the frame problem as *the* major stumbling block to the success of early AI. In 2005 he reported that pioneering AI researcher Marvin Minsky had recently acknowledged that AI had been brain-dead since the early 1970s when it encountered the problem of commonsense knowledge (Dreyfus 2005, 48; Minsky in an interview with McHugh 2003). Or as Jerry Fodor had likewise recognized, in a passage also cited by Dreyfus:

> The problem ... is to get the structure of an entire belief system to bear on individual occasions of belief fixation. We have, to put it bluntly, no computational formalisms that show us how to do this, and we have no idea how such formalisms might be developed ... In this respect, cognitive science hasn't even *started*; we are literally no farther advanced than we were in the darkest days of behaviorism ... If someone—a Dreyfus, for example—were to ask us why we should even suppose that the digital

computer is a plausible mechanism for the simulation of global cognitive processes, the answering silence would be deafening. (Fodor 1983, 128–29; cited in Dreyfus 2005, 48)

Many years earlier, the well-known psychologist, Jerome Bruner, had expressed his dissatisfaction with the tenets of cognitive science when he remarked:

> Very soon, computing became the model of the mind, and in place of the concept of meaning there emerged the concept of computability. Cognitive processes were equated with the programs that could be run on a computational device, and the success of one's efforts to "understand," say, memory or concept attainment, was one's ability realistically to simulate such human conceptualizing or human memorizing with a computer program . . . This new reductionism provided an astonishing libertarian program for the new cognitive science that was being born . . . One did not have to truck with . . . meaning at all . . . There could be no place for "mind" in such a system—"mind" in the sense of intentional states like believing, desiring, intending, grasping a meaning. The cry soon rose to ban such intentional states from the new science. (Bruner 1990, 6–7)

Just so, "situated cognition" theorists proceeded as if their job was to remedy flaws in the ways in which Bargh's direct perception-behavior or Prinz's ideomotor theories explained the sensitivity of priming responses to the meaning of the situational contexts, while adhering to explanations based on hypothetical information-processing and action-control mechanisms. They did not confront the basic question of how those non-semantic, non-intentional information-processing mechanisms could give rise to the intentions and meaning that inhered in the actions of the persons whose responses they were studying. Indeed, there were compelling reasons for doubting that it was possible to do so within the terms of analysis proposed by Loersch and Payne or any of the researchers on either side of the debate over priming.[4]

---

4. An example is a paper by Schröder and Thagard (2013) in which the authors proposed three information-processing and action control mechanisms, including ideomotor mechanisms, operating at the psychological, cultural, and biological-neuronal levels to account for priming effects, mixing appeals to the combination of semantic meaning

From this perspective, the picture of action that began to emerge under the general name of *situated cognition* appears superficially close to but was fundamentally remote from Bavelas's handling of postural imitation as a form of intentional, interpersonal communication, and Fridlund's comparable treatment of facial and postural signaling. Situated-cognition theorists appear to have been unaware of both these researchers' pioneering work. In the case of both Bavelas and Fridlund, intentionality was taken for granted as a capacity in human and many nonhuman forms of life that could not be broken down into component parts and given a mechanical-causal explanation in terms of putative internal mental representations modeled on computational theories. Rather, Bavelas and Fridlund focused on the communicative interactions of the whole animal, human or nonhuman, in their more or less natural settings, and their explanations remained at the descriptive level of intentional, interpersonal communication (Leys 2017, 270–300, 361–64).

However, what can be said positively of the theorists of situated cognition is that they raised new questions about the plasticity and flexibility of priming behaviors in response to situational contingencies in terms that challenged Bargh's more mechanical approach. In doing so they contributed to the overall reckoning with Bargh's work that was precipitated when Doyen et al. (2012) reported that they had been unable to reproduce his iconic elderly priming experiment. It is to Doyen et al.'s intervention and the ensuing controversy over priming that I turn in the next chapter.

---

and hypothetical neuronal processes in the brain in terms that Dreyfus long ago labeled "gibberish" (Dreyfus 1979, 179). Moreover, the authors appeared unable to imagine that many of the actions they called automatic and characterized as unintentional might be the result of conflicting intentions, such as when people start an affair even though they believe in faithfulness, to take one of the Schröder and Thagard's own examples. It seems implausible, to say the least, that an action such as starting an affair could be carried out unintentionally, unconsciously, and automatically, but that is what Schröder and Thagard (2013) appeared to propose. Payne, Brown-Ianuzzi, and Loersch (2016) cited Schröder and Thagard's paper as a sign of the progress being made in establishing theoretical frameworks capable of making priming predictions. But it could be objected that all Schröder and Thagard had done was to translate the fact that people respond in complex ways to the situations and environments in which they live into the language of hypothetical information-processing systems and mechanisms.

7

The Fate of Priming

> Replication of others' findings and results is an activity that is rarely practiced! Only in exceptional circumstances is there any reward to be gained by repeating another's work. Science reserves its highest honours for those who do things first, and a confirmation of another's work merely confirms that the other is prizeworthy... It is only when the existence of some phenomenon is cast into doubt that attempts are made to use replicability as a test.
> —H. M. COLLINS (1985, 19–20)

> When adjustments to ward off apparent falsifications become excessive, the research program is degenerating.
> —P. E. MEEHL (1992, 715)

Doyen et al.'s (2012) Failed Replication and Its Aftermath

The take-home lesson of the developments I have described in the previous chapter was that priming outcomes were hard to predict and that attempts to replicate experimental findings were likely to fail. If, in principle, many contextual factors could influence priming reactions, perhaps it was true that, as Katzko argued and Bargh admitted, it was merely a matter of luck if a researcher hit upon a dependent variable, such as walking, that happened to express the stereotype that was being primed. A similar experiment with another group of participants or at another laboratory at a later time might not be able to reproduce a previous finding because of subtle differences in the participants and/or the priming situation.

Moreover, although prior to 2012 experts in the field had accepted that "semantic" priming effects were robust, some researchers had begun to question the kinds of behavioral priming effects that had been reported by Bargh and his colleagues. In semantic priming, reading a word such as *doctor* causes participants to respond more quickly to a lexically related target word, such as *nurse*, when it is presented shortly afterward. Such semantic priming effects had been replicated in hundreds of experiments with impressive statistical power, within-subject comparisons, and a large number of repeated measures (Pashler, Coburn, and Harris 2012). More controversial were the *behavioral* priming effects whose study Bargh had pioneered. Semantic priming effects were largely held to last for only a very brief period of time, a matter of seconds, whereas social psychologists were reporting effects that lasted minutes, hours, and even in some cases days after exposure to priming stimuli, results that caused a certain suspicion and bewilderment among researchers (Higgins and Eitam 2014, 23).

Furthermore, we have seen that, traditionally, social psychologists had assumed that primes influenced behavior through the mediation of an individual's understanding of or ideas about the situation. Bargh and his colleagues emphasized instead the unintentional, unconscious, and automatic character of priming. Yet, as reported by Bower (2012), researchers had begun to question whether the methods typically used to assess participants' awareness of the influence of primes on their behavior were adequate to test whether the primes exerted their effects entirely without participants' consciousness and intention.

It is against the background of these several developments that Doyen et al.'s (2012) failed replication of Bargh, Chen, and Burrows's iconic elderly priming experiment and its impact must be assessed. In this chapter I propose to examine some of the details of the dispute generated by Doyen et al.'s publication. There is now a huge literature on the replication crisis in psychology that Doyen et al.'s publication helped precipitate, much of it rightly concerned with the methodological and statistical weaknesses of experimental practices in the field. My interests are somewhat different. In particular, I plan to focus on the intellectual strategies adopted by the different parties to the dispute to shore up their competing theoretical claims. As we shall see, when faced with reports of multiple replication failures, Bargh and like-minded colleagues did not abandon their positions. Instead, they pursued various arguments in order to defend the validity of their experimental findings and their theories.

In 2012, a team of Belgian psychologists announced that they had been unable to replicate the most iconic behavioral priming experiment of all, Bargh, Chen, and Burrows's (1996) elderly priming study. With the provocative title "Behavioral Priming: It's All in the Mind, but Whose Mind?" Doyen et al. began their article by noting the central role played by Bargh, Chen, and Burrows's (1996) "seminal" elderly priming study in consolidating the claim that behavior was determined by unconscious determinants (Doyen et al. 2012). The researchers gave three reasons for attempting to replicate Bargh, Chen, and Burrows's (1996) experiment:

1. Only two replication attempts had been made so far, and these were problematic in various ways (citing Aarts and Dijksterhuis 2002 and Cesario, Plaks, and Higgins 2006).

2. In social psychology, it was widely assumed that high-level priming could occur automatically and outside conscious awareness. But that assumption conflicted with cognitive-neuroscience evidence suggesting that semantic processing required top-down attention to the prime and bottom-up stimulus strength, a pattern typically associated with conscious awareness. This evidence suggested that the salience of a concept such as "being old" seemed too weak to automatically prime a behavior that was, in any case, only indirectly related to old age in the absence of contextual cues relevant to that trait.

3. There were several methodological weaknesses in Bargh, Chen, and Burrows's elderly priming experiment. Doyen et al. observed that the confederate who timed the walking speeds in that experiment had been unaware whether the participant belonged to the elderly priming condition or not, a precaution designed to ensure that the experiment followed double-blind procedures. But according to them no such precautionary measures had been reported concerning the experimenter himself, who administered the word-sorting task to the participants. Doyen et al. noted in this regard that numerous studies had shown that an experimenter's expectations could influence participants' behavior, even in highly controlled environments (Doyen et al. 2012, 2). They therefore suggested that in Bargh, Chen, and Burrows's study, the experimenter who administered the word-sorting task could have been aware of whether the participants were in the prime condition or not and could have tuned his behavior accordingly. "Thus," they concluded, "given the fact that subtle cues can influence behavior, controlling for the experimenter's expectations appears to be essential" (Doyen et al. 2012, 2).

In addition, Doyen et al. questioned Bargh, Chen, and Burrows's use of a handheld stopwatch to measure the participants' walking speed, a timing method that required special precautions that appeared to have been lacking. Finally, Doyen et al. criticized the debriefing methods used by Bargh, Chen, and Burrows to evaluate whether the participants were aware of the purpose of the study, or of the fact that the words used in the scrambled-sentence task were related to the concept of old age.

Based on these concerns, Doyen et al. described two experiments designed to replicate Bargh, Chen, and Burrows's original experiment, but with certain variations. A total of 150 French-speaking Belgian participants took part in Doyen et al.'s experiments, in which the researchers used direct or best-fit French translations of Bargh, Chen, and Burrows's old-age-related priming words. In his angry response to Doyen et al.'s paper, Bargh accused Doyen et al. of failing to check whether their participants possessed the same stereotype of the elderly as that of Bargh, Chen, and Burrows's (1996) participants (Bargh 2012b). But, in fact, in attempting to match Bargh, Chen, and Burrows's experiment, Doyen et al. found French substitutes for Bargh's English priming words using the most frequent answers given in an online survey in which eighty participants had provided adjectives related to the concept of old age; the researchers regarded this as one way to evaluate stereotypes. In addition, in Doyen et al.'s experiments strict double-blind procedures were followed, including the use of randomly recruited student experimenters who had no prior expectations regarding participant behavior and no prior knowledge of the experiment, and who remained blind to condition. In order to minimize their potential influence on priming outcomes, the student experimenters were also required to follow a precise script when interacting with the participants. The scrambled-sentence-test words were enclosed in an envelope so as to keep the experimenters unaware of condition.

In the first experiment, in order to measure the speed of walking, Doyen et al. substituted for the handheld stopwatch in Bargh, Chen, and Burrows's (1996) original experiment a hidden automatic-timing device. This device took the form of infrared sensors automatically triggered by the participants when they walked along a specific length of the corridor on leaving the lab. This change in method was justified on the grounds that an "objective" method for measuring walking speeds was less susceptible to "subjective" bias than a handheld stopwatch watch.[1] The debriefing,

---

[1]. In another failed replication of Bargh, Chen, and Burrows's (1996) elderly priming study conducted in 2008 and posted in 2011 to the online repository Psych File Drawer, in order to measure the participants' walking speeds, Pashler, Harris, and Coburn replaced

which occurred before the participants' reached the exit, involved the use of the funnel debriefing procedure to assess their awareness of the primes themselves, any changes in their walking speeds, or the link between the scrambled-sentence task and their own walking speeds on leaving the laboratory. The debriefing also probed the participants' suspicions regarding the purpose of the experiment.

Experiment 1 showed no significant difference in walking speeds between primed and unprimed participants. Four of the participants in the prime condition reported that the scrambled words were related to the stereotype of old age; and on a forced-choice test the primed group chose among four pictures that of an old person above chance level, whereas the unprimed group chose equally among the four pictures. Ninety-six percent of the participants reported that they could not establish a connection between the scrambled-word task and their subsequent behavior. In sum, using strict double-blind procedures but replacing the handheld stopwatch with infrared sensors to measure participants' walking speeds, Doyen et al. were unable to replicate the walking effects observed by Bargh, Chen, and Burrows. Their results suggested that the use of a handheld stopwatch in Bargh, Chen, and Burrows's (1996) original study had introduced a subjective, experimenter bias that was eliminated when an impersonal, "objective" method was employed instead.

Based on these negative findings, Doyen et al. set out to investigate whether, as Chartrand and Bargh (1999) themselves had suggested in their studies of the Chameleon Effect (Doyen et al. 2012, 2), primed subjects tended to imitate the experimenters' expectancy behaviors. It seemed plausible to the researchers that the experimenters' expectations about

---

the handheld watch with hidden Nike digital-timing cones that automatically triggered on and off as the participant walked along the corridor on leaving the laboratory. They also took extra steps to ensure that the experimenter remained blind to condition, because they felt that in the original experiment it was not clear whether the experimenter and the confederate who timed the participants' walking pace by hand had been blind to condition throughout the experiment. The finding was that participants in the elderly priming condition actually walked faster, not more slowly, than subjects in the neutral priming condition, although the difference was not statistically significant (Pashler, Harris, and Coburn 2011; see also Chambers 2017, 13–14). I note that Bargh, Chen, and Burrows did not say whether the face of the handheld stopwatch was visible to the confederates who were measuring the participants' speed of walking. If it was, it could either have made the confederates' walking-speed measurements more anchored to the actual passage of time, or, if they were driven to please Bargh above all and had been influenced by his expectations in some way, it might have made them ensure the biased results. One would need an offshoot study to determine this question.

primed participants' walking speed could alter the experimenters' own behavior, resulting in slower interactions and gestures. Those alterations might then be unconsciously communicated to the participants, who would copy them in a kind of self-fulfilling prophecy, as Rosenthal had earlier suggested in his well-known discussions of experimenter-expectancy effects (Doyen et al. 2012, Rosenthal 1966). In this way, experimenters' expectations might act as an amplifier to the effects of the primes.

Experiment 2 was based on these possibilities. Fifty new participants took part in the experiment, and in addition another ten participants were recruited as experimenters. The same design and procedures were used as in Experiment 1, with two further modifications:

1. The experimenters' expectations about the behavior of the primed participants were manipulated. One half of the experimenters were told that the primed participants would walk more slowly as a result of the primes; the other half were told that participants would walk more quickly. Each experimenter tested five participants randomly assigned to the primed or the unprimed condition. Experimenters' expectations were shaped through a one-hour briefing and "persuasion" session prior to the first participant's session (Doyen et al. 2012, 3). In addition, the first participant tested was a confederate who had been "covertly instructed to act in the manner expected by the experimenter." Crucially, participants' condition (that is, primed or unprimed) was made salient to the experimenter (Doyen et al. 2012, 3). As in Experiment 1, experimenters were instructed to follow a script in order to standardize their interactions with the participants and not reveal to the latter the anticipated effects of the primes.

2. The other modification was that, as in Experiment 1, in Experiment 2 infrared sensors were used to measure participants' walking speeds ("objective timing"). But in Experiment 2, the sensors were presented to the experimenters as experimental hardware that was unreliable and that needed further calibration. The experimenters were therefore asked to measure the participants' walking time with a handheld stopwatch ("subjective timing").

The results of Experiment 2 showed that, according to the experimenters' "subjective" timing, primed participants walked significantly more slowly than the unprimed participants, when tested by an experimenter who had been manipulated to expect this result. Slower primed-participant walking speeds occurred regardless of whether walking times were measured "subjectively," with a handheld watch, or "objectively," with infrared sensors. Here, Bargh, Chen, and Burrows's (1996) original finding of slower walking after elderly priming was confirmed, but only because the experimenters expected that result. But the slower walking speeds were reversed in the case of experimenters who had been led to expect that primed participants would walk more quickly than the unprimed participants. However, when walking speeds were measured objectively with the infrared beam, there was no difference in walking speed between primed and unprimed participants. Doyen et al. attributed the reverse-priming effect on walking speed, observed only when experimenters were manipulated to expect faster walking speeds and used a handheld watch, to errors committed by the experimenters "because they expected the need to capture a fast event and hence tended to be inaccurate in stopping the watch" (Doyen et al. 2012, 6). Evidence collected from a forced-choice questionnaire demonstrated that the primed group, over both experimenters' conditions, chose the picture of an old person above chance levels, whereas the unprimed group showed no such result. Ninety-five percent of the participants in the primed condition stated that they had detected no link between the scrambled-sentence task and their subsequent walking behavior.

Doyen et al.'s conclusions from their experiments were, first, that when double-blind procedures and an objective method of recording walking speeds were employed, Bargh, Chen, and Burrows's claims regarding the automatic effects of priming on walking speeds were not confirmed. Second, they concluded that Bargh, Chen, and Burrows's findings *were* confirmed when—and only when—experimenters were led to expect that primed participants would walk more slowly. But Doyen et al. argued that their findings could not be explained solely in terms of Rosenthal's notion of the self-fulfilling character of expectancy effects. They held this view because, according to the "objective" infrared-beam measurement of walking speeds, primed participants did *not* walk faster simply because the experimenter testing them expected that they would do so. This finding suggested that neither primes alone nor expectancy per se were sufficient to produce the effects: there had to be some sort of *alignment* between primes and experimental cues, such as the experimenters' behavior, for such responses to occur. In the absence of such an alignment, the effects were not observed: when primes relating to old age were conjoined with an experimenter expecting to observe faster walking speed, no effect on actual walking speed was detected as measured objectively by infrared chronometry.

Doyen et al. also stressed that, according to their findings, most of the participants primed with the scrambled-sentence task were aware of the social category with which they had been primed, suggesting that the students, who were performing the experiment as part of a psychology course, had a higher degree of awareness of the primes than previous priming researchers might have realized. They also noted that a good proportion of the participants who actually exhibited a slower walking speed were aware of their walking response. "Whether automatic behavioral priming can occur without awareness remains unclear," the authors wrote (Doyen et al. 2012, 6). They also noted the congruence between their findings regarding the influence of experimenters' beliefs on the participants' behavior and the recent findings by Cesario, Plaks, and Higgins (2006) and Loersch and Payne (2011) to the effect that primed behaviors were sensitive to the contexts in which they took place. Doyen et al. concluded that

> Experimenters' expectations seem to provide a favorable context to [*sic, for*] the behavioral expression of the prime. Obviously, this interpretation remains tentative, as we do not know how this process operates. However, it is likely that experimenters who expect their participants to walk slower behave differently than those who expect their participants to walk faster and that such behavioral cues are picked up by participants.
>
> In conclusion, although automatic behavioral priming seems well established in the social cognition literature, it seems important to consider its limitations. In line with our result it seems that these methods need to be taken as an object of research per se before using it can be considered as an established phenomenon. (Doyen et al. 2012, 6)

Doyen et al.'s article appeared in January 2012, and was followed the same month by a *National Geographic* blog post by well-regarded science journalist Ed Yong, linking Doyen et al.'s findings about the influence of experimenters' expectations to the notorious case of the horse Clever Hans, who had solved math problems by picking up the correct response from the very subtle movements of his owner (Yong 2012a). Yong credited Doyen et al. for showing that, in the case of Bargh, Chen, and Burrows's classic elderly priming experiment at least, "it's not the words that create the effect. It's the *experimenter's expectations*" (Yong 2012a; his emphasis). Yong emphasized that Doyen et al. had not accused Bargh's team of simply making up their results to fit what they had expected: "Rather, their expectations affected *their behavior*, which then affected the volunteer's behavior. The volunteers were still being primed albeit by the experimenters rather than the word tasks" (Yong 2012a; his emphasis). He quoted

Doyen as stating: "'Our results don't completely rule out the possibility of unconscious priming, but they point to the fact that the (generally weak) effects may also be influenced by many other factors that are almost never controlled in such studies.'" Yong also cited Doyen on the importance of replication experiments. "'The need for independent replications of important results as those of Bargh cannot be overstated,'" Doyen was quoted as saying. "'The literature relies far too much on findings that have been produced using different methods dating back to 30 or 40 years ago'" (Yong 2012a).

Bargh responded angrily on March 5 in a *Psychology Today* blog post in which he criticized Doyen and his colleagues for various technical mistakes, questioned their competency, excoriated them for publishing in a journal that he claimed lacked adequate procedures for peer review, and rejected their conclusions (Bargh 2012a).[2] Instead of treating the differences between his own results and those of Doyen et al. as a problem that needed to be addressed, he reacted as if Doyen et al. and Yong had attacked him personally. Chief among his complaints was the implication that he and his colleagues had failed to observe adequate double-blind procedures and that unregulated experimenter expectations had therefore contaminated their findings. He countered that, as the experimenter in the original elderly priming study, he had been completely blind to the experimental condition of both primed and unprimed participants. He reported that he had never witnessed the priming manipulation (the scrambled-sentence test). He had packed envelopes with the two different scrambled-word tasks (tasks with elderly-related words or tasks with neutral words), had selected envelopes at random to give to participants, had led the participants to the test room, had briefed them, and had left them to finish the word task.

Doyen et al. had suggested that, during this procedure of handing out envelopes, the experimenter (Bargh) could have seen which set of priming conditions the participants received, and might have tuned his or her behavior accordingly, but Bargh vehemently denied that this was the case.[3]

---

2. Bargh subsequently deleted this blog post, but archived copies are available online.

3. Yong asked: "Could the experimenter have known what the experiment was about, even though Bargh asserts that they were blind?" Yong noted that in the comments section of Bargh's post, psychologist Matt Craddock observed that the experimenter was also responsible for prepackaging the various tasks in their packets, and so had ample time to study the materials. Yong commented: "This is the first of several inconsistencies in Bargh's interpretation of his own study" (Yong 2012b).

Nor, he stated, did he himself conduct the measurements of walking speed, which were carried out by a graduate student posing as the next participant, who sat waiting with her coat on her lap and surreptitiously started and stopped the stopwatch. There was no way, Bargh asserted, that experimenter expectations or any other form of experimenter bias could have influenced the original findings. "We were fully aware of this potential problem at the time," he declared, "and took every precaution to make sure it did not contaminate or spuriously produce our results" (Bargh 2012a).[4]

As more than one commentator observed, a lot depended on how Bargh and his team had actually behaved in the test room. Although it might be said in justification of Bargh's methods that he and his co-authors had followed the rather minimal standards in place in 1996 for reporting laboratory procedures, it is also the case that certain details remained unclear.[5] In any case, Bargh had no answer to the fact that, using rigorous

---

4. One of Bargh's charges against Doyen et al. (2012) was that the latter had called the participants' attention to how to walk down the hall on leaving the laboratory, which would tend to make them aware of the issue of walking speed and hence to interfere with the expression of automatic processes. Bargh wrote that Doyen et al.'s experimenter "called the participant's attention to walking down the hallway after the experiment, by giving them instructions to 'go straight down the hall on leaving.'" Bargh claimed that Bargh, Chen, and Burrows (1996) had not done this; rather, they "let the participant leave in the most natural way" (Bargh, 2012a). Yong pointed out, however, that Doyen et al.'s paper did not contain the words Bargh attributed to them, but merely stated that "'participants were clearly directed to the end of the corridor.'" Yong commented: "It is not clear how this differs from Bargh's own study in which Bargh, Chen, and Burrows had stated that "'the experimenter told the participant that the elevator was down the hall'" (Yong 2012b). Dijksterhuis subsequently (2014) repeated Bargh's complaint (2012a) that Doyen et al. (2012) had drawn attention to the dependent variable of walking speed by giving the participants explicit instructions to walk down the corridor in ways that could have aroused their suspicions about the purpose of the experiment, thereby attenuating the priming effects — a criticism that had already been rejected by Yong (2012b).

5. Thus, another of Bargh's (2012a) criticisms was that Doyen et al. (2012) had used too many of the elderly priming words in their priming manipulation: he noted that Doyen et al. had apparently used an elderly-related word in all thirty of their scrambled-sentence items, whereas, he asserted, in his methods recommendations for conducting priming experiments (Bargh and Chartrand 2000), he had suggested using only around ten or twelve critical primes out of the thirty total items. His argument was that using too many primes of the same category or theme could cause the participants to consciously notice the category or theme, an eventuality that might eliminate or reverse the predicted priming effect. But it is not clear from Bargh, Chen, and Burrows's (1996) description of their methods how the priming words for the elderly were distributed in their own scrambled-sentence packets. Moreover, as Yong (2012b) pointed out, Bargh's complaint contradicted Bargh and Ferguson (2000), which stated that, if there were too many primes, participants would be more likely to perform as expected because of demand effects — not that too

double-blind procedures and an objective timing method, his original findings concerning slower walking speeds in participants primed with words associated with old age had failed to replicate.[6] In a second posting Bargh emphasized the fact that back in 1996 he and his team had made sure to conduct both exact (or direct) and conceptual replications of their elderly priming findings, and had waited to publish their experiments until conceptual replications had been obtained in other laboratories unaffiliated with his own. Bargh suggested that the reason his elderly priming study had become such a focus of the replication debate was because there was a dislike of the notion of unconscious processes. This antipathy went back at least to Freud, but since the 1950s it had also manifested itself in fears of brainwashing, mind control, and subliminal advertising (Bargh 2012b).

Bargh's heated response to Doyen et al.'s findings and the tumultuous controversy that then ensued have been extensively discussed.[7] As I noted in the introduction, Kahneman wrote a letter to *Nature* urging Bargh and his colleagues to restore the credibility of the priming field by collectively acknowledging and confronting the problem of replication; the letter inflamed an already explosive situation (Kahneman 2012). In the wake of the failed replication of Bargh, Chen, and Burrows's iconic experiment, there followed many unsuccessful attempts to replicate other priming studies, such as the well-known experiment on the priming of intelligent behavior by Bargh's Dutch colleague Ap Dijksterhuis. The details of these several failed replications can be followed in numerous publica-

---

many primes would make the effect evaporate. By that reasoning, Yong suggested, Doyen's participants should have shown an even stronger priming response. More generally, Chambers (2017, 62) noted that the absence of methodological precision in the description of experiments allowed researchers to criticize any failed replication for not following some unpublished but apparently crucial detail of the original.

6. Bargh also protested that in "in the Doyen et al. study but not in ours the experimenter was also the timer of how slowly the participant walked down the hallway. We instead had been very careful to keep the experimenter separate from any data collection" (2012a). The implication of Bargh's objection was that, because in Doyen et al.'s experiment the experimenters were allowed to collect the data concerning the participants' walking speeds, the influence of their expectations was not controlled for, as it was in the original experiment in which the walking speed was measured by a confederate and not the experimenter himself or herself. But Bargh's complaint does not address the fact that in Experiment 1, when double-blind procedures and infrared sensors measured walking speeds, not handheld stopwatches, no effect of the primes was detected.

7. Doyen et al. were taken aback by the severity of Bargh's reaction to their paper. Bartlett reported that, although they did not feel that his critiques of their methods were valid, they tried the experiment again, taking Bargh's concerns into account. "It still didn't work" (Bartlett 2013).

tions.[8] But Bargh himself did not try to replicate his own experiments, as Kahneman had suggested he ought to do.

No doubt Bargh suffered a reputational setback owing to the publication of Doyen et al.'s failed replication of his famous experiment.[9] It was reported that, in the immediate wake of the controversy, Bargh's efforts to obtain funding for the study of clinical applications of priming failed (Bower 2012, 29). As a pattern of non-replication of priming experiments began to emerge, the entire field of priming came to be considered suspect. Nevertheless, Bargh stubbornly defended his work. He refused to retract the results of his other priming experiments when these were shown to be non-replicable (Bargh and Shalev 2012; Donnellan, Lucas, and Cesario 2015; Simons 2014; Chambers 2017, 66, 80–81). He reiterated his claims for the unintentional and unconscious nature of priming responses, as did some of his former students (for example, Ferguson and Mann 2014). Bargh and like-minded colleagues pointed to evidence of priming effects in real-life contexts and to functional-imaging findings ostensibly demonstrating the brain regions involved in priming, and they unapologetically continued to cite as valid priming results that had failed to replicate. In the process Bargh seamlessly accommodated his views to those of Cesario and others who had adopted a situational approach to priming. In this way, he minimized the theoretical differences between his original, direct perception-behavior account of priming and Cesario's and others' more contextual approach (see for example Bargh et al. 2012; Bargh 2014b).

In 2017, Bargh published *Before You Know It: The Unconscious Reasons We Do What We Do*, a book for the general public in which he presented the results of research on priming without acknowledging that many of the most well-known findings, including his own, had been cast into doubt, and without replying to incisive critiques of his experiments (his book was

---

8. In a very large literature, see Pashler, Coburn, and Harris 2012; Pashler, Rohrer, and Harris 2013; Shanks et al. 2013; Bargh 2014a; Bargh and Shalev 2012; 2015; Cesario 2014; Cesario and Jonas 2014; Dijksterhuis 2014; Dijksterhuis, van Knippenberg, and Holland 2014; Dijksterhuis et al. 2014; Donnellan, Lucas, and Cesario 2015; Doyen et al. 2014; Ferguson and Mann 2014; Higgins and Eitam 2014; Klein et al. 2014b; Loersch and Payne 2014; Molden 2014a; 2014b; Newell and Shanks 2014b; Simons 2014; Stroebe and Strack 2014; Wheeler, DeMarree, and Petty 2014; Nosek et al. 2015; Open Science Collaboration 2015; Spellman 2015; Barsalou 2016; Eitam and Higgins 2016; Strack and Schwarz 2016; Stroebe 2016; Chambers 2017; Nelson, Simmons, and Simonsohn 2018; Zwaan et al. 2018; Camerer et al. 2018; Chabris et al. 2019; Chivers 2019; Ritchie 2020.

9. See Fetterman and Sassenberg 2015 and Ebersole, Axt, and Nosek 2016 for discussions of the reputational consequences of failed replications among scientists.

severely criticized by reformers; for example, Schimmack 2017). Tellingly, in a sign that the psychology establishment continued to esteem Bargh's work and was prepared to rally behind him, in 2014 the American Psychological Association awarded him a prestigious award for his research contributions (Bargh 2014c). Moreover, in 2016 a group of prominent psychologists, which included well-known researcher Daniel T. Gilbert at Harvard University, asserted that a study undertaken by the Open Science Collaboration (2015) claiming that the reproducibility of psychological science was surprisingly low was statistically flawed; the group argued that the data were consistent with the view that, on the contrary, the reproducibility of psychological science was quite high (Gilbert et al. 2016). Forty-four authors involved in the Open Science Collaboration wrote a rebuttal, accusing Gilbert's group of statistical errors and unwarranted inferences (Anderson et al. 2016; see also Lakens 2016; Srivastava 2016). It seemed that psychologists could not agree about the basic methods required for arriving at the truth.

Hidden Moderators: "The Ultimate Attribution Error"?

One of the most frequent defenses adopted by priming researchers committed to defending their claims against reform-minded critics was that subtle, unidentified "moderators" must have played decisive roles in facilitating priming effects in ways that were hard to detect and that made replications unlikely to succeed. On the one hand, psychology reformers demanding better research practices endorsed Popper's view that an "effect" that could not be directly reproduced did not qualify as a scientific discovery. Thus Rolf Zwaan et al. (2018) argued:

> Repeatability is an essential component of science. A finding is arguably not scientifically meaningful until it can be replicated with the same procedures that produced it in the first place . . . [T]here are no substantive and methodological arguments against direct replication. In fact, replication is an important instrument for theory building. It should therefore be made a mainstream component of psychological research. (Zwaan et al. 2018, 13)

On the other hand, the same reformers also accepted that a single replication failure could not be considered definitive against any specific body of scientific research. As Zwaan et al. (2018) also observed, if a finding could not be reproduced, this fact did not necessarily lead to a wholesale falsification of the theory from which the original prediction had been derived:

Under Lakatos' notion of *sophisticated falsificationism*, an auxiliary hypothesis can be formulated, which enables the expanded theory to accommodate the troublesome result. If more falsifications arise, however, and even more auxiliary hypotheses must be formulated to account for the unsupported predictions, problems begin to accrue for the theory. This *strategic retreat* (Meehl 1990) can cause a research program to become *degenerative*... If, on the other hand, the auxiliary hypotheses are empirically successful, the program acquires greater explanatory power and is deemed *progressive*. Thus, replications are an instrument for distinguishing progressive from degenerative research programs. (Zwaan et al. 2018, 2, citing Lakatos 1970, their emphases; and Meehl 1990b)

Under this rationale, Bargh gained some leeway in his efforts to stem the damage to his reputation. Original findings could be defended by appealing to the role of auxiliary hypotheses, hay could be made from disagreements among researchers over methodological issues, and there were disputes about the value of direct versus conceptual replication, and even about whether a replication crisis existed at all.

And in fact, in many ways Bargh's response to the failed replication of his and colleagues' priming experiments did exemplify the Kuhnian or Meehlian insight that scientists tend to cling to their positions when confronted with "anomalies," appealing when necessary to ad hoc subsidiary hypotheses to defend their views. According to Kuhn this tendency was especially characteristic of the social sciences, which had yet to attain the status of "normal" science in his sense of the term (Kuhn 1970b). As I have already noted, by this he meant there was no fundamental research exemplar or core canon of reproducible results governing the field, as was the case in the basic sciences, but rather a plethora of research enterprises and theoretical claims, with frequent clashes about fundamentals.[10] As Christopher Ferguson and Moritz Heene observed in this regard:

The aversion to the null and the persistence of publication bias and denial of the same, renders a situation in which psychological theories are virtually unkillable. Instead of rigid adherence to an objective process of

---

10. In a discussion of the value and importance of direct replication, Alexander and Moors argued that the poor replication record in psychology was symptomatic of "pre-paradigmatic" science (Alexander and Moors 2018, 13).

replication and falsification, debates within psychology too easily degenerate into ideological snowball fights, the end result of which is to allow poor quality theories to survive indefinitely, ... [T]he entire discipline risks a slide toward the unfalsifiable. (Ferguson and Heene 2012, 559)

This comment captures the essence of the priming problem. To defend the validity of their claims, priming researchers frequently appealed to the by-now-familiar idea that replication failures might be due to various hidden moderators or variables, unidentified in their original experiments but able to interfere with replication attempts. Thus, in the wake of Doyen et al.'s failed replication of Bargh, Chen, and Burrows's elderly priming experiment, Cesario (2014) criticized those who argued that it ought to be possible to identify invariant priming effects that could be consistently and easily obtained by any researcher in the world, in any lab, in any context, and with any participant population. He did not doubt the essential importance of replication in science. Indeed, in 2013 he was quoted as saying that, although he was sympathetic to the argument that the existence of moderators made priming experiments difficult to replicate, he also thought that the argument only went so far. "'At some point,'" he observed, "'it becomes excuse-making. We have to have some threshold where we say that [the effect] doesn't exist'" (Bartlett 2013; see also Bartlett 2014).[11] But Cesario also maintained that, because of the sensitivity of priming effects to variations in experimental conditions and subject populations, inferences that could be drawn from replication results were inevitably ambiguous. It was simply unfortunate, from his point of view, that priming researchers still lacked theories "specifying the precise contingencies that lead to such variation" (Cesario 2014, 40). He was confident, however, that with time those theories would be developed.

But would they? Or did the logic of the claim for the role of moderators in priming outcomes imply that no theories would ever be able to

---

11. Cesario remarked:

My suspicion is that, more often than not, a researcher is accidentally hitting on the right level of an important moderating variable ... as to obtain a priming effect ... And when researchers do not get the "right" combination of variables, the failures end up in the file drawer ... [P]riming researchers cannot appeal endlessly to "unknown moderation" without doing the work to provide evidence for such moderation. At some point, the evidence may shift, and it would be more reasonable to conclude that the original effect was wrong or was so specific as to be rendered meaningless. (Cesario 2014, 44)

identify all the contingencies involved in priming experiments, given the almost infinite number of such potential variables in the different cultures, populations, and laboratories in which such replications were likely to be attempted?

Already prior to 2012, Wheeler and DeMarree had identified as many as sixteen moderators capable of influencing some aspect of the perception-behavior pathway (Wheeler and DeMarree 2009). As the controversy over priming developed steam, the appeal to the importance of moderators in influencing priming outcomes was a common alibi among researchers convinced of the truth of priming effects. Thus, Dijksterhuis argued that criticism of behavioral priming experiments was "largely overblown" (Dijksterhuis 2014, 72), denied that the field was infested with false positives, rejected as an illusion the importance of direct replication, and emphasized instead the value of research investigating the influence of hitherto unidentified contextual-situational moderators on priming outcomes. Similarly, Bargh appealed to the role of moderators to explain why one of his studies, ostensibly demonstrating that holding a warm cup of coffee promoted interpersonal warmth, had failed to replicate (Williams and Bargh 2008; Chabris et al. 2019; Schimmack 2019).[12] Loersch and Payne's Situated Inference Model (Loersch and Payne 2011, 2014); Wheeler, DeMarree, and Petty's Active-Self explanation (Wheeler, DeMarree and Petty. 2007; 2014); Cesario and Jonas's Resource Computational Model (RCM) (2014); Higgins and Eitam's Relevance of a Representation theory (ROAR) (2014); Barsalou's (2016) Situated Conceptualization theory: the soup of competing theories and acronyms cluttering the field suggests that psychologists were driven to announce their own theories rather than deal with existing ones—theories they designed to accommodate the now widely accepted fact that priming effects did not conform to Bargh's original direct perception-behavior model but depended on a multiplicity of mostly unidentified controlling factors.

Doyen et al. skeptically observed in this regard that with so many

---

12. As reported by Schimmack (2019), Bargh suggested that the replication attempt had failed to reproduce the exact warmth of the coffee required to produce the predicted result. Schimmack observed, however, that Bargh had overlooked the fact that his original study produced only weak evidence for the effect, and that accordingly to claim that holding a warm cup of coffee would impact people's experience of warmth or their behavior would require studies with larger samples and more convincing evidence. But as far as I know, Bargh himself made no attempt to replicate his original study with better sample sizes or better methodological controls.

possible moderators playing a role, it was unsurprising if priming effects were hard to reproduce. He and his colleagues suggested that most priming studies were too underpowered to detect even medium-sized effects of the prime and were "massively underpowered to detect an interaction of that effect with one or more moderators" (Doyen et al. 2014, 27). The proliferation of moderators led Locke to ask somewhat plaintively: "Does every primed action depend on different moderators and/or traits? . . . Would a full theory of behavioral priming have to include thousands of moderators?" (Locke 2015, 412).

In a related vein, Leif Nelson and colleagues suggested that the burden of proof regarding the influence of moderators on priming was on the researcher who advocated the least plausible claim: it was not sufficient for a researcher confronted by a failed replication to suggest the possible role of unidentified moderators without being willing to make "*testable claims about the circumstance(s) under which the effect is expected to replicate and, therefore, the circumstances under which a failure to replicate would be informative . . .* If critics of a replication cannot specify conditions under which the effect is expected to replicate, then they are not making a scientific claim" (Nelson, Simmons, and Simonsohn 2018, 521, citing Lakatos 1970; their emphasis). Applying such a standard to Bargh would have meant that, if he believed that certain moderators explained why replications of various of his own priming experiments had failed, he ought to be able to specify a set of circumstances he thought would yield the effect. But Bargh was not willing to do so. Similarly, Ulrich Schimmack characterized the attribution of replication failures to hidden moderators as "the ultimate attribution error of social psychologists." He argued: "It makes them conduct study after study in the search for a predicted outcome without realizing that a few successes among many failures are expected simply due to chance alone. To avoid realizing the fragility of these successes, they never repeat the same study twice. The ultimate attribution error has enabled social psychologists to deceive themselves and others for decades" (Schimmack 2018).

The Historical Sensitivity of Priming Outcomes

In one of the more provocative papers claiming that unknown moderators explain replication failures, yet another hitherto-neglected variable was proposed: the *language* of the priming words used in Bargh's elderly priming experiment. In 2014, Stroebe and Strack argued that contextual differences mattered when replications were attempted. People's beliefs differed in different cultures and even over time in the same culture, so the meaning of primes changed(Stroebe and Strack 2014). The authors speculated in this regard that, even though Doyen et al. (2012) had attempted to faithfully replicate Bargh, Chen, and Burrows's (1996) original elderly priming procedures, their replication attempt might have failed because the French translations of the words Bargh, Chen, and Burrows had used in their scrambled-sentence test to prime their participants had different meanings in Belgium, where the replication attempt had taken place (Stroebe and Strack 2014, 62). On this and related grounds, Stroebe and Strack argued that the direct replications of the kind now being widely performed, including the attempted replication by Doyen et al. (2012), were uninformative unless researchers could demonstrate that their replications constituted rigorous tests of the postulated underlying theoretical constructs or mechanisms involved. "Even multiple failures to replicate an established finding would not result in a rejection of the original hypothesis," Stroebe and Strack claimed, "if there are multiple studies that supported the hypothesis" (Stroebe and Strack 2014, 64–68). In their view, only conceptual replications mattered. They claimed that the most effective strategy for resolving conflicts between competing explanations for the same psychological phenomena was to search for the variables determining the conditions under which theories applied. As I already noted: according to Stroebe and Strack, the claim that there was a replication crisis had been greatly exaggerated (Stroebe and Strack 2014, 59).

In 2015, Michael Ramscar, Cyrus Shaoul, and R. Harald Baayen lent support to Stroebe and Strack's (2014) argument about the difference language made to replication attempts. We have seen that in their replication of Bargh, Chen, and Burrows's study in Belgium, Doyen et al. (2012) had translated, or found French equivalences for, the English words in the scrambled-sentence test Bargh and his team (1996) had used to prime their participants. But Ramscar and his colleagues objected:

> Doyen et al. appear to assume that the language a priming study is conducted in is not an important factor in research, or indeed, in replication... [T]here is reason to believe that this assumption is mistaken: Bargh et al.'s prime set (like the materials used in many priming studies) utilizes a high proportion of English adjectives, however the frequencies and distribution of adjectives varies [*sic*, vary] considerably across languages... and adjectives appear to play very different functional roles

in discourse depending on the language in question. (Ramscar, Shaoul, and Baayen 2015, 16–17)

In David Trafimow and Brian Earp's (2016) summary of Ramscar, Shaoul, and Baayen's (2015) argument:

> Adjectives in English tend to precede nouns, and therefore prime them, much more frequently than do adjectives in French. Importantly, this pattern holds true for the specific adjectives used in the Bargh et al. (1996) study compared to those in the Doyen et al. (2012) replication attempt. According to Ramscar et al. (2015), the average frequency of the English items used in the Bargh et al. study in a large English corpus was "far higher" ... than that of the French items used by Doyen et al. in a similar French corpus ... In other words, "when it comes to their experience of encountering the [adjectives] in the prime sets in contexts where they actually served as primes to nouns ... we can expect that the subjects in Bargh et al.'s study will have had something [on] the order of six times more experience" ... than the participants in Doyen et al.'s study. Accordingly, the adjectives used in the Bargh et al. study could be expected to serve as much stronger primes of the targeted elderly stereotype. (Trafimow and Earp 2016, 545)

Ramscar, Shaoul, and Baayen (2015) spelled out the implications of their argument: because the primes in Doyen et al.'s replication were far less powerful than those in Bargh, Chen, and Burrows's original experiment, it was not surprising that the former researchers had failed to obtain the results that Bargh and his team had obtained. Ramscar and his colleagues therefore concluded that it was impossible for anyone to directly replicate Bargh, Chen, and Burrows's elderly priming experiment when using French instead of English priming words: "Failed replication attempts in other languages that are conducted using naïve translations of materials in other languages can only be seen as scientifically uninformative, and something of a waste of time and resources" (Ramscar, Shaoul and Baayen 2015, 21).

More radically, Ramscar and his team suggested that the efficacy of Bargh, Chen, and Burrows's priming words, including the word *old*, had also declined significantly since 1996 in the United States. In sum, not only could priming studies not be expected to replicate across languages but they might also fail to replicate within the same language over time, including even across an individual's lifespan. Therefore, to try and conduct a direct replication of Bargh, Chen, and Burrows's 1996 experiment in America in 2015 in America would be something of a "fool's errand." The problem that priming research had to face, Ramscar and his colleagues commented, "is not that the field doesn't replicate its findings often enough, but rather that, as they are currently employed, the approaches that some researchers in psychology have borrowed from the natural sciences may not be appropriate to the phenomena they study at the level that [they] actually study them" (Ramscar, Shaoul, and Baayen 2015, 13, 27).

In other words, according to Ramscar and his co-authors, the reason priming studies could not be expected to replicate was because cultural contexts trumped everything else. In short, *the objects of concern to social psychologists were radically contingent and historical.*

This argument was precisely the one Stroebe and Strack (2014) had made the year before when they had proposed that a major problem with direct replication was that the variables in priming experiments were culturally and socially mediated. Experiments undertaken at one point in time with a specific population were not likely to succeed when performed at another time with another population: "Although the experimenter has control over the prime, this is not true for the concept it activates. People differ in their beliefs about the elderly. Furthermore, different beliefs are differently accessible in different contexts . . . Therefore, the same prime can activate different concepts in different people and/or under different conditions" (Stroebe and Strack 2014, 62). Stroebe and Strack (2014) had suggested that this nuance was probably why Doyen et al.'s (2012) attempt to replicate Bargh, Chen, and Burrows's elderly priming study had failed: there were too many differences between the beliefs of the students who had participated in Bargh and colleagues' original elderly priming experiment and Doyen et al.'s participants in Belgium twenty years later. Indeed, with life expectancies increasing every year and people staying active much longer, the construct of "walking slowly" might no longer form part of the elderly stereotype all those years later, even in New York.[13]

It is striking that in support of their argument Stroebe and Strack

---

13. It is also worth noting another implication of Stroebe and Strack's (2014) arguments, namely, that beliefs and concepts (including unconscious meanings and intentions) were a crucial dimension of people's responses to priming situations, in ways that would seem to contradict Bargh's claims for the non-intentional, automatic character of priming reactions. But they did not address the status of those beliefs and intentions.

appealed to the work of Kenneth Gergen, who in 1973 had famously rejected the claims of social psychology to the status of a natural science on the grounds that the events it studied were culturally variable and unstable (Gergen 1973). Moreover, as discussed in chapter 2, in a 1989 conference Gergen had directly challenged the positivist approach of Stroebe and others precisely on the grounds of the historicity of psychological phenomena (Gergen 1989; Rijsman and Stroebe 1989; Stroebe and Kruglanski 1989). But now Stroebe and Strack (2014) appealed to Gergen's views to support their arguments concerning the cultural sensitivity of priming outcomes. As they commented: "This was one of the major arguments that Gergen (1973) used to argue that 'social psychology is primarily an historical inquiry. Unlike the natural sciences, it deals with facts that are largely nonrepeatable and which fluctuate markedly over time'" (Stroebe and Strack 2014, 68 n2).

Yet Stroebe and Strack seemed indifferent to the implications that Gergen had drawn from this claim. They omitted Gergen's next remarks suggesting that social psychology was not a cumulative science. Gergen had continued: "Principles of human interaction cannot readily be developed over time because the facts on which they are based do not generally remain stable. Knowledge cannot accumulate in the usual scientific sense because such knowledge does not generally transcend its historical boundaries" (Gergen 1973, 310). On this basis, Gergen had concluded that, because empirical research was based on historically situated observations of constantly changing patterns of human action, the attempt to establish general laws of human conduct abstracted from the historical situation were doomed to fail. In other words, in alignment with the arguments of Peter Winch (2008) and other critics of the social sciences before him, Gergen had proposed that psychology could not be made to fit the norms of the natural sciences. It followed that, according to him, completely different social-constructionist or hermeneutical approaches in psychology were called for.

This problem was precisely the one confronting priming research: if contextual factors played such an important role in priming outcomes, the predictive and explanatory validity of the priming model could be realized only within very narrow sets of restrictive conditions and could not be generalized beyond them. In short, as Edwin Gantt, J. P. Lindstrom, and R. Williams (2017) put the point, there was a lack of fit between the positivist-experimental methodologies of the kind that informed most contemporary research in social psychology and the social-constructionist, hermeneutic approaches of Gergen and others that were more attentive to the meaning of the everyday actions of human beings in their particular historical, situated contexts. From the perspective of Gantt, Lindstrom, and Williams (2017), the idea that human behaviors could be understood as automatic responses to impersonal, essentially nonsocial, lawlike forces emanating from the external world was a mistake.

But Stroebe himself did not draw this conclusion from Gergen's work. In another paper of 2016, Stroebe addressed the topic of the epistemological status of psychology in order to explicitly refute Gergen's radical conclusions. Stroebe here repeated the arguments he and Strack (2014) had made two years earlier against the value of direct replication of the kind being carried out by reformers in several multi-lab replication endeavors. He suggested that such efforts were not informative because failures to replicate did not prove that the original findings were invalid (Stroebe 2016, 140). This argument led him to turn once again to Gergen's (1973) response to the earlier crisis in social psychology, this time in order to distance his position from Gergen's.

Stroebe seized on Gergen's remark that social phenomena "'may vary considerably in the extent to which they are subject to historical change,'" and that we "'must think . . . in terms of a *continuum of historical durability*, with phenomena highly susceptible to historical influence at one extreme and the more stable processes at the other'" (Gergen 1973, 318; his emphasis; quoted by Stroebe 2016, 140). Gergen had suggested in this connection that phenomena "closely tied to physiological *givens*" (Gergen 1973, 318) were the least susceptible to historical modifications. But Stroebe argued that in addition to such physiological givens, certain "*basic psychological processes*" were likewise insensitive to cultural alteration (Stroebe 2016, 140; my emphasis). He identified the "anchoring effect" as such a basic psychological process, namely, the tendency of people to rely on the first piece of information they receive when making decisions.[14] Stroebe suggested that, although over time people's changing knowledge might influence their responses to the anchoring prime, the anchoring process itself remained unaffected. "In terms of Gergen's 'continuum of

---

14. The anchoring effect occurs when, to take one familiar example, car salesmen prime or "anchor" their price negotiations with customers by naming a price well above the market value of the car, so that when a deal is cut it seems to buyers that they are getting a bargain—a behavioral effect that is usually attributed to the unconscious influence of the anchor.

historical durability,'" he argued, "this is an example of a process at the durable end" (Stroebe 2016, 140).[15]

Stroebe contrasted such "basic psychological processes" as the anchoring effect with social psychological phenomena that depended partly on social learning and were as such sensitive to historical changes. Thus, Stroebe suggested that the other extreme of Gergen's "continuum of historical durability" was epitomized by a set of priming experiments by Travis Carter (2011), co-authored by a former student of Bargh's, Melissa Ferguson, and Ran Hassin. The experiments purported to show that a single exposure to the American flag led both Republican and Democratic voters in the United States to shift toward Republican beliefs, attitudes, and voting behaviors. What made the experiments especially striking, not to say notorious, was the claim that some of the priming effects lasted for eight months after exposure to the prime—a much greater length of time than semantic priming researchers were used to observing in their experiments.

One of Carter, Ferguson, and Hassin's (2011) American-flag experiments had recently failed to replicate in a Many Labs replication effort

---

15. To explain the anchoring effect itself, Stroebe adopted the "selective accessibility" hypothesis of Strack and Mussweiler (1997). According to this hypothesis, participants compare the target of judgment to the anchor value by applying a hypothesis-consistent test strategy (the Selectivity Hypothesis), with the result that the accessibility of anchor-consistent evidence is selectively increased, a process that is held to depend on a memory search. Stroebe noted that the fact that different participants might be more or less knowledgeable about the task at hand in ways that might affect their estimates would have no influence on the anchoring effect itself. That is why he considered the anchoring mechanism to be a basic psychological process lying at the durable end of Gergen's historical continuum (Stroebe 2016, 140). It is worth noting in this connection, however, that the causal mechanisms underlying the anchoring effect are still not fully understood. See Furnham and Boo (2011) for a discussion of the view that multiple mechanisms may be involved.

Moreover, Stroebe (2016) made no reference to a paper of Newell and Shanks (2014b) who, in an analysis of the anchoring literature, had not disputed the reality of anchoring effects but had challenged the standard claim of priming researchers that the influence of anchoring was the result of low-level, unconscious, automatic processes. Instead, they had concluded: "Anchors have narrow effects on behavior with little transfer across judgments, these effects can be controlled, and deliberate engagement with the anchor is a prerequisite for obtaining influences on later judgments. We question whether priming studies reveal evidence for the sort of automatic and consequential mental processes that are commonly proposed" (Newell and Shanks 2014b, 88). In short, Newell and Shanks appeared to question whether the anchoring effect constituted a "basic psychological process" in Stroebe's sense of the concept.

(Klein et al. 2014a). Carter and colleagues had been consulted regarding the Many Labs replication attempts, and they had not disputed the fact that their original findings could not be reproduced. But they had explained the replication failure by suggesting that changing political conditions had altered the outcome. They had observed in this regard that their original experiment had been run in 2009 (actually in the spring of 2010; see Carter, Ferguson, and Hassin 2011, 1016), a year after Barack Obama had been sworn in as president, and much had changed since then (Ferguson, Carter, and Hassin 2014, 301). In other words, Carter and his team had defended their original findings on the grounds that the priming phenomena they had studied were too sensitive to their specific political-historical context to be directly reproducible in a different context. As they had remarked: "Our original study tested the influence of an American flag on Americans' support for American political policies. There is nothing in the paper to suggest that this effect could be transplanted to other countries" (Ferguson, Carter, and Hassin 2014, 299, 302).[16] Stroebe echoed Ferguson and her colleagues' conclusion: "As Ferguson et al. (2014) argued, this is basically a historical effect, namely that at a certain time in American history, American citizens became more conservative, when primed with the American flag" (Stroebe 2016, 140).

Stroebe went on to suggest that historical forces could "also affect the dependent measure, even in experiments that test basic psychological pro-

---

16. Because of differences between in-lab versus online samples and other variables in the Many Labs replication attempts, Ferguson, Carter, and Hassin regarded the replication attempt as a form of conceptual replication rather than a direct replication (2014). But if this was the case, then for Ferguson and her team the outstanding question was: Why had that conceptual replication failed? They were sure the answer would be found. If, as seemed clear, replication failures were due to the dynamic influence of cultural variables or moderators, then what was needed was a revision of the original priming theories to accommodate this fact, and Ferguson, Carter, and Hassin claimed to be working on just such a revision (2014, 299). In a follow-up paper several years later, Ferguson and colleagues reported the findings of a meta-analysis of all published and unpublished studies from their own laboratories, in order to evaluate the priming effect of the American flag on political attitudes. They concluded that the American-flag primes did produce politically conservative shifts in attitude during the initial time period when the experiments were originally conducted. They attributed the subsequent decline in the effect of the flag to zero in the ensuing years, as documented by many later studies that did not show the effect, to alterations in the meaning of the flag, owing to changes in political and social culture. The researchers conceded, however, that they could not rule out other interpretations, including the view that the original finding of the influence of a brief exposure to an image of the American flag on political attitudes was a false positive (Carter et al. 2020).

cesses" (Stroebe 2016, 140). It was perhaps unfortunate that he chose to illustrate this particular claim with the Facial Feedback mechanism, which he treated as a "basic psychological process" that was immune to historical alteration. The Facial Feedback mechanism, or rather the Facial Feedback Hypothesis, had had a long and contested history. It postulates that people's facial movements and expressions influence their emotional experience (see Buck 1980; Ekman 1982; Izard 1990; Laird 1984; Matsumoto 1987; and Tourangeau and Ellsworth 1979; Coles, Larsen, and Lench 2019 provides a recent overview of the literature). In support of his views regarding the status of the Facial Feedback Hypothesis, Stroebe cited a well-known experiment by Fritz Strack, Leonard Martin, and Sabine Stepper. (1988). In Strack and colleagues' experiment, participants were instructed to hold a pen in their mouth in ways that either inhibited or facilitated the movement of certain facial muscles. The students were coached to either hold the pen in their mouths with clenched teeth, thereby producing the expression of a smile, or to hold the pen in their mouths by pursing their lips, which was incompatible with contracting the muscles that are used in smiling. The hypothesis was that feedback from the smile expression would make the participants happier—as measured by their degree of amusement when viewing cartoons—than those who held the pen with their lips puckered. The hypothesis appeared to be confirmed when the participants who held the pen in their teeth in the smile position rated a set of cartoons from Gary Larson's well-known *The Far Side* sketches as funnier than the participants who held the pen with puckered lips did.

Relying on the validity of Strack and his team's experiment, Stroebe proposed that while the basic facial-feedback mechanism itself was unaffected by the changing context, the dependent variable in Strack, Martin, and Stepper's (1988) study—namely, the participants' emotional response to seeing funny cartoons—could well be influenced by alterations in cultural norms: "Whereas their [Strack et al.'s 1988] manipulation of facial activity should not be affected by historical change, it is unlikely that the cartoons, which German students found moderately funny in the late 80ies, would still be considered funny today" (Stroebe 2016, 140).

In fact, Strack himself had used precisely this argument to explain a recent failed attempt to replicate his "seminal" experiment feedback of 1988. In a preregistered replication study, E. J. Wagenmakers et al. had attempted to replicate Strack, Martin, and Stepper's (1988) study in experiments carried out in seventeen laboratories in eight countries involving nearly two thousand participants, but the team had been unable to reproduce Strack and colleagues' findings in a statistically compelling fashion.[17] The replicators had used a different set of cartoon images as the dependent variable, but they had nevertheless used a set taken from the same comic strip used by Strack, Martin, and Stepper in their original experiment (1988): Gary Larson's *The Far Side* (Wagenmakers et al. 2016, 919). Wagenmakers et al. had pretested the selected cartoons with a large sample of university students to make sure that the images met the same standard of being "moderately funny" as in the original experiment. Although Strack himself had volunteered his experiment for the replication attempts, had provided the original cartoon publication and other materials, and had had input during the early stages of the protocol development, he had found fault with the replication: "Despite the obtained ratings of funniness, it must be asked if Gary Larson's *The Fire Side* cartoons that were iconic for the zeitgeist of the 1980s instantiated similar psychological conditions 30 years later. It is indicative that one of the four exclusion criteria was participants' failure to understand the cartoons" (Strack 2016, 929).[18] In other words, like Stroebe, Strack had attributed the replication failure chiefly to changes in

---

17. More specifically, Wagenmakers et al. (2016) reported that nine out of the seventeen outcomes were consistent with the original findings (albeit in a much weaker form), but eight were in the opposite direction, while overall there was no significant effect—with the result that the Facial Feedback Hypothesis was called into question (see also Engber 2016). In 2017, Strack criticized the influence of Registered Replication Reports such as that of Wagenmakers et al. (2016) on the field of social psychology, on the grounds that subtle and fragile effects were too easily dismissed as untrue if they failed to replicate and because a probabilistic model of significance testing falsely promised a direct path from data to truth in ways that undermined basic research. "When it comes to basic research," Strack argued, "the strength of an effect is much less relevant because basic science is not about demonstrating or generalizing effects but about testing theories" (Strack 2017, 2). Nelson, Simmons, and Simonsohn (2018) argued, however, that it was essential for those who were not convinced by a failure to replicate their experiment to make testable claims about the conditions under which the effect was expected to replicate, and hence about the circumstances in which a failure to replicate would be informative. On this basis, Nelson, Simmons, and Simonsohn argued that, if Strack thought the cartoons used in Wagenmakers et al.'s (2016) replication attempts were no longer effective, he ought to specify alternatives that could be expected to work. "If the critics of a replication cannot specify conditions under which the effect is expected to replicate, then they are not making a scientific claim," Nelson and his team observed (2018, 521), citing Lakatos 1970.

18. As observed by Engber (2016), Strack had raised this issue with Wagenmakers at the start of the project, but his concern had been ignored. Engber (2016) reports many interesting details about the efforts involved in Wagenmakers et al.'s multi-lab replication attempt, as well as about Strack's critical response to the outcome. As Engber notes, even before the publication of Wagenmakers et al.'s findings, Strack had denied the value of direct replications of this kind (Stroebe and Strack 2014).

the historical conditions that had occurred between his original experiment and Wagenmakers et al.'s multi-lab efforts, and on that basis had justified holding on to his claims regarding the Facial Feedback Hypothesis.[19]

Another change Wagenmakers et al. (2016) had made to Strack, Martin, and Stepper's (1988) original experiment was to provide instructions to participants on a computer screen without the experimenter present, a procedure that was introduced in an effort to eliminate experimenter expectancy or demand effects. In their original experiment, Strack and his team (1988) had seated the participants, four at a time, in separate cubicles designed to prevent communication between them but that allowed them to communicate with the experimenter through an open space. The risk of the arrangement was that the experimental test could be confounded with implicit suggestions to the participants about how they should act, especially since the experimenter, who was Strack himself, had demonstrated to the participants in person the correct technique for holding the pen in the teeth-clenched position versus holding it in the lips-pursed condition.

In fact, experimenter demand was one among several confounds Alan Fridlund had identified in an earlier critique of Strack, Martin, and Stepper's (1988) and related facial-feedback experiments and of the importance these researchers attached to the notion of facial feedback itself. In particular, Fridlund had emphasized the role of implicit sociality and demand effects in such facial-feedback experiments. As he had skeptically commented:

---

19. In addition, Strack faulted Wagenmakers et al. for using a video camera to ensure that the pens were held as instructed, a deviation from the original experiment (Strack 2016, 929). Strack, Martin, and Stepper (1988) had argued that the facial-feedback process occurred outside awareness. Accordingly, Strack now suggested that the use of video cameras to record the participants' facial movements might have caused them to feel a degree of self-consciousness that interfered with their emotional reactions. See also Strack (2017) for his further comments on the failed replication of his facial-feedback experiment. Noah, Schul, and Mayo (2018) reported that, according to Wagenmakers, the use of the video camera was suggested to the replicators by a facial-feedback expert who reviewed the experimental protocol in advance. Noah, Shul, and Mayo (2018) investigated the facial-feedback effect in two replication conditions, one with and the other without a video camera, and confirmed Strack, Martin, and Stepper's findings of a feedback effect in the no-camera condition, an effect that was eliminated if a camera was used, though the evidence for the effect of the presence of the video camera was marginal. However, in a meta-analysis of the facial-feedback literature, Coles, Larsen, and Lench reported that the use of overt video recordings produced no difference in facial-feedback effects: facial-feedback effects were small both when participants were aware and when they were unaware of the video recording (2019, 638).

In these studies the experimenter is actually a director, and the subject a Stanislavski actor who "slips into role." The actor-subject may indeed be using sensations from the face to assume role, as he would his gestures or tone of voice, for example, were he so coached. But it is the role or "set" taken in the given social context that determines the emotion, not the displays themselves, whether facial or otherwise ... Seen in this way, simulation manipulations are ... pure dramaturgy (Fridlund 1994, 179)[20]

Fridlund had gone on to identify several other artifacts and confounds that had marred such facial-feedback experiments, noting that although researchers had attempted to control for them, it was not clear that they had succeeded (Fridlund 1994, 180–82). Fridlund's criticisms included the following points:

1. The claim that mimicking specific facial expressions automatically produced the corresponding emotional experience assumed, on the basis of Ekman's Basic Emotion Theory, that there existed such a direct, brain-mediated face-emotion relationship. Yet people often deceived others with their facial expressions (see my chapter 5 for a discussion of the Basic Emotion Theory).

2. People frequently made expressions that were contrary to mimicry accounts, as when they responded submissively to a threatening face.

3. The Facial Feedback Hypothesis implied that there ought to be a spiral of unrestrained happiness in others each time someone smiled, or a spiral of melancholy whenever someone started crying, but such effects did not occur.

---

20. Fridlund noted that this performative, dramaturgical analysis might be especially applicable to an experiment by Ekman, Levenson, and Friesen (1983) in which "many of the subjects were *actors*, and the directed facial actions were obtained using a 'coach' (i.e., a director) and a mirror. Together, these make for an audience and thus a performance" (Fridlund 1994, 179n6; his emphasis). In the same way, Strack, Martin, and Stepper (1988) "directed," which is to say suggested, the required facial postures to the participants in their experiment by demonstrating to them in person the correct ways to hold the pen in their mouths. Regarding Strack, Martin, and Stepper's (1988) finding that in their experiment, participants who puckered their lips rated the cartoons less amusing than those who clenched their teeth in a smiling expression, Fridlund had moreover commented: "I suspect that subjects felt sillier putting on a forced grin than puckering. Moreover, from a performative perspective, Strack et al. merely used a prop (the felt-tip pen) to lead subjects to smile in the experimental situation, and higher amusement ratings would be consistent with the subjects' performances. The Strack et al. study is also dubious ecologically: if the findings were general, then humans would find pleasure in neither kissing nor playing brass instruments" (Fridlund 1994, 180n7).

4. Facial-feedback theorists who favored mimicry accounts typically ignored Bavelas et al.'s findings (already discussed in chapter 5) showing that "empathic" faces were only weakly related to listeners' affect in the first place but were, rather, communicative performances.

In short, according to Fridlund, the elusive and fragile results of facial-feedback experiments were not due to a hypothetical feedback mechanism but were the effect of context-dependent, social-communicative interactions and mediations. His critique of the Facial Feedback Hypothesis had been published in 1994 but subsequent researchers had largely ignored his criticisms. However, Wagenmakers et al.'s (2016) failed replication of Strack, Martin, and Stepper's 1988 experiment, in which experimental demand effects were controlled for, implicitly reinforced Fridlund's skepticism about the validity of the facial feedback effect, making Stroebe's treatment of facial feedback as a "basic psychological process" problematic. Moreover, it is not clear that more recent attempts to assess the validity of the Facial Feedback Hypothesis have managed to eliminate all possible confounds. The most significant of such recent attempts is the multi-lab Many Smiles Collaboration, in which Nicholas Coles, Jeff Larsen, and Heather Lench have teamed up to determine the best ways to evaluate the Facial Feedback Hypothesis (Coles, Larsen, and Lench 2019; 2022). Twenty-one labs in over nineteen countries have performed experiments designed to test the hypothesis, hoping thereby to settle once and for all whether there is any facial-feedback effect. The undertaking has produced evidence that facial mimicry and a voluntary facial-action task can both amplify and initiate feelings of happiness, although the reported effects are small, suggesting that facial feedback is not the primary source of emotional experience, as several researchers have claimed. Moreover, the evidence for facial-feedback effects is inconclusive when facial feedback is manipulated using Strack and colleagues' pen-in-mouth task. Coles, Larsen, and Lench (2019; 2022) themselves have commented that it is unclear why facial-feedback effects are not observed in the pen-in-teeth task that Strack, Martin, and Stepper had designed in their 1988 study.

The Many Smiles Collaboration thus appears to support the Facial Feedback Hypothesis in a limited way. But many questions remain concerning the status of the hypothesized facial feedback mechanism, especially about whether unidentified confounds are responsible for the very varied effects observed even in recent experiments. Moreover, Fridlund's previous questions about the role of social mediation in facial-feedback experiments could well be asked about the Many Smiles Collaboration experiments. For one thing, as Fridlund has observed (personal communication, September 20, 2022), since no effort was made by Coles and his team to control for various kinds of social mediation, the observed effects ought not to be attributed to facial feedback itself but only to the fact that participants had been asked to make certain faces.

Against this background, it seems fair to say that Stroebe's attempt to refute Gergen's pessimistic conclusions concerning the possibility of establishing a natural-science approach in social psychology rested on rather slender evidence that the facial-feedback mechanism was the kind of "basic psychological process" that he took it to be and was accordingly immune to historical influence. As he observed in this regard: "I would therefore disagree with Gergen['s] (1973) conclusion that 'the continued attempt to build general laws of social behavior seems misdirected, and the associated belief that knowledge of social interaction can be accumulated in a manner similar to the natural sciences appears unjustified' . . . [T]he fact that different cartoons are considered [less?] funny today than three decades ago does not invalidate the general finding of the study of Strack et al. (1988)" (Stroebe 2016, 140).

Not surprisingly, on the grounds that the argument for the importance of contextual sensitivity meant that experimental lines of inquiry would be rendered immune from independent verification, several reformers rejected the entire argument central to Stroebe that, at the extreme, contextual variables were so influential as to render direct replications of little value. Reformers replied that, on balance, context sensitivity was *not* a serious problem for direct-replication attempts. For them, the fact that many such attempts, carried out under various conditions in different laboratories, had produced the same outcomes proved that contextual differences were not of decisive importance (Klein et al. 2014a, 142; see also Simonsohn 2017; Trafimow 2017; Zwaan et al. 2018).

But scientists who accepted the idea of the context sensitivity of priming tended to reject direct replication as unhelpful. Instead, they adopted a variety of ways to accommodate the fact of cultural variation without abandoning the requirements of experimental science. Here again, appeal was made to the importance of various moderators or boundary conditions in the production of priming effects. For example, Aiyana Willard, Azim Shariff, and Ara Norenzayan explained a failed replication (Gomes and McCullough 2015) of their claims for the influence of religious primes on prosocial behavior by pointing to new evidence suggesting that religious primes promoted prosocial behavior only among religious believers, not among nonbelievers (Willard, Shariff, and Norenzayan 2016; Shariff and Norenzayan 2007; 2015; see also Locke 2015). Similarly, Gary Latham, a professor of management and a recent convert to the importance of Bargh's automaticity model of subconscious priming, reported positive results from both laboratory experiments and field studies, suggesting that future research should investigate the role of moderators in influencing priming behaviors (Latham 2016). Greenfield (2017) took the argument one step further when she rejected entirely the emphasis on replication as the gold standard in psychological science, shifting attention instead to the fact of sociodemographic and cultural change itself as the crucial motor of behavior. She criticized Klein et al. (2012) for treating the social context as if it were merely an interfering factor or "noise" in experiments that ought to be controlled or assessed so that it could be ruled out. She suggested instead that the various historical changes should be considered the "independent variables" on which behavior depended; as such, these changes should be made the basis on which theoretically based predictions of behavior change ought to be proposed and general explanatory laws and mechanisms derived. According to Greenfield, the chief interest of failed replications was simply that they told researchers about the changes that had occurred between the original experiment and present conditions.[21]

For his part, Stroebe concluded his comments on Gergen's views by arguing that one of the best ways to shore up priming claims scientifically was not only to undertake conceptual replications designed to test underlying theories but also to perform meta-analyses that, by combining results from multiple studies, could calculate overall effect sizes and the reliability of priming outcomes (Stroebe 2016, 140–41).[22] He cited Evan Weingar-

---

21. But would it be possible to formulate general laws of human social behavior if the context of those behaviors constantly changed? Greenfield seemed to think so, on the grounds that social and cultural change produced systematic shifts in behavior. One certain prediction that followed from her analysis was that replications in social psychology were likely to fail. Greenfield noted that a paper by Van Bavel et al. (2016) had confirmed the influence of contextual sensitivity on replication outcomes. Van Bavel et al. (2016) had investigated the role of social context empirically, suggesting that contextual sensitivity in psychology experiments was associated negatively with replication success: the more culturally sensitive an original experiment was rated, the less likely it was to be replicated. See also Schweinsberg et al. (2016).

22. Stroebe regarded meta-analytic methods, which permitted the statistical integration of the results of independent studies, as a more economical and methodologically advanced alternative to mass replication. He argued that even if results seemed to be inconsistent, with some replications producing nonsignificant findings, the overall effect might still be statistically significant. He acknowledged that one serious disadvantage

ten et al.'s conclusion, drawn from 133 studies of the effects of priming on behavior and goal pursuits, that a small priming effect was robust across methodological procedures and was only minimally biased by the publication of positive versus negative results (Weingarten et al. 2016a; 2016b; see also Fabrigar and Wegener 2016). But here, too, opinions about the value of meta-analyses differed. On the one hand, Schimmack, a prolific blogger and the scourge of many established psychologists for their many methodological failures, made use of meta-analyses using sophisticated statistical procedures to demonstrate over and over again why so many classical experiments in social psychology failed to replicate (see for example Schimmack 2017; 2018; 2019; 2021; 2022b; Schimmack, Heene, and Kesavan 2017). On the other hand, some equally committed reformers, such as Nelson, Simmons, and Simonsohn 2018, were skeptical about most statistical solutions to publication bias, arguing that meta-analytic methods actually increased the prevalence of false-positive results.[23]

"There might be deep and substantive limits to both the replicability and the generalizability of . . . social priming effects"

What tended to go unremarked in discussions of the problems of psychology were the more pessimistic implications of findings concerning the contextual-cultural sensitivity of priming for theory development. If priming effects were so historically and situationally sensitive, how would it be possible to develop general laws or systematic predictions about behav-

---

of meta-analyses was that their conclusions could be affected by the publication bias of selectively reporting only positive findings. Nevertheless, he suggested that meta-analyses presented a much better picture of the replicability of social psychological research than that provided by replication research (Stroebe 2016, 140–41).

23. For general discussions of how reliance on statistical methods to identify patterns of aggregate data can give a false picture of the true situation, see also Danziger 1990 and Ritchie 2020; for specific meta-analyses that have failed to confirm claims for the behavioral effects of "romantic priming" and money priming, see Shanks et al. 2015 and Lodder et al. 2019. Meehl reminded his readers that in his classic text (1938) Skinner had not performed any statistical significance tests. The argument, as summarized by Meehl, was: "*If I describe my study so that you can replicate my results, and enough of you do so, it doesn't matter whether any of us did a significance test; whereas if I describe my study in such a way that the rest of you cannot duplicate my results, others will not believe me, or use my findings to corroborate or refute a theory, even if I did reach statistical significance*" (Meehl 1990b, 138; his emphasis). Meehl added: "So if my work is replicable, the significance test is unnecessary; if my work is not replicable, the significance test is useless" (Meehl 1990b, 138; cited by Iso-Ahola 2017, 7).

ior? Researchers might be able to identify the moderators that influenced priming outcomes in certain specific cultural settings, involving specific participant populations at specific times and places, but how could the findings be extended to other situations, other participant populations, and other times?

It is striking that most social psychologists shied away from confronting that question.

For example, the contributors to a special journal issue on priming, edited by Strack and Schwarz (2016), criticized the old model of priming, associated especially with the work of Bargh. But they did not take the argument for the contextually sensitive or situated character of priming responses to what might have seemed to be its logical conclusion. On the one hand, Strack and Schwarz disputed Bargh's claims for the automatic effects of primes, arguing that the human mind was sensitive and flexible enough to behave strategically in order to block any influence from the environment if it seemed unreliable (Strack and Schwarz 2016; see also Kleiman et al. 2015). In effect, they reintroduced into their discussion the influence of human meaning, intentionality, and belief that Bargh had previously attempted to eliminate from his analysis of priming. As they observed:

> While early research . . . emphasized the importance of a concept's applicability to the target information, subsequent research showed that even highly applicable concepts are not used when they seem to come to mind for the 'wrong reason' . . . Further highlighting the socially contextualized nature of information use, people deliberately disregard accessible and applicable information when its use would violate Gricean norms of cooperative conversational conduct . . . [T]he early expectation that high accessibility of a given applicable concept would affect judgment and behavior in identical ways across different contexts needed to be qualified. The lessons that emerged are consistent with the situated, context-sensitive, and pragmatic nature of human thinking . . . [I]ndividuals' immediate context is embedded in a broader context of culture . . . and language . . . adding additional complexity to *what* comes to mind and *when* and *how* it is. (Strack and Schwarz 2016, iv–v; their emphases)[24]

---

24. For how people may block or inhibit the effect of primed concepts on their behavior, see the report of experiments demonstrating the way in which dispositional or contextual distrust produced strategic responses to specific sources (Kleiman et al. 2015).

Similarly, in his contribution to the same journal issue, Barsalou made the situated nature of human behavior the key to his analysis of the problems of priming. He observed that one reason it was difficult to define social priming was because any aspect of a social situation could be a prime or a primed response, leading him to question the usefulness of the very concept. "The generality of this process," he wrote, "suggests that social priming is not a meaningful category and should not be viewed as a coherent phenomenon" (Barsalou 2016, 8). He also argued that the moderator issue was much more extreme than had been imagined, because

> virtually any element of a situation can modulate social priming, not just those noted so far in the literature. Many previous reviews have documented the exquisite sensitivity of cognition and behavior to the presence of detailed contextual information . . . Thus, it should not be surprising that social priming reflects this exquisite sensitivity as well [. . .] Given the diverse situational experience that people have, both in the past and in the current moment, it seems likely that diverse responses to a prime will occur regularly. (Barsalou 2016, 9)

But what if, as Barsalou argued, any aspect of a social situation could function as a prime, such that the very concept of social priming was no longer meaningful? It would then be hard to imagine a theoretical framework capable of making predictions about the effect of a prime that could be generalized beyond a very specific cultural, situational, and time-limited context. The fact that Barsalou theorized priming responses as packages of "multimodal" responses resulting from multimodal inferences or simulations did not, as such, indicate how general priming laws could be identified.

Yet neither Strack and Schwarz nor Barsalou were willing to draw the implications that seemed to follow from their views, namely, that if the phenomena of interest in priming studies were not replicable or generalizable, then the hope of establishing priming studies on a firm scientific footing appeared doomed. Instead, Strack and Schwarz ended their 2016 discussion of priming with a comment that would surely have appeared far too bland to psychology's more radically skeptical critics, such as Gergen:

> As the contributions to this issue illustrate, priming research has developed far beyond cognitive psychology's early models of semantic accessibility . . . One of the messages learned is that main effects of mere

semantic accessibility are not to be expected once one moves beyond the simplicity of lexical decision tasks and related experimental paradigms. Understanding the processes underlying judgment and decision making requires close attention to the interplay of declarative and experiential information and their use in their social, linguistic, and cultural contexts. (Strack and Schwarz 2016, vi)

Barsalou concluded his paper on a similarly cautious note, observing: "Clearly, however, much remains to be learned about how the situated conceptualization framework operates. Indeed, we currently understand little about the framework in any depth or with any certainty" (Barsalou 2016, 10).

Even Ramscar, whose 2015 paper I discussed above, did not appear to think his arguments regarding the historical sensitivity of priming phenomena had radical implications for the future of scientific research. In his own paper in Strack and Schwarz's special issue of 2016 on social priming, Ramscar repeated his argument that, at the limit, the sensitivity of lexical meaning to historical change meant that all direct replications of priming studies involving learned information were destined to fail. Indeed, according to him even conceptual replications were vulnerable to the same inescapable fact of historical and cultural mutation: "Because in practice all replications of learned priming effects are conceptual replications, and because any attempt at a conceptual replication must use items that provide the learned information relevant to an effect, many so-called 'failures to replicate' will simply reflect the fact that this information is not a fixed property of items, but rather is subject to constant cultural change" (Ramscar 2016, 82–83).

In short, Ramscar claimed that, in the absence of methods for determining what the information was that produced a priming effect, or for determining that the same information was available to the population in a replication, all learned priming effects were unfalsifiable and—as Stroebe and Strack had argued (2014)—also uninformative. Ramscar even suggested that experimental approaches to priming were misguided: "For many areas of priming research, the development of a quantitative, mechanistic account of why a given stimulus primes a given behavior is probably a tall order; raising questions about whether research in these areas is best observed by the quantitative framework of experimentation in which their results are currently reported" (Ramscar 2016, 83). The only solution he could suggest in order to salvage this seemingly dire situation was that priming researchers could make use of the formal models developed by linguistics that permitted the relationships between primes and behaviors to be estimated, or they could deploy models developed by linguists like himself and his colleagues that allowed the effects of primes to be simulated (Ramscar et al. 2013; Baayen, Hendrix, and Ramscar 2013; Baayen and Ramscar 2015)—a rather tall order for priming researchers not trained in the linguistic field.[25] Even as Ramscar admitted that the scientific models he himself advocated had their drawbacks, he nevertheless clung to the hope that these or other ones would serve to further the cause of priming research. "Although all of these models have limitations," he wrote, "it is to be hoped that either they—or their future developments—can move priming research toward a point where studies test and refine the predictions of well-specified scientific models, and away from cataloging what are otherwise transient cultural effects" (Ramscar 2016, 83).

But psychologist Barry Schwartz came to a different conclusion: he argued that if priming results were so tied to their specific historical situation, place, and time, then generalizations were impossible—and priming research could not conform to the requirements of the experimental natural sciences. Indeed, according to Schwartz his argument applied to all the social sciences. Roberta Klatzky and J. David Creswell (2014) had attempted to shed light on the problem of replicability in priming research by arguing that the unreliability of social priming effects was not due to sloppy research methods but to the fact that such effects were multiply determined and stochastic in character. By analogy with research demonstrating the complexity of cross-modal perceptual effects, they therefore emphasized the fundamental indeterminacy of priming outcomes. But Klatzky and Creswell had also suggested that once priming effects were understood on a probabilistic model, research could move ahead with confidence: "Thus, although the thrust of the present argument is to explain why social priming effects are vulnerable, the same approach also

---

25. Ramscar and his colleagues used advanced-learning models and statistical techniques to search enormous databases of words and phrases in order to simulate what an older brain had to do to retrieve a word. They had argued that larger data sets, of the kind humans acquire as they age, need longer search times, but that this fact had nothing to do with cognitive decline, as was standardly assumed. It was merely due to the fact that compared to young people, old brains and minds had larger pools of words and phrases that needed to be searched. These claims drew media attention but also criticism: researchers were not persuaded by Ramscar's arguments, because they thought there was good evidence that the minds and brains of adults did tend to decline with age in ways that undercut Ramscar et al.'s approach. See Ramscar et al. 2013 (451); Carey 2014; and Brink 2014.

suggests why a range of effect sizes might be possible," they had stated. "The model . . . suggests that experiments that systematically manipulate contextual cues are likely to be particularly informative, as it proposes that context has multiple effects" (Klatzky and Creswell 2014, 56).

But in a commentary in which he praised Klatzky and Creswell for their "thoughtful" paper, Schwartz suggested that these researchers had failed to recognize the drastic implications of their own arguments. Their contribution, he proposed, raised the possibility that there might be "deep and substantive limits to both the replicability and the generalizability of many of the phenomena that most interest psychologists"—including the phenomena of social priming (Schwartz 2015, 404). Schwartz based his argument on Fodor's characterization of the "Central Systems" as those systems of the cognitive apparatus that were responsible for deliberation, reason, and thinking (Fodor 1983, 101ff) (these were the central systems that cognitive scientists had called the "executive" systems). As Schwartz noted, whereas Fodor had postulated the existence of "input modules" in the mind which were informationally encapsulated in the sense that they could only respond to certain types of information, he had argued that there were no limits to the kinds of information relevant to the central systems. For the central cognitive system, as Schwartz formulated Fodor's claims:

> Anything might be relevant to the interpretive problem at hand, and thus the central system is wide open to all kinds of influences. But just for this reason, according to Fodor, we cannot have a science of central systems. Because context always matters, and because every context is in some sense unique, there are no lawful generalizations about central systems to be had, except, perhaps, for generalizations so abstract that they yield little in the way of predictions in specific situations [. . .] So, according to Fodor, although it might be possible to develop a history of central systems, just as we have a history of science, we can't expect to develop a science of central systems. (Schwartz 2015, 404–5)

Or as he also observed:

> What I want to suggest is that, in light of Fodor's characterization of central systems, a good deal more might be lost than just determinism. In effect, Klatzky and Creswell are suggesting that when it comes to the controversial social priming literature, potentially anything is relevant. People's associative chains are different, their cultures are different,

what they happen to be paying attention to changes from one person to another and one moment to another. Almost anything can happen—even if priming is real. This seems to be a lot like Fodor's central system in operation. And if it is, Klatzky and Creswell's ingenious attempt to rescue social priming from the skeptics is perhaps being achieved at a high price—relinquishing the chance to develop a science of social priming, as opposed to a kind of history of social priming. (2015, 405)

Indeed, Schwartz argued that strict replication, under tight laboratory control, was not so much validating a phenomenon as it was distorting it by "preventing the various factors that might affect the central system from exerting their influence. In other words, the success of strict replication might give us an erroneous picture of how robust a phenomenon is outside the laboratory." It followed that "the kinds of powerful generalizations that psychological scientists look for might not be available when it comes to at least certain kinds of priming effects. This need not mean that they are capricious, random, or unintelligible. But it will likely mean that they are unpredictable, and thus often unreplicable—*as a feature, not a bug*." Schwartz added: "And it should be pointed out that the issue does not stop with social priming effects ... The possibilities I raise here could apply quite broadly to aspects of affective science, to moral judgment and moral action, to memory, to decision making, to the influence of culture on cognition and social interaction, and who knows what more" (Schwartz 2015, 406; my emphasis).

It is hardly surprising that on this basis Schwartz would invoke Gergen's name, but with very different conclusions from those reached by Stroebe in 2016:

As Gergen (1973) pointed out many years ago, in a paper aptly titled 'Social Psychology as History,' many of the phenomena that psychologists are most interested in understanding might be largely the province of ... central systems.

In his very thoughtful book, *Time's Arrow, Time's Cycle*, Stephen J. Gould (1987) distinguished between processes in nature that are repeatable ('time's cycle') and processes that are historical ('time's arrow'). Gould regarded the theory of evolution as the paradigm case of a science that is essentially historical ... Gould was hardly suggesting that because evolutionary theory is historical, it could not be scientific. What he was suggesting, however, was that, to capture evolutionary processes, we need a different model of science than the one handed down by physics. We need explanation, not prediction. Exactly the same might be true when it comes to understanding the operation of the central system, and social priming effects might be an illustration of how prediction can fail us. (Schwartz 2015, 407)

It is not clear, however, what Schwartz thought the implications of his position were for the field of psychology itself. He did not offer any further comments on Gergen's social-constructionist solution to the problem posed by the historicity of psychological knowledge. He seemed to suggest that, although psychology should give up its efforts to be an experimental science on the model of the basic sciences, it could still be regarded as a historical science like geology or the science of evolution, domains of inquiry that were less amenable to experimentation but could still generate explanations and general laws. But if psychologists could not do experiments, what could they do? What would count as the equivalent in psychology of studying the different layers of soil or the history of stars and planets? Did Schwartz propose a return to the survey methods of the sociologist? To ask a Kuhnian question, what would an established researcher train a beginning social psychologist to do?

In fact, as Gergen had made clear long before, if psychology were to abandon its claims to be an experimental science, the field would have to change quite drastically. This prospect was also recognized by Jan Smedslund (2015), Gantt et al. (2017), and other reforming researchers who understood the implications of the claim that, as a historical enterprise, psychology could not be successfully modeled on the experimental paradigm that had guided its fortunes, for good or ill, since its earliest modern foundations.[26] It is not surprising, then, that the majority of psychologists refused to take the route proposed by such critics. But if they assumed the extreme contextual sensitivity of psychological data these critics suggested, it was hard to conceive how they could advance the field by sticking to their usual cognitive-science assumptions and experimental practices.

---

26. For example, in their defense of a hermeneutical approach to the study of psychology, Gantt, Lindstrom, and Williams argued that the two problems of situational specificity and the impossibility of formulating general laws of human social behavior rendered "unworkable" the positivist approach to social psychology, associated with the work of Hempel and Popper (Gantt, Lindstrom, and Williams 2016, 135).

"Behavioral Priming: It's All in the Mind, but Whose Mind?"

8

One of the seven wonders of psychology is that so striking a phenomenon as hypnosis has been neglected. Some psychologists literally do not believe in it, but consider it a hoax, an act put on by a cooperative stooge. The majority of psychologists admit that hypnosis is an actual phenomenon, but they have not worked with it and do not quite trust anyone who has. Unfortunately, in spite of its remarkable effects, few psychologists have any good idea what hypnosis is or what to use it for.
—**G. A. MILLER**, **E. GALANTER**, and **K. H. PRIBRAM** (1960, 103–4)

It should be clear that demand characteristics cannot be eliminated from experiments; all experiments will have demand characteristics, and these will always have some effect . . . [R]esponse to the demand characteristics is not merely conscious compliance. When we speak of "playing the role of a good experimental subject," we use the concept analogously to the way in which Sarbin (1950) describes role playing in hypnosis: namely, largely on a nonconscious level.
—**M. T. ORNE** (1962, 779)

Hypnotic responsiveness [is] more concerned with genuine, internal alterations in perception, cognition, and subjective experience than with behavioral compliance to external demand characteristics.
—**K. S. BOWERS** (1992, 258)

Experimenter Expectancy

Perhaps the most contentious, and to Bargh the most objectionable, claim Doyen et al. (2012) made in their assessment of his famous elderly priming experiment was that uncontrolled experimenter expectancy or demand characteristics probably influenced his priming outcome. We have seen that Bargh indignantly rejected the idea outright, insisting that all the required double-blind procedures had been followed and that consequently expectancy effects could not have played any role in the results. In the aftermath of Doyen et al.'s findings, researchers carrying out replications of some of the well-known priming experiments were careful to introduce double-blind methods to control for such expectancy effects, even in cases where the original scientists had failed to report their use (for example, Pashler, Coburn, and Harris 2012). And there were suggestions by some investigators, who could not replicate certain priming experiments, that uncontrolled expectancy effects might have affected the original findings (for example, Lynott et al. 2014, 220).[1]

Moreover, it emerged in the wake of Doyen et al.'s (2012) failed replication of Bargh's elderly priming experiment that concern for the problem of experimenter bias and demand characteristics had dramatically declined in the previous decades, because researchers thought the problem had largely been solved. As Olivier Klein and his team (which included Doyen) reported in an article published later in 2012, since the studies by Orne, Rosenthal, and others in the 1960s and 1970s there had been a steady decrease in interest in these topics (Klein et al. 2012).[2] In a survey of the contents of two prominent psychology journals between 1965 and 2010, Klein and his colleagues documented the lack of information regarding the presence of the experimenters during the laboratory sessions, or details concerning how the experiments were presented to the participants, as well as the absence of thorough debriefing methods for probing the participants' knowledge of the purposes of the studies.

---

1. Lynott et al. (2014) commented on the role of expectancy effects in the course of reporting their failure to replicate an experiment by Williams and Bargh (2008) ostensibly proving that holding a coffee cup containing warm coffee primed participants to judge target individuals as having warmer personalities, as compared to participants who held a cold beverage.

2. Klein had been one of the co-authors of Doyen et al. 2012, just as Doyen was a co-author of Klein et al. 2012.

Klein et al. identified several reasons for the decline of attention to expectancy effects and demand characteristics during the previous decades. These included the following (Klein et al. 2012, 576–77):

1. *Automatization*. Klein et al. suggested that the chief reason why contemporary psychologists had become less interested in demand characteristics and experimenter bias was because of the "automatization" of experimental procedures. In most recent experiments, participants had little direct contact with the experimenter because they typically interacted with a computer that displayed standardized instructions. In their pioneering studies, Rosenthal and Rosnow (2009 [1969]) had anticipated this development. Klein et al. pointed out, however, that computerized procedures did not necessarily eliminate experimental demand. Participants might still conform to what they regarded as the experimenter's expectations as communicated through the computer or in other ways, and they might also detect the purpose of manipulations and respond accordingly.

2. *Types of Dependent Variables and Stimuli*. Klein et al. suggested that another reason for the decline of interest in experimental demand and demand characteristics might be the type of dependent variables studied by contemporary researchers. Most experiments no longer relied on self-reports, as they had in the past, but on behavioral measures that might be more difficult to manipulate and that therefore might be viewed as neutralizing expectancy effects. However, Klein et al. suggested that even here caution was in order with respect to demand characteristics.

3. *Changes in Psychologists' Topics of Interest*. The authors proposed that perhaps the kinds of research topics of interest to today's psychologists involved processes that were less likely to be influenced by experimenter expectancies and demand effects than those studied in the early 1960s.

4. *Habits*. Another, more positive explanation for the decline of concern with experimenter expectancy and demand effects was that researchers tended to be better trained in avoiding their pitfalls than they had been in the past. In fact, Klein et al. noted, researchers had become so well trained that they tended to believe that precautions to avoid such influences were entrenched in current best practices and did not deserve to be described in detail any longer. But as the explosive replication controversy made clear, it remained an open question to what extent researchers were successfully employing double-blind procedures and other necessary experimental controls in priming and related experiments.

5. *Journal Space.* It was possible that competition for journal space and the increased reliance on short reports had forced authors to reduce the method sections of their papers to a minimum, thus omitting information relevant to the control of expectancy and demand effects.

6. *Encapsulated View of Cognition.* Finally, Klein et al. suggested that there might be a further, "deeper," reason why interest in experimenter bias and demand effects had declined so dramatically over the previous decades. This reason was that the rise of the cognitive neurosciences had promoted a view of cognitive processes as "wholly dependent on and encapsulated in neural processes that take place within the confines of the brain." From Klein et al.'s perspective, this approach meant that investigators tended to forget that "the brain [or mind] is itself in constant interaction not only with the world, but also with other people," with the consequence that there was a tendency to underestimate the contextual affordances and constraints influencing participants' reactions (Klein et al. 2012, 577).[3] Klein et al. also argued that psychologists' tendency to give neurally driven accounts of behavior relegated social influence to the status of a "mere noise" that needed to be controlled or eliminated, instead of recognizing the importance of social influences even on phenomena thought to be automatic—as when it was shown that Stroop effects were affected by social influences.

Klein et al.'s critique of the "encapsulated" view of cognition was consistent with those of the "situated-cognition" theorists: not enough attention was being paid to the social context in which experiments were being conducted. Instead of regarding contextual influences as inherent in an individual's perceptions and actions, cognitive neuroscientists too readily treated contextual influences as secondary additions that merely moderated the mental processes that were of more fundamental interest. In line with the work of Smith and Semin (2004), Cesario et al. (2010), and Loersch and Payne (2011), whose work we encountered in chapter 6,

---

3. Earlier, Klein (2009) had argued that the transition from a reason-based explanation of behavior, in terms of intentions and motivations, to a neurobiological explanation, posed ethical problems, quoting Webel and Stigliano as remarking: "If electrical charges between brain cells are what we once called the 'self', and holding to terms like 'self' or 'agency' is merely a matter of social convenience, then our actions are simply whatever scientific laws follow from those electrical charges. One should not then attribute action or motive to anyone, or consequently hold a person responsible for their conduct" (Webel and Stigliano 2004, 84).

Klein et al. argued that the situated-cognition perspective altered conceptions of experimenter expectancy and demand characteristics by making them integral features of the experimental context, rather than treating them as pollutants of the "real" underlying mechanisms.

On this basis, Klein et al. (2012) assessed the role of expectancy and demand features in Bargh, Chen, and Burrows's (1996) elderly priming experiment, expanding on the analysis already given in Doyen et al.'s (2012) paper. Klein et al. did not argue that Bargh and his colleagues' results were merely the effect of experimenter demand. They accepted Bargh's assurance that in the original study the experimenter had been blind to the priming condition of the participants. On the other hand, when using an "objective" infrared beam to measure walking speed, Doyen et al. (2012) had been unable to reproduce Bargh, Chen, and Burrows's findings. Klein et al. (2012) therefore proposed that a more expansive understanding of the contextual factors shaping priming responses was needed. They suggested that what influenced the participants' responses in the case of Doyen et al.'s replication attempts was not just the priming process but the priming process in concert with the situational affordances of the experiment, including specifically the presence of an experimenter who had been deliberately manipulated to believe that his or her participants would walk more slowly. Klein et al. explained:

> The participant leaves the lab following an injunction from the experimenter. In the perception-behavior model, we would expect slower walking speeds regardless of whether the participant leaves the laboratory following such an injunction or in response to any other contextual stimulus. If we take a more situated perspective, the presence of this injunction and the person issuing it may be crucial to the understanding of the process. It may also shape the cues used by the participant to regulate walking speed. Given that the injunction is made by the experimenter, the latter's behavior may constitute a cue. In this way, nonverbal mimicry (Chartrand and Bargh, 1999) may for example be part of the explanation for the reduced walking speed in Doyen et al.'s replication . . .
>
> More generally, Doyen et al.'s (2012) results are compatible with the existence of priming effects: It is just that the primes are presented in a social context that either also acts as a congruent prime or not. Thus, experimenters who believe their participants will walk slower may act in a manner that is congruent with these expectations (e.g., moving and

speaking more slowly). Such behavior may be unconsciously picked up by participants, who would then unwittingly adapt their own behavior to that of experimenters. (Klein et al. 2012, 579)

In short, Klein et al. did not deny the existence of behavioral priming but maintained that it operated very differently depending on the social context in which it took place, a context that accordingly had to be taken into account in evaluating the effects of primes.

Klein et al. ended their paper by offering several practical recommendations for controlling or minimizing sources of bias. These recommendations echoed others already proposed much earlier by Orne and Rosenthal, but they also included the use of more-detailed debriefing methods to gain insight into the participants' expectations and knowledge about the purpose of experiments. Klein et al. also stressed the need for researchers to supply far more information about their experimental procedures in their published papers than was the norm at present, and crucially to design experiments in ways that made the social context more relevant to the process being studied.[4] They concluded, however, by remarking that it would never be possible to control all possible influences on experiments: the expectations and beliefs of both experimenters and participants could not be simply turned off but were an inherent component of the experimental situation. Moreover, experimenters and participants might be unaware of the influence of their beliefs and expectations on the outcome of their procedures. Klein et al. observed in this regard that the case of Clever Hans was exemplary in this respect: "Neither Van [*sic, Von*] Osten (his owner) nor the horse were aware of the cues they respectively emitted and used so as to endow Hans with seemingly extraordinary mathematical skills" (Klein et al. 2012, 582). Accordingly, the best that scientists could do was explore such sources of "bias" in a systematic manner.

---

4. Gilder and Heerey (2018) subsequently focused on the issue of double-blind procedures in priming experiments. They emphasized, as had Klein et al., that in many articles in the priming literature, double-blind experimental designs were not explicitly described, noting also that the authors of several classical priming experiments had failed to use double-blind methods. Gilder and Heerey demonstrated that if double-blind procedures were used in a famous priming experiment on the influence of high or low power assignments, the original findings were not replicated. But when experimenter beliefs and expectations about which primes participants had received were manipulated, experimenter belief rather than the prime condition altered the participants' responses. Gilder and Heerey surmised that the original experimenters must have unwittingly conveyed their beliefs to the participants by subtle changes in their behavior.

What Explains Experimenter Expectancy and Demand Effects?

It is interesting that neither Doyen et al. (2012) nor Klein et al. (2012) had much to say about the nature of human "influence," which is to say, how an experimenter's expectations are transmitted to their primed subjects. As Doyen et al. remarked, "We do not know how this process operates" (Doyen et al. 2012, 6). Likewise, Klein et al. quoted expectancy researcher Robert Rosenthal as stating that "'problems of experimenter effects have not been solved yet'" (Klein et al. 2012, 581, citing Rosenthal and Rosnow 2009, ix). Doyen et al. and Klein et al. merely followed Rosenthal in suggesting that expectancy appeared to involve the communication of subtle cues emanating from the experimenter's behavior.[5] In the passage quoted above, Klein et al. (2012) cited Chartrand and Bargh's (1999) paper on the Chameleon Effect in order to suggest that the participants' mimicry of the experimenter's behaviors might in part explain the reduced walking speeds observed in Doyen et al.'s priming replication. Since the experimenters had been manipulated to believe that their participants would walk more slowly, they might have unconsciously conveyed their expectations by subtle alterations in their actions and behaviors, changes to which the participants had mimetically responded.[6] Klein et al. also cited an ear-

---

5. Friedman (1967) commented on the difficulty of understanding how expectancies were transmitted. See also Barber and Silver (1968) for a discussion of eleven possible ways in which experimenter expectations and desires might influence research results, including the role of intentional or unintentional linguistic, paralinguistic, and kinetic cues. A common complaint among peer commentators on Rosenthal and Rubin's (1978) paper summarizing the results of 345 experiments investigating interpersonal expectancy effects was the authors' failure to even consider the expectancy transmission process. One commentator also noted the paradox that, at the very time social psychologists were collecting masses of data and formulating theories about disturbances in social perception and judgment, as well as deficiencies in information processing practices (of the kind seen in attribution studies), students were discouraged from directly studying the related phenomenon of experimenter bias, because, it was suggested, the latter threatened the integrity of the experimental process itself. See Adair 1978 and Adair 1973.

6. In their attempted replication of Bargh, Chen, and Burrows's elderly priming study, in addition to citing Rosenthal 1966 and Chartrand and Bargh 1999, Doyen et al. (2012) cited two other studies relevant to the topic of the influence of experimenter expectations on experimental results: Conty et al. 2010; and Kay et al. 2004. Conty et al.'s paper documented the powerful, automatic effect of eye contact on the responses of subjects during the performance of the Stroop interference task, the implication presumably being that even something as simple as the experimenter's unregulated gaze could communicate his or her expectations to participants. Kay et al.'s paper, which included Bargh as a co-author, concerned the influence of material objects common to business, such as briefcases or

lier paper by Harris and Rosenthal (1985) which had identified thirty-one behavioral variables influencing interpersonal expectancy effects, such as smiles, eye contact or gaze, head nods, touch, and other nonverbal cues. But there was still a great deal of uncertainty about how expectancy effects were transmitted.

The most influential sources on the topic were of course the well-known studies of Rosenthal and Martin Orne. Klein et al.'s (2012) references to Rosenthal's discussion of experimenter expectancy and Orne's studies of experimental compliance testify to the continuity between post–2012 crisis worries about the potential impact of experimental expectancy and the importance of the contributions to the topic by these much earlier researchers (Klein et al. 2012, 572–73, citing Rosenthal and Rosnow 2009; and Orne 1962). The classical explanation for the communication of an experimenter's influence on experimental participants and the compliance of the subject with such implicit demands was of course suggestion, and it was in the context of debates about the nature of hypnosis and suggestion that the first studies of experimenter expectancy and experimental demand by Rosenthal and Orne had taken place.

Broadly speaking, ever since the 1950s researchers had been divided into two opposing camps over how to explain hypnotic phenomena. According to the social psychological explanation proposed by Theodore Sarbin, Theodore Barber, William Coe, Nicholas Spanos, and others, hypnotic responses were the result of the hypnotized subject's intention to perform the hypnotic role (Sarbin 1950; Sarbin and Coe 1972; Barber 1969; Barber and Silver 1968; Spanos 1986). For these researchers, the characteristic signs of the hypnotic state—the apparent lack of consciousness; experience of involuntariness, in which a paralysis of the limbs is combined with a puppetlike responsiveness to the hypnotist's commands; insensitivity to pain; and posthypnotic amnesia—were the product of strategic, goal-directed behaviors in which hypnotized subjects personified what they believed to be the appropriate identity of the "good" hypnotic subject. In other words, the subject intentionally adopted the persona of the passive, compliant somnambulistic person according to culturally determined ideas about how hypnotic subjects ought to behave. On this interpretation, the hypnotized subjects' actions were not the result of con-

---

boardroom tables, on subsequent behavior, where the participants' expectations regarding such objects appeared to influence their actions, although the authors did not address the topic of the effect of experimenter expectancy on participants' behaviors.

scious role-playing but of an apparently unconscious intention to perform the hypnotic role in in appropriate way.[7]

The fact that in the majority of subjects, characteristic posthypnotic amnesia could be lifted or breached on the command of the hypnotist was cited as evidence that the hypnotic enactment was indeed just a performance, albeit one in which subjects were sincerely immersed—they weren't faking their roles but "genuinely" simulating them. One consequence of the role-playing theory was an emphasis on the continuity between hypnotic compliance and related behaviors observed in non-hypnotized, awake persons. To cite the statement that appears as one of the epigraphs to this chapter, Orne applied the role-playing thesis to the psychology of the experimental situation when he observed: "Response to the demand characteristics is not merely conscious compliance. When we speak of 'playing the role of a good experimental subject,' we use the concept analogously to the way in which Sarbin (1950) describes role playing in hypnosis: namely, largely on a nonconscious level" (Orne 1962, 779).[8] The implication was that the participant's compliance with experimenter expectancy was an unconscious, intentional response. Although Rosenthal's views on the nature of expectancy are less clear, we can say that, with reference to Orne's researches, Rosenthal treated the influence of the experimenter's expectations on experimental subjects as the result of some kind of unconscious, largely nonverbal communication between them (Rosenthal 1963).[9] Moreover, it is worth remembering that, from Orne's

---

7. For a detailed discussion of Freud's and Sandor Ferenczi's struggles with hypnotic suggestion, imitation, and memory, as well as Janet's work on automatism and hypnosis and related developments, see Leys 2000; in a very large literature on the topic see also Borch-Jacobsen 1988; Hacking 1995; and Lachapelle 2011.

8. Orne remarked:

It is entirely compatible with my view to describe hypnosis as Sarbin (1950) does: a role which is played with such conviction as to become totally compelling to the individual. It would be essential for the individual to experience the role as real and not to be consciously acting a part ... Equally acceptable and, in my view, operationally indistinguishable from my formulation, is to describe hypnosis as a 'believed-in imagining' (Sarbin and Coe, 1972). The crucial point in such a formulation is that the individual for the time being becomes unable to distinguish between his fantasy and other life experiences. (Orne 1980, 37)

9. Note also that Rosenthal used several different names for experimenter expectancy. "In various places, Rosenthal has labeled this effect as the experimenter bias effect, the experimenter expectancy effect, the experimenter outcome-orientation effect, and the 'Clever Hans Phenomenon.' We will henceforth label this effect simply the experimenter bias effect" (Barber and Silver 1968, 2).

point of view, expectancy effects—which is to say, suggestive influences—were an ineliminable aspect of the experimental situation, and also, presumably, of everyday human life. As he wrote in a passage quoted in the epigraphs to this chapter: "It should be clear that demand characteristics cannot be eliminated from experiments; all experiments will have demand characteristics, and these will always have some effect . . . [T]echniques designed to study the effect of demand characteristics need to take into account that these effects result from the subject's *active* attempt to respond appropriately to the *totality* of the experimental situation" (Orne 1962, 779; his emphasis).

But for "special-state" or "dissociation" theorists of hypnosis, the role-playing interpretation of hypnotic behavior was inadequate. Thus Ernest Hilgard (1986 [1977]) rejected the idea that people intentionally enacted the role of the hypnotic subject by complying with the hypnotist's suggestions, even if they were unaware that they were doing so. Instead, he argued that the characteristic signs of hypnotism in highly hypnotizable individuals were the result of genuine alterations in the subjects' psychological state. According to him, when subjects were hypnotized, they were precipitated into a special mental condition in which individual consciousness was dissociated into separate consciousnesses or selves, with barriers of amnesia dividing them. He therefore conceptualized the hypnotized person's behavior as the product of a secondary personality whose actions could not be fully controlled by the primary "executive" consciousness. The fact that in highly susceptible persons, posthypnotic amnesia could *not* be breached or lifted, even when the subject was commanded to remember what had happened, was one of the pieces of evidence that lent support to the dissociation position.

The debate between role-playing versus dissociation theorists concerning the nature of hypnosis remained unresolved. Each camp was able to draw on evidence that the other camp found difficult to explain, with the result that the arguments oscillated back and forth without resolution. In this context, it is interesting that, even prior to Doyen et al.'s (2012) and Klein et al.'s (2012) proposals that experimenter expectancy had influenced the outcome of Bargh, Chen, and Burrows's elderly priming experiment, Bargh himself had drawn attention to the similarity between the effects of priming and those of hypnotic suggestion. In particular, he had made use of the work on hypnosis by theorist Kenneth Bowers, who had recently offered a particular version of the "special-state" or dissociation theory (see especially Spanos 1986 for a discussion of the issues in dispute between the two camps). It is to Bowers's account of hypnotic dissociation that I now turn.

Kenneth Bowers's "Dissociated Control" Theory of Hypnosis

In the years before 2012, several investigators had pointed to an ambiguity in "special-state" or dissociation theories of hypnosis. The ambiguity concerned whether the control of movement during hypnosis remained within the person at some level or whether the hypnotist directly manipulated the suggested behaviors. Since some special-state theorists accepted that hypnotic actions were genuinely involuntary, but also held that the hypnotized subject's "executive" retained some measure of control, it seemed to follow that hypnotized subjects intentionally carried out actions without being aware that they were doing so. But some theorists felt this proposition posed a serious theoretical difficulty. As prominent hypnosis researchers Irving Kirsch and Steven Jay Lynn put the concern: "How can people be unaware of their intentions? Is not the idea of an unconscious intention an oxymoron, as Bowers (1992) has suggested?" (Kirsch and Lynn 1998, 102).[10]

Hypnosis researcher Kenneth Bowers, to whom Kirsch and Lynn here referred, had recently proposed a "dissociated-control" model of hypnosis that was designed to address that alleged oxymoron. Bowers's critical move was to insist on a distinction between actions that were performed "on purpose" versus those that were done "with a purpose."[11] According to him, only actions performed "on purpose" were intentional, with the result that he regarded as unintentional all the familiar actions people performed on a daily basis "with a purpose" but in an apparently automatic and unconscious way. He thus proposed a more or less hard-and-fast

---

10. Kirsch and Lynn (1998) referred here to Bowers's comment on the work of Bargh and others that "Lynn and Rhue (1991, p. 611) have recently raised the possibility that behavior can result from unconscious intentions and strategies. By the old hard and fast distinction, an unconscious strategy would be an oxymoron. If the notion of unconscious intentions and strategies catches on, it will be interesting to see how and in what sense they differ from dissociated control" (Bowers 1992, 264 n6). In their paper, Lynn and Rhue cited role-playing theorists such as Sarbin and Spanos in commenting, "There seems to be a growing recognition that subjects can intend to respond to suggestions and have suggested experiences, yet may not necessarily be conscious of the contextual determinants and cognitive operations that shape their hypnotic experiences" (Lynn and Rhue 1991, 611).

11. For a tribute to the work of Kenneth Bowers (1937–1996) after his premature death, see Kihlstrom (1998a).

dichotomy between conscious-intentional and unconscious-unintentional actions (Bowers and Davidson 1991, 106–7).[12] On this basis, he proposed a "dissociated-control" model of hypnosis according to which hypnotic induction caused a dissociation between the individual's executive processes, which regulated conscious-intentional actions, and the subsystems, which subserved unconscious, unintentional behaviors.

From Bowers's point of view, the behavior of hypnotized subjects could be regarded as goal-directed, in that they carried out the hypnotist's suggestions "with a purpose," but they were not performed "on purpose," which is to say intentionally and voluntarily, because control over hypnotic behaviors was disconnected or dissociated from the higher-level, executive control of the conscious self. His argument was that hypnotized subjects did not lose all control, since they performed quite complex actions in response to the hypnotist's suggestions. They only lost the kind of control that was exercised by high-level executive plans and intentions (Bowers and Davidson 1991, 107). As Bowers argued in favor of his "neo-dissociative" approach to hypnosis and against the role-playing theory:

> A neo-dissociative model of mind is better equipped than a social-psychological model to deal with the complexities of hypnosis, and of human behavior generally. It recognizes . . . that behavior can be more automatically activated than strategically enacted. In particular, . . . emphasis on human behavior as purposeful and goal directed does not distinguish between goal-directed behavior that serves a purpose, and goal-directed behavior that is performed on purpose. It is this distinction that permits goal directed behavior to be dissociated from a person's conscious plans and intentions. (Bowers 1992, 253)

According to Bowers, "dissociated control" was especially evident in various "action slips." For example, he explained that in the case of someone who dials a more familiar telephone number than the consciously intended one, "a subsystem of control has been activated—more, perhaps, by vagrant thoughts of a close friend than by conscious plans and intentions" (Bowers and Davidson 1991, 108). Of course, these were the

---

12. Whether a clean line can be drawn between these two categories of actions in the way Bowers proposed is debatable. Some of his examples are questionable, as when he wrote that when we go to the bathroom on waking in the middle of the night, our actions are unintentional (Bowers and Davidson 1991, 106).

kinds of "parapraxes" or slips that Freud had viewed as motivated by unconscious intentions. But like Bargh in this regard, and based on the same post-Freudian interpretations and sources on the topic, Bowers conceptualized such actions as strictly unintentional—unintentional *because* they were performed unconsciously and automatically. Accordingly, Bowers challenged Spanos's role-playing theory of hypnosis by asserting that

> not everything people do or achieve is consciously intended, initiated, or controlled . . . The possibility for such "dissociated control" . . . in everyday life is particularly well revealed in various mental lapses, but is the basis for hypnotic responsiveness as well. Such dissociated control of thought and behavior depends on a hierarchical model of mind, which assumes—quite reasonably, we think—that different cognitive control systems can operate in relative independence of each other . . . Spanos's evident disdain for dissociation is more and more a rearguard action that is unresponsive to current developments in cognitive psychology. (Bowers and Davidson 1991, 135)

The "current developments in cognitive psychology" that Bowers had in mind included the work of Posner and Snyder (1975) and others on the existence of independent information-processing channels for conscious executive functions and unconscious automatic functions, work that had also informed Bargh's approach to automaticity. It is therefore not surprising that, as Kirsch and Lynn noted, Bowers's "dissociated control" theory of hypnosis was in keeping with work at the "cutting edge" of the cognitive sciences, specifically, with Bargh's work. As they observed: "A major strength of dissociated control theory is that it has drawn attention to contemporary work on the automatic triggering of behavioral responses and the importance of that work to the task of explaining hypnotic phenomena" (Kirsch and Lynn 1998, 110, citing Bargh 1994).[13]

Moreover, just as Bargh (2005) had compared the behavior of primed participants to that of frontal-lobe patients (see chapter 4), so Bowers had similarly proposed that hypnotized subjects manifested the same behaviors seen in frontal-lobe patients, such as motor paralysis and excessive

---

13. In spite of his criticisms of the "automaticity juggernaut" (Kihlstrom 2008), Kihlstrom likewise emphasized the distinction between automatic and executive processes and hence legitimized the notion of the dissociation of consciousness in hypnosis and related states, such as automatic processes (Kihlstrom 2015, 2–3).

"irritability" (Woody and Bowers 1994, 70–73). (In fact, it seems possible that Bargh [2005] derived his ideas about the similarities between frontal-lobe patients and priming responses from Bowers's work.)[14] These behaviors included a tendency to perseveration: like frontal-lobe patients, hypnotized individuals exhibited a reduced capacity to overcome routine responses and to cope with novel problem-solving demands.

Bowers acknowledged that invoking the theory of dissociated control "might just seem to postpone the problem of explaining hypnotic responding, rather than really solving it" (Woody and Bowers 1994, 58), by which I take him to mean that his explanation still left unclear *why* hypnotic commands caused the hypothesized cognitive dissociation. In trying to strengthen his arguments on this point, he resorted to the same model of attention proposed by Norman and Shallice (1986) to which Bargh had also appealed (Dijksterhuis, Bargh, and Miedema 2000, 37; see also my discussion in chapter 4). According to that model, there were two complementary control systems for the initiation and regulation of action. The idea was that in the case of well-learned, habitual, or automatic tasks, an autonomous channel of processing, which Norman and Shallice called the "contention-scheduling system," could usually carry out the required activities without the need for conscious attentional control. But when the required action was complex, or when a routine behavior had to be overcome, then a second-order "supervisory attentional system" intervened. As Bowers explained, the supervisory attentional system had access to its own "relatively unique information, including the individual's goals and intentions" (Woody and Bowers 1994, 60), such that, like a CEO of a company who did not directly execute an action but through his authority managed what went on, the individual had the phenomenal experience of will and the intentional control that was otherwise lacking in the lower-level systems. But when the supervisory system was not monitoring the lower-level systems, the action was experienced as, and appeared to be, automatic (Woody and Bowers 1994, 60).

---

14. Bargh (2005) cited Woody and Bowers (1994), who did not mention Lhermitte's work but cited Norman and Shallice's (1986) discussion of the "supervisory attentional system" in relation to frontal-lobe functions. Norman and Shallice (1986) cited Lhermitte, Derouesne, and Signoret (1972) on the psychology of frontal-lobe patients. Moreover, in addition to citing Lhermitte (1986) on the environmental dependency syndrome (Bargh 2005, 37), Bargh also cited Woody and Sadler (1998), in which the authors cited the same Lhermitte (1986) paper (Bargh 2005, 45, 48).

Applying these ideas to the apparent absence of volition and tendency to automaticity in hypnotized subjects, Bowers postulated that hypnosis weakened or disabled the operation of the higher-level supervisory system, with the result that the hypnotized subject became dependent on the lower-level system of control. "According to this conception," Woody and Bowers argued,

> hypnosis results in a genuine change in the control of behavior—namely, the hypnotized individual is especially dependent on the contention-scheduling level of control, and this control can not be modulated readily in a willful manner. One should keep in mind that routine control of action can occur without the intervention of the supervisory system (the one weakened by hypnosis), for instance, with action that is triggered directly by environmental stimuli and coactive schemas. Control at the level of the contention-scheduling system, then, would be what is meant—in the language of the neo-dissociation theory of hypnosis—by "subsystems of control," which may be "directly activated." (Woody and Bowers 1994, 61)

The authors reinforced these claims by comparing the effects of hypnosis to the effects of a drug that weakened the integrative mechanisms that normally coordinated the various systems of control (Woody and Bowers 1994, 58). Referring to Stevenson's famous novel, *Dr. Jekyll and Mr. Hyde*, in which Dr. Jekyll drank a serum that turned him into his second self, Mr. Hyde, Woody and Bowers remarked:

> The notion that hypnosis weakens higher integrative functioning has an extremely important implication: hypnosis alters not just the experience of behavior, but how it is *controlled*. Let us refer . . . to the Stevenson story . . . The effect of the drug, which we may think of for the present purposes as an analogue of hypnosis, is not simply to provide Jekyll with some novel experiences, but to release patterns of behavior that would have been entirely suppressed when in his normal state. (Woody and Bowers 1994, 57; their emphasis)

Bowers's comparison between the effects of a drug and the effects of hypnosis served the purpose of suggesting that the hypnotized subject's dissociation was comparable to a drug-induced state and, as such, was a materially caused condition rather than an intentional action of the kind proposed by Spanos and others.[15]

"The question 'Why' has and yet has not application"

Whether any of Bowers's proposals actually succeeded in explaining hypnosis is highly doubtful. In a sense, all he had done was to translate the mystery of hypnotic influence into the technical language of cognitive science, and hence to present his "dissociated control" theory as a new, up-to-date scientific approach. We might put it that his arguments were driven as much by his cognitive-science commitments as by the clinical and experimental evidence, the interpretation of which in any case remained a topic of contestation.

The interest for us of Bowers's work, however, is that he offered a strictly causal explanation of hypnotic phenomena. By this I mean the following. In her book *Intention*, aspects of which I discussed in chapter 2, Elizabeth Anscombe famously defined intentional action as a form of description that makes the question "why" (as in "Why did you do that?") the relevant question. As she put it: "Intentional actions . . . are the ones to which the question 'Why' is given application" (2000 [1957], ¶16, 24). But Anscombe went on to note that there were cases in which the question "Why" was not refused application, but the answer was: "I don't know why I did it." She suggested that this answer was appropriate in the case of actions in which "some special reason seems to be demanded, and one has none" (Anscombe 2000[1957], ¶17, 25). She continued:

> "I don't know why I did it" may be said by someone who does not *discover* that he did it; he is quite aware as he does it; but he comes out with this expression as if to say "It is the sort of action in which a reason seems requisite." As if there were a reason, if only he knew it; but of course that is not the case in the relevant sense; even if psychoanalysis persuades him to accept something as his reason, or he finds a reason in a divine or diabolical plan or inspiration, or a causal explanation in his having been previously hypnotized. (Anscombe 2000 [1957], ¶17, 26; her emphasis)

---

15. It is worth mentioning that, as Miller, Galanter, and Pribram observed, the hypnotist's speech (words or commands) played an important role in hypnotic induction (Miller, Galanter, and Pribram 1960, 106), a point that does not seem to have concerned Bowers when he compared the effect of hypnosis on behavior to the effect of a drug on Dr. Jekyll.

To which she added:

> I myself have never wished to use these words in this way, but that does not make me suppose them to be senseless. They are a curious intermediary case: the question "Why?" has and yet has not application; it has application in the sense that it is admitted as an appropriate question; it lacks it in the sense that the answer is that there is no answer. (Anscombe 2000 [1957], ¶17, 26)

One way to interpret Anscombe's brief remarks would be to say that, in the case of psychoanalysis, there is a sense in which individuals may not know the reason for their actions but could become convinced, as a result of psychoanalytic treatment, that they had previously been driven by repressed reasons that they now accept as their own. In other words, they might become convinced that they had had unconscious reasons which have now been brought into consciousness and in this way have become available to them as their reasons for having felt and acted in some way.

But Anscombe appeared to believe that in the case of hypnosis, individuals don't actually have reasons at all: her remarks suggest that in her view hypnosis is a strictly causally determined condition. This may be why people are attracted to and yet have a difficult time with hypnosis. They treat "I reached for the bread because I was hungry" and "I reached for the bread because I was hypnotized" as if they were versions of the same kind of explanation, the difference between them being mainly epistemological (for example, they might not know or remember that they had been hypnotized). As we have seen, this view of hypnosis as a form of intentional action was adopted by several prominent hypnosis researchers in the form of "role-playing" theory. But for Anscombe, these two explanations are different. They are not different because one is more automatic than the other (there is a considerable amount of automaticity in reaching for the bread). They are different because, in the case of psychoanalysis, subjects might come to accept certain reasons as their own.[16] But in the case of hypnosis the notion of reason is irrelevant. On Anscombe's causal account, even if someone knew very well that she had been hypnotized

---

16. However, Anscombe's use of the word *persuasion* to describe how a person might come to provide a reason for her actions implies that the person's reason had been "suggested" to her by the psychoanalyst and, accordingly, could not properly be considered her own, authentic reason.

and remembered everything about it, she still wouldn't have a reason for reaching for the bread.

In a recent commentary on this "very difficult passage" in Anscombe's *Intention*, John Schwenkler proposes that we can understand Anscombe's remarks as concerned with the phenomena of self-ignorance that are "often discussed under the headings of repression, self-deception, the Freudian unconscious, and so on." He observes that while we say of such cases of self-ignorance that they involve a failure to understand or appreciate the reasons why we think and do things, "we do not think of this as *mere* ignorance," as with our ignorance of the causes of a reflex (2019, 45). Thus, explaining someone's behavior in a Freudian manner is not like giving "'a causal explanation that [the agent] does not know.'" Nor, he argues, is it like ignorance of the "reasons" of a hypnotist, a divine planner or diabolical manipulator—"for the reasons that explain one's behavior here are supposed to be *one's own*. That is precisely why these are not described *straightforwardly* as cases where a person is ignorant of why she acts as does. As Anscombe says, we only speak of them *as if* this were so" (Schwenkler 2019, 45, citing Anscombe 2000 [1957], ¶17, 25).

Schwenkler goes on to comment that what makes these cases so hard to pin down is that the status of the putative reason-giving explanation of an action is generally tied to the agent's capacity to give such an explanation herself. But the agent in these cases seems unable to do so—although, as he notes, in the psychoanalytic case, the subject's ignorance may only be partial, owing to a psychological dysfunction, such as the "repression" of something that the individual "knows" at some level (Schwenkler 2019, 46).[17] But, he adds,

> to the extent that such ignorance *does* seem to be total, and the agent can become aware of her reason *only* in a third-personal way, we lose our handle on its *really* having been *her* reason—and, perhaps, *her* intentional action—after all. Here, Anscombe says, we have "a curious intermediary case: the question 'Why' has and yet has not application; it has

---

17. For a good start on these "puzzling" phenomena, Schwenkler (2019, 45) recommends an article by Eric Marcus (2019) in which, with reference to Anscombe's *Intention*, the author argues that people are not really unaware of their apparently unconscious (repressed?) intentions, it's just that they deceive themselves into thinking themselves unaware because of their desire to avoid painful feelings. Surprisingly, Marcus does not refer to either Freud or psychoanalysis; nor does he address the question of hypnosis and its relation to psychoanalysis.

application in the sense that it is admitted as an appropriate question; it lacks it in the sense that it has *no answer*" . . . No doubt this leaves a great deal more to be said. But doing this would be a project for another occasion. (Schwenkler 2019, 46; his emphasis)

Schwenkler focuses his discussion on the psychoanalytic but not the hypnotic case. But one thing more that *can* be said in connection with the hypnotic case is that for Bowers the reason the question "Why" is applicable in the case of the hypnotized subject yet has no answer is precisely because the hypnotic induction is a causally induced state, as Anscombe also appeared to believe: According to Bowers, hypnosis causes a dissociation between the person's "executive" functions—which is to say, her conscious-intentional functions—and her unconscious automatic subsystems. The dissociation leaves the subject in a condition rather like a patient who intentionally submits to anesthesia in order to undergo an operation, but afterward can't remember anything of what occurred during her medicated state because the anesthesia rendered her completely unconscious. The result is that in principle the hypnotized person can't give a reason for her hypnotic actions: the reasons she provides are fabrications designed to rationalize what is to her an otherwise unreasonable, inexplicable performance.[18]

---

18. In an interesting discussion of the relation between forms of automaticity such as taking a photograph and intentionality, Charles Palermo makes use of a distinction Anscombe makes between an "action" and a "description," according to which "a man may know that he is doing a thing under one description, and not under another" (Anscombe 2000 [1957], 11). Thus, according to Anscombe, a person may do something that under one description is intentional, but under another description is unintentional. On this basis, Palermo proposes that, under the influence of hypnosis, the agent initiates intentional actions that are disconnected from her ability to describe herself as the agent of the actions she performs. He comments of the automatic writing that a spirit medium performs on a planchette that "generally, I think we want to speak of an automatic act as automatic if we are tempted to note some disconnection (or disconnections) between our intentions in performing it and the description under which we act. Automatism is our way of describing the capacity (or incapacity) in the agent that produces the disconnection between the agent's intentions and descriptions. Sometimes that (in)capacity looks like a pathology (say, somnambulism), sometimes like a special talent or sensitivity (spirit mediumship), but sometimes it looks like a technique, as in the case of photography or of surrealist psychic automatism" (Palermo 2014, 171). If I understand Palermo's arguments correctly, his interpretation of hypnotically induced automaticity as a form of intentional action is congruent with that of the "social-role" theorists of hypnosis, who likewise interpreted the hypnotic performance as intentional; his account therefore acknowledges the inseparability between intention and automaticity that is a major theme of my book. But according to

It would be interesting to know why Anscombe held to a causal view of hypnosis. We learn from various sources that in 1948, several years before she published *Intention*, Anscombe consulted a hypnotist in order to give up smoking. But it seems she had nothing more to say about the topic (and almost immediately after her hypnotic treatment resumed her lifelong smoking habit).[19] For my purposes, however, the interest of Anscombe's views about hypnosis lies in the fact that, as we have seen, in the 1990s Bowers and colleagues would have agreed with her judgment concerning its causal status. We could put it that in 1957 Anscombe adopted a causal explanation of hypnosis of the kind that many years later Bowers and like-minded researchers also advocated on the basis of their research on the topic. The whole point of Bowers's "dissociated-control" approach to hypnosis was to counteract the role-playing theory according to which, even if hypnotized subjects appeared to behave completely passively, involuntarily, and unconsciously in compliance with the hypnotist's suggestions, their actions were really intentional and strategic. For Bowers, rather, hypnotic responses were causally induced unconscious, unintended behaviors that were triggered by the loss of executive control consequent on the hypnotic induction.

---

my reading, Palermo's interpretation of hypnotic automaticity is at odds with Anscombe's interpretation of hypnosis as a causally induced state.

19. Lipscomb reports that Anscombe "fled" to Ireland to see Wittgenstein because her emotional relationship with the philosopher and novelist Iris Murdoch had reached some sort of crisis, but also because of symptoms of nicotine withdrawal after having undergone hypnosis in order to give up smoking. In addition, Anscombe was working "feverishly" on a late draft of her first philosophical publication. Lipscomb quotes Anscombe as stating in an unpublished notebook of reminiscences about Wittgenstein: "'I visited [Wittgenstein] in Dublin in 1948 in need of . . . help and advice because of a matter that was troubling me . . . I had certainly got into a queer state of mind, partly assisted by my having employed a hypnotist to help me give up smoking; this had been partly successful . . . but [I] was beset by a troubling obsession and by insomnia.'" Wittgenstein told her to resume smoking (Lipscomb 2022, 123). Hayes provides the further detail that Wittgenstein advised Anscombe to consult "his former student and friend Maurice O'Connor ('Con') Drury, who, after war service in the Royal Army Medical Corps, had taken a post in psychiatry at St. Patrick's Hospital . . . Drury helped restore her sleep through his good sense and friendliness. Long term, he advised—as did Wittgenstein—that she resume smoking. She left Dublin much refreshed." (Hayes 2020, 43–44). For further details about Anscombe's crisis over her relations to Murdoch, see Lipscomb 2022. Wittgenstein, who had tried hypnosis in 1913, also adopted a causal view of the phenomenon, comparing his experience of it to being anesthetized. See Von Wright 1990 (54); McGuiness 1988 (171); and Baker 2003 (424).

Bargh on Priming and Hypnosis

In the context of these developments, it is not surprising that Bowers's causal theory of hypnosis caught Bargh's attention for the light it seemed to throw on the effects of priming, which could also seem surprising and, indeed, somewhat uncanny. So far as I have been able to determine, Bargh first mentioned the connection between hypnosis and primed behavior in 1999, when he and Chartrand compared the subject's unconscious tendency to imitation to Hilgard's causal account of the hypnotic response (Chartrand and Bargh 1999, 906, citing Hilgard 1965), a comparison that made priming effects the result of dissociation between conscious and automatic processes.[20] Bargh mentioned the connection between priming and hypnosis again, with reference to the work of both Hilgard and Bowers, when he attempted to "demystify" the idea of the nonconscious control of behavior. "People are often unaware of the reasons and causes of their own behavior," he stated. "In fact, recent experimental evidence points to a deep and fundamental dissociation between conscious awareness and the mental processes responsible for one's behavior; many of the wellsprings of behavior appear to be opaque to conscious access." The purpose of his paper was thus to bring together various lines of research demonstrating two principles: "that an individual's behavior can be directly caused by the current environment, without the necessity of an act of conscious choice or will; and that this behavior can and will unfold without the person being aware of its external deter-

---

20. Thus, Chartrand and Bargh commented that their views were "in harmony with Hilgard's (1965) account of hypnotic suggestion. According to Hilgard, the directives given by the hypnotist are first perceived by the person being hypnotized, and then, because of the suspension of the will that is characteristic of the hypnotic state, passive effects of perception on action are left free to operate. In other words, the suggestions made by the hypnotist have a direct automatic effect on behavior because of the abdication of conscious control by the hypnotized person." Chartrand and Bargh he characterized the response as an "instance of James's (1890) ideomotor action effect in which the ideation is externally induced by the hypnotist" (1999, 906). Chartrand and Bargh (1999) also cited Wegner and Wheatley (1999) at this juncture, in which, with reference to hypnotic effects and other phenomena, the latter argued that conscious will is an illusion: "The real causes of human action are unconscious, so it is not surprising that behavior could often arise—as in automaticity experiments—without the person having conscious insight into its causation" (Wegner and Wheatley 1999, 490). Wegner and Wheatley aligned their claims with Nisbett and Wilson's (1977) skeptical conclusions regarding the ability of individuals to identify the true reasons for their actions and behaviors (Wegner and Wheatley 1999, 481).

minant." He declared that "the classic phenomenon" demonstrating a dissociation between conscious will and behavior was hypnosis (Bargh 2005, 37–38, 39, 48).

Just like priming, he argued, hypnosis had long been seen as magical and mysterious but was now part of mainstream medicine—as, for example, when it served as an alternative to anesthesia for inducing analgesia. He quoted the role-playing theorists of hypnosis Sarbin and Coe as remarking in this connection how the behaviors induced by hypnosis violated expectations about the normal limits of human behavior: "'This aspect of the hypnotic situation creates surprise and puzzlement. *How can we account for the apparent magnitude of response to such a benign stimulus? How can only a verbal request bring about so dramatic a change as analgesia to the surgeon's scalpel?*'" (Bargh 2005, 48; Sarbin and Coe 1972, 17; their emphasis). But for Bargh the answer to that question lay not in role-playing approaches associated with the work of Sarbin, Coe, Spanos, and others but in "dissociation" theories of the kind advocated by Hilgard and Bowers. "The various modern theories of hypnosis, such as those of Hilgard (1986 [1977]), Woody and Bowers (1994), and Kihlstrom (e.g., 1998[b]) are dissociation theories of one sort or another," he observed (Bargh 2005, 48), adding:

> Woody and Bowers argued that hypnosis may alter not just the self-perception of the control of one's behavior but the actual nature of that control (dissociated control theory). In this theory, highly hypnotizable people's subsystems of control may be relatively directly or automatically accessed, without being governed by higher level executive control as much as they normally would.
>
> There are obvious parallels between hypnotic and priming phenomena and. . . . neuropsychological research . . . supports the notion of dissociated will or control in hypnosis as well as in priming effects. In both cases, the will is apparently controlled from outside, by external forces. (Bargh 2005, 49)

Bargh acknowledged that there were also differences between priming and hypnotic phenomena. In particular, he noted that, according to the evidence, only about 15 percent of people were so deeply hypnotizable that they could carry out posthypnotic suggestions, whereas any randomly selected group of normal participants could easily be primed. He offered the following explanation for this difference:

The reason for this difference may lie in the participants' relative degrees of knowledge of the potential influence of the hypnotic suggestion versus the prime: in the former situation, one is certainly aware of the intent of the hypnotist to make one behave in a certain way, but in the priming situation one is not. The latter thus enables a more passive influence of the environment: it also allows a cleaner dissociation between awareness of what one is doing or trying to do, and one's actual actions. (Bargh 2005, 49)

Bargh's statement is ambiguous. One way of reading it is to assume that he equated the role of the experimenter in priming studies with that of the hypnotist, implying that the actions of primed participants were due to the influence of the experimenter's beliefs and expectations, just as the behaviors of hypnotized subjects were due to the hypnotist's suggestions and commands. But this reading would contradict everything Bargh had had to say about the sources of priming behavior, which he had always traced to the direct influence of the priming words, not to the suggestions of the experimenter. Moreover, Bowers had explicitly argued that hypnotic responsiveness was not a matter of compliance to the demands of the hypnotist but the consequence of authentic changes in the subject's cognitive apparatus. In a statement cited as an epigraph to this chapter, he had stated: "*Hypnotic responsiveness [is] more concerned with genuine, internal alterations in perception, cognition, and subjective experience than with behavioral compliance to external demand characteristics*" (Bowers 1992, 258; my emphasis).

Similarly, for Bargh it was the exposure to the priming words associated with old age that had directly "activated" his participants' stereotypes of the elderly, causing them to walk more slowly than unprimed participants. The response had nothing to do with the experimenter's intentions or expectations. Rather, just as, according to Bowers, the performances of highly hypnotizable subjects were unintentional, unconscious, and nonvolitional because of the effects of dissociation, so also, according to Bargh, the actions of priming participants were genuinely unintentional, unconscious, and nonvolitional because of the direct, causal influence of the priming words and the participants' responses. By viewing the main determinant of human behavior as unconscious priming, and by defining the latter as a variant of hypnotic suggestion (see also Bargh 2006), Bargh thus appeared to normalize the hypnotic state as an everyday, causally induced condition of dissociation in ways that Anscombe (and perhaps even Bowers himself) would not have done.

Priming and Expectancy Effects

To return to the replication crisis of 2012: I am not claiming that Bargh's causal approach to hypnosis succeeded in disarming Doyen et al.'s (2012) suggestion that uncontrolled experimenter-expectancy effects—which is to say, implicit experimenter beliefs and demand characteristics—might have influenced the outcome of his elderly priming experiment. But I am suggesting that Bargh's assumptions about the perception-behavior mechanism responsible for priming effects could have led him to underestimate the need for vigilance concerning the potential impact of the experimenter's beliefs and expectations on priming results. Because he interpreted priming effects, like hypnotic responses, as the result of a direct link between the perception of the priming words and the resulting behavioral outcome, he ignored the influence of cues inhering in the larger laboratory setting, including the potential influence of the experimenter on participants' behavior.

To make this observation is not to deny that in their elderly priming experiment Bargh, Chen, and Burrows (1996) might have followed proper protocols for controlling the influence of the person in the form of experimental expectancy effects, as he claimed they had. Although, as noted in chapter 7, it was hard to be sure about this matter from their published report, Bargh insisted that he and his co-researchers had used effective double-blind methods. However, it is revealing that when Doyen et al. (2012) employed strict double-blind procedures in their replication of Bargh, Chen, and Burrows's study, they were unable to confirm the original findings. It is also seems telling that when Doyen et al. (2012) manipulated experimenter beliefs concerning the priming condition of the participants, the results demonstrated the influence of expectancy effects.

Moreover, in a recent study that attempted to replicate claims concerning the influence of social-power priming words on participant behavior, Gilder and Heerey (2018) reported that an initial conceptual replication of one experiment, involving rigorous double-blind methods, failed to find evidence of the expected power-priming effect on a task performance. But when, in a series of conceptual and direct replications of earlier well-known priming experiments, they manipulated both the priming condition and the experimenters' beliefs about the priming condition, they found that the experimenters' knowledge of which primes participants had received significantly altered the participants' behavior. One of Bargh's experiments (Smith and Bargh 2008) was included in these replication experiments, and Gilder and Heerey reported that in this case their findings "strongly supported the experimenter-belief-only model" (2018, 411). The implication was that Smith and Bargh had failed to adequately control for the influence of such experimenter beliefs.

Gilder and Heerey observed that although the researchers undertaking the experiments, who were advanced students in the field of psychology, obtained the experimental results predicted on the basis of their beliefs about the participants' prime condition, none of them thought that those beliefs had affected their behavior when they were instructing the participants. But when Gilder and Heerey examined the relationship between participants' ratings of the experimenters in terms of various traits and experimenter beliefs, they found statistically significant effects for several of those traits. Thus, in general, when experimenters believed that their participants were in the high-power prime condition, the participants rated the experimenters as more trustworthy, friendlier, and sometimes more attractive than the experimenters who believed their participants were in the low-power condition. Gilder and Heerey concluded that "experimenters' prior beliefs shaped participants' target-task behavior, likely via subtle changes in experimenter behavior" (Gilder and Heerey 2018, 412). They recommended that research findings should be treated skeptically unless the authors reported the use of double-blind procedures in which it was impossible for experimenters to become aware of participants' conditions during the collection of data.[21]

But my argument is that it was not just methodological concerns such as these that contributed to the crisis over Bargh's famous elderly priming study. Another factor was the way in which Bargh's theoretical presuppositions about the direct perception-behavior link seem to have encouraged him to neglect the wider social setting of his priming experiments. It's as if Bargh thought that the influence of the person in the form of the experimenter's expectations and beliefs could be ignored in priming experiments, not only because the experimenters purportedly deployed adequate methodological controls, but because according to his automa-

---

21. Gilder and Heerey reported that none of the experimenters, masters students, or advanced undergraduates, charged with conducting the experiments thought that their beliefs about the participants' priming condition had affected their participants' behavior after the latter had been given instructions. Yet the results clearly showed that experimenter beliefs had been transmitted in ways that influenced the participants' responses. Gilder and Heerey concluded on the basis of their findings that the experimenters transmitted their expectations in different ways (2018, 412).

ticity theory, the only thing that really mattered was the simple unfolding sequence of events: the participant's exposure to the priming words, the ensuing activation of the participant's "internal" stereotype representations or constructs, and the resulting behavioral response. Bargh's direct perception-behavior model of priming excluded attention to the myriad other situational cues that might influence participants' behaviors, clues that, according to Klein et al. (2012), included even the tone of voice, body language, and nonverbal mimicry of the experimenter when issuing an injunction to participants to leave the laboratory at the end of the experiment. In sum, Bargh, Chen, and Burrows (1996) had had too restricted an understanding of the total environmental affordances of the laboratory situation when performing their famous elderly priming study, affordances that likely included the subtle and implicit cues stemming from the persons involved in carrying out the study.

The larger question raised by the influence of experimenter beliefs and expectations on experimental outcomes, however, was whether psychologists were justified in thinking that, with strict double-blind and other methods, such beliefs and expectations could be excluded from the laboratory situation, or whether such beliefs and expectation were, instead, a constitutive and hence ineliminable feature of every experimental interaction, as Orne had argued (Orne 1962, 776). Given that experimenters might be convinced that their beliefs played no role in shaping experimental outcomes and that, according to Orne, participants' attempts to comply with the experimenter's real or imagined beliefs might be unconscious, it was unclear how such beliefs and demand effects could ever be managed or brought fully under control.[22]

The Long Legacy of Nisbett and Wilson (1977): What Is Consciousness For?

The discussion and analyses I have so far provided leave a further question raised by Bargh's views about priming and hypnosis. If he was correct about the pervasiveness of unconscious priming processes in human

---

22. Gilder and Heerey did not claim that their results invalidated priming research generally, because they had not shown that all priming tasks might fail under double-blind conditions. "Indeed," they commented, "reports suggest that priming may work when no experimenter is present (e.g., online)" (2018, 415. It seems unlikely, however, that participant expectations or demand characteristics can be entirely excluded even from online experiments.

action and behavior, what was the function of consciousness? Was it merely an epiphenomenon, as Libet (1985) and so many other researchers had concluded? Did consciousness play no role at all in human behavior?

The topic is of timeless interest, of course, but it took on added importance among cognitive psychologists when Bargh and others made the case for the supposed advantages of unconscious automaticity. Indeed, Doyen et al. (2014) argued that the most important question looming over priming research was whether primes could influence behavior in the absence of consciousness. "This is both the most important question and the most controversial one," they observed, with important implications for concepts of free will, personal responsibility, and the mind-body problem. The question also remained controversial for many scientists because establishing empirically the absence of awareness was fraught with methodological and epistemological complications (Doyen et al. 2014).

This point was precisely the message of Newell and Shanks's article the same year in the influential journal *Behavioral and Brain Sciences* (Newell and Shanks 2014a).[23] Newell and Shanks rejected the idea that people's actions are typically caused by unconscious influences, leaving them without knowledge or insight into their own reasons when they make decisions. They suggested that not enough care had been taken in pursuing the "seductions" of the unconscious to warrant the extreme claims that had been made for its importance by advocates of Unconscious Thought Theory and priming researchers such as Bargh.

In particular, Newell and Shanks argued that experimenters who claimed that unconscious determinants were pervasive in human action had often failed to use adequate techniques for evaluating the awareness of experimental participants, or had neglected to consider artifac-

---

23. During the debates over replication, Newell and Shanks emerged as among the most outspoken critics of priming claims. Thus Shanks et al. (2013) reported that in nine experiments with 475 participants, they had been unable to replicate Dijksterhuis and van Knippenberg's (1998) famous experiment on the influence of priming words associated with intelligence on subsequent behavior. They argued that conscious thoughts were by far the most important drivers of performance and that, if unconscious influences existed at all, they had limited effects. They further suggested that the most plausible explanation for the findings of Dijksterhuis and van Knippenberg and related studies was that the effects were false positives. Subsequently, Dijksterhuis and van Knippenberg's (1998) experiment was the subject of a massive direct-replication effort involving multiple laboratories in Europe and the United States, none of which found any overall difference between primed and unprimed conditions. See O'Donnell et al. (2018) and Dijksterhuis (2018) for the latter's response to these findings.

tual explanations for "landmark" results. According to them, some of the findings used to argue for the importance of unconscious influences on decision-making and in priming experiments were due to the shortcomings of commonly used tests for measuring awareness. Newell and Shanks proposed that in experimental situations, measures of awareness had to meet four criteria: *reliability*, meaning assessments should not be influenced by experimental demands or social desirability; *relevance*, meaning assessments should target only information relevant to the behavior; *immediacy*, meaning assessments should be made concurrently or as soon as possible; and *sensitivity*, meaning assessments should be made under optimal retrieval conditions, for example, that the same cues were used for measuring awareness as for eliciting the behavior (Newell and Shanks 2014a, 4). In their judgment, however, these criteria had rarely been met in the decision-making or priming literature. Indeed, Doyen et al. had already argued that the standard "funnel" debriefing method of assessing participants' awareness of the influence of primes on their behavior was faulty in several ways: (a) the test of awareness was delayed rather than immediate; (b) it relied on verbal reports that might not be sufficiently sensitive; (c) it might not be reliable because it could be influenced by experimental demands; and (d) it might not be relevant if verbal reports did not implicate the same processes assumed to be unconscious (Doyen et al. 2014, 22). These researchers maintained that when probes of awareness were more reliable, relevant, immediate, and sensitive, greater evidence for conscious awareness was revealed.

Newell and Shanks traced the willingness of so many experimental psychologists to endorse the idea of the importance of unconscious influences on behavior to the work of Nisbett and Wilson (1977), who had claimed that people typically lacked insight into their own mental processes and hence into the reasons for their actions. Newell and Shanks's paper thus testifies to the enduring legacy of that paper in the cognitive sciences. It will be recalled that Nisbett and Wilson (1977) had suggested that subjects were better at reporting *what* they were thinking and feeling than *why* they were, or how cognitive contents influenced their thought and feelings, because the latter processes were the product of unconscious, unintentional cognitive processes that were unavailable to introspection or consciousness (Nisbett and Wilson 1977). The argument surfaced regularly in priming research (for example, Loersch and Payne 2012, 241). More than thirty years later Newell and Shanks still found it necessary to revisit the arguments that Nisbett and Wilson had made so many years before. They essentially rehearsed criticisms that had already been voiced numerous times over the years, concluding that, in many of the sorts of situations cited by Nisbett and Wilson, "we do in fact have introspective access to our conscious mental states, and the verbal reporting of these states conveys privileged information about the causes of our behavior" (Newell and Shanks 2014a, 5).[24]

Not only did Newell and Shanks critique the debriefing methods Bargh, Chen, and Burrows (1996) had used in their elderly priming experiment for assessing participants' awareness of the purpose of the experiment. They cast doubt on claims that supposedly automatic processes of the kind observed in habitual actions were cognitively immune from top-down attentional influences, suggesting that very few of such processes were truly uncontrollable. In addition, they questioned the importance attached to unconscious processes in dual-system theories such as those of Kahneman and others. They suggested that when experimental participants were given adequate opportunities to report their awareness of the factors influencing their behavior, there was little if any explanatory role to be played by phenomenologically inaccessible unconscious processes (Newell and Shanks 2014a, 17). The authors concluded that the evidence for unconscious influences on decision-making and related behaviors was weak, and that many of the key research findings either demonstrated directly that behavior was under conscious control or could plausibly be explained without recourse to the notion of unconscious influences.[25]

---

24. It will be remembered that in the much-discussed "stockings" experiment, subjects had been asked to choose between four sets of stockings that were arranged in a row from left to right and were in fact identical; the participants tended to favor the rightmost pair of stockings, leading Nisbett and Wilson (1977) to conclude that the position of the stockings alone was the decisive cause of their choice. From Newell and Shanks's perspective, asking the subjects about the influence of position failed the relevance criterion, because, as Smith and Miller (1978) had argued long ago, the position of the stockings was almost certainly not an immediate cause of their choices but at best as a distal cause or factor. Newell and Shanks argued that the participants' choices were more likely a function of using a sequential comparison process involving the decision rule that, if a current item is no worse than the previous one, then it makes sense to prefer the current item—a rule that would result in most of the participants preferring the rightmost pair of stockings. To establish the role of position, Newell and Shanks argued, Nisbett and Wilson would have had to show that the participants denied employing a sequential comparison process, which they had failed to do (Newell and Shanks 2014a, 5).

25. In a related paper on the anchoring process, Newell and Shanks questioned whether priming studies revealed adequate evidence for the sort of automatic mental processes of the kind Bargh had proposed. They concluded by remarking that "there are few

It could be argued, as some commentators did, that in their zeal to downplay the importance of unconscious cognitive processes, Newell and Shanks risked throwing the baby out with the bathwater (for example, Finkbeiner and Coltheart 2014; and Ingram and Prochnowik 2014).[26] Indeed, it could be argued that Newell and Shanks risked assuming the same stark dualism between consciousness and nonconsciousness that had informed Bargh's work on automaticity all along, with the result that they forced an unnatural choice between the two processes. It is interesting in this regard that the authors commented on the remarkably minor role debates about the meaning of the terms *consciousness* and *awareness* themselves had played in recent research (Newell and Shanks 2014a, 15). The same criticism could be leveled at Newell and Shanks. They rejected talk of "brains" making decisions as a form of category mistake, because consciousness was a property of persons, not neural networks (Newell and Shanks 2014a, 2, 15). But they were themselves more concerned with making sure the right methods were used to assess the causal impact of consciousness than with offering conceptual clarifications, and they followed standard cognitive-science usage in thematizing the role of consciousness in terms of information processing and decision-making.

It took the philosopher Louise Antony, in her comment on Newell and Shanks's paper, to make the point that what was at stake conceptually in their discussion of consciousness was the role of reasons and intentions in the explanation of human actions. As she remarked: "An ongoing debate

---

(if any) truly automatic or unconscious processes, nor is activation a passive and obligatory phenomenon" (Newell and Shanks 2014b, 105).

26. Hogarth (2014, 31) expressed surprise that Newell and Shanks had not explored the topic of automatic processes in more detail. Newell and Shanks replied:

> We do not dispute that the acquisition of many physical or perceptual-motor skills involves a period in which people are acutely aware of their movements, and that when such skills are mastered, they are executed with very shallow phenomenological experience. However, just because we allocate very little attention to and engage in minimal monitoring of the mental operations involved in performing perceptual-motor skills, it does not follow that such skills are controlled and executed unconsciously. A relevant example comes from studies of ball catching. Although this ability is often highlighted as a paradigmatic case of a skill outside conscious control, detailed analyses of what people know about the cues they use to decide whether to advance or retreat to intercept and catch a ball reveal surprisingly rich and accurate information... Thus, while we agree with Hogarth that it can be difficult to prove or disprove the role of unconscious influences in such skills, those studies that have tried to do so provide evidence that falls far short of demonstrating independence from conscious control. (Newell and Shanks, 2014a, 47)

in the philosophy of mind concerns the status of our everyday, 'folk psychological' explanations of human actions—explanations that advert to the agents' intentions and goals. It is part of this folk picture that in cases where people do act for some particular reason, they know what that reason is." It was this last claim that Nisbett and Wilson and theorists such as Bargh had denied when they had suggested not only that we might frequently be wrong about the reasons for our actions but that we might be wrong in thinking we had any reasons at all, so that our ordinary attributions of intentions were "explanatorily otiose"—an argument Antony rejected (Antony 2014, 19–20).[27]

Many of the researchers invited to comment on Newell and Shanks's paper welcomed the latter's effort to restore balance in the assessment of the respective contributions of conscious and unconscious processing in human cognition and decision-making. Not surprisingly, though, Unconscious Thought theorists Dijksterhuis and his colleagues fought back with a sharply worded attack, accusing critics of basing their arguments on what Dijksterhuis et al. considered a biased sampling of the literature and impoverished theoretical assumptions. They conceded that strong early claims, such as the proposal that it was best "'to leave decisions to the unconscious'" were, in retrospect, "naïve," indeed that unconscious thought effects were "far from robust" (Dijksterhuis et al. 2014, 25). Nevertheless, they accused Newell and Shanks of failing to do justice to the dozens of experiments proving the importance of unconscious thought, and of ignoring many experiments they deemed were fully compatible with Newell and Shanks's awareness criteria. A few other researchers likewise disagreed with Newell and Shanks's principal claims (for example, Hassin and Milyavsky 2014). The debate was by no means over, as Newell and Shanks continued to clash with priming researchers over the role of unconscious processes in decision-making and related actions.[28] In sum, psychologists remained divided over the role of consciousness in decision-making—which is to say the role of intentions and reasons.

---

27. But as a self-declared naturalist in the philosophy of mind, Antony did not accept the contrast McDowell (2009) made between the space of reasons and the space of nature (as defined by the modern sciences).

28. For example, Newell and Shanks (2014b) interpreted the "situated cognition" theorists Loersch and Payne as having reintroduced into cognitive psychology the role of consciousness and intentionality in priming responses that Bargh's theories had rejected, only to have Loersch and Payne repudiate such an interpretation of their priming views. See Loersch and Payne 2014; Payne, Brown-Iannuzzi, and Loersch 2016; and Shanks 2017.

Consciousness as Rationalization

The same year Newell and Shanks's (2014a) article appeared, in a target paper in the same influential journal Julie Huang and Bargh implicitly rebutted Newell and Shank's criticisms by arguing that, when people offered reasons for their behavior, they did not provide good-faith, post-hoc explanatory accounts with sufficient accuracy but gave reasons that were mere rationalizations. They therefore continued the very line of thinking derived from Nisbett and Wilson (1977) that Newell and Shanks had just condemned: for Huang and Bargh, consciousness was powerless to cause or control anything, because people's actions were determined by unconscious, unintentional goal pursuits automatically triggered by situational factors. One might put it that Huang and Bargh arguments epitomized Bargh's skepticism about the role of intentionality and agency in human action.

The main purpose of Huang and Bargh's paper was to suggest that people's "goal pursuits" operated "as if" they were "selfish" (for earlier statements of the thesis see Bargh, Green, and Fitzsimons 2008; Bargh and Huang 2009; Huang and Bargh 2011). By this claim they meant that, like Richard Dawkins's "selfish" genes (Dawkins 1976), certain goals pursued their own interests independently of, and sometimes in conflict with, the conscious goals of individuals themselves. As Huang and Bargh put the point: "As multiple goals within a single individual operate autonomously, becoming activated, operating, and turning off with achievement of their associated end-states, a person's behaviors and judgments will continue to vary as a function of which goals are most motivating. To an outsider, that person's behavior may appear inconsistent over time and, at extremes, even contrary to his or her general self-interests" (Huang and Bargh 2014, 132). Those goal constructs took the form of internal mental representations of "desired" end states (Huang and Bargh 2014, 124), each one of which "egotistically" vied for dominance over all the others—constructs that were themselves passively activated by situational-environmental stimuli.

Although the selection process by which certain goals prevailed over others was not clear, for Huang and Bargh the important point was that the automatic pursuit of goals happened in the absence of consciousness and intention. In effect the authors treated individuals as passengers in their own airplanes with no access to the cockpit. "The use of the term 'unconscious,'" they announced, "highlights the *unintentional* nature of the process, along with a lack of awareness of its underlying causes and processes" (Huang and Bargh 2014, 124; their emphasis). According to them, research on the influence of situational variables in determining behavior; Nisbett and Wilson's (1977) claims regarding the limits of people's introspective awareness of the causes of their actions and the fabricated nature of their ostensible reasons; dual-process models of the mind proposed by Kahneman and others; the findings of priming research; and Lhermitte's account of the tendency to uncontrolled imitation in frontal-lobe patients—all suggested that commonsense intuitions regarding the requirement of consciousness and intentions in pursuing goals were false (Huang and Bargh 2014, 123). Huang and Bargh did not deny that some goal pursuits could operate consciously. But according to their evolutionary account, unconscious goal pursuits were the phylogenetically primordial phenomena. In fact, they argued that it was because unconscious processes had evolved in nonhuman animals before conscious ones that these processes not only took the form of less centralized, distributed motivational systems capable of causing adaptive behaviors, but dominated behavior.

From my perspective, the chief interest of Huang and Bargh's paper concerns their ideas about the function of consciousness itself. A major theme of their article was that temporarily active goals could produce outcomes for individuals that appeared inconsistent over time or contrary to the person's interests. In support of their claims regarding the apparent inconsistencies arising when a person's overall goals conflicted with unintentionally triggered goal pursuits, Huang and Bargh cited an experiment (Bargh, Green, and Fitzsimons 2008) in which participants had been asked to evaluate a videotaped, enacted interview of a candidate's suitability for the job of either restaurant waiter or newspaper crime reporter. The idea behind the choice of those jobs was that the desired personality characteristics of a waiter (deferential and polite) and a crime reporter (tough and aggressive) were "opposites" of each other (Huang and Bargh 2014, 132). In the control condition, participants had merely been told that they were watching two people getting reacquainted. During the videotaped interview, the conversation had been interrupted by a person named Mike, who had behaved either politely or aggressively. After viewing the videotapes, the participants had been given a surprise impression task in which they had been asked to rate Mike, rather than the job candidates on whom they had been consciously focused. As Bargh, Green, and Fitzsimons had reported, the participants viewing the videotapes of the waiter interview and the control condition had liked Mike significantly more if he was polite rather than rude, but in a reversal, participants watching videotapes of the reporter interview had liked rude Mike more than polite Mike.

Bargh and his co-authors (2008) had described these results as surprising because, as shown by the participants' ratings in the control condition, people did not normally like rude or aggressive people. But the experiments appeared to show that people liked offensive people if their traits were valued within a currently active goal pursuit—even if, as in this experiment, the consciously intended focus of that goal pursuit had not been Mike but an entirely different person, the interviewee. Bargh, Green, and Fitzsimons (2008) had further suggested that the conflict between conscious intentions and unconscious goal pursuits made people appear inconsistent over time and, at the extreme, even contrary to an individual's general self-interests. In short, as Huang and Bargh summarized the implications of these experiments: "Even the goals one intends to pursue, and of which one is aware, are capable of producing information processing and behavioral effects consistent with the goal's agenda but not necessarily with the individual's self-related values and/or overall interests, thus potentially leading to unintended consequences of intended (conscious) pursuits" (Huang and Bargh 2014, 132). (But who was the "individual" here? The authors' appeal to the idea of the "individual" with her own values and interests and pursuing her own goals potentially in conflict with unconsciously triggered goal pursuits was incoherent within the terms of their analysis. This is because according to them, people lacked any kind of central self or overarching capacity for conscious control but were merely constellations of multiple, autonomous goal constructs that regulated actions.)[29]

---

29. Their experiments, Bargh, Green, and Fitzsimons (2008) wrote, "demonstrate that goals to evaluate a job applicant for either a waiter or a crime reporter position also shape impressions of incidental bystanders in the situation, such that the bystander is later liked or disliked not on his own merits, but on how well his behavior matches the criteria consciously applied in evaluating the job applicant" (Bargh et al. 2008, 534). Even assuming that Bargh, Green, and Fitzsimons's (2008) findings could be replicated, the interpretation they offered was based on several questionable assumptions. These assumptions included: the positing of a simplistic opposition between the aggressivity required of a crime reporter (as if a reporter pursuing a story does not have to be polite sometimes in order to get an interview) and the politeness of a waiter (as if a waiter doesn't have to be aggressive sometimes, as when dealing with an unruly customer); the idea that the participants could have judged Mike on his "own merits," when he was presumably a stranger and all they had to go on in judging him was his behavior in the context of the experiment; the

So again, the question posed was: If consciousness had developed belatedly in the evolution of purposive behaviors and indeed appeared to lack a direct, causative role in action, what function did it serve? The answer, Huang and Bargh maintained, was that as a latecomer to events that were largely (or wholly?) determined by unconscious goal pursuits, consciousness had evolved to manage publicly observed inconsistencies in behavior by making up reasons after the fact for actions over which the organism or "individual" had no control. Huang and Bargh further claimed that those concocted reasons served the purpose of helping individuals put a positive spin on their situationally triggered behaviors, because that is what survival required. As they argued:

> When examining behavior from the perspective of the individual, people can appear inconsistent by thinking, feeling, and acting in a contradictory fashion over time . . . These inconsistencies . . . pose a problem for individuals in a social world in which trust and predictability of behavior are at a premium and are essential for positive, cooperative relations with one's peers . . . Thus we note . . . that several recent accounts of the purpose of conscious thought have argued that it evolved (was selected for as an adaptive advantage) in order to manage these same public inconsistencies that are produced by selfish-goal operations (Baumeister and Masicampo 2010; Mercier and Sperber 2011; see also Gazzaniga 1984).

Huang and Bargh added:

> The conscious self, in this view, is not so much involved in the guidance of our purposive behavior so much as it is in the business of producing rationalizations and socially acceptable accounts for the actions produced at the goal level. Tetlock (2002) has argued that our accountability to others was so important over evolutionary time that we evolved the "politician" (or "defense attorney") social mindset in order to maintain good relations within our group . . . That's no small potatoes: not being able to explain or justify any negative outcomes one was involved in to

---

notion that the participants' evaluation of Mike as likeable when he behaved aggressively in the context of their assessment of the interviewee's suitability for the job of crime reporter was surprising, given that the interviewee's aggressive behavior in the videotaped investigative-reporter interview condition set up its own contextual norm in which aggressivity was called for, and the participants might therefore have been comfortable with Mike's behavior in that setting; and so on.

one's peers could come at the cost of ostracism or worse; being able to give a plausible positive account would thus have strong survival value . . . In assigning this valuable politician role to conscious thought and the conscious self, room is thus made for autonomous goal processes as the proximal determinant of human judgment and behavior. (Huang and Bargh 2014, 134)

It's as if, for Huang and Bargh, our ordinary lives are largely, perhaps entirely, carried out in a state of automaticity, and we are all the better for this automaticity because our unconscious processes unerringly function in adaptive ways—as if diplomacy came automatically.[30]

In making these claims, Huang and Bargh (2014) appeared to turn the thought of Tetlock (2002) and Mercier and Sperber (2011) in a radical direction those authors had not intended. Although these latter authors had attributed various functions to consciousness, such as its role in argumentation, none of them had suggested that consciousness (or reasoning) served only rhetorical purposes without regard to the epistemic goal of searching for the truth. Mercier and Sperber (2011) had suggested that the chief purpose of consciousness was to produce argumentation as such, rather than to function as a device exclusively devoted to the search for the truth. But they had rejected the view that reasoning had a merely rhetorical function, a point Huang and Bargh (2014) appear to have lost sight

---

30. I note that claims for the importance of the situation in producing a pervasive automaticity in everyday life have been taken up by many philosophers committed to exploring the implications of empirical findings in psychology for moral philosophy and who have proposed alternatives to reason explanations of human action. The topic has produced a contentious debate that lies outside the compass of this book, but for a sense of the arguments and scope of the literature, see Harman 1999; Sabini and Silver 2005; Spurrett, Ross, and Stephens 2007; Doris 2002; and Enfield and Kockelman 2017. In line with such developments, philosophers Washington and Kelly replied to Huang and Bargh (2014) by accepting the validity of the latters' arguments about the role of selfish goals in human behavior (Washington and Kelly 2014; see also Washington and Kelly 2016). Citing the work of Dennett (2003) and Clark (2008) on the social, embodied, and dispersed nature of cognition, Washington and Kelly suggested that skepticism about human agency and responsibility, based on the threat posed by the disintegration of the mind into numerous "selfish" cognitive subsystems systems operating independently of each other and of consciousness, could be countered by appealing to notions of distributed agency (Shapiro 2007) or of "pre-intentional" self-governing systems (Ismael 2007; 2011). For a superb critical account of the invention of the legal concept of corporate personhood and the problems of authorial intention and moral accountability associated with the notion of distributed agency, see Siraganian 2019; 2020.

of. As Mercier and Sperber had replied to commentators who had misconstrued their views on this point:

> The misunderstanding we are most eager to correct consists in attributing to us the view that reasoning has only rhetorical rather than both rhetorical *and* epistemic goals. We didn't argue that reasoning is designed only to find arguments in order to persuade others ... We don't hold that epistemic goals should be poorly served by reasoning or that mere rhetoric is all it takes to influence people. Nor does it follow from our account that people should hardly ever change their mind ... On the contrary, reason evolved in part to make people change their mind by giving *good* reasons to do so. (Mercier and Sperber 2011, 95; their emphasis)

As for Tetlock, here too Huang and Bargh (2014) appear to have overreached. As an alternative to the then-dominant functionalist assumptions that depicted people either as intuitive scientists animated by epistemic goals or as intuitive economists motivated by utilitarian aims, Tetlock (2002) had proposed three different functionalist frameworks for inquiry into how people make decisions. One of these frameworks treated individuals as "pragmatic politicians" who seek to be accountable to key constituencies in their lives, motivating them to look for the approval and respect of those important to them. But Tetlock did not regard seeking approval as people's only motive and, moreover, he stated that accountability required that individuals needed to be cognitively equipped with "good reasons for their opinions." It therefore seems unlikely that he would have endorsed Huang and Bargh's use of his ideas to support the claim that people seek to maintain good relations with others at all costs, or that they merely offer rationalizations for their views. As Tetlock had remarked, although his model assigned a central role to the approval motive "it does not elevate that motive to sovereign regulator of all conduct" (Tetlock 2002, 455). He had also rejected the views of those who endorsed functionalist theories of evolutionary or dual-process models that treated decision-making as the product of mindless automaticity. More generally, Tetlock had argued on empirical and logical-philosophical grounds — of the kind, as he had noted, that philosopher John Searle had raised in his famous Chinese Room thought experiment in objecting to the reduction of intentional states to the workings of a computer program — against the full-scale reductionism associated with evolutionary psychology that Huang and Bargh were advocating (Tetlock 2002, 465–67).

But it was not in Bargh's nature to dodge radical positions. Several commentators rejected the analogy between selfish genes and selfish goals and raised other criticisms of Huang and Bargh's (2014) overall argument. But Bargh stuck to his guns. Indeed, in another paper the same year, Roy Baumeister, a former critic of Bargh's claim that consciousness played no causal role in behavior (for example, Baumeister and Sommer 1997), joined forces with Bargh to argue that the sole function of consciousness was to supplement behaviors that were normally carried out by unconscious, automatic processes. As they argued:

> Our preferred metaphor would be that consciousness is akin to a fancy navigational system. Unconscious processes mostly drive the car, but occasionally they do not know how to get where they want to go, so they consult the navigational system, which can perform calculations that the driver cannot ... The driver is thus better off, and more likely to reach the destination, because of having used the navigational system, although the navigational system does not directly move or steer the car. Its influence is purely advisory—but quite adaptive and valuable.
>
> In that view, consciousness is not needed for perceiving and understanding the immediate environment, nor is it responsible for the direct execution of action. But (among other things) consciousness can mentally simulate various possible courses of action and their likely, anticipated consequences. The unconscious can use these simulations in deciding what to do and in carrying out these plans for action. The result may well be superior outcomes that are more adaptive and successful than what would have happened had the person simply responded unconsciously to the situation, without consciously imagining various courses of action. (Baumeister and Bargh 2014, 37–38)

Baumeister and Bargh went on to argue that the chief role of consciousness was to provide support for unconscious processes by virtue of its ability to communicate between, and integrate, the various systems of the mind-brain. According to them, the communicative function of consciousness included crucially the capacity for speech or language, of which the most important feature was the ability of humans to generate simulated and imagined narrative scenarios of various kinds as alternatives to present reality. Unconscious processes, they argued, had evolved to guide behavior in adaptive ways in the moment, so that conscious processes could be freed to "time-travel" into the past or future, "comparing present events or past occurrences through memory processes, and making plans for future circumstances . . . Conscious thoughts are therefore very useful in coordinating past, present, and future, such as when contemplation of future goals influences present selection of actions" (Baumeister and Bargh 2014, 43)—although how exactly consciousness exerted its influence on unconscious processes remained something of a mystery.

Baumeister and Bargh included reasoning among the advantages that the evolution of consciousness had conferred on humans over other animals. However, for them the importance of reasoning was not its ability to discover and communicate the truth but rather its ability to make arguments regardless of the truth. Appealing to Mercier and Sperber's (2011) suggestion that flaws in human reasoning were only defects if one assumed that the purpose of reasoning was a "solipsistic," dispassionate search for the truth, Baumeister and Bargh proposed that reasoning evolved primarily for the sake of arguing, in which case flaws in reasoning appeared not as a weakness but as "helpful to the cause of survival" (Baumeister and Bargh 2014, 45). With reference also to Tetlock's (2002) views, Baumeister and Bargh suggested that people functioned less like intuitive scientists than "intuitive lawyers who want to argue for their position" (Baumeister and Bargh 2014, 46). From this perspective, so-called confirmation bias, according to which one paid more attention to evidence supporting one's ideas than to contradictory evidence, was not a failing but a sign that biased reasoning served an adaptive function. The authors even appeared to take Mercier and Sperber's (2011) suggestion that, among other functions, reasoning served the purpose of detecting the shortcomings of other people's arguments, as evidence that reasoning was not motivated by the search for truth so much as the urge to best one's adversaries, regardless of the truth.

Baumeister and Bargh concluded their line of argument in a statement that deserves to be quoted at length:

> There would seem to be clear adaptive advantages in being able to argue in one's own defense within one's social group, as argued in Tetlock's (2002) model of evolved social mindsets. Take as a starting point Gazzaniga's (1985) prescient idea based on hypnosis, as well as early neuroscientific research, that impulses to action arise unconsciously and are then interpreted consciously to form a coherent narrative account of what one is doing and why. He noted that people's behavior under posthypnotic suggestion, in which they found themselves down on all fours because

of the hypnotist's command, or getting up from the chair and leaving the room, found immediate rational explanations and justifications ("I lost an earring down here"; "I'm thirsty and want to get some water").[31] One can imagine how helpful to maintaining one's good graces with one's group, back in the day when ostracism was a certain death sentence, it would be to have readily to hand a positive spin for whatever one was doing or had just done. Without this ready explanation and ability to communicate it effectively, one would be seen as personally responsible and as having intended all the accidental mishaps (spilling the jar of water on the long walk back from the well, falling asleep and letting the sheep wander away, picking some poisonous berries on a foraging run) that can occur to any of us given the vagaries and uncertainties of life. Indeed, given the strong evidence of the correspondence bias or fundamental attribution error, each of us would be likely seen as intending each of these bad outcomes, and situational or circumstantial causes would tend to be dismissed by the group. Thus, we can see a clear case for the adaptive, survival value of being able to . . . argue effectively for a positive, pro-group version of whatever one has just done. (Baumeister and Bargh 2014, 46)

What this passage appears to claim is that, if we weren't able to rationalize our actions, we would find ourselves accused of fully intending, and hence of being responsible for, all the behaviors or "accidental mishaps" we perform but of which we are not the agent, because those actions have been automatically triggered by the conditions of our situation. We humans are not personally selfish, our goal constructs are: they egoistically pursue their ends without regard to our "own" intentions and desires (in fact, we don't have a self, understood as a central source of agency). Under the circumstances, the best we can hope to do is, like hypnotized subjects, to confabulate reasons for our actions after the fact in order to make us appear rational, thereby legitimizing ourselves in the eyes of our social group.

Baumeister and Bargh were hardly alone in treating the function of consciousness in this way. To take one example, the same well-known psy-

---

31. I have been unable to locate a reference to the behavior of posthypnotic subjects in Gazzaniga (1985). In an earlier reference to the same Gazzaniga text, Bargh and Barndollar (1996, 463) attributed the case of the rationalizations of posthypnotic subjects not to Gazzaniga but to Hilgard (1986 [1977]) and Searle (1992).

chologist, Timothy Wilson, who co-authored with Nisbett the famous paper "Telling More Than We Can Know" (1977), published a book in 2002 on the adaptive unconscious in which he likewise argued that confabulation was intrinsic to consciousness. Citing the tendency of individuals to invent excuses for their strange posthypnotic behaviors and the tendency to rationalization that Gazzaniga had observed in his split-brain patients, Wilson had followed Gazzaniga's lead in suggesting that "our conscious selves often do not know the causes of our responses and thus have to confabulate reasons" (Wilson 2002, 99). Indeed, according to Wilson, people's explanations of their own actions were "no more accurate than the casual reports of strangers" (Wilson 2002, 113)—which is to say not very accurate at all.[32]

What are we to make of such claims? In an obvious sense Baumeister, Bargh, and Wilson offered a dire picture of consciousness and social life, one in which the function of human reason is limited to the invention of excuses for behaviors over which people have no control, and to do so in ways designed to conform to the requirements of the relevant social group. Baumeister and Bargh's evolutionary model of consciousness thus made adaptation and conformity to the norms of society the function of all human consciousness and communication. One feels like protesting: If the function of consciousness is to produce rationalizations, why should readers ever believe the claims these authors (consciously?) make about the nature of consciousness itself? Isn't it naïve of them not to realize that their radical skepticism about the possibility of ever determining the truth about anything discredits their own ideas?

But we should not be surprised by their picture of the function of consciousness, because it expressed the logic of the cognitive sciences to which the authors were committed. Ever since Nisbett and Wilson (1977) had proposed that people are not good at detecting the causes of their own behavior or that of others, the assault on intentionality and meaning had been a basic feature of cognitive psychology. To cite Bargh's remark

---

32. The claim that consciousness fabricates reasons after the fact has a long pedigree. Several decades earlier, in his study of "Alien Hand" syndrome, Nielsen (1963) argued the same point (cf. Wegner and Wheatley 1999). We find the same idea in Hayles's recent (2014) argument that the "cost" of consciousness is that of constant confabulation. Although Freud also emphasized the tendency of human mind to unconscious fantasy, he believed that the tendency could be managed and controlled by insights gained through the psychoanalytic process, whereas Hayles and like-minded theorists appear to believe that the confabulations of consciousness are constitutive and incurable.

made more than twenty years earlier and with which I began this book: "In the attempt to address the ways in which the mind worked in conjunction with the environment, cognitive science did not need to invoke concepts such as consciousness, intention, or free will" (Bargh and Ferguson 2000, 928).

Conclusion: The Two Camps

What conclusions can one draw from the developments I have charted in this book? Since 2012, debates over the value of replication and the status of psychology as a science, and more specifically over the validity of priming results, have been intense and ongoing, and it would be rash to offer firm predictions about their outcome. But the broad contours of those debates can be discerned. At the most general level, the situation today is as it has been in the past, one in which there is a fundamental divide between those who accept the idea that psychology is and ought to be studied by the methods of the natural sciences, versus those who reject what they regard as the substantive or methodological reductionism implied or entailed by that approach. The sticking point for the latter group of critics concerns meaningful, intentional human action, the nature of which they believe requires several reorientations in the field. That divide has surfaced with great regularity over the years, with no resolution in sight. It will be remembered that, in a conference of 1988 devoted precisely to the problem of the "two psychologies," discussed at the close of chapter 2, the two sides—as represented by Zajonc and Stroebe among others on one side and Gergen and Harré on the other—could not find a meeting of minds.[1]

---

1. I note in this regard that accepting the fundamental importance of intentionality in human life does not mean that all experimentation is ruled out, as the important studies of Bavelas and Fridlund clearly attest. But it does mean that the answer to the question of how people and nonhuman animals behave is to be found in studying their interactions in their more-or-less natural social settings, without recourse to explanations based on the existence of hypothetical mental representations or causal entities and processes. In short, it means staying on a descriptive level and eschewing the search for internal, putative cognitive-neural mechanisms. See Leys 2017, 365–66.

But Gergen and Harré represented the minority position in that earlier debate. In the modern period, the majority view has always been that psychology is and ought to emulate the established natural sciences. The disagreements among most psychologists today are therefore more narrowly focused on determining the best methods for achieving that goal. On this topic, as Schimmack (2021) has pointed out, researchers are divided into two camps: one camp, represented mostly by younger scientists, believes that direct replication, involving the preregistration of experiments, larger sample sizes, better experimental controls, improved statistical methods, and so on, are crucial. The other camp, represented mostly by older, more established researchers, several of whose classic experiments have failed to replicate, defends the status quo and denies that psychology is in trouble.[2] There is little love lost between these two groups, as the continuing clashes between them demonstrate.

The reformers are optimistic about the future: they point to the various changes that, through their initiatives, psychology has undertaken to improve its practices, changes that they view as distinct progress. The other camp, represented by psychologists such as Bargh, Stroebe, Strack, Schwarz, Gilbert, and others, argues against the value of direct replication in favor of the usefulness of conceptual replication; denies that questionable research practices have undermined the validity of published results; and, as reformer Schimmack has commented, "continue to rely on published studies as credible empirical evidence" (Schimmack 2021). For the reformers, self-correction through exact, replicable experiments is the key feature that distinguishes science from the humanities and other fields. For them, the refusal of the other camp to accept this need for self-correction through direct replication stamps social psychology as a "para-science" (Schimmack 2021).

An exchange in 2017 epitomizes the stand-off between the two sides. In response to the announcement that Roy Baumeister's well-known "ego-depletion effect" had failed to replicate, Seppo Iso-Ahola used the

---

2. See Zwaan et al.'s (2018) arguments in favor of making direct replication mainstream, with commentaries by leading researchers in the field, among whom Strack and Stroebe were almost alone in questioning the value of direct replication and in criticizing as "negligible" the theoretical knowledge gained by these means. Strack and Stroebe even argued that the onus should be on replicators, not the original researchers, to identify the reasons why effects did not replicate (Strack and Stroebe 2018). See also Nosek et al.'s (2022) valuable overview of the replication literature and findings since 2010.

argument that psychological phenomena vary across time, persons, and situations to suggest that the importance of direct replication had been overstated.[3] It followed for him that it was never possible to declare that certain psychological phenomena, such as the ego-depletion effect, were nonexistent or not real. "Psychological phenomena exist to a varying degree," Iso-Ahola wrote,

> with variation occurring between and within them. Some of them are stronger and more consistent in their appearance and influence across time, situations and groups than others. It would be a mistake, however, to conclude that the former are more important than the latter, because they all are part of the psychological landscape helping explain the human condition and behavior . . . Thus, some phenomena may appear less consistently across situations and yet be equally important as substantive phenomena. In short, inter-phenomenon differences have little relevance regarding the non-existence of a given phenomenon. (Iso-Ahola 2017, 2)

Iso-Ahola extended his argument to priming:

> On one hand, behavioral reactions can easily be produced by subtle nonconscious cues at one time in one specific situation, such as speaking softly after being exposed to a library picture (for a review of research, see Custers and Aarts, 2010; Baumeister et al., 2011 [*see Baumeister, Masicampo, and Vohs 2011*]; Kahneman, 2011; Bargh, 2014a [*see Bargh 2014a*]). On the other, unless the individual conditions (e.g., a way of thinking) and social contexts are identical in other circumstances, the same unconscious social influences may not materialize at all (Bargh, 2014a) [*see Bargh 2014a*]. This would not mean that priming effects are weak but instead, that they are sensitive to subtle changes in the social environment. In fact, a long line of experimental research has shown that various forms of priming influence not only participants' reactions in laboratory tasks but people's behaviors in everyday life (Bargh, 2014b

---

3. The ego-depletion effect refers to the idea that an exertion of self-control impairs or depletes subsequent self-control behaviors. Several recent studies have cast doubt on the replicability of the effect. In a large literature, see Baumeister et al. 1998; Baumeister 2002; Baumeister and Vohs 2007, 2016; Hagger et al. (2016); Schimmack 2016; Vohs et al. 2021.

[*see Bargh 2014b*]; Molden, 2014 [*see Molden 2014c*]). However, the subtle nature and changing influences of psychological phenomena create methodological difficulties for research and also increase the likelihood of unjustified conclusion about phenomena's non- existence. (Iso-Ahola 2017, 3).[4]

Iso-Ahola also supported his opinion that no psychological phenomenon could ever be declared nonexistent by appealing to Meehl's famous "crud factor" principle, according to which "everything is correlated with everything, more or less" (Meehl 1990b, 123). "This, of course, means that the null hypothesis is never true," Iso-Ahola argued:

> That "everything influences everything" also means that psychological phenomena do not represent stand-alone effects but rather, are related to other effects. This in turn means that a manipulation of the focal independent variable affects, either by enhancing or reducing, other causal independent variables even in randomized experiments ... Such uncontrolled causal factors can produce negative results. Taken together, the nature of psychological phenomena as subtle and correlated effects on one hand and their confounded manipulation in laboratories on the other, make it impossible to ever declare them non-existent. (Iso-Ahola 2017, 3)

On the face it, this argument was a rather blatant misuse of Meehl's point, which was the exact opposite of Iso-Ahola's. According to Meehl, the "crud factor" meant that, in the absence of better statistical and other

---

4. It strikes me as naïve of Iso-Ahola to defend the validity of priming experiments on the grounds that they have been published in prestigious journals, as if the refereeing by prominent researchers guaranteed the absence of publication bias (2017, 3). He also faulted Doyen et al. (2012) for substituting a laser beam for a handheld stopwatch in their attempt to replicate Bargh, Chen, and Burrows's elderly priming study—perhaps implying that Doyen et al.'s concerns about subjective bias in measuring the participants' walking speeds was unwarranted. He even said that Doyen et al.'s description of the primed participants' slow walking in Bargh, Chen, and Burrows's original experiment as a "methodological artifact" was undeserved. "While more accurate measures are desirable," Iso-Ahola wrote, "they cannot eliminate other important reasons for failures to replicate, such as changes in the human mind and instructions given to participants from one study to another" (Iso-Ahola 2017, 6). (See also Iso-Ahola 2020, in which he again endorsed Bargh's priming findings but conceded that some laboratory experiments had failed to replicate them.) In a subsequent paper Iso-Ahola thanked Bargh among others for his helpful comments on earlier drafts (Iso-Ahola 2020, 13).

methods, most of the correlations observed in psychology, especially social psychology, were uninterpretable or simply meaningless (Meehl 1990a; 1990b; see also Ferguson and Heene 2021, 620). As such, Meehl viewed the crud factor as one of several obstacles to sound scientific practice, obstacles that called for various statistical and methodological remedies, of which making more precise falsifiable predictions was one.

There has recently been a resurgence of interest in Meehl's notion of the crud factor in psychological research, owing to the ways in which the increasing availability of large data sets has raised questions about how to interpret small effect sizes. In their useful review of this development, Amy Orben and Daniël Lakens have observed that the crud factor has become a "convenient tool for psychologists to use to disregard unwanted results, even though the presence of the crud factor should be a large inconvenience for the discipline" (Orben and Lakens 2020, 238). The authors argue that "prediction of any nonzero effect has almost no risk of being falsified if the crud factor plays a role, so researchers need to carefully consider, and preferably to specify in advance, what would falsify their prediction" (Orben and Lakens 2020, 245). For these and other researchers in the reformer camp, the task is not to treat every observed correlation as potentially real, as Iso-Ahola recommends, but rather to clarify the definition of the crud factor, or to counter the overreliance on tiny effect sizes by introducing estimates below which effect sizes should not be interpreted as supporting a hypothesis (Orben and Lakens 2020; Ferguson and Heene 2021).

Orben and Lakens argue that the future of psychology lies in reforming its practices so that it better conforms to the experimental standards in the more established sciences. In a somewhat sympathetic yet critical comment on Iso-Ahola's argument, Trafimow has adopted a similar view:

> In the end, we must decide whether or not we wish psychology to be a science. If so, it follows that empirical victories and defeats must be reproducible, though much fun can be had arguing about precisely what we mean by "replicate." In contrast, to the extent that we fail to insist on reproducible findings, it becomes increasingly difficult to distinguish psychology from religion, philosophy, and so on. Psychology is not physics, and there are problems that are unique to the social sciences, but that is no justification for abandoning the requirement that findings be replicable, nor failing to keep an open mind that some proposed entities might not exist even if published in top journals, any more than the

luminiferous ether or phlogiston exist (to the best of our current knowledge, of course) . . . [T]here is much that is wrong with how psychologists conduct their research and even think about their research, that can be improved dramatically. Making improvements is to be preferred over questioning whether we can do it. (Trafimow 2017)

Trafimow's statement can stand as an epitome of the reformers' belief that psychology's status as a science stands or falls on its commitment to replication as the sine qua non of good practice. One is reminded here of Kuhn's remark that "no theory that was not *in principle* testable could function or cease to function adequately when applied to scientific puzzle solving" (Kuhn 1970b, 248). Through their emphasis on direct (and conceptual) replication as a nonnegotiable feature of the scientific enterprise, the reformers appear to have demonstrated beyond a reasonable doubt that (a) past laboratory practices of psychologists have frequently been so sloppy as to produce numerous false-positive results, especially in priming research, and (b) that when methods have been improved, many findings, especially priming results, have been shown to be false. As a result, the reformers have dealt a serious blow to priming as a phenomenon.[5]

In 2012, Kahneman had warned priming researchers that a train wreck was coming, but as he noted ten years later, the social psychologists had simply "circled the wagons and developed a strong antipathy for the replicators." He therefore concluded that priming research was a failed enterprise, observing:

There were essentially no takers for my suggestion that priming researchers should proactively replicate each other's work. This eventually convinced me that they did not have real confidence. They believed

---

5. See also Schimmack, Heene, and Kesavan (2017) for a discussion of the low replicability index (the R-Index) of the priming experiments by Bargh and others cited by Kahneman in his 2011 book *Thinking, Fast and Slow*. In 2022, Schimmack included behavioral priming in a list of "false psychology" topics that lacked empirical evidence (2022a). As noted in a "replicability audit" of Bargh's published results, by 2019 confidence in social priming had substantially decreased, as reflected in Bargh's declining citation counts (Schimmack 2019). However, Schafmeister (2021) has reported that neither positive nor negative replication results have significantly influenced citation patterns in leading psychology journals, suggesting that replications do not constitute a hoped-for self-correcting mechanism in science.

their findings were true, but they were not quite sure they could replicate them, and they didn't want to take the risk . . . *[B]ehavioral priming research is effectively dead.* (Kahneman 2022; my emphasis)

If, as Kahneman says, priming research is dead, then my hope is that this book will serve as a useful postmortem.

Appendix:
Bargh on Unconscious Intentionality

In a paper of 2018, David Melnikoff and Bargh challenged the dual-process typology that had long dominated the cognitive sciences. As they remarked, many researchers claimed that there existed two types of psychological processing. In their description:

> One (Type 1) is triggered by the stimulus so it does not require the intention that it occur; it cannot be controlled (stopped or altered) once it has started; it is efficient, using minimal working capacity; and it requires little conscious awareness. The other type (Type 2) requires an intention that it occurs and thus cannot be triggered directly by the stimulus; its operation can be controlled (stopped and/or altered) after starting; it is relatively inefficient, occupying limited processing resources and thus interfering with other ongoing mental tasks; and it occurs consciously, so one is phenomenally aware of the process and can verbally report on it. (Melnikoff and Bargh 2018a, 281)

As Melnikoff and Bargh remarked, dual-process theories had been enormously popular, shaping empirical and theoretical work in a wide range of subjects and fields even as they had also generated considerable criticism. In the introduction I noted that Kahneman had framed his book *Thinking, Fast and Slow* (2011) in terms of "System 1" and "System 2," of which System 1 was responsible for efficient, automatic processes of the kind studied in Bargh's priming experiments, while System 2 was responsible for conscious, deliberate (or intentional) processes(Kahneman 2011).

Although in the past Bargh had sometimes been credited with rejecting the idea that automatic and controlled (or intentional) processes were mutually exclusive processes (for example, Moors and De Houwer 2006, 299), I think it is fair to say that prior to 2018 he had not raised substantial concerns about the coherence of dual-process theories. Or perhaps it is more accurate to say that he had sometimes raised tentative questions about the validity of such theories (for example, Hassin, Bargh, and Zimerman 2009, 33), but at other times had appeared to presuppose their soundness (for example, Huang and Bargh 2014, 123).[1] More generally, we have seen that, again and again throughout his career, Bargh had characterized automatic behaviors as unconscious and unintentional and had contrasted them with conscious-intentional processes.

It is all the more striking, then, that in 2018 Melnikoff and Bargh attacked dual-process theories on the grounds that the features ostensibly associated with two different information-processing systems did not line up together in the way such a dual typology required. As they declared:

> In fact, the alignment requirement has never been tested. The reader will not find a single statistic pertaining to the degree of correspondence between processing features. No attempt has been made to estimate the probability of a process being intentional given that it is conscious versus unconscious, or the probability of a process being controllable given that it is efficient versus inefficient, and so forth. For all we know, Type 1 features (e.g., unconsciousness) are no likelier to occur with other Type 1 features (e.g., unintentional) than they are to occur with Type 2 features (e.g., intentional). Likewise, it could be the case that Type 2 features (e.g., consciousness) are no likelier to occur with other Type 2 features (e.g., intentional) than they are to occur with Type 1 features (e.g., unintentional). The basic tenet of the Type 1/Type 2 distinction—that the attributes within each category are aligned—simply has not been demonstrated. (Melnikoff and Bargh 2018a, 282)[2]

1. As I discussed at the end of chapter 4, in 2009 Bargh and colleagues had made a note of what they called the "quasi-contradiction" of dual-process theories that occurred if, as seemed to be the case, automatic processes of the kind usually associated with System 1 in dual-process theories were capable of flexibility, a feature usually associated with System 2. At the time, they could not resolve this contradiction (Hassin, Bargh, and Zimerman 2009, 33).

2. In fact, as Melnikoff and Bargh subsequently reported, Kahneman acknowledged that his System 1 and System 2 model of human decision-making was just a convenient fiction (Melnikoff, Bargh, and Wood 2021, 4). See also the subsequent exchange between Pennycook et al. (2018) and Melnikoff and Bargh (2018b).

The aim of Melnikoff and Bargh's article was to demonstrate the truth of their claims by offering examples in which the properties ostensibly associated exclusively with only one or the other of the two systems were in fact combined together in ways denied by such dual-process theories. Their first example concerned the misalignment between intentionality and consciousness. They observed:

> We start with phenomena that are intentional yet able to operate without conscious monitoring. Such misalignments are common because consciousness and intentionality are affected differently as information processing becomes more routinized [citing, among other references, Bargh and Morsella 2008] . . . Specifically, routinization can make processing less reliant on conscious attention without affecting whether it requires an intention to be executed. A skilled typist, for example, does not need to consciously monitor their typing, but will never start plucking away at their keys without intending to type something in the first place . . . *Driving, typing, playing piano, and many other skills can also be practiced to the point that they can operate unconsciously while remaining completely intentional* activities. (Melnikoff and Bargh 2018a, 285; my emphasis)

In light of Bargh's reiterated claims concerning the non-intentionality of primed behaviors and other forms of automaticity, such a statement amounted to a rather dramatic revision of his previously stated position. Several aspects of Melnikoff and Bargh's statements are striking in this regard. The authors acknowledged that they were by no means the first to challenge dual-systems theories, citing many of the most prominent critiques in the literature. But they offered a subtle misrepresentation of Bargh's own previous views in order to make it seem that his position had always been congruent with the opinions of researchers who had questioned the validity of such dual-process typologies.

It is true that, as I have already noted, at the start of his career Bargh had argued against treating the features usually associated with automaticity as if they formed a unity or were correlated together. He had observed that, as had been claimed by Logan and Cowan (1984), most processes that were usually considered to be automatic, such as typing, driving, and walking, were actually highly controlled in that they were intentional and stoppable (Bargh 1989, 6; Bargh 1994). But, as I have demonstrated in this book, over time Bargh came to treat automatic actions as unconscious and unintentional—indeed unintentional *because* they were unconscious.

To take one example, in the passage just quoted above, Melnikoff and Bargh (2018a) cited a paper by Bargh and Morsella (2008) as supporting their claim that routinized skills may operate unconsciously while remaining intentional. But in that 2008 article, Bargh and Morsella had asserted the opposite view. They had written:

> For most of human history, only the concepts of conscious thought and intentional behavior existed. In the 1800s, two very different developments—hypnotism and evolutionary theory—both pointed to the possibility of *unconscious, unintended* causes of human behavior. But nearly two centuries later, contemporary psychological science remains wedded to a conscious-centric model of the higher mental processes . . .
>
> We propose an alternative perspective, in which *unconscious processes are defined in terms of their unintentional nature* and the inherent lack of awareness is of the influence and effect of the triggering stimuli and not of the triggering stimuli (because nearly all naturally occurring stimuli are supraliminal). By this definition of the unconscious, which is the original and historic one, contemporary social cognition research on priming and automaticity effects have shown the existence of sophisticated, flexible, and adaptive unconscious behavior guidance systems. (Bargh and Morsella 2008, 78; my emphasis)

This statement is one among many that could be adduced—and many have been cited in this book—as evidence that Bargh had long held the view that automatic actions, such as the behavior of primed participants or the performance of learned skills, were unintentional.

In addition to obfuscating where exactly Bargh had previously stood on these issues, Melnikoff and Bargh (2018a) made some problematic statements about the nature of intentionality itself. They stated:

> There are at least two flavors of intentionality . . . One, which we simply call intentional, describes any process that is activated by a goal to perform that particular process. Examples include hugging, singing, eating, and so forth. Alternatively, a process can be goal dependent. Such processes are activated directly by external stimuli (so they are not purely intentional) but only in the presence of a relevant processing goal (so they are not purely unintentional). For instance, when a driver

slams their foot on the break [*sic, brake*], they do something that was initiated directly by an external stimulus, like a stop sign or brake lights. However, this process is dependent on having a goal to drive safely in the first place. If that same person were exposed to the same stimulus while walking down the street or attempting to cause a massive car wreck, the seemingly unintentional process would not occur. This is unlike purely unintentional processes such as evaluation, stereotyping, and word reading, which do not require a processing goal, as well as purely intentional processes such as hugging, singing, and eating, which cannot be activated directly by external stimuli. This in-between form of intentionality is simply a square peg that does not fit into the round hole of the "two types" framework. (Melnikoff and Bargh 2018a, 289)

Not only does Bargh here quietly revise the account he had previously given of sudden braking at a stop sign (or red light) as an automatic, unintentional action (see chapter 4), the distinctions Melnikoff and Bargh propose in this statement do not make sense. Intentional actions cannot be separated into "pure" versus "impure" types. All intentional actions are saturated with automatisms; they all involve an in-mixing of automatic and intentional processes. To take one example, think of the automatisms involved in eating. Melnikoff and Bargh categorize eating as a strictly intentional action on the grounds that it "cannot be activated directly by external stimuli" (Melnikoff and Bargh 2018a, 289). What they seem to mean by this claim is that we don't automatically eat some edible thing the moment we see it. And of course, they are correct: we tend to decide what to eat. But it is also the case that eating entails numerous automatic processes, such as swallowing, which we don't consciously decide to perform. The same is true of hugging and singing, which depend on many automatic actions and processes. Driving is no different in this regard.

Melnikoff and Bargh's use of the term "purely" for the kinds of intentionality involved in eating, hugging, and singing is a marker of their idea that certain intentional actions are entirely independent of any forms of automaticity. But to hold this idea is to metaphysicalize intentionality. What defines eating, hugging, singing—and driving—as intentional actions is that they are all forms of behavior that are responsive to the question *why*, which is to say that they are all actions we perform for a reason. The mistake Melnikoff and Bargh make is to think that one can treat the intentionality of driving as different from the other kinds of action simply because we learn to brake at a stop sign or red light according to the rules and conventions of driving. But what the example of driving really shows is something different, namely, that our habitual actions may well be performed below the threshold of awareness and may contain "automatic" (or routinized) aspects, but nonetheless they remain intentional: they don't become unintentional merely because with practice they become automatic and don't require our conscious attention.

It would be interesting to know what led Bargh at this late point in his career to focus on the question of unconscious intentionality. In one subtle sign of a change of viewpoint, in their joint paper on the function of consciousness four years earlier, already discussed in chapter 8, Baumeister and Bargh (2014) had equated unconscious goal pursuits with intentionality in ways that appeared to contradict Bargh's prior statements on the topic. They had observed that

> *conscious* and *unconscious processes* have been distinguished historically in terms of several different features (e.g., Bargh 1994) — awareness, intentionality, efficiency, and controllability, with the former two at the heart of the terms in common usage. However, because of mounting evidence that motivations and goal pursuits (roughly speaking, intentionality) operate unconsciously in much the same way as they operate consciously ... the intentionality (purposive, goal-oriented) quality no longer differentiates conscious and unconscious processes. Thus, it is the awareness and reportability of a mental process that most clearly distinguish between what is considered a conscious versus an unconscious mental process or experience. (Baumeister and Bargh 2014, 35–36; their emphases).

But Baumeister and Bargh had made these remarks only in passing and did not provide any further elaboration, although in line with Nisbett and Wilson (1977) and other researchers, they emphasized that the case for the unconscious causation of behavior was "overwhelming." This paper by Bargh and Baumeister was the same one in which, as I discussed in chapter 8, they went on to suggest that consciousness functioned merely to rationalize behaviors over which the individual had no genuine control.[3]

---

3. The only other reference by Bargh to the idea that mental processes could be both unconscious and intentional that I have been able to find prior to 2018 occurred in a 1996 publication in which he observed: "The unconscious can ... in principle, be a source of intentions and goals independently from conscious intents and purposes ... To our minds,

There are also hints that the post-2012 debate over the validity of behavioral priming results may have had something to do with stimulating renewed attention to issues of intentionality. For example, also in 2014 Ferguson, Bargh's former student then at Cornell University, and Thomas Mann co-authored a paper in a special issue of a journal devoted to the debate over the replicability of priming results (Ferguson and Mann 2014). The authors defended Bargh against what they characterized as "poorly specified critiques of 'social' priming" that threatened to "ostracize robust findings" and stunt "exciting new investigations into when and how unintentional influences occur" (Ferguson and Mann 2014, 33). In an attempt to clarify the meaning of the terms *behavioral* or *goal* priming, Ferguson and her co-author focused on the role of intentionality. They observed that

> in social psychology, priming usually refers to the *unintentional* influence of some prime on some target, even if the person can explicitly remember the prime itself. . . . Note that an assumption of a lack of intention refers to a characteristic of the process of how the prime influences the target, and such an assumption is not strictly needed for the basic phenomenon of a prime affecting the processing of the target. And yet, almost all of the priming work in social psychology assumes, and tests, that the influence of the prime is unintentional (e.g., see Bargh and Ferguson, 2000). This may be due to the long history of interest in social psychology in whether people act in "knowing" versus unknowing ways (e.g., Bargh and Chartrand 1999; Nisbett and Wilson, 1977; Wilson, 2002), and thus there has been great emphasis on whether people *realize* that a prime affected their judgment, attitude or behavior. However, there is great variability in social psychological research in the ways in which intentionality is conceptualized and measured . . . and it remains unclear what aspects of intentionality are implicated in the priming research under scrutiny. (Ferguson and Mann 2014, 35; their emphasis)

This statement is interesting. Ferguson and Mann correctly state that the fundamental assumption in behavioral priming had been that the effects of primes were unintentional, and they attribute that assumption not only to Bargh and Chartrand (1999), but also to Wilson (2002), and Nis-

---

the unconscious intention is just as 'intentional' as . . . the momentary conscious goal" (Bargh and Barndollar 1996, 464–465). But the statement hangs, and the authors' overall account of unconscious intentionality in this paper was marred by several confusions.

bett and Wilson's famous (or infamous) paper on attribution (Nisbett and Wilson 1977).[4] But in the same passage quoted above, the authors also observe that the assumption of the lack of intentionality in priming was "not strictly needed." Their remark simply hangs. The authors merely add that "the ambiguity surrounding the definitional terms is a serious issue that almost completely prohibits any clear discussion of the problems, because it precludes inducing the commonalities among the examples"—and then announce that, all the same, in the remainder of their article, "we put these definitional issues aside" (Ferguson and Mann 2014, 35–36). It therefore appears that for these authors the definitional status of intentionality was too difficult for them to confront, even as they presented it as one of the fundamental issues at stake in the priming field. It is worth noting that Ferguson and Mann did not cite any philosophical works on the status of the concept of intentionality when addressing the topic.

Nor did Bargh handle the issue of intentionality any better, as we have just seen. His reputation as a researcher had largely been based on his claim that automatic behaviors were unintentional actions that were directly triggered by priming stimuli of whose influence subjects were completely unaware. But he now asserted that unconscious processes could be intentional. Did this mean that he still believed that primed behaviors were unintentional actions? Melnikoff and Bargh (2018a) did not say.

The topic of unconscious intentionality also attracted the attention of certain other researchers at this time. For example, in the course of raising some "inconvenient questions" about the usual attribution of efficiency, inevitability, and non-intentionality to automatic actions, in 2018 Trafimow suggested that the attempt to define skilled actions in terms of an opposition between conscious, intentional processes versus unconscious, non-intentional processes could not be sustained. Specifically, he questioned whether it made sense to describe as unintentional those habitual behaviors of the kind labeled "action slips," such as when, in an example he provided, one day he intended to turn right when driving his car but turned left instead, because that was the turn he routinely made when driving to work (Trafimow 2018, 383–85). The implication of Trafimow's remarks on this point was that these action slips were better characterized as on a continuum with the intentional actions from which they had

---

4. In another paper a few years later, Ferguson and Cone linked the claim for the non-intentionality of priming effects to the desire on the part of Bargh and others to challenge the dominant view that behavior was intentionally and consciously chosen (2021, 39).

derived, although he deliberately ignored the issue of consciousness and accordingly did not directly address the status of habits as *unconscious* intentional actions (Trafimow 2018, 379).

In recent publications, philosopher Markus Schlosser has tackled the question of unconscious intentionality directly by noting the conundrum that results when, in dual-system (or dual-process) theories, intentional actions are aligned with consciousness in System 2 processing, whereas automatic actions are aligned with the lack of intention in System 1 processing. The trouble, he argues, is that such an opposition makes it impossible to characterize the automatic actions of the kind studied in priming experiments as intentional in character. "Is the philosophical account of intentional action compatible with the dual-system theory?" he asks. "If we simply identify intentional actions with consciously controlled System 2 outputs, we face the unpalatable conclusion that most of our behavior is not intentional, provided that most of our behavior is automatic and driven by System 1, as claimed in the empirical literature. We face, then, the further question of *how much* of our behavior can qualify as intentional within the dual-system framework" (Schlosser 2019b, 35–36; his emphasis). Or as he also observes: "If one simply claimed that intentional action requires conscious intention, without further qualification, one could not accommodate the apparent intentionality of habitual actions, and one would once again face the undesirable conclusion that most of our actions are not intentional" (2019b, 42).

To avoid such an undesirable conclusion, Schlosser defends the idea of unconscious intentions (Schlosser 2019b, 36–37). On that basis, he argues that most of the automatic behaviors Bargh had described as unintentional in the past — unintentional *because* they are unconscious — are in fact "derivatively" intentional because they originate in intentional actions that have become habitual through practice and because, as such, they remain potentially sensitive to the agents' beliefs about how their goals can be achieved.

Although, for reasons I explained in the introduction, I think aspects of Schlosser's arguments are misguided, this fact doesn't detract from the interest of his suggestions concerning the existence of unconscious intentionality itself, especially since he applies those arguments to the phenomenon of priming. The significant issue is whether cognitive psychologists such as Bargh, whose work he cites (though he does not mention Melnikoff and Bargh 2018a), have been correct in their interpretation of automatic processes as wholly unintentional in nature. Schlosser considers five cases in which behavior is influenced by the activation of social stereotypes in five different ways, with varying degrees of consciousness. His aim is to cover the full range of actions from automatic and unconscious goal pursuits to conscious and deliberate actions. His basic position is that if an action is clearly habitual and has the right history of habit formation, it qualifies as derivatively intentional even if it occurs without the subject's conscious attention. If there is no history of habit formation—of which he thinks acquiring social stereotypes by mere exposure to them in the sociocultural environment is an example—then Schlosser is inclined to think such automatic behaviors are not intentional.[5]

Bargh and Chartrand (1999) had titled one of their papers on the pervasiveness of automaticity in everyday life "The Unbearable Automaticity of Being," which I have borrowed for the title of chapter 4 (Bargh and Chartrand 1999). In using this phrase, they meant that it might be "unbearable" to have to accept the idea that most of daily life was driven by unintentional, automatic, unconscious processes. Yet this is what they claimed the empirical evidence demonstrated. Schlosser, however, ended his article by arguing with reference to Bargh and Chartrand's claims that, on the contrary, "the findings from the empirical research on automaticity are not so 'unbearable' after all, because they do not undermine the assumption that most of our everyday behavior can qualify as intentional" (Schlosser 2019b, 54).

---

5. As I observed in the introduction (note 10), Schlosser accepts a version of the "standard" theory of intentional action associated with the work of Davidson, rather than Anscombe's approach to intentionality. Thus, he believes intentionality can be explained in causal terms. Like many others committed to a causal analysis of intentionality, Schlosser (2019a) thinks that intentional actions are the product of internal mental states having the right representational contents. Accordingly, his approach is compatible with that of cognitive psychology's treatments of cognition, which also explain mentation in causal terms as the product of internal mental representations. But a detailed discussion of Schlosser's arguments lies outside the scope of this book.

References

Aarts, H., and A. Dijksterhuis. 2000a. "Habits as Knowledge Structures: Automaticity in Goal-Directed Behavior." *Journal of Personality and Social Psychology* 78, no. 1: 53–63. https://doi.org/10.1037//0022-3514.78.1.53.

Aarts, H., and A. Dijksterhuis. 2000b. "The Automatic Activation of Goal-Directed Behavior: The Case of Travel Habit." *Journal of Environmental Psychology* 20, no. 1: 75–82. https://doi.org/10.1006/jevp.1999.0156.

Aarts, H., and A. Dijksterhuis. 2002. "Category Activation Effects in Judgment and Behaviour: The Moderating Role of Perceived Comparability." *British Journal of Social Psychology* 41, no. 1: 123–38. https://doi.org/10.1348/014466602165090.

Aarts, H., and A. Dijksterhuis. 2003. "The Silence of the Library: Environment, Situational Norm, and Social Behavior." *Journal of Personality and Social Psychology* 84, no. 1: 18–28. https://doi.org/10.1037/0022-3514.84.1.18.

Abelson, R. P. 1981. "Psychological Status of the Script Concept." *American Psychologist* 36, no. 7: 715–29. https://doi.org/10.1037/0003-066X.36.7.715.

Acker, F. 2008. "New Findings on Unconscious versus Conscious Thought in Decision Making: Additional Empirical Data and Meta-Analysis." *Judgment and Decision Making* 3, no. 4: 292–303. https://doi.org/10.1017/S1930297500000863.

Ackerman, J. M., and J. A. Bargh. 2010. "Two to Tango: Automatic Social Coordination and the Role of Felt Effort." In *Effortless Attention: A New Perspective in the Cognitive Science of Attention and Action*, edited by B. Bruya, 335–71. Cambridge, MA: MIT Press.

Adair, J. G. 1973. *The Human Subject: The Social Psychology of the Psychological Experiment*. Boston, MA: Little, Brown and Company.

Adair, J. G. 1978. "Open Peer Commentary on Rosenthal and Rubin (1978)." *Behavioral and Brain Sciences* 3: 386–87.

Adair, J. G. 1991. "Social Cognition, Artifact and the Passing of the So-Called Crisis in Social Psychology." *Canadian Psychology* 32, no. 3: 445–50. https://doi.org/10.1037/h0079016.

Adair, J. G., and B. Spinner. 1981. "Subjects' Access to Cognitive Processes: Demand Characteristics and Verbal Report." *Journal for the Theory of Social Behaviour* 11, no. 1: 31–52. https://doi.org/10.1111/j.1468-5914.1981.tb00021.x.

Adams, G., S. Estrada-Villalta, D. Sullivan, and H. R. Markus. 2019. "The Psychology of Neoliberalism and the Neoliberalism of Psychology." *Journal of Social Issues* 75, no. 1: 189–216. https://doi.org/10.1111/josi.12305.

Aizerman, M. A. 1963. *Theory of Automatic Control*. New York: Pergamon Press.

Alda, A. December 16, 2009. "Web-Exclusive Video: Social Mimicry and Positive Feelings." *The Human Spark*, 5:00, video. https://www.pbs.org/wnet/humanspark/featured/web-exclusive-video-social-mimicry-and-positive-feelings/326/.

Alexander, D. M., and P. Moors. 2018. "If We Accept That Poor Replication Rates Are Mainstream." *Behavioral and Brain Sciences* 41: 13–14. https://doi.org/10.1017/s0140525x18000572.

Allport, A. 1993. "Attention and Control: Have We Been Asking the Wrong Questions? A Critical Review of Twenty-Five Years." In *Attention and Performance XIV: Synergies in Experimental Psychology, Artificial Intelligence, and Cognitive Neuroscience*, edited by D. E. Meyer and S. Kornblum, 183–218. Cambridge, MA: MIT Press.

Allport, A. 2008. "The Ups and Downs of Cognitive Psychology: Attention and Other 'Executive Functions.'" In *Inside Psychology: A Science Over 50 Years*, edited by P. Rabbitt, 13–26. New York: Oxford University Press.

Anderson, C. J., S. Bahník, M. Barnett-Cowan, F. A. Bosco, J. Chandler, C. R. Chartier, and F. Cheung et al. 2016. "Response to Comment on 'Estimating the Reproducibility of Psychological Science.'" *Science* 351, no. 6277: 1037. https://doi.org/10.1126/science.aad9163.

Anscombe, G. E. M. 2000 (1957). *Intention*. Cambridge, MA: Harvard University Press.

Anscombe, G. E. M. 1979. "Under a Description." *Noûs* 13, no. 2: 219–33.

Antony, L. 2014. "Degraded Conditions: Confounds in the Study of Decision Making." *Behavioral and Brain Sciences* 37, no. 1: 19–20. https://doi.org/10.1017/S0140525X13000629.

Austin, J. L. 1961. *Philosophical Papers*. Oxford: Oxford University Press.

Baayen, R. H., P. Hendrix, and M. Ramscar. 2013. "Sidestepping the Combinatorial Explosion: Towards a Processing Model Based on Discriminative

Learning." *Language and Speech* 56: 329–47. https://doi.org/10.1177/0023830913484896.

Baayen, R. H., and M. Ramscar. 2015. "Abstraction, Storage and Naive Discriminative Learning." In *Handbook of Cognitive Linguistics*, edited by E. Dabrowska and D. Divjak, 99–120. Berlin: De Gruyter Mouton.

Baddeley, A. D. 1986. *Working Memory*. London: Oxford University Press.

Baddeley, A. D., S. D. Sala, and T. W. Robbins. 1996. "Working Memory and Executive Control." *Philosophical Transactions of the Royal Society of London: Series B, Biological Sciences* 351, no. 1346: 1378–88. https://doi.org/10.1093/acprof:oso/9780198524410.003.0002.

Baker, G., ed. 2003. *The Voices of Wittgenstein: The Vienna Circle. Ludwig Wittgenstein and Friedrich Waismann*. London: Routledge.

Bakhurst, D. 2011. *The Formation of Reason*. Oxford: Wiley-Blackwell.

Bakhurst, D. 2016a. "Introduction: Exploring the Formation of Reason." *Journal of Philosophy of Education* 50, no. 1: 76–83.

Bakhurst, D. 2016b. "Response to Rödl, Standish and Derry." *Journal of Philosophy of Education* 50, no. 1: 123–29.

Bakhurst, D., and S. G. Shanker, eds. 2001. *Jerome Bruner: Language, Culture, and Self*. London: Sage.

Bakker, M., A. van Dijk, and J. M. Wicherts. 2012. "The Rules of the Game Called Psychological Science." *Perspectives on Psychological Science* 7, no. 6: 543–54. https://doi.org/10.1177/1745691612459060.

Barber, T. X. 1969. *Hypnosis: A Scientific Approach*. New York: Van Nostrand Reinhold.

Barber, T. X., and M. J. Silver. 1968. "Fact, Fiction, and the Experimenter Bias Effect." *Psychological Bulletin* 70, no. 6: 1–29. https://doi.org/10.1037/h0026724.

Bargh, J. A. 1982. "Attention and Automaticity in the Processing of Self-Relevant Information." *Journal of Personality and Social Psychology* 43, no. 3: 425–36. https://doi.org/10.1037/0022-3514.43.3.425.

Bargh, J. A. 1984. "Automatic and Conscious Processing of Social Information." In *Handbook of Social Cognition*, vol. 3, edited by R. S. Wyer Jr. and T. K. Srull, 1–41. Hillsdale, NJ: Lawrence Erlbaum Associates.

Bargh, J. A. 1989. "Conditional Automaticity: Varieties of Automatic Influence in Social Perception and Cognition." In *Unintended Thought*, edited by J. S. Uleman and J. A. Bargh, 3–51. New York: Guilford Press.

Bargh, J. A. 1990a. "Auto-Motives: Preconscious Determinants of Social Interaction." In *Handbook of Motivation and Cognition*, vol. 2, edited by E. T. Higgins and R. M. Sorrentino, 93–130. New York: Guilford Press.

Bargh, J. A. 1990b. "Goal ≠ Intent: Goal-Directed Thought and Behavior Are Often Unintentional." *Psychological Inquiry* 1, no. 3: 248–51.

Bargh, J. A. 1992. "The Ecology of Automaticity: Toward Establishing the

Conditions Needed to Produce Automatic Processing Effects." *American Journal of Psychology* 105, no. 2: 181–99. https://doi.org/10.2307/1423027.

Bargh, J. A. 1994. "The Four Horsemen of Automaticity: Awareness, Intention, Efficiency, and Control in Social Cognition." In *Handbook of Social Cognition: Basic Processes; Applications*, 2nd ed., edited by R. S. Wyer Jr. and T. K. Srull, 1–40. Hillsdale, NJ: Lawrence Erlbaum Associates.

Bargh, J. A. 1997. "The Automaticity of Everyday Life." In *The Automaticity of Everyday Life: Advances in Social Cognition*, edited by R. S. Wyer Jr., 1–61. Mahwah, NJ: Lawrence Erlbaum Associates.

Bargh, J. A. 1999. "The Cognitive Monster: The Case against the Controllability of Automatic Stereotype Effects." In *Dual-Process Theories in Social Psychology*, edited by S. Chaiken and Y. Trope, 361–82. New York: Guilford Press.

Bargh, J. A. 2003. "Why We Thought We Could Prime Social Behavior." *Psychological Inquiry* 14, no. 3: 216–18. https://doi.org/10.1080/1047840X.2003.9682882.

Bargh, J. A. 2005. "Bypassing the Will: Towards Demystifying the Nonconscious Control of Social Behavior." In *The New Unconscious*, edited by R. R. Hassin, J. S. Uleman, and J. A. Bargh, 37–58. Oxford: Oxford University Press.

Bargh, J. A. 2006. "What Have We Been Priming All These Years? On the Development, Mechanisms, and Ecology of Nonconscious Social Behavior." *European Journal of Social Psychology* 36, no. 2: 147–68. https://doi.org/10.1002/ejsp.336.

Bargh, J. A. 2011. "Unconscious Thought Theory and Its Discontents: A Critique of the Critiques." *Social Cognition* 29, no. 6: 629–47. https://doi.org/10.1521/soco.2011.29.6.629.

Bargh, J. A. March 5, 2012a. "Nothing in Their Heads." *Psychology Today* (blog). https://osf.io/bgb3c.

Bargh, J. A. March 23, 2012b. "Angry Birds." *Psychology Today* (blog). Archived at https://etiennelebel.com/documents/ss/Bargh-02-March-23-2012-second-response.pdf.

Bargh, J. A. May 11, 2012c. "Priming Effects Replicate Just Fine, Thanks." *Psychology Today* (blog). https://www.psychologytoday.com/us/blog/the-natural-unconscious/201205/priming-effects-replicate-just-fine-thanks.

Bargh, J. A. January 2014a. "Our Unconscious Mind." *Scientific American* 310, no. 1: 30–37. https://static.scientificamerican.com/sciam/cache/file/C33250D3-EFD8-43E9-91DDFB4690A6236D.pdf.

Bargh, J. A. July 2014b. "The Historical Origins of Priming as the Preparation of Behavioral Responses: Unconscious Carryover and Contextual Influences of Real-World Importance." *Social Cognition* 32: 209-24. https://doi.org/10.1521/soco.2014.32.supp.209.

Bargh, J. A. November 2014c. "Award for Distinguished Scientific Contributions (2014)." *American Psychologist* 69, no. 8: 727–29. http://doi.org/10.1037/a0037574.

Bargh, J. A. 2017. *Before You Know It: The Unconscious Reasons We Do What We Do*. New York: Touchstone.

Bargh, J. A., and K. Barndollar. 1996. "Automaticity in Action: The Unconscious as Repository of Chronic Goals and Motives." In *The Psychology of Action: Linking Cognition and Motivation to Behavior*, edited by P. M. Gollwitzer and J. A. Bargh, 457–81. New York: Guilford Press.

Bargh, J. A., and T. L. Chartrand. 1999. "The Unbearable Automaticity of Being." *American Psychologist* 54, no. 7: 462–79. https://doi.org/10.1037/0003-066X.54.7.462.

Bargh, J. A., and T. L. Chartrand. 2000. "Studying the Mind in the Middle: A Practical Guide to Priming and Automaticity Research." In *Handbook of Research Methods in Social and Personality Psychology*, edited by H. T. Reis and C. M. Judd, 311–44. New York: Cambridge University Press.

Bargh, J. A., M. Chen, and L. Burrows. 1996. "Automaticity of Social Behavior: Direct Effects of Trait Construct and Stereotype Activation on Action." *Journal of Personality and Social Psychology* 71, no. 2: 230–44. https://doi.org/10.1037/0022-3514.71.2.230.

Bargh, J. A., and M. J. Ferguson. 2000. "Beyond Behaviorism: On the Automaticity of Higher Mental Processes." *Psychological Bulletin* 126, no. 6: 925–45. https://doi.org/10.1037//0033-2909.126.6.925.

Bargh, J. A., and P. M. Gollwitzer. 1994. "Environmental Control of Goal-Directed Action." In *Integrative Views of Motivation, Cognition, and Emotion: Nebraska Symposium on Motivation*, vol. 41, edited by W. D. Spaulding, 71–124. Lincoln: University of Nebraska Press.

Bargh, J. A., P. M. Gollwitzer, A. Lee-Chai, K. Barndollar, and R. Trötschel. 2001. "The Automated Will: Nonconscious Activation and Pursuit of Behavioral Goals." *Journal of Personality and Social Psychology* 81, no. 6: 1014–27. https://doi.org/10.1037/0022-3514.81.6.1014.

Bargh, J. A., M. Green, and G. Fitzsimons. 2008. "The Selfish Goal: Unintended Consequences of Intended Goal Pursuits." *Social Cognition* 26, no. 5: 534–54. https://doi.org/10.1521/soco.2008.26.5.534.

Bargh, J. A., and J. Y. Huang. 2009. "The Selfish Goal." In *The Psychology of Goals*, edited by G. B. Moskowitz and H. Grant, 127–50. New York: Guilford Press.

Bargh, J. A., and E. Morsella. 2008. "The Unconscious Mind." *Perspectives on Psychological Science* 3, no. 1: 73–79. https://doi.org/10.1111/j.1745-6916.2008.00064.x.

Bargh, J. A., and P. Pietromonaco. 1982. "Automatic Information Processing and Social Perception: The Influence of Trait Information Presented

Outside of Conscious Awareness on Impression Formation." *Journal of Personality and Social Psychology* 43, no. 3: 437–49. https://doi.org/10.1037/0022-3514.43.3.437.

Bargh, J. A., and I. Shalev. 2012. "The Substitutability of Physical and Social Warmth in Daily Life." *Emotion* 12, no. 1: 154–62. https://doi.org/10.1037/a0023527.

Bargh, J. A., and I. Shalev. 2015. "On the Association between Loneliness and Physical Warmth-Seeking through Bathing: Reply to Donnellan et al. (2014) and Three Further Replications of Bargh and Shalev (2012) Study 1." *Emotion* 15, no. 1: 120–23. https://doi.org/10.1037/Emo0000014.

Bargh, J. A., K. L. Schwader, S. E. Hailey, R. L. Dyer, and E. J. Boothby. 2012. "Automaticity in Social Cognitive Processes." *Trends in Cognitive Sciences* 16, no. 12: 593–605. http://dx.doi.org/10.1016/j.tics.2012.10.002.

Bargh, J. A, and J. S. Uleman. 1989. "Introduction." In *Unintended Thought*, edited by J. S. Uleman and J. A. Bargh, xiii–xxvi. New York: Guilford Press.

Barsalou, L. W. 1992. *Cognitive Psychology: An Overview for Cognitive Scientists*. Hillsdale, NJ: Lawrence Erlbaum Associates.

Barsalou, L. W. 2016. "Situated Conceptualization Offers a Theoretical Account of Social Priming." *Current Opinion in Psychology* 12, no. 6: 6–11. https://doi.org/10.1016/j.copsyc.2016.04.009.

Bartlett, T. January 30, 2013. "Power of Suggestion." *Chronicle of Higher Education*. https://chronicle.com/article/power-of-suggestion.

Bartlett, T. June 23, 2014. "Replication Crisis in Psychology Turns Ugly and Odd." *Chronicle of Higher Education*. https://chronicle.com/article/replication-crisis-in-psychology-research-turns-ugly-and-odd.

Bates, D. 2015. "Insight in the Age of Automation." In *Genealogies of Genius*, edited by D. McMahon and J. Chaplin, 153–69. New York: MacMillan Palgrave.

Bates, D. 2020. "The Political Theology of Entropy: A Katechon for the Cybernetic Age." *History of the Human Sciences* 33, no. 1: 109–27. https://doi.org/10.1177/0952695119864237.

Bateson, M., D. Nettle, and G. Roberts. 2006. "Cues of Being Watched Enhance Cooperation in a Real-World Setting." *Biological Letters* 2, no. 3: 412–14. https://doi.org/10.1098/rsbl.2006.0509.

Baumeister, R. F. 1984. "Choking under Pressure: Self-Consciousness and Paradoxical Effects of Incentives on Skillful Performance." *Journal of Personality and Social Psychology* 46, no. 3: 610–20. https://doi.org/10.1037/0022-3514.46.3.610.

Baumeister, R. F. 2002. "Ego Depletion and Self-Control Failure: An Energy Model of the Self's Executive Function." *Self and Identity* 1, no. 2: 129–36. https://doi.org/10.1080/152988602317319302.

Baumeister, R. F., and J. A. Bargh. 2014. "Conscious and Unconscious: Toward an Integrative Understanding of Human Mental Life and Action." In *Dual-Process Theories of the Social Mind*, edited by J. W. Sherman, B. Gawronski, and Y. Trope, 35–49. New York: Guilford Press.

Baumeister, R. F., E. Bratslavsky, M. Muraven, and D. M. Tice. 1998. "Ego-Depletion: Is the Active Self a Limited Resource?" *Journal of Personality and Social Psychology* 74, no. 5: 1252–65. https://doi.org/10.1037//0022-3514.74.5.1252.

Baumeister, R. F., and E. J. Masicampo. 2010. "Conscious Thought Is for Facilitating Social and Cultural Interactions: How Mental Simulations Serve the Animal-Culture Interface." *Psychological Review* 117, no. 3: 945–71. https://doi.org/10.1037/a0019393.

Baumeister, R. F., E. J. Masicampo, and K. D. Vohs. 2011. "Do Conscious Thoughts Cause Behavior?" *Annual Review of Psychology* 62: 331–61. https://doi.org/10.1146/annurev.psych.093008.131126.

Baumeister, R. F., and C. J. Showers. 1986. "A Review of Paradoxical Performance Effects: Choking under Pressure in Sports and Mental Tests." *European Journal of Social Psychology* 16: 361–83. https://doi.org/10.1002/ejsp.2420160405.

Baumeister, R. F., and K. L. Sommer. 1997. "Consciousness, Free Choice, and Automaticity." In *The Automaticity of Everyday Life: Advances in Social Cognition*, vol. 10, edited by R. S. Wyer Jr., 75–81. Mahwah, NJ: Lawrence Erlbaum Associates.

Baumeister, R. F., and K. D. Vohs. 2003. "Social Psychology Articles from the 1980s and 1990s: Some New Classics and Overlooked Gems." *Psychological Inquiry* 14, nos. 3–4: 193–95.

Baumeister, R. F., and K. D. Vohs. 2007. "Self-Regulation, Ego Depletion, and Motivation." *Social and Personality Psychology Compass* 1, no. 1: 115–28. https://doi.org/10.1111/j.1751-9004.2007.00001.x.

Baumeister, R. F., and K. D. Vohs. 2016. "Misguided Effort with Elusive Implications." *Perspectives on Psychological Science* 11, no. 4: 574-75. https://doi.org/10.1177/1745691616652878.

Bavelas, J. B. 1990a. "Some Problems with Linking Goals with Discourse." In *Understanding Face-to-Face Interaction: Issues Linking Goals and Discourse*, edited by K. Tracy, 119–30. Hillsdale, NJ: Lawrence Erlbaum.

Bavelas, J. B. 1990b. "Behaving and Communicating: A Reply to Motley." *Western Journal of Speech Communication* 54, no. 4: 593–602. https://doi.org/10.1080/10570319009374362.

Bavelas, J. B. 1995. "Gestures Specialized for Dialogue." *Personality and Social Psychology Bulletin* 21, no. 4: 394–405. https://doi.org/10.1177/0146167295214010.

Bavelas, J. B. 1998. "Theoretical and Methodological Principles of the Equivocation Project." *Journal of Language and Social Psychology* 17, no. 2: 183–99. https://doi.org/10.1177/0261927X980172003.

Bavelas, J. B. 2007. "Face-to-Face Dialogue as a Micro-Social Context: The Example of Motor Mimicry." In *Gesture and the Dynamic Dimension of Language*, edited by S. D. Duncan, J. Cassell, and E. T. Levy, 127–46. Amsterdam: John Benjamins Publishing Company. https://doi.org/10.1075/gs.1.15bav.

Bavelas, J. B. 2013. "Fifty Years of the Interactional View: An Interview with Janet Bavelas." Interview by Mark McKergow. *InterAction* 5, no. 2: 92–116.

Bavelas, J. B., A. Black, N. Chovil, C. R. Lemery, and J. Mullett. 1988. "Form and Function in Motor Mimicry: Topographic Evidence That the Primary Function Is Communicative." *Human Communication Research* 14, no. 3: 275–99. https://doi.org/10.1111/j.1468-2958.1988.tb00158.x.

Bavelas, J. B., A. Black, C. R. Lemery, and J. Mullett. 1986. "'I *Show* How You Feel': Motor Mimicry as a Communicative Act." *Journal of Personality and Social Psychology* 50, no. 2: 322–29. https://doi.org/10.1037/0022-3514.50.2.322.

Bavelas, J. B., A. Black, C. R. Lemery, and J. Mullett. 1987. "Motor Mimicry as Primitive Empathy." In *Empathy and Its Development*, edited by N. Eisenberg and J. Strayer, 317–38. Cambridge: Cambridge University Press.

Bavelas, J. B., and N. Chovil. 1997. "Faces in Dialogue." In *The Psychology of Facial Expression*, edited by J. Russell and J. M. Fernandez-Dols, 334–46. Cambridge: Cambridge University Press.

Bavelas, J. B., and N. Chovil. 2000. "Visible Acts of Meaning: An Integrated Message Model of Language in Face-to-Face Dialogue." *Journal of Language and Social Psychology* 19, no. 2: 163–94. https://doi.org/10.1177/0261927X00019002001.

Bavelas, J. B., and L. Coates. 1992. "How Do We Account for the Mindfulness of Face-to-Face Dialogue?" *Communication Monographs* 59, no. 3: 301–5. https://doi.org/10.1080/03637759209376271.

Beck, L. W. 1975. *The Actor and the Spectator*. New Haven, CT: Yale University Press.

Bem, D. 2011. "Feeling the Future: Experimental Evidence for Anomalous Retroactive Influences on Cognition and Affect." *Journal of Personality and Social Psychology* 100, no. 3: 407–25. https://doi.org/10.1037/a0021524.

Berg, E. A. 1948. "A Simple Objective Technique for Measuring Flexibility in Thinking." *Journal of General Psychology* 39: 15–22. https://doi.org/10.1080/00221309.1948.9918159.

Berkowitz, L. 1984. "Some Effects of Thoughts on Anti- and Prosocial Influences of Media Events: A Cognitive-Neoassociation Analysis." *Psychological Bulletin* 95, no. 3: 410–27. https://doi.org/10.1037/0033-2909.95.3.410.

Besnard, J., P. Allain, G. Aubin, V. Chauviré, F. Etcharry-Bouyx, and D. Le Gall.

2011. "A Contribution to the Study of Environmental Dependency Phenomena: The Social Hypothesis." *Neuropsychologia* 49, no. 12: 3279–94. https://doi.org/10.1016/j.neuropsychologia.2011.08.001.

Besnard, J., P. Allain, G. Aubin, F. Osiurak, V. Chauviré, F. Etcharry-Bouyx, and D. Le Gall. 2010. "Utilization Behavior: Clinical and Theoretical Approaches." *Journal of the International Neuropsychological Society* 16, no. 3: 453–62. https://doi.org/10.1017/S1355617709991469.

Blair, I. V. 2002. "The Malleability of Automatic Stereotypes and Prejudice." *Personality and Social Psychology Review* 6, no. 3: 242–61. https://doi.org/10.1207/S15327957PSPR0603_8.

Bongers, K. C. A., and A. Dijksterhuis. 2009. "Consciousness as a Trouble-Shooting Device? The Role of Consciousness in Goal-Pursuit." In *Oxford Handbook of Human Action*, edited by E. Morsella, J. A. Bargh, and P. M. Gollwitzer, 589–604. Oxford: Oxford University Press.

Borch-Jacobsen, M. 1988. *The Freudian Subject*. Stanford, CA: Stanford University Press.

Bower, B. 2012. "The Hot and Cold of Priming: Scientists Are Divided on Whether Unnoticed Cues Can Influence Behavior." *Science News* 181, no. 10: 26–29.

Bowers, K. S. 1992. "Imagination and Dissociation in Hypnotic Responding." *International Journal of Clinical and Experimental Hypnosis* 40, no. 4: 253–75. https://doi.org/10.1080/00207149208409661.

Bowers, K. S., and T. M. Davidson. 1991. "A Neodissociative Critique of Spanos's Social-Psychological Model of Hypnosis." In *Theories of Hypnosis: Current Models and Perspectives*, edited by S. J. Lynn and J. W. Rhue, 105–43. New York: Guilford Press.

Brandt, M. J., H. Ijzerman, A. Dijksterhuis, F. J. Farach, J. Geller, R. Giner-Sorolla, J. A. Grange, J. R. Spies, and A. van't Veer. 2014. "The Replication Recipe: What Makes for a Convincing Replication?" *Journal of Experimental Social Psychology* 50: 217-24.

Brass, M., H. Bekkering, and W. Prinz. 2001. "Movement Observation Affects Movement Execution in a Simple Response Task." *Acta Psychologica* 106, nos. 1–2: 3–22. https://doi.org/10.1016/s0001-6918(00)00024-x.

Bratman, M. E. 1987. *Intention, Plans, and Practical Reason*. Cambridge, MA: Harvard University Press.

Brentano, F. 1874. *Psychologie Vom Empirischen Standpunkt*. Leipzig, Germany: Duncker and Humblot.

Brett, N. 1981. "Human Habits." *Canadian Journal of Philosophy* 11, no. 3: 357–76. https://doi.org/10.1080/00455091.1981.10716309.

Brewer, M. B., V. Dull, and L. Lui. 1981. "Perceptions of the Elderly: Stereotypes as Prototypes." *Journal of Personality and Social Psychology* 41: 656–70. https://doi.org/10.1037/0022-3514.41.4.656.

Brink, S. January 29, 2014. "An Aging Brain Is Still Pretty Smart." *National Geographic*. https://www.nationalgeographic.com/science/article/140128-aging-brain-memory-cognitive-decline-neurology.

Briskman, L. B. 1972. "Is a Kuhnian Analysis Applicable to Psychology?" *Science Studies* 2, no. 1: 87–97. https://doi.org/10.1177/030631277200200103.

Bruner, J. S. 1990. *Acts of Meaning*. London: Sage.

Bruner, J. S. 1992. "On Searching for Bruner." *Language and Communication* 12, no. 1: 75–78. https://doi.org/10.1016/0271-5309(92)90012-X.

Buck, R. 1980. "Nonverbal Behavior and the Theory of Emotion: The Facial Feedback Hypothesis." *Journal of Personality and Social Psychology* 38: 811–24. http://dx.doi.org/10.1037/0022-3514.38.5.811.

Buck, R. 1984. *The Communication of Emotion*. New York: Guilford Press.

Buck, R. 1991. "Social Factors in Facial Display and Communication: A Reply to Chovil and Others." *Journal of Nonverbal Behavior* 15, no. 3: 155–61. https://doi.org/10.1007/BF01672217.

Buss, A. R. 1978. "Causes and Reasons in Attribution Theory: A Conceptual Critique." *Journal of Personality and Social Psychology* 36, no. 11: 1311–21. https://doi.org/10.1037/0022-3514.36.11.1311.

Buss, A. R. 1979. "On the Relationship Between Causes and Reasons." *Journal of Personality and Social Psychology* 37, no. 9: 1458–61. https://doi.org/10.1037/0022-3514.37.9.1458.

Callard, F. 2022. "Replication and Reproduction: Crises in Psychology and Academic Labour." *Review of General Psychology* 26, no. 2: 199–211. https://doi.org/10.1177/10892680211055660.

Camerer, C. F., A. Dreber, F. Holzmeister, H. Teck-Hua, J. Huber, M. Johannesson, and M. Kirchler et al. 2018. "Evaluating the Replicability of Social Science Experiments in *Nature* and *Science* between 2010 and 2015." *Nature Human Behavior* 2: 637–44. https://doi.org/10.1038/s41562-018-0399-z.

Carey, B. January 27, 2014. "The Older Mind May Just Be a Fuller Mind." *New Old Age* (*New York Times* blog). http://newoldage.blogs.nytimes.com/2014/01/27/the-older-mind-may-just-be-a-fuller-mind.

Carlisle, C. 2010. "Between Freedom and Necessity: Félix Ravaisson on Habit and the Moral Life." *Inquiry* 53, no. 2: 123–45.

Carlisle, C. 2014. *On Habit*. New York: Routledge.

Carnap, R. 1953. "The Two Concepts of Probability." In *Readings in the Philosophy of Science*, edited by H. Feigl and M. Brodbeck, 438–55. New York: Appleton-Century-Crofts.

Carr, D. J. Z. 2020. "'Ghastly Marionettes' and the Political Metaphysics of Cognitive Liberalism: Anti-Behaviorism, Language, and the Origins of Totalitarianism." *History of the Human Sciences* 33, no. 1: 147–74. https://doi.org/10.1177/0952695119874009.

Carroll, J. S., and J. W. Payne, eds. 1976. *Cognition and Social Behavior*. Hillsdale, NJ: Lawrence Erlbaum Associates.

Carter, T. J., M. J. Ferguson, and R. R. Hassin. 2011. "A Single Exposure to the American Flag Shifts Support toward Republicanism up to 8 Months Later." *Psychological Science* 22, no. 8: 1011–18. https://doi.org/10.1177/0956797611414726.

Carter, T. J., G. Pandrey, N. Bolger, R. R. Hassin, and M. J. Ferguson. 2020. "Has the Effect of the American Flag on Political Attitudes Declined over Time? A Case Study of the Historical Context of American Flag Priming." *Social Cognition* 38, no. 6: 489–520. https://doi.org/10.1521/soco.2020.38.6.489.

Carver, C. S., R. J. Ganellen, W. J. Froming, and W. Chambers. 1983. "Modeling: An Analysis in Terms of Category Accessibility." *Journal of Experimental Social Psychology* 19, no. 5: 403–21. https://doi.org/10.1016/0022-1031(83)90019-7.

Cesario, C. 2014. "Priming, Replication, and the Hardest Science." *Perspectives on Psychological Science* 9, no. 1: 40–48. https://doi.org/10.1177/1745691613513470.

Cesario, J., and K. J. Jonas. 2014. "Replicability and Models of Priming: What a Resource Computation Framework Can Tell Us about Expectations of Replicability." *Social Cognition* 32: 124–36. https://doi.org/10.1521/soco.2014.32.supp.124.

Cesario, J., J. E. Plaks, and E. T. Higgins. 2006. "Automatic Social Behavior as Motivated Preparation to Interact." *Journal of Personality and Social Behavior* 90, no. 6: 893–910. https://doi.org/10.1037/0022-3514.90.6.893.

Cesario, J., J. Plaks, N. Hagiwara, C. Navarette, and E. T. Higgins. 2010. "The Ecology of Automaticity: How Situational Contingencies Shape Action Semantics and Social Behavior." *Psychological Science* 21, no. 9: 1311–17. https://doi.org/10.1177/0956797610378685.

Chabris, C. F., P. R. Heck, J. Mandart, D. J. Benjamin, and D. J. Simons. 2019. "No Evidence That Experiencing Physical Warmth Promotes Interpersonal Warmth: Two Failures to Replicate Williams and Bargh (2008)." *Social Psychology* 50, no. 2: 127–32. https://doi.org/10.1027/1864-9335/a000361.

Chambers, C. 2017. *The Seven Deadly Sins of Psychology: A Manifesto for Reforming the Culture of Scientific Practice*. Princeton, NJ: Princeton University Press.

Chartrand, T. L., and J. A. Bargh. 1996. "Automatic Activation of Impression Formation and Memorization Goals: Non-Conscious Goal Priming Reproduces Effects of Explicit Task Instructions." *Journal of Personality and Social Psychology* 71, no. 3: 464–78. https://doi.org/10.1037/0022-3514.71.3.464.

Chartrand, T. L., and J. A. Bargh. 1999. "The Chameleon Effect: The Perception-

Behavior Link and Social Interaction." *Journal of Personality and Social Psychology* 76, no. 6: 893–910. https://doi.org/10.1037/0022-3514.76.6.893.

Chartrand, T. L., and J. A. Bargh. 2002. "Nonconscious Motivations: Their Activation, Operation, and Consequences." In *Self and Motivation: Emerging Psychological Perspectives*, edited by A. Tesser, D. A. Stapel, and J. W. Woods, 13–41. Washington, DC: American Psychological Association. https://doi.org/10.1037/10448-001.

Chartrand, T. L., and A. N. Dalton. 2009. "Mimicry: Its Ubiquity, Importance, and Functionality." In *Oxford Handbook of Human Action*, edited by E. Morsella, J. A. Bargh, and P. M. Gollwitzer, 458–83. New York: Oxford University Press.

Chartrand, T. L., and V. Jeffers. 2003. "Consequences of Automatic Goal Pursuit and the Case of Nonconscious Mimicry." In *Responding to the Social World: Implicit and Explicit Processes in Social Judgments and Decisions*, edited by J. P. Forgas, K. D. Williams, and W. von Hippel, 290–305. Philadelphia, PA: Psychology Press.

Chartrand, T. L., and J. L. Lakin. 2013. "The Antecedents and Consequences of Human Behavioral Mimicry." *Annual Review of Psychology* 64: 285–308. https://doi.org/10.1146/annurev-psych-113011-143754.

Chartrand, T. L., W. W. Maddux, and J. L. Lakin. 2005. "Beyond the Perception-Behavior Link: The Ubiquitous Utility and Motivational Moderators of Nonconscious Mimicry." In *The New Unconscious*, edited by R. R. Hassin, J. D. Uleman, and J. A. Bargh, 334–61. Oxford: Oxford University Press.

Chartrand, T. L., and R. van Baaren. 2009. "Human Mimicry." *Advances in Experimental Social Psychology*, vol. 41, edited by M. P. Zanna, 219–74. https://doi.org/10.1016/S0065-2601(08)00405-X.

Chen, M., T. L. Chartrand, A. Y. Lee-Chai, and J. A. Bargh. 1998. "Priming Primates: Human and Otherwise." *Behavioral and Brain Sciences* 21, no. 5: 685–86. https://doi.org/10.1017/S0140525X98231748.

Cheng, C. M., and T. L. Chartrand. 2003. "Self-Monitoring without Awareness: Using Mimicry as a Nonconscious Affiliation Strategy." *Journal of Personality and Social Psychology* 85, no. 6: 1170–79. https://doi.org/10.1037/0022-3514.85.6.1170.

Chivers, T. December 12, 2019. "A Theory in Crisis." *Nature* 576: 200–202.

Choi, S., and M. Fara. 2018. "Dispositions." In *The Stanford Encyclopedia of Philosophy* (Spring 2021), edited by E. N. Zalta. https://plato.stanford.edu/archives/spr2021/entries/dispositions/.

Chovil, N. 1991. "Social Determinants of Facial Displays." *Journal of Nonverbal Behaviors* 15, no. 3: 141–54. https://doi.org/10.1007/BF01672216.

Chovil, N., and A. J. Fridlund. 1991. "Why Emotionality Cannot Equal Sociality: Reply to Buck." *Journal of Nonverbal Behavior* 15, no. 3: 163–67. https://doi.org/10.1007/BF01672218.

Clark, A. 2008. "Soft Selves and Ecological Control." In *Distributed Cognition and the Will*, edited by D. Spurrett, D. Ross, H. Kincaid, and L. Stephens, 101–22. Cambridge, MA: MIT Press.

Clark, A. 2009. "Perception, Action, and Experience: Unraveling the Golden Braid." *Neuropsychologia* 47: 1460–68. https://doi.org/10.1016/j.neuropsychologia.2008.10.020.

Cohen-Cole, J. 2014. *The Open Mind: Cold War Politics and the Sciences of Human Nature*. Chicago: University of Chicago Press.

Coles, N. A., J. T. Larsen, and H. C. Lench. 2019. "A Meta-Analysis of the Facial Feedback Literature: Effects of Facial Feedback on Emotional Experience Are Small and Variable." *Psychological Bulletin* 145, no. 6: 610–51. http://dx.doi.org/10.1037/bul0000194.

Coles, N. A., J. T. Larsen, and H. C. Lench. 2022. "A Multi-Lab Test of the Facial Feedback Hypothesis by the Many Smiles Collaboration." *Nature Human Behavior* 6: 1731–42. https://doi.org/10.1038/s41562-022-01458-9.

Collins, H. M. 1985. *Changing Order: Replication and Induction in Scientific Practice*. Chicago: University of Chicago Press.

Conty, L., D. Gimmig, C. Belletier, N. George, and P. Huguet. 2010. "The Cost of Being Watched: Stroop Interference Increases under Concomitant Eye Contact." *Cognition* 115, no. 1: 133–39. https://doi.org/10.1016/j.cognition.2009.12.005.

Cordaro, D., A. J. Fridlund, D. Keltner, and J. A. Russell. 2015. "Debate: Keltner and Cordaro vs. Fridlund vs. Russell." In *Emotion Researcher*, the International Society for Research on Emotions Sourcebook for Research on Emotion and Affect, edited by A. Scarantino. http://emotionresearcher.com.

Crivelli, C., and A. J. Fridlund. 2018. "Facial Displays Are Tools for Social Influence." *Trends in Cognitive Sciences* 22, no. 5: 388–99. https://doi.org/10.1016/j.tics.2018.02.006.

Crowther-Heyck, H. 1999. "George A. Miller, Language, and the Computer Metaphor of Mind." *History of Psychology* 2, no. 1: 37–64.

Custers, R., and H. Aarts. 2010. "The Unconscious Will: How the Pursuit of Goals Operates Outside of Conscious Awareness." *Science* 329 (5987): 47–50. https://doi.org/10.1126/science.1188595.

Dalton, A, N., T. L. Chartrand, and E. J. Finkel. 2010. "The Schema-Driven Chameleon: How Mimicry Affects Executive and Self-Regulatory Resources." *Journal of Personality and Social Psychology* 98, no. 4: 605–17. https://doi.org/10.1037/a0017629.

Danziger, K. 1988. "On Theory and Method in Psychology." In *Recent Trends in Theoretical Psychology*, edited by W. J. Baker, L. P. Mos, H. V. Rappard, and

H. Stam, 87–94. New York: Springer-Verlag. https://doi.org/10.1007/978-1-4612-3902-4_9.

Danziger, K. 1990. *Constructing the Subject: Historical Origins of Psychological Research*. Cambridge: Cambridge University Press.

Danziger, K. 2000. "Making Social Psychology Experimental: A Conceptual History, 1920–1970." *Journal of the History of the Behavioral Sciences* 36, no. 4: 329–47. https://doi.org/10.1002/1520-6696(200023)36:4%3C329::aid-jhbs3%3E3.0.co;2-5.

Daston, L. 2009. "Science Studies and the History of Science." *Critical Inquiry* 35: 798–813.

Davidson, D. 1963. "Actions, Reasons, and Causes." Reprinted in Davidson, *Essays on Actions and Events*, 2nd ed. (Oxford: Oxford University Press, 2001): 3–19.

Davidson, D. 1970. "Mental Events." Reprinted in Davidson, *Essays on Actions and Events*, 2nd ed. (Oxford: Oxford University Press, 2001): 207–27.

Davidson, D. 1971. "Agency." Reprinted in Davidson, *Essays on Actions and Events*, 2nd ed. (Oxford: Oxford University Press, 2001): 43–61.

Davidson, D. 1980. *Essays on Action and Events*. 1st ed. Oxford: Oxford University Press.

Davidson, D. 2001. *Essays on Actions and Events*. 2nd ed. Oxford: Oxford University Press.

Davis, J., J. Redshaw, T. Suddendorf, M. Nielsen, S. Kennedy-Constantini, J. Oostenbroek, and V. Slaughter. 2021. "Does Neonatal Imitation Exist? Insights from a Meta-Analysis of 336 Effect Sizes." *Perspectives on Psychological Science* 16, no. 6: 1 373–97. https://doi.org/10.1177/1745691620959834.

Dawkins, R. 1976. *The Selfish Gene*. Oxford: Oxford University Press.

Deese, J. 1965. *The Structure of Associations in Language and Thought*. Baltimore, MD: Johns Hopkins University Press.

De Neys, W. 2021. "On Dual- and Single-Process Models of Thinking." *Perspectives on Psychological Science* 16, no. 6: 1412–27. https://doi.org/10.1177/1745691620964172.

Dennett, D. 1969. *Content and Consciousness*. London: Routledge and Kegan Paul.

Dennett, D. 1982. "Beyond Belief." In *Thought and Object*, edited by A. Woodfield, 1–95. Oxford: Clarendon Press.

Dennett, D. 1987. *The Intentional Stance*. Cambridge, MA: MIT Press.

Dennett, D. 1998. "Reflections on Language and Mind." In *Language and Thought: Interdisciplinary Themes*, edited by P. Carruthers and J. Boucher, 284–94. Cambridge: Cambridge University Press.

Dennett, D. 2003. *Freedom Evolves*. New York: Penguin.

Despret, V. 2015a. "Who Made Clever Hans Stupid?" *Angelaki* 20, no. 2: 77–85. https://doi.org/10.1080/0969725X.2015.1039843.

Despret, V. 2015b. *Hans, Le Cheval Qui Savait Compte*. Paris: Seuil.
Dijksterhuis, A. 2004. "Think Different: The Merits of Unconscious Thought in Preference Development and Decision Making." *Journal of Personality and Social Psychology* 87, no. 5: 586–98. https://doi.org/10.1037/0022-3514.87.5.586.
Dijksterhuis, A. 2014. "Welcome Back Theory!" *Perspectives on Psychological Science* 9, no. 1, 72–75. https://doi.org/10.1177/1745691613513472.
Dijksterhuis, A. 2018. "Reflection on the Professor-Priming Replication Report." *Perspectives on Psychological Science* 13, no. 2: 295–96. https://doi.org/10.1177/1745691618755705.
Dijksterhuis, A., and J. A. Bargh. 2001. "The Perception-Behavior Expressway: Automatic Effects of Social Perception on Social Behavior." In *Advances in Experimental Social Psychology*, vol. 33, edited by M. P. Zanna, 1–40. New York: Academic Press.
Dijksterhuis, A., J. A. Bargh, and J. Miedema. 2000. "Of Men and Mackerels: Attention, Subjective Experience, and Automatic Social Behavior." In *The Message Within: The Role of Subjective Experience in Social Cognition and Behavior*, edited by H. Bless and J. P. Forgas, 37–51. Philadelphia, PA: Psychology Press.
Dijksterhuis, A., T. L. Chartrand, and H. Aarts. 2007. "Effects of Priming and Perception on Social Behavior and Goal Pursuit." In *Social Psychology and the Unconscious: The Automaticity of Higher Mental Processes*, edited by J. A. Bargh, 51–131. New York: Psychology Press.
Dijksterhuis, A., and L. F. Nordgren. 2006. "A Theory of Unconscious Thought." *Perspectives on Psychological Science* 1, no. 2: 95–109. https://doi.org/10.1111/j.1745-6916.2006.00007.x.
Dijksterhuis, A., R. Spears, T. Postmes, D. A. Stapel, W. Koomen, A. van Knippenberg, and D. Scheepers. 1998. "Seeing One Thing and Doing Another: Contrast Effects in Automatic Behavior." *Journal of Personality and Social Psychology* 75, no. 4: 862–71. https://doi.org/10.1037/0022-3514.75.4.862.
Dijksterhuis, A., and A. van Knippenberg. 1998. "The Relation between Perception and Behavior, or How to Win a Game of Trivial Pursuit." *Journal of Personality and Social Psychology* 74, no. 4: 865–77. https://doi.org/10.1037/0022-3514.74.4.865.
Dijksterhuis, A., A. van Knippenberg, and R. W. Holland. 2014. "Evaluating Behavior Priming Research: Three Observations and a Recommendation." In *Understanding Priming Effects in Social Psychology*, edited by D. C. Molden, 205–17. New York: Guilford Press.
Dijksterhuis, A., A. van Knippenberg, R. W. Holland, and H. Veling. 2014. "Newell and Shanks' Approach to Psychology Is a Dead End." *Behavioral and Brain Sciences* 37, no. 1: 25–26. https://doi.org/10.1017/S0140525X1300068X.

Doise, W. 1989. "Constructivism in Social Psychology." *European Journal of Social Psychology* 19, no. 5: 389–400. https://doi.org/10.1002/ejsp.2420190507.

Donnellan, K. S. 1967. "Reasons and Causes." In *Encyclopedia of Philosophy*, vol. 7, edited by P. Edwards, 85–88. New York: Macmillan.

Donnellan, M. B., R. E. Lucas, and J. Cesario. 2015. "On the Association between Loneliness and Bathing Habits: Nine Replications of Bargh and Shalev (2012) Study 1." *Emotion* 15, no. 1: 109–15. https://doi.org/10.1037/a0036079.

Doris, J. M. 2002. *Lack of Character*. Cambridge: Cambridge University Press.

Doyen, S., O. Klein, C.-L. Pichon, and A. Cleeremans. 2012. "Behavioral Priming: It's All in the Mind, but Whose Mind?" *PLoS ONE* 7, no. 1: article e29081. https://doi.org/10.171/journal.pone.0029081.

Doyen, S., O. Klein, D. J. Simons, and A. Cleeremans. 2014. "On the Other Side of the Mirror: Priming in Cognitive and Social Psychology." *Social Cognition* 32 (supplement): 12–32. https://doi.org/10.1521/soco.2014.32.supp.12.

Dretske, F. (1973). "Perception and Other Minds." *Noûs* 7, no. 1: 34–44.

Dreyfus, H. L. 1979. *What Computers Still Can't Do: A Critique of Artificial Reason*. Cambridge, MA: MIT Press.

Dreyfus, H. L. 2005. "Overcoming the Myth of the Mental: How Philosophers Can Profit from the Phenomenology of Everyday Expertise." *Proceedings and Addresses of the American Philosophical Association* 79, no. 2: 47–65.

Dreyfus, H. L. 2007a. "The Return of the Myth of the Mental." *Inquiry: An Interdisciplinary Journal of Philosophy* 50, no. 4: 352–65. https://doi.org/10.1080/00201740701489245.

Dreyfus, H. L. 2007b. "Response to McDowell." *Inquiry: An Interdisciplinary Journal of Philosophy* 50, no. 4: 371–77. https://doi.org/10.1080/00201740701489401.

Dreyfus, H. L. 2013. "The Myth of the Pervasiveness of the Mental." In *Mind, Reason, and Being in the World: The McDowell-Dreyfus Debate*, edited by J. Schear, 15–40. London: Routledge.

Duffy, K. A., and T. L. Chartrand. 2015. "Mimicry: Causes and Consequences." *Current Opinion in Behavioral Science* 3: 112–16. http://dx.doi.org/10.1016/j.cobeha.2015.03.002.

Duffy, K., and T. L. Chartrand. 2017a. "From Mimicry to Morality: The Role of Prosociality." In *Moral Psychology: Virtue and Character*, edited by W. Sinnott-Armstrong and C. B. Miller, 439–64. Cambridge, MA: MIT Press. https://doi.org/10.2307/j.ctt1n2tvzm.33.

Duffy, K., and T. L. Chartrand. 2017b. "Reply to Goodwin and Nahmias." In *Moral Psychology: Virtue and Character*, edited by W. Sinnott-Armstrong and C. B. Miller, 489–96. Cambridge, MA: MIT Press. https://doi.org/10.2307/j.cttln2tvzm.36.

Dupuy, J.-P. 2009. *On the Origins of Cognitive Science: The Mechanization of Mind*, translated by M. B. DeBevoise. Cambridge, MA: MIT Press.

Earp, B. D., and D. Trafimow. 2015. "Replication, Falsification, and the Crisis in Confidence in Social Psychology." *Frontiers in Psychology* 6, no. 621: 1–11. https://doi.org/10.3389/fpsyg.2015.00621.

Ebersole, C. R., J. R. Axt, and B. A. Nosek. 2016. "Scientists' Reputations Are Based on Getting It Right, Not Being Right." *PloS Biology* 14, no. 5: article e1002460. https://doi.org/10.1371/journal.pbio.1002460.

Edwards, P. N. 1996. *The Closed World: Computers and the Politics of Discourse in Cold War America*. Cambridge, MA: MIT Press.

Eilan, N., and J. Roessler. 2003. "Agency and Self-Awareness: Mechanism and Epistemology." In *Agency and Self-Awareness*, edited by J. Roessler and N. Eilan, 1–47. Oxford: Clarendon Press.

Eitam, B., and E. T. Higgins. 2016. "From Reaction ('Priming') to Motivated Selection: Changing Conceptualizations of Accessibility." *Current Opinion in Psychology* 12: 55–62. http://doi.org/10.1016/j.copsyc.2016.05.017.

Ekman, P. 1982. *Emotion in the Human Face*. 2nd ed. Cambridge: Cambridge University Press.

Ekman, P., R. J. Davidson, and W. V. Friesen. 1990. "The Duchenne Smile: Emotional Expression and Brain Physiology. II." *Journal of Personality and Social Psychology* 58, no. 2: 342–53.

Ekman, P., R. W. Levenson, and W. V. Friesen. 1983. "Autonomic Nervous System Activity Distinguishes among the Emotions." *Science* 221, no. 4616: 1208–10. https://doi.org/10.1126/science.6612338.

Elio, R., ed. 2002. *Common Sense, Reasoning and Rationality*. Oxford: Oxford University Press.

Enfield, N. J., and P. Kockelman, eds. 2017. *Distributed Agency*. New York: Oxford Academic.

Engber, D. August 28, 2016. "Sad Face: Another Classic Finding in Psychology—That You Can Smile Your Way to Happiness—Just Blew Up. Is It Time to Panic Yet?" *Slate*. https://www.slate.com/articles/health_and_science/cover_story/2016/08/can_smiling_make_you_happier_maybe_maybe_not_we_have_no_idea.html.

Erdelyi, M. 1990. "Issues in the Study of Unconscious Defense Processes: Discussion of Horowitz's Comments, with Some Elaborations." In *Psychodynamics and Cognition*, edited by M. H. Horowitz, 81–94. Chicago: University of Chicago Press.

Erickson, P., J. Klein, R. Daston, R. Lemov, T. Sturm, and M. D. Gordin. 2013. *How Reason Almost Lost Its Mind: The Strange Career of Cold War Rationality*. Chicago: University of Chicago Press.

Eronen, M. I., and L. F. Bringmann. 2021. "The Theory Crisis in Psychology: How to Move Forward." *Perspectives on Psychological Science* 16, no. 4: 779–88. https://doi.org/10.1177/1745691620970586.

Evans, J. St. B. T. 2008. "Dual-Processing Accounts of Reasoning, Judgment, and Social Cognition." *Annual Review of Psychology* 59: 255–78. https://doi.org/10.1146/annurev.psych.59.103006.093629.

Evans, J. St. B. T., and K. Frankish, eds. 2009. *In Two Minds: Dual Processes and Beyond*. New York: Oxford University Press.

Fabrigar, L. L., and D. T. Wegener. 2016. "Conceptualizing and Evaluating the Replication of Research Results." *Journal of Experimental Social Psychology* 66: 68–80. https://doi.org/10.1016/j.jesp.2015.07.009.

Faye, C. 2012. "American Social Psychology: Examining the Contours of the 1970s Crisis." *Studies in History and Philosophy of Science Part C: Studies in History of Biological and Biomedical Sciences* 43, no. 2: 514–21. https://doi.org/10.1016/j.shpsc.2011.11.010.

Feldman Barrett, L. 2006. "Are Emotions Natural Kinds?" *Perspectives on Psychological Science* 1, no. 1: 25–58. https://doi.org/10.1111/j.1745-6916.2006.00003.x.

Felski, R. 2015. *The Limits of Critique*. Chicago: University of Chicago Press.

Felski, R. 2020. *Hooked: Art and Attachment*. Chicago: University of Chicago Press.

Ferguson, C. J., and M. Heene. 2012. "A Vast Graveyard of Undead Theories: Publication Bias and Psychological Science's Aversion to the Null." *Perspectives on Psychological Science* 7, no. 6: 555–61. https://doi.org/10.1177/1745691612459059.

Ferguson, C. J., and M. Heene. 2021. "Providing a Lower-Bound Estimate for Psychology's 'Crud Factor': The Case of Aggression." *Professional Psychology: Research and Practice* 52, no. 6: 620–26. https://doi.org/10.1037/pro0000386.

Ferguson, M. J., and J. A. Bargh. 2004. "How Social Perception Can Automatically Influence Behavior." *Trends in Cognitive Sciences* 8, no. 1: 33–39. https://doi.org/10.1016/j.tics.2003.11.004.

Ferguson, M. J., T. J. Carter, and R. R. Hassin. 2014. "Commentary on the Attempt to Replicate the Effect of the American Flag on Increased Republican Attitudes." *Social Psychology* 45, no. 4: 299–311.

Ferguson, M. J., and J. Cone. 2013. "The Mind in Motivation: A Social Cognitive Perspective on the Role of Consciousness in Goal Pursuit." In *The Oxford Handbook of Social Cognition*, edited by D. Carlston, 476–96. New York: Oxford University Press.

Ferguson, M. J., and J. Cone. 2021. "The Role of Intentionality in Priming." *Psychological Inquiry* 32, no. 1: 38–40. https://doi.org/10.1080/1047840X.2021.1889839.

Ferguson, M. J., and T. C. Mann. 2014. "Effects of Evaluation: An Example of Robust 'Social' Priming." *Social Cognition* 32 (supplement): 33–46. https://doi.org/10.1521/soco.2014.32.supp.33.

Fetterman, A. K., and K. Sassenberg. 2015. "The Reputational Consequences of Failed Replications and Wrongness Admission among Scientists." *PloS ONE* 10, no. 12: e0143723. https://doi.org/10.1371/journal.pone.0143723.

Fiedler, K. 2017. "What Constitutes Strong Psychological Science? The (Neglected) Role of Diagnosticity and A Priori Theorizing." *Perspectives on Psychological Science* 12, no. 1: 46–61. https://doi.org/10.1177/1745691616654458.

Fiedler, K., and M. Hütter. 2014. "The Limits of Automaticity." In *Dual-Process Theories of the Social Mind*, edited by J. W. Sherman, B. Gawronski, and Y. Trope, 497–513. New York: Guilford Press.

Finkbeiner, M., and M. Coltheart. 2014. "Dismissing Subliminal Perception because of Its Famous Problems Is Classic 'Baby with the Bathwater.'" *Behavioral and Brain Sciences* 37, no. 1: 27. https://doi.org/10.1017/S0140525X13000708.

Fischer A. H., D. Becker, and L. Veenstra. 2012. "Emotional Mimicry in Social Context: The Case of Disgust and Pride." *Frontiers in Psychology* 3: 1–9. https://doi.org/10.3389/fpsyg.2012.00475.

Fishback, A., and M. J. Ferguson. 2007. "The Goal Construct in Social Psychology." In *Social Psychology: Handbook of Basic Principles*, vol. 2, edited by A. W. Kruglanski and E. T. Higgins, 490–515. New York: Guilford Press.

Fiske, S. T. 1989. "Examining the Role of Intent: Toward Understanding Its Role in Stereotyping and Prejudice." In *Unintended Thought*, edited by J. S. Uleman and J. A. Bargh, 253–83. New York: Guilford Press.

Fiske, S. T. 2003. "The Discomfort Index: How to Spot a Really Good Idea Whose Time Has Come." *Psychological Inquiry* 14, nos. 3–4, 203–8.

Fitts, P. M., and M. I. Posner. 1967. *Human Performance*. Belmont, CA: Brock-Cole.

Flanagan, O. 1991. *Varieties of Moral Personality: Ethics and Psychological Realism*. Cambridge, MA: MIT Press.

Fleissner, J. L. 2009. "Symptomatology and the Novel." *Forum on Fiction* 42: 387–92.

Flis, I. 2019. "Psychologists Psychologizing Scientific Psychology: An Epistemological Reading of the Replication Crisis." *Theory and Psychology* 29, no. 2: 158–81. https://doi.org/10.1177/0959354319835322.

Flis, I. 2022. "The Function of Literature in Psychological Science." *Review of General Psychology* 26, no. 2: 146–56. https://doi.org/10.1177/10892680211066466.

Fluck, W. 2019. "The Limits of Critique and the Affordances of Form: Literary

Studies after the Hermeneutics of Suspicion." *American Literary History* 31, no. 2: 229–48.
Fodor, J. A. 1983. *The Modularity of Mind*. Cambridge, MA: MIT Press.
Förster, J., N. Liberman, and R. S. Friedman. 2009. "What Do We Prime? On Distinguishing between Semantic Priming, Procedural Priming, and Goal Priming." In *Oxford Handbook of Human Action*, edited by E. Morsella, J. A. Bargh, and P. Gollwitzer, 173–93. Oxford: Oxford University Press.
Frey, J. 2013. "Analytic Philosophy of Action: A Very Brief History." *Philosophical News* 7: 50–58.
Fridlund, A. J. 1991. "Sociality of Solitary Smiling: Potentiation by an Implicit Audience." *Journal of Personality and Social Psychology* 60, no. 2: 229–40. https://doi.org/10.1037/0022-3514.60.2.229.
Fridlund, A. J. 1994. *Human Facial Expression: An Evolutionary View*. San Diego, CA: Academic Press.
Fridlund, A. J. 1997. "The New Ethology of Human Facial Expressions." In *The Psychology of Facial Expression*, edited by J. A. Russell and J. M. Fernández-Dols, 103–29. Edinburgh: Cambridge University Press. https://doi.org/10.1017/CBO9780511659911.007.
Fridlund, A. J., and J. A. Russell. 2006. "The Functions of Facial Expressions: What's in a Face?" In *The Sage Handbook of Nonverbal Communication*, edited by V. Manusov and M. L. Patterson, 299–319. Washington, DC: Sage Publications, Inc.
Fridlund, A. J., J. P. Sabini, L. E. Hedlund, J. A. Schaut, J. I. Shenker, and M. J. Knauer. 1990. "Social Determinants of Facial Expressions during Affective Imagery: Displaying to the People in Your Head." *Journal of Nonverbal Behavior* 14: 113–37.
Fried, M. 1990. *Courbet's Realism*. Chicago: University of Chicago Press.
Fried, M. 2006. "Absorbed in the Action." *Artforum International* 45, no. 1: 333–35, 398.
Fried, M. 2012. *Flaubert's "Gueuloir": On Madame Bovary and Salammbô*. New Haven, CT: Yale University Press.
Friedman, N. 1967. *The Social Nature of Psychological Research: The Psychological Experiment as a Social Interaction*. New York: Basic Books.
Furnham, A., and H. C. Boo. 2011. "A Literature Review of the Anchoring Effect." *Journal of Socio-Economics* 40, no. 1: 35–42. https://doi.org/10.1016/j.socec.2010.10.008.
Gadenne, V. 1989. "Does Introducing the Social Require Eliminating the Mental? A Commentary on Rom Harré: 'Metaphysics and Methodology: Some Prescriptions for Social Psychological Research.'" *European Journal for Social Psychology* 19, no. 5: 455–61.
Gallese, V. 2011. "The Two Sides of Mimesis: Mimetic Theory, Embodied Simulation, and Social Identification." In *Mimesis and Science: Empirical*

Research on Imitation and the Mimetic Theory of Culture and Religion, edited by S. R. Garrels, 87–108. East Lansing: Michigan State University Press.

Gantt, E. E., J. P. Lindstrom, and R. Williams. 2017. "The Generality of Theory and the Specificity of Social Behavior: Contrasting Experimental and Hermeneutic Social Science." *Journal for the Theory of Social Behaviour* 47, no. 2: 130–53. https://doi.org/10.1111/jtsb.12111.

Garfinkel, H. 1967. *Studies in Ethnomethodology*. Englewood Cliffs, NJ: Prentice-Hall.

Gazzaniga, M. S. 1984. *The Social Brain*. New York: Basic Books.

Gazzaniga, M. S. 1985. *The Ethical Brain*. New York: Dana Press.

Gendler, T. S. 2008a. "Alief and Belief." *Journal of Philosophy* 105, no. 10: 634–63.

Gendler, T. S. 2008b. "Alief in Action (and Reaction). *Mind and Language* 23, no. 5: 552–85.

Gendler, T. S. 2010. *Intuition, Imagination, and Philosophical Methodology*. Oxford: Oxford University Press.

Gendler, T. S. 2012. "Intuition, Imagination, and Philosophical Methodology: Summary." *Analysis Reviews* 72, no. 4: 759–64.

Gergen, K. J. 1973. "Social Psychology as History." *Journal of Personality and Social Psychology* 26, no. 2: 309–20. https://doi.org/10.1037/h0034436.

Gergen, K. J. 1982. *Toward Transformation in Social Knowledge*. New York: Springer.

Gergen, K. J. 1989. "Social Psychology and the Wrong Revolution." *European Journal of Social Psychology* 19, no. 5: 463–84. https://doi.org/10.1002/ejsp.2420190513.

Gergen, K. J., and M. M. Gergen. 1981. "Causal Attribution in the Context of Social Explanation." In *Perspectives on Attribution Research and Theory*, edited by D. Gorlitz, 195–211. Cambridge, MA: Ballinger Publishing Company.

Geroulanos, S., and L. Weatherby. 2020. "Cybernetics and the Human Sciences." *History of the Human Sciences* 33, no. 1: 3–11. https://doi.org/10.1177/0952695119887098.

Gervais, W. M. 2021. "Practical Methodological Reform Needs Good Theory." *Perspectives on Psychological Science* 16, no. 4: 827–43. https://doi.org/10.1177/1745691620977471.

Gigerenzer, G. 1991. "How to Make Cognitive Illusions Disappear: Beyond 'Heuristics and Biases.'" *European Review of Social Psychology* 2: 83–115. https://doi.org/10.1093/acprof:oso/9780195153729.003.0012.

Gigerenzer, G. 2010. "Personal Reflections on Theory and Psychology." *Theory and Psychology* 20, no. 6: 733–43. https://doi.org/10.1177/0959354310378184.

Gigerenzer, G. 2018. "Statistical Rituals: The Replication Delusion and How

We Got There." *Advances in Methods and Practices in Psychological Science* 1, no. 2: 198–218. https://doi.org/10.1177/2515245918771329132.

Gigerenzer, G., and T. Regier. 1996. "How Do We Tell an Association from a Rule? Comment on Sloman (1996)." *Psychological Bulletin* 119, no. 1: 23–26. https://doi.org/10.1037/0033-2909.119.1.23.

Gilbert, D. T. 1989. "Thinking Lightly about Others: Automatic Components of the Social Inference Process." In *Unintended Thought*, edited by J. S. Uleman and J. A. Bargh, 189–211. New York: Guilford Press.

Gilbert, D. T., G. King, S. Pettigrew, and T. D. Wilson. 2016. "Comment on 'Estimating the Reproducibility of Psychological Science.'" *Science* 351, no. 6277: 1037. https://doi.org/10.1126/science.aad7243.

Gilder, T., and E. A. Heerey. 2018. "The Role of Experimenter Belief in Social Priming." *Psychological Science* 29, no. 3: 403–17. https://doi.org/10.1177/0956797617737128

Ginet, C. 2001. "Reasons Explanations of Action: Causalist versus Noncausalist Accounts." In *Oxford Handbook of Free Will*, edited by R. Kane, 386–405. Oxford: Oxford University Press.

Gjorgjioska, M. A., and A. Tomicic. 2019. "The Crisis in Social Psychology under Neoliberalism: Reflections from Social Representations Theory." *Journal of Social Issues* 75, no. 1: 169–88. https://doi.org/10.1111/josi.12315.

Gladwell, M. 2005. *Blink: The Power of Thinking without Thinking*. New York: Little, Brown and Company.

Goertzen, J. R. 2008. "On the Possibility of Unification: The Reality and Nature of the Crisis in Psychology." *Theory and Psychology* 18, no. 6: 829–52. https://doi.org/10.1177/0959354308097260.

Goffman, E. 1969 (1959). *The Presentation of Self in Everyday Life*. London: Penguin Press.

Gollwitzer, P. M. 1993. "Goal Achievement: The Role of Intentions." *European Review of Social Psychology* 4, no. 1: 141–85. https://doi.org/10.1080/14792779343000059.

Gomes, C. M., and M. E. McCullough. 2015. "The Effects of Implicit Religious Primes on Dictator Game Allocations: A Preregistered Replication Experiment." *Journal of Experimental Psychology: General* 144, no. 6: e94-e104. https://doi.org/10.1037/xge0000027.

González-Vallejo, C., G. D. Lassiter, F. S. Bellezza, and M. J. Lindberg. 2008. "'Save Angels Perhaps': A Critical Examination of Unconscious Thought Theory and the Deliberation-without-Attention Effect." *Review of General Psychology* 12, no. 3: 282–96. https://doi.org/10.1037/a0013134.

Goodale, M. A., and A. D. Milner. 1991. "A Neurological Dissociation between Perceiving Objects and Grasping Them." *Nature* 349: 154–56.

Goodale, M. A., and A. D. Milner. 1992. "Separate Visual Pathways for Perception and Action." *Trends in Neuroscience* 15, no. 1: 20–25. https://doi.org/10.1016/0166-2236(92)90344-8.

Goodale, M. A., and A. D. Milner. 2003. *Sight Unseen*. Oxford: Oxford University Press.

Goodale, M. A., and A. D. Milner. 2008. "Two Visual Systems Re-Viewed." *Neuropsychologia* 46, no. 3: 774–85. https://doi.org/10.1016/j.neuropsychologia.2007.10.005.

Goodwin, G. P. 2017. "Prosociality Is Not Morality." In *Moral Psychology, Volume V: Virtue and Character*, edited by W. Sinnott-Armstrong and C. Miller, 465–75. Cambridge, MA: MIT Press.

Gould, S. J. 1987. *Time's Arrow, Time's Cycle: Myth and Metaphor in the Discovery of Geological Time*. Cambridge, MA: Harvard University Press.

Grahek, I., M. Schaller, and J. L. Tackett. 2021. "Anatomy of a Psychological Theory: Integrating Construct-Validation and Computational-Modeling Methods to Advance Theorizing." *Perspectives on Psychological Sciences* 16, no. 4: 803–15. https://doi.org/10.1177/1745691620966794.

Grandy, R. E., and R. Warner. 2021. "Paul Grice." In *The Stanford Encyclopedia of Philosophy* (Fall 2023), edited by E. N. Zalta and U. Nodelman. https://plato.stanford.edu/archives/fall2023/entries/grice/.

Greenfield, P. M. 2017. "Cultural Change over Time: Why Replicability Should Not Be the Gold Standard in Psychological Science." *Perspectives on Psychological Science* 12, no. 5: 762–71. https://doi.org/10.1177/1745691617707314.

Greenwald, A. G. 1970. "Sensory Feedback Mechanism in Performance Control: With Special Reference to the Ideomotor Mechanism." *Psychological Review* 77: 73–99.

Greenwald, A. G. 1971. "On Doing Two Things at Once: Time Sharing as a Function of Ideomotor Compatibility." *Journal of Experimental Psychology* 94: 52–57.

Greenwald, A. G., and R. M. Banaji. 1995. "Implicit Social Cognition: Attitudes, Self-Esteem, and Stereotypes." *Psychological Review* 102, no. 1: 4–27. https://doi.org/10.1037/0033-295X.102.1.4.

Greenwood, J. D. 1999. "Understanding the 'Cognitive Revolution' in Psychology." *Journal of the History of the Behavioral Sciences* 35, no. 1: 1–22. https://doi.org/10.1002/(SICI)1520-6696(199924)35:1<1::AID-JHBS1>3.0.CO;2-4.

Grice, H. P. 1975. "Logic and Conversation." In *Syntax and Semantics*, vol. 3, *Speech Acts*, edited by P. Cole and J. L. Morgan, 41–58. New York: Academic Press.

Guilhot, N. 2011. "Cyborg Pantocrator: International Relations Theory from Decisionism to Rational Choice." *Journal of the History of the Behavioral Sciences* 47, no. 3: 279–301. https://doi.org/10.1002/jhbs.20511.

Guilhot, N. 2020. "Automatic Leviathan: Cybernetics and Politics in Carl Schmitt's Postwar Writings." *History of the Human Sciences* 33, no. 1: 128–46. https://doi.org/10.1177/0952695119864244.

Hacking, I. 1983. *Representing and Intervening*. New York: Cambridge University Press.

Hacking, I. 1995. *Rewriting the Soul: Multiple Personality and the Sciences of Memory*. Princeton, NJ: Princeton University Press.

Hagger, M. S., N. L. D. Chatzisarantis, H. Alberts, C. O. Anggono, C. Batailler, A. R. Birt, and R. Brand et al. 2016. "A Multilab Preregistered Replication of the Ego-Depletion Effect." *Perspectives on Psychological Science* 11, no. 4: 546–73. https://doi.org/10.1177/1745691616652873.

Harman, G. 1999. "Moral Philosophy Meets Social Psychology: Virtue Ethics and the Fundamental Attribution Error." *Proceedings of the Aristotelian Society* 91, no. 3: 315–31.

Harré, R. 1970. "Powers." *British Journal for the Philosophy of Science* 21, no. 1: 81–101.

Harré, R. 1989. "Metaphysics and Methodology: Some Prescriptions for Social Psychological Research." *European Journal of Social Psychology* 19, no. 5: 439–53.

Harré, R. 1993 (1979). *Social Being*. Oxford: Blackwell.

Harré, R., and E. H. Madden. 1975. *Causal Powers: A Theory of Natural Necessity*. Totowa, NJ: Rowman and Littlefield.

Harré, R., and P. F. Secord. 1972. *The Explanation of Social Behavior*. Totowa, NJ: Littlefield, Adams and Co.

Harris, L., and Associates. 1975. *The Myth and Reality of Aging in America*. Washington, DC: National Council on Aging.

Harris, M. J., and R. Rosenthal. 1985. "Mediation of Interpersonal Expectancy Effects: 31 Meta-Analyses." *Psychological Bulletin* 97, no. 3: 363–86. https://doi.org/10.1037/0033-2909.97.3.363.

Harvey, J. H., and J. A. Tucker. 1979. "On Problems with the Cause-Reason Distinction in Attribution Theory." *Journal of Personality and Social Psychology* 37, no. 9: 1441–46. https://doi.org/10.1037/0022-3514.37.9.1441.

Hasher, L., and R. T. Zacks. 1979. "Automatic and Effortful Processes in Memory." *Journal of Experimental Social Psychology: General* 108, no. 3: 356–88. https://doi.org/10.1037/0096-3445.108.3.356.

Hassin, R. R. 2005. "Nonconscious Control and Implicit Working Memory." In *The New Unconscious*, edited by R. Hassin, J. Uleman, and J. A. Bargh, 196–222. New York: Oxford University Press.

Hassin, R. R., J. A. Bargh, and S. Zimerman. 2009. "Automatic and Flexible: The Case of Nonconscious Goal Pursuit." *Social Cognition* 27, no. 1: 20–36. https://doi.org/10.1521/soco.2009.27.1.20.

Hassin, R. R., and M. Milyavsky. 2014. "But What If the Default Is Defaulting?" *Behavioral and Brain Sciences* 37, no. 1: 29–30.

Hassin, R. R., J. S. Uleman, and J. A. Bargh, eds. 2005. *The New Unconscious.* Oxford: Oxford University Press.

Hatfield, E., J. T. Cacioppo, and R. L. Rapson. 1994. *Emotional Contagion.* Cambridge: Cambridge University Press.

Hatfield, E., L. Bensman, P. D. Thornton, and R. L. Rapson. 2014. "New Perspectives on Emotional Contagion: A Review of Classic and Recent Research on Facial Mimicry and Contagion." *Interpersona: An International Journal on Interpersonal Relationships* 8, no. 2: 159–79. https://doi.org/10.5964/ijpr.v8i2.162.

Hayes, J. 2020. "G. E. M. Anscombe: Irish-Born Philosopher." *History Ireland* 28, no. 5: 42–44. https://www.jstor.org/stable/10.2307/26934660.

Hayles, N. K. 2014. "Cognition Everywhere: The Rise of the Cognitive Nonconscious and the Costs of Consciousness." *New Literary History* 45, no. 2: 199–220.

Hayles, N. K. 2016a. "The Cognitive Nonconscious." *Critical Inquiry* 42, no. 4: 783–808.

Hayles, N. K. 2016b. "Cognitive Assemblages." *Critical Inquiry* 43, no. 1: 32–55.

Hayles, N. K. 2017. *Unthought: The Power of the Cognitive Nonconscious.* Chicago: University of Chicago Press.

Hayles, N. K. 2019. "Can Computers Create Meanings? A Cyber/Bio/Semiotic Perspective." *Critical Inquiry* 46: 32–55.

Heider, F. 1944. "Social Perception and Phenomenal Causality." *Psychological Review* 51, no. 6: 358–74. https://psycnet.apa.org/doi/10.1037/h0055425.

Heider, F. 1958. *The Psychology of Interpersonal Relations.* New York: Wiley.

Hess, U., R. Banse, and A. Kappas. 1995. "The Intensity of Facial Expression Is Determined by Underlying Affective State and Social Situation." *Journal of Personality and Social Psychology* 69, no. 2: 280–88. https://doi.org/10.1037/0022-3514.69.2.280.

Hess, U., and A. Fischer. 2013. "Emotional Mimicry as Social Regulation." *Personality and Social Psychology Review* 17, no. 2: 142–57. https://doi.org/10.1177/1088868312472607.

Hess, U., and A. Fischer. 2014. "Emotional Mimicry: Why and When We Mimic Emotions." *Social and Personality Psychology Compass* 8, no. 2: 45–57. https://doi.org/10.1111/spc3.12083.

Hess, U., and A. Fischer, eds. 2017. *Emotional Mimicry in Social Context.* Cambridge: Cambridge University Press.

Hess, U., and S. Hareli. 2016. "The Impact of Context on the Perception of Emotions." In *The Expression of Emotion: Philosophical, Psychological, and Legal Perspectives,* edited by C. Abell and J. Smith, 199–218.

Cambridge: Cambridge University Press. https://doi.org/10.1017/CBO9781316275672.010.

Hess, U., and S. Hareli. 2017. "The Social Signal Value of Emotions: The Role of Contextual Factors in Social Inferences Drawn from Emotion Displays." In *The Science of Facial Expression*, edited by J. A. Russell and J. M. Fernández-Dols, 375–93. Oxford: Oxford University Press. https://doi.org/10.1093/acprof:oso/9780190613501.003.0020.

Hess, U., and S. Hareli. 2018. "On the Malleability of the Meaning of Contexts: The Influence of Another Person's Emotion Expressions on Situation Perception." *Cognition and Emotion* 32, no. 1: 185–91. https://doi.org/10.1080/02699931.2016.1269725.

Hess, U., P. Philippot, and S. Blairy. 1998. "Facial Reactions to Emotional Facial Expressions: Affect or Cognition?" *Cognition and Emotion* 12, no. 4: 509–31. https://doi.org/10.1080/026999398379547.

Heyck, H. 2015. *Age of System: Understanding the Development of Modern Social Science*. Baltimore, MD: Johns Hopkins University Press.

Higgins, E. T., and B. Eitam. 2014. "Priming . . . Shmiming: It's about Knowing *When* and *Why* Stimulated Memory Representations Become Active." *Social Cognition* 32: 225–42. https://doi.org/10.1521/soco.2014.32.supp.225.

Higgins, E. T., W. S. Rholes, and C. R. Jones. 1977. "Category Accessibility and Impression Formation." *Journal of Experimental Social Psychology* 13, no. 2: 141–54. https://doi.org/10.1016/S0022-1031(77)80007-3.

Hilgard, E. R. 1965. *Hypnotic Susceptibility*. New York: Harcourt, Brace and World.

Hilgard, E. R. 1986 (1977). *Divided Consciousness: Multiple Controls in Human Thought and Action*. New York: Wiley.

Himmelbach, M., R. Boehme, and H. O. Karnath. 2012. "20 Years Later: A Second Look at DF's Motor Behavior." *Neuropsychologia* 50, no. 1: 139–44. https://doi.org/10.1016/j.neuropsychologia.2011.11.011.

Hogarth, R. M. 2014. "Automatic Processes, Emotions, and the Causal Field." *Behavioral and Brain Sciences* 37, no. 1: 31–32. https://doi.org/10.1017/S0140525X13000757.

Holland, R. W., M. Hendriks, and H. Aarts. 2005. "Smells Like Clean Spirit: Nonconscious Effects of Scent on Cognition and Behavior." *Psychological Science* 16, no. 9: 689–93. https://doi.org/10.1111/j.1467-9280.2005.01597.x.

Holler, J., and K. Wilkin. 2011. "Co-Speech Gesture Mimicry in the Process of Collaborative Referring during Face-to-Face Dialogue." *Journal of Nonverbal Behavior* 35, no 2: 133–53. https://doi.org/10.1007/s10919-011-0105-6.

Hommel, B. 2019. "Binary Theorizing Does Not Account for Action Control." *Frontiers in Psychology* 10: 2542. https://doi.org/10.3389/fpsyg.2019.02542.

Hommel, B., and R. W. Wiers. 2017. "Towards a Unitary Approach to Human Action Control." *Trends in Cognitive Sciences* 21, no. 12: 940–49. http://doi.org/10.1016/j.tics.2017.09.009.

Hornsby, J. 1997a. "Dennett's Naturalism." In *Simple Mindedness: In Defense of Naïve Naturalism in the Philosophy of Mind*, 168–84. Cambridge, MA: Harvard University Press.

Hornsby, J. 1997b. *Simple Mindedness: In Defense of Naïve Naturalism in the Philosophy of Mind*. Cambridge, MA: Harvard University Press.

Hornsby, J. 1998. "Dualism in Action." *Royal Institute of Philosophy Supplement* 43: 377–401.

Hornsby, J. 2004. "Agency and Actions." In *Agency and Action*, edited by J. Hyman and H. Steward, 1–23. Cambridge: Cambridge University Press.

Hornsby, J. 2011. "Actions in Their Circumstances." In *Essays on Anscombe's Intention*, edited by A. Ford, J. Hornsby, and F. Stoutland, 105–27. Cambridge, MA: Harvard University Press.

Hornsby, J. 2015. "Causality and 'The Mental.'" *Humana Mente Journal of Philosophical Studies* 8, no. 29: 125–40.

Hsee, C. K., E. Hatfield, J. G. Carlson, and C. Chemtob. 1990. "The Effect of Power on Susceptibility to Emotional Contagion." *Cognition and Emotion* 4: 327–40. https://doi.org/10.1080/02699939008408081.

Huang J. Y., and J. A. Bargh. 2011. "The Selfish Goal: Self-Deception Occurs Naturally from Autonomous Goal Operation." *Behavioral and Brain Sciences* 34, no. 1: 27–28. http://dx.doi.org/10.1017/S0140525X1000258X.

Huang, J. Y., and J. A. Bargh. 2014. "The Selfish Goal: Autonomously Operating Motivational Structures as the Proximate Cause of Human Judgment and Behavior." *Behavioral and Brain Sciences* 37, no. 2: 121–35. https://doi.org/10.1017/S0140525X13000290.

Hughes, B. M. 2018. *Psychology in Crisis*. London: Palgrave Macmillan.

Hull, J. G., L. B. Slone, K. B. Meteyer, and A. R. Matthews. 2002. "The Nonconsciousness of Self-Consciousness." *Journal of Personality and Social Psychology* 83, no. 2: 406–24. https://doi.org/10.1037/0022-3514.83.2.406.

Hutchins, E. 1995. *Cognition in the Wild*. Cambridge, MA: MIT Press.

Hutchinson, P., R. Read, and W. Sharrock. 2008. *There is No Such Thing as A Social Science: In Defence of Peter Winch*. London: Routledge.

Iaccarino, L., S. Chieffi, and A. Iavarone. 2014. "Utilization Behavior: What Is Known and What Has to Be Known?" *Behavioral Neurology*: article 297128. https://doi.org/10.1155/2014/297128.

Ingram, G. P. D, and K. Prochownik. 2014. "Restrictive and Dynamic Conceptions of the Unconscious: Perspectives from Moral and Developmental Psychology." *Behavioral and Brain Sciences* 37, no. 1: 34–35. https://doi.org/10.1017/S0140525X13000782.

Ioannidis, J. P. A. 2005. "Why Most Published Research Findings Are False." *PloS Medicine* 2, no. 8: 124. https://doi.org/10.1371/journal.pmed.0020124.

Ioannidis, J. P. A. 2012. "Why Science Is Not Necessarily Self-Correcting." *Perspectives on Psychological Science* 7, no. 6: 645–54. https://doi.org/10.1177/1745691612464056.

Ioannidis, J. P. A. 2014. "How to Make More Published Research True." *PloS Medicine* 11, no. 10: e1001747. https://doi.org/10.1371/journal.pmed.1001747.

Isen, A. M., and G. A. Diamond. 1989. "Affect and Automaticity." In *Unintended Thought*, edited by J. S. Uleman and J. A. Bargh, 124–52. New York: Guilford Press.

Ismael, J. 2007. *The Situated Self*. New York: Oxford University Press.

Ismael, J. 2011. "Self-Organization and Self-Governance." *Philosophy of the Social Sciences* 41, no. 3: 327–51. https://doi.org/10.1177/0048393110363435.

Iso-Ahola, S. E. 2017. "Reproducibility in Psychological Science: When Do Psychological Phenomena Exist?" *Frontiers in Psychology* 8: 1–16. https://doi.org/10.3389/fpsyg.2017.00879.

Iso-Ahola, S. E. 2020. "Replication and the Establishment of Scientific Truth." *Frontiers in Psychology* 11: article 2183. https://doi.org/10.3389/fpsyg.2020.02183.

Izard, C. E. 1990. "Facial Expressions and the Regulation of Emotions." *Journal of Personality and Social Psychology* 58, no. 3: 487–98. https://doi.org/10.1037/0022-3514.58.3.487.

James, William. 1950 (1890). *The Principles of Psychology*. 2 vols. New York: Dover.

Jeannerod, M., and P. Jacob. 2005. "Visual Cognition: A New Look at the Two-Visual Systems Model." *Neuropsychologia* 43, no. 2: 301–12. https://doi.org/10.1016/j.neuropsychologia.2004.11.016.

Jennings, C. D. 2012. "The Subject of Attention." *Synthese* 189, no. 3: 535–54. https://doi.org/10.1007/s11229-012-0164-1.

Johnston, W. A., and V. J. Dark. 1986. "Selective Attention." *Annual Review of Psychology* 37: 43–75. https://doi.org/10.1146/annurev.ps.37.020186.000355.

Jones, E. E. 1976. "How Do People Perceive the Causes of Behavior? Experiments Based on Attribution Theory Offer Some Insights into How Actors and Observers Differ in Viewing the Causal Structure of Their Social World." *American Scientist* 64, no. 3: 300–305.

Jones, E. E., and K. E. Davis. 1965. "A Theory of Correspondent Inferences: From Acts to Dispositions." In *Advances in Experimental Social Psychology*, edited by L. Berkowitz, 219–66. New York: Academic Press.

Jones, E. E., and V. A. Harris. 1967. "The Attribution of Attitudes." *Journal of Experimental Social Psychology* 3, no. 1: 1–24. https://doi.org/10.1016/0022-1031(67)90034-0.

Jones, E. E., and R. E. Nisbett. 1972. "The Actor and the Observer: Divergent Perceptions of the Causes of Behavior." In *Attribution: Perceiving the Causes of Behavior*, edited by E. E. Jones, D. E. Kanhouse, H. H. Kelley, R. E. Nisbett, S. Valin, and B. Wiener, 79–94. Hillsdale, NJ: Lawrence. Erlbaum Associates.

Julian, J. S., M. M. Chun, and K. Nakayama. 1997. "Attentional Requirements in a 'Pre-Attentive' Search Task." *Nature* 387: 805–7. https://doi.org/10.1038/42940.

Kahneman, D. 2011. *Thinking, Fast and Slow*. New York: Farrar, Straus and Giroux.

Kahneman, D., to colleagues. September 26, 2012. "A Proposal to Deal with Questions about Priming Effects." *Nature*. https://www.nature.com/news/polopoly_fs/7.6716.1349271308!/suppinfoFile/Kahneman%20Letter.pdf.

Kahneman, D. 2022. "Adversarial Collaboration." EDGE lecture. https://www.edge.org/adversarial-collaboration-daniel-kahneman.

Kahneman, D., and A. Tversky. 1973. "On the Psychology of Prediction." *Psychological Review* 80, no. 4: 237–51. https://doi.org/10.1037/h0034747.

Katzko, M. W. 2002. "The Rhetoric of Psychological Research and the Problem of Unification in Psychology." *American Psychologist* 57, no. 4: 262–70. https://doi.org/10.1037/0003-066X.57.4.262.

Katzko, M. W. 2006. "A Study of the Logic of Empirical Arguments in Psychological Research: 'The Automaticity of Social Behavior' as a Case Study." *Review of General Psychology* 10, no. 3: 210–28. https://doi.org/10.1037/1089-2680.10.3.210.

Kay, A., S. C. Wheeler, J. A. Bargh, and L. Ross. 2004. "Material Priming: The Influence of Mundane Physical Objects on Situational Construal and Competitive Behavioral Choice." *Organizational Behavior and Human Decision Processes* 95: 83–96. https://doi.org/10.1016/j.obhdp.2004.06.003.

Kelley, H. H. 1967. "Attribution Theory in Social Psychology." In *Nebraska Symposium on Motivation*, vol. 15, edited by D. Levine, 192–238. Lincoln: University of Nebraska Press.

Kelley, H. H. 1973. "The Processes of Causal Attribution." *American Psychologist* 28, no. 2: 107–28. https://doi.org/10.1037/h0034225.

Keren, G. 2013. "A Tale of Two Systems: A Scientific Advance or a Theoretical Stone Soup? Commentary on Evans and Stanovich." *Perspectives on Psychological Science* 8, no. 3: 257–62. https://doi.org/10.1177/1745691613483474.

Keren, G., and Y. Schul. 2009. "Two Is Not Always Better Than One: A Critical Evaluation." *Perspectives on Psychological Science* 4, no. 6: 533–50. https://doi.org/10.1111/j.1745-6924.2009.01164.x.

Kihlstrom, J. F. 1987. "The Cognitive Unconscious." *Science*, new series 237: 1445–52. https://doi.org/10.1126/science.3629249.

Kihlstrom, J. F. 1998a. "Attributions, Awareness, and Dissociation: In Memoriam Kenneth S. Bowers, 1937–1996." *American Journal of Clinical Hypnosis* 40, no. 3: 194–205. https://doi.org/10.1080/00029157.1998.10403426.

Kihlstrom, J. F. 1998b. "Dissociations and Dissociation Theory in Hypnosis: Comment on Kirsch and Lynn (1998)." *Psychological Bulletin* 123, no. 2: 186–91. https://doi.org/10.1037/0033-2909.123.2.186.

Kihlstrom, J. F. 2004. "Is There a 'People Are Stupid' School in Social Psychology?" *Behavioral and Brain Sciences* 27, no. 3: 348. https://doi.org/10.1017/S0140525X04420081.

Kihlstrom, J. F. 2008. "The Automaticity Juggernaut—or, Are We Automatons after All?" In *Are We Free? Psychology and Free Will*, edited by J. Baer, J. C. Kaufman, and R. F. Baumeister, 155–80. Oxford: Oxford University Press.

Kihlstrom, J. F. 2015. "Dynamic versus Cognitive Unconscious." In *The Encyclopedia of Clinical Psychology*, edited by R. L. Cautin and S. O. Lilienfield, 1–8. John Wiley and Sons, Inc. https://doi.org/10.1002/9781118625392.wbecp275.

Kirsch, I., and S. J. Lynn. 1998. "Dissociation Theories of Hypnosis." *Psychological Bulletin* 123, no. 1: 100–15. https://doi.org/10.1037/0033-2909.123.1.100.

Kirschenbaum, M., L. Siraganian, H. Bajohr, S. Perlow, R. Raley, R. Samolsky, T. Shoemaker, A. Vee, A. Gil, C. Bassett, K. Kraus, T. Underwood, S. Knapp, W. B. Michaels, and N. K. Hayles. June 27, 2023. "Again Theory: A Forum on Language, Meaning, and Intent in the Time of Stochastic Parrots." *In the Moment* (Critical Inquiry blog). https://critinq.wordpress.com/2023/06/26/again-theory-a-forum-on-language-meaning-and-intent-in-the-time-of-stochastic-parrots/.

Klatzky, R., and J. D. Creswell. 2014. "An Intersensory Interaction Account of Priming Effects—And Their Absence." *Perspectives on Psychological Science* 9, no. 1: 49–58. https://doi.org/10.1177/1745691613513468.

Kleiman, T., N. Sher, A. Elster, and R. Mayo. 2015. "Accessibility Is a Matter of Trust: Dispositional and Contextual Distrust Blocks Accessibility Effects." *Cognition* 142: 333–44. https://doi.org/10.1016/j.cognition.2015.06.001.

Klein, O. 2009. "From Utopia to Dystopia: Levels of Explanation and the Politics of Social Psychology." *Pyschologica Belgica* 49, nos. 2–3: 85–100. https://doi.org/10.5334/pb-49-2-3-85.

Klein, O., S. Doyen, C. Leys, P. A. M. de S. da Gama, S. Miller, L. Questienne, and A. Cleeremans. 2012. "Low Hopes, High Expectations: Expectancy Effects and the Replicability of Behavioral Experiments." *Perspectives on Psychological Science* 7, no. 6: 572–84. https://doi.org/10.1177/1745691612463704.

Klein, R. A., K. A. Ratcliff, M. Vianello, R. B. Adams Jr., S. Bahník, M. J. Bernstein, and K. Bocian et al. 2014a. "Investigating Variation in Replicability: A 'Many Labs' Replication Project." *Social Psychology* 45, no. 3: 142–52. https://doi.org/10.17605/OSF.IO/WX7CK.

Klein, R. A., K. A. Ratcliff, M. Vianello, R. B. Adams Jr., S. Bahník, M. J. Bernstein, and K. Bocian et al. 2014b. "Theory Building through Replication: Response to Commentaries on the 'Many Labs' Replication Project." *Social Psychology* 45, no. 4: 307–11. https://doi.org/10.1027/1864-9335/a000202.

Klein, S. B. 2014. "What Can Recent Replication Failures Tell Us about the Theoretical Commitments of Psychology?" *Theory and Psychology* 24, no. 3: 326–38. https://doi.org/10.1177/0959354314529616.

Kline, R. R. 2015. *The Cybernetics Moment: Or Why We Call Our Age the Information Age*. Baltimore, MD: Johns Hopkins University Press.

Kline, R. R. 2020. "How Disunity Matters to the History of Cybernetics in the Human Sciences in the United States, 1940–80." *History of the Human Sciences* 33, no. 1: 12–35. https://doi.org/10.1177/0952695119872111.

Knuf, L., G. Aschersleben, and W. Prinz. 2001. "An Analysis of Ideomotor Action." *Journal of Experimental Psychology: General* 130, no. 4: 779–98. https://doi.org/10.1037/0096-3445.130.4.779.

Kraut, R. E., and R. E. Johnson. 1979. "Social and Emotional Messages of Smiling: An Ethological Approach." *Journal of Personality and Social Psychology* 37:1539–53. https://doi.org/10.1037/0022-3514.37.9.1539.

Kruglanski, A. W., and G. Gigerenzer. 2011. "Intuitive and Deliberate Judgments Are Based on Common Principles." *Psychological Review* 118, no. 1: 97–109. https://doi.org/10.1037/a0020762.

Krumhuber, E. G., K. U. Likowski, and P. Weyers. 2014. "Facial Mimicry of Spontaneous and Deliberate Duchenne and Non-Duchenne Smiles." *Journal of Nonverbal Behavior* 38: 1–11. https://doi.org/10.1007/s10919-013-0167-8.

Kuhn, T. S. 1970a. *The Structure of Scientific Revolutions*. Chicago: University of Chicago Press.

Kuhn, T. S. 1970b. "Reflections on My Critics." In *Criticism and the Growth of Knowledge*, edited by Imre Lakatos and Alan Musgrave, 231–78. Cambridge: Cambridge University Press.

LaBerge, E. J., and S. J. Samuels. 1974. "Toward a Theory of Automatic Information Processing in Reading." *Cognitive Psychology* 6, no. 2: 293–323. https://doi.org/10.1016/0010-0285(74)90015-2.

Lachapelle, S. 2011. *Investigating the Supernatural: From Spiritism and Occultism to Psychical Research and Metaphysics in France, 1853–1931*. Baltimore, MD: Johns Hopkins University Press.

LaFrance, M. 1979. "Nonverbal Synchrony and Rapport: Analysis by the Cross-

Lag Panel Technique." *Social Psychology Quarterly* 42, no. 1: 66–70. https://doi.org/10.2307/3033875.

LaFrance, M. 1982. "Posture Mimicry and Rapport." In *Interaction Rhythms: Periodicity in Communicative Behavior*, edited by M. Davis, 279–98. New York: Human Sciences Press.

LaFrance, M., and M. Broadbent. 1976. "Group Rapport: Posture Sharing as a Nonverbal Indicator." *Group Organization Studies* 1, no. 3: 328–33. https://doi.org/10.1177/105960117600100307.

Laird, J. D. 1984. "The Real Role of Facial Response in the Experience of Emotion: A Reply to Tourangeau and Ellsworth, and Others." *Journal of Personality and Social Psychology* 47, no. 4: 909–17. https://doi.org/10.1037/0022-3514.47.4.909.

Lakatos, I. 1970. "Falsification and the Methodology of Scientific Research Programmes." In *Criticism and the Growth of Knowledge*, edited by I. Lakatos and A. Musgrave, 91–196. Cambridge: Cambridge University Press.

Lakens, D. March 6, 2016. "The Statistical Conclusions in Gilbert et al (2016) Are Completely Invalid." *20% Statistician* (blog). https://daniellakens.blogspot.com/2016/03/the-statistical-conclusions-in-gilbert.html.

Lakin, J. L. 2006. "Automatic Cognitive Processes and Nonverbal Communication." In *The Sage Handbook of Nonverbal Communication*, edited by In V. Manusov and M. J. Patterson, 59–77. Thousand Oaks, CA: Sage. https://doi.org/10.4135/9781412976152.n4.

Lakin, J. L., and T. L. Chartrand. 2003. "Using Nonconscious Behavioral Mimicry to Create Affiliation and Rapport." *Psychological Science* 14, no. 4: 334–39. https://doi.org/10.1111/1467-9280.14481.

Lakin, J. L., T. L. Chartrand, and R. M. Arkin. 2008. "I Am Too Just Like You: Nonconscious Mimicry as an Automated. Behavioral Response to Social Exclusion." *Psychological Science* 19, no. 8: 816–22. https://doi.org/10.1111/j.1467-9280.2008.02162.x.

Lakin, J. L., V. E. Jefferis, C. M. Cheng, and T. L. Chartrand. 2003. "The Chameleon Effect as Social Glue: Evidence for the Evolutionary Significance of Nonconscious Mimicry." *Journal of Nonverbal Behavior* 27, no. 3: 145–62. https://doi.org/10.1023/A:1025389814290.

Langer, E. J. 1978. "Rethinking the Role of Thought in Social Interaction." In *New Directions in Attribution Research*, vol. 2, edited by J. H. Harvey, W. J. Ickes, and R. F. Kidd, 35–58. Hillsdale, NJ: Lawrence Erlbaum Associates.

Langer, E. J., A. Blank, and B. Chanowitz. 1978. "The Mindlessness of Ostensibly Thoughtful Action: The Role of 'Placebic' Information in Interpersonal Interaction." *Journal of Personality and Social Psychology* 36, no. 6: 635–42. https://doi.org/10.1037/0022-3514.36.6.635.

Langer, E. J., and C. Weinman. 1981. "When Thinking Disrupts Intellectual Performance: Mindfulness on an Overlearned Task." *Personality and Social Psychology Bulletin* 7, no. 2: 240–43. https://doi.org/10.1177 /014616728172009.

Lashley, K. S. 1951. "The Problem of Serial Order in Behavior." In *Cerebral Mechanisms in Behavior: The Hixon Symposium*, edited by L. A. Jeffress, 112–36. New York: Wiley.

Lassiter, G. D., M. J. Lindberg, C. González-Vallejo, F. S. Bellezza, and N. D. Phillips. 2009. "The Deliberation-without-Attention Effect: Evidence for Artifactual Interpretation." *Psychological Science* 20, no. 6: 671–75. https://doi.org/10.1111/j.1467-9280.2009.02347.x.

Latham, G. P. 2016. "Goal Setting: A Possible Theoretical Framework for Examining the Effect of Priming Goals on Organizational Behavior." *Current Opinion in Psychology* 12: 85–88. https://doi.org/10.1016/j.copsyc.2016 .07.005.

Latour, B. 1996. "On Actor-Network Theory: A Few Clarifications." *Soziale Welt* 47: 369–81. http://transnationalhistory.net/interconnected/wp -content/uploads/2015/05/Latour-Actor-Network-Clarifications.pdf.

Latour, B. 2000. "When Things Strike Back: A Possible Contribution of "Science Studies" to the Social Sciences." *British Journal of Sociology* 51, no. 1: 107–23. https://doi.org/10.1111/j.1468-4446.2000.00107.x.

Latour, B. 2004. "Why Has Critique Run Out of Steam? From Matters of Fact to Matters of Concern." *Critical Inquiry* 30: 225–48.

Lavin, D. 2015. "Action as a Form of Temporal Unity: On Anscombe's 'Intention.'" *Canadian Journal of Philosophy* 45, no. 5: 609–29. https://doi.org /10.1080/00455091.2015.1125589.

Lazarus, R. S. 1999. "The Cognition-Emotion Debate: A Bit of History." In *Handbook of Cognition and Emotion*, edited by T. Dalgleish and M. J. Power, 3–19. London: John Wiley and Sons.

Le Bon, G. 1895. *The Crowd: A Study of the Popular Mind*. New York: Viking.

Leahey, T. H. 1992. "The Mythical Revolutions of American Psychology." *American Psychologist* 47, no. 2: 308–18. https://doi.org/10.1037/0003 -066X.47.2.308.

Leander, N. P., T. L. Chartrand, and J. A. Bargh. 2012. "You Give Me the Chills: Embodied Reactions to Inappropriate Amounts of Behavioral Mimicry." *Psychological Science* 23, no. 7: 772–79. https://doi.org/10.1177 /0956797611434535.

Leander, N. P., T. L. Chartrand, and W. Wood. 2011. "Mind Your Mannerisms: Behavioral Mimicry Elicits Stereotype Conformity." *Journal of Experimental Social Psychology* 47, no. 1: 195–201. https://doi.org/10.1016/j.jesp.2010 .09.002.

Leighton, J., G. Bird, C. Orsini, and C. Heyes. 2010. "Withdrawn: Social Attitudes Modulate Automatic Imitation." *Journal of Experimental Social Psychology* 46: 905–10. https://doi.org/10.1016/j.jesp.2009.04.014.

Lewis, M. 1990. "The Development of Intentionality and the Role of Consciousness." *Psychological Inquiry* 1, no. 3: 231–47. https://doi.org/10.1207/s15327965pli0103_13.

Lewis-Kraus, G. 2023. "Big Little Lies." *New Yorker* 99, no. 32: 40–53.

Leys, R. 1993. "Mead's Voices: Imitation as Foundation, or, the Struggle against Mimesis." *Critical Inquiry* 19: 277–307. Baltimore, MD: Johns Hopkins University Press.

Leys, R. 2000. *Trauma: A Genealogy*. Chicago: Chicago University Press.

Leys, R. 2012. "Trauma and the Turn to Affect." In *Trauma, Memory, and Narrative in the Contemporary South African Novel*, edited by E. Mengele and M. Borzaga, 3–28. Amsterdam: Rodopi.

Leys, R. 2014. "'Both of Us Disgusted in *My* Insula': Mirror Neuron Theory and Emotional Empathy." In *Science and Emotions after 1945*, edited by F. Biess and D. Gross, 67–95. Chicago: University of Chicago Press.

Leys, R. 2017. *The Ascent of Affect: Genealogy and Critique*. Chicago: University of Chicago Press.

Leys, R. 2020. *Newborn Imitation: The Stakes of a Controversy*. Cambridge: Cambridge University Press.

Leys, R., and R. B. Evans. 1990. *Defining American Psychology: The Correspondence between Adolf Meyer and Edward Bradford Titchener*. Baltimore, MD: Johns Hopkins University Press.

Lhermitte, F. 1983. "'Utilization Behavior' and Its Relation to Lesions of the Frontal Lobes." *Brain* 106: 237–55. https://doi.org/10.1093/brain/106.2.237.

Lhermitte, F. 1986. "Human Autonomy and the Frontal Lobes. Part II: Patient Behavior in Complex and Social Situations: The 'Environmental Dependency Syndrome.'" *Annals of Neurology* 19: 335–43. https://doi.org/10.1002/ana.410190405.

Lhermitte, F., J. Derouesne, and J.-L. Signoret. 1972. "Analyse Neuropsychologique du Syndrome Frontale." *Revue Neuropsychologique* 127, no. 4: 415–40.

Lhermitte, F., P. Pillon, and M. Serdaru. 1986. "Human Autonomy and the Frontal Lobes. Part I: Imitation and Utilization Behavior: A Neuropsychological Study of 75 Patients." *Annals of Neurology* 19: 326–34. https://doi.org/10.1002/ana.410190404.

Libet, B. 1985. "Unconscious Cerebral Initiative and the Role of Conscious Will in Voluntary Action." *Behavioral and Brain Sciences* 8: 529–66. https://doi.org/10.1017/S0140525X00044903.

Lieberman, M. D., D. Schreiber, and K. Ochsner. 2003. "Is Political Cognition Like Riding a Bicycle? How Cognitive Neuroscience Can Inform Research on Political Thinking." *Political Psychology* 24, no. 4: 681–704. https://doi.org/10.1046/j.1467-9221.2003.00347.x.

Lipscomb, B. J. B. 2022. *The Women Are Up to Something: How Elizabeth Anscombe, Philippa Foot, Mary Midgley, and Iris Murdoch Revolutionized Ethics.* Oxford: Oxford University Press.

Locke, D., and D. Pennington. 1982. "Reasons and Other Causes: Their Role in Attribution Processes." *Journal of Personality and Social Psychology* 42, no. 2: 212–23. https://doi.org/10.1037/0022-3514.42.2.212.

Locke, E. A. 2015. "Theory Building, Replication, and Behavioral Priming: Where Do We Need to Go from Here?" *Perspectives on Psychological Science* 10, no. 3: 408–14. https://doi.org/10.1177/1745691614567231.

Lodder, P., H. H. Ong, and R. P. P. P. Grasman, and J. M. Wicherts. 2019. "A Comprehensive Meta-Analysis of Money Priming." *Journal of Experimental Psychology* 148, no. 4: 688-712. http://dx.doi.org/10.1037/xge0000570.

Loersch, C., and B. K. Payne. 2011. "The Situated Inference Model: An Integrative Account of the Effects of Primes on Perception, Behavior, and Motivation." *Perspectives on Psychological Science* 6, no. 3: 234–52. https://doi.org/10.1177/1745691611406921.

Loersch, C., and B. K. Payne. 2012. "On Mental Contamination: The Role of (Mis) Attribution in Behavior Priming." *Social Cognition* 30, no. 2: 241–52. https://doi.org/10.1521/soco.2012.30.2.241.

Loersch, C., and B. K. Payne. 2014. "Situated Inferences and the What, Who, and Where of Priming." *Social Cognition* 32: 137–51. https://doi.org/10.1521/soco.2014.32.supp.137.

Loersch, C., and B. K. Payne. 2016. "Demystifying Priming." *Current Opinion in Psychology* 12: 32–36. https://doi.org/10.1016/j.copsyc.2016.04.020.

Logan, G. D. 1985. "Skill and Automaticity: Relations, Implications, and Future Directions." *Canadian Journal of Psychology* 39, no. 2: 367–86. https://doi.org/10.1037/h0080066.

Logan, G. D., and W. B. Cowan. 1984. "On the Ability to Inhibit Thought and Action: A Theory of an Act of Control." *Psychological Review* 91, no. 3: 295–327. https://doi.org/10.1037/0033-295X.91.3.295.

Lombardi, W. J., E. T. Higgins, and J. A. Bargh. 1987. "The Role of Consciousness in Priming Effects on Categorization: Assimilation Versus Contrast as a Function of Awareness of the Priming Event." *Personality and Social Psychology Bulletin* 13, no. 3: 411–29. https://doi.org/10.1177/0146167287133009.

Lowe, E. J. 2011. "How *Not* to Think of Powers: A Deconstruction of the 'Dispositions and Conditionals' Debate." *Monist* 94, no. 1: 19–33.

Lynn, S. J., and J. W. Rhue. 1991. "Hypnosis Theories: Themes, Variations, and Research Directions." In *Theories of Hypnosis: Current Models and Perspectives*, edited by S. J. Lynn and J. W. Rhue, 601–26. New York: Guilford Press.

Lynott, D., K. S. Corker, J. Wortman, L. Connell, M. B. Donnellan, R. E.

Lucas, and K. O'Brien. 2014. "Replication of 'Experiencing Physical Warmth Promotes Interpersonal Warmth' by Williams and Bargh (2008)." *Social Psychology* 45, no. 3: 216–22. https://doi.org/10.1027/1864-9335/a000187.

Mackenzie, B. D. 1972. "Behaviorism and Positivism." *Journal of the History of the Behavioral Sciences* 8: 222–31.

Macrae, C. N., G. V. Bodenhausen, A. B. Milne, L. Castelli, A. M. Schloerscheidt, and S. Greco. 1998. "On Activating Exemplars." *Journal of Experimental Social Psychology* 34, no. 4: 330–54. https://doi.org/10.1006/jesp.1998.1353.

Macrae, C. N., and L. Johnston. 1998. "Help, I Need Somebody: Automatic Action and Inaction." *Social Cognition* 16, no. 4: 400–17. https://doi.org/10.1521/soco.1998.16.4.400.

Mahoney, M. J. 1985. "Open Exchange and Epistemic Progress." *American Psychologist* 40, no. 1: 29–39. https://doi.org/10.1037/0003-066X.40.1.29.

Maier, M., F. Bartos, T. D. Stanley, D. R. Shanks, A. J. L. Harris, and E-J. Wagenmakers. 2022. "No Evidence for Nudging after Adjusting for Publication Bias." *Proceedings of the National Academy of Sciences* 119, no. 32: e2200300119. https://doi.org/10.1073/pnas.2200300119.

Makel, M. C., J. A. Plucker, and B. Hegarty. 2012. "Replications in Psychology Research: How Often Do They Really Occur?" *Perspectives on Psychological Science* 7, no. 6: 537–42. https://doi.org/10.1177/1745691612460688.

Malle, B. F. 2006a. "Of Windmills and Straw Men: Folk Assumptions of Mind and Action." In *Does Consciousness Cause Behavior? An Investigation of the Nature of Volition*, edited by S. Pockett, W. P. Banks, and S. Gallagher, 207–31. Cambridge, MA: MIT Press. https://doi.org/10.7551/mitpress/9780262162371.003.0012.

Malle, B. F. 2006b. "The Actor-Observer Asymmetry in Causal Attribution: A (Surprising) Meta-Analysis." *Psychological Bulletin* 132, no. 6: 895–919. https://doi.org/10.1037/0033-2909.132.6.895.

Malle, B. F. 2008. "Fritz Heider's Legacy: Celebrated Insights, Many of Them Misunderstood." *Social Psychology* 39, no. 3: 163–73. https://doi.org/10.1027/1864-9335.39.3.163.

Malle, B. F., and W. Ickes. 2000. "Fritz Heider: Philosopher and Psychologist." In *Portraits of Pioneers in Psychology*, vol. 4, edited by G. A. Kimble and M. Wertheimer, 195–214. Washington, DC: American Psychological Association.

Malle, B. F., J. Knobe, M. J. O'Laughlin, G. E. Pearce, and S. E. Nelson. 2000. "Conceptual Structure and Social Functions of Behavior Explanations: Beyond Person-Situation Attributions." *Journal of Personality and Social Psychology* 79, no. 3: 309–26. https://doi.org/10.1037/0022-3514.79.3.309.

Mandelbaum, E. 2010. "The Architecture of Belief: An Essay on the Unbearable Automaticity of Being." PhD diss., University of North Carolina at Chapel Hill. https://philarchive.org/rec/MANTAO-26.

Mandelbaum, E. 2013. "Against Alief." *Philosophical Studies* 2013, no. 1: 197–211. https://doi.org/10.1007/s11098-012-9930-7.

Mandelbaum, E. 2014. "Thinking Is Believing." *Inquiry: An Interdisciplinary Journal of Philosophy* 57, no. 1: 55–96. https://doi.org/10.1080/0020174X.2014.858417.

Mandler, G. 1975. *Mind and Emotion*. New York: Wiley.

Marcus, E. 2019. "Reconciling Practical Knowledge with Self-Deception." *Mind* 128: 1205–25. https://doi.org/10.1093/mind/fzy061.

Masterman, M. 1970. "The Nature of a Paradigm." In *Criticism and the Growth of Knowledge*, edited by I. Lakatos and A. Musgrave, 59–89. Cambridge: Cambridge University Press.

Matsumoto, D. 1987. "The Role of Facial Response in the Experience of Emotion: More Methodological Problems and a Meta-Analysis." *Journal of Personality and Social Psychology* 52, no. 4: 769–74. https://doi.org/10.1037/0022-3514.52.4.769.

McArthur, L. A. 1972. "The How and What of Why: Some Determinants and Consequences of Causal Attribution." *Journal of Personality and Social Psychology* 22, no. 2: 171–93. https://doi.org/10.1037/h0032602.

McClure, J. 1983. "Telling More Than They Can Know: The Positivist Account of Verbal Reports and Mental Processes." *Journal for the Theory of Social Behaviour* 13, no. 1: 1110–27. https://doi.org/10.1111/j.1468-5914.1983.tb00466.x.

McCullough, K. C., M. J. Ferguson, C. C. K. Kawada, and J. A. Bargh. 2008. "Taking a Closer Look: On the Operation of Nonconscious Impression Formation." *Journal of Experimental Social Psychology* 44, no. 3: 614–23. https://doi.org/10.1016/j.jesp.2007.02.001.

McDowell, J. 1994a. *Mind and World*. Cambridge, MA: Harvard University Press.

McDowell, J. 1994b. "The Content of Perceptual Experience." *Philosophical Quarterly* 44, no. 175: 190–205. https://doi.org/10.2307/2219740.

McDowell, J. 2007a. "What Myth?" *Inquiry: An Interdisciplinary Journal of Philosophy* 50, no. 4: 338–51. https://doi.org/10.1080/00201740701489211.

McDowell, J. 2007b. "Response to Dreyfus." *Inquiry: An Interdisciplinary Journal of Philosophy* 50, no. 4: 366–70. https://doi.org/10.1080/00201740701489351.

McDowell, J. 2009. "Naturalism in the Philosophy of Mind." In *The Engaged Intellect: Philosophical Essays*, 257–75. Cambridge, MA: Harvard University Press.

McDowell, J. 2013. "The Myth of the Mind as Detached." In *Mind, Reason, and Being in the World: The McDowell-Dreyfus Debate*, edited by J. K. Schear, 41–58. London: Routledge.

McGuinness, B. 1988. *Wittgenstein: A Life. Young Wittgenstein 1889–1921*. Berkeley: University of California Press.

McHugh, J. 2003. "Why A.I. Is Brain-Dead." *Wired*. https://www.wired.com/2003/08/why-a-i-is-brain-dead.

McIntosh, R. D., and T. Schenk. 2009. "Two Visual Systems for Perception and Action: Current Trends." *Neuropsychologia* 47, no. 6: 1391–96. https://doi.org/10.1016/j.neuropsychologia.2009.02.009.

McTavish, D. G. 1971. "Perceptions of Old People: A Review of Research Methodologies and Findings." *Gerontologist* 11, no. 4: 90–102. https://doi.org/10.1093/geront/11.4_Part_2.90.

Meehl, P. E. 1967. "Theory Testing in Psychology and Physics: A Methodological Paradox." *Philosophy of Science* 34, no. 2: 103–15. https://doi.org/10.1086/288135.

Meehl, P. E. 1978. "Theoretical Risks and Tabular Asterisks: Sir Karl, Sir Ronald, and the Slow Progress of Soft Psychology." *Journal of Consulting and Clinical Psychology* 46, no. 4: 806–34. https://doi.org/10.1037/0022-006X.46.4.806.

Meehl, P. E. 1990a. "Why Summaries of Research on Psychological Theories Are Often Uninterpretable." *Psychological Reports* 66, no. 1: 195–244. https://doi.org/10.2466/PR0.66.1.195-244.

Meehl, P. E. 1990b. "Appraising and Amending Theories: The Strategy of Lakatosian Defense and Two Principles That Warrant It." *Psychological Inquiry* 1: 108–41. https://doi.org/10.1207/s15327965pli0102_1.

Meehl, P. E. 1992. "Philosophy of Science: Help or Hindrance?" *Psychological Reports* 72, no. 3: 707–33. https://doi.org/10.2466/pr0.1993.72.3.707.

Mele, A. R. 1997. "Agency and Mental Action." *Philosophical Perspectives* 11: 231–49. https://doi.org/10.1111/0029-4624.31.s11.11.

Mele, A. R. 2009. *Effective Intentions: The Power of Conscious Will*. Oxford: Oxford University Press.

Melnikoff, D. E., and J. A. Bargh. 2018a. "The Mythical Number Two." *Trends in Cognitive Sciences* 22, no. 4: 280–93. https://doi.org/10.1016/j.tics.2018.02.001.

Melnikoff, D. E., and J. A. Bargh. 2018b. "The Insidious Number Two." *Trends in Cognitive Science* 22, no. 8: 668–69. https://doi.org/10.1016/j.tics.2018.05.005.

Melnikoff, D. E., J. A. Bargh, and W. Wood. 2021. "Editorial: On the Nature and Scope of Habits and Model-Free Control." *Frontiers in Psychology* 12: 1–6. https://doi.org/10.3389/fpsyg.2021.760841.

Meltzoff, A. N., and M. K. Moore. 1977. "Imitation of Facial and Manual Gestures by Human Neonates." *Science* 198: 75–78. https://doi.org/10.1126/science.198.4312.75.

Meltzoff, A. N., and M. K. Moore. 1983. "Newborn Infants Imitate Adult Facial Gestures." *Child Development* 54, no. 3: 702–9. https://doi.org/10.2307/1130058.

Meltzoff, A. N., and M. K. Moore. 2002. *The Imitative Mind: Development, Evolution, and Brain Bases*. Cambridge: Cambridge University Press.

Mercier, H., and D. Sperber. 2011. "Why Do Humans Reason? Arguments for an Argumentative Theory." *Behavioral and Brain Sciences* 34, no. 2: 57–74. https://doi.org/10.1017/S0140525X10000968.

Messenger, K. 2021. "The Persistence of Priming: Exploring Long-Lasting Syntactic Priming Effects in Children and Adults." *Cognitive Science* 45: e13005. https://doi.org/10.1111/cogs.13005.

Michaels, W. B. 2016a. "'I Do What Happens': Anscombe and Winogrand." *Nonsite.org* 19.

Michaels, W. B. 2016b. "Anscombe and Winogrand, Danto and Mapplethorpe: A Reply to Dominic McIver Lopes." *Nonsite.org* 19.

Michaels, W. B. 2019. "Blind Time (Drawing with Anscombe)." *REAL: Yearbook of Research in English and American Literature* 35: 49–60.

Michaels, W. B. 2020. "Eyes Wide Shut: Anscombe/Action/Art." *Nonsite.org* 32. https://nonsite.org/eyes-wide-shut-anscombe-action-art/.

Michaels, W. B. 2022. "What One Does: Rainer/Aristotle/Welling." *Nonsite.org* 38. https://nonsite.org/what-one-does-rainer-aristotle-welling/.

Milgram, S. 1974. *Obedience to Authority: An Experimental View*. London: Tavistock.

Miller, G. A. 1956. "The Magical Number Seven, Plus or Minus Two: Some Limits on Our Capacity for Processing Information." *Psychological Review* 63, no. 2: 81–97. https://doi.org/10.1037/h0043158.

Miller, G. A. 1962. *Psychology: The Science of Mental Life*. New York: Harper and Row.

Miller, G. A., E. Galanter, and K. H. Pribram. 1960. *Plans and the Structure of Behavior*. New York: Holt, Rinehart and Winston, Inc.

Mindell, D. A. 2002. *Between Human and Machine: Feedback, Control, and Computing before Cybernetics*. Baltimore, MD: Johns Hopkins University Press.

Mirowski, P. 2018. "The Future(s) of Open Science." *Social Studies of Science* 48, no. 2: 171–203. https://doi.org/10.1177/0306312718772086.

Mischel, W. 1968. *Personality and Assessment*. New York: Wiley.

Mischel, W. 1969. "Continuity and Change in Personality." *American Psychologist* 24: 1012–18. https://doi.org/10.1037/h0028886.

Mischel, W. 1971. *Introduction to Personality*. New York: Holt, Rinehart and Winston.

Mischel, W. 1997. "Was the Cognitive Revolution Just a Detour on the Road to Behaviorism? On the Need to Reconcile Situational Control and Personal Control." In *The Automaticity of Everyday Life*, edited by R. S. Wyer Jr., 181–86. Mahwah, NJ: Lawrence Erlbaum Associates.

Molden, D. C. 2014a. "Understanding Priming Effects in Social Psychology: What Is 'Social Priming' and How Does It Occur?" *Social Cognition* 32:1–11. https://doi.org/10.1521/soco.2014.32.supp.1.

Molden, D. C. 2014b. "Understanding Priming Effects in Social Psychology: An Overview and Integration." *Social Cognition* 32: 243–49. https://doi.org/10.1521/soco.2014.32.supp.243.

Molden, D. C., ed. 2014c. *Understanding Priming Effects in Social Psychology*. New York: Guilford Press.

Mole, C. 2009. "Attention." *The Stanford Encyclopedia of Philosophy* (Winter 2021), edited by E. N. Zalta. https://plato.stanford.edu/archives/win2021/entries/attention/.

Monsell, S. 1996. "Control of Mental Processes." In *Unsolved Mysteries of the Mind: Tutorial Essays in Cognition*, edited by V. Bruce, 93–148. Hove, East Sussex, UK: Lawrence Erlbaum Associates.

Montero, B. 2010. "Does Bodily Awareness Interfere with Highly Skilled Movement?" *Inquiry: An Interdisciplinary Journal of Philosophy* 53, no. 2: 105–22. https://doi.org/10.1080/00201741003612138.

Montero, B. 2013. "A Dancer Reflects." In *Mind, Reason, and Being-in-the-World: The McDowell-Dreyfus Debate*, edited by J. K. Schear, 303–19. London: Routledge.

Moors, A. 2014. "Examining the Mapping Problem in Dual Process Models." In *Dual Process Theories of the Social Mind*, edited by J. W. Sherman, B. Gawronski, and Y. Trope, 20–34. New York: Guilford Press.

Moors, A., and J. De Houwer. 2006. "Automaticity: A Theoretical and Conceptual Analysis." *Psychological Bulletin* 132, no. 2: 297–326. https://doi.org/10.1037/0033-2909.132.2.297.

Moors, A., and J. De Houwer, J. 2007. "What Is Automaticity? An Analysis of Its Component Features and Their Interrelations." In *Social Psychology and the Unconscious: The Automaticity of Higher Mental Processes*, edited by J. A. Bargh, 11–50. New York: Psychology.

Morawski, J. 2015. "Epistemological Dizziness in the Psychology Laboratory: Lively Subjects, Anxious Experimenters, and Experimental Relations, 1950–1970." *Isis* 106, no. 3: 567–97. https://doi.org/10.1086/683411.

Morawski, J. 2019. "The Replication Crisis: How Might Philosophy and Theory of Psychology Be of Use?" *Journal of Theoretical and Philosophical Psychology* 39, no. 4: 218–38. https://doi.org/10.1037/teo0000129.

Morawski, J. 2020. "Psychologists' Psychologies of Psychologists in a Time of Crisis." *History of Psychology* 23, no. 2: 176–98. https://doi.org/10.1037/hop0000140.

Morawski, J. 2022. "How to True Psychology's Objects." *Review of General Psychology* 26, no. 2: 157–71. https://doi.org/10.1177/10892680211046518.

Morsella, E., T. C. Dennehy, and J. A. Bargh. 2013. "Voluntary Action and the Three Forms of Binding in the Brain." In *Decomposing the Will*, edited by A. Clark, J. Kiverstein, and T. Vierkant, 183–98. Oxford: Oxford University Press. https://doi.org/10.1093/acprof:oso/9780199746996.003.0010.

Motley, M. M. 1985. "Slips of the Tongue." *Scientific American* 25, no. 3: 116–27. https://doi.org/10.1038/scientificamerican0985-116.

Motyl, M., A. P. Demos, T. S. Carsel, B. E. Hanson, Z. J. Melton, A. B. Muller, and J. P. Prims et al. 2017. "The State of Social and Personality Science: Rotten to the Core, Not So Bad, Getting Better, or Getting Worse?" *Journal of Personality and Social Psychology* 113, no. 1: 34–58. https://doi.org/10.1037/pspa0000084.

Moutsopoulou, K., C. Pfeuffer, A. Kiesel, Q. Yang, and F. Waszak. 2019. "How Long Is Long-Term Priming? Classification and Action Priming in the Scale of Days." *Quarterly Journal of Experimental Psychology* 72, no. 5: 1183–99. https://doi.org/10.1177/1747021818784261.

Muscovi, S. 1989. "Preconditions for Explanation in Social Psychology." *European Journal of Social Psychology* 19, no. 5: 407–30.

Nahmias, E. 2014. "Is Free Will an Illusion? Confronting Challenges from the Modern Mind Sciences." In *Moral Psychology: Free Will and Moral Responsibility*, vol. 4, edited by W. Sinnott-Armstrong, 1–25. Cambridge, MA: MIT Press. https://doi.org/10.7551/mitpress/9780262026680.003.0002.

Nahmias, E. 2017. "The Dark Side of Mimicry: Comments on Duffy and Chartrand." In *Moral Psychology, Virtue and Character*, vol. 5, edited by W. Simmott-Armstrong and C. Miller, 477–87. Cambridge, MA: MIT Press.

Navarro, D. J. September 2020. "Paths in Strange Places: A Comment on Preregistration." *PsyArXiv*. https://doi.org/10.31234/osf.io/wxn58.

Nehaniv, C. L., and K. Dautenhahn. 2002. "The Correspondence Problem." In *Imitation in Animals and Artifacts*, edited by K. Dautenhahn and C. L. Nehaniv, 41–61. Cambridge, MA: MIT Press. https://doi.org/10.7551/mitpress/3676.001.0001.

Neisser, U. 1967. *Cognitive Psychology*. Englewood Cliffs, NJ: Prentice-Hall, Inc.

Nelson, L. D., J. P. Simmons, and U. Simonsohn. 2018. "Psychology's Renaissance." *Annual Review of Psychology* 69: 511–34. https://doi.org/10.1146/annurev-psych-122216-011836.

Nelson, N. C., J. Chung, K. Ichikawa, and M. M. Malik. 2022. "Psychology Exceptionalism and the Multiple Discovery of the Replication Crisis." *Review of General Psychology* 26, no. 2: 184–98. https://doi.org/10.1177/10892680211046508.

Neumann, R., and F. Strack. 2000. "'Mood Contagion': The Automatic Transfer of Mood Between Persons." *Journal of Personality and Social Psychology* 79, no. 2: 211–23. https://doi.org/10.1037/0022-3514.79.2.211.

Newell, B. R., and T. Rakow. 2011. "Revising Beliefs about the Merit of Unconscious Thought: Evidence in Favor of the Null Hypothesis." *Social Cognition* 29, no. 6: 711–26. https://doi.org/10.1521/soco.2011.29.6.711.

Newell, B. R., and D. R. Shanks. 2014a. "Unconscious Influences on Decision Making: A Critical Review." *Behavioral and Brain Sciences* 37, no. 1: 1–61, with peer commentary. https://doi.org/10.1017/S0140525X12003214.

Newell, B. R., and D. R. Shanks. 2014b. "Prime Numbers: Anchoring and Its Implications for Theories of Behavior Priming." *Social Cognition* 32: 88–108. https://doi.org/10.1521/soco.2014.32.supp.88.

Newell, B. R., K. Y. Wong, and J. C. Cheung. 2009. "Think, Blink, or Sleep on It? The Impact of Modes of Thought on Complex Decision Making." *Quarterly Journal of Experimental Psychology* 62, no. 4: 707–32. https://doi.org/10.1080/17470210802215202.

Newstead, S. E. 2000. "Are There Two Different Types of Thinking?" *Behavioral and Brain Sciences* 23: 690–91. https://doi.org/10.1017/S0140525X0049343X.

Nielsen, T. I. 1963. "Volition: A New Experimental Approach." *Scandinavian Journal of Psychology* 4: 225–30.

Nisbett, R. E., C. Caputo, P. Legant, and J. Maracek. 1973. "Behavior as Seen by the Actor and as Seen by the Observer." *Journal of Personality and Social Psychology* 27, no. 2: 154–64. https://doi.org/10.1037/h0034779.

Nisbett, R. E., and L. Ross. 1980. *Human Inference: Strategies and Shortcomings of Social Judgment*. Englewood Cliffs, NJ: Prentice-Hall, Inc.

Nisbett, R. E., and T. D. Wilson. 1977. "Telling More Than We Can Know: Verbal Reports of Mental Processes." *Psychological Review* 84, no. 1: 231–59. https://doi.org/10.1037/0033-295X.84.3.231.

Noah, T., T. Schul, and R. Mayo. 2018. "When Both the Original Study and Its Failed Replication Are Correct: Feeling Observed Eliminates the Facial Feedback Effect." *Journal of Personality and Social Psychology* 114, no. 5: 657–64. https://doi.org/10.1037/pspa0000121.

Nordgren, L. F., and A. Dijksterhuis. 2011. "Introduction: Still Thinking Different." *Social Cognition* 29, no. 6: 625–28. https://doi.org/10.1521/soco.2011.29.6.625.

Norenzayan, A., and N. Schwarz. 1999. "Telling What They Want to Know: Participants Tailor Causal Attributions to Researchers' Interests." *European Journal of Social Psychology* 29: 1011–20. https://doi.org/10.1002/(SICI)1099-0992(199912)29:8<1011::AID-EJSP974>3.0.CO;2-A.

Norman, D. A. 1981. "Categorization of Action Slips." *Psychological Review* 88, no. 1: 1–15. https://doi.org/10.1037/0033-295X.88.1.1.

Norman, D. A., and T. Shallice. 1986. "Attention to Action: Willed and Automatic Control of Behavior." In *Consciousness and Self-Regulation*, edited by R. Davidson, G. Schwartz, and D. Shapiro, 1–18. New York: Plenum.

Nosek, B. A., G. Alter, G. C. Banks, D. Borsboom, S. D. Bowman, S. J. Breckler, and S. Buck et al. 2015. "Promoting an Open Research Culture: Author Guidelines for Journals Could Help to Promote Transparency, Openness, and Reproducibility." *Science* 348, no. 6242: 1422–25. https://doi.org/10.1126/science.aab2374.

Nosek, B. A., T. E. Hardwicke, H. Moshontz, A. Allard, K. S. Corker, A. Dreber, and F. Fidler et al. 2022. "Replicability, Robustness, and Reproducibility in Psychological Science." *Annual Review of Psychology* 73: 719–48. https://doi.org/10.1146/annurev-psych-020821-114157.

Nuttin, J. M., Jr. 1989. "Proposal for a Heuristic Quasi-Social Analysis of Social Behavior: The Case of Harlow's 'Nature of Love.'" *European Journal of Social Psychology* 19, no. 5: 371–83. https://doi.org/10.1002/ejsp.2420190505.

O'Connor, T. 2003. "Agent Causation." In *Free Will*, edited by G. Wilson, 257–84. Oxford: Oxford University Press.

O'Donnell, M., L. N. Nelson, E. Ackerman, B. Aczel, A. Akhtar, S. Aldrovandi, and N. Alshaif et al. 2018. "Registered Replication Report: Dijksterhuis and van Knippenberg (1998)." *Perspectives on Psychological Science* 13, no. 2: 268–94. https://doi.org/10.1177/1745691618755704.

Open Science Collaboration. 2015. "An Open, Large Scale, Collaborative Effort to Estimate the Reproducibility of Psychological Science." *Perspectives on Psychological Science* 7, no. 6: 657–60. https://journals.sagepub.com/doi/epub/10.1177/1745691612462588.

Orben, A., and D. Lakens. 2020. "Crud (Re)Defined." *Advances in Methods and Practices in Psychological Science* 3, no. 2: 238–47. https://doi.org/10.1177/2515245920917961.

Orne, M. 1962. "On the Social Psychology of the Psychological Experiment: With Particular Reference to Demand Characteristics and their Implications." *American Psychologist* 17: 776–83. https://doi.org/10.1037/h0043424.

Orne, M. 1980. "On the Construct of Hypnosis." In *Handbook of Hypnosis and Psychosomatic Medicine*, edited by G. D. Burrows and L. Dennerstein, 29–51. Amsterdam: Elsevier Press.

Orne, M. 2009. "Demand Characteristics and the Concept of Quasi-Controls." In *Artifacts in Behavioral Research*, edited by R. Rosenthal and R. L. Rosnow, 110–37. Oxford: Oxford University Press.

Osman, M. 2004. "An Evaluation of Dual-Process Theories of Reasoning." *Psychonomic Bulletin and Review* 11, no. 6: 988–1010. https://doi.org/10.3758/bf03196730.

Osman, M. 2013. "A Case Study: Dual-Process Theories of Higher Cognition—Commentary on Evans and Stanovich (2013)." *Perspectives on Psychological Science* 8, no. 3: 248–52. https://doi.org/10.1 77/1745691613483475.

Palermo, C. 2014. "Automatism." *Critical Inquiry* 41: 167–77.

Palermo, D. S. 1971. "Is a Scientific Revolution Taking Place in Psychology ?" *Science Studies* 1, no. 2: 135–55. https://doi.org/10.1177/030631277100100202.

Parkinson, B. 2005. "Do Facial Movements Express Emotions or Communicate Motives?" *Personality and Social Psychology Review* 9, no. 4: 278–311. https://doi.org/10.1207/s15327957pspr0904_1.

Parkinson. B. 2011. "Interpersonal Emotional Transfer: Contagion and Social Appraisal." *Social and Personality Psychology Compass* 5, no. 5: 428–39. https://doi.org/10.1111/j.1751-9004.2011.00365.x.

Parkinson, B., A. H. Fischer, and A. S. R. Manstead, eds. 2005. *Emotion in Social Relations: Cultural, Group, and Interpersonal Processes*. New York: Psychology Press.

Parkinson, B., and G. Simons. 2012. "Worry Spreads: Interpersonal Transfer of Problem-Related Anxiety." *Cognition and Emotion* 26, no. 3: 462–79. https://doi.org/10.1080/02699931.2011.651101.

Pashler, H., N. Coburn, and C. R. Harris. 2012. "Priming of Social Distance? Failure to Replicate Effects on Social and Food Judgments." *PloS ONE* 7, no. 8: e42510. https://doi.org/10.1371/journal.pone.0042510.

Pashler, H., and C. R. Harris. 2012. "Is the Replicability Crisis Overblown? Three Arguments Examined." *Perspectives on Psychological Science* 7, no. 6: 531–36. https://doi.org/10.1177/1745691612463401.

Pashler, H., C. Harris, and N. Coburn. 2011. "Elderly Related Words Prime Slow Walking (#15)." *Psych File Drawer*. Archived at https://web.archive.org/web/20170118054159/http://www.psychfiledrawer.org/replication.php?attempt=MTU%3D.

Pashler, H., D. Rohrer, and C. R. Harris. 2013. "Can the Goal of Honesty Be Primed?" *Journal of Experimental Social Psychology* 49: 959–64. https://doi.org/10.1016/j.jesp.2013.05.011.

Payne, B. K., J. L. Brown-Iannuzzi, and C. Loersch. 2016. "Replicable Effects of Primes on Human Behavior." *Journal of Experimental Psychology: General* 145, no. 10: 1269–79. https://doi.org/10.1037/xge0000201.

Payne, J. W., A. Samper, J. R. Bettman, and M. F. Luce. 2008. "Boundary Conditions on Unconscious Thought in Complex Decision Making." *Psychological Science* 19, no. 11: 1118–23. https://doi.org/10.1111/j.1467-9280.2008.02212.x.

Pennycook, G., W. De Neys, J. St. B. T. Evans, K. E. Stanovich, and V. A. Thompson. 2018. "The Mythical Dual-Process Typology." *Trends in Cognitive Sciences* 22, no. 8: 667–68. https://doi.org/10.1016/j.tics.2018.04.008.

Pentland, A. 2008. *Honest Signals: How They Shape Our World*. Cambridge, MA: MIT Press.

Perdue, C. W., and M. B. Gurtman. 1990. "Evidence for the Automaticity of Ageism." *Journal of Experimental Social Psychology* 26, no. 3: 199–216. https://doi.org/10.1016/0022-1031(90)90035-K.

Peters, R. S. 1958. *The Concept of Motivation*. London: Routledge and Kegan Paul.

Pockett, S., W. P. Banks, and S. Gallagher, eds. 2006. *Does Consciousness Cause Behavior?* Cambridge, MA: MIT Press.

Ponari, M., M. Conson, N. P. D'Amico, D. Grossi, and L. Trojano. 2012. "Mapping Correspondence between Facial Mimicry and Emotion Recognition in Healthy Subjects." *Emotion* 12, no. 6: 1398–403. https://doi.org/10.1037/a0028588.

Posner, M. I., and C. R. R. Snyder. 1975. "Attention and Cognitive Control." In *Information Processing and Cognition: The Loyola Symposium*, edited by R. L. Solso, 55–85. Hillsdale, NJ: Lawrence Erlbaum Associates.

Posnock, R. 2016. "Review of R. Felski, *The Limits of Critique*." *ALH Online Review* 6: 1–4.

Prinz, W. 1987. "Ideomotor Action." In *Perspectives on Perception and Action*, edited by H. Heuer and A. F. Sanders, 47–73. Hillsdale, NJ: Lawrence Erlbaum Associates.

Prinz, W. 1990. "A Common Coding Approach to Perception and Action." In *Relationships Between Perception and Action*, edited by O. Neumann and W. Prinz, 167–201. Berlin: Springer-Verlag.

Prinz, W. 1997a. "Explaining Voluntary Action: The Role of Mental Content." In *Mindscapes: Philosophy, Science, and the Mind*, edited by Martin Carrier and Peter K. Machamer, 153–75. Pittsburgh, PA: University of Pittsburgh Press.

Prinz, W. 1997b. "Perception and Action Planning." *European Journal of Cognitive Psychology* 9, no. 2: 129–54.

Prinz, W. 2002. "Experimental Approaches to Imitation." In *The Imitative Mind: Development, Evolution, and Brain Bases*, edited by Andrew N. Meltzoff and W. Prinz, 143–62. Cambridge: Cambridge University Press.

Prinz, W. 2005. "An Ideomotor Approach to Imitation." In *Perspectives on Imitation: From Neuroscience to Social Science. Vol. 1. Mechanisms of Imitation and Imitations in Animals*, edited by S. Hurley and N. Chater, 141–56. Cambridge, MA: MIT Press.

Proulx, T., and R. D. Morey. 2021. "Beyond Statistical Ritual: Theory in Psychological Science." *Perspectives on Psychological Science* 16, no. 4: 671–81. https://doi.org/10.1177/17456916211017098.

Ramanathan, S., and A. L. McGill. 2007. "Consuming with Others: Social Influences on Moment-to-Moment and Retrospective Evaluations of Experience." *Journal of Consumer Research* 34, no. 4: 506–24. https://doi.org/10.1086/520074.

Ramscar, M. 2016. "Learning and the Replicability of Priming Effects." *Current Opinion in Psychology* 12: 80–84. https://doi.org/10.1016/j.copsyc.2016.07.001.

Ramscar, M., P. Hendrix, B. Love, and H. Baayen. 2013. "Learning Is Not Decline: The Mental Lexicon Is a Window into Cognition across the Lifespan." *Mental Lexicon* 8, no. 3: 450–81. https://doi.org/10.1075/ml.8.3.08ram.

Ramscar, M., C. Shaoul, and R. H. Baayen. 2015. "Why Many Priming Results Don't (and Won't) Replicate: A Quantitative Analysis." Working paper. Eberhard Karls University, Germany. https://www.sfs.uni-tuebingen.de/~mramscar/papers/Ramscar-Shaoul-Baayen_replication.pdf.

Reason, J. T. 1984. "Lapses of Attention in Everyday Life." In *Varieties of Attention*, edited by R. Parasuraman and R. D. Davies, 515–49. Orlando, FL: Academic Press.

Reason, J. T., and K. Mycielska. 1982. *Absentminded? The Psychology of Mental Lapses and Everyday Errors*. Englewood Cliffs, NJ: Prentice-Hall.

Regan, J. E. 1981. "Automaticity and Learning: Effects of Familiarity on Naming Letters." *Journal of Experimental Psychology: Human Perception and Performance* 7: 180–95.

Rid, T. 2016. *Rise of the Machines: A Cybernetic History*. New York: W. W. Norton.

Rijsman, J., and W. Stroebe. 1989. "The Two Psychologies, or Whatever Happened to the Crisis?" *European Journal of Social Psychology* 19, no. 5: 339–343. https://doi.org/10.1002/ejsp.2420190502.

Rindzevičiūtė, E. 2016. *The Power of Systems: How Policy Sciences Opened Up the Cold War World*. Ithaca, NY: Cornell University Press.

Ritchie, S. 2020. *Science Fictions: How Fraud, Bias, Negligence, and Hype Undermine the Search for Truth*. New York: Henry Holt and Company.

Robbins, B. 2017. "Not So Well Attached." *Proceedings of the Modern Language Association* 132, no. 2: 371–76.

Rödl, S. 2016. "Education and Autonomy." *Journal of the Philosophy of Education* 50, no. 1: 84–97.

Roessler, J., and N. Eilan. 2003. *Agency and Self-Awareness: Issues in Philosophy and Psychology*. Oxford: Clarendon Press.

Rosenthal, R. 1963. "On the Social Psychology of the Psychological Experiment: The Experimenter's Hypothesis as Unintended Determinant of Experimental Results." *American Scientist* 51, no. 2: 268–83.

Rosenthal, R. 1966. *Experimenter Effects in Behavioral Research*. New York: Appleton-Century-Crofts.

Rosenthal, R., and R. L. Rosnow, eds. 2009 (1969). *Artifacts in Behavioral Research*. Oxford: Oxford University Press.

Rosenthal, R., and D. B. Rubin. 1978. "Interpersonal Expectancy Effects: The First 345 Studies." *Behavioral and Brain Sciences* 1, no. 3: 377–415. https://doi.org/10.1017/S0140525X00075506.

Ross, L. 1977. "The Intuitive Psychologist and His Shortcomings: Distortions in the Attribution Process." *Advances in Experimental Psychology* 10: 173–220. https://doi.org/10.1016/S0065-2601(08)60357-3.

Rossetti, Y., L. Pisella, and R. D. McIntosh. 2017. "Rise and Fall of the Two Visual Systems Theory." *Annals of Physical and Rehabilitation Medicine* 60, no. 3: 148–54. https://doi.org/10.1016/j.rehab.2017.02.002.

Rotella, A., A. M. Sparks, S. Mishra, and P. Barclay. 2021. "No Effect of 'Watching Eyes': An Attempted Replication and Extension Investigating Individual Differences." *PloS ONE* 16, no. 10: e0255531. https://doi.org/10.1371/journal.pone.0255531.

Russell, J. A., and J. M. Fernández-Dols, eds. 1997. *The Psychology of Facial Expression*. Cambridge: Cambridge University Press.

Rychlak, J. F. 1990. "Is a Levels Model of Intention Just Another Mixed Model?" *Psychological Inquiry* 1, no. 3: 265–67. https://doi.org/10.1207/s15327965pli0103_20.

Rychlowska, M., E. Cañadas, A. Wood, E. G. Krumhuber, A. Fischer, and P. M. Niedenthal. 2014. "Blocking Mimicry Makes True and False Smiles Look the Same." *PloS ONE* 9, no. 3: e90876. https://doi.org/10.1371/journal.pone.0090876.

Ryle, G. 1949. *The Concept of Mind*. London: Hutchinson's Universal Library.

Sabini, J., M. Siepmann, and J. Stein. 2001. "The Really Fundamental Attribution Error in Social Psychological Research." *Psychological Inquiry* 12, no. 1: 1–15. https://doi.org/10.1207/S15327965PLI1201_01.

Sabini, J., and M. Silver. 1980. "Baseball and Hot Sauce: A Critique of Some Attributional Treatments of Evaluation." *Journal of the Theory of Social Behaviour* 10, no. 2: 83–95. https://doi.org/10.1111/j.1468-5914.1980.tb00008.x.

Sabini, J., and M. Silver. 1981a. "Introspection and Causal Accounts." *Journal of Personality and Social Psychology* 40, no. 1: 171–79. https://doi.org/10.1037/0022-3514.40.1.171.

Sabini, J., and M. Silver. 1981b. "Evaluations in Commonsense Thought: A Reply to Weary and Harvey." *Journal for the Theory of Social Behaviour* 11, no. 1: 99–106. https://doi.org/10.1111/j.1468-5914.1981.tb00026.x.

Sabini, J., and M. Silver. 1983. "Dispositional vs. Situational Interpretations of Milgram's Obedience Experiments: 'The Fundamental Attribution Error.'" *Journal for the Theory of Social Behaviour* 13, no. 2: 147–54. https://doi.org/10.1111/j.1468-5914.1983.tb00468.x.

Sabini, J., and M. Silver. 2005. "Lack of Character? Situationism Critiqued." *Ethics* 115, no. 3: 535–62. https://doi.org/10.1086/428459.

Saling, L. L., and J. G. Phillips. 2007. "Automatic Behaviour: Efficient Not Mindless." *Brain Research Bulletin* 73, nos. 1–3: 1–20. https://doi.org/10.1016/j.brainresbull.2007.02.009.

Sarbin, T. R. 1950. "Contributions to Role-Taking Theory: I. Hypnotic Behavior." *Psychological Review* 57, no. 5: 255–70. https://doi.org/10.1037/h0062218.

Sarbin, T. R., and W. C. Coe. 1972. *Hypnosis: A Social Psychological Analysis of Influence Communication*. New York: Holt, Rinehart and Winston.

Satiya, K. 2018. "Intention." In *The Stanford Encyclopedia of Philosophy* (Fall 2018), edited by E. N. Zalta. https://plato.stanford.edu/archives/fall2018/entries/intention/.

Schafmeister, F. 2021. "The Effect of Replications on Citation Patterns: Evidence from a Large-Scale Reproducibility Project." *Psychological Science* 32, no. 10: 1537–48. https://doi.org/10.1177/09567976211005767.

Schear, J. K., ed. 2013. *Mind, Reason, and Being-in-the-World: The McDowell-Dreyfus Debate*. London: Routledge.

Scheel, A. M., L. Tiokhin, P. M. Isager, and D. Lakens. 2021. "Why Hypothesis Testers Should Spend Less Time Testing Hypotheses." *Perspectives on Psychological Science* 16, no. 4: 744–55. https://doi.org/10.1177/1745691620966795.

Schenkler, B. R. 1974. "Social Psychology and Science." *Journal of Personality and Social Psychology* 29, no. 1: 1–15. https://doi.org/10.1037/h0035668.

Schimmack, U. 2012. "The Ironic Effect of Significant Results on the Credibility of Multiple-Study Articles." *Psychological Methods* 17, no. 4: 551–66. https://doi.org/10.1037/a0029487.

Schimmack, U. April 18, 2016. "Replicability Report No. 1: Is Ego-Depletion a Replicable Effect?" *Replicability-Index*. https://replicationindex.com/2016/04/18/is-replicability-report-ego-depletionreplicability-report-of-165-ego-depletion-articles/.

Schimmack, U. November 28, 2017. "'Before You Know It' by John Bargh: A Quantitative Book Review." *Replicability-Index*. https://replicationindex.com/2017/11/28/before-you-know-it-by-john-a-bargh-a-quantitative-book-review/.

Schimmack, U. January 5. 2018. "Why the Journal of Personality and Social Psychology Should Retract Article DOI: 10.1037/a0021524 'Feeling the Future: Experimental Evidence for Anomalous Retroactive Influences on Cognition and Affect.'" *Replicability-Index*. https://replicationindex.com/2018/01/05/bem-retraction/.

Schimmack, U. March 17, 2019. "Replicability Audit of John A. Bargh." *Replicability-Index*. https://replicationindex.com/2019/03/17/raudit-bargh/.

Schimmack, U. December 30, 2020. "A Meta-Scientific Perspective on 'Thinking: Fast and Slow.'" *Replicability-Index*. https://replicationindex.com/2020/12/30/a-meta-scientific-perspective-on-thinking-fast-and-slow.

Schimmack, U. June 4, 2021. "Incidental Anchoring Bites the Dust." *Replicability-Index*. https://replicationindex.com/2021/06/04/incidental-anchoring-audit/.

Schimmack, U. February 13, 2022a. "False Psychology Glossary." *Replicability-Index*. https://replicationindex.com/2022/02/13/false-psychology-glossary/.

Schimmack, U. February 16, 2022b. "Unconscious Thought Theory in Decline." *Replicability-Index*. https://replicationindex.com/2022/02/16/rr22-unconscious-thought/.

Schimmack, U., M. Heene, and K. Kesavan. February 2, 2017. "Reconstruction of a Train Wreck: How Priming Research Went Off the Rails." *Replicability-Index*. https://replicationindex.com/2017/02/02/reconstruction-of-a-train-wreck-how-priming-research-went-of-the-rails/.

Schlosser, M. E. 2011. "Agency, Ownership, and the Standard Theory." In *New Waves in the Philosophy of Action*, edited by J. Aguilar, A. Buckareff, and K. Frankish, 13–31. Basingstoke: Palgrave Macmillan.

Schlosser, M. E. 2012. "Causally Efficacious Intentions and the Sense of Agency: In Defense of Real Mental Causation." *Journal of Theoretical and Philosophical Psychology* 32, no. 3: 135–60. https://doi.org/10.1037/a0027618.

Schlosser, M. E. 2019a. "Agency." In *The Stanford Encyclopedia of Philosophy* (Winter 2019), edited by E. N. Zalta. https://plato.stanford.edu/archives/win2019/entries/agency/.

Schlosser, M. E. 2019b. "Dual-System Theory and the Role of Consciousness in Intentional Action." In *Free Will, Causality, and Neuroscience*, edited by B. Feltz, M. Missal, and A. C. Sims, 35–56. Leiden: Brill. https://doi.org/10.1163/9789004409965_004.

Schmidt, S. 2009. "Shall We Really Do It Again? The Powerful Concept of Replication Is Neglected in the Social Sciences." *Review of General Psychology* 13, no. 2: 90–100. https://doi.org/10.1037/a0015108.

Schneider, W., and R. F. Shiffrin. 1977. "Controlled and Automatic Human Information Processing: I. Detection, Search, and Attention." *Psychological Review* 84, no. 1: 1–66. https://doi.org/10.1037/0033-295X.84.1.1.

Schröder, T., and P. Thagard. 2013. "The Affective Meanings of Automatic Social Behaviors: Three Mechanisms That Explain Priming." *Psychological Review* 120, no. 1: 255–80. https://doi.org/10.1037/a0030972.

Schwartz, B. 2015. "On Klatzky and Creswell (2014): Saving Social Priming Effects but Losing Science as We Know It?" *Perspectives on Psychological Science* 10, no. 3: 404–7. https://doi.org/10.1177/1745691614567717.

Schweinsberg, M., N. Madan, M. Vianello, S. A. Sommer, J. Jordan, W. Tierney, and E. Awtrey et al. 2016. "The Pipeline Project: Pre-Publication Independent Replications of a Single Laboratory's Research Pipeline." *Journal of Experimental Social Psychology* 66: 55–67. https://doi.org/10.1016/j.jesp.2015.10.001.

Schwenkler, J. 2019. *Anscombe's Intention: A Guide*. Oxford: Oxford University Press.

Schwenkler, J. 2020. "The World and the Will: On the Problem of Photographic Agency." *Nonsite.org* 32.

Schwitzgebel, E. 2019. "Introspection." In *The Stanford Encyclopedia of Philosophy* (Winter 2019), edited by E. N. Zalta. https://plato.stanford.edu/archives/win2019/entries/introspection/.

Searle, J. 1983. *Intentionality: An Essay in the Philosophy of Mind*. Cambridge: Cambridge University Press.

Searle, J. 1984. *Minds, Brains and Science*. Cambridge, MA: Harvard University Press.

Searle, J. 1992. *The Rediscovery of the Mind*. Cambridge, MA: MIT Press.

Sedgwick, E. K. 2003. *Touching Feeling: Affect, Pedagogy, Performativity*. Raleigh, NC: Duke University Press.

Segal, S. J., and C. N. Cofer. 1960. "The Effect of Recency and Recall on Word Association." *American Psychologist* 15, no. 7: 451.

Sehon, S. S. 2000. "An Argument against the Causal Theory of Action Explanation." *Philosophy and Phenomenological Research* 60, no. 1: 67–85.

Shallice, T. 1988. *From Neuropsychology to Mental Structure*. Cambridge: Cambridge University Press.

Shallice, T., and P. W. Burgess. 1993. "Supervisory Control of Action and Thought Selection." In *Attention: Selection, Awareness and Control*, edited by A. Baddeley and L. Weiskrantz, 171–87. Oxford: Oxford Clarendon Press.

Shallice, T., P. W. Burgess, F. Schon, and D. M. Baxter. 1989. "The Origins of Utilization Behavior." *Brain* 112: 1587–98.

Shanker, S. G. 1992. "In Search of Bruner." *Language and Communication* 12, no. 1: 53–74. https://doi.org/10.1016/0271-5309(92)90011-W.

Shanker, S. G. 1993. "Locating Bruner." *Language and Communication* 13, no. 4: 239–63. https://doi.org/10.1016/0271-5309(93)90029-M.

Shanker, S. G. 1998. *Wittgenstein's Remarks on the Foundations of AI*. London: Routledge.

Shanks, D. R. 2017. "Misunderstanding the Behavior Priming Controversy: Comment on Payne, Brown-Iannuzzi, and Loersch (2016)." *Journal of Experimental Psychology: General* 146, no. 8: 1216–22. https://doi.org/10.1037/xge0000307.

Shanks, D. R., B. R. Newell, E. H. Lee, D. Balakrishnan, L. Ekelund, Z. Cenac,

F. Kavvadia, and C. Moore. 2013. "Priming Intelligent Behavior: An Elusive Phenomenon." *PloS ONE* 8, no. 4: e56515. https://doi.org/10.1371/journal.pone.0056515.

Shanks, D. R., M. A. Vadillo, B. Riedel, A. Clymo, S. Govind, N. Hickin, and A. J. F. Tamman, and L. M. C. Puhlmann. 2015. "Romance, Risk, and Replication: Can Consumer Choices and Risk-Taking Be Primed by Mating Motives?" *Journal of Experimental Psychology* 144, no. 6: e142-58. https://doi.org/10.1037/xge0000116.

Shannon, C. E. 1948. "A Mathematical Theory of Communication." *Bell System Technical Journal* 27, no. 3: 379–423. https://doi.org/10.1002/j.1538-7305.1948.tb01338.x.

Shapiro, L. 2007. "The Embodied Cognition Research Programme." *Philosophy Compass* 2, no. 2: 338–46. https://doi.org/10.1111/j.1747-9991.2007.00064.x.

Shariff, A. F., and A. Norenzayan. 2007. "God Is Watching You: Priming God Concepts Increases Prosocial Behavior in an Anonymous Economic Game." *Psychological Science* 18, no. 9: 803–9. https://doi.org/10.1111/j.1467-9280.2007.01983.x.

Shariff, A. F., and A. Norenzayan. 2015. "A Question of Reliability or of Boundary Conditions? Comment on Gomes and McCullough (2015)." *Journal of Experimental Psychology: General* 144, no. 6: e105-e106. https://doi.org/10.1037/xge0000111.

Sharrock, W., and R. Read. 2002. *Kuhn: Philosopher of Scientific Revolution*. Cambridge: Polity Press.

Shevrin, H., and S. Dickman. 1980. "The Psychological Unconscious: A Necessary Assumption for All Psychological Theory?" *American Psychologist* 35, no. 5: 421–34. https://doi.org/10.1037/0003-066X.35.5.421.

Shiffrin, R. M. 1997. "Attention, Automatism, and Consciousness." In *Scientific Approaches to Consciousness*, edited by J. D. Cohen and J. W. Schooler, 49–64. Hillsdale, NJ: Lawrence Erlbaum Associates.

Shiffrin, R. M., and R. M. Nosofsky. 1994. "Seven Plus or Minus Two: A Commentary on Capacity Limitations." *Psychological Review* 101, no. 2: 357–61. https://doi.org/10.1037/0033-295X.101.2.357.

Shiffrin, R. M., and W. Schneider. 1977. "Controlled and Automatic Human Information Processing: II. Perceptual Learning, Automatic Attending, and a General Theory." *Psychological Review* 84, no. 2: 127–90. https://doi.org/10.1037/0033-295X.84.2.127.

Shin, Y. K., R. W. Proctor, and E. J. Capaldi. 2010. "A Review of Contemporary Ideomotor Theory." *Psychological Bulletin* 136: no. 6: 943–74. https://doi.org/10.1037/a0020541.

Simmons, D. 2016. "Imposter Syndrome: A Reparative History." *Engaging Science, Technology and Society* 2: 106–27.

Simons, D. J. 2014. "The Value of Direct Replication." *Perspectives on Psychological Science* 9, no. 1: 76–80. https://doi.org/10.1177/1745691613514755.

Simonsohn, U. 2013. "Just Post It: The Lesson from Two Cases of Fabricated Data Detected by Statistics Alone." *Psychological Science* 24, no. 10: 1875–88. https://doi.org/10.1177/0956797613480366.

Simonsohn, U. October 20, 2017. "'Many Labs' Overestimated the Importance of Hidden Moderators." *Data Colada* (blog). http://datacolada.org/63.

Singal, J. 2021. *The Quick Fix: Why Fad Psychology Can't Cure Our Social Ills*. New York: Farrar, Straus and Giroux.

Siraganian, L. 2019. "Distributing Agency Everywhere: TV Critiques Postcritique." *American Studies* 6, no. 4: 595–616.

Siraganian, L. 2020. *Modernism and the Meaning of Corporate Persons*. Oxford: Oxford University Press.

Siraganian, L. 2021. "Against Theory, Now with Bots! On the Persistent Fallacy of Intentionless Speech." *Nonsite.org* 36.

Skinner, B. F. 1938. *The Behavior of Organisms: An Experimental Analysis*. New York: Appleton-Century.

Smedslund, J. 2015. "Why Psychology Cannot Be an Empirical Science." *Integrative Psychological and Behavioral Science* 50: 185–95. https://doi.org/10.1007/s12124-015-9339-x.

Smith, E. R., and F. D. Miller. 1978. "Limits on Perception of Cognitive Processes: A Reply to Nisbett and Wilson." *Psychological Review* 85, no. 4: 355–62. https://doi.org/10.1037/0033-295X.85.4.355.

Smith, E. R., and G. R. Semin. 2004. "Socially Situated Cognition: Cognition in Its Social Context." In *Advances in Experimental Social Psychology*, vol. 36, edited by M. P. Zanna, 53–117. Amsterdam: Elsevier Academic Press. https://doi.org/10.1016/S0065-2601(04)36002-8.

Smith, E. R., and G. R. Semin. 2007. "Situated Social Cognition." *Current Directions in Psychological Science* 16, no. 3: 132–35. https://doi.org/10.1111/j.1467-8721.2007.00490.x.

Smith, N. H. 2013. "Rationality and Engagement: McDowell, Dreyfus, and Zidane.'" *Hegel Bulletin* 34, no. 2: 159–80.

Smith, P. K., and J. A. Bargh. 2008. "Nonconscious Effects of Power on Basic Approach and Avoidance Tendencies." *Social Cognition* 26, no. 1: 1–24. https://doi.org/10.1521/soco.2008.26.1.1.

Spanos, N. 1986. "Hypnotic Behavior: A Social-Psychological Interpretation of Amnesia, Analgesia, and 'Trance Logic.'" *Behavioral and Brain Sciences* 9, no. 3: 449–67. https://doi.org/10.1017/S0140525X00046537.

Spellman, B. A. 2015. "A Short (Personal) History of Revolution 2.0." *Perspectives on Psychological Science* 10, no. 6: 886–99. https://doi.org/10.1177/1745691615609918.

Spurrett, D., H. Ross, and L. Stephens. 2007. *Distributed Cognition and the Will*. Cambridge, MA: MIT Press.

Srivastava, S. March 3, 2016. "Evaluating a New Critique of the Reproducibility Project." *Hardest Science* (blog). https://thehardestscience.com/2016/03/03/evaluating-a-new-critique-of-the-reproducibility-project/.

Srull, T. K., and R. S. Wyer Jr. 1979. "The Role of Category Accessibility in the Interpretation of Information about Persons: Some Determinants and Implications." *Journal of Personality and Social Psychology* 37, no. 10: 1660–72. https://doi.org/10.1037/0022-3514.37.10.1660.

Srull, T. K., and R. S. Wyer Jr. 1980. "Category Accessibility and Social Perception: Some Implications for the Study of Person Memory and Interpersonal Judgments." *Journal of Personality and Social Psychology* 38, no. 6: 841–56. https://doi.org/10.1037/0022-3514.38.6.841.

Stam, H. J., H. L. Radtke, and I. Lubek. 2000. "Strains in Experimental Social Psychology: A Textual Analysis of the Development of Experimentation in Social Psychology." *Journal of the History of the Behavioral Sciences* 36, no. 4: 365–82. https://doi.org/10.1002/1520-6696(200023)36:4<365::AID-JHBS5>3.0.CO;2-S.

Stanovich, K. E., and R. F. West. 2000. "Individual Differences in Reasoning: Implications for the Rationality Debate?" *Behavioral and Brain Sciences* 23, no. 5: 645–65. https://doi.org/10.1017/s0140525x00003435.

Steele, C. M., and J. Aronson. 1995. "Stereotype Threat and the Intellectual Test Performance of African Americans." *Journal of Personality and Social Psychology* 69, no. 5: 797–811. https://doi.org/10.1037/0022-3514.69.5.797.

Steele, R. S., and J. G. Morawski. 2002. "Implicit Cognition and the Social Unconscious." *Theory and Psychology* 12, no. 1: 37–54. https://doi.org/10.1177/0959354302121003.

Stein, B. E., and M. A. Meredith. 1993. *The Merging of the Senses*. Cambridge, MA: MIT Press.

Stein, B. E., T. R. Stanford, and B. A. Rowland. 2014. "Development of Multisensory Integration from the Perspective of the Individual Neuron." *Nature Reviews Neuroscience* 15, no. 8: 520–35. https://doi.org/10.1038/nrn3742.

Stel, M., and A. van Knippenberg. 2008. "The Role of Facial Mimicry in the Recognition of Affect." *Psychological Science* 19, no. 10: 984–85. https://doi.org/10.1111/j.1467-9280.2008.02188.x.

Stiegler, B. 2016. *Automatic Society: Vol. I. The Future of Work*. Translated by D. Ross. Malden, MA: Polity Press.

Stock, A., and C. Stock. 2004. "A Short History of Ideo-Motor Action." *Psychological Research* 68, nos. 2–3: 176–88. https://doi.org/10.1007/s00426-003-0154-5.

Storms, L. H. 1958. "Apparent Backward Association: A Situational Effect."

Journal of Experimental Psychology 55, no. 4: 390–95. https://doi.org/10.1037/h0044258.

Stoutland, F. 2011. "Introduction: Anscombe's *Intention* in Context." In *Essays on Anscombe's Intention*, edited by A. Ford, J. Hornsby, and F. Stoutland, 1–32. Cambridge, MA: Harvard University Press.

Strack, D. 2017. "From Data to Truth in Psychological Science: A Personal Perspective." *Frontiers in Psychology* 8: article 702. https://doi.org/10.3389/fpsyg.2017.00702.

Strack, D., and T. Mussweiler. 1997. "Explaining the Enigmatic Anchoring Effect: Mechanisms of Selective Accessibility." *Journal of Personality and Social Psychology* 73, no. 3: 437–46. https://doi.org/10.1037/0022-3514.73.3.437.

Strack, F. 2016. "Reflections on the Smiling Registered Replication Report." *Perspectives on Psychological Science* 11, no. 6: 929–30. https://doi.org/10.1177/1745691616674460.

Strack, F., L. L. Martin, and S. Stepper. 1988. "Inhibiting and Facilitating Conditions of the Human Smile: A Non-Obtrusive Test of the Facial Feedback Hypothesis." *Journal of Personality and Social Psychology* 54, no. 5: 768–77. https://doi.org/10.1037/0022-3514.54.5.768.

Strack, F., and N. Schwarz. 2016. "Editorial Overview: Social Priming: Information Accessibility and Its Consequences." *Current Opinion in Psychology* 12: iv–vii. https://doi.org/10.1016/j.copsyc.2016.11.001.

Strack, F., and W. Stroebe. 2018. "What *Have* We Learned? What *Can* We Learn?" *Behavioral and Brain Sciences* 41: e151. https://doi.org/10.1017/S0140525X18000870.

Strick, M., A. Dijksterhuis, M. W. Bos, A. Sjoerdsma, R. van Baaren, and L. F. Nordgren. 2011. "A Meta-Analysis on Unconscious Thought Effects." *Social Cognition* 29, no. 6: 738–62. https://doi.org/10.1521/soco.2011.29.6.738.

Strickland, L., F. E. Aboud, and K. G. Gergen, eds. 1976. *Social Psychology in Transition*. New York: Springer.

Stroebe, W. 2016. "Are Most Published Social Psychological Findings False?" *Journal of Experimental Social Psychology* 66: 134–44. http://doi.org/10.1016/j.jesp.2015.09.017.

Stroebe, W., and A. W. Kruglanski. 1989. "Social Psychology at Epistemological Cross-Roads: On Gergen's Choice." *European Journal of Social Psychology* 19, no. 5: 485–89. https://doi.org/10.1002/ejsp.2420190514.

Stroebe, W., and F. Strack. 2014. "The Alleged Crisis and the Illusion of Exact Replication." *Perspectives on Psychological Science* 9, no. 1: 59–71. https://doi.org/10.1177/1745691613514450.

Stroebe, W., M. S. Stroebe, K. Gergen, and M. Gergen. 1982. "The Broken

Heart: Reality or Myth?" *OMEGA: Journal of Death and Dying* 12, no. 2: 87–106. https://doi.org/10.2190/ECNA-PE1C-KCYK-TTJ3.

Sturm, T., and A. Mülberger. 2012. "Crisis Discussions in Psychology—New Historical and Philosophical Perspectives." *Studies in History and Philosophy of Biological and Biomedical Sciences* 43, no. 2: 425–33. https://doi.org/10.1016/j.shpsc.2011.11.001.

Sutton, John. 2007. "Batting, Habit and Memory: The Embodied Mind and the Nature of Skills." *Sport in Society: Cultures, Commerce, Media, Politics* 10, no. 5: 763–86. https://doi.org/10.1080/17430430701442462.

Szollosi, A., and C. Donkin. 2021. "Arrested Theory Development: The Misguided Distinction Between Exploratory and Confirmatory Research." *Perspectives on Psychological Science* 16, no. 4: 717–24. https://doi.org/10.1177/1745691620966796.

Szollosi, A., D. Kellen, D. J. Navarro, R. Shiffrin, I. van Rooij, T. Van Zandt, and C. Donkin. 2020. "Is Preregistration Worthwhile?" *Trends in Cognitive Sciences* 24, no. 2: 94–95. https://doi.org/10.1016/j.tics.2019.11.009.

Szucs, D., and J. P. A. Ioannidis. 2017. "Empirical Assessment of Published Effect Sizes and Power in the Recent Cognitive Neuroscience and Psychological Literature." *PloS Biology* 15, no. 3, article e2000797. https://doi.org/10.1371/journal.pbio.2000797.

Tarde, G. 1903. *The Laws of Imitation*. Translated by E. C. Parsons. New York: H. Holt and Company.

Taylor, C. 1964. *The Explanation of Behaviour*. London: Routledge and Kegan Paul.

Tetlock, P. E. 2002. "Social Functionalist Frameworks for Judgment and Choice: Intuitive Politicians, Theologians, and Prosecutors." *Psychological Review* 109, no. 3: 451–71. https://doi.org/10.1037/0033-295X.109.3.451.

Thaler, R. H., and C. R. Sunstein. 2021. *Nudge: The Final Edition*. Penguin Books.

Thompson, M. 2008. *Life and Action: Elementary Structures of Practice and Practical Thought*. Cambridge, MA: Harvard University Press.

Tourangeau, R., and P. C. Ellsworth. 1979. "The Role of Facial Response in the Experience of Emotion." *Journal of Personality and Social Psychology* 37: 1519–31. https://doi.org/10.1037/0022-3514.37.9.1519.

Trafimow, D. 2017. "Commentary: Reproducibility in Psychological Science: When Do Psychological Phenomena Exist?" *Frontiers in Psychology* 8: 918. https://doi.org/10.3389/fpsyg.2017.00918.

Trafimow, D. 2018. "The Automaticity of Habitual Behaviors: Inconvenient Questions." In *The Psychology of Habit: Theory, Mechanisms, Change, and Contexts*, edited by B. Verplanken, 379–95. Heidelberg: Springer. https://doi.org/10.1007/978-3-319-97529-0_21.

Trafimow, D., and B. D. Earp. 2016. "Badly Specified Theories Are Not Responsible for the Replication Crisis in Social Psychology: Comment on Klein." *Theory and Psychology* 26, no. 4: 540–48. https://doi.org/10.1177/0959354316637136.

Tversky, A., and D. Kahneman. 1973. "Availability: A Heuristic for Judging Frequency and Probability." *Cognitive Psychology* 5, no. 2: 207–32. https://doi.org/10.1016/0010-0285(73)90033-9.

Tversky, A., and D. Kahneman. 1974. "Judgement under Uncertainty: Heuristics and Biases." *Science*, new series 185, np. 4157: 1124–31. https://doi.org/10.1126/science.185.4157.1124.

Uleman, J. S. 1999. "Spontaneous versus Intentional Inferences in Impression Formation." In *Dual Process Theories in Social Psychology*, edited by S. Chaiken and Y. Trope, 141–60. New York: Guilford Press.

Uleman, J. S. 2005. "Introduction: Becoming Aware of the New Unconscious." In *The New Unconscious*, edited by R. R. Hassin, J. S. Uleman, and J. A. Bargh, 7. New York: Oxford University Press.

Van Baaren, R. B., D. A. Fockenberg, R. W. Holland, L. Janssen, and A. van Knippenberg. 2006. "Effect of Mood on Nonconscious Mimicry." *Social Cognition* 24, no. 4: 426–37. https://doi.org/10.1521/soco.2006.24.4.426.

Van Baaren, R. B., R. W. Holland, B. Steenaert, and A. van Knippenberg. 2003a. "Mimicry for Money: Behavioral Consequences of Imitation." *Journal of Experimental Social Psychology* 39, no. 4: 393–98. https://doi.org/10.1016/S0022-1031(03)00014-3.

Van Baaren, R. B., L. Janssen, T. L. Chartrand, and A. Dijksterhuis. 2009. "Where Is the Love? The Social Aspects of Mimicry." *Philosophical Transactions of the Royal Society, B: Biological Sciences* 364: 2381–89. https://doi.org/10.1098/rstb.2009.0057.

Van Baaren, R. B., W. W. Maddux, T. L. Chartrand, C. de Bouter, and A. van Knippenberg. 2003b. "It Takes Two to Mimic: Behavioral Consequences of Self-Construals." *Journal of Personality and Social Psychology* 84, no. 5: 1093–102. https://doi.org/10.1037/0022-3514.84.5.1093.

Van Bavel, J. J., P. Mende-Siedlecki, W. J. Brady, and D. A. Reinero. 2016. "Contextual Sensitivity in Scientific Reproducibility." *Proceedings of the National Academy of Sciences* 113, no. 23: 6454–59. https://doi.org/10.1073/pnas.1521897113.

Van Langenhove, L. 2021. "Towards the Spoken World Theory: The Contribution of Rom Harré to Advancing Social Theory." *Journal for the Theory of Social Behaviour* 51, no. 2: 273–90. https://doi.org/10.1111/jtsb.12288.

Vogel, G. 2011. "Psychologist Accused of Fraud on 'Astonishing Scale.'" *Science* 334, no. 6056: 579. https://doi.org/10.1126/science.334.6056.579.

Vohs, K. D., N. L. Mead, and M. R. Goode. 2006. "The Psychological Consequences of Money." *Science* 314, no. 5802: 1154–56. https://doi.org/10.1126/science.1132491.

Vohs, K. D., B. J. Schmeichel, S. Lohmann, Q. F. Gronau, A. J. Finley, S. E. Ainsworth, and J. L. Alquist et al. 2021. "A Multisite Preregistered Paradigmatic Test of the Ego-Depletion Effect." *Psychological Science* 32, no. 10: 1566–81. https://doi.org/10.1177/0956797621989733.

Von Wright, G. H., ed. 1990. *A Portrait of Wittgenstein as a Young Man: From the Diary of David Hume Pinsent, 1912–1914*. Oxford: Basil Blackwell.

Wagenmakers, E. J., T. Beek, L. Dijkhoff, Q. F. Gronau, A. Acosta, R. B. Adams Jr., and D. N. Alboun et al. 2016. "Registered Replication Report: Strack, Martin, and Stepper (1988)." *Perspectives on Psychological Science* 11, no. 6: 917–28. https://doi.org/10.1177/1745691616674458.

Wallach, L., and M. A. Wallach. 1994. "Gergen against the Mainstream: Are Hypotheses in Social Psychology Subject to Empirical Test?" *Journal of Personality and Social Psychology* 67, no. 2: 233–42. https://doi.org/10.1037/0022-3514.67.2.233.

Wang, Y., and A. F. C. Hamilton. 2014. "Why Does Gaze Enhance Mimicry? Placing Gaze-Mimicry Effects in Relation to Other Gaze Phenomena." *Quarterly Journal of Experimental Psychology* 67, no. 4: 747–62. https://doi.org/10.1080/17470218.2013.828316.

Wang, Y., R. Newport, and A. F. C. Hamilton. 2011. "Eye Contact Enhances Mimicry of Intransitive Hand Movements." *Biological Letters* 7, no. 1: 7–10. https://doi.org/10.1098/rsbl.2010.0279.

Warren, N. 1971. "Is a Scientific Revolution Taking Place in Psychology?—Doubts and Reservations." *Science Studies* 1, nos. 3-4: 407–13. https://doi.org/10.1177/030631277100100307.

Warren, N. 1974. "Normal Science and the Normal Standards of Scholarly Debate." *Science Studies* 4, no. 2: 195–97. https://doi.org/10.1177/030631277400400207.

Warroquier, L., D. Marchiori, O. Klein, and A. Cleeremans. 2009. "Methodological Pitfalls of the Unconscious Thought Paradigm." *Judgment and Decision Making* 4, no. 7: 601–10. https://doi.org/10.1017/S1930297500001169.

Washington, N., and D. Kelly. 2014. "Should an Individual Composed of Selfish Goals Be Held Responsible for Her Actions?" *Behavioral and Brain Sciences* 37, no. 2: 158–59. https://doi.org/10.1017/S0140525X13002185.

Washington, N., and D. Kelly. 2016. "Who's Responsible for This? Moral Responsibility, Externalism, and Knowledge about Implicit Bias." In *Implicit Bias and Philosophy, Volume 2: Moral Responsibility, Structural Injustice, and Ethics*, edited by M. Brownstein and J. Saul, 10–36. Oxford: Oxford University Press.

Watson, D. 1982. "The Actor and the Observer: How Are Their Perceptions of Causality Divergent?" *Psychological Bulletin* 92, no. 3: 682–700. https://doi.org/10.1037/0033-2909.92.3.682.

Watzlawick, P., J. H. Beavin, and D. D. Jackson. 1967. *Pragmatics of Human Communication: A Study of Interactional Patterns, Pathologies, and Paradoxes*. New York: Norton.

Webel, C., and T. Stigliano. 2004. "Are We 'Beyond Good and Evil'? Radical Psychological Materialism and the 'Cure' for Evil." *Theory & Psychology* 14, no. 1: 81–103. https://doi.org/10.1177/0959354304040199.

Wegner, Daniel M. 1994. "Ironic Processes of Mental Control." *Psychological Review* 101, no. 1: 34–52. https://doi.org/10.1037%2F0033-295x.101.1.34.

Wegner, D. M. 2002. *The Illusion of Conscious Will*. Cambridge, MA: MIT Press.

Wegner, D. M., and J. A. Bargh. 1997. "Control and Automaticity in Social Life." In *The Handbook of Social Psychology*, edited by D. T. Gilbert, S. T. Fiske, and G. Lindzey, 446–96. Boston, MA: McGraw-Hill.

Wegner, D. M., and T. P. Wheatley. 1999. "Apparent Mental Causation: Sources of the Experience of Will." *American Psychologist* 54, no. 7: 480–92. https://doi.org/10.1037/0003-066X.54.7.480.

Weimer, W. B. 1974. "The History of Psychology and Its Retrieval from Historiography: 1. The Problematic Nature of History." *Science Studies* 4, no. 3: 235–58. https://doi.org/10.1177/030631277400400302.

Weimer, W. B., and D. S. Palermo. 1973. "Paradigms and Normal Science in Psychology." *Science Studies* 3, no. 3: 211–44. https://doi.org/10.1177/030631277300300301.

Weimer, W. B., and D. S. Palermo. 1974. "Standards, Scholarship, and Debate: A Rejoinder to Warren." *Science Studies* 4, no. 2: 198–200. https://doi.org/10.1177/030631277400400208.

Weingarten, E., Q. Chen, M. McAdams, J. Yi, J. Hepler, and D. Albarracin. 2016a. "On Priming Action: Conclusions from a Meta-Analysis of the Behavioral Effects of Incidentally-Presented Words." *Current Opinion in Psychology* 12: 53–57. https://doi.org/10.1016/j.copsyc.2016.04.015.

Weingarten, E., Q. Chen, M. McAdams, J. Yi, J. Hepler, and D. Albarracin. 2016b. "From Primed Concepts to Action: A Meta-Analysis of the Behavioral Effects of Incidentally Presented Words." *Psychological Bulletin* 142, no. 5: 472–97. http://dx.doi.org/10.1037/bul0000030.

Westen, D. 1999. "The Scientific Status of Unconscious Processes: Is Freud Really Dead?" *Journal of the American Psychoanalytic Association* 47, no. 4: 1061–106. https://doi.org/10.1177/000306519904700404.

Wheeler, S. C., and K. G. DeMarree. 2009. "Multiple Mechanisms of Prime-to-Behavior Effects." *Social and Personality Compass* 3, no. 4: 566–81. https://doi.org/10.1111/j.1751-9004.2009.00187.x.

Wheeler, S. C., K. G. DeMarree, and R. E. Petty. 2007. "Understanding the Role of the Self in Prime-to-Behavior Effects: The Active-Self Account." *Personality and Social Psychology Review* 11, no. 3: 234–61. https://doi.org/10.1177/1088868307302223.

Wheeler, S. C., K. G. DeMarree, and R. E. Petty. 2014. "Understanding Prime-to-Behavior Effects: Insights from the Active-Self Account." In *Understanding Priming Effects in Social Psychology*, edited by D. C. Molden, 114–28. New York: Guilford Press.

Wheeler, S. C., and R. E. Petty. 2001 "The Effects of Stereotype Activation on Behavior: A Review of Possible Mechanisms." *Psychological Bulletin* 127, no. 6: 797–826. https://doi.org/10.1037/0033-2909.127.6.797.

White, P. A. 1980. "Limitations on Verbal Reports of Internal Events: A Refutation of Nisbett and Wilson and of Bem." *Psychological Review* 87, no. 1: 105–12. https://doi.org/10.1037/0033-295X.87.1.105.

White, P. A. 1988. "Knowing More about What We Can Tell: 'Introspective Access' and Causal Report Accuracy 10 Years Later." *British Journal of Psychology* 79, no. 1: 13–45. https://doi.org/10.1111/j.2044-8295.1988.tb02271.x.

White, P. A. 1991. "Ambiguity in the Internal/External Distinction in Causal Attribution." *Journal of Experimental Social Psychology* 27, no. 3: 259–70. https://doi.org/10.1016/0022-1031(91)90015-X.

Wicker, B., C. Keysers, J. Plailly, J. P. Royet, V. Gallese, and G. Rizzolatti. 2003. "Both of Us Disgusted in *My* Insula: The Common Neural Basis of Seeing and Feeling Disgust." *Neuron* 40, no. 3: 655–64. https://doi.org/10.1016/S0896-6273(03)00679-2.

Wiener, N. 1948. *Cybernetics: Or Control and Communication in the Animal and the Machine*. Cambridge, MA: MIT Press.

Wiggins, B. J., and C. D. Christopherson. 2019. "The Replication Crisis in Psychology: An Overview for Theoretical and Philosophical Psychology." *Journal of Theoretical and Philosophical Psychology* 39, no. 4: 202–17. https://doi.org/10.1037/teo0000137.

Wilensky, R. 1983. *Planning and Understanding*. Reading, MA: Addison-Wesley.

Willard, A. K., A. F. Shariff, and A. Norenzayan. 2016. "Religious Priming as a Research Tool for Studying Religion: Evidentiary Value, Current Issues, and Future Directions." *Current Opinion in Psychology* 12: 71–75. https://doi.org/10.1016/j.copsyc.2016.06.003.

Williams, L. E., and J. A. Bargh. 2008. "Experiencing Physical Warmth Promotes Interpersonal Warmth." *Science, NS* 322, no. 5901: 606–7. https://doi.org/10.1126/science.1162548.

Wilson, G. 1989. *The Intentionality of Human Action*. Stanford, CA: Stanford University Press.

Wilson, T. D. 2002. *Strangers to Ourselves: Discovering the Adaptive Unconscious*. Cambridge, MA: Harvard University Press.

Wilson, T. D., and J. W. Schooler. 1991. "Thinking Too Much: Introspection Can Reduce the Quality of Preferences and Decisions." *Journal of Personality and Social Psychology* 60, no. 2: 181–92. https://doi.org/10.1037/0022-3514.60.2.181.

Winch, P. 2008 (1958). *The Idea of a Social Science and Its Relation to Philosophy*. London: Routledge.

Wiseman, R. 2016. *Anscombe's Intention*. London: Routledge.

Wiseman, R. 2017. "What Am I and What Am I Doing?" *Journal of Philosophy* 17, no. 1410: 536–50.

Wittgenstein, L. 1953. *Philosophical Investigations*. New York: Macmillan.

Woody, E. Z., and K. S. Bowers. 1994. "A Frontal Assault on Dissociated Control." In *Dissociation: Clinical, Theoretical and Research Perspectives*, edited by S. J. Lynn and J. W. Rhue, 52–79. New York: Guilford Press.

Woody, E., and P. Sadler. 1998. "On Reintegrating Dissociated Theories: Comment on Kirsch and Lynn (1998)." *Psychological Bulletin* 123, no. 2: 192–97. https://doi.org/10.1037/0033-2909.123.2.192.

Wu, W. 2014. *Attention*. London: Routledge.

Yong, E. January 18, 2012a. "Primed by Expectations: Why a Classic Psychology Experiment Isn't What It Seemed." *Not Exactly Rocket Science* (blog). https://www.discovermagazine.com/mind/primed-by-expectations-why-a-classic-psychology-experiment-isnt-what-it-seemed.

Yong, E. March 12, 2012b. "A Failed Replication Draws a Scathing Personal Attack from a Psychology Professor." *Not Exactly Rocket Science* (blog). https://www.nationalgeographic.com/science/article/failed-replication-bargh-psychology-study-doyen.

Yong, E. May 16, 2012c. "Replication Studies: Bad Copy." *Nature* 485, no. 7398: 298–300. https://doi.org/10.1038/485298a.

Yong, E. July 3, 2012d. "The Data Detective." *Nature* 487, no. 7405: 18–19. https://doi.org/10.1038/487018a.

Yong, E. October 3, 2012e. "Nobel Laureate Challenges Psychologists to Clean Up Their Act." *Nature*. https://doi.org/10.1038/nature.2012.11535.

Young, M. F., J. M. Kulikowich, and S. A. Barab. 1997. "The Unit of Analysis for Situated Assessment." *Instructional Science* 25, no. 2: 133–50.

Zajonc, R. B. 1980. "Feeling and Thinking: Preferences Need No Inferences." *American Psychologist* 35, no. 2: 151–75. https://doi.org/10.1037/0003-066X.35.2.151.

Zajonc, R. B. 1989. "Styles of Explanation in Social Psychology." *European Journal of Social Psychology* 19, no. 5: 345–68. https://doi.org/10.1002/ejsp.2420190503.

Zammito, J. 2004. *A Nice Derangement: Post-Positivism from Quine to Latour.* Chicago: University of Chicago Press.

Zbrodoff, N. J., and G. D. Logan. 1986. "On the Autonomy of Mental Processes: A Case Study of Arithmetic." *Journal of Experimental Psychology: General* 115, no. 2: 118–30. https://doi.org/10.1037/0096-3445.115.2.118.

Zwaan, R. A., A. Etz, R. E. Lucas, and M. B. Donnellan. 2018. "Making Replication Mainstream." *Behavioral and Brain Sciences* 41: e120. https://doi.org/10.1017/S0140525X1700.

Index

Aarts, H., 176, 178, 230
Abelson, Robert, 106
Ackerman, 2010, 175n7
action, intention in relation to, 26–28, 79–80, 89. *See also* skilled actions
action slips, 29–30, 278–79, 324–25
actions of the will, 21
Active-Self, 243
adaptation: automaticity and, 143, 158–59, 167–68, 171; mimicry and, 167–68, 171, 182; priming research and, 219; the unconscious and, 30, 61, 160, 204–5, 304–5, 307
agency: automaticity in relation to, 5, 20–23; cognitive psychology and, 225–27; conceptions and theories of, 88–89, 138–39; and the problem of the disappearing agent, 86; rejection of, 138–39; of subjects in experiments, 75n. *See also* agent causation; intention/intentionality; moral responsibility
agent causation, 83–89
AI. *See* artificial intelligence

Alda, Alan, 202–3
Allen, Woody, *Zelig*, 165
American Psychological Association, 240
analysis of variance (ANOVA), 51–52, 52n
anchoring effects, 249–50, 249n, 250n
Anscombe, Elizabeth, 27, 27n, 36, 38, 63–64, 73n, 78–85, 81n12, 87, 149, 153, 282–86, 285n, 286n18, 286n19, 326n
Antony, Louise, 296–97
Arendt, Hannah, 24
Ariely, Daniel, 9n9
Aristotle, 73, 213
Arkin, Robert, 172
artificial intelligence (AI), 117, 225
attention: Anscombean approach to, 149; conceptions and theories of, 102, 149–50, 280; controlling role of, 144–49; effect of, on performance of skilled/habitual actions, 24, 154–57; focal, 145, 151; selective, 143, 148–49. *See also* consciousness; mind
attribution bias, 50, 67

attribution theory, 40–66; actors and observers in, 53–54, 74–75, 75n; aim of, 34; on conscious and unconscious processes, 35, 57–62, 105–6; criticisms of, 68–78; growth of, 53–57; Heider's contribution to, 41–46; Jones and Davis's contribution to, 46–50; Kelley's contribution to, 50–53; Nisbett and Wilson's contribution to, 57–62; personal vs. situational causes in, 46–56, 63, 69, 72n2, 101–2; social psychology and, 35, 40–41, 52, 57, 61–62; stages of attribution, 49. See also causes; decision-making

audience effects, 178, 189–90, 196n19, 201

Austin, John, 71, 72

automaticity: agency in relation to, 5, 20–23; Bargh's theory of, 3–4, 7, 21, 24, 34, 36, 57–62, 97–98, 107–10, 112–20, 131–35, 216–17, 239, 260, 289, 291–92, 318; completion of processes as feature of, 22, 29, 104n, 108, 133, 158; consciousness and intention in relation to, 1, 3–5, 7, 20–24, 30, 30–33, 152–53, 158, 293–308, 321–22, 325–26; control and, 107–15, 143–57; Dreyfus and, 24–26; features of, 22, 107–8, 112–14, 113n10; flexibility and context sensitivity of, 29, 37–38, 158–63, 221, 239; goal-dependent, 109; graded approach to, 22, 110–12, 110n; history of interest in, 21, 101; hypnotically induced, 285n; mimicry and, 26, 36–37, 164–68, 176–80, 192–93; nonautomatic processes in relation to, 103–4, 104n, 107, 110–12, 137–38, 158, 162–63, 207, 279; perception as instigator of, 3, 32, 36–37, 97, 121–24, 128, 131, 133, 165, 183–85, 193, 202, 204, 217, 219, 221; postconscious, 109; preconscious, 109; Prinz's theory of, 121–24, 128, 166; skepticism about, 7; skilled actions and, 152–57, 168; unconscious, 39, 104–5, 143, 209, 279, 285, 293, 318. See also automaticity of everyday life; Bargh, John

automaticity of everyday life: Bargh's claims for, 5, 21, 32, 34, 36, 131, 135–36, 140, 142–43, 168, 209, 302, 326; criticisms of claims for, 24, 134–35, 326

auto-motive theory, 3, 116–18, 124, 128, 131, 140

autonomy, of processes, 108–10, 109n7, 158

availability heuristic, 60

Baayen, R. Harald, 245–46
Baddeley, Alan, 143
Bakhurst, David, 94n23
Barber, Theodore, 274
Barber, T. X., 273n5
Bargh, John: automaticity theory of, 3–4, 7, 21, 24, 34, 36, 57–62, 97–98, 107–10, 112–20, 131–35, 216–17, 239, 260, 289, 291–92; awards and honors for, 240; background of, 76, 98–99; *Before You Know It*, 239; "The Chameleon Effect" (with Tanya Chartrand), 165, 182, 273; and control of automatic behavior, 143–52; criticisms of/challenges to, 5–7, 10–11, 18, 24, 31–33, 37, 97–98, 134–35, 207, 210–44, 243n12, 260, 268n1, 271–72, 290–91, 295; and critiques of rationality, intention, and con-

sciousness in behavioral analysis, 7, 13, 26, 32–34, 39, 54, 57, 101–2, 114–15, 134, 136–38, 142, 209, 293–308; defenses of research of, 37, 118, 140, 168, 183–85, 214–15, 217–19, 226, 229, 231, 236–39, 268, 323 (*see also* moderators); development of priming research of, 36, 97–120; "feisty" period of, 21, 36, 131; on flexibility and context sensitivity of automatic behaviors, 29, 37–38, 158–63; and foundational issues of priming research, 13, 20–34; and hypnosis, 7, 31–32, 38, 276, 287–89, 287n; and mimicry, 164–203; reputation of, 239–41, 314n, 324; and skilled actions, 152–57; the unconscious as conceived by, 30–31, 209, 298–99; and Unconscious Thought Theory, 209. *See also* auto-motive theory; elderly priming experiment; priming research

Barsalou, Lawrence, 132, 217, 243, 261–62

Basic Emotion Theory, 171, 174, 189, 191, 191n15, 191n16, 193–95, 255

Bateson, Melissa, 198–99

Baumeister, Roy, 304–7, 310, 322

Bavelas, Janet, 36–37, 164, 168–80, 182, 187–92, 188n, 189n13, 194, 198n, 199–200, 202, 220n, 227, 256, 309n

Behavioral Ecology View, 174–75, 175n7, 191n16, 193–95

behavioral priming, 229

behaviorism: automaticity theory likened to, 23, 97–98, 132–34, 140; cognitive psychology/science vs., 22, 65n6, 97, 140; criticisms of, 76

Bem, Daryl, 6

Berkowitz, Leonard, 128

bias: attribution, 50, 67; confirmation, 8, 213, 305; publication, 312n

biased rationality, 13

Blair, Irene, 221

Bower, Bruce, 1, 229

Bowers, Kenneth, 267, 276–82, 286–89

brain, as site for cognitive processes, 270

brain structures, 145–46

Bratman, M. E., 162n15

Brentano, Franz, 116

Brett, Nathan, 158

Brown-Ianuzzi, J. L., 227n

Bruner, Jerome, 88n17, 226

Buck, Ross, 171, 173, 201

Burgess, P. W., 145

Burrows, Lara, 2–3, 5, 7–8, 11, 18, 31, 36, 37, 128–30, 146, 165, 205, 210–13, 216, 221–22, 229–38, 245–47, 271, 290, 292, 295. *See also* elderly priming experiment

Buss, Allan, 72–75, 75n, 88

bystander research, 119, 134

capacity, cognitive, 102–3, 103n4, 107, 207

Carlisle, Clare, 158

Carnap, Rudolf, 42, 85

Carpenter, William, 101, 121, 123

Carroll, John S., 54

Carter, Travis, 250–51, 251n

Cartesian dualism, 79, 82n13

causes: Anscombe-Davidson disagreement about, 79–84, 86–87, 120; intention vs., 35–36, 88, 227; reasons vs., 35–36, 43–45, 62–66, 69–84, 87–88, 270n; role of, in attribution, 35–36, 42–44. *See also* agent causation; attribution theory; event causation; explanations

Cesario, Joseph, 12–13, 193, 221–23, 230, 235, 239, 242, 242n, 243, 270
Chambers, C., 238n5
Chameleon Effect, 165–67, 181–82, 193, 202–3, 232, 273
Chartrand, Tanya, 26, 36, 124, 139, 164–203, 197n21, 198n, 202n26, 215, 232, 287, 287n, 323, 326; "The Chameleon Effect" (with John Bargh), 165, 182, 273
Chen, Mark, 2–3, 5, 7–8, 11, 18, 31, 36, 37, 128–30, 146, 165, 205, 210–13, 216, 221–22, 229–38, 245–47, 271, 290, 292, 295. *See also* elderly priming experiment
Chovil, Nicole, 175, 200–201
Christopherson, Cody, 14
Clever Hans, 6–7, 235, 272
Coburn, N., 231–32n
Coe, William, 274, 288
Cofer, C. N., 100
cognition. *See* mind; rationality/reasons; situated cognition
cognitive dissonance theory, 76–77
cognitive psychology: and agency, 225–27; Bargh and, 97; behaviorism vs., 65n6, 97, 140; conception of consciousness in, 23; conception of goals in, 28–29; conception of intention in, 26–28; conception of the mind in, 25, 35; criticisms of, 93–94; critiques of, 69; and determinism, 132; and information-processing model of the mind, 28–29, 35, 102. *See also* cognitive science
cognitive science: and automaticity theory, 20, 22–24, 33; conception of consciousness in, 23, 32–33; conception of intention in, 26–28; conception of the unconscious in, 30–31; criticisms of, 88n17, 117, 226; development of, 22; elimination of the role of the person by, 32; and information-processing model of the mind, 48, 54, 57–58, 61, 64, 97. *See also* cognitive psychology
Cohen-Cole, J., 65n6
Cold War, 34
Coles, Nicholas, 254n, 256–57
Collins, Harry, 11, 228
conceptual replication, 8, 8n8, 166, 238, 241, 245, 251n, 262, 290, 310, 314
Cone, J., 324n
confirmation bias, 8, 213, 305
consciousness: attribution theory and, 35, 57–62, 105–6; automaticity in relation to, 1, 3–5, 7, 20–24, 30–33, 153, 158, 293–308; degrees of, 21; diminishment of role of, 7, 32–34, 39, 105–6, 134, 136–39, 142–43, 293–97; intentions in relation to, 172, 191n16, 296–97, 319; limitations of, 101, 102, 207; rationalization as function of, 32–33, 38–39, 299–308, 322; System 2 processing and, 5n4, 102; the unconscious in relation to, 207, 277–78, 296–97, 322. *See also* attention; control; executive mental processes; intention/intentionality; mind; rationality/reasons
contagion. *See* mimicry
context sensitivity: automaticity and, 29, 37–38, 158–63, 221, 239; Bargh's disregard for, 291–92; mimicry and, 26, 193–96; priming research and, 37–38, 223–26, 247–66, 311–12; replication and, 247–66, 258n21. *See also* interpersonal/social phenomena; moderators

control: absence of, as feature of automaticity, 22, 32–33, 107; alleged loss of, through conscious attention, 24, 154–57; attention's role in, 144–49; automaticity and, 107–15, 143–57; conventional assumption of, over our thoughts and behaviors, 20, 55; diminishment of role of, 23–24, 32–33, 61–62, 102–5; exerted by the environment, 125–28, 140–43; hypnosis and, 276–82; nonconscious sources of cognitive, 136–39; of stereotype effects, 114, 147–48. See also consciousness; executive mental processes; intention/intentionality
Conty, L., 273n6
correspondence problem, 122
correspondent inference theory, 49–50
Cowan, W. B., 107–8, 319
Craddock, Matt, 236n3
Creswell, J. David, 263–65
critique, 15–18
crowd behavior, 146
Crowther-Heyck, Hunter. See Heyck, Hunter
crud factor, 312–13
Crury, Maurice O'Connor, 286n19
cybernetics, 22, 24, 28, 28n, 137

Danziger, Kurt, 92n, 189n13
Dark, Veronica, 148–49
Daston, Lorraine, 19
Davidson, Donald, 64, 73n, 79–84, 86–87, 87n, 120, 162, 162n15, 326n
Davis, Keith E., 46–50, 52
Dawkins, Richard, 174
decision-making: influences on, 5n5; limitations in the human capacity for, 24, 34, 54, 56–62, 102, 114; unconscious processes in, 205–6, 208–9, 297. See also attribution theory; evaluations; rationality/reasons
De Houwer, Jan, 107–11, 119–20
demand characteristics: controlling for, 7, 32n, 101, 254, 256, 268, 272, 292; decreasing attention paid to, 268–71; explanations of, 220, 220n, 273–77; as influence on experimental outcomes, 7, 65n6, 90, 237n5, 254, 290. See also experimenter expectancy
DeMarree, Kenneth, 217–18, 243
Dennett, Daniel, 118, 149–51
determinism: Bargh and, 98, 136, 137n, 139–40; behaviorism and, 132, 140; cognitive psychology and, 132, 139, 140; Prinz and, 124n15; in science, 124n15, 139
deviant causal chains, 79n9, 87n
Dijksterhuis, Ap, 130, 141n, 148, 151–52, 154–58, 166, 176–80, 183–84, 204–10, 212, 214, 216, 230, 237n4, 238, 243, 293n, 297
direct replication, 8, 8n8, 12, 238, 240–41, 241n, 243, 247, 249, 251n, 253n18, 257, 262, 290, 293n, 310–11, 310n, 314
disappearing agent problem, 86
dispositions: attribution theory and, 84–86, 88; defined, 44; intentions in relation to, 47; personal vs. environmental, 44–46; rating of, 48–49; role of, in attribution theory, 44–49; situations in relation to, 46–53; skepticism about, 54n2. See also person
dissociation theory of hypnosis, 31, 167–68, 276–82, 285n, 286–88
Doise, Wille, 91

Donnellan, K. S., 73, 73n, 75
double-blind procedures, 8, 33, 234, 236, 238, 268, 272n, 290–92
Doyen, Stéphane, 5–6, 8, 9n9, 11, 32, 37–38, 213, 229–39, 237n4, 238n6, 238n7, 243–46, 268, 271, 273, 273n6, 290, 293–94, 312n
Dreyfus, Hubert, 24–26, 117, 156, 225, 227n
dualism. *See* Cartesian dualism
dual-process/system theories: of attention, 102; automaticity theory and, 22, 111–12, 113n10; Bargh's criticisms of, 317–19; distinct systems in, 21, 103, 112n, 158, 162–63, 207, 295; intentionality and, 317–19, 325; Systems 1 and 2 model as, 5, 5n4, 317. *See also* mind; System 1 mental processes; System 2 mental processes
Duffy, Korrina, 197, 197n21, 199, 202n26
Durkheim, Émile, 71

Earp, Brian, 246
ego-depletion effect, 311, 311n
Eilan, Naomi, 149
Eitam, B., 243
Ekman, Paul, 171, 173, 174, 189, 191, 191n15, 191n16, 193–95, 200, 255, 255n. *See also* Basic Emotion Theory
elderly priming experiment, 1–8, 9n9, 18, 31–32, 36, 37, 128–30, 146, 165, 205, 210–14, 216, 221–22, 229–38, 245–47, 271, 273n6, 290–91, 295
emotion, and mimicry, 171, 174, 187–202
environmental dependency syndrome, 141, 141n
Erdelyi, Matthew Hugh, 61

ethics. *See* moral responsibility
evaluations, 69–71, 139–40
event causation, 83–87
everyday language. *See* ordinary language
everyday life. *See* automaticity of everyday life
evolution, 145–46, 186, 209, 265–66, 301, 303, 305, 307
executive mental processes: automatic processes in relation to, 23, 104, 143–48; diminishment of role of, 23, 36, 115–16; hypnosis in relation to, 276–82, 285; resistant to exact scientific description, 264–65. *See also* attention; consciousness; control
experimenter expectancy: controlling for, 8, 32n, 254, 268, 271, 272, 290–92; decreasing attention paid to, 268–71; explanations of, 220, 220n, 273–77, 273n5; as influence on experimental outcomes, 6–7, 31–33, 64–65, 65n6, 90, 230, 232–35, 237, 254, 268, 272n, 273, 274, 289–92, 291n; nature of, 38; synonyms for, 275n9. *See also* demand characteristics
experiments: automatization of, 269; contrasting approaches to, 91–92n; in intentionality-oriented practice of psychology, 309n; preregistration of, 9, 14–15; subjects/participants in, 75n. *See also* demand characteristics; experimenter expectancy; research
explanations: by appeal to rules, 68–69, 74, 77–78, 84, 87–91, 153n; personal vs. sub-personal levels of, 150–51; rational vs. causal-mechanical, 35–36, 43–45, 47, 62–66, 69–84, 87–88; of

unconscious behavior, 284. *See also* causes
exposure effect, 99

facial displays and mimicries, 37, 165, 168–80, 182, 187–202, 188n, 191n16. *See also* Facial Feedback Hypothesis
Facial Feedback Hypothesis, 252–57, 253n17, 254n
falsification, 11, 240–41
Faye, C., 65n6
feedback, 22–23, 137
Felski, Rita, 17
Ferguson, Christopher, 241–42
Ferguson, Melissa, 137–38, 237n5, 250, 251, 251n, 323–24, 324n
Feyerabend, Paul, 94
Fiedler, Klaus, 113, 148
file drawer problem, 8, 8n8
Fischer, Agneta, 194–97, 196n19
Fiske, Susan, 114
Fitts, P. M., 154
Fitzsimons, G., 299–300, 300n
Fleissner, Jennifer, 16n
Flis, Ivan, 13–14
focal attention, 145, 151
Fodor, Jerry, 109, 184, 225–26, 264–65
Foucault, Michel, 17
fraud, 6, 9n9
free will, 124n15, 132, 136, 138, 180, 293
Freud, Sigmund, 16n, 30–31, 33, 60–61, 209, 238, 279, 307n
Fridlund, Alan, 174–75, 175n6, 175n7, 178, 182, 188n, 190–95, 191n16, 199–202, 227, 254–57, 255n, 309n
Fried, Michael, 156–57, 157n12
Friedman, N., 273n5
Friesen, W. V., 255n

frontal-lobe functioning, 30, 140–43, 141n, 160, 279–80
functionalism, 303
fundamental attribution error, 54–55, 69

Gadenne, V., 94
Galanter, Eugene, 22, 26–27, 117, 267, 282n
Gallese, Vittorio, 182
Gantt, Edwin, 248–49, 266
Garfinkel, Harold, 71, 90
Gazzaniga, M. S., 305–7
generalizability, of priming research, 185, 213, 248, 259–65
Gergen, Kenneth, 79, 91–94, 94n23, 248–50, 257–58, 261, 265–66, 309–10
Gigerenzer, Gerd, 13, 52n, 56, 213–14
Gilbert, Daniel, T. E., 105, 240
Gilder, T., 272n, 290–91, 291n
Gino, Francesca, 9n9
goals: automatic activation of, 115–18, 133, 137; conceptions of, 28; environment triggering pursuit of, 124–28; intentions in relation to, 28–29, 119–20, 119n, 124–28, 136, 162, 186, 320–21; the unconscious and, 209, 298–99
Goffman, Erving, 90
Gollwitzer, Peter, 28, 116, 124–29
González-Vallejo, C., 207
Gordon, Douglas, *Zidane* (with Philippe Parreno), 156, 157n12
Gould, Stephen J., 265–66
Green, M., 299–300, 300n
Greenfield, P. M., 258, 258n21
Grice, H. P., 220, 220n

habits, 21, 158. *See also* skilled actions
Hamilton, Antonia, 198–200
Hareli, Shlomo, 194

HARKing (hypothesizing after the results are known), 8, 8n8
Harré, Rom, 75–78, 88–94, 309–10
Harris, C., 231–32n
Harris, M. J., 274–75
Harris, Victor, 49–50
Hassin, Ran, 158–63, 250, 251n
Hayes, J., 286n19
Hayles, N. Kathleen, 28n, 157n13, 307n
Heene, Moritz, 241–42
Heerey, E. A., 272n, 290–91, 291n
Hegarty, B., 12n
Heidegger, Martin, 117
Heider, Fritz, 40–46, 50, 64, 73
Herbart, Friedrich, 121
Hess, Ursula, 194–97, 196n19
Heyck, Hunter, 23, 24
Heyes, Cecilia, 186n
Higgins, E. Tory, 100–101, 114, 221–23, 230, 235, 243
Hilgard, Ernest, 167–68, 276, 287–88, 287n
Holler, Judith, 198–99
Hornsby, Jennifer, 79–86, 150
Huang, Julie, 298–304
Hull, J. G., 217
Human Spark, The (television show), 202–3
Hume, David, 27, 76, 80–81, 86–89, 88n16
Hütter, Mandy, 113, 148
hypnosis: Anscombe and, 283–84, 286, 286n18, 286n19; Bargh and, 7, 31–32, 38, 276, 287–89, 287n; dissociation theory of, 31, 167–68, 276–82, 285n, 286–88; executive functions in relation to, 276–82, 285; ideomotor action and, 121, 123; priming compared to, 6–7, 31–32, 167–68, 279–80, 288–89; role-playing theory of, 31, 274–76, 278–79, 283, 285n, 288; speech as factor in, 282n; Wittgenstein and, 286n19
hypotheses testing, 14–15

ideomotor action, 121–24, 131, 166, 226
imitation. *See* mimicry
implementation intentions, 125–26
inferences, in making attributions, 34, 40–41, 47–49, 56
information, 28, 28n
information-processing model of the mind: attention's place in, 149; Bargh and, 36, 117, 139; behavioral analysis according to, 28–29, 35, 36, 38; capacity models, 107; cognitive psychology and, 28–29, 35, 102; cognitive science and, 48, 54, 57–58, 61, 64, 97; criticisms of, 77; and goal/intentions/purposes, 117; priming research and, 226n; situated cognition and, 225; thinking and, 48, 54, 56; unconscious processes in, 31, 35, 57–58, 61–62
intention/intentionality: action in relation to, 26–28, 79–80, 89; Anscombe's theory of, 27, 27n, 63–64, 78–83, 81n12, 153, 282–85, 285n, 326n; automaticity in relation to, 3, 7, 20–24, 30, 32–33, 152, 321–22, 325–26; causal-mechanical attributions vs., 35–36, 88, 227; cognitive science and, 22; conceptions and theories of, 26–28, 118–19; consciousness in relation to, 172, 191n16, 296–97, 319; Davidson's theory of, 79–83, 326n; debates over, 20–21, 61; diminishment of role of, 7, 26, 57, 134, 136–38; dispositions in relation to, 47; dual-process/system

theories and, 317–19, 325; goals in relation to, 28–29, 119–20, 119n, 124–28, 136, 162, 186, 320–21; as hidden/private, 23, 26–27, 48; priming research as challenge to theories stressing, 3, 7, 20, 32, 114; psychoanalysis and, 282–85; System 2 mental processes reliant on, 5n4; unconscious, 30, 113, 113n11, 163, 277–78, 317–26; "why" questions and, 27, 27n, 43, 63, 282–85, 321. *See also* agency; consciousness; control; implementation intentions; meaning; moral responsibility; rationality/reasons

interpersonal/social phenomena: attribution theory and, 41–47; communicative function of, 26, 36–37, 164, 168–76; individualistic emphasis as obstacle to understanding, 189n13; mimicry as, 31, 164–203; the mind/thinking as, 68–69, 84, 94, 270; mirror neurons and, 181–82; rules as, 68–69, 84; social psychology debates concerning, 64–65; the unconscious as, 31. *See also* context sensitivity

introspection: attribution theory and, 35, 57–62; criticisms of, 11n, 57n, 67–68; limitations on, 38, 57–62, 67

Iowa Gambling Task, 160–61
Iso-Ahola, Seppo, 310–13, 312n

James, William, 29, 101, 121, 123–24
Janet, Pierre, 101
Jennings, C. D., 149
Johnson, Robert, 189–90
Johnston, L., 215–16
Johnston, Lucy, 144–46

Johnston, William, 148–49
Jonas, K. J., 243
Jones, Carl, 100–101
Jones, Edward E., 46–50, 52–56, 54n2, 70, 74–75, 91, 101
journal editorial bias, 8
judgment. *See* attribution theory; decision-making; evaluations

Kahneman, Daniel, 4–5, 5n5, 6n, 7, 21, 54, 56, 60, 102, 207, 213, 238–39, 295, 299, 314–15
Katzko, Michael, 210–14, 228
Kay, A., 273n6
Kelley, Harold E., 50–53, 63, 70
Keren, G., 112, 162
Kihlstrom, John, 61, 98, 133, 136, 288
Kirsch, Irving, 277, 279
Klatzky, Roberta, 263–65
Klein, Olivier, 139n, 258, 268–74, 270n, 292
Knoblauch, Chuck, 156
Kraut, Robert, 189–90
Krebs, John, 174
Kruglanski, A. W., 94–95
Kuhn, Thomas, 10, 10–11n12, 11, 14, 19, 65, 76, 94, 241, 314

Lacan, Jacques, 16n
Lakatos, Imre, 10, 11, 241
Lakens, Daniël, 313
Lakin, Jessica, 172, 176, 179–80, 185–86, 191n16, 197n21, 198, 198n
Langer, Ellen, 104–7, 114, 132
Larsen, Jeff, 254n, 256–57
Larson, Gary, *The Far Side*, 252–53
Lashley, Karl, 100
Latham, Gary, 258
Latour, Bruno, 17–18
Laycock, Thomas, 121
Lazarus, Richard, 99
Le Bon, G., 146

Leighton, J., 186–87n
Lench, Heather, 254n, 256–57
Levenson, R. W., 255n
Lewis, Michael, 118–19
Lhermitte, F., 30, 140–43, 141n, 299
Lhermitte's syndrome, 141
Libet, Benjamin, 138, 180, 293
Lieberman, M. D., 139n
Lindstrom, J. P., 248–49
linguistics, 263
Lipscomb, B. J. B., 286n19
Locke, E. A., 244
Loersch, Chris, 223–26, 227n, 235, 243, 270, 297n28
Logan, G. D., 109n, 110, 155, 155n10, 319
logical positivism, 42
Lombardi, W. J., 114
Lotze, Hermann, 121
Lowe, E. J., 85–86
Lubek, I., 91–92n
Lynn, S. J., 277n10
Lynn, Steven Jay, 277, 279
Lynott, D., 268n1

Macrae, C. Neil, 144–46, 211–12, 215–16
Madden, Edward, 89
Maddux, W. W., 179–80, 197n21
Makel, M. C., 12n
Malle, Bertram, 55
Mandelbaum, Eric, 66n7
Mandler, George, 58
Mann, Thomas, 323–24
Many Labs, 250–51
Many Smiles Collaboration, 256–57
Marcus, Eric, 284n
Martin, Leonard, 252–56, 255n
Matched Motor Hypothesis, 194–95
Mayo, R., 254n
McDowell, John, 25, 84, 94n23, 150–51, 156

McGill, Ann, 198–99
Mead, George Herbert, 71
meaning: attribution theory and, 70–71, 74; as concern of social psychology, 14, 63; as concern of the social sciences, 36, 63; post-critical approaches to, 17; "why" questions and, 77. *See also* intention/intentionality
Meehl, Paul, 9–10, 10n11, 65, 228, 241, 259n23, 312–13
Melnikoff, David, 317–21, 324
Meltzoff, Andrew, 122, 128, 165
mental states. *See* dispositions; mind
Mercier, H., 302–3, 305
meta-analyses, 258–59, 258n22
Meyer, Adolf, 57n
Michaels, Walter Benn, 18n17, 29n, 79n8, 81n12
Miedema, J., 148, 151–52, 154–58, 216
Milgram, Stanley, 23–24, 65
Miller, F. D., 295n24
Miller, George, 22, 26–27, 58, 102, 117, 207, 267, 282n
mimicry: as automatic behavior, 26, 36–37, 164–68, 176–80, 192–93; Bargh's and Chartrand's work on, 26, 36–37, 164–203, 215; contextual sensitivity of, 26, 193–96; correspondence problem and, 122; emotion and, 171, 174, 187–202; evolutionary behavior and, 146; eye contact's effect on, 167–72, 176–78, 187–88, 188n12, 189n14, 194, 196n19, 197–99, 198n22, 201; facial, 165; as intentional-strategic communication, 26, 36–37, 164, 168–80, 182, 186–87n, 187–91, 194, 196–202, 222; limits of, 182–86; misconstrual of Bavelas's experiments and arguments on, 175–80, 187–

88, 188n, 194, 197, 198n; newborns', 122–23, 128, 131, 165, 180; perception as instigator of, 121–22, 165; Prinz's ideomotor theory and, 121–22; research supporting automaticity of, 180–82; social affiliation resulting from (not as goal of), 167, 202n26; solitary, 173–75, 178–80, 191–92; between strangers, 166–67
mind: and cognitive decline, 263n; cognitive science theories of, 22; contents vs. processes of, 57–58, 67–68, 104, 294; as hidden/private, 23, 26–27, 31, 48, 136–37n; intention's role/place in, 26–28; modular structure of, 184; role of, in performance of skilled actions, 24–26, 139, 152–57, 155n10; as social/interpersonal, 84. *See also* capacity, cognitive; consciousness; dual-process/system theories; executive mental processes; information-processing model of the mind; person; rationality/reasons; situated cognition; System 1 mental processes; System 2 mental processes; unconscious, the; Unconscious Thought Theory
Minsky, Marvin, 225
mirror neurons, 181–82
Mischel, Walter, 54n2, 134–35
moderators: in automaticity, 36, 187n; examples of, 183–85; in mimicry, 164–65, 183–85, 215; in priming experiments, 37–38, 184–85, 216–18, 240–44, 257–58, 261. *See also* context sensitivity
modules, 184
Molière, 213–14

Montero, B., 154
Moore, M. Keith, 122, 128, 165
Moors, Agnes, 107–12, 119–20
moral responsibility, 39, 270n, 302n
Morawski, Jill, 15–18, 16n, 18n, 65n6, 75n
Morsella, E., 320
Moscovici, Serge, 91
motivations, in making attributions, 54, 54n3, 56
Murdoch, Iris, 286n19
Mussweiler, T., 250n

naïve psychology, 42, 43, 46, 50–51
naturalism: and conceptions of the mind, 25, 64, 84; and intention, 83–84
Navarro, Danielle, 14–15
Neisser, Ulric, 23, 58, 115, 143
Nelson, Leif, 244, 253n17, 259
Nettle, Daniel, 198–99
Neumann, Roland, 179
Newell, Ben, 208, 225, 250n, 293–98, 293n, 295n24, 296n26
Newport, Roger, 198–200
Nielsen, T. I., 307n
Nisbett, Richard, 48, 53–56, 54n2, 74–75, 101; "Telling More Than We Can Know" (with Timothy Wilson), 34–35, 38, 41, 57–62, 64, 66–68, 70–72, 87, 89, 104, 130, 287n, 294–97, 295n24, 299, 307, 322–24
Noah, T., 254n
Nordgren, Loran, 204, 206–8, 210
Norenzayan, Ara, 219–20, 220n, 257
Norman, Donald, 143–44, 146, 149, 151, 280
nudges, 5n5
null hypothesis, 8, 8n8, 10n11, 65, 208, 312
Nuttin, Jozef M., 91

objectivist epistemologies, 14
Ochsner, K., 139n
O'Connor, Timothy, 89
one-to-many problem, 37, 209–15, 218
Open Science Collaboration, 240
Orben, Amy, 313
ordinary language, 28–29, 28n, 41–42, 71, 73
Orne, Martin, 32n, 64, 90, 220, 220n, 267, 268, 272, 274–76, 275n8, 292

Palermo, Charles, 285n
Parkinson, Brian, 193–94
Parreno, Philippe, *Zidane* (with Douglas Gordon), 156, 157n12
participant compliance, 31–32, 65
Pashler, H., 231–32n
Payne, B. Keith, 223–26, 227n, 235, 243, 270, 297n28
Payne, John W., 54
perception: automatic behaviors activated by, 3, 32, 36–37, 97, 121–24, 128, 131, 133, 165, 183–85, 193, 202, 204, 217, 219, 221; goals activated by, 28; mental representations in relation to, 133n; mimicry and, 121–22, 165; Prinz's ideomotor theory and, 121–24
person: attribution theory and, 43–56, 62–63, 101; Bargh's elimination of the role of, 23, 32, 115–16, 132–33; cognitive science's elimination of the role of, 25; as concern of psychology, 77; naturalistic theories on the role of, 25. *See also* consciousness; dispositions; mind; rationality/reasons; unconscious, the
personality theory, 158
Peters, R. S., 73
Petty, R. E., 243
Pflueger, Otto, 6

Phillips, J. G., 109n, 155n10
Piaget, Jean, 118
Plaks, J. E., 193, 221–23, 230, 235
Plucker, J. A., 12n
Polanyi, Michael, 59
Popper, Karl, 11, 240
positivism, 76, 89, 91, 133, 248
Posner, M. I., 143, 154, 279
post-critique, 17
powers, causal, 81, 84, 86, 88–89
Pribram, Karl, 22, 26–27, 117, 267, 282n
priming: defined, 1, 99; experimenter expectancy and, 290–92; first uses of the term, 100; hypnosis compared to, 6–7, 31–32, 167–68, 279–80, 288–89; semantic, 4, 229; semantic priming, 229. *See also* priming research
priming research: basic assumptions in, 20–34; complexity of, 12–13; controversies about, 5–7, 32, 213, 221–23, 228–66, 293n, 314–15; cultural/context sensitivity of, 37–38, 223–26, 247–66, 311–12; examples of, 4; experimenter expectancy and, 290–92; flourishing of, 180; generalizability of, 185, 213, 248, 259–65; history of, 15, 18–20, 97, 100; information-processing model of the mind and, 226n; moderators in, 37–38, 184–85, 216–18, 240–44, 257–58, 261; one-to-many problem in, 37, 209–15, 218; status of, 10, 12–13, 38, 261; typical experiment in, 99–100. *See also* Bargh, John; elderly priming experiment; replication; research
Prinz, W., 36
Prinz, Wolfgang, 121–24, 124n15, 128, 131, 166, 221, 226

probabilistic reasoning, 13, 49, 56, 60, 263–64
psychoanalysis, and intentionality, 282–85. *See also* Freud, Sigmund
psychology: basic issues in, 20–21; debates about research in, 7–14; as a historical undertaking, 13–14, 91, 265–66; replication in, 12n; scientific status of, 19, 65, 91, 266, 309–10, 313–14; and theory, 13, 15–16, 213. *See also* naïve psychology; social psychology
publication bias, 312n

Radtke, H. L., 91–92n
Rakow, Tim, 208
Ramanathan, Suresh, 198–99
Ramscar, Michael, 245–46, 262–63, 263n
rationality/reasons: causes vs., 35–36, 43–45, 62–66, 69–84, 87–88, 139n, 270n; Cold War ideal of, 34; critiques of, in behavioral analysis, 13, 26, 32–34, 39, 54, 56–58, 101–2, 204–5; diminishment of role of, 13, 54, 57, 101–2; intention in relation to, 27, 27n, 63; post-hoc role of, for automatic behaviors, 32–33, 38–39, 298–308, 322; role of, in performance of skilled / habitual actions, 24–26. *See also* biased rationality; decision-making
reflexes, 21n
reform, of research practices, 9, 13–14, 240–41, 310, 313–14
Regan, J. E., 110
relativism, 18–19
reparative reading, 16–18
replication: controversies about, 5, 6n, 7–14, 33, 37–38, 240–59, 253n17, 262–66; crisis concerning (2012), 7–18, 37–38, 229, 245, 290; cultural / context sensitivity of, 247–66, 258n21; failures of, for Bargh's experiments, 5–8, 11, 18, 32, 37–38, 66, 212–13, 217, 221, 229–41, 245–47, 268, 273n6, 290; failures of, for Dijksterhuis's experiment, 207–8, 238, 293n; importance of, 235, 240–42, 259n23; language as factor in, 244–47; multi-laboratory efforts for, 9; of priming research, 130, 228, 238–39, 244–59, 262–66, 290, 314–15, 314n (*see also* failures of, for Bargh's experiments); in psychology, 12n, 240; in social psychology, 13; in the social sciences, 12–13. *See also* conceptual replication; direct replication
representativeness heuristic, 60
research: economic pressures on, 12; fraud in, 6, 9n9; reform proposals for, 9, 13–14, 240, 310, 313–14; skepticism about, 8–9; sloppy, 9n9, 11; status of, in scientific enterprise, 10. *See also* experiments; priming research; replication
researchers' degrees of freedom, 8, 8n8
Resource Computational Model, 243
Retraction Watch Database, 9n9
Rholes, Williams, 100–101
Rhue, J. W., 277n10
Rijsman, John, 91, 95
Roberts, Gilbert, 198–99
Roessler, James, 149
role-playing theory of hypnosis, 31, 274–76, 278–79, 283, 285n, 288
Rosenthal, Robert, 64, 90, 233, 234, 268, 269, 272–75, 273n5
Rosnow, R. L., 269
Ross, Lee, 40–41, 54–56, 101

Rubin, D. B., 273n5
rules: explanation of action by appeal to, 68–69, 74, 77–78, 84, 87–91, 153n; intention and meaning central to, 74, 77–78, 87–88; social/public nature of, 68–69, 84, 90–91
Rychlak, Joseph, 118–19
Ryle, Gilbert, 42, 73, 74, 136–37n, 137
Ryle, Tommy, 69–70

Sabini, John, 68–72, 84, 88
Saling, L. L., 109n, 155n10
sample sizes, 8, 9
Sarbin, Theodore, 274–75, 288
Schafmeister, F., 314n
Schimmack, Ulrich, 243n12, 244, 259, 310
Schlosser, Markus, 87, 87n, 163, 325–26, 326n
Schneider, W., 143
Schreiber, D., 139n
Schröder, T., 226–27n
Schul, T., 254n
Schul, Y., 162
Schumacher, Michael, 212
Schwartz, Barry, 263–66
Schwarz, Norbert, 219–20, 220n, 260–62
Schwenkler, John, 153, 284–85
science: debates about research in, 9, 9n9; maturation process of, 11n; psychology in relation to, 19, 65, 93, 266, 309–10, 313–14; social psychology in relation to, 14, 64–65, 248–49, 257; social sciences in relation to, 11n, 36, 65, 87–88, 93, 241, 265–66. See also research
science and technology studies (STS), 16–18

scripts, 105–6
Searle, John, 118, 303
Secord, P. F., 75–78, 88–90
Sedgwick, Eve, 16–17, 17n
Segal, S. J., 100
selective attention, 143, 148–49
selectivity, of responses, 215–16
self-reports, 57–58, 67, 89, 102n3, 269
semantic priming, 4, 229
Semin, Gun, 219, 221, 223, 270
Shallice, Tim, 141n, 143–46, 149, 151, 280
Shanker, S. G., 153n
Shanks, David, 225, 250n, 293–98, 293n, 295n24, 296n26
Shannon, C. E., 28, 28n
Shaoul, Cyrus, 245–46
Shariff, Azim, 257
Shiffrin, Richard, 143, 207
Silver, Maury, 68–72, 84, 88, 273n5
Simmons, Dana, 17n
Simmons, J. P., 253n17, 259
Simonsohn, U., 253n17, 259
Siraganian, Lisa, 27n, 28n
situated cognition, 218–24, 223–27, 270–71, 297n28
Situated Conceptualization, 243
Situated Inference Model, 243
situationism, 23–24, 72n2, 98, 134
skilled actions, conscious vs. unconscious performance of, 24–26, 59, 139, 152–57, 168, 324–25. See also habits
Skinner, B. F., 132, 259n23
slips. See action slips
sloppy research practices, 9n9, 11
Smedslund, Jan, 266
Smeesters, Dirk, 6
Smith, Eliot, 219, 221, 223, 270
Smith, E. R., 295n24

Smith, P. K., 290–91
Smith, W. John, 174
Snyder, C. R. R., 143, 279
Social Cognition (journal), 208
social constructivism, 91, 93, 94n23
social psychology: attribution theory and, 35, 40–41, 52, 57, 61–62; conceptions and theories of the mind in, 48, 54; crisis of, 64–65, 87–96; criticisms of, 71–78, 89–91, 93–94; goals and scientific status of, 14, 64–65, 248–49, 257; Heider and, 42, 46; as a historical undertaking, 14, 247–49, 265–66; paradigms of, 64–65, 76–77, 89–91, 95–96; reasons vs. causes debate in, 63–64; replication in, 13; research in, 1, 4, 6. *See also* priming research; psychology
social sciences: replication in, 12–13; scientific status of, 11n, 36, 65, 87–88, 93, 241, 265–66. *See also* social psychology
Spanos, Nicholas, 274, 279, 288
special-state theory, 31
Sperber, D., 302–3, 305
Srull, T. K., 101
Stam, H. J., 91–92n
Stapel, Diederik, 6, 9n9
statistical methods, 258n22, 259, 259n23, 313
Stepper, Sabine, 252–56, 255n
stereotypes: controllability/malleability of, 114, 147–48, 221; of the elderly, 1–3, 2n, 211, 216, 218, 231; primes' evocation of, 1–3; representativeness heuristic reliant on, 60
Stevenson, Robert Louis, *Dr. Jekyll and Mr. Hyde*, 281

Stiegler, B., 24
Stigliano, T., 270n
stockings experiment, 58–59, 62, 295n24
Storms, L. H., 100
Strack, Fritz, 179, 244–45, 247–49, 247n, 250n, 252–57, 253n17, 253n18, 254n, 255n, 260–62, 310n
Stroebe, Wolfgang, 91, 94–95, 244–45, 247–53, 247n, 250n, 257–59, 258n22, 262, 265, 309, 310n
Stroop effect, 103, 104n, 273n6
subliminal exposure, 97, 99–101. *See also* priming research
Sunstein, Cass R., 5n5
symptom, concept of, 16n
System 1 mental processes, 5, 5n4, 5n5, 102, 162, 317. *See also* mind; unconscious, the
System 2 mental processes, 5, 5n4, 5n5, 102, 317. *See also* consciousness; mind

tacit knowledge, 59
Tarde, G., 146
Taylor, Charles, 73
Tetlock, P. E., 302–3, 305
Thagard, P., 226–27n
Thaler, Richard H., 5n5
thinking. *See* decision-making; evaluations; information-processing model of the mind; mind; rationality/reasons
Thompson, Michael, 84
Titchener, Edward Bradford, 57n
Tomkins, Sylvan, 171, 174
Trafimow, David, 246, 313–14, 324–25
traits. *See* dispositions
transparency, 15
Tversky, Amos, 54, 56, 60, 102, 213

Uleman, J. S., 113n10, 131
unconscious, the: adaptive functions of, 30, 61, 160, 204–5, 304–5, 307; attribution theory and, 35, 57–62, 105–6; Bargh on the role of, 7, 30–33, 39, 104–5, 115, 142, 209, 293, 318, 320; behavior influenced by, 33–34; conceptions and theories of, 30–31, 58, 60–61, 102–3, 209; consciousness in relation to, 207, 277–78, 296–97, 322; and decision-making, 205–6, 208–9, 297; and goals, 209, 298–99; information-processing model of, 31, 35, 57–58, 61–62; intentionality and, 30, 113, 113n11, 163, 277–78, 317–26; as social/interpersonal, 31; System 1 processing and, 5n4, 102
Unconscious Thought Theory, 37, 180, 204–9, 293, 297
utilization behaviors, 141n

van Baaren, Rick, 189–92, 194–95
Van Bavel, J. J., 258n21
van Knippenberg, A., 130, 166, 212, 214, 293n

Wagenmakers, E. J., 252–56, 253n17, 253n18, 254n
Wang, Yin, 198–200
"watching eyes" experiments, 198, 200n
Webel, C., 270n
Wegner, Daniel, 128, 136–37, 180, 287n
Weiner, Norbert, 137
Weingarten, Evan, 258–59
Westen, Drew, 154

Wheatley, T. P., 287n
Wheeler, S. Christian, 217–18, 243
"why" questions: attribution theory and, 45, 47, 58–59, 63–66; dual answers to, 78; intention and, 27, 27n, 43, 63, 282–85, 321; meaning and, 77
Wiggins, Bradford, 14
Wilensky, Robert, 117–18
Wilkin, Katie, 198–99
Willard, Aiyana, 257
Williams, L. E., 268n1
Williams, R., 248–49
Wilson, Timothy, 158, 307; "Telling More Than We Can Know" (with Richard Nisbet), 34–35, 38, 41, 57–62, 64, 66–68, 70–72, 87, 89, 104, 130, 287n, 294–97, 295n24, 299, 307, 322–24
Winch, Peter, 64, 73, 87–88, 88n16, 248
Wisconsin Card Sorting Task, 159–60
Wiseman, Rachel, 63
Wittgenstein, Ludwig, 36, 48, 64, 68, 71, 72, 73n, 74, 87, 117, 153n, 286n19
Woody, E. Z., 288
Wyer, R. S., Jr., 101

Yong, Ed, 6–7, 235–36, 236n3, 237n4, 238n5

Zajonc, Robert, 76–77, 89, 91–93, 96, 98–99, 139, 309
Zbrodoff, N. J., 109n
Zidane, Zinédine, 156–57, 157n12
Zimerman, S., 158–63
Zizek, Slavoj, 16n
Zwaan, Rolf, 240, 310n